The Critical Edge

Critical Thinking for Reading and Writing

The Critical
Edge

Critical Thinking
for Reading and
Writing

Vincent E. Barry
Bakersfield College

Harcourt Brace Jovanovich College Publishers
Fort Worth   Philadelphia   San Diego
New York   Orlando   Austin   San Antonio
Toronto   Montreal   London   Sydney   Tokyo

Publisher *Ted Buchholz*
Acquisitions Editor *Jo-Anne Weaver*
Project Editor *Catherine Townsend*
Production Manager *Milt Sick*
Art & Design Supervisor *John Ritland*
Cover Illustration *Terry Widener*
Text Design *Paula Goldstein*

Library of Congress Cataloging-in-Publication Data

Barry, Vincent E.
   The critical edge : critical thinking for reading and writing /
Vincent E. Barry.
      p.   cm.
   Includes index.
   ISBN 0-03-047522-8
   1. Critical thinking — Study and teaching (Secondary) — United
States. 2. Critical thinking — Study and teaching (Higher) — United
States. 3. Reading (Secondary) — United States. 4. Reading (Higher
education) — United States. 5. English language — Composition and
exercises — Study and teaching (Secondary) — United States.
6. English language — Composition and exercises — Study and teaching
(Higher) — United States.   I. Title.
LB1590.3.B369   1992
428.4'071'1 — dc20   91-32031
                                                        CIP

ISBN: 0-03-47522-8

Address for Editorial Correspondence
Harcourt Brace Jovanovich, Publishers, 301 Commerce Street, Suite 3700, Fort Worth, TX 76102

Address for Orders
Harcourt Brace Jovanovich, Publishers, 6277 Sea Harbor Drive, Orlando, FL 32887
1-800-782-4479, or 1-800-433-0001 (in Florida)

Printed in the United States of America

2 3 4 5   016   9 8 7 6 5 4 3 2 1

For **Fred Rue Jacobs,**
bluffing his way through poetry

Preface
for Instructors

I have a secret dread. A recurring nightmare of sorts. Let me share it with you.

It's the end of the term and a mysterious stranger has come to examine my students. The examination involves essays on contemporary issues. The questions seem simple and straightforward enough. What are the essays' main ideas? their supporting details? their key unexpressed assumptions? There is also an evaluative part. It calls for critical inspection of the authors' reasoning and for an overall assessment. And finally, there is a section that invites students to join the issue by constructing an extended argument of their own. Pretty tame stuff, actually, the stuff that critical thinking is made of — understanding, analyzing, and evaluating argumentative rhetoric; constructing well-reasoned and developed arguments. In fact, so seemingly benign and fair is the test that I'm actually eager for its start. I can hardly wait for my students to strut their stuff, as it were, to demonstrate their critical thinking skills to this interloper.

Then something goes terribly wrong. Students mistake main ideas for subordinate ones. They confuse conclusions with premises; reconstruct wildly irrelevant premises; and generally misinterpret and distort the passages. I cringe and wilt as even the most obvious of logical errors elude them.

There. Now you know. My secret dread is no secret anymore. Neither is the impulse behind this book: *To help students apply critical thinking skills to extended arguments, their own as well as those of others.* A rather pedestrian goal, I admit — one shared by many teachers of critical thinking and informal logic. But, as is true of many other goals, the challenge lies not in the conception, but in the execution.

Actually, I've harbored this goal for a long time. And for just as long, I believed I was pretty much attaining it. The mistake I made—the one revealed by the *mysterious stranger*—was in assuming that students would and could automatically transfer to extended arguments what they learned from studying short specimen arguments. But this glib assumption is belied by the organization, structure, and rhetoric of the argumentative essay—not to mention its sheer length and level of sophistication. Multi-paragraph arguments can test the logical and analytical skills of even the best students. For those struggling, such discourse can be mind-numbing. No matter the state and stage of their critical faculties, all students can benefit from explicit instruction on the role of critical thinking in extended arguments, and from exposure to them. *The Critical Edge* attempts to achieve this in the context of (1) helping students bring some order or structure to their thinking, and (2) providing them ample opportunities to sharpen their logical and analytical powers.

As for disciplining their thinking, I have attempted to provide students with adequate conceptual understanding of some basic issues in critical thinking and informal logic. In order to facilitate this, I've minimized the jargon, maximized the examples and illustrations, and adopted what I hope is a lively, engaging writing style. *Of special note are the bite-size modules into which the chapters are divided.* This should not only make the material more digestible to students, but allow instructors to pinpoint assignments, as well as to delete material. Although there is a linear development of topics within chapters, customizing the coverage will in no way compromise the integrity of a chapter or thwart comprehension. Beyond this, a recurring device to help conceptual understanding are the "Speaking of . . . " boxes featured in many of the modules. These basically show the practical implications or extensions of a module's content. The "In Brief" inserts, on the other hand, highlight a module's key points; and the post-module exercises test for both conceptual understanding and application.

As for providing students ample opportunities for sharpening their critical thinking skills, I'm reminded of the old saw about the three most important factors in ensuring the success of a new business: location, location, location. Using similar exaggeration to make a point, I'm tempted to say that the three most important factors for developing critical thinking skills are practice, practice, practice. This explains the text's massive amount and variety of exercises and learning aids presented in the end-of-chapter sections called "Improving Performance." "Improving Performance" sections typically consist of four categories of activities:

(1) *Summary-Test Questions.* A bank of true-false, multiple choice questions that both summarize and test on the chapter content. (Any questions that might pertain to deleted modules can easily be ignored.)

(2) *Critical Thinking Applications.* Situations, problems, or passages that require an application of logical and analytical skills. These skills usually relate to the chapter's content.

(3) *Point/Counterpoint: Essays for Analysis.* Here a contemporary issue is identified and explained. A relevant resolution is expressed and then addressed in two essays that take opposing viewpoints. Each essay is

followed by a number of questions, some of which test comprehension, but most of which exercise a variety of critical thinking skills, including organizing and structuring, comprehending, analyzing, comparing, and evaluating. Since many of the questions tie in with the chapter's content, students can readily see how authors make use of the very skills that they themselves are learning.

(4) *Related Theme Topics.* A handful of topics dealing with the issue are suggested in hope that students will join the dialogue by constructing argumentative essays of their own. Far from being a tack-on, this section is a natural outgrowth of the "Writing with Reason" modules that appear in selected chapters. The purpose of these modules is to help students transfer critical thinking skills to arguments of their own. These forays into argument formulation certainly aren't intended as a full-blown study of rhetoric. But they do address a woefully neglected and important aspect of the study of critical thinking: the construction and presentation of one's own arguments.

The foregoing should be enough to distinguish this text from others in the field. But some additional coverage differences, of kind or degree, merit note:

—More than most other texts, this one attempts to join logic and rhetoric, a classical predilection abandoned during the Renaissance when logic and rhetoric were separated. This union seems especially felicitous for mastering extended arguments, although, admittedly, it won't accommodate formalistic approaches.

—Quite often an argument's key elements are buried in the underbrush of rhetoric and syntax. The aforementioned rhetorical focus, together with numerous exercises, should help students sort things out.

—Although in contemporary rhetoric the line between argument and persuasion often is blurred and indistinct, there is nonetheless a theoretical difference that seems worth keeping in mind in responding to ordinary argumentative essays. I employ the classical distinction between deliberative and forensic oration; avoid categorically rejecting all persuasive devices; and suggest "rational persuasion" as a practical goal of argumentative discourse.

—What is said can't be separated from how it is said. And how something is said can't be separated from its structure and organization. In order to sensitize students to how an extended argument is assembled, I've included a module on outlining.

—Although fallacy recognition is an important part of argument evaluation, sometimes label-slapping substitutes for mature analysis. I've attempted to discourage this tendency by framing fallacies—both informal and formal—in the broader criteria-hallmarks of a good argument: acceptable and relevant premises that provide sufficient support for a conclusion. Similarly, where it could be rendered artfully, I treat a particular fallacy as a manifestation of a more general flaw in the reasoning process.

—General statements, both universal and nonuniversal, play major roles in extended arguments. Authors attempt to establish and apply them. But they don't always express these general statements; they merely imply them, leaving the audience to "fill them in," as it were. Reconstructing such statements can daunt even the most seasoned of analysts. I use a discussion of general statements as an entree into the topic of argument reconstruction, which in turn I associate with the construction of valid syllogisms. I've also tried to enrich the discussion of general statements by showing how their misapplication produces invalid arguments.

— Generalizations are handled as arguments offered in support of general statements. Not only are criteria for evaluating generalizations covered, but also the formulation and practical impact of generalizations, as well as the difference between inductive and noninductive generalizations.

— Since some of the standardized tests students take involve analogy problems, this topic is covered. Also presented are some practical strategies for responding to arguments from analogy.

In the end, I hope that *The Critical Edge* lives up to the promise of its title, whose meaning is intentionally multi-layered. I hope it encourages *careful* and *exact* evaluation, and that it convinces readers of the *crucial* and *decisive* role of effective thinking in everyday life. And I hope that students acquire a high degree of *sharpness* in their thinking, and that, for their time and effort, they gain an *advantage* in the lifelong quest for understanding, truth, and meaning.

If readers do acquire "the critical edge" as a result of using this text, they, like I, will have many individuals to thank, including the numerous authors in the field of logical and critical thinking whose work helped shape this one. A very special thanks goes to these professors whose generosity of mind and spirit saved readers from the effects of my high crimes and misdemeanors: Anthony Adams, Tennessee State University; Judith Barad, Indiana State University; Mark Battersby, Capilano College; Linda Bomstad, California State University, Sacramento; Robert Boyd, Texas Christian University; Steve Giambrone, University of Southwestern Louisiana; Paul Haanstad, University of Utah; Elton Hall, Oxnard College; Lutz Kramer, Rogue Community College; John Nolt, University of Tennessee; Walter O'Briant, University of Georgia.

I'm also indebted to the people at Harcourt Brace Jovanovich, especially to philosophy editor Jo-Anne Weaver and her assistant Tracy Napper and Project Editor Catherine Townsend for their confidence and support, and to Carol Paschal of the Bakersfield College library for her assistance in preparing the instructor's manual. And let's not forget the *mysterious stranger,* to whose rebuke this book is response.

3 The Language of Argument   89

Introduction   89

MODULE 3.1 _____

Functions of Language   90
Informative Function   90
Directive Function   90
Expressive Function   92
Ceremonial Function   92
Performative Function   92
   Exercises on the Functions of Language   93
Mixed Functions of Language   93
   Exercises on the Mixed Functions of Language   94
The Intended Functions of Discourse   95
   Evaluating Discourse   96

MODULE 3.2 _____

Categories of Argument Language   97
Premise and Conclusion Indicators   98
   Exercises on Premise and Conclusion Indicators   100
Qualifiers   102
Intensifiers   103
Discounts   104
Asides   106
   Exercises on Categories of Argument Language   110

MODULE 3.3 _____

Writing with Reason: Achieving Argument Coherence   112
   Exercises on Achieving Coherence   116
Improving Performance   117
   Summary-Test Questions for Chapter 3   117
   Critical Thinking Applications   118
   Point/Counterpoint: Essays for Analysis   124
      Issue: *Human Nature and Violence*   124
      RESOLVED: Humans are by nature aggressive and violent.   124
      Humans Are Born Violent by Sigmund Freud   125
      Humans Learn Violence by René Dubos   127
      Basic Humanity vs. Base Behavior by Roderic Gorney   130
   Related Theme Topics   133

4 Meaning and Definition   134

Introduction   134

MODULE 4.1 _____

Word Meaning   134

Definitions   136
Denotative Definitions   136
Lexical or Logical Definitions   136
Persuasive Definitions   137
Stipulative Definitions   137
Theoretical Definitions   138
   Exercises on Definition   143
Ambiguity and Vagueness   144
   Exercises on Ambiguity and Vagueness   146

MODULE 4.2 _____
Disputes   147
Verbal Disputes   147
Factual Disputes   147
Evaluative Disputes   148
Interpretive Disputes   148
Theoretical Disputes   148
   Exercises on Disputes   151

MODULE 4.3 _____
Writing with Reason: Developing Extended Definitions   153
Providing Historical Background   154
Keying on One Element   154
Finding the Common Element   155
Distinguishing Terms   155
Improving Performance   156
   Summary-Test Questions for Chapter 4   156
   Critical Thinking Applications   159
   Point/Counterpoint: Essays for Analysis   161
      Issue: *The Proper Limits of Individual Freedom*
      RESOLVED: Burning the flag as a political protest is a form of free speech
         protected by the Constitution.   161
      On Liberty by John Stuart Mill   162
      The Supreme Court's Decision Barring Prosecution in Flag Protest   163
   Related Theme Topics   169

PART 2   ARGUMENT EVALUATION   171

5 Linguistic Confusion I: Rhetorical Fallacies   173

Introduction   173

MODULE 5.1 _____
Semantic Ambiguity   174
Abuse of Vagueness   176
   Exercises on Semantic Ambiguity and Abuse of Vagueness   177

MODULE 5.2 _____
Slanting through the Use of Emotive Language   178

MODULE 5.3 _____
Misuse of Jargon   182
Abuse of Euphemism   183

MODULE 5.4 _____
Assumption-Loaded Labels   186
False Dilemma   189
  Exercises on Assumption-Loaded Labels and False Dilemma   831

MODULE 5.5 _____
Begging the Question   193
  Exercises on Begging the Question   195
Question-Begging Definition   196
Complex or Loaded Questions   198
Rhetorical Questions   199

MODULE 5.6 _____
Rhetorical Inconsistency   201
Distinction without a Difference   203
  Exercises on Distinction without a Difference   204
Improving Performance   204
  Summary-Test Questions for Chapter 5   204
  Critical Thinking Applications   206
  Point/Counterpoint: Essays for Analysis   212
    Issue: *The Death Penalty*
    RESOLVED: The death penalty is justified on grounds of retribution.   212
    Deserved Retribution by Ernest van den Haag   213
    All-Embracing Affect of the Death Penalty by John Cole Vodicka   218
  Related Theme Topics   225

6 Linguistic Confusion II: Fallacies of Ambiguity   227
Introduction   227

MODULE 6.1 _____
Equivocation   227
  Exercises on Equivocation   229
Amphiboly   230
  Exercises on Amphiboly   232

MODULE 6.2 _____
Accent   233
Innuendo   234
  Exercises on Accent and Innuendo   237

MODULE 6.3

Composition   **238**

Division   **239**

Exercises on Composition and Division   239

MODULE 6.4

Hypostatization   **241**

Exercises on Hypostatization   242

Improving Performance   **243**

Summary-Test Questions for Chapter 6   243

Critical Thinking Applications   244

Point/Counterpoint: Essays for Analysis   248

Issue: *Pornography*

RESOLVED: In general, pornography should not be controlled.   248

The Dangers of Antipornography Legislation by Jerome Frank   249

The Need for Antipornography Legislation by Janella Miller   257

Related Theme Topics   263

7   Fallacies of Irrelevance   264

Introduction   **264**

MODULE 7.1

Ad Hominem Appeals   **265**

Abusive Ad Hominem   265

Circumstantial Ad Hominem   268

Well Poisoning   269

Two Wrongs Make a Right   272

Exercises on Ad Hominem Appeals   274

MODULE 7.2

Emotional Appeals   **278**

Mob Appeal   279

Appeal to Pity   284

Appeal to Fear   285

Exercises on Emotional Appeal   288

MODULE 7.3

Diversion   **291**

Red Herring   291

Straw Argument   293

Exercises on Diversion   294

Improving Performance   **295**

Summary-Test Questions for Chapter 7   295

Critical Thinking Applications   298

Point/Counterpoint: Essays for Analysis   303

Issue: *Abortion*
RESOLVED: Extreme tactics are justified to stop abortions.   303
Closed: 99 Ways To Stop Abortion by Joseph Scheidler   304
Antiabortion Violence on the Rise: How Far Will It Go? by
    Lisa Cronin Wohl   309
Related Theme Topics   317

PART 3   TYPES OF ARGUMENT   319

8 Generalizations I: Formulation and Extension   321

Introduction   321

MODULE 8.1
General Statements   321
Generalizations   323
Inductive Generalizations   323
Noninductive Generalizations   324
    Exercises on Inductive and Noninductive Generalizations   327

MODULE 8.2
Forming and Applying Generalizations   328
    Exercises on Forming and Applying Generalizations   329

MODULE 8.3
General Statements in Syllogisms   330
Categorical Syllogisms   330
    Exercises on Categorical Syllogisms   333
Invalidity and Misapplied General Statements   334
    Exercises on Invalidity and Misapplied General Statements   338

MODULE 8.4
Conditional Syllogisms   339
    Exercises on Conditional Syllogisms   344

MODULE 8.5
Disjunctive Syllogisms   345
    Exercises on Disjunctive Syllogisms   348

MODULE 8.6
General Statements as Warrants   349
    Exercises on Filling in Warrants   356

MODULE 8.7
**Writing with Reason: Supporting and Extending General
    Statements   358**
Improving Performance   363

Summary-Test Questions for Chapter 8   363
Critical Thinking Applications   368
Point/Counterpoint: Essays for Analysis   368
  Issue: *Teenage pregnancies*
  RESOLVED: There should be parental notice laws.   368
  Safeguarding the Welfare of Young Women by Louise Cox   369
  *Shattering the Dreams of Young Women: The Tragic Consequences of
    Parental Involvement Laws* by American Civil Liberties Union   374
Related Theme Topics   381

9   Generalizations II: Evaluation   382

Introduction   382

MODULE 9.1 _____
Observation   385
Exercises on Observation   389

MODULE 9.2 _____
Representativeness   389
Sample Size   390
Typicality   391
Some Basic Questions for Evaluating Polls and Surveys   392

MODULE 9.3 _____
Handling Statistical Evidence   394
Evaluative Questions   395
Exercises on Handling Statistical Evidence   399

MODULE 9.4 _____
Fallacies of Missing Evidence   400
Hasty Generalization   400
Misapplied Generalization   401
Exercises on Hasty and Misapplied Generalizations   403
Neglect of Relevant Evidence   405
Three Guidelines for Uncovering Neglected Evidence   407
Exercises on Neglect of Relevant Evidence   410

MODULE 9.5 _____
Authority as Evidence   412
Two Questions for Evaluating Authority   412
The Appeal to Popularity   414
The Appeal to Tradition   417
Exercises on Authority   418

MODULE 9.6 _____
**Additional Evaluation Strategies: Checking for Consistency and
    Tracing Implications   420**
Checking for Consistency   421

Tracing Implications   424

MODULE 9.7 _____

Writing with Reason: Developing the Argument of Opinion   425
Defending the Opinion-Generalization   425
Adjusting the Opinion   427
Improving Performance   428
   Summary-Test Questions for Chapter 9   428
   Critical Thinking Applications   431
   Point/Counterpoint: Essays for Analysis   434
      Issue: *Euthanasia*
      RESOLVED: Living wills should be used and respected.   434
      Withhold Treatment by Judith Areen   434
      Living Will or Death Warrant? by George A. Kendall   439
   Related Theme Topics   446

10 Arguments from Comparison and Analogy   448

Introduction   448

MODULE 10.1_____

Comparison and Contrast   450
   Exercises on Comparison and Contrast   453
Faulty Comparisons   453
Incomplete Comparison   453
Selective Comparison   454
False Dilemma   455
   Exercises on Faulty Comparisons   455

MODULE 10.2_____

Analogy   457
Analogy Problems   458
   Exercises on Analogy Problems   459
Uses of Analogy   460

MODULE 10.3_____

Arguments from Analogy   462
   Exercises on Arguments from Analogy   463

MODULE 10.4_____

Responding to Analogies   465
   Exercises on Responding to Analogies   468

MODULE 10.5_____

**Writing with Reason: Developing the Argument from Comparison
   or Analogy   470**
Subject-by-Subject Method   471
Point-by-Point Method   472

Improving Performance   473
   Summary-Test Questions for Chapter 10   473
   Critical Thinking Applications   476
   Point/Counterpoint: Essays for Analysis   478
      Issue: *World Hunger*
      RESOLVED: The survival of rich nations depends on their not assisting
        poor ones.   478
      Lifeboat Ethics: The Case Against Helping the Poor by Garrett Hardin   478
      Population and Food: Metaphors and the Reality by William N. Murdoch
        and Allan Oates   485
   Related Theme Topics   490

11   Causal Arguments   491

Introduction   491

MODULE 11.1
Causal Arguments and Explanations   492
   Exercises on Causal Arguments and Explanations   497

MODULE 11.2
Causes as Antecedent Conditions   500
   Exercises on Causes as Antecedent Conditions   503

MODULE 11.3
Confusion in Causal Reasoning   504
Confusing a Cause with an Antecedent   504
Confusing Cause with the Whole of Which It Is a Part   505
Confusing Cause with Correlation   510
   Exercises on Confusion in Causal Reasoning   514

MODULE 11.4
Writing with Reason: Developing Causal Arguments   519
Chronological Order of Causes   520
Order of Importance   521

Improving Performance   523
   Summary-Test Questions for Chapter 11   523
   Critical Thinking Applications   528
   Point/Counterpoint: Essays for Analysis   529
      Issue: *Drugs*
      RESOLVED: Decriminalization is the way to stop the escalating drug
        problem.   529
      Nothing Else Has Worked: Abolish the Prohibitions by Robert W. Sweet   530
      Legitimizing Enslavement Will Not Reduce Its Harm by Midge Decter   534
   Related Theme Topics   538

Suggested Answers to Starred Exercises   540
Index   596

PART 1

Argument and its Expression

1

The Argument:
An Overview

INTRODUCTION

"Does anybody know who Alyssa Smith is?" Professor Morales asked the students in his ethics class.

"Sure," someone said, "she's the baby that just got the liver transplant."

Professor Morales congratulated the student on keeping abreast of current events. The day before, the media happily reported that the twenty-one-month-old girl had endured more than twenty hours of highly experimental surgery. In fact, the operation was the first ever performed in the United States that involved the use of a *living* donor organ. In the past, surgeons had been implanting parts of cadaver livers into children needing transplants for survival. The advantage of taking an organ from a living donor is that, because it's "fresher," it reduces the chances that the recipient's body will reject it.

"Does anyone know who donated the portion of liver that little Alyssa received?" Morales asked.

"Her mother," another student said.

"Wouldn't a stranger's have done just as well?"

"No," came the reply, "There would have been a greater chance of rejection."

"So, what you're saying," Professor Morales said, "is that because little Alyssa received a part of her mother's liver, she has a better chance of surviving than if she'd received, say, the tissue from a stranger."

The class agreed.

Morales then asked the class to imagine a hypothetical situation.

"Suppose that you're a parent of a child just like Alyssa Smith. The surgeons inform you that fully half of the children awaiting liver transplants die before an appropriate donor organ can be located. They also explain, as you just correctly did, that the portion of the liver from a living relative would greatly increase your child's chances of survival. What would you do?"

The room exploded with opinions. It seemed that everyone wanted to speak at once. After awhile, the question "What *would* you do?" evolved into "What *should* you do?" — the discussion turned from psychology to ethics.

As the class drew to a close, Professor Morales said, "Okay, for the next class I want you to write an essay dealing with this case. I want you to show me that cases like Alyssa Smith's raise serious moral concerns."

One student, Pam Wentworth, couldn't wait to plunge into the assignment, and for good reason: Five years earlier, her infant brother died before an acceptable liver donor could be located for him.

After giving the assignment some thought and doing a little research, Pam composed the following essay:

The Morality of Medical *Miracles*

Although all of us can rejoice at the amazing surgery that has given little Alyssa Smith a new lease on life, we tend to overlook the serious moral aspects of cases like hers. Far from being merely medical "miracles," the use of organs from living, related donors raises a knot of ethical problems.

First, imagine the emotional state of parents who learn that their baby is suffering from a life-threatening disease. Add to this that the only way to save the child is to replace a vital organ, such as a liver. Then, just for good measure, introduce the fact that in all likelihood no such organ will be found before the child succumbs. Faced with this bleak prospect, the parents would probably fall apart. They'd be overcome by such grief and panic that they'd do anything for their child.

This is precisely what my family had to deal with five years ago when we learned that my baby brother Timothy needed a liver transplant to live. My parents were literally overwhelmed with grief and desperation. The emotional roller-coaster that we were on for a year is indescribable. We would have done anything to save Timothy's life. To see him languishing day after day as surgeons frantically and, as it turned out, unsuccessfully searched for a liver donor was a wrenching experience I wouldn't want anyone to go through. My parents would have done anything to save Timothy's life, including giving up their own.

Now, can we really believe that such distraught parents are rational enough to make a free decision when a surgeon tells them: "Well, there is one thing you can do that might extend your child's life. You can give him a piece of your own liver"? My parents certainly would not have been. They would have leapt at the chance to save their son.

But even if such parents can make a free, voluntary decision, is it right to ask them to? Just think of the enormous guilt that would hit a parent who refused. It would be a rare parent, indeed, who could live with the guilt of standing idly by and letting his or her child die. So, even if a voluntary, free choice is possible in these cases, we have no way of knowing that parents who consent, consent *freely*. I suppose what I'm implying is that asking a parent to donate an organ is really compelling them to, because only a rare parent could say no, even if that's what he or she really wanted to do.

And speaking of consent, the notion of *informed* consent has always been a basic part of medical ethics. Do we really think that Alyssa Smith's mother had any real idea what risks she was taking, or that she cared, when the surgeons suggested that she be a donor? Did she really know what might happen.to her during all those hours of surgery? The fact is that Mrs. Smith not only gave up part of her liver, but also lost her spleen when surgeons damaged it accidentally during surgery.

But even if the problem of free and informed consent can be overcome, there's the question of the financial fairness of this kind of surgery, as well as the use of scarce medical resources. It's estimated that about 700 children are born each year who need a liver transplant to survive. Certainly all of us wish that all these unfortunate children could receive new livers. But the cost of this would exceed $200 million. Furthermore, doctors say that only about two-thirds of these children will survive a year after surgery. That means we're spending more than $200 million a year to save 461 children—almost a half-million dollars per child. And remember, that's to keep the child alive for one year.

Obviously life is important. No price can be placed on it. Wealthy parents probably would spend whatever it cost to keep their child with them for a month, let alone a year. But it's not the parents of these children who are picking up the bill—it's society. And that means we have $200 million less for other pressing health care problems, for example, the shamefully high infant mortality rate in the United States. Just imagine how much more good that money would do if it was distributed among the states with the highest infant mortality rates in order to improve obstetric and pediatric care for women and children at high risk. Clearly, women and children who might well lead long and productive lives are being shortchanged when the money and resources they need are being used to carry off a so-called medical miracle.

Does the question of high-tech care for a handful of children raise moral questions? Absolutely. Chief among them are the issues of informed consent, financial fairness, and the distribution of scarce medical resources.

Pam certainly did what Professor Morales asked. She wrote an essay which attempts to convince the audience of a point of view. In other words, she wrote an **extended argument.**

✗ An extended argument is a multi-paragraph essay (or speech) in which the central aim is to be rationally persuasive. Its goal is to persuade an audience to accept a particular viewpoint by appealing to the audience's reason, as opposed to its emotion. Pam attempted to convince her audience that transplanting organs from living, related donors raises moral concerns.

Open a newspaper, turn to an opinion/editorial page, peruse a magazine, attend a political rally, listen to a policy address, or take a college course, and chances are you will meet the extended argument. You will hear someone deliver a "speech of conviction" or you will read an article whose main purpose is to convince you rationally the author's position is correct. It is through the extended argument that we confront the most significant of contemporary issues and related disputes. In fact, so pervasive is this form of discourse that the mastery of it is vital to making sense of our complicated world. Beyond this, understanding the extended argument can be a powerful tool for self-discovery. For when we engage the ideas and thought processes of others, we indirectly crystallize and refine our own.

What is required to make sense of this most common form of discourse, the extended argument? You could probably list a lot of things—reading skills, adequate vocabulary, some familiarity with the topic, general interest, and so on—but your list might omit an absolutely vital element: good critical thinking skills.

What is critical thinking? Let's try to answer this question by first asking a few others about Pam's essay. What exactly is Pam trying to say? What is her main idea? Do you accept it or not? Why? Has she convinced you? Perhaps you're undecided. Is there something about her essay that has left you unable to endorse or reject what she says? Would additional material help you decide?

We probably cannot provide satisfactory answers to any of these questions without good critical thinking skills. The reason is that **critical thinking is a process of carefully determining whether to accept, reject, or suspend judgment about what someone says. It is also a process that emphasizes a rational basis for beliefs and provides a set of standards for analyzing, testing, and evaluating them.** In short, critical thinking helps us understand and react intelligently to arguments such as Pam's. It also helps us clarify our own beliefs and articulate them effectively.

The connection that we have made between critical thinking and extended arguments such as Pam's has been deliberate; a key goal of this book is to help you transfer the critical thinking skills you will be learning to extended arguments. That is why essays appear at the end of each chapter (except the first). Typically, these essays deal with controversial topics such as burning the flag, legalizing drugs, or requiring teenagers to notify their parents before having an abortion. However, knowing how to construct your own extended arguments is as important as knowing how to analyze someone else's; for this reason, guidelines for composing argumentative essays are interspersed throughout the text.

A good place to begin our study is with the goal of extended argument: *rational* persuasion. Authors (that is, writers or speakers) of extended arguments try to bring the audience to a belief by using arguments that, taken together, constitute a logical appeal to the audience's sense of reason. In short, they are trying to convince the audience. This, of course, calls for audience cooperation. This cooperation consists of an intellectual temperament of open-mindedness and impartiality. No argument, however powerfully reasoned in the abstract, can move a closed mind. An audience that is unwilling to suspend its own presuppositions and biases while considering an opposed (or even unopposed) viewpoint not only frustrates the function of extended argument but effectively denies its own beliefs a rational basis.

What about Pam's essay—does it rationally persuade? Are we convinced by it? Notice that the question is not whether we agree with Pam's point of view. We may agree with her viewpoint, but remain unconvinced by her reasoning. In fact, we may think that she has offered up a mix of irrelevancy and presumption that provides anything but a rational basis for her viewpoint—even though we share her belief that using organs from living, related donors raises moral questions. Or, we may judge that her arguments, on balance, have made a logical case for this belief. In the final analysis, whether or not Pam has succeeded in convincing us should depend on whether she has presented acceptable arguments. Has she? When is an argument, any argument, an acceptable one? To answer this question, we need an understanding of the general nature of arguments.

Trying to illuminate the anatomy and structure of argument from studying essays is somewhat awkward. Fortunately, we can learn the basics of argument by initially studying short arguments—ones as brief as two sentences and no longer than a paragraph or two. Short arguments are really microcosms of long ones. This is why this opening chapter uses short argument as a springboard to our study of extended argument. In learning about the ingredients and logical structure of the short argument—and in establishing evaluative criteria for it—we will be indirectly acquiring the necessary tools for thinking about extended arguments.

MODULE 1.1

ARGUMENTS

An argument is a group of propositions, one of which, supposedly, follows logically from the others, which are offered as support for it. This definition contains three features of an argument:

Feature 1: *An argument consists of propositions or claims—statements that are either true or false.* "Washington D.C. is the capital of the United States," "The South won the Civil War," "Vitamin C can cure the common cold." The first statement is true, the second is false, the third is highly questionable—but each of them is a proposition, that is, a statement that's either true or false. In contrast, questions ("What time is it?" "Is there a cure for cancer?" "Who first circumnavigated the world?"), exclamations ("Hurrah!" "Good grief, Charlie Brown!" "What, no dessert?"), and commands ("Do your homework," "Vote," "Practice safer sex,") in their base form are not propositions; they are neither true nor false.

Feature 2: *An argument consists of a* group *of propositions or claims—that is, more than one.* The following single statements are *not* arguments: "You should have voted Republican in the last election," "Abortion should be permitted," "The United States must maintain a strong defense," "Extraterrestrial life exists," "Anyone who minimizes the value of a college education is unwise." Combined with at least one additional proposition, however, they may become part of an argument, as in "A woman has a moral right to decide whether or not to carry a fetus to term. Therefore, abortion should be permitted"; or "A college education is vital to survival and prosperity. So, anyone who minimizes the value of a college education is unwise."

Feature 3: *In any argument, the propositions or claims are so related that one of them is intended to be supported by the others.* For example, let's say a friend of yours claims that using fluoride helps prevent cavities. You are skeptical. "Why should I believe that?" you ask her. "Because," she replies, "a study recently conducted at a leading university proves it." Notice that your friend is giving you a reason for accepting her claim that using fluoride can help prevent cavities. She is offering an argument. The reason she is giving may or may not be a good one for accepting her claim, but that is another issue. Whether or not the reason is good, she is offering one in support of the proposition that using fluoride prevents cavities. Therefore, she is arguing. Arguments contain reasons or evidence for claims.

Again, suppose that in attempting to make a case for capital punishment, you argue:

> **Capital punishment deters crime, and whatever deters crime should be legalized. Therefore, capital punishment should be legalized.**

You are giving reasons for legalizing capital punishment. You are attempting to demonstrate the acceptability of legalizing capital punishment on the basis of two pieces of evidence or reasons. You offer these reasons because the ultimate claim — the legalization of capital punishment — is in question. You need to convince your audience. You attempt to convince the audience by offering reasons in support of your claim that capital punishment should be legalized.

Keeping in mind this logical relationship among the statements in an argument helps us not to confuse arguments with nonarguments. Consider, for example, this group of propositions:

> **Toyotas are popular cars in America.**
>
> **The Hyundai is a recent import from Korea.**
>
> **Volkswagens are popular autos among younger drivers.**

What we have here is simply a group of propositions that are loosely connected by their interest in foreign cars. It is very hard to imagine that someone would be proposing the acceptability of one of these statements on the basis of the acceptability of the others. On the other hand, suppose someone says:

> **Whatever is popular in America is popular worldwide.**
>
> **Toyotas are very popular in America.**
> _____
> **Therefore, Toyotas must be popular overseas.**

Speaking of . . .

Propositions

Some Kinds of Propositions

One of the most important things to understand about propositions is that they can perform different roles and say different things, even though they may look alike. A good way to remember this is to think about the ambiguity of the verb form "to have." Examine the following sentences and consider some of the differences in what they say.

1. George has a chainsaw.
2. George has a drinking problem.
3. George has an article in *Reader's Digest.*
4. George has great parties.
5. George has a mean streak.

If the differences among these propositions are not obvious to you, ask the question, "What does he do with it?" after each one. It becomes clear that the only one he can "do" anything with is the chainsaw. Only proposition 1 is about George actually "having" or owning anything. Proposition 2 makes a statement about George's condition, while proposition 3 makes a statement about something George has done. Proposition 4 makes a statement about something George does regularly, and proposition 5 makes a statement about one of George's qualities or attributes.

There are many other ways propositions differ. Look at them in comparison with each other and ask, "What different kinds of statements do they amount to?" Consider, for instance, these two propositions:

1. San Diego is in southern California.
2. San Diego is a lovely city.

It's clear that proposition #1 states a *fact* about San Diego, whereas proposition #2 states a *judgment* about San Diego. This is an important distinction . . .

(From **Real Writing: Argumentation, Reflection, Information** by Walter H. Beale. Copyright © 1982 by Scott, Foresman and Company. Reprinted by permission of Harper Collins Publishers)

Why do you think it is important to be clear about what a proposition is saying?

Clearly, the first two statements are offered as reasons for accepting the third statement. Stated another way, the third statement supposedly follows logically from the first two statements.

Sometimes arguments are confused with simple explanations. For example, suppose that you and I are wondering why a mutual friend, Kathy, looks far healthier and more fit than we have ever seen her. You suggest that it is the vacation she has just taken. "Kathy looks a lot better since she took a vacation," you say. You are not trying to support the claim that Kathy looks better. That is not in question; we both agree on that. What you are offering is not an argument, but an explanation. You are merely trying to explain *why* Kathy looks better; you are not trying to show or prove or convince me *that* she does.

Suppose you and a companion go to the airport to pick up a friend, only to discover that his flight has been delayed. When you ask the ticket agent about the delays, she replies: "The flight's been delayed because bad weather has forced the pilot to take an alternative route." The agent is not offering an argument, but an explanation. She is not attempting to demonstrate that the flight has been delayed — that has already been established. She is simply giving an *explanatory* reason (as opposed to an *argumentative* reason) that accounts for the delay.

On the other hand, if, after hearing the explanation, you say to your companion, "Since the flight's been delayed, we better call the restaurant and cancel our reservation," you would be offering support for the wisdom of informing the restaurant. You would be arguing.

A basic difference between arguments and nonarguments, then, is one of interest or purpose. If we are interested in establishing the truth or believability of a statement and offer reasons for it, then we are arguing. However, if we regard the truth of a statement as nonproblematic and are interested, perhaps, in explaining or clarifying it, then we are not arguing.

IN BRIEF When a statement comes with supporting reasons, the statement, together with the reasons, constitutes an argument.

EXERCISES ON ARGUMENTS*

1. Explain in terms of an argument's 3 key features why the following passages are or are not arguments.
   A. Capital punishment should be legalized.
   B. The game has been postponed because of rain.
   C. Not vote? Why, that's as un-American as spitting on the flag. Of course, we should vote.
   D. Because fossil fuels are limited, it's important that we devise alternative energy sources.
   E. The defendant had the opportunity, motive, and means to commit the murder. There can be no doubt of his guilt.

---

*Answers to asterisked exercises appear in the back of the textbook.

F.   Elms are found throughout America. Cherry blossoms bloom in Washington in spring. Redwoods are found in California.
2.   Construct an argument for each of the following topics: abortion, gun control, pornography, testing for drugs in the work place.

THE "WHAT" AND "WHY" OF ARGUMENTS

Every argument expresses a point of view that, presumably, is supported. Arguments tell not only *what* arguers believe but *why*.

What arguers believe is the conclusion of the argument; *why* they believe it is the premise. **Conclusions are the judgments or inferences that supposedly follow logically from the premises; premises are the reasons that are given to support the conclusion.**

Here are some examples of arguments, with conclusions in boldface and premises in italics.

1. **Capital punishment should be abolished** *because it does not deter crime.*
2. *On the whole, college graduates get the best paying jobs.* **So, one would be wise to complete college.**
3. *Abortion can have serious psychological effects on the mother. And having an unwanted child also has serious psychological consequences.* **Either way, an abortion decision raises serious psychological questions.**
4. *Since it was made expressly for students,* **the film on AIDS must be educational.** *Also, it's been endorsed by the National Education Association.*

What makes the italicized statements premises is that they are being used as evidence in an argument. What makes the boldface statements conclusions is that they supposedly are being supported by the premises.

IN BRIEF   Premises are statements whose truth presumably is already established. Conclusions are statements whose truth someone is attempting to establish by means of a logical argument.

Notice that it is *not* the stated order of the statements that determines how they function in an argument. In example 1, the conclusion is stated first. In examples 2 and 3, it comes last. In example 4, the conclusion comes in the middle. **Whether a statement is a premise or conclusion is determined by how it is used in the argument, not by where it occurs.**

The terms *premise* and *conclusion* are relative. The same statement can be a premise in one argument and a conclusion in another, as in the following arguments:

All deciduous trees lose their leaves.

Elms are deciduous.
_____
Therefore, **elms lose their leaves.**

Elms lose their leaves.

The tree outside the classroom is an elm.
_____
Therefore, the tree outside the classroom will lose its leaves.

It is also possible to have two completely different arguments, using exactly the same statements, as in:

All mothers are females.

Alice is a mother.
_____
So, **Alice is a female.**

All mothers are females.

Alice is a female.
_____
So, **Alice is a mother.**

In the first argument, "Alice is a mother" functions as a premise and "Alice is a female" as a conclusion. However, in the second argument, "Alice is a mother" functions as a conclusion, whereas "Alice is a female" functions as a premise.

How do we know which statement in an argument is the conclusion, and which is the premise? This question deserves very close examination because it is at the root of all successful argument analysis.

MODULE 1.2

CONCLUSIONS AS MAIN IDEAS

Sometimes, students have trouble getting a handle on the notion of *conclusion.* As a result, they experience difficulty finding conclusions in arguments. Perhaps introducing the notion of *main idea* can help ease this difficulty.

You are probably familiar with the term *main idea* from your composition courses. The main idea of an essay corresponds roughly with the key claim that a writer is making amidst all the claims that make up the essay. The main idea is the writer's whole purpose or intention for composing the essay. It is what the essay is all about, what ties it together, what gives it purpose and direction. The main idea is the writer's overriding concern—the idea that, above all else, the writer wants to convey to the audience. The conclusion of an argument is nothing more than its main idea.

Just as understanding a writer's main idea is vital to understanding what has been written, understanding an arguer's main idea or conclusion is crucial to understanding the argument. If we miss the arguer's main idea or conclusion, we cannot identify evidence or evaluate how well the evidence supports that main idea; we cannot determine whether the arguer's reasoning is good or not so good because we cannot establish the *line* of reasoning. In short, identifying the main idea or conclusion is the key that unlocks the whole argument.

The specimen arguments we have considered so far have been made intentionally easy, unlike the extended arguments which can test the mettle of even the most seasoned of analysts. But no matter what an argument's nature is—easy or hard, short or long, simple or complex, nontechnical or specialized—identifying its main idea basically requires two skills: **(1) locating the argument's main idea** and **(2) precisely defining it.**

Locating the Main Idea

It is true that conclusions often come at the end of an argument, as in:

> **Since completion of logic is required of all graduates, and I wish to graduate, I must take logic.**

However, the expressed order of the statements, as we have seen, does not determine the logical structure of the argument. The conclusion or main idea can appear anywhere in the argument. For example, observe the location of the conclusion in three versions of an argument:

1. Since Marie is a logic student, and all logic students are bright, **Marie must be bright.**
2. **Marie must be bright.** After all, she's a logic student, and all logic students are bright.
3. It follows that, because she is a logic student, **Marie must be bright,** for all logic students are bright.

IN BRIEF   Whether a statement is a conclusion (or premise) is determined by how it is used, not by where it happens to occur in the argument.

Although brief arguments like these rarely pose problems of conclusion identification, extended arguments do, because main ideas can be camouflaged in the underbrush of rhetoric, subordinate ideas, asides, and the like. If you learn to observe carefully, you can pick up clues to the author's main idea. Specifically, train yourself to do the following:

1. Look for words that signal conclusions. Authors will often signal the conclusion of their arguments with words such as:

therefore	hence
thus	as a result
consequently	it follows that
so	

Be alert to the presence of words that may signal logically certain conclusions, such as:

certainly
necessarily
must

Also be alert to words that may signal logically probable conclusions, such as:

probably	it is reasonable to suppose that
in all likelihood	it's a good bet that
chances are	

2. Look for words that signal premises. Because isolating premises can implicitly locate a conclusion, watch for words that signal premises. There are an array of these, as follows.

General Area Premise Signals — words or phrases that indicate the general area of the passage where you will likely find the premise, such as:

since	consider the following
because	the following reasons
for	after all
for the reason that	inasmuch as
this follows from	insofar as
this is why *[what precedes the phrase is the premise]*	

Specific Premise Signals — words or phrases that help point out specific individual premises, such as:

a. words used for numbering premises:
   first . . .
   second . . .
   third . . .

2. words used for indicating the accumulation of different considerations related to the same conclusion:

for one thing . . . for another	in addition
furthermore	also
moreover	and

3. Words used to contrast considerations related to the same conclusion:

however	despite this
nevertheless	but

3. Ask yourself: What is the author trying to prove? *The best way to identify an argument's main idea is to determine what the author is trying to prove, establish, demonstrate, or make a case for.* This calls for *making sense* of what someone is saying.

Making sense of what someone is saying is not governed by hard-and-fast, mechanical, decision criteria. In part, it calls for a close inspection of the physical context of a message, for example, time, place, and circumstances. It also requires examination of the linguistic context — signal words, syntax, punctuation, and so on. In the end, *making sense* calls for reflection and deliberation that ultimately leads to a decision about which of several interpretations is the most plausible, given the physical and linguistic environment of the message. With extended, multiparagraph arguments, this process can be long and involved, but nonetheless vital to understanding and evaluating them.

As we know from having just considered signal words, the author's language provides initial clues to the author's intent. But effective appraisal of the language environment of longer arguments usually requires more than merely spotting signal words. Moreover, signal words can themselves be misleading.

For example, a signal word may be separated from the argument element it indicates, as with the conclusion signal "so" in the following argument:

The game has been rained out. So, since postponements are rescheduled, **we can expect to play this game at a later date.**

More importantly, as we saw earlier, words such as *since* or *because* do not always indicate the presence of a premise, or, by implication, a conclusion. Compare, for example, these two uses of *since,* one in an argument, the other in a nonargument:

Argument: **Beth should receive the award,** *since* her performance was the best.

Nonargument: **Beth's performance has improved** *since* she started running regularly.

In the first passage, "since" functions to logically connect premise and conclusion. In the second passage, however, it functions as a temporal connective to relate two events in time sequence. The point is that signal words and other linguistic aspects of a passage serve as important initial clues in helping us make sense of what someone says, but cannot be blindly relied upon to indicate conclusions or premises.

It is important to distinguish between *making sense* of what authors say and knowing *for certain* what they mean. Rarely do authors come right out and say, "This is what I mean . . ." or "my main idea is . . ." or something along the same lines. Rarely, if ever, are authors available to ask: "Exactly what are you getting at?" Therefore, we are left only with various contextual clues and our own interpretive faculties to use in deciding which of several candidates is the author's main idea. Our job, then, is not to establish with 100 percent certainty what authors exactly mean, for only they know that (or should); rather, it is to establish the author's *most likely* meaning, using the clues they give and we gather, together with our own well-considered appraisal.

To illustrate, consider three versions of the same argument. Suppose someone is trying to establish that a particular quantitative relationship holds between two things, based on a known quantitative relationship that holds between each of these two and some third thing. Thus, the person argues:

A is greater than B. B is greater than C. Therefore, A is greater than C.

In this instance, the arguer's use of "therefore" leaves no doubt as to her main idea or conclusion: "A is greater than C." Now, suppose that the person presented the argument this way:

A is greater than B. B is greater than C. A is greater than C.

Although the arguer deletes the signal word *therefore,* the *sentence arrangement* provides a sufficient measure of guidance to again infer the conclusion is "A is greater than C."

Neither the signal word *therefore* nor the order of the statements is what determines the main idea or conclusion; rather, it is the *internal relationship* that exists among the statements—that third key feature of an argument discussed earlier. The conclusion signal and sentence order help us discern this relationship, they do not create it. They are devices authors use to make the intended meaning clear, to preclude ambiguity, and to make themselves understood. Even without these clues, the same internal relationship would hold among the statements. Thus:

B is greater than C. A is greater than C. A is greater than B.

In this case, no verbal or syntactical clues are provided. If we had to determine what the arguer's main idea is, strictly on the basis of these three statements, we should still say that it is "A is greater than C." Why? Because, of the alternatives, it expresses the most plausible internal relationship among the statements. It simply makes more sense than either of the other main idea possibilities, "A is greater than B" or "B is greater than C." These are less plausible because they do not follow from the premises. In other words, even if:

> B is greater than C, and
>
> A is greater than C, it doesn't necessarily follow that
>
> A is greater than B.

Even if:

> A is greater than B, and
>
> A is greater than C, it doesn't necessarily follow that
>
> B is greater than C.

In contrast, if:

> A is greater than B, and
>
> B is greater than C, then
>
> A must be greater than C.

Of course, it is possible that the arguer did not intend this version at all. Maybe the arguer intended to establish that A is greater than B or that B is greater than C. That is possible; we do not know for sure. But, again, *trying to determine* what an arguer is attempting to prove is *not* identical to *knowing absolutely* what the arguer is attempting to prove. Making sense of what someone says is *not* an exercise in mind-reading, but in detection. It is a matter of discovering the most logical internal relationship among the statements asserted; this sometimes requires a good deal of flexible, as well as critical, thinking.

Now, you may be thinking: "Making sense of what someone says seems to require techniques of argument evaluation. After all, we just said that 'A must be greater than C' logically follows from the premises, whereas neither of the other two alternatives does." You are right. Argument analysis and argument evaluation often depend on each other. Where very few linguistic clues are given, determining the arguer's main idea — making sense of what he says — requires inspecting relationships among the various candidates for premise and conclusion in order to determine which most logically follows from which. It is precisely for this reason — to minimize any ambiguity and incoherence, any audience confusion about intended meaning or interpretation — that good writers use appropriate signals, syntax, punctuation, and sentence and paragraph arrangement. They realize that it is infinitely better to have someone understand and, perhaps, disagree with them, than not to understand them at all.

Here are two additional examples of arguments devoid of language clues to their conclusions:

> **Jane is concerned about the widespread use of drugs in public schools.
> Jane has children in public school.**

Which of the two statements is the arguer intending to prove?

1. Jane is concerned about the widespread use of drugs in public schools, because *she has children in public schools.*

or

2. Jane has children in public schools, because *she is concerned about the widespread use of drugs in public schools.*

Statement 1 makes better sense, because having children in public schools counts as evidence or a reason for being concerned about the widespread use of drugs in the schools. But in statement 2, the fact that Jane is concerned about the widespread use of drugs in public schools does not provide any evidence to establish that Jane has children, let alone children in public schools.

> Domestically, health, education, and welfare issues demand a larger share of the U.S. tax dollar. This is a good time for the United States to start cutting its defense spending.

Which of the following two versions of this argument likely reflects what the author is trying to say:

1. This is a good time for the United States to start cutting its defense spending, because *domestically, health, education, and welfare issues demand a larger share of the U.S. tax dollar.*
2. Domestically, health, education, and welfare issues demand a larger share of the U.S. tax dollar, because *this is a good time for the United States to start cutting its defense spending.*

The italicized portion of argument 1 provides a reason for the wisdom of reducing U.S. defense spending. In contrast, the italicized portion of argument 2 does not offer support for the claim that domestic needs are increasing.

Subarguments   Sometimes, an argument may contain a mini- or subargument within the main argument. For example, the argument about U.S. defense spending might have included this subargument:

> *AIDS, cancer, and other diseases are sweeping the United States.* Further-more, *test scores indicate that U.S. public school students lag behind their counterparts in other countries in math and science.* And *the social security system, not to mention other social welfare programs, is sorely in need of reform.* So, **clearly, health, education, and welfare issues demand a larger share of the U.S. tax dollar.**

Notice that the premise of the earlier argument is the conclusion (boldface) of this subargument, which has three explicit premises (italicized). This miniargument might have been integrated into the final main argument as follows:

AIDS, cancer, and other diseases are sweeping the United States. Furthermore, test scores indicate that U.S. public school students lag behind their counterparts in other countries in math and science. And the social security system, not to mention other social welfare programs, is sorely in need of reform. So, clearly, health, education, and welfare issues demand a larger share of the U.S. tax dollar. Therefore, **this is a good time for the United States to start cutting its defense spending.**

The argument's *main* idea, its *main* conclusion, is the last sentence. The sentence that immediately precedes it functions as a premise for this conclusion. It contains the conclusion signal "so," because it is the conclusion of the subargument, not the main argument. It is an intermediate or *transitional* conclusion that is functioning as a premise in the main argument. The presence of numerous subarguments makes analyzing and evaluating essays especially challenging.

EXERCISES ON LOCATING THE MAIN IDEA*

1. Using punctuation and signals as clues to missing elements, fill in the blanks of each of the following argument skeletons with either "P" (for premise), "TC" (for transitional conclusion), and "C" (for main conclusion). Then write an argument in the given pattern.
   A. _____ and _____ . So, _____ .
   B. _____ , because _____ and _____ .
   C. Inasmuch as _____ , _____ , for _____ .
   D. Since _____ , as _____ , _____ ; for _____ .
   E. _____ for the reasons that _____ and _____ .
      Thus, because _____ , _____ .
2. Assume that each of the following passages is an argument. Show the most plausible relationship among the statements by rewriting the passage in the pattern provided. Then explain why your interpretation of the main idea makes better sense than any other alternative.
   A. Capital punishment deters crime. Capital punishment should be legalized.
      _____ ,
      because _____ .
   B. Pornography doesn't contribute to sex crimes. Pornography shouldn't be restricted.
      Since _____ , _____ .
   C. A college education affects one's earning potential. Research shows that college graduates make more money in a lifetime than non-college graduates.
      _____ , for
      _____ .
   D. This new diet won't help me lose weight. No diet I've ever tried has worked.
      _____ .
      So, _____ .

E. Sexually promiscuous people have a greater chance of getting AIDS than people who aren't sexually promiscuous. AIDS is a sexually transmitted disease. People who use condoms run less risk of getting AIDS than people who don't.

_____ ,

because _____

and _____ .

F. It's no business of the government if a person wants to commit suicide. Laws prohibiting suicide are indefensible. Whether or not people should be able to inflict harm on themselves is strictly their own affair.

_____ ,

because _____ ,

since _____ .

G. Parents need to be careful about imposing punishment and bestowing rewards on children. Too quickly giving rewards can set up the parent for blackmail. Deferring punishment can be a sign of weakness.

_____ ,

for _____

and _____ .

H. There are no natural rights. Social anthropologists report that the rights accorded persons vary from society to society and even within a society over a period of time.

Since _____ ,

as _____ ,

it follows that _____ .

I. When the civil-rights movement began in the early 1950s, the South had a lock on leadership positions in the U.S. Senate. That made Congressional leadership in the assault on racial discrimination highly improbable. Whatever progress blacks, and women for that matter, have made in attaining equal rights with white males, they can thank the Supreme Court for. Without the resolute backing of the Supreme Court, there could have been no civil-rights revolution as we know it.

_____ ,

because _____ ,

because, _____ ,

because _____ .

Precisely Defining the Main Idea

Once you have isolated the main idea, it is important to define it exactly. In general, this calls for an inspection of the breadth of the author's claim — how broad or limited it is — which requires an examination of the language used. Since we will consider the language of argument elsewhere, we will confine our remarks here to the role played by various kinds of words and phrases in defining the main idea.

Quantifiers   _Quantifiers are words or phrases that indicate how many of something the author has in mind._ We have many words that indicate _universal_ quantification: *all, every, no, never, any, whatever, wherever, whenever,* and the like. Similarly, we have words that indicate *partial* quantification or some number less than all: *some, a few, many, most, several, a lot, sometimes, occasionally,* and statistical references, such as *forty-four percent* or *one-third.* There is obviously a big difference in the sweep of the claims:

> *Some* trees are deciduous.
>
> *All* trees are deciduous

> or

> *Many* citizens are voters.
>
> *Every* citizen is a voter.

> or

> The United States and the Soviet Union have *sometimes* been allies.
>
> The United States and the Soviet Union have *never* been allies.

The first statement of each pair is true, the second is false. Overlooking the quantitative clues authors provide, we can misinterpret the breadth of their main idea. The same applies to qualifiers and intensifiers.

Qualifiers *Qualifiers are terms that specify the degree of force or probability.* Among the most common qualifiers are: *maybe, perhaps, possibly, likely, probably, there's a chance, typically, usually, generally,* and *may* (which, incidentally, indicates more likelihood than *might*).

Intensifiers *Intensifiers are terms used to express something that we believe is incontrovertible.* Among the most common: *surely, certainly, no doubt, obviously, simply, undoubtedly, obviously, unquestionably.* Again, there is a big difference in the claims:

1. The student has a 3.5 GPA. Therefore, she will *surely* get into the medical school of her choice.
2. The student has a 3.5 GPA. Therefore, she will *probably* get into the medical school of her choice.
3. The student has a 3.5 GPA. Therefore, she *may* get into the medical school of her choice.

The conclusion of the first argument is the least cautious, and is not acceptable, because not all students with a 3.5 GPA get into the medical school of their choice. The conclusion of the second argument is more cautious, but is still too strong, since many such students fail to be admitted to their preferred medical school. The conclusion of the third argument is most guarded and is supported by the evidence.

Descriptive Phrases Just as important as the preceding terms are descriptive words and phrases that circumscribe the author's conclusion. No listing of these is possible, but a few examples should give you an idea of what to look for.

Most American professional racing cars have stochastic fuel-injection.

Notice that in this statement the author refers to *"American professional racing"* cars. So it would be incorrect to apply the assertion to production-line vehicles or to non-American racing cars. And, of course, the author further qualifies the statement with "most."

Of all the major brands available in the greater metropolitan area, none offers you faster pain relief than Formula Y.

Although ads like this sound rather boastful, their precise claims are rather modest. First, this ad's claim is expressly restricted to a comparison of *"major brands available,"* and within a specific geographical area at that ("the greater metropolitan area"). Second, the ad does not assert that Formula Y provides the fastest pain relief, only relief *as fast as* the other major brands available. Third, the ad makes no claim about the degree or duration of pain relief, only how fast the product will take effect compared to other major brands. And, of course, it says nothing about the actual take-effect time, only that none of the others takes effect more quickly.

EXERCISES ON PRECISELY DEFINING THE MAIN IDEA*

1. Identify the quantifier, qualifier, or intensifier in the following statements.
   A. Some Americans are highly materialistic.
   B. There might be a tax increase next year.
   C. There's a considerable difference between knowing something and knowing that you know it.
   D. The clerk, perhaps, can tell you where the odd sizes are located.
   E. A lot of citizens don't vote.
   F. The United States must reduce its trade imbalance.
2. Write a stronger version of sentence A, then an even stronger version.
   Strong version: _____
   Stronger still: _____
3. For sentence B, substitute:
   An equivalent word for "might":
   A stronger word for "might":
4. For sentence C, substitute:
   A weaker word for "considerable":
   A synonym for "considerable":
5. Which of the following words are equivalent to "perhaps" in sentence D?
   might, could, probably, possibly, likely, maybe, undoubtedly, surely
6. Write two equivalent versions of sentence F that do not use "must."

7. Write a stronger, then a weaker, version of sentence E by substituting appropriate words for "A lot."
8. Each of the following passages contains more than one argument. Identify the main and subarguments.
   A. Capital punishment should be abolished because it does not deter crime. This was recently demonstrated by an exhaustive university study.
   B. Capital punishment should be legalized because it does deter crime, as many would-be murderers have themselves said. Whatever deters crime should be legal.
   C. The longer elected officials hold office the more likely it is that they will become corrupt. The reason is that power corrupts and over time officeholders get more and more powerful. Therefore, there should be a limit to the number of years any elected official may serve.
   D. Smoking can kill. But it's also expensive and offensive. Statistics show that nonsmokers increasingly object to the smoker's violation of their right to breathe smoke-free air. So, the prudent person shouldn't smoke.
   E. Humans are fallible, so they will make mistakes. Since mistakes are unintentional, it's clear that human fallibility often mocks our best laid plans.
   F. None of us left to ourselves can attain all we desire. That's why societies are necessary. But societies cannot survive without compromise and cooperation. Hence, each of us must strive to see things from the other fellow's viewpoint.
   G. In a democracy, the people exercise government in person. But in a republic, they express their will through representatives. Clearly, then, the United States is a republic. The only way to preserve and enrich democratic freedoms in a republic is for the people to be educated enough to select representatives wisely. There's no question, therefore, that Americans ought to take education most seriously.

MODULE 1.3

THE LOGICAL FUNCTION OF PREMISES

Premises, as we know, are the elements in an argument that provide evidence for the conclusion. When we locate the argument's conclusion or main idea, we indirectly isolate its premises. So, in discussing conclusions, we have indirectly addressed premises as well. Still, it will prove helpful to make some general observations about how premises function in argument.

There are many types of premises. We have already met some premises that are the conclusions of subarguments. Premises may be principles, rules, or definitions that supposedly provide a basis for the conclusion. They can take the form of personal observation, expert testimony, or common knowledge.

In theory, premises can function to provide a basis for a conclusion in one of two main ways: as data or warrant. It is not always easy, or necessary for that matter, to distinguish these functions clearly in arguments. Indeed, it is not uncommon for reasonable people to disagree on the precise logical function of a premise in a particular argument, owing to the ambiguity embedded in the argument's logical structure. Still, the better you understand how premises *can* function, the keener a student of argument you will be. With that in mind, let's briefly illustrate these two logical functions of premises.

We'll begin with this simple argument, containing two premises (italicized):

> *Frank dropped a course last semester. He also failed to maintain a GPA of 2.5.* Therefore, **Frank will be placed on probation.**

The premises here function as data offered in support of the conclusion. Let's take *data* **to mean the evidence, assumptions, or assertions that provide a basis for a conclusion.**

But how does the conclusion of this argument follow from these two pieces of data? How is it that Frank will be placed on probation since he dropped a course and did not maintain a 2.5 GPA? There is nothing in the *stated* premises that makes the conclusion either logically necessary or probable. Yet, obviously, the arguer believes that the data do lead logically to the conclusion. Why does she think that?

Questions like these, in effect, are asking for an additional premise that expresses how the arguer moved logically from the data to the conclusion. In other words, a warrant. You're probably familiar with the term *warrant* in the context of *license* or *permit*. A search warrant, for example, is a legal license or permit for a search. If you insist that the authorities who want to search your home produce a search warrant, you are asking them for proof of legal authorization to conduct such a search. **When a premise functions as a warrant, it is stating the grounds on which a move from data to conclusion is thought to be permitted or authorized, logically speaking.**

A warrant-functioning premise, then, shows how the arguer arrived at the conclusion from the data. Usually a warrant states a general, lawlike relationship between data and conclusion, as in this example:

All humans are mortals.

I am a human.
_____
Therefore, I am a mortal.

The premise "All humans are mortals" expresses a lawlike relationship between humans and mortals and, therefore, between datum ("I am a human") and conclusion ("I am a mortal").

It is important to think very carefully about an argument's warrant because it shows how the conclusion follows from the data presented. What makes warrants especially tricky is that they are usually implied rather than stated. In order to evaluate a person's reasoning and argument, we need to actually state the warrant.

How might the warrant be stated in the argument concerning placing Frank on probation? One way would be to say:

(Dropping a course and not maintaining a 2.5 GPA are sufficient grounds for probation.)

Notice that we placed the warrant in parentheses because it was implied, but not stated. Of course, we could state the warrant alternatively, as for example:

(Any student who drops a course and doesn't maintain a 2.5 GPA will be placed on probation.)

or

(If a student drops a course and doesn't maintain a 2.5 GPA, he or she will be placed on probation.)

However stated, the warrant makes the arguer's line of reasoning explicit. It shows how and why she drew the inference she did. Indeed, we can portray the arguer's reasoning and argument as follows, where (D) stands for data, (C) for conclusion, (W) for warrant, and an arrow (→) for the direction of the reasoning:[1]

(D) Frank dropped a course last semester.

(D) Frank failed to maintain a GPA of 2.5.

→ **(C)** Frank will be placed on probation.

    (W) (Dropping a course and failing to maintain a 2.5 GPA are sufficient grounds for probation.)

Of course, sometimes it is not the warrant, but the datum that is unexpressed. For example, suppose someone formulated the argument this way:

(W) Dropping a course and failing to maintain a 2.5 GPA are sufficient grounds for probation.

→ Frank will be placed on probation.

The clear implications here are the *data* that Frank dropped a course and failed to maintain a 2.5 GPA. These data represent unexpressed premises in the argument.

One reason authors so often imply, rather than state premises, is that the premise is too obvious or uncontroversial to state. For example, you say to a friend:

Joan must be a good student. After all, she was recently admitted to Harvard Medical School.

---

[1]See Stephen Toulmin, *The Uses of Argument* (Cambridge, England: Cambridge University Press, 1958).

Your implied warrant is obvious: "Only good students get admitted to Harvard," or something like that. So evident is the warrant that your friend unconsciously comprehends it. That is why he does not respond: "I don't follow you. Why do you say Joan's a good student simply because she got into Harvard?" (People who have to ask questions like this rarely have acquaintances going to Harvard!)

Other times, however, premises are implied not because they are obvious and incontestable, but because the arguer may not be fully aware of them. Take, for example, an argument that was recently expressed by a student in a classroom:

Capital punishment should be legalized because it deters crime.

Upon hearing this argument, another student asked the arguer: "Do you really believe that any punishment that deters crime should be legalized? For example, if maiming deterred theft, ought we maim thieves? If burning at the stake deterred arson, ought we burn arsonists at the stake?" The first student bristled up. "I never said that!" he protested, "You're twisting my words!" In fact, his warrant was precisely what his antagonist said it was. Thus:

(D) Capital punishment deters crime.   →   **(C)** Capital punishment should be legalized.

(W) (If a punishment deters crime, it should be legalized.)

The arguer did not fully realize what he was implicitly assuming until his audience pointed it out to him—and then he wasn't sure if he accepted his own assumption.

Beyond this, arguers sometimes intentionally suppress premises because, if stated, the premises would render the argument clearly specious. Most advertising is like this. Consider the ad that would have us use a product or vote for a candidate because some celebrity endorsement implies that we should buy, use, or vote for whatever or whomever the celebrity endorses. Thus:

(D) Famous Celebrity endorses product.   →   **(C)** You should buy product.

(W) (Whatever Famous Celebrity endorses, you should buy.)

Perhaps you are beginning to sense that unexpressed premises call for special attention. You are right, they do, especially in argumentative essays. Before we can evaluate the reasoning behind an argument, we need to make implied premises explicit.

IN BRIEF   The flaws in many arguments reside in premises that are implied, not stated.

When arguers anticipate questions about the truth of their premises, or wish to establish a premise as uncontroversial, they offer *backing* for it. **Backing is premise support.** We can illustrate backing by modifying our original example about Frank as follows:

> Frank dropped a course last semester. He also failed to maintain a GPA of 2.5. *His official transcript shows that he earned a 2.2.* Therefore, Frank will be placed on probation.

The italicized statement provides evidence or support for the assertion that Frank did not maintain a 2.5. Thus, letting (B) stand for backing, we can represent the argument as follows:

(D) Frank dropped a course last semester.

(D) Frank failed to maintain a GPA of 2.5. $\rightarrow$ (C) Frank will be placed on probation.

(B) His official transcript shows that
     he earned a 2.2.

    (W) (Dropping a course and failing to maintain a
     2.5 GPA are sufficient grounds for probation.)

Notice that (B), together with the (D) it supports, forms a miniargument within the main argument.

Thus, a statement expressing premise support can be considered a premise of a mini- or subargument for a transitional conclusion (which, in this case, is "Frank failed to maintain a GPA of 2.5.") As such, it will always function as datum or warrant. Here the backing ("His official transcript shows that he earned a 2.2.") is a datum.

IN BRIEF   Premises function as either datum or warrant. In either case, the premise of an argument may be implied rather than expressed. Stating its missing premises is an important part of understanding an argument.

MODULE 1.4

VALID AND INVALID ARGUMENTS

Logicians ordinarily distinguish between two complementary modes of reasoning, deductive and inductive. *A deductive argument is one whose premises are intended to provide conclusive support for the conclusion.* In contrast, *an inductive argument is one whose premises are intended to provide some, but not conclusive, support for the conclusion.* For example, suppose the treasurer of a club presents this argument:

> Every member present has paid her dues.
>
> Tess is a member who's present.
> _____
> Therefore, Tess has paid her dues.

Or this one:

> If a club member has paid dues, she can vote.
>
> Tess has paid her dues.
> _____
> Therefore, Tess can vote.

Most likely the treasurer is regarding the premises of these arguments as providing conclusive support for her conclusions. In other words, it is hard to imagine that she would welcome, in the case of the first argument, the following interpretation:

> **Even if every member present has paid her dues and Tess is a member who is present, Tess may** *not* **have paid her dues.**

So these two arguments are examples of *deductive* arguments. On the other hand, let's say she offered these arguments:

> Tess hasn't missed a meeting all year.
> _____
> So, she'll be present at the next meeting.

or

> At this time last year we'd met one-third of our new membership goal.
>
> This year we've met 90 percent.
> _____
> Therefore, this year we'll meet our membership goals sooner than we did last year.

In these arguments, the treasurer most probably would regard her premises as providing *something less than conclusive support* for her conclusion. Thus, it is possible that Tess may *not* be present at the next meeting and that the club may *not* attain its goal any sooner than it did the previous year. Of course, the treasurer would not think either of these outcomes is likely, and she would probably say that her premises were not intended to rule out these possibilities. By this account, then, these two arguments are inductive.

In the preceding examples, the difference between deductive and inductive arguments was relatively obvious. But many of the arguments that we read and write cannot be so easily distinguished. Consider, for example, this argument:

The only trains that stop at this station are express trains.
_____
So, I guess all express trains stop at this station.

Is this a deductive or inductive argument? Does the arguer regard the premise ("The only trains that stop at this station are express trains") as conclusive evidence for accepting his conclusion ("I guess all express trains stop at this station")? Or does he regard the premises as providing something less than conclusive support for the conclusion? Without asking him, we cannot be sure. In fact, if he were asked, he might not even know exactly what relationship he is intending to establish between premise and conclusion.

Although we cannot be sure of the arguer's intentions, we can definitely say that *at best* the stated premise provides some, but not conclusive, support for the conclusion. Even if only express trains stop at the station, it does not mean that *all* express trains do. Since the premise does not rule out this possibility, it cannot be providing conclusive support for the conclusion, but something less than that.

Fortunately, in everyday arguments, we rarely need to draw the often difficult to discern distinction between deductive and inductive arguments. But basic, good argument analysis always requires an effort to determine whether the premises provide conclusive or something less than conclusive support for a conclusion.

A valid argument is one whose premises do provide conclusive support for the conclusion. In a valid argument, then, it is logically impossible to deny the argument's conclusion, while, at the same time, accepting its premises. In other words, the truth of the premises logically guarantees or provides absolutely conclusive support for the conclusion.

Here's an example of a valid argument:

All club members are licensed drivers.

Tess is a club member.
_____
Therefore, Tess is a licensed driver.

To call this argument valid simply means that on the assumption that the premises are true, the conclusion necessarily follows. The truth of the premises, in other words, logically guarantees the truth of the conclusion. We can imagine no additional facts, events, or conditions that, while being consistent with these premises, could deny this conclusion.

It is important to realize that **the validity of an argument does *not* depend on the actual truth of the premises.** Suppose, for example, that

P is greater than Q, and

Q is greater than R.

What would you infer about the relationship between P and R? Clearly, P must be greater than R. But you do not know whether the premises are actually true. In fact, you do not even know what P, Q, and R stand for—you do not need to. *If* P is greater than Q, and *if* Q is greater than R, conclusive support is provided for saying P must be greater than R.

Since the validity of an argument does not depend on the actual truth of its premises, it is possible for a valid argument to contain false premises, as in:

All Supreme Court justices are females.

Madonna is a Supreme Court justice.

Therefore, Madonna is a female.

Even though its premises are absurd, this argument is valid. Why? Because, logically speaking, it is impossible to accept its premises while rejecting its conclusion.

IN BRIEF   To test the validity of an argument, ask yourself: "Can I logically assert the premises and deny the conclusion without contradicting myself?" If you cannot, the premises provide absolutely conclusive support for the conclusion—which means the argument is valid.

Even though the preceding argument is valid, you would not likely be persuaded by it because its premises are obviously untrue. Thus, a valid argument is not necessarily a *sound* argument. For a valid argument to be sound, it must contain true or acceptable premises, as in:

All mothers are females.

The "First Lady," Mrs. Bush, is a mother.

Therefore, the "First Lady," Mrs. Bush, is a female.

This argument is valid—its premises provide conclusive support for its conclusion. It also contains true premises. Therefore, this argument is not only valid, it is sound. So, we use the word *sound* to refer to valid arguments that contain true premises.

IN BRIEF   A valid argument is not necessarily a sound argument. If a valid argument contains one or more false premises, it is unsound. Only if a valid argument has true premises is it sound. Conversely, a sound argument is a valid argument that has true premises.

Let's rejoin our club treasurer as she presents the following argument:

Tess didn't miss a single meeting last year.

And she hasn't missed one so far this year.

So, I'm confident that she'll show up for this meeting.

The premises of this argument provide something less than conclusive support for the conclusion. So the argument is invalid. But that does not mean the treasurer does not know what she is talking about or that her argument has no merit. It only means that Tess may not show up, even though she attended all of last year's meetings and all of this year's so far. This is a possibility, but an unlikely one. It is far more likely that Tess *will* turn up. In other words, assuming their truth, the premises provide solid grounds — although, admittedly, not absolutely conclusive ones — for the treasurer's conclusion.

So, although the argument is invalid, it is still relatively strong. The premises lend considerable weight to the conclusion. In other words, the conclusion is unlikely to be false, given the premises. **The defining feature of a strong (as opposed to a *valid*) argument, then, is that if the premises are assumed true, the conclusion is unlikely to be false.**

Clearly, *strong* is a term that admits of degrees. Thus, invalid arguments can be spoken of as *relatively* strong or weak depending on how likely the premises show the conclusion to be. For example, if the treasurer received a call from Tess saying she was on her way, that would greatly strengthen the argument. On the other hand, if earlier in the day Tess was called away by a medical emergency, that could very well weaken it.

Consider the following argument:

The first apple I withdrew from this basket containing 500 apples was sour.

The second apple I withdrew also was sour.

Therefore, most of the apples in this basket are sour.

This is a relatively weak argument because the premises by themselves do not show the conclusion to be likely. As the number of sour apples in the sample increased, so too would the strength of the argument. So, whereas *valid* is an absolute term, *strong* and *weak* are relative terms. An argument is either valid or not. If it is invalid, it may be relatively strong or weak depending on how likely the premises show the conclusion to be.

IN BRIEF   Whereas *valid* is an absolute term, *strong* and *weak* are relative terms. An argument is either valid or not, and no one argument is "more valid" than another. If an argument is invalid, it is relatively strong or weak depending on how likely the premises show the conclusion to be.

Recall that the actual truth of the premises has no bearing on the validity of an argument. Similarly, the actual truth of the premises of an *invalid* argument has no bearing on the argument's relative strength. Consider, for example, this argument expressed in symbols:

Almost all X are Y.

Z is X.

Therefore, Z is probably Y.

This is a very strong argument, regardless of what X, Y, and Z stand for and the actual truth of the premises. By the same token, an invalid argument can have *true* premises but be weak. Thus, even if it is true that two apples from a basket of 500 are sour, it does not provide much support for concluding that most of the remaining 498 are sour.

Earlier, we distinguished between *valid* and *sound,* we now need a term to refer to arguments that are not only strong but also have true premises — that term is *justified.* Thus, *a strong argument that has true premises is justified.* For an invalid argument to be justified, it must have true premises that are strong enough to make its conclusion more likely true than false. An invalid argument that contains one or more untrue premises or premises that are not strong enough to support the conclusion is unjustified.

We can summarize the key terms and concepts in the preceding analysis as follows:

1. *A valid argument is one whose premises, when assumed true, provide conclusive support for its conclusion.*
2. *A sound argument is a valid argument with actually true premises.*
3. *The terms* sound *and* unsound *should be used only with reference to valid arguments.*

In contrast:

1. *An invalid argument is one whose premises provide some, but not conclusive, support for the conclusion.*
2. *A relatively strong argument is an argument whose premises, when assumed true, make it unlikely that the conclusion is false.*
3. *A justified argument is a strong argument with actually true premises.*
4. *The terms* justified *and* unjustified *should be used only with reference to invalid arguments.*

EXERCISES ON VALID AND INVALID ARGUMENTS*

1. Are the following arguments valid or invalid? If valid, say whether they are sound. If invalid, explain why you do or do not think they are justified.

Sample: All those who smoke have healthy lungs. Wally's lungs must be healthy because he's a chain smoker.

Analysis: Valid, because it's logically impossible to assert the premises and deny the conclusion. If we accept that smokers have healthy lungs, and that Wally is a chain smoker, then it necessarily follows that Wally's lungs are healthy. Of course, one of the premises is false, but that has no bearing on the validity of this argument. The premises do provide conclusive support for the conclusion. Unsound, because one of the premises ("All those who smoke have healthy lungs") is untrue.

Sample: Smokers run serious health risks. Wally runs serious health risks. It follows that Wally is a smoker.

Analysis: Invalid, because it is possible that Wally runs serious health risks — for example, by drunk driving or eating lots of fatty foods and never exercising — and yet not smoke. Even if this argument's premises are true, they provide no direct evidence for saying Wally is a smoker. So this is a weak, unjustified argument.

A. The right to life is irrevocable. What's irrevocable should be safeguarded by law. Thus, there should be laws guaranteeing the right to life.

B. Some businesspeople are philanthropists, and some philanthropists are politicians. It follows that some politicians are businesspeople.

C. Because musicians don't use drugs, and only drug users are poor and uneducated, no musician is poor and uneducated.

D. Sally can't be qualified because, if she were, she should have passed the test, but she didn't.

E. The battery must be faulty because the ignition works, and either the battery or the ignition is faulty.

F. Surely it has rained, because if it hadn't, the streets wouldn't be wet, but they are.

G. If pornography threatens society, it should be strictly controlled. But pornography doesn't threaten society. So, it shouldn't be controlled.

H. Some fruits are green. Some fruits are apples. Therefore, some fruits are green apples.

2. For the purposes of this exercise, assume that the premises of each of the following arguments are true. Given that assumption, do you think that the conclusion supported by the premises is: (A) true beyond a reasonable doubt, (B) probably true, (C) possibly true or false?

A. Professor Smith isn't in class. So, he is in his office.

B. On five previous math tests, Louise has averaged a B. So she fully expects to get a B on the next one.

C. There won't be a female umpire in the major leagues next season since there hasn't ever been one.

D. We can conclude that oxygen was present in the building for the simple reason that the building burned.

E. I'm sure I'll like the next Disney production. I've never seen one yet that I haven't enjoyed.

F. There are far more male physicists than female. It follows that there's something about females that leaves them ill-equipped to do physics.

G. Even though Killer said he was too sick to attend football practice, Merlin says he saw him at the mall with his girlfriend during practice. "They were having a good old time." When I asked Merlin how Killer looked he said, "Never better." Killer lied to us about being too sick to practice.

H. The Nielsens notice that the more their kids watch TV, the worse grades they get. The less they watch TV, the better their grades. The Nielsens conclude that the kids' grades are being influenced by their TV habits.

I. I read a sober analysis of the stock market in the *Wall Street Journal* today. It seconds the warning that a lot of brokerage houses are issuing: Avoid stocks right now. What's more, the federal reserve's planning to raise interest rates, which will dry up a lot of the money businesses need to expand and do research. It's pretty clear, I think, that this isn't a good time to invest in the market.

3. For any of the above conclusions that you answered B or C, state two additional facts that would have the effect of strengthening the argument, then state two additional facts that would weaken it.

MODULE 1.5

EVALUATING ARGUMENTS

Presumably, when we argue, we wish to argue well. When we read or hear arguments such as Pam Wentworth's, we want to be able to distinguish strong ones from weak ones. In short, as writers and readers, we want arguments that are acceptable.

When is an argument acceptable? The preceding discussion clearly implies that an argument is acceptable when, in the case of a valid argument, it is sound; or when, in the case of an invalid argument, it is justified. While acceptable in theory, these criteria raise some practical difficulties owing to their reliance on truth and, in the case of invalid arguments, relativity of inductive strength.

For example, we know that only arguments with true premises can be sound or justified, but are we to require *absolute* truth of arguments? If so, then we are effectively branding many arguments unacceptable (that is, unsound or unjustified) because the absolute truth of a statement is achingly difficult to establish. It is a safe bet that very few arguments could pass muster if they were required to contain premises that were true in a strict or absolute sensc. If, on the other hand, we require something less than absolute truth of arguments, then inevitably we are drawn into the problems associated with "relative strength."

Furthermore, we have learned that a whole category of arguments needs to be justified before they are, logically speaking, acceptable. Only if such arguments have true premises sufficient to support their conclusions are they justified. But how much support is "sufficient"? Clearly, we cannot say for sure. It depends on the particular argument. Some conclusions will require more support than others.

These problems suggest that the truth and relative-strength tests for arguments need some amendment to be of more practical use. The three question-strategies that follow, then, are an informal application of what is implied in the notions of soundness and justifiedness.

Testing for Acceptability: Three Basic Questions

Acceptable arguments have premises that are *acceptable* and *relevant*, and *provide adequate support* for their conclusion.[2] A solid, basic test of any argument, therefore, consists of asking three questions: (1) Are the premises acceptable? (2) Are the premises relevant? (3) Do the premises provide adequate support for the conclusion? If the answer is "Yes" to *each* of these questions, the argument is acceptable; if the answer is "No" to *any one* of them, it is unacceptable.

Question 1: Are the premises acceptable?   We are using "acceptable" instead of "true" for two reasons. One reason relates to the aforementioned philosophical problems embedded in the notion of truth. A second reason deals with the social environment of most arguments.

When we argue, we use what we purport to know (premises) as a basis for proving something (conclusion). We, in effect, say to our audience: "If you accept my premises, logically you must accept my conclusion." The audience may accept our premises, then examine the logical quality of our argument — that is, see whether the conclusion does logically follow the premises. Or, they can question the premises by asking: "What if there are good reasons to believe that the premises, in fact, aren't acceptable?" In either case, agreement on the conclusion requires acceptance of the premises.

Under what conditions are premises acceptable? The following guidelines should prove useful in the initial stages of argument evaluation. *In general,* the following kinds of premise statements are acceptable.[3]

1. *Statements of common knowledge.*
   Examples: "AIDS is a sexually communicable disease," "Humans need oxygen to survive," "Dinosaurs once roamed the earth."
2. *Statements invoking experts whose views represent a consensus of expert opinion.*
   Example: "Smoking is hazardous to one's health," when the opinion of the Surgeon General, for example, is used as backing for that statement.

---

[2]See Trudy Govier, *A Practical Study of Argument* (Belmont, CA: Wadsworth Publishing, 1985).
[3]See Edward Damer, *Attacking Faulty Reasoning,* 2nd ed. (Belmont CA: Wadsworth Publishing, 1987), pp. 11–15.

3. *Statements of observations made under satisfactory conditions and by reliable observers.*
   Example: "The more accurately we determine an electron's location, the more uncertain we are of its velocity." This statement reflects the findings of physicists based upon carefully controlled experiments.
4. *Statements of reasonable assumption or based upon reasonable assumption.*
   Examples: "Most people wish to live a long life," "A person with motive, means, and opportunity is a prime suspect in a crime."
5. *Statements of first-person experience.*
   Examples: "I have a toothache," "This milk tastes sour to me," "I believe that a depression is just around the corner." Note that what is acceptable in the last statement is that the speaker holds that belief, and *not* that a depression is, in fact, imminent.
6. *Statements that are true on grounds of word meaning.*
   Examples: "Humans are mammals," or "A triangle has three sides."
7. *Statements whose truth is logically necessary.*
   Example: "The flower is either a rose or not a rose," "This plane, curved figure cannot be both a circle and a noncircle."
8. *Statements that are integral parts of a deductive system, such as geometry.*
   Example: "The sum of the interior angles of a triangle is equal to two right angles."

These guidelines suggest a complementary list of statements that are *not* acceptable as premises:

1. *Statements that flout common knowledge.*
   Example: "AIDS can be transmitted through a handshake."
2. *Statements invoking dubious experts or questionable opinion.*
   Example: "Vitamin C can cure cancer," when the opinion of, say, some nutritionist is given as backing for that statement. Note that it is not the fact that the nutritionist makes the claim or holds the belief that is being rejected. Rather, it is the authoritative grounds for the claim, thus the claim itself, that are unacceptable. Unacceptable because the weight of expert opinion either rejects or seriously questions the belief.
3. *Statements of observations made under unsatisfactory conditions or by unreliable observers.*
   Example: "I have strep throat," when that claim is based on no more than my experiencing a sore throat. Only clinical observation—a throat culture—can determine the presence of strep.
4. *Statements of or based upon dubious assumptions.*
   Examples: "Women make better nurses than men," or "Men make better engineers than women."
5. *Statements as disputable as the conclusions they allegedly support.*
   Examples: "Abortion is murder" as a reason for prohibiting abortion, "Ancient cave drawings reflect familiarity with acrodynamic principles" as a reason for asserting that the earth was once visited by astronaut gods.

6. *Statements that clash with other statements in the same argument.*
   Example: In the summer of 1981, after Israel's Prime Minister Menachem Begin ordered the bombing of Beirut, Lebanon, the United States decided to withhold shipment of F-16 fighter planes to Israel. Defending the administration's decision, Deputy Secretary of State William Clark said: "Mr. Begin is without question making it difficult to assist Israel. Our commitment is not to Mr. Begin but to the nation he represents." But if the U.S. commitment was to Israel, why should any action of Begin's have made it difficult to assist Israel? Clark's are conflicting statements.

7. *Statements that are ambiguous, vague, self-contradictory, or otherwise unintelligible.*
   Example: "This two-day seminar will open you to the wonders of the contemporary experience of modern High-Tech Serendipity Meditation, as your seminar leader and originator of the High-Tech Serendipity Meditation Experience personally conducts this expansive program, demonstrating the power and potential of this contemporary meditative technology."

The forthcoming chapters will deepen your understanding of these guidelines. At this point, it is enough for you to acquire general familiarity with the guidelines and gain a sensitivity to premise acceptability as an important criterion of good arguments.

Question 2: Are the premises relevant?   To see what premise relevancy involves, let's join a couple as they leave a supermarket after spending $150 in ten minutes on groceries. As they are pushing two cartfuls of groceries to their parked car, the disgruntled husband mutters to his wife: "Can you believe it? A 150 bucks in ten minutes! I'm telling you, inflation is out of control."

The husband reasons as follows:

(D) We spent $150 in ten minutes on groceries. $\rightarrow$ (C) Inflation is
out of control.

Now, the datum is acceptable. The couple did, in fact, spend $150 on groceries in ten minutes. But it is irrelevant to the conclusion, because inflation is not measured by how long it takes to spend money, but rather by the money's purchasing power compared to some previous time. The husband should be comparing what they have just paid for their groceries with what they would have paid, say, three years before. If he did and discovered that the identical purchases would have cost perhaps twenty percent less, then he would have a relevant basis for his claim.

A *premise is relevant if it is the sort required to establish the point at issue.* Relevant premises support or provide reasons for accepting the conclusion. An irrelevant premise is disconnected from the conclusion it purports to demonstrate. It may appear to bear directly on the conclusion, or its proponent may believe it does; but in fact it is not the kind of evidence required to establish the point.

IN BRIEF   Since a premise is relevant only if it makes a difference to the conclusion, ask yourself: "Is this the sort of evidence needed to establish *this* conclusion?" If yes, the premise is relevant. If no, it is not.

Speaking of . . .

Argument Evaluation

Reading Critically

If (the reader of an argument) is a critical reader, he will ask two questions about a piece of argumentative prose: Is the evidence good? Is the reasoning (correct)? In answering the first question he will be helped immeasurably, of course, if he has read and thought about the subject, if he himself has some command of the facts and some acquaintance with the recognized authorities in the field. But without this knowledge he still can make (reliable) judgments about the evidence on which the writer's conclusions are based. He can see how well the writer's statements are substantiated. Some of them may be unsubstantiated, or practically so: "leading scientists agree," or "as psychologists tell us," or "the facts are well known," or "experiments have proven" is not equivalent to quoting scientists, psychologists, facts, or results of specific experiments. . . . The reader can also recognize the citing of irrelevant authority—Thomas Jefferson, for example, quoted to support an argument against national health insurance, or a famous chemist quoted on old age pensions, or a prominent businessman on modern art. Persons competent in one field are not necessarily authorities in another. Finally, a reader can make some judgment of the evidence by asking himself how much of it there is, and whether the writer seems to have minimized or ignored evidence on the other side.

   In answering the second question—Is the reasoning (correct)?—the reader is aided by a knowledge of logic. Frequently, while reading or listening to argument, one has an elusive sense of illogic in the thinking, a feeling of something's-wrong-but-I-can't-put-my-finger-on-it. A knowledge of two kinds of logical thinking called *induction* and *deduction*, and of the common errors in logic, called *fallacies*, makes it easier to detect weaknesses in reasoning and also to recognize and to practice sound reasoning.

(Newman and Genevieve Birk, *Understanding and Using English*)

Question 3: Do the premises provide adequate support for the conclusion?
Even though a premise is acceptable and relevant, it may not provide adequate
support for the conclusion. Recall the basket of apples. Although acceptable and
relevant, a sample of two sour apples is simply too small to support a conclusion that
most of the apples are sour. There are all sorts of ways that premises fail to support
their conclusions adequately. They may provide evidence based on too small or
unrepresentative samples, overlook significant details, or ignore contradictory
evidence.

EXERCISES ON EVALUATING ARGUMENTS

Portray the structure of the following arguments, using D, B, C, and W. Then
indicate whether you think the premises are relevant and acceptable and provide
sufficient grounds for the conclusion. In some cases, it may be necessary to qualify
your answer.

1. Since oxygen is necessary for life, it follows that humans cannot be deprived of
   oxygen very long without suffering irreparable brain damage.
2. Jeff must register for the draft because he's eighteen years old, and all
   eighteen-year-olds must register.
3. The current administration will cause a recession. It is, after all, Republican.
4. A study of prison inmates shows that most heroin addicts first used pot. Since
   smoking pot clearly leads to hard core drug addiction, many of today's young
   people will be tomorrow's heroin addicts, because they smoke pot.
5. A square has four sides and this polygon has four sides. It must be a square.
6. Inasmuch as Suzie is a child of a broken home, she'll surely develop emotional
   problems. Studies consistently show that children of broken homes tend to have
   more emotional problems than children of unbroken homes. Besides, Suzie's
   family has a history of mental illness.
7. "... the (Reagan) tax cuts will result in higher deficits than would have occurred
   had the Democrats stayed in office. The result will be blistering inflation. The
   federal deficits for the last half of the 1970s totalled $310 billion. Without the tax
   cuts, they would have totalled at least twice that amount for the first half of the
   1980s. With the cuts, they will probably total $800 billion for that period. ...." (John
   Pugsley, "The Deficits Deepen: An Economic Program Disintegrates." *Common
   Sense,* December 13, 1981. p. 4.)
8. "A recent five-year study at a major electronics company indicates that getting
   fired may have a lot to do with overreaching. Among 2,000 technical, sales
   and managerial employees who were followed during their first five years with
   the company, the 173 people who eventually were fired started out with much
   higher expectations of advancement than either the 200 people who left
   voluntarily or the people who remained. On a questionnaire given during their
   first week on the job, more than half the people who were fired within the

first two years ranked themselves among the top 5% of typical people in their job category. Only 38% of those who stayed with the company ranked themselves that highly." (Berkeley Rice, "Aspiring to a Fall." *Psychology Today,* March 1980. p. 25.)

IMPROVING PERFORMANCE

SUMMARY-TEST QUESTIONS FOR CHAPTER 1*

Each chapter of this text concludes with a battery of questions that are intended as both a summary and a test of the chapter's content. Try to answer the questions without referring to the chapter. If you get stuck, by all means consult the appropriate pages for material that will help you answer correctly. After you complete the summary-test, check your answers with those in the back of the textbook. If you miss questions, restudy the relevant part of the chapter.

1. "An argument is a group of sentences arranged in a particular sequence." True or False?
2. Which of the following is *not* a feature of an argument?
   A. true propositions
   B. true or false statements
   C. more than one proposition
   D. a logical relationship among the propositions
3. A proposition is (DEFINE) _____ .
   Another word for *proposition* is _____ .
4. Which of the following assertions is a proposition?
   A. Michael Dukakis won the 1988 presidential election.
   B. Two atoms of hydrogen and one oxygen combine to form water.
   C. The title of this textbook is *The Challenge of Argument.*
   D. Who can run for the U.S. Senate?
   E. The United States and Japan were allies during World War II.
   F. Most Germans desire a reunification of the two Germanys.
   G. Woody Allen wrote *Hamlet.*
5. Which of the following must a passage exhibit to be an argument?
   A. Premises that precede conclusions
   B. Coherent logical development from true premises to true conclusions
   C. Premises that are acceptable and relevant and that adequately support the conclusion
   D. Coherent logical development regardless of the acceptability, relevancy, or adequacy of the premises
6. "The concert has been delayed because the band hasn't arrived yet." Is this an argument? Explain.
7. True or False?
   A. The location of a statement in an argument determines whether it is a premise or conclusion.

B. The terms *premise* and *conclusion* are relative.

C. Conclusions always come after premises.

D. How a proposition functions in an argument determines whether it is a premise or conclusion.

E. Premises and conclusions are always introduced by signal words.

F. In an argument, the statement that immediately follows a word like *so* or *therefore* is the conclusion.

G. The terms *inference, judgment,* and *main idea* are rough equivalents for *conclusion.*

H. Both conclusion and premises can be considered an argument's assumptions.

I. Warrants function like logical "permits" or "authorization" to move from data to conclusion.

J. Unexpressed premises are not significant.

8. Which word does not belong with the others?

A. for

B. hence

C. insofar as

D. as

9. True or False?

A. "In a valid argument, it is logically impossible to deny a conclusion while, at the same time, accepting the premises."

B. Such an argument would have deductive certainty.

10. A sound argument

A. is always valid.

B. always has true premises.

C. may be invalid.

D. A and B

E. B and C

11. Can a valid argument have false premises? If so, illustrate. Can a relatively strong argument have false premises?

12. Which of the following terms does not belong with the others?

A. valid

B. logical certainty

C. logically necessary

D. logically justified

E. There are no exceptions; each of the preceding terms describes a good argument.

13. Is the following argument valid? Explain.

All mothers are females.

Jane is a female.

———————

Therefore, Jane is a mother.

14. An invalid argument is an argument (complete the sentence) ————————

————————————————————————————————— .

15. Match the terms in the left column with the proper ones in the right column.

A. intensifier
B. qualifier
C. deductive certainty
D. inconclusive support
E. argument
F. license or permit
G. conclusion
H. "after all"
 I. "as a result"
 J. universal quantifier

1. conclusion signal
2. "any"
3. invalid
4. main idea
5. valid
6. demonstration
7. warrant
8. premise signal
9. "perhaps"
10. "obviously"

16. What is the best way to identify an argument's conclusion?

17. Which of the numbered statements in the following argument is the main conclusion?

1

Since a college education increases one's earning potential, it follows,

2

since we'll continue to pursue a higher standard of living, that the demands for

3   4

college admissions will intensify, thereby raising the costs of a college education.

18. Identify the mini- or subargument embedded in the preceding argument.

19. Expressing the conclusion last, arrange the following statements into a coherent unit.

A. TV coverage, however, focuses on what's visually appealing and dramatic.
B. That's why a political campaign should be issue-oriented.
C. TV isn't an effective medium for conducting a political campaign.
D. Otherwise, there can't be an intelligent expression of the popular will.
E. A case in point, the 1988 presidential elections.
F. A democracy can only work if the people are informed.
G. Recall Dukakis riding atop an army tank and Bush nuzzling babies and flanked by police officers.

20. Several candidates for missing premise are presented for the following argument. Which is best? Why?

The Argument: Since critical thinking is fast becoming a part of a child's early education, we can expect the next generation of college students to be better readers and writers.

The Possible Warrants:

A. Critical thinking didn't use to be part of a child's early education.
B. Learning to think critically inevitably makes one a better reader and writer.
C. Some students' reading and writing improves as their critical thinking skills improve.
D. Improving critical thinking usually improves reading and writing.
E. College students who can read and write well can be expected to have good critical thinking skills.

21. True or False?
    A. A good argument may be invalid.
    B. An invalid argument may be justified.
    C. A valid argument is always a sound argument.
    D. An argument with an unacceptable premise may be valid.
    E. An argument with an irrelevant premise can never be acceptable.
    F. A justified argument always has acceptable and relevant premises that provide adequate grounds for the conclusion.
    G. A sound argument always has acceptable and relevant premises that provide adequate grounds for the conclusion.
22. Evaluate the following arguments in terms of: A. *unacceptable premise,* B. *irrelevant premise,* C. *inadequate premise for establishing the conclusion.* Indicate all that apply. *Choose D if the argument is acceptable.*
    A. All apples are fruits and some fruits are sweet. It follows that at least some apples are sweet.

    B. Many teenage marriages end in divorce.

       Jim and Tammy, who recently married, are teenagers.
       _____

       Thus, Jim and Tammy's marriage will end in divorce.

    C. Since females usually make better elementary teachers than do males, Wendy probably will make a better elementary teacher than will Harry.

    D. All humans are mortal.

       The creature standing before me is mortal.
       _____

       So, surely the creature standing before me must be a human.

    E. Most people support capital punishment. So, despite what some say, capital punishment probably deters crime.
23. Construct (1) a valid argumernt, (2) an invalid argument, (3) a sound argument, (4) a justified argument. Which of the preceding arguments is/are acceptable?

CRITICAL THINKING APPLICATIONS

1. **From the propositions that follow the passage, select the one that represents the main idea.**
   Politicians are mainly concerned with their own survival. In contrast, artists are concerned with revealing truth. This means that artistic vision precedes political practice. Consider, for example, the age of industrialization in Western Europe. While politicians and governmental leaders were celebrating the triumph of the machine with laws designed to ensure its survival, painters, writers, and musicians were responding to and cataloguing the horrors ushered in by the Industrial Revolution.

    A. Artists are idealists, politicians pragmatists.

    B. Politicians aren't responsive to the needs of people.

    C. Artists would make good leaders.

    D. Political practice lags behind artistic vision.

    E. The Industrial Revolution was a dreadful time for the average person.

2. Since all dogs that I have ever known could bark, it follows that the next dog I will see can bark.

    Which of the following arguments most closely parallels the reasoning of the preceding argument?

    A. Since some dogs will chase a stick, it follows that the next dog I see will probably chase a stick.

    B. Every cat I've ever encountered has run when frightened. So, an animal that runs when frightened is probably a cat.

    C. Since all depressed people I've ever known were also alcoholics, there must be something in alcohol that depresses some people.

    D. Because every society has a version of the "Golden Rule," the idea of fair play must be innate in humans.

    E. Since I've never had fun on a blind date, I won't have fun on tonight's blind date.

3. Not everyone agreed with the U.S. military intervention in the Mid-East in the wake of Iraq's invasion of Kuwait in August of 1990. One party who opposed the U.S. military presence in Saudi Arabia asked: "Are we supposed to send in our troops every time a country gets invaded?"

    This question can be criticized because it

    A. assumes the United States should send in troops every time a country is invaded.

    B. substitutes emotion for reason.

    C. implies disloyalty to an action that was overwhelmingly popular.

    D. ignores the issue at hand.

    E. assumes the United States should *not* send in troops when a country is invaded.

4. If Pete comes to the restaurant, Warren will leave the restaurant. If Warren leaves the restaurant, either Ray or Sam will ask Aimee out. If Aimee is asked out by either Ray or Sam, and Warren leaves the restaurant, Aimee accepts. But if Aimee is asked out by either Ray or Steve, and Warren doesn't leave the restaurant, Aimee doesn't accept the date.

    If Warren does not leave the restaurant, which of the following propositions can be validly deduced from the information given?

    A. Ray asks Aimee out.

    B. Sam asks Aimee out.

    C. Aimee refuses to go out with either Ray or Sam.

    D. Pete doesn't come to the restaurant.

    E. Aimee leaves the restaurant.

5. Whenever some of the supervisors are present, and all of the clerks are pleasant, all of the customers are pleased.

    Some of the supervisors are present, but some of the customers are not pleased.

Which of the following conclusions can be validly deduced from these two statements?

A. Some of the supervisors are not present.
B. Some of the customers are pleased.
C. None of the clerks is pleasant.
D. All of the clerks are pleasant.
E. Some of the clerks are not pleasant.

6. "I recently bumped into a fellow who claimed he belonged to a unique club called 'Liars Unlimited.' When I asked him what was unique about the club, he said, 'You can't believe anything a club member says because we always lie.' 'Always?' I asked him. 'Absolutely,' he assured me. I told him that I found what he said intriguing, though I had no intention of believing it."

Which of the following best describes the author's reaction?

A. It was rather rude, since the fellow was really doing him a service by alerting him to a club full of liars.
B. It was paradoxical, because in discounting what the fellow said, he in effect relied on it.
C. It was understandable, because the fellow admitted that he always lied.
D. It was rash, because the fellow should have been given a chance to explain what he meant.
E. It was typical of how most people would respond to such a weird claim.

7. Crickets are usually heard in this part of town on summer evenings when the temperature is at least 75 degrees Fahrenheit. No crickets can be heard tonight.

Which of the following would logically complete an argument with the preceding premises?

 I. So, the temperature must be lower than 75 degrees.
 II. So, the temperature probably is lower than 75 degrees.
 III. So, there are no crickets in this part of town.

A. I only
B. II only
C. III only
D. I and III only
E. II and III only

8. The principal of a high school reports to the school board that there are far fewer pregnancies and incidences of venereal disease among students who take Sex Education 101 than among students who don't take that course. The board concludes that the best way to keep its students from getting pregnant or contracting venereal disease is to have them take the course.

The board's conclusion is based on which of the following warrants?

 I. The students from the course who were sampled didn't get pregnant or contract a venereal disease.
 II. All high school students should be required to take a sex education course.
 III. Taking the course mainly accounts for the differences in the pregnancy and venereal disease rates.

A. I only
B. II only

    C. III only

    D. II and III only

    E. I, II, and III

9. Suppose the board decides to pursue these findings further and investigates the cases of fifty students who are either pregnant or who have a venereal disease. **Which of the following possible findings would weaken the original conclusion?**

    I. Some of the students did not take Sex Education 101.

    II. Some of the students did take Sex Education 101.

    III. Some of the students are currently taking Sex Education 101.

    A. I only

    B. II only

    C. I and II only

    D. II and III only

    E. I, II, and III

10. All books on philosophy are kept in the Social Science room.

    No novels are kept in the Social Science room.

    Every book kept in the Social Science room is catalogued.

    If all the preceding propositions are true, which of the following must also be true?

    A. All the books in the Social Science room deal with philosophy.

    B. No novels are philosophy books.

    C. Some philosophy books are catalogued.

    D. No books in the Social Science room are novels.

    E. All books on philosophy are catalogued.

11. Attorney: According to your father's will, the first male born to his first wife is the first in line to inherit his entire estate.

    Daughter: That's preposterous! My sister and I are my father's only children.

    Attorney: Indeed you are. And if you'd permit me to continue, you'd learn that your father left his entire estate to you.

    Daughter: I don't understand.

    The daughter is confused because she has misinterpreted the will to mean which of the following?

    I. Only sons can inherit the father's estate.

    II. Her father had more than one wife.

    III. Her father had more than one child.

    A. I only

    B. II only

    C. III only

    D. I and II

    E. I, II, and III

12. At the start of a tennis tournament, six contestants—Chris, Stefi, Boris, Martina, Jimmy, and Ivan—are to be ranked first (highest) through sixth (lowest), though not necessarily in that order. During the tournament, players can challenge only someone ranked immediately above or below them. Chris is ranked above Stefi. Jimmy is ranked above both Boris and Martina. Ivan is ranked two places above

Boris. And Chris is ranked either third or fourth. **Based on these assumptions, which of the following is a *possible* initial ranking from highest to lowest?**
   A. Jimmy, Boris, Ivan, Chris, Martina, Stefi
   B. Ivan, Stefi, Boris, Chris, Jimmy, Martina
   C. Ivan, Martina, Boris, Jimmy, Chris, Stefi
   D. Jimmy, Ivan, Chris, Boris, Martina, Stefi
   E. Jimmy, Ivan, Boris, Chris, Martina, Stefi
13. If, at the outset, Ivan is ranked first, then:
   A. Jimmy must be ranked second.
   B. Boris must be ranked second.
   C. Chris must be ranked third.
   D. Stefi must be ranked fifth.
   E. Martina must be ranked sixth.
14. If, at the outset, Chris is ranked third, then:
   A. Jimmy must be ranked first.
   B. Ivan must be ranked second.
   C. Stefi must be ranked fourth.
   D. Martina must be ranked fourth.
   E. Martina must be ranked sixth.
15. If, at the outset, Ivan is ranked third, and he makes the first challenge, whom could he *possibly* play in the first match?
   A. Chris and Boris only
   B. Chris and Martina only
   C. Boris and Jimmy only
   D. Martina and Jimmy only
   E. Chris, Boris, and Jimmy
16. If Chris makes the first challenge of the tournament, and it is against Boris, all of the following must be true *except:*
   A. Ivan is ranked first.
   B. Jimmy is ranked second.
   C. Boris is ranked third.
   D. Chris is ranked fourth.
   E. Martina is ranked fifth.
17. If Jimmy makes the first challenge of the tournament, and it is against Ivan, then with regard to the initial rankings:
   A. Ivan must be ranked first.
   B. Jimmy must be ranked third.
   C. Chris must be ranked third.
   D. Boris must be ranked fourth.
   E. Stefi must be ranked fifth.

2

The Extended Argument

INTRODUCTION

Having learned something about how arguments work in general, we will now examine the extended or multiparagraph argument, also known as the argumentative essay. Before beginning, however, it will prove useful to draw some theoretical distinctions between argument and a rhetorical form with which it is closely linked, persuasion.

Both rhetorical forms trace their roots to two distinct, though related, forms of discourse popular in ancient Athens. One was the *deliberative oration,* taught by Aristotle (384–322 B.C.) and others, which was a speech form for proposals made in the Athenian Senate. This form consisted of a carefully controlled, scrupulously logical approach to a public issue or policy, the purpose of which was to convince the senators of the reasonableness of the orator's position. This is not to say that the speakers lacked passion for their view; however, their purpose was not to incite emotion through inflammatory rhetoric, but to stimulate free and open inquiry. In appealing to the rationality, rather than the emotions, of their audience, speakers adhered to a strict logical format in presenting their ideas. We will consider this classical organization of extended argument later in this chapter.

Away from the senate, in the law courts of Athens, another kind of discourse was practiced. Used by defense lawyers, the purpose of *forensic oration* was to gain the acquittal of a defendant. Given this goal, lawyers did not feel bound by the logical, objective constraints of deliberative oration. An acquittal was an acquittal, whether gained by rational or emotional means. Predictably, Athenian lawyers developed a repertoire of rhetorical tricks to win their cases, for example, introducing irrelevancies, arousing feelings of patriotism, confusing the source of an idea with the idea itself, and so on. These devices, which Aristotle first catalogued in his *Rhetoric,* still resound in the practice of trial law. And they turn up in speeches and essays whose purpose it is to move an audience to some action. Because these devices frequently infiltrate extended arguments today, we must become familiar with them, which we will do in the second part of this book.

Like argument, persuasion attempts to win assent to a belief or proposal. It also relates the proofs or evidence for the main idea to a proposed action. Thus, persuasion generally presents evidence as motives for taking some action.

In its pure form, argument does not do this. The arguer claims to convince the audience, for example, that German reunification is desirable, but does not ask them to take steps to achieve it. Persuasion, by contrast, not only cites reasons for German reunification but also attempts to stimulate the audience to a definite action that will promote it. In the abstract, then, persuasion aims to win consent as well as assent.

Because persuasion is basically an appeal to will, it employs certain characteristics that either are absent or downplayed in argument. For example, keying on the audience's will requires that writers and speakers be especially mindful of how their audience views them. They must appear to be someone of good sense and goodwill, and especially someone with whom an audience can identify. The author of effective persuasion realizes the audience will be won over not by reasons and explanations, but by *persona,*[1] which refers to the role or identity assumed by the author. Beyond this, persuasion invites a heightened emotional and imaginative delivery, again because the aim is to provoke action.

Because forensic oration was developed to cause the audience to act, it is tempting to associate all persuasion with illicit manipulation. But ideal persuasion is not deliberately illogical. Rather, it is based on a simple fact of human nature: People are more likely to be aroused to action if given more motivation than logic. Thus, the best persuasion contains a judicious blend of logic and emotion. It combines reason with motivation—it appeals to both intellect and will, head and heart.

In theory, then, argument and persuasion can be differentiated by purpose and technique. **The purpose of an argument is to establish the acceptability of a claim wholly on the basis of a supporting body of logically related, incontrovertible statements.** On the other hand, **persuasion aims to make an audience think or act in accordance with the author's will.** This is why persuasion is associated with audience *consent* as well as *assent.*

So much for the theoretical distinctions between argument and persuasion. In practice, many extended arguments blur these theoretical distinctions. They have a persuasive function—they aim at the audience's will as well as its intelligence. They

---

[1] *Persona* comes from the Latin word for the masks worn by actors in ancient classical drama to immediately classify their roles for the audience. Accordingly, a smiling mask signaled a comic character, a sorrowful mask a tragic character.

are not merely bloodless exercises in cold logic. Although they are erected on a rational base, they often make circumspect use of emotional techniques and, thus, become examples of what might be called *logical persuasion.*

Logical persuasion is not easy to accomplish. In my passion, say, for German reunification, I can easily disregard the matter of my argument—for instance, by introducing irrelevancies and questionable assumptions, by distorting or suppressing evidence, or by substituting emotion for reason and hoping that you, my audience, do the same. I may also get careless with my language usage, for example, by employing vague or ambiguous terms or rhetorical techniques that will have the effect of persuading you illogically. I may not even be conscious of what I am doing in the way that advertisers, publicists, political campaign managers, and other professional persuaders deliberately intend to win consent by whatever means necessary. Indeed, some of the most persuasive rhetoric emanates from those rabidly convinced they are right, for sincere belief can pass as reasoned conviction among a logically naïve audience.

Because persuasive devices are embedded in so many of today's argumentative essays, we need to take a close look at those devices elsewhere in our study. But first, it is important to have a clear idea of the anatomy of the argumentative essay. With that behind us, we can better distinguish between licit and illicit persuasive devices that turn up in argumentative essays.

In fact, you already know quite a bit about extended arguments, because they contain all the elements of a short argument: signal words, premises (data and warrants), premise support or backing, unexpressed premises, and, of course, conclusions. Indeed, the extended argument can be viewed as a string of shorter arguments, all of which support a main idea or ultimate conclusion. Moreover, understanding the organization or logical structure of an argumentative essay is similar to understanding the structure of a short argument. Each requires that you grasp the logical relationships of support between individual structural elements, the most important of which is the conclusion.

A typical argumentative essay serves up many points, some of which are main points because they support the thesis. Other details serve as minor points; that is, backing or support for the main points. Still other details function to support these minor points. Embedded in an argumentative essay, then, are smaller or miniarguments, in contrast with the essay's main argument. So, understanding the organization or logical structure of the argumentative essay usually involves analysis on several levels of detail. In analyzing an argumentative essay, it is best to start with the main argument, which we will presently learn consists of thesis and main points. Having profiled the main argument of the essay, which you will learn how to do in this chapter, it is easier to key on the details of embedded miniarguments.

One final point before we begin. Since a well-constructed argumentative paragraph is really a microcosm of a well-constructed extended argument, we can learn a great deal about the logical structure of an argumentative essay from studying argumentative paragraphs. This explains why—in addition to economy—argumentative paragraphs are used abundantly in this chapter to illustrate the structure of argumentative essays.

Speaking of . . .

Logical Persuasion

Save Europe by Uniting Europe

Shortly after World War II, Winston Churchill delivered an address entitled "Save Europe by Uniting Europe." In this speech, Churchill not only cited reasons for uniting war-torn Europe, but stimulated his audience to take action to this end, namely, founding an organization in Great Britain for a united Europe. Notice how, in the excerpt that follows, the reasons Churchill gives for European unity also function as motives for action. Thus, he appeals to honor, shame, pride, and other feelings in order to provoke action.

Are the states of Europe to continue forever to squander the first fruits of their toil upon the erection of new barriers, military fortifications, tariff walls, and passport networks against one another?

Are we Europeans to become incapable, with all our tropical and colonial dependencies, with all our long created trading connections, with all that modern production and transportation can do, of even averting famine from the mass of our peoples? Are we all, through our poverty and our quarrels, forever to be a burden and a danger to the rest of the world? Do we imagine that we can be carried forward indefinitely upon the shoulders—broad though they be—of the United States?

The time has come when these questions must be answered. This is the hour of our choice, and surely the choice is plain. If the peoples of Europe resolve to come together and work together for mutual advantage, to exchange blessings instead of curses, they still have it in their power to sweep away the horrors and miseries which surround them and to allow the streams of freedom, happiness, and abundance to begin again their healing flow.

This is the supreme opportunity, and, if it be cast away, no one can predict that it will ever return or what the resulting catastrophe will be.

In my experience of large enterprises, it is often a mistake to try to settle everything at once. Far off, on the skyline, we can see the peaks of the Delectable Mountains. But we cannot tell what lies between us and them.

We know where we want to go, but we cannot foresee all the stages of the journey or plan our marches as in a military operation. We are not acting in the field of forces, but in the domain of opinion. We cannot give orders. We can only persuade.

I will therefore explain in general terms where we are and what are the first things we have to do. We have now at once set on foot an organization in Great Britain to promote the cause of united Europe and to give this idea the prominence and vitality the minds of our fellow countrymen to such an extent that it will affect their actions and influence the course of natural policy.

MODULE 2.1

THESIS

In Chapter 1, we saw that an argument has a conclusion or main idea. So do extended arguments.

The conclusion or main idea of an extended argument is termed its thesis. The thesis is what the essay is all about, its central point. The thesis gives an essay purpose and direction. Without a thesis, an essay would be a tangle of unrelated sentences and paragraphs.

Identifying an essay's thesis is crucial to evaluating the essay because support material—evidence or premises—can only be assessed according to whether they advance the thesis. As is true of the conclusion of any argument, a thesis may appear anywhere in an essay, although usually it is at the beginning or end. Furthermore, a thesis may be expressed directly or only suggested. Even though the location of a thesis is not fixed, and a thesis may not be directly expressed, keenly inspecting an essay for its *topic* and the author's *attitude* toward the topic can help us discover an essay's thesis. Let's see how.

Topic

Like every other piece of writing, an extended argument is about someone or something. That someone or something is the essay's topic. **The topic, then, is the central subject of the essay.**

Consider, for example, these two paragraphs:

Example 1: There is nothing in the biorhythm theory that contradicts scientific knowledge. Biorhythm theory is totally consistent with the fundamental tenet of biology which holds that all life consists of discharge and creation of energy, or, in biorhythmic terms, an alternation of positive and negative phases. In addition, given that we are subject to a host of smaller but nonetheless finely regulated biological rhythms, it seems reasonable that longer rhythms will also come with play.

The topic here is biorhythm theory—that is the *something* the paragraph is about.

Example 2: The life of Frank Lloyd Wright as an an architect could well serve as the point of departure for a discussion of what is both right and what is wrong with Americans. I do not say "with American judgment" or "American critical taste," for much more is involved than that. Wright, like the land of which he was a product, was full of promises, potential talents which by their very prodigality endangered their predecessors. Talents require discipline, and the greater the talents, the greater the discipline required. What is talent? It is involvement. But involvement is not enough. What is necessary for substantive achievement is disciplined involvement, the devotion to the critical and systematic, the skillful organization of one's potentialities.

Essentially this means the sharpening of one's wits on the whetstone of all the best that has been said, written, and done in the field of one's major interest. Genius can afford to take shortcuts. Frank Lloyd Wright not only considered himself to be a genius, but also imperiously demanded of others that they be in fealty bound to his own valuation of himself—a valuation to which most Americans readily accede. Americans like their geniuses to be flamboyant, especially when they are homespun, as Frank Lloyd Wright was, the "Prairie Genius," a gross national product, if ever there was one. (Ashley Montagu, *The American Way of Life.*)

The topic here is Frank Lloyd Wright—that's *who* the paragraph is about.

EXERCISES ON IDENTIFYING TOPICS

1. Read the following two paragraphs, then select the topic of each from among the choices given.
    A. U.S. prisons are a failure. First, they don't rehabilitate anyone. Second, they don't so much punish as provide free room and board. Third, they further alienate those with well-established antisocial tendencies. Fourth, they bring criminals together, thereby allowing them to swap information and refine their unseemly crafts.
        1. Rehabilitation of criminals
        2. The causes of crime
        3. Alternatives to incarceration
        4. U.S. prisons
    B. When we cheat impersonal corporations, we indirectly cheat our friends and ourselves. Department of Commerce data show that marketplace theft raises the cost of what we buy by more than two percent. Doctors who collect Medicare and Medicaid money for unnecessary treatments cost the average taxpayer several hundred dollars a year. The same applies to veterans who collect education money but who do not attend school.
        1. Crooked doctors
        2. Dishonest veterans
        3. Marketplace theft
        4. Cheating corporations
2. Read each of the following two paragraphs and state the topic of each.
    A. It was about this time I conceived the bold and arduous project of arriving at moral perfection; I wished to live without committing any fault at any time, and to conquer all that either natural inclination, custom, or company might lead me into. As I knew, or thought I knew, what was right and wrong, I did not see why I might not *always* do the one and avoid the other. But I soon found I had undertaken a task of more difficulty than I had imagined: while my attention was taken up, and employed in guarding against one fault, I was often surprised by another: habit took the advantage of inattention; inclination was sometimes too strong for reason. I concluded at length that the mere speculative conviction, that it was our interest to be completely virtuous, was not sufficient to prevent our slipping; and that the contrary habits must be

broken, and good ones acquired and established, before we can have any dependence on a steady uniform rectitude of conduct. (*Autobiography* of Benjamin Franklin.)

B.   "Philanthrophy," so (Henry David) Thoreau wrote, "is almost the only virtue which is sufficiently appreciated by mankind . . . the kind uncles and aunts of the race are more esteemed than its true spiritual fathers and mothers. I once heard a reverend lecturer on England, a man of learning and intelligence, after enumerating his scientific, literary and political worthies, Shakespeare, Bacon, Cromwell, Milton, Newton and others, speak next of her Christian heroes, whom, as if his profession required it of him, he elevated to a place far above all the rest, as the greatest of the great. They were Penn, Howard and Mrs. Fry. Everyone must feel the falsehood and cant of this. The last were not England's best men and women; only, perhaps, her best philanthropists." This is a tough-minded opinion. It is stated with characteristic exaggeration. But at least there is something to be said for those who do their best even though they do not see at the moment just what practical good it is going to do for the common man. (Joseph Wood Krutch, *If You Don't Mind My Sayin' So.*)

THESIS PROPOSITION

The authors of the preceding selections obviously had something to say about their topics. **What an author is trying to say about a topic that is special or unique is the essay's thesis or main idea,** which is equivalent to the conclusion of a short argument. So, when we identify an essay's topic and the author's attitude toward it, we have identified the essay's thesis.

IN BRIEF   Taken together, the topic and the author's attitude toward it make up the thesis of an essay.

A statement of an essay's thesis or main idea is called a **thesis proposition.** Sometimes writers will express a thesis proposition directly at or near the beginning of the essay. That is the writer's way of preparing the reader's mind to understand what is to follow.

In the previous examples, Example 1 contained the thesis proposition: "There is nothing in the biorhythm theory that contradicts scientific knowledge." Notice that the topic is biorhythm theory, and the author's feeling is that biorhythm theory is compatible with scientific knowledge. In Example 2, the thesis proposition was: "The life of Frank Lloyd Wright as an architect could well serve as the point of departure for a discussion of what is both right and what is wrong with Americans." The topic is Frank Lloyd Wright; the author believes that Wright's life illustrates what is right and wrong with Americans.

> **IN BRIEF**   A thesis proposition is a statement composed of the topic of the essay and the author's attitude toward the topic.

EXERCISES ON IDENTIFYING THESIS PROPOSITIONS*

Underline the thesis proposition of each of the following paragraphs.

A. Threats to the environment are threats to national security. When careless, unscrupulous corporations and government agencies permit chemical pollution in our communities, that's a threat to our security. No punishments likely to deter polluters — such as long prison terms — ever seem to be levied for these crimes against the future. Here, if anywhere, we are coddling criminals — showing more concern for the polluters than the rights of the victims. Cleaning up their mess will cost hundreds of billions of dollars. Not cleaning it up will cost far more. . . . (Carl Sagan and Ann Druyan, "Give Us Hope," *Parade,* November 27, 1988.)

B. The educational system takes over where cultural myths, Freudian folklore, and the media leave off in depressing a girl's aspirations and motivations. All along, she's taught to accept a double standard for success and self-esteem: It's marriage and motherhood for girls, while it's education and career for boys. She's pushed to be popular, date, and marry young (more than half of all American women are married before the age of twenty-one). Success in school only inhibits her social life. Intellectual striving, a necessity for academic success, is considered competitively aggressive; that is unnatural and unladylike behavior, since the essence of femininity she has learned, is repressing aggressiveness. Telling her she thinks like a man is a backhanded compliment, which is discouraging if she has tried to be a woman using her brains, not sex, in the classroom and office. (Paula Stern, "The Womanly Image: Character Assassination through the Ages," *The Atlantic Monthly,* March 1970.)

C. During the past four years, (paleontologist Jack) Horner has collaborated with a French paleontologist, Armand de Ricqles, on an analysis of the differences between the growth structure of endothermic and ectothermic bone. Detailed examinations of microthin sections of bone from nestling and juvenile dinosaurs, modern birds and crocodiles, reveal a remarkable similarity between bird and dinosaur bone. Horner attributes this to the fact that both are fast-growing. "Fast-growing bone has a lot of vascular canals, which are rich with blood, and a woven structure around them," he says. "You see very few of these canals in crocodile bones." Crocodile bone is marked with arrenst lines, thick banks indicative of slow growth. "You don't see those lines on dinosaur bone," Horner says. (Virginia Morell, "The Sociable Dinosaur," *Science Illustrated,* March 11, 1988.)

Unexpressed Thesis Propositions

Sometimes writers never directly express a thesis proposition, but merely suggest it. On those occasions, you need to use the clues the writer gives in the form of detail, including the verbal expressions that we examined in Chapter 1. The clues indicate the topic and what the author is saying about it.

As practice in how to infer a thesis proposition from the clues given, read the following passage, then choose the statement from among those provided that you think best states the writer's main idea or thesis. Remember, select the statement that best expresses the topic of the passage and the author's attitude toward the topic.

> There is a sexually transmitted disease with a very long incubation period that is life threatening, and incurable. AIDS? No, syphilis prior to 1945. It was defeated by routine epidemiologic techniques. Everyone was tested when hospitalized, married, or inducted into the Armed Forces until the affected were identified, counseled, and all contacts followed up. Prior to this public health effort, syphilis filled one-half of the hospital beds in the United States, just as AIDS will do in five years unless the Federal Government changes it lackadaisical attitude. Syphilis never had civil rights. Why is AIDS different? What about the rights of health care workers who frequently are not informed of those with ARC or AIDS, but are required to work with infected body fluids without giving informed consent?

1. Prior to 1945, syphilis was an incurable, life-threatening disease.
2. The Federal Government has been lackadaisical in its attitude toward AIDS.
3. AIDS is like syphilis.
4. Everyone should be tested for AIDS.
5. We need to apply routine epidemiological techniques in the battle against AIDS.

The correct answer is statement 5. It identifies the topic, AIDS, and what the author is saying about it. Statement 1 is a fact in the paragraph but it is too specific to be the main idea. It does not identify the topic. Statement 2 is an opinion in the paragraph, but the Federal Government is not what the paragraph is about—AIDS is. The author feels the Federal Government's attitude toward AIDS is "lackadaisical" because it is not subjecting target groups to AIDS screening. Statement 3 is implied, but the point of comparing syphilis and AIDS is to make the larger point that we need to approach AIDS in the same manner as we approached syphilis. Statement 4 is far too general. Statement 5 is what the paragraph is about.

IN BRIEF   Unless you can correctly identify the thesis of an essay, you can make no progress in analyzing or evaluating the essay. This means that you must identify the thesis proposition, if it is expressed directly; or clearly formulate it, if it is implied. In its formulation, the thesis proposition should be a general statement of the essay's content, but not so general that it exceeds what is stated or implied.

EXERCISES ON UNEXPRESSED THESIS PROPOSITIONS*

1. Read each of the following paragraphs, then choose the statement that best expresses its thesis. Explain why your choice is the best of the alternatives presented.

A. The first serious study of the behavior of simians — including their behavior in the wild — was made in Indonesia by Alfred Russel Wallace, the co-discoverer of evolution by natural selection. Wallace concluded that a baby orangutan he studied behaved exactly like a human child in similar circumstances. In fact, orangutan is a Malay phrase meaning not ape but man of the woods. Teuber recounted many stories told by his parents, pioneer German ethologists who founded and operated the first research station devoted to chimpanzee behavior on Tenerife in the Canary Islands early in the second decade of this century. It was here that Wolfgang Kohler performed his famous studies of Sultan, a chimpanzee genius who was able to connect two rods in order to reach an otherwise inaccessible banana. On Tenerife, also, two chimpanzees were observed maltreating a chicken: one would thrust at it with a piece of wire it concealed behind its back. The chicken would retreat but soon allow itself to approach once again — and be beaten once again. Here is a fine combination of behavior sometimes thought to be uniquely human: cooperation, planning a future course of action, deception and cruelty. It also reveals that chickens have a very low capacity for avoidance learning. (Carl Sagan, *The Dragons of Eden.*)
   1. Wallace, Kohler, and Teuber conducted studies on simian behavior.
   2. It appears that chimpanzees can reason.
   3. Chimpanzees are probably smarter than chickens.
   4. Chimpanzees exhibit human behavior.
   5. Chimpanzees resemble humans.
B. Language is usually used to communicate a fairly specific message ("The redcoats are coming"). Most linguistic theories treat just this aspect of language. Language may also be used to communicate the speaker's attitude toward the message *("John got some more overtime,"* or *"Poor John has to work overtime")* and the speaker's attitude toward the listener ("Get dem crates over here," "Please move those boxes over here"). It may, in addition, be used as a tool to establish social contact ("Hello, this is the Internal Revenue Service office calling"), or to fill awkward silences once social contact has been made (most conversations about the weather fall into this category). (Peter H. Fries, *Tagamemics.*)
   1. Language is a good example of random behavior.
   2. Linguists treat only a single aspect of language.
   3. People use language to achieve some goal.
   4. Language is a form of communication.
C. "Virile females" have various attributes, but the one most lovely to R. J. Reynolds Tobacco Company is that they are minimally educated. According to a company marketing memo, virile females are 18 to 20, have no education beyond high school, work in entry-level service or factory jobs, wear jeans and knit tops, watch "Roseanne," enjoy such events as motorcycle races, tractor pulls, monster truck competitions. Virile females are the market segment targeted by the new brand "Dakota," which may be promoted by Dakota-sponsored "Nights of the Living Hunks" and male strip shows . . . Targeted marketing, a common tactic, is . . . considered disgusting when the

targeted group is picked because it is badly educated and informed, and hence manipulable, and the product being marketed is injurious. But senior executives who set the tobacco companies' marketing strategies do not have daughters who fit the "virile female" profile. One wonders: Do the executives' daughters smoke? If so, are the executives pleased? If so, are they not strange parents? (George Will, "Public Policy Is Too Soft on Cigarette Pushers.")

1. "Virile females" are badly educated.
2. Cigarette company executives are moral hypocrites.
3. Targeting a group for marketing because the group is manipulable is reprehensible.
4. "Virile females" are easy to manipulate in the marketplace.

D. One of the most unkillable human instincts is the urge to learn, and C-SPAN is the place to satisfy that itch. In some ways, C-SPAN is the fulfillment of an old journalistic dream—great newspaper editors have always tried to get their reporters to write stories that would let the reader see what happened. C-SPAN DOES IT. This is the answer for those who believe the media are biased. You don't have to take Dan Rather's word for what happened or what was said—you can watch it for yourself. It's enough to make you wonder whether journalism has any function left, except to synopsize for those who haven't the time to spend hours listening. But, "objective journalism," which is, of course, never truly objective, is so unsatisfactory. To present facts without their context is to leave facts meaningless. Anyone can listen to a Congressional debate on C-SPAN, but it turns out only the knowledgeable can appreciate one . . . (Molly Ivins, "You Don't Have To Rely on The Brokaw/Jennings/Rather Versions," *TV Guide,* December 3, 1985.)

1. C-SPAN effectively lets viewers know what's happened.
2. C-SPAN is objective journalism.
3. Facts out of context are meaningless.
4. One needs to be informed to appreciate C-SPAN.

2. Assume that each of the following passages is an argument. You will notice that they do not directly express a thesis proposition, but merely suggest it. By making use of the details and verbal expressions given, try to construct a plausible thesis proposition for each argument. Remember, a thesis proposition should include the topic and the writer's attitude toward the topic.

A. Today a good education is crucial to getting a good job. It's also necessary to keep abreast of rapidly changing events. Beyond this, a good education is a person's best hedge against boredom and dissatisfaction in old age.

B. When police officers pose as prostitutes or drug sellers, they're trying to entrap people who have not yet committed a crime. They're also encouraging crime. But the basic function of the police is neither to target people before a crime is committed nor to encourage the commission of a crime.

C. Advertisers say that consumers aren't much influenced by ads. Yet, they spend hundreds of millions of dollars a year trying to get people to buy their products. Not only do TV commercials exhibit the latest cinematic techniques, but often include the endorsements of well-paid movie stars and sports figures.

Furthermore, when even the Federal Communications Commission attempts to regulate TV ads, marketing agencies cry, "Freedom of speech!"

D. Without the Fairness Doctrine rule, the business motivations of broadcasters might overwhelm the public interest in the airing of public issues. Broadcasters might only air views with which they agree if they are freed from complying with the rule. Because they are privileged to use the public's airwaves, broadcasters must serve the public interest, including the providing of balanced, fair programming. (Ford Rowan, *Broadcast Fairness.*)

E. When I was a kid in the '60s, I grew up listening to rock n' roll songs. But there were others who attacked these songs because they thought rock n' roll music was going to destroy America's youth. They would show Elvis Presley shakin' only above the waist on television, and they would burn the records of the Beatles. Well these censorship efforts were eventually turned back, and my generation turned out OK. (Anthony T. Podesta, *Houston Post,* October 16, 1986.)

MODULE 2.2

MAIN POINTS

The second component of the argumentative essay is its main points. Every argumentative essay has **main points, which are principal support assertions offered to advance the thesis.** The main points, the argument's *premises,* are a crucial part of an extended argument, for they underpin the thesis.

Since evaluating an extended argument consists chiefly in inspecting the relationship between premises and thesis, we must pay close attention to an essay's main points. It is usually not difficult to identify the main points of an extended argument, especially of a tightly organized one. But even when the essay is loosely ordered, a close reading of the paragraphs and awareness of the connection between them usually reveals the essay's main points.

A thesis proposition functions as a compass to direct a reader to an essay's main points. The reader can often determine from the thesis proposition the kind of supporting details that will follow—facts, examples, comparisons or contrasts, cause and effect situations, sequence of events, and other common developmental patterns. In this way, a thesis proposition serves to prepare the reader's mind for what is to follow and, thus, helps the reader follow the author's argument and line of reasoning.

To see how a thesis proposition suggests the kind of supporting details or main points that will follow, let's consider some hypothetical thesis propositions:

Thesis Proposition: It's a good idea to get a college education nowadays.
What Will Likely Follow: *Facts* that support acquiring a college education.

Thesis Proposition: Going away to college has advantages, but it also has distinct disadvantages.

What Will Likely Follow: *Contrasting* advantages and disadvantages of going away to college.

Thesis Proposition: Although children go through several stages in cognitive development, it's not until the last stage, the formal stage, that they are able to do high-level abstract reasoning.

What Will Likely Follow: *Sequence* of stages that children go through in learning how to do high-level abstract reasoning.

Thesis Proposition: Drinking enough water daily is an important factor in weight control.

What Will Likely Follow: Development of a *causal relation* between drinking water and weight control.

Of course, as we have learned, thesis propositions frequently go unexpressed. Still, an accurate construction of the thesis proposition functions as a reliable guide to the essay's main points because, when accurately formulated, it effectively prepares the mind to home-in on the writer's key points. Indeed, this is precisely why formulating unexpressed thesis propositions is so important. Once you have identified the essay's main idea, you can more easily recognize the support material that is offered for it, because you are anticipating it.

EXERCISES ON IDENTIFYING MAIN POINTS

1. State what you think will likely follow these thesis propositions (TP). Choose from among facts, examples, comparison/contrast, sequence of events, cause and effect situations, or a combination of these.

    SAMPLES:

    TP: *TV violence leads to real-life violence.*

    What Will Likely Follow: *Development of a* **causal** *relation between TV and real-life violence.*

    TP: *In many significant ways, women today are no more liberated than they were twenty-five years ago.*

    What Will Likely Follow: Facts *and* **examples** *that show important ways women are no more emancipated today than they were a quarter century ago.*

    A. *TP:* Recreation can be a signal for eating.
       What Will Likely Follow:
    B. *TP:* Overeating is an overture to many serious, even life-threatening diseases.
       What Will Likely Follow:
    C. *TP:* The meaning of Christmas has become thoroughly perverted.
       What Will Likely Follow:

D. *TP:* The explosion of the space shuttle *Challenger,* which killed seven astronauts, could have been avoided.
   What Will Likely Follow:

E. *TP:* Women don't approach problems the way men do.
   What Will Likely Follow:

F. *TP:* The accident must have occurred in the following way.
   What Will Likely Follow:

G. *TP:* The HIV virus, of itself, does not account for AIDS.
   What Will Likely Follow:

H. *TP:* Business is a lot like poker.
   What Will Likely Follow:

I. *TP:* Expressing emotion isn't the only function of poetry.
   What Will Likely Follow:

J. *TP:* The chimpanzee definitely exhibits human intelligence.
   What Will Likely Follow:

K. *TP:* Football is much like war.
   What Will Likely Follow:

L. *TP:* Television may be primarily a medium of entertainment, but it's also educational.
   What Will Likely Follow:

2. The main points of each of the following paragraphs are developed in a variety of ways, which are identified for you. Read each of the paragraphs, then (1) state its thesis or main idea, and (2) its premises or main points. (Do not forget to make use of verbal clues and details in identifying the thesis.)

A. **Facts:** Ethical decision-making in an organization does not occur in a vacuum. As individuals and as managers, we formulate our ethics (i.e., that standard of "right" and "wrong" behavior that we set for ourselves) based upon family, peer, and religious influences, our past experiences, and our own unique value systems. In making ethical decisions within the organizational context, many times there are situational factors and potential conflicts of interest that further complicate the process.

B. **Facts:** Swanscombe man represents a distinct advance over his fossil predecessors, although the extent of the advance has been debated. Examination of the three fragments and reconstructions based on them indicate that he had a large brain; his cranial capacity is estimated at about 1,300 cubic centimeters, which . . . lies well within the modern range. Furthermore, there is a general suggestion of rounded and expanded skull contours somewhat like modern man's. These features have been interpreted as evidence for an apparent evolutionary leap, the sudden appearance of a man who was nearly fully modern. On the other hand, the relatively low brain case and certain other characteristics suggest that the specimen may be a less advanced form intermediate between *Homo erectus* and modern man. (John E. Pfeiffer, *The Emergence of Man.*)

C. **Example:** Even when the historical tide is low, a particular group of doers may emerge in exploits that inspire awe. Shrouded in the mists of the eighth century, long before the cathedrals, Viking seamanship was a wonder of daring, stamina, and skill. Pushing relentlessly outward in open boats, the Vikings sailed south, around Spain to North Africa and Arabia, north to the top of the world, west across unchartered seas to American coasts. They hauled their boats overland from the Baltic to make their way down Russian rivers to the Black Sea. Why? We do not know what engine drove them, only that it was part of the human endowment. (Barbara Tuchman, "Humanity's Better Moments," *American Scholar,* Autumn, 1980.)

D. **Comparison and Contrast:** Years of watching and comparing bright children and non-bright or less bright, have shown that they are very different kinds of people. The bright child is curious about life and reality, eager to get in touch with it, embrace it, unite himself with it. There is no wall, no barrier between him and life. The dull child is far less curious, far less interested in what goes on and what is real, more inclined to live in a world of fantasy. The bright child likes to experiment, to try things out. He lives by the maxim that there is more than one way to skin a cat. The dull child is usually afraid to try at all. It takes a good deal of urging to get him to try even once; if that try fails, he's through. (John Holt, *How Children Fail.*)

E. **Cause and Effect, Facts:** Many more inmates should be paroled, for prison experience unquestionably boosts the chances that an offender will break the law again. In one experiment, conducted by the California Youth Authority, a group of convicted juvenile delinquents were given immediate parole and returned to their homes or foster homes wherein they got intensive care from community parole officers. After five years, only 28 percent of the experimental group have had their paroles revoked, compared to 52 percent of a comparable group that was locked up after conviction.

F. **Comparison:** Of course, there are other reasons besides its bizarre forms of punishment that the Islamic system of justice seems uncivilized to the Western mind. One is the absence of due process. Another is the long list of offenses — such as drinking, blasphemy, adultery, profiteering, and so on — that can bring on conviction and punishment. A third is all the ritualistic mumbo-mumbo in pronouncements of Islamic law. Even in these matters, however, a little cultural modesty is called for. The vast majority of American criminals are convicted and sentenced as a result of plea bargaining, in which due process plays almost no role. It has been only a half century since a wave of religious fundamentalism stirred this country to outlaw the consumption of alcoholic beverages. Most states still have laws imposing austere constraints on sexual conduct. Only two weeks ago the *Washington Post* reported that the FBI has spent two-and-a-half-years and untold amounts of money to break up a nationwide pornography ring. Flogging the clients of prostitutes, as the Pakistanis did, does seem silly. But only a few months ago Mayor Koch of New York was proposing that clients caught in his own city have their names broadcast by radio stations. We are not so far advanced in such matters as we often like to think. (Stephen Chapman, "The Prisoners' Dilemma," *The New Republic,* March 8, 1980.)

ORGANIZATION

The third element of an extended argument is its organization, which refers to its structure. Like any other essay form, the extended argument typically has a beginning, middle, and end, or what commonly are termed an *introduction, body,* and *conclusion.*

In its classic form, an extended argument's introduction includes necessary background, a statement of the issue or problem, a method of approach, and a thesis proposition. The body attempts to establish the thesis by presenting main points and other supporting details and sometimes attempts to refute opposing arguments. The conclusion summarizes or restates the essential argument. Thus, the classic structure of an argumentive essay can be portrayed as follows:

INTRODUCTION	Necessary background
	Statement of issue or problem
	Approach to issue or problem
	Thesis proposition
BODY	Main points and other details that support thesis
	Possibly a refutation of opposing viewpoints
CONCLUSION	Summary or restatement of thesis

It is worth noting that this is a paradigm or model format. In fact, writers frequently depart from this classic structure for stylistic or rhetorical effect. For example, sometimes an author will plunge directly into the body and hold off asserting the thesis until the very end. Other times, the author may omit a refutation of opposing viewpoints. On still other occasions, authors will quickly dispatch some of these ingredients, perhaps by merely alluding to a problem or issue that they assume their audience is generally familiar with. Nevertheless, most argumentative essays reflect the classic model enough to make it worth remembering as you journey through what may be a highly complex essay.

IN BRIEF Knowing how an extended argument is typically structured helps us to follow the development of ideas. It provides a kind of map to keep us oriented to thesis and main points, and it helps us avoid confusing nonessential information—for example, background—with essential information—for example, main points.

Deductive and Inductive Organization

In addition to this classic framework for setting up an essay, it is useful to keep in mind the deductive and inductive organization that writers follow in developing their arguments. These methods of ensuring the logical development of ideas, which sometimes are combined in a single essay, can be considered another aspect of an essay's organization.

Briefly, in a deductively organized essay, one or several premises are presented and a series of deductions are made from them. In other words, the author shows what the premises imply. The thesis, therefore, is an inference drawn from an application of some broad assumptions.

As an example of a deductively organized argument, let's consider this excerpt from an essay expressing opposition to reverse discrimination — showing women and minority members preferential treatment. Notice how the author sets up a general statement (in **bold** print), and relates particular cases to it in order to draw her conclusion (*italicized*):

> Now, if justice (Aristotle's justice in the political sense) is equal treatment under law for all citizens, what is injustice? **Clearly, injustice is the violation of that equality, discrimination for or against a group of citizens, favoring them with special immunities and privileges or depriving them of those guaranteed to the others.** When . . . employers refuse to hire blacks in white-collar jobs, when Wall Street will only hire women as secretaries with new titles . . . we have examples of injustice, and we work to restore the equality of the public realm by ensuring that equal opportunity will be provided in such cases in the future. But of course, when the employers . . . *favor* women and blacks, the same injustice is done. Just as the previous discrimination did, this reverse discrimination violates the public equality which defines and destroys the rule of law for the areas in which these favors are granted. To the extent that we adopt a program of discrimination, reverse or otherwise, justice in the political sense is destroyed . . . Logically, the conclusion is simple enough: *"All discrimination is wrong prima facie because it violates justice, and that goes for reverse discrimination too."* (Lisa Newton, "Reverse Discrimination as Unjustified.")

In contrast to a deductive essay, one that is organized inductively moves in the reverse order, from a series of facts and details to a general conclusion based on them. The inductive order is especially useful when one's purpose is to convince the audience of rather controversial assertions — for example, "Capital punishment should be legalized," or "The United States should have a national health insurance program that guarantees all citizens health care and services despite their ability to pay," or "Public schools are not adequately preparing young people to survive in a highly technological society." Audiences may greet such controversial assertions of value or social policy with prejudice and distrust. In order to overcome audience resistance, authors often will try to win over the audience slowly, point by point, deliberately turning its attention to the evidence, which is allowed to speak for itself. In an inductive development of ideas, the support material usually is presented first; then, in the final paragraph or two, the general conclusion — the thesis — is drawn. Ideally, having seen the evidence, members of the audience will change their minds or at least be receptive to the controversial conclusion.

Here is an example of inductive order in an essay dealing with seal hunting:

> A sealer who recently returned from a seal hunting expedition described the voyage as "the most bloodthirsty thing I've ever seen." And he has

Speaking of . . .

Deductive Organization

The Declaration of Independence

The Declaration of Independence is a classic example of deductive organization: setting up general statements, relating particular cases to them, and then drawing conclusions. Thus, at the outset, Thomas Jefferson writes:

> We hold these truths to be self-evident, that all men are created equal, that they are endowed by their Creator with certain unalienable Rights, that among these are Life, Liberty, and pursuit of Happiness. That to secure these rights, Governments are instituted among Men, deriving their just powers from the consent of the governed—That whenever any Form of Government becomes destructive of these ends, it is the Right of the People to alter or to abolish it, and to institute new Government, laying its foundation on such principles and organizing its powers in such form, as to them shall seem most likely to affect their Safety and Happiness. Prudence, indeed, will dictate that Governments long established should not be changed for light and transient causes; and accordingly all experience hath shown that mankind are more disposed to suffer, while evils are sufferable, than to right themselves by abolishing the forms to which they are accustomed. But when a long train of abuses and usurpations, pursuing invariably the same Object, evinces a design to reduce them under absolute Despotism, it is their right, it is their duty, to throw off such Government, and to provide new Guards for their future security—

> Such has been the patient sufferance of these Colonies; and such is now the necessity which constrains them to alter their former Systems of Government. The history of the present King of Great Britain is a history of repeated injuries and usurpations, all having in direct object the establishment of an absolute Tyranny over these States. To prove this, let Facts be submitted to a candid world . . .

Having presented a series of basic principles, Jefferson then documents particular cases of tyrannical policies and conduct imposed on the Colonies by King George III of Great Britain. Thus, he establishes a logical basis for *deducing*:

> We, therefore, the Representatives of the United States of America, in General Congress, Assembled, appealing to the Supreme Judge of the world for the rectitude of our intentions, do, in the Name, and by Authority of the good People of these Colonies, solemnly publish and declare, that these United Colonies are, and of Right ought to be Free and Independent States; that they are Absolved from all allegiance to the British Crown, and that all political connection between them and the State of Great Britain is and ought to be totally dissolved; and that as Free and Independent States, they have full Power to levy war, conclude Peace, contract Alliances, establish Commerce, and to do all other Acts and things which Independent States may of right do—

> And for the support of this Declaration, with a firm reliance on the protection of divine Providence, we mutually pledge to each other our Lives, our Fortunes, and our sacred Honor.

traveled the world for many years. The seaman reported that the crew at times became so incensed about the appalling shipboard conditions that they literally vented their anger on the baby harp seals, skinning many of them alive. In an interview with a local television station, he stated further: "When the sealers saw a fishery officer approaching, they'd bash in the skulls of the seals so the officer wouldn't know they'd been skinned alive."

Of course, there are those who insist that killing harp seals is no different from killing cattle. Don't believe it. Unlike cattle, which are not an endangered species and are killed for human consumption, the vanishing baby harp seal is killed for fashion.

Beyond this, profits from sealing never reach the pockets of those directly involved. Nor do they contribute significantly to local economies. For example, of the $6 million gained from sealing last year, less than .2 percent of the annual Newfoundland Gross Provincial income was derived from sealing. Of that $6 million only $800,000 or about 13 percent went to 2,750 landspersons involved in the "hunt." The remaining went to only 25 percent of those involved. Where did the rest of the profits end up? In the coffers of large ship owners and European, mainly Norwegian, companies who convert pelts into apparel.

Let's stop kidding ourselves. This is no "hunt"—it's a slaughter. And it must be stopped.

MODULE 2.3

OUTLINING

The basic challenge in understanding an argumentative essay is identical to that posed by the short argument. Recall that, with short arguments, we must identify four key elements: conclusion, data, support, and warrants. The thesis of an essay is equivalent to the conclusion of a short argument; and the main points, which often are supported, are equivalent to the premises.

A good way to understand an extended argument is to outline it. Outlining explicitly identifies the logic of the relationships between thesis and supporting details and, thus, prepares us to evaluate the essay.

In constructing outlines, we will follow the conventional format according to which Roman numerals (for example, I, II, III, and so on) represent main points or premises; capital letters (A, B, C, and so on) and Arabic numbers (1, 2, 3, and so on) represent supporting details. Additionally, we will use parentheses to indicate unexpressed elements. Here is what the skeleton of such an outline looks like:

THESIS: Thesis Proposition

I. Statement of First Main Point	+ (Statement, if necessary)
A. Statement of First Piece of Support	+ (Statement, if necessary)
B. Statement of Second Piece of Support	+ (Statement, if necessary)
and so on	
II. Statement of Second Main Point	+ (Statement, if necessary)
A. Statement of First Piece of Support	+ (Statement, if necessary)
B. Statement of Second Piece of Support	+ (Statement, if necessary)

And so forth until all main points, supporting details, and significant missing elements are expressed.

Let's apply this format to a short sample essay, which we will present, then outline.

Why Businesses Fail

When a business fails, management is usually blamed. No doubt, management does share part of the responsibility. But what about the employees? Rarely is the employee's role in a business failure explored.

In fact, employee theft of money or merchandise translates into lost profits for a business. Research shows that one-third of all employees are "high risk." This means that, at a growth rate of 10% per year, as estimated by the Commerce Department, business losses due to employee dishonesty are at epidemic proportions.

Moreover, about 15% of all employees have a history of violent emotional instability. Employee vandalism is a good example. Many employees view sabotage of company equipment or merchandise as a way of "getting back" at a company. Similarly, employee assaults on customers or fellow workers aren't uncommon. And who can be held legally responsible? Employers. Beyond this are the numerous incidents of employee mood swings that can certainly disrupt not only the employee's productivity but other workers' as well.

Then there's the drug problem. Recent research projects the cost of drug abuse to industry at several billion dollars per year and increasing. Approximately 25% of all prospective employees have definitely abused marijuana and about 10% have a history of using other illegal drugs on a regular basis. These various forms of drug abuse translate into more absenteeism, less initiative, poor attention, more accidents, and decreased productivity.

Taken together, employee dishonesty, violent emotions, instability, and drug abuse threaten the survival of a business by undercutting its profits.

The author of this essay argues *inductively* that employee theft, emotional instability, and drug abuse contribute to business failures. In order to establish this thesis, he offers evidence for establishing both that these problems exist and that they are costly to business. Although brief, this essay does roughly follow the classic structure. Its introduction, the first paragraph, sets up the issue and foreshadows the thesis by identifying the topic, which is the employee's role in business failures. (The author also alludes to an opposing viewpoint in the first paragraph.) The second, third, and fourth paragraphs constitute the body, which presents support for the thesis that is explicitly stated in the fifth paragraph.

The essay could be outlined as follows:

THESIS: Employee dishonesty and emotional instability can significantly contribute to a business failure.
I. Employee theft means lost profits.
  A. 1/3 of all employees are "high risk."
  B. Commerce Department estimates theft at 10% a year.
II. Employee emotional instability means lost profits.
  A. Vandalism is costly.
  B. Assaults on customers, for which employers can be held legally responsible, aren't uncommon.
  C. Mood swings hurt productivity.
III. Employee drug use means lost profits.
  A. Drug abuse costs business several billion dollars per year in absenteeism, lost initiative, poor attention, accidents, and low productivity.
  B. About 25% of all prospective employees abuse marijuana regularly.
  C. About 10% use illegal drugs regularly. + ("Regular use" of marijuana or other illegal drugs makes employees inefficient and unproductive.)

Although no two analysts will ever construct identical outlines, they should generally agree on two basic elements of any essay under discussion: its thesis and its support. Filling in missing elements can be problematic. What you may find controversial, I may not, and vice versa. For example, I filled in a warrant about drugs because I am curious about the evidence for saying that marijuana and other unspecified illegal drugs used regularly lead to problems such as absenteeism and accidents. (It is also unclear what the author means by "regular use," but the expressed premises themselves raise this question.) The other unstated assumptions seem so obvious and noncontroversial that they are hardly worth expressing. For example, under IA ("One-third of all employees are 'high risk'"), clearly the warrant is "High risk employees probably will steal." I do have questions about the meaning of "high risk," and how "high risk" is determined, but the stated premise itself provokes these questions, so there is no need to express the warrant. Similarly, under IB ("Commerce Department estimates theft at 10% a year"), the author obviously is assuming that this figure is accurate and that it translates into lost profits. If I wish to question the figure, I can—without making the assumption explicit.

At any rate, this outline would give us a handle on the essay. We would now have a relatively good idea of what the author is saying, and we would be poised to evaluate the essay. In fact, this particular outline is detailed enough for use without having to refer to the essay.

> **IN BRIEF**   Evaluating argumentative essays is always a tricky business. A good outline simplifies the evaluation process by providing it the necessary focus. That is why outlining is a skill worth cultivating.

MODULE 2.4

WRITING WITH REASON: CONSTRUCTING EXTENDED ARGUMENTS

One of the best ways to improve our own thinking and sharpen our analysis of other people's reasoning and arguments is to construct arguments of our own. When we formulate our own arguments, we deepen our understanding of the very elements that we are inspecting in the arguments of others. Constructing our own arguments, then, makes us more acute critics of what we read and hear—it sharpens our reasoning and powers of analysis.

Beyond this, probably few of us are content merely to play the critic in life. We want to be *actors* as well as *reactors*—that is, participants in, as well as critics of, the passing scene. We want to express our ideas and have them taken seriously—at school, at work, in the community, and so on. In fact, we often are required to, for example, when we must write a paper for a college course or make a presentation at work. If our ideas are to be taken seriously, we need to present them in a clear, orderly, and compelling way. In other words, we need to know how to construct good arguments of our own.

Obviously everything you are learning about arguments in this book applies equally to everyone's arguments, your own included; but what you are learning does not automatically transfer to your own creations. You and I can know a lot about correct argument. Armed with that knowledge, we can become trenchant critics of the arguments we encounter every day. However, this does not guarantee that we can construct good arguments of our own, any more than knowing music theory, for example, automatically makes a good musician. In fact, it is far easier to criticize a product—even criticize it well and fairly—than to turn out a good product. (Just think of all the good movie critics around, not a single one of whom has ever written a first-rate screenplay.)

So, occasionally taking time out to apply what we are learning to our own arguments serves two important purposes. First, it makes us better critics by immersing us in the process of reasoning and arguing. Second, it speaks to our own desire and need for effective expression of ideas. This explains why "Writing With Reason" sections, such as this one, are included in selected chapters of this textbook. They are not intended to substitute for a formal study of rhetoric, but to help you transfer what you are learning to the construction of your own arguments.

Although, in this limited space, we cannot exhaustively apply all of this chapter's content to writing essays, we will point out some of the major applications. For economy, we will confine our remarks to thesis and main points.

Formulating the Thesis Proposition

To begin, let's recall that in an argumentative essay, you are basically trying to prove something. Obviously, you would not try to prove what has already been established, for example, "Millions of Americans smoke cigarettes," or "Nearly half the households in the United States are supported primarily by working women," or "The spirochete causes syphilis." Statements like these are easily confirmed or refuted. The ease with which they can be evaluated precludes the need—and certainly the wisdom—of constructing essays to demonstrate their truth.

In contrast, some statements are so disputable, controversial, or opinionated that they lend themselves to elaboration. "Many films today subtly attempt to justify violence directed against women," "Experimenting on animals is immoral," "The earth has been visited by extraterrestrials," "Too much money is being spent on exotic medical technology and not enough on basic, maintenance health care" and similar statements need supporting details before anyone can be reasonably expected to accept them. In other words, they are arguable. What you are trying to prove is in question—that is why you are trying to prove it. What you are offering as evidence is either not in question or is easily established.

IN BRIEF   A thesis proposition should be arguable. This means it should be sufficiently controversial that its acceptability depends on a body of supporting details.

Arguable Statements   Assertions that make good thesis propositions generally fall into five categories: statements about meaning, value, consequences, policy, and fact.

1. Statements about meaning. Statements about meaning are focused on how we define or interpret something.   For example, what is meant by concepts and terms such as *pornography, equal opportunity, the just state, death, equal opportunity, the common good,* and *mental incompetence* have exercised numerous authors of countless essays and books. The reason is that their meanings are open to diverse interpretations with varying, sometimes conflicting, social implications.

2. Statements about value. Statements about value express an assessment of worth.   For example, "Abortion is never right," "Tom Cruise is a better actor than Sean Penn," "Democracy is the best form of government." Although value statements in morality, the arts, politics, religion and other areas can rarely be argued conclusively, they do make for spirited argument.

3. Statements about consequences. Statements about consequences express causal patterns involved in certain ideas and actions. Thus, "'Head Start' programs reduce the number of high school drop-outs," "Capital punishment deters crime," "Passage of the Equal Rights Amendment will have the effect of denying women certain privileges," or "The U.S. invasion of Panama in January 1990 set back U.S.-Latin relations thirty years." Such statements are really responses to "what if" questions. "What if there are 'Head Start' programs?" "What if there's an Equal Rights Amendment?" and so on. In fact, they are often stated that way as thesis propositions: "If there are 'Head Start' programs, the number of high school drop-outs will decline" or "If the Equal Rights Amendment passes, women will lose certain privileges."

4. Statements about social policy. Statements about social policy deal with courses of actions, guiding principles, or procedures that individuals or groups should adopt. Thus, "Capital punishment should be legalized," "Corporate responsibility needs to include more than making profit," "Tenure for teachers should be abolished," "Prisoners should be permitted conjugal visits," and the like.

5. Statements about fact. Statements about fact are intended as reports of actual states of affairs in the present or past or probable states of affairs in the future. It may seem odd to include such statements in our classification of arguable assertions. After all, we just agreed that there's nothing disputable about the factual statements "Millions of Americans smoke cigarettes," "Nearly half the households in the United States are supported primarily by working women," or "The spirochete causes syphilis." It is not that these are statements of fact that makes them unworthy as thesis propositions, but that they are statements of easily confirmed facts.

Many statements purporting to be facts actually are quite controversial. For example, "The United States induced Saddam Hussein to invade Kuwait," "Lee Harvey Oswald did not act alone in assassinating John F. Kennedy," or "Shakespeare did not write all of the plays and sonnets attributed to him." We could not reasonably expect an audience to accept such statements without considerable supporting details. So, controversial statements that purport to be facts can make stimulating thesis propositions.

Generally speaking, writers employ one of these five types of statements in formulating their thesis propositions; of course, in developing their essays, they often use a combination. Thus, you might construct an extended argument whose thesis is "Gun control should be mandatory in every state" (a policy statement). In supporting your thesis, you might stipulate what you mean by "gun" and "gun control" (meaning), point out that certain states with gun control have relatively low rates of handgun-related crimes (fact), discuss the social merit of gun control (consequences), and insist that failure to enact such legislations is socially irresponsible (value). Nevertheless, the statement that provides your essay purpose and direction—the thesis proposition—is a policy statement. Your task, therefore, would be to demonstrate the wisdom of this policy.

Writing the Thesis Proposition

Although there is no one way to write a thesis proposition, the following steps provide a logical approach to this important part of the process of constructing the argumentative essay.

Step 1: Decide on a subject.   The subject is your broad area of concern or interest. For example, "Education in the United States," "The Electoral Process," "Drugs," "Feminism," "The Penal System," "Organized Religion," or "Conflict between the Generations." Often in college, instructors select the subject for you. Let's say, for example, that a business professor assigns you a 600-word essay on the subject of advertising. "What about advertising?" you wonder. What indeed! Advertising is far too broad and unwieldy a subject to handle in a mere 600 words (although some students might consider that book length). Before making any progress, then, you must identify some aspect of advertising that is manageable within the prescribed format. (Of course, this also applies to subjects that you yourself might choose.)

Step 2: Identify possible topics.   The "What about advertising?" question you asked is a groping for a topic, which is an aspect of the subject. Obviously, subjects can spawn numerous topics. For example:

Subject	Possible Topics
Baseball	Salaries of players
	The Pete Rose case
	The 1990 "lockout"
Education	The high costs of college
	Shortcomings in public schools
	Misplaced priorities
Religion	The decline of institutional religion
	Influence of politics
	Conflicts with science
Advertising	Relationship to the law
	Deceptive practices
	Impact on the economy

At this stage, then, you are brainstorming—identifying as many possible aspects of a subject you can. From this list, you will choose the topic to write about.

Step 3: Select and limit the topic.   With a list of topics in hand, you should then select one you want to write about, and limit it. The second part of this step—limiting the topic—is very important. If you do not limit your topic, it can overwhelm you. The proper limits of a topic usually are determined by essay length. The topics we have listed could be, and have been, the subjects of books. So, to tackle any of them in, say, a 600–1000-word essay would be unwise. They need trimming. Here are some scaled-down versions for the topics dealing with the subject of "Advertising."

Possible Topics	**Limited Topics**
Relationship to the law	The impact on big business of three landmark decisions in consumer law
Deceptive practices	The use of ambiguity to sell aspirin, toothpaste, and mouthwash
Impact on the economy	Effects of advertising on retail prices of alcoholic and nonalcoholic beverages

It is worth noting that the suggested limited topics contain a most common and effective method for controlling an essay—*dividing it into parts.* Thus, the first limited topic refers to *three* landmark decisions; the second refers to *aspirin, toothpaste,* and *mouthwash;* the third to *alcoholic* and *nonalcoholic* beverages. These divisions tell you precisely what your essay will cover, even the order of coverage (for example, aspirin, *then* toothpaste, *then* mouthwash). By the same token, your audience knows what you will discuss and even how (for example, *examples* of ambiguity in selling aspirin, toothpaste, and mouthwash). All of this prepares their minds for what will follow. It sets up the logical arrangement of your presentation.

Step 4: Determine your attitude toward the topic.　　Earlier, we saw that a thesis consists of a topic and the author's attitude toward it. Determining your attitude will help you zero in on what you are trying to establish. For example, you may be *fearful* of the impact of the three landmark decisions; *critical* of the use of ambiguity to sell aspirin, toothpaste, and mouthwash; or *convinced* of the significant effects of advertising costs on the retail prices of alcoholic and nonalcoholic beverages. In crystalizing your attitude, remember the nature of arguable assertions. Thus, your fear about the three legal decisions springs from a concern about *consequences,* your criticism of ambiguity probably relates to *value* or *policy,* and your conviction about the impact of advertising costs reflects some ultimate assertion of *fact* and perhaps *value* ("significant" implies a value assertion).

Step 5: Write the thesis proposition.　　This step consists of wedding topic and attitude in a single statement. Again, keep in mind what kind of statement you want to make (for example, consequences, value, social policy, and so on). This will ensure sharp focus. Here are some possibilities for the topic we have set up:

Limited Topic	Author's Attitude
Three landmark decisions in consumer law	Fearful of impact on big business

Thesis Proposition
Three landmark decisions in consumer law spell big
　　trouble for big business. (*Statement of value*)
or
Unless modified, three landmark decisions in consumer
　　law could seriously undercut the interests of big
　　business. (*Statement of value*)

Limited Topic	Author's Attitude
Use of ambiguity to sell aspirin, toothpaste, and mouthwash	Critical of

Thesis Proposition

Stricter regulations are needed to control the widespread use of ambiguity to sell aspirin, toothpaste, and mouthwash. (*Statement of policy*)

or

Employing ambiguity to sell aspirin, toothpaste, and mouthwash is reprehensible. (*Statement of value*)

Limited Topic	Author's Attitude
Effects of advertising on the retail prices of alcoholic and nonalcoholic beverages	Convinced of significance

Thesis Proposition

Even a cursory look at the pricing structure of alcoholic and nonalcoholic beverages reveals the enormous effects of advertising costs. (*Statement of fact and value*)

or

Make no mistake about it: Consumers pay dearly for the costs of advertising alcoholic and nonalcoholic beverages. (*Statement of fact and value*)

Step 6. Test the thesis proposition.   After writing your thesis statement, check it for focus. You want to make sure your topic and viewpoint are crystal clear. One way to ensure this is to have someone else read it. Ask the person, "What do you think I'm trying to prove (or demonstrate or establish or convince my audience of)?" If the reply corresponds with your purpose, you are ready to outline your essay. If not, then back to the drawing board!

EXERCISES ON WRITING A THESIS PROPOSITION

Following the six steps just discussed, write a thesis proposition for each of the following subjects:

1. Safe Sex
2. Junk Foods
3. The Plight of the Homeless
4. College Curricula
5. American Foreign Policy
6. Restoring Cities
7. Animal Rights

Speaking of . . .

Constructing Extended Arguments

The Internalized Reader

Talking to yourself as you walk down the street may earn you some hard stares, but talking to yourself as you plan and write an essay will likely earn you higher grades.

To write well, we need to become a little "schizoid." We need to construct an adult equivalent to the fantasy playmate children sometimes create. Let's give this imaginary creature a fancy name: the "Internalized Reader."

What does the Internalized Reader (I.R.) do? Mainly, he or she asks doubting questions, challenges our generalizations, and demands more evidence.

"Who says?" I.R. questions. "Aren't you overstating a bit there? I.R. challenges. "How about a couple of examples to make the point clear?" I.R. demands.

Listen. And obey. I.R. is your friend. I.R. is on your side. I.R. wants to save you from mistakes that will confuse, alienate, or anger real readers in the real world.

Effective writing, like effective speaking, is not a monologue but a dialogue — an interaction between two people, the writer and the reader. In conversations, this is obvious. The person we're speaking with nods, shakes his or her head, frowns, smiles, leans forward or away, questions, objects, and requests clarification — dialogue.

When people read an essay or report we've written, they do precisely the same thing, only mentally rather than out loud. They mentally frown in disagreement, shake their heads in puzzlement, wish for a clarifying example, and so forth. The dialogue is taking place, just as in conversation, but it's taking place at two separate points in time rather than at a single point in time as in conversation.

In order to communicate clearly and persuasively, we need to bring our future readers into our minds as we write, watching for frowns and head shakes, listening for requests for clarification. In short, we need to answer the future readers' objections and see their confusion as we write. But we can't do that unless we have a reader inside our brains to converse with as we write. Hence the writer's best friend: Internalized Reader.

(Ray Kytle, *Clear Thinking for Composition*, McGraw-Hill, Inc., 1977. Reprinted by permission of McGraw-Hill, Inc.)

8. Allocation of Scarce Medical Resources
9. Presidential Elections

Developing Support Materials

Just as effective reading requires identification of an essay's main points, writing good argumentative essays calls for developing main points to support the thesis. A main piece of support basically is answering a "why" or "how" question that you are asking in your thesis. For example, "*Why* are stricter regulations needed to control the widespread use of ambiguity to sell aspirin, toothpaste, and mouthwash?" Or, "*How* does even a cursory look at the pricing structure of alcoholic and nonalcoholic beverages reveal the enormous effect of advertising costs?" If you train yourself to ask the why or how question of your thesis, you will avoid including irrelevant material in your essay. Stated another way, by answering the why or how question, you ensure premises that logically demonstrate the thesis.

You can enlist several sources in assembling support material. One is *observations,* which are close, first-hand studies of scenes, people, objects, and events outside you. Another good source of evidence is *personal experience,* that is, what goes on *inside* you. Personal experience is your consciousness of thoughts, ideas, and involvement with incidents, persons, places, and things. The views of others who have studied the subject, *informed opinion,* is a third, rich source for developing reasons and evidence for a thesis. And *organized research* — the systematic sifting of evidence from records, reports, and other printed sources — is a fourth source of material. Having assembled these materials, you can then select the most salient points and organize them in an outline along the lines previously discussed.

IN BRIEF   Draw on observations, personal experience, informed opinion, and organized research for materials to support your thesis. Select the most effective points and, if necessary, shore them up with support material that you again cull from these sources. When you have gathered enough support for your thesis, organize it into an outline, which is the blueprint of the essay.

IMPROVING PERFORMANCE

SUMMARY-TEST QUESTIONS FOR CHAPTER 2*

1. "The following terms are synonymous: thesis, main idea, main point, conclusion." True or False? Explain.
2. The topic of an essay is

    A. its central subject.
    B. its thesis.
    C. the writer's attitude.
    D. A and B
    E. A, B, and C

3. A thesis consists of _____ and _____ .
4. What is a thesis proposition? Is it always stated in an essay? If not, how can you determine it?
5. Which of the following statements would lend itself to development in an extended argument? Explain.

    A. Millions of Americans are overweight.
    B. People can communicate with one another over great distances without using any of the usual means of communication.
    C. Among people over fifty-five, more women than men have dangerously high cholesterol.
    D. Sabbaticals would prove worthwhile in business.
    E. Many of today's movies glorify violence.

6. Which of the following terms does not belong with the others?

    A. main points
    B. thesis
    C. warrants
    D. data

7. How would you expect the following paragraph to be developed: by comparison, contrast, cause and effect, or a combination? "Another problem facing a beekeeper is getting to know a newly arrived hive and getting it to know him, a delicate problem that calls for much tact. The process somewhat resembles that of a young man becoming acquainted with a sensitive, slightly suspicious, young lady. . . ."
8. What composes an essay that follows the classic organization format?
9. Are the following statements necessarily true?

    A. Background always appears in an essay.
    B. A thesis proposition is always expressed in the introduction of an essay.
    C. Essays always include a refutation of opposing viewpoints.
    D. Essays not organized in the classic form are always deficient.
    E. A good argumentative essay always has a thesis proposition, but it is not necessarily expressed.

10. "In a deductively organized essay, the author lays out basic assumptions and then relates particular cases to them. But in an inductively

organized essay, the author moves from a series of facts and details to a general conclusion based on them. You'll never find a mix of these methods in an essay." Would you agree with all three assertions in this passage? If not, explain.

11. Name a classic example of deductive organization.

12. Fill in the blanks of the following outline with the appropriate term: unexpressed support, thesis proposition, or main point.

_____

  I. _____
    A. _____   + (_____)
    B. _____

13. Is it always necessary to express an unexpressed premise (that is, main point or support) in an outline? If not, when should you?

14. In the following outline specimens, warrants are provided for main points. Do you think the warrant was worth making explicit or not? Explain.

A. **THESIS PROPOSITION: Capital punishment deters crime.**

  I. A study has shown that where   +   (If the rate of violent crime
  capital punishment has been   increases after a punishment
  discontinued, the rate of violent   is discontinued, that proves
  crime has increased.   that the punishment is a
                                                            deterrent.)
                                              +   (The study is reliable.)

B. **THESIS PROPOSITION: Making job applicants take honesty exams is unfair.**

  I. It threatens privacy.   +   (What threatens privacy is always
                                                  unfair.)

C. **THESIS PROPOSITION: ULTRA-BRIGHT toothpaste helps control tartar.**

  I. A study at a leading university
  shows that people who used   +   (Any study conducted at a leading
  ULTRA-BRIGHT had far less   university is reliable.)
  tartar build-up than those
  who did not use ULTRA-
  BRIGHT.

D. **THESIS PROPOSITION: Baseball commissioner Bart Giamatti was right in banning Pete Rose from baseball for life.**

  I. Rose was a notorious gambler.   +   (Professional baseball players
                                                              should be banned from the game
                                                              for gambling.)

E. **THESIS PROPOSITION: Many women don't find rape the heinous crime it is.**

  I. A sizeable number of rape   +   (A rape victim who does not
  victims never report the rape   report being raped docs not
  to the authorities.   consider rape to be a heinous
                                                          crime.)

CRITICAL THINKING APPLICATIONS

Read the following passages carefully, then answer the questions that accompany them.

1. Parochial schools attempt to impart religious instruction as well as general education. This explains why officials of these schools are concerned to teach what they consider proper religious values in the relationships between the sexes. As a result, many religious school systems still segregate boys and girls in separate institutions. In so doing, the administrators are convinced they're protecting their charges from temptation. In fact, this policy may be having the opposite effect. Segregated grouping tends to make students preoccupied with sex and even encourages viewing members of the opposite sex as sex objects. It also sends out a sinister message — that sex is evil.

Which of the following sentences provides the most logical continuation of this paragraph?

    A. School administrators should recognize that parochial education is misguided.
    B. School administrators should include sex education in their schools.
    C. School administrators obviously are misinformed about the effect of segregating the sexes.
    D. School administrators should no longer insist upon separate schools for boys and girls.
    E. School administrators may be unwittingly developing in students the very attitudes they wish to discourage.

2. Many of us today complain about the high cost of legal services, courts costs, and the like. In some cities, lawyers are charging as much as $200 an hour and merely filing papers can cost thousands. What few of us realize is that in the earliest stages of common law, you couldn't have your case heard unless you first paid the court a fee, and then only if your case fit a prescribed form for which there existed a writ. As time passed, judges invented new forms, which increased the number of cases, and, of course, revenues.

Which of the following is the conclusion most strongly suggested by this paragraph?

    A. Early judges were money-grubbers.
    B. People are ill-informed about the economics of law.
    C. It's outrageous that people have to pay to get justice.
    D. Economics has always played a significant role in legal and judicial practice.
    E. We shouldn't be so critical of the high costs of legal services.

3. We assume that the right to property is guaranteed by the Constitution. In fact, the protections offered by the Fifth Amendment are, at best, tenuous. While it's

true that the Fifth Amendment prohibits the government from arbitrarily seizing private property, it does permit it to take private property for public use with compensation. The rub is that it's the government – not the property owner – that defines both private property and fair compensation.

Which of the following is the point that the author is leading up to?

A. The Constitution is a sham.
B. The government uses the Constitution to seize private property.
C. The Constitution needs to be amended.
D. The protections afforded by the Fifth Amendment with respect to private property are subject to government interpretation.
E. In fact, there is no such thing as private property.

4. Efficiency experts typically attempt to improve office productivity by applying rather complex methodology. They will divide production procedures into discrete work tasks, then analyze them. They will then study the organization of those tasks and recommend to management ways to speed production – for example, by relocating office equipment, rescheduling employee breaks, or removing duplication of steps of processes. Although I'm sure this all has a sound scientific basis, it can be costly, time-consuming, and disruptive. In my office, I have found a simple and direct way to improve employee efficiency, which no efficiency expert has ever suggested. Lower the room temperature. I have found that as the temperature drops, worker productivity increases. Thus, the optimum office temperature seems to be around 68 degrees. So long as the room temperature doesn't fall below 68 degrees, my office workers grow increasingly productive as the temperature drops.

The passage leads most naturally to which of the following conclusions?

A. Efficiency experts do little to increase office productivity.
B. Occasionally restructuring office tasks improves productivity.
C. Office workers seem most efficient at 68 degrees.
D. The temperature-efficiency formula is applicable to all office work.
E. Sometimes seemingly complex problems have rather simple solutions.

Questions 5–10 deal with the following essay. Questions 5–7 require that you complete sentences by choosing the most appropriate word or phrase from the alternatives given after the essay.

Smokers often claim that they have a "right" to smoke wherever and whenever they choose. There are no conceivable circumstances, they imply, under which the law might legitimately prohibit their smoking. This position is indefensible.

If the concept of a "right" means anything, it means that one person's freedom of action is limited by ____5____ . Now, it doesn't take a genius to realize that smoking in certain situations presents a clear and present danger. Obvious examples would be: smoking in a crowded theater, around flammable materials, or during take-off in an airplane. Who would seriously argue that the pleasure of the smoker in these situations outweighs the potential harm to others?

But people can be injured in ways other than the obvious ones just cited. The long-term harm of inhaling so-called secondary smoke is well documented. The mild discomfort that a restaurant diner might feel as a direct result of another diner's smoking, although trivial, is nevertheless a harm that the smoker causes. Similarly, the lingering smell of cigarette smoke that permeates a hotel room after a smoker has vacated it is not life-endangering, ____6____ it is obnoxious to the nonsmoking occupant. It is true that in cases like these, certainly the last two, the harm is so trivial that we automatically and rightly strike the balance in favor of the smoker. But the very recognition that a balance of freedom is and should be struck indicts the smoker's claim to an absolute right to smoke.

When smokers talk about the "right" to smoke, then, they should reflect on the nature of a right. Yes, smokers have a right to smoke, but only when and where ____7____ .

5. A. statutes
   B. the Constitution
   C. the rights of other persons not to smoke
   D. the rights of nonsmokers to be free of the disgusting fumes of tobacco smoking
   E. the interest of any other person to not be injured or inconvenienced by that action.

6. A. and
   B. but
   C. for
   D. while
   E. even though

7. A. they are permitted by law
   B. no one else is present
   C. no one is offended by their act
   D. their interest in smoking outweighs the interest of other persons in their nonsmoking
   E. they can ensure that no other persons will be even slightly inconvenienced by their smoking

8. **The author's main strategy in developing his argument is to**

   A. cite details which are not generally known.
   B. show the evils of smoking.

C. clarify and define a key concept.
D. prove that smokers are inconsiderate.
E. demonstrate that laws need to be passed to restrict smoking.

9. **Which of the following is a main point in the argument?**

A. Smoking in crowded theaters, around flammable materials, and during take-offs in an airplane present clear and present dangers.
B. The lingering smell of cigarette smoke in a hotel room is offensive to nonsmokers.
C. Smoking in certain situations presents a clear and present danger.
D. Secondary smoke can be dangerous to the health of nonsmokers.
E. Smoking in a restaurant can be offensive to nonsmokers.

10. **Which of the following, if it were omitted, would most weaken the author's argument?**

A. Examples of the dangers of tobacco smoke
B. Examples of the trivial negative effects of tobacco smoke
C. A definition of a "right"
D. An acknowledgement that at times a balance of freedom is struck in the smoker's favor
E. Expression of a smoker's conception of a "right" to smoke

As computers increasingly dominate our lives, a question of once merely academic interest has begun to intrigue the popular mind. Can computers reason? Reasoning involves drawing logical conclusions from a given set of facts. Clearly reasoning often goes awry. Humans frequently draw fallacious conclusions — conclusions that are not supported by the evidence. Now, we can find the help we need to avoid logical errors.

There's a computer program, ERA (Elegant Reasoning Assistant), that solves a problem by drawing conclusions from given data about the problem. The program can't learn or self-analyze but it can draw logical conclusions flawlessly. It employs basic principles of correct reasoning, but, more importantly, accesses sophisticated logical strategies that often elude us humans.

ERA basically works by using sophisticated techniques to discover a contradiction between goal and assumptions. Thus, one inputs a set of assumptions together with a contradictory statement that a goal is unreachable. If ERA finds no contradiction between the goal statement and the set of assumptions, then we know instantly that we must rethink the relationship between our assumptions and our goal statement. For example, if the problem is to test the safety system that will automatically shut down a nuclear reactor when instruments indicate a problem, ERA is told that the system will not shut the reactor down under those circumstances. If ERA discovers a contradiction between the goal statement and the system's design assumptions, then we know that this aspect of the reactor's design has been proved satisfactory.

The beauty of ERA is not that it replaces human reasoning. Rather it augments it—it frees the mind to engage deeper, far more complex ideas. The ideas, when even partially formulated, can then be checked by ERA.

11. **Which of the following topics best reflects the content of this passage?**

    A. Scientific applications of computers
    B. Some applications of ERA
    C. Assisting human reasoning
    D. Replacing human reasoning with computer reasoning
    E. The present role of artificial intelligence

12. **The author's attitude toward the topic of this passage can best be described as**

    A. cautious.
    B. fearful.
    C. skeptical.
    D. reluctant.
    E. optimistic.

13. **The author is primarily concerned with**

    A. giving an overview of recent developments in artificial intelligence.
    B. demonstrating the limitations of human reasoning.
    C. selling ERA.
    D. recommending a solution.
    E. refuting a common misconception.

14. **Which of the following sentences provides the most logical continuation of the last paragraph?**

    A. In this way, many of the common errors in human reasoning can be avoided.
    B. The chief use for ERA at present is for electronic circuit design validation.
    C. Thus, ERA has many nontechnical applications.
    D. In this way, ERA "unclutters" the mind.
    E. In other words, ERA can detect contradictions in human reasoning.

15. **Which of the following is a main point expressed in the development of the passage?**

    A. Humans frequently reason fallaciously.
    B. ERA can draw logical conclusions flawlessly.
    C. ERA cannot learn to self-analyze.
    D. ERA can be used to ensure the safety of nuclear reactors.
    E. ERA uses the principle of contradiction to detect flaws in human reasoning.

POINT/COUNTERPOINT: ESSAYS FOR ANALYSIS

Issue: *Privacy in the Workplace*

RESOLVED: Personality tests should be used as pre-employment screens.[2]

Background: In 1988, the United States Supreme Court outlawed polygraph (lie detector) tests as pre-employment screens, but by no means has this completely relieved the tension between organizations and private interest. Organizations often feel compelled to take actions for self-defense or self-preservation that clash with individual rights of privacy.

David Ewing has devoted considerable research to life within organizations. In the following excerpt from his book, *Freedom Inside the Organization: Bringing Civil Liberties to the Workplace,* Mr. Ewing sets the stage for the two opposed viewpoints concerning personality tests that are presented immediately afterward.

From: **Freedom Inside the Organization***

David Ewing

According to an old Chinese saying, the buyer needs a thousand eyes, the seller but one. Personnel officials apparently have another version of this thought. Some of them say: the employer needs a thousand eyes, the employee but one.

However, neither this philosophy nor present law sits well with the public mood. It is becoming increasingly obvious that Americans, old and young alike, object to the no-privacy-is-good-policy tradition. Former Supreme Court Justice William O. Douglas once said, "The right to be let alone is indeed the beginning of all freedom." This statement comes close to mirroring the national mood.

For instance, many national legislators are disturbed by reports that there are nearly 900 federal data banks containing more than 1.25 billion records with personnel information about individuals. The U.S. Senate Government Operations Committee and other Congressional committees have shown dismay over the sharing of information that goes on among federal agencies. Various groups of experts have been studying ways to control this situation. The Pentagon, after complaints about information filed on discharged military personnel, has agreed to omit from discharge papers certain coded data that previously permitted prospective employers to identify misfits, drug abusers, and alcoholics.

Universities and schools face a similar change in attitudes. Responding to college students' complaints about secret information in their files, Congress in 1974 enacted a law giving students the right to inspect their records. In that same year, a schoolteacher who lost her job after the school superintendent, without her consent, obtained a doctor's report

---

[2]A *resolution* is a formal statement of a decision or expression of an opinion put before an audience. The pairs of chapter-ending essays in this text present opposing viewpoints on some resolution, which we will signal by the word *resolved.*

that she was pregnant, went to court and got reinstated. The federal court held that her privacy could not thus be invaded.

In the business sector the wind has been blowing in the same direction. Reacting to employees' complaints about alleged invasions of their privacy, unions have been protesting more vigorously. . . . Traditionally, the law has favored employer attitudes of "the less employee privacy, the better." Thus, the personnel records of employees are not confidential. Authorities agree that the constitutional concept of a right to privacy has had little influence on personnel relations. Even when an employer misuses personal information about an employee and the employee is fortunate enough to find out, the way to a remedy can be very difficult. (From *Freedom Inside the Organization* by David W. Ewing. Copyright (c) 1977 by David W. Ewing. Reprinted with permission of the publisher, Dutton, an imprint of New American Library, a division of Penguin Books USA, Inc.)

1. What is the thesis proposition of the essay?
2. What kind of statement is the thesis proposition?
3. Identify the author's main points.
4. What sources does the author use in establishing his thesis?
5. Do you think the essay is roughly organized along the classic model? Explain.
6. Explain the author's use of inductive reasoning in his presentation.
7. Construct an outline of the essay, following the format developed in this chapter.

The Best Insurance against Problem Workers*

Faced with economic downturns, spiralling costs, and tight margins, today's employers must exercise special care in hiring. By some estimates, annual losses to U.S. companies due to employee-related problems reach about $25 billion annually. The best defense against such losses is careful screening of job applicants. And the best way to ensure honest, reliable employees is by subjecting them to a pre-employment personality test.

Understandably, employers are concerned about the legality of such tests. But there are no antidiscrimination laws that prohibit the use of personality screens. Indeed, the Federal Equal Employment Opportunity Commission's (EEOC) "Uniform Guidelines on Employee Selection Procedures" expressly states that tests which measure "psychological traits" are permissible. Also, Section 703(h) of Title VII of the Civil Rights Act of 1964 sanctions the use of professionally developed personality tests.

But are such tests valid? Do they accurately predict dishonesty, violent behavior, and drug use? Absolutely.

Several approaches have been used to validate them. In one, scores on a professionally developed personnel inventory were compared to actual admissions made in pre-employment polygraph examinations. (This was conducted before the polygraph was outlawed as a pre-employment screen.) Dishonesty, violence, and drug-use scales correlated highly with actual admitted behavior involving these three workplace problems. In another test, consisting of anonymously sampled college students, scores from attitude scales reliably correlated with these students' admitted weekly alcohol consumption rates, semiannual intoxication rates, and the number of alcohol-related problems they had at home or on the job. In still another test, the violence scales of a personality test accurately predicted the amount of on-the-job damage and waste and correlated with the number of arguments with and assaults on managers, co-workers and customers the employees were involved in.

Of course, no matter how valid or reliable a test, it's impractical if it's not cost effective. But employers should keep in mind that the average American business, depending on the industry, loses between 2–5 percent of gross sales per year due to internal shrinkage. By helping employers select low-risk workers, a good psychological test prevents theft and constant turnover, thereby paying for itself in a short time.

So, although employee dishonesty, aggression, and drug use pose a formidable challenge for today's employers, they are not insurmountable problems. The wise employer can keep these problem workers out of the workplace by identifying them before they're hired through a professionally developed pre-employment personality test.

A Workplace Outrage

Statistics report an alarming reality in the contemporary American workplace: American business loses billions of dollars a year due to employee theft, violent behavior, and drug use. That employers are profoundly concerned about this is altogether understandable. That they have the right to protect their property from such workers is indisputable. But are personality tests the answer?

A typical test consists of a battery of questions such as the following: "How strong is your conscience?" "How often do you feel guilty?" "Do you always tell the truth?" "Do you occasionally have thoughts you wouldn't want made public?" "Does everyone steal a little?" "Have you ever been so intrigued by the cleverness of a thief that you hoped the person would escape detection?" Depending on the question, applicants are asked to answer: "far more than average," "more than average," "average," or "definitely yes," "probably yes," "uncertain," "probably no," "definitely no."

Now surely a fundamental part of the validity of any survey is that its language is clear and precise enough for all respondents to interpret the questions in roughly the same way. Otherwise, the results are simply identifying an individual's self-perceptions in regard to his or her own subjective interpretations. But it's most doubtful that even the makers of these tests can specify what's to be considered "average," "less than average," "slightly less than average," and so on. If they do, why don't they state what they mean, so that the respondents can accurately judge themselves? Lacking clarity, such questions invite job applicants to evaluate themselves according to standards of their own making. In what sense such a device can yield "valid and reliable" results is puzzling, to say the least.

Moreover, a big part of these tests consists of a behavioral history of applicants who are asked to reveal the nature, frequency, and quantity of specific drug use, if any. They also must indicate if they have ever engaged in drunk driving, illegal gambling, selling or using pot and other controlled substances, traffic violations, forgery, vandalism, rape, arson, and a lot of other unseemly or illegal conduct. Applicants must also state their opinions about the social acceptance of drinking alcohol and using other drugs. Such inquiries obviously are intended to expose to others one's innermost thoughts, attitudes, values, and ideas. In a word, they're invasions of privacy, not to mention possible violations of the constitutional right to be protected from self-incrimination.

Of course, proponents of these tests argue that no one's privacy is being invaded, since applicants are free to refuse to take the test. But the ability to refuse to take such a test is more of theory rather than of choice. If applicants really want the job, they must take the test. In other words, they're coerced into cooperating with others who would invade their privacy. They are hardly "free to refuse."

Undoubtedly, some would admit these psychological tests do invade privacy but insist that, in the light of the epidemic of employee dishonesty and destructive behavior, such invasions are justifiable. But not even the staunchest champion of these tests would claim they are 100 percent reliable. Even if these tests are reliable 90 percent of the time, that means that 100 out of 1,000 job applicants will be mislabeled. Among these 100 could well be decent individuals. So, such a procedure doesn't only offend privacy, it's downright unfair because it handicaps good applicants seeking employment.

Certainly employers must respond to the myriad costly threats posed by unsavory workers. But personality tests that are of questionable reliability, insult privacy, and mock fair play, aren't the answer.

1. What is the thesis of each argument? What kind of statement is it (that is, value, policy, and so on)?
2. Point out the classic elements in the organization of each essay.
3. Explain how each argument is developed inductively.
4. Construct an outline of each essay.
5. Using D (for data), B (for backing), and C (for conclusion), represent the argument expressed in paragraphs 3 and 4 of the first essay and the one expressed in paragraph 3 of the second essay.

RELATED THEME TOPICS

1. In all but two states, company managers are free to monitor employees' conversations on company telephones without telling the employees. The two exceptions are California, which requires a beeper to be used on monitored phones, and Georgia, where the Public Service Commission requires that monitored phones be marked with a bright orange label and that monitoring supervisors obtain licenses. *Write an argumentative essay (between 600 and 1,000 words) in which you either defend or reject the practice of monitoring employee conversations on company telephones without informing the employees. Keep in mind the guidelines presented in this chapter concerning determining your attitude toward the topic, writing a clear thesis proposition that is controversial or opinionated, developing support materials, and outlining. Remember that you are attempting to establish the acceptability of your position.*

2. In a small New York town, a bank teller was called in one day by his supervisor and told that various customers had noticed him at a local bar early in the morning. The teller confirmed his presence in the bar, but pointed out that he always came to work on time and did his job. But what would the bank's customers think, the supervisor asked him? After all, it was a small town and people talk. When the teller refused to change his habits, he was fired. Applying for unemployment compensation, the teller argued that his dismissal was not due to disobedience because the bank had no right to run his private life. The unemployment agency did not agree. It ruled that when an employee's behavior affects the organization's image, controls such as the ones the bank imposed were justified. *Pretend that you are the bank teller. Write an essay in which you argue your case of unfair dismissal. Alternatively, pretend you are the bank supervisor and write an essay defending the dismissal.*

3

The Language
of Argument

INTRODUCTION

All arguments are expressed in language. Unless we understand the language of an argument, we cannot understand the argument itself. We cannot analyze or evaluate it nor can we construct good arguments of our own.

The language of short arguments usually is nonproblematic. If we understand the meaning of its words, we can usually understand the argument. However, the same cannot be said of the longer, multiparagraph arguments in which writers typically present numerous mini- or subarguments embedded in the main argument.

Given its length and complexity, the extended argument—in contrast to the short argument—challenges the writer to ensure unity, coherence, logic, and intelligbility. Good essayists are mindful of this challenge and employ a variety of linguistic devices to meet it—for example, words that show logical relationships, qualify assertions, or downplay some facts while intensifying others. Sensitivity to these devices is basic to the whole process of critical analysis; insensitivity to them is perhaps the single most important factor for readers' not understanding, let alone evaluating insightfully, what they read. This is why, in this chapter, we will examine some of the more common linguistic devices that extended arguments contain. A knowledge of them will help make you a more intensive reader.

MODULE 3.1

FUNCTIONS OF LANGUAGE

Unless we understand how language functions in general, we stand little chance of understanding its function in a particular argument. So, a good place to begin our overview of the language of argument is with some observations about how language generally functions. Although language serves many functions, we will emphasize five: the informative, directive, expressive, ceremonial, and performative.

Informative Function

The informative function of language refers to language used to communicate information, which in this context includes misinformation. This is usually accomplished by formulating statements of truth value, that is, statements that are either true or false, for example:

AIDS is a sexually transmitted disease. (T)
The earth's atmosphere appears to be heating up. (T)
Shakespeare wrote a number of novels. (F)

Of course, a statement may be serving the informative function of language even if we do not know whether it is true. For example, "In the early 1800s, astronomers lacked tables and charts that give the positions of the various planets" or "Geneticists Salvador Luria and Max Delbruck didn't demonstrate the importance of molecular biology in solving a major problem concerning the production of mutations in living organisms." Although you may not know that the first statement is true and the second false, you do know that both are the kinds of statements that are either true or false. They have truth value. Language used to affirm or deny propositions, or present arguments, is said to be serving the informative function of language.

> **IN BRIEF**   Since arguments consist of true or false statements (that is, propositions), premises and conclusions always serve the informative function of language.

Directive Function

If someone asked you whether the assertion "Shut the door" was true, you would be puzzled, because commands have no truth value. "Shut the door," "Put on a sun screen when you go to the beach on a sunny day," "Buckle up for safety," and the like are not intended to communicate information but to cause some action.

Speaking of . . .

Intensive Reading

Reading for Love and Profit

No doubt, you already have had some practice in intensive reading, even though you may not have known it at the time. Mortimer Adler, in *How to Read a Book,* illustrates:

> If we consider men and women generally, and apart from their professions or occupations, there is only one situation I can think of in which they almost pull themselves up by their bootstraps, making an effort to read better than they usually do. When they are in love and are reading a love letter, they read for all they are worth. They read every word three ways: they read between the lines and in the margins; they read the whole in terms of the parts, and each part in terms of the whole; they grow sensitive to context and ambiguity, to insinuation and implication; they perceive the color of words, the odor of phrases, and the weight of sentences. They may even take the punctuation into account. Then, if never before or after, they read.

But the necessity for close reading is not confined to affairs of the heart, or even to college assignments, for that matter. As Professor Richard T. Altick points out:

> Uncritical reading habits cost us money. When we read an advertisement in a magazine or newspaper, we are being influenced to buy something. The art of writing advertising copy is based wholly upon the skillful use of language specially chosen to subtly flatter us, to whet our interest, to entice us to think we need something which we often really don't need. How often do we buy a product on the strength of the advertiser's persuasion when we should have bought another brand which is both cheaper and better? We are prone to forget that the product which is most attractively packaged in words may well be inferior to other brands. If you question this, spend a half hour sometime with the current report of one of the consumers' research organizations, which dispassionately rank various brands on the basis of laboratory tests.

(Richard D. Altick, *Preface to Critical Reading.*)

Can you think of an occasion where you paid a price in money, time, embarrassment, or the like for not reading closely?

Language used to cause or prevent action is said to serve a directive function.

Commands are not the only example of directive use of language; requests are, too. When a teacher asks a student, "Are you prepared for the test?" she is *requesting* an answer. It is as if she said, *"Tell me* whether you're prepared for the test."

> **IN BRIEF**   Since commands and requests have no truth value, in their
> base form they are never premises or conclusions. However, they frequently
> appear in passages containing arguments.

Expressive Function

Expressive language is language used to vent or arouse feelings or emotions.
Poetry provides the clearest examples of expressive language, as illustrated by this
selection from T. S. Eliot's "The Hollow Men":

> We are the hollow men
> We are the stuffed men
> Leaning together
> Headpiece filled with straw, Alas!
> Our dried voices, when
> We whisper together
> Are quiet and meaningless
> As wind in dry grass
> Or rats' feet over broken glass
> In our dry cellar. . . .

Such poetry serves up graphic description and powerful insights into the human
condition. But it is not primarily intended to inform us of any fact or theory about the
world. The poet wishes to express deep emotions and attitudes, rather than
knowledge.

Expressive language is not confined to poetry, however. When you cheer "Right
on!" or console "That's too bad," or murmur affectionately "Honey," or mutter the
expletive "Damn!" you are also using language expressively.

Ceremonial Function

**Ceremonial language is language used on special occasions for special
ritualistic purpose.** The marriage ceremony is a classic example of the ceremonial
use of language. The language of legal documents and religious ceremonies also fall
into the category of ceremonial language. So do the reflexive words of greeting we use
daily—"How are you?" or "How are you doing?" or "What's happening?" or "How's
it going?" and the like.

Performative Function

**The performative function of language refers to language, the utterance of
which, in appropriate circumstances, actually effects what it appears to
report.** For example, when a baseball umpire shouts "You're out!" the player is out.

(An umpire once rightly told a contentious baserunner, "You ain't nothing 'til I say so.") And when the parties to a legal contract sign their names on the proverbial dotted line, they have effected a legally binding agreement. The list of performative words includes *apologize, agree, accept,* and *guarantee.*

EXERCISES ON THE FUNCTIONS OF LANGUAGE*

1. Discuss the function of the language in the following passages. (When a passage contains two sentences, comment on both.)
   A. Sacramento is the nation's capital.
   B. U.S. Senators serve a two-year term.
   C. When is the next election?
   D. Twenty percent of the homeless are alcoholics.
   E. Paris is a city in France.
   F. Water consists of two atoms of hydrogen and one of oxygen.
   G. "Shut the door. I'm cold."
   H. "Congratulations!"
   I. "She was a phantom of delight, when first she came upon my sight." (William Wordsworth)
   J. "I now pronounce you husband and wife."
   K. "For many years Trisomy 21 was believed directly and simply correlated to maternal age. Was that correct?"
   L. The field of molecular biology is today one that receives considerable attention. But it's actually a very young science, its beginning going back only to the 1940s.
2. Write five sentences that serve the informative function of language.

MIXED FUNCTIONS OF LANGUAGE

Language, of course, is a subtle and frequently elusive medium of communication. It is often more than what it appears to be. In other words, language can, and commonly does, serve a combination of functions, especially in extended arguments.

As an example of the mixed functions of language, consider the frequently studied poem "Shine, Perishing Republic" by the American poet Robinson Jeffers (1887–1962):

> I sadly smiling remember that the flower fades to make
>   fruit, the fruit rots to make earth.
> Out of the mother; and through the spring exultances,
>   ripeness and decadence; and home to the mother.
> You making haste haste on decay; not blameworthy; life
>   is good, be it stubbornly long or suddenly
> A mortal splendor: meteors are not needed less than
>   mountains: shine, perishing republic.

But for my children, I would have them keep their
    distance from the thickening center; corruption
Never has been compulsory, when the cities lie at the
    monster's feet there are left the mountains.
And boys, be in nothing so moderate as in love of man,
    a clever servant, insufferable master.
There is the trap that catches noblest spirits, that
    caught — they say — God, when he walked on earth.

This poem not only expresses an attitude and deep feeling, it also is packed with information, as professors K. L. Knickerbocker and H. Willar Reninger point out in the following commentary:

> Students of Jeffers recognize this basic pattern of belief in this area as something like this: Civilizations have always risen and inevitably fallen, this cycle always moving from east to west. . . . Why do civilizations fall? Freedom and wealth are irreconcilable, according to Jeffers, because man is driven by desire (self-love) to achieve power over his fellow man, and he will sell his freedom to achieve it. Men and their nations therefore travel the cycle of freedom, desire, wealth, loss of freedom, and ruin. Men then travel westward — as the Pilgrims and others did in the early seventeenth century; they fight to regain their freedom, win it, and travel the cycle to ruin once more. The implication is clear: America is next.[1]

Given this interpretation, the poem can also be said to use directive use of language by intending to cause us to value freedom over any other value.

    Similarly, the sermon of a televangelist may be directive, intended to cause us to believe and behave in a certain way. However, when dressed in fiery rhetoric, it also expresses and elicits strong feelings, thus serving the expressive function. In addition, it could include factual material, thus serving the informative function.

    By the same token, language used primarily to transmit information may serve other functions. For example, I have before me a book that is described variously as "imaginative," "provocative," "daring," "absorbing," "fascinating," and "great fun." Sounds like a novel, doesn't it? In fact, the work being described is a book dealing with the evolution of human intelligence. Amidst the welter of information the author provides on the human brain, he also transmits his own contagious enthusiasm (expressive use of language) and, in effect, bids readers to reflect upon, even verify his conclusion for themselves (directive function).

EXERCISES ON THE MIXED FUNCTIONS OF LANGUAGE

What language functions — informative, directive, expressive, ceremonial, or performative — are most likely intended to be served by each of the following passages? Be alert to mixed functions.

---

[1] K. L. Knickerbocker and H. Willar Reninger, *Interpreting Literature,* 5th ed. (New York: Holt, Rinehart and Winston, 1974), pp. 312–313.

1. Good words are worth much and cost little.
2. Happy families are all alike.
3. Don't count your chickens before they're hatched. (Aesop's *Fables*)
4. To everything there is a reason, and a time to every purpose under heaven.
5. Whoever shall smite thee on thy right cheek, turn to him the other also.
6. Familiarity breeds contempt.
7. Thou shalt give life for life, eye for eye, tooth for tooth and hand for hand.
8. Don't put off 'til tomorrow what you can do today.
9. Prepare today for the wants of tomorrow.
10. Make hay while the sun shines.
11. Never send to know for whom the bell tolls. It tolls for thee. (John Donne, "Meditation," 1624)
12. There's a skeleton in every house. (William Makepeace Thackeray)
13. Don't cut off your nose to spite your face.
14. *Caveat emptor!* (Let the buyer beware!)
15. Don't look a gift horse in the mouth.
16. No Man is an island, entire of itself; Everyman is a piece of the continent, a part of the main. (John Donne, "Meditation," 1624)
17. Ask not what your country can do for you; ask what you can do for your country. (President John F. Kennedy, *Inauguration Address,* 1961)
18. It is nought good a slepyng hound to wake. (Geoffrey Chaucer, *Troilus and Criseyde,* late fourteenth century)
19. No man is wise enough by himself. (Plautus)
20. Nurture your mind with great thoughts. (Benjamin Disraeli)
21. "What can we do when hope is gone?"
    The words leapt like a leaping sword:
    "Sail on! Sail on! Sail on! and on!" (Joaquin Miller, "Columbus")
22. What is this life if, full of care,
    We have no time to stand and stare? (William Henry Davies)

THE INTENDED FUNCTIONS OF DISCOURSE

You cannot always tell from the grammatical structure of a passage what its intended function is. For example, pretend that you and a friend are caught in a traffic jam on the way to a concert. As the minutes tick by and the traffic inches forward, you glimpse at your watch and say: "Would you believe we're going to be late?"

While using the interrogative form to frame your utterance, clearly you are not asking your friend for information. You are not requesting that your friend confirm or deny that you are going to be late. Rather, your question functions to convey (1) information (you will be late), and (2) exasperation about this fact. The first function is informative, the second expressive. Thus, an interrogative is not always a directive use of language. It may be functioning informatively or expressively, or both, as in this case.

Again, suppose that you are attending a party at which your state senator happens to be present. You have developed a sharp dislike of the senator's political philosophy and intend to campaign against her re-election. During the affair, an acquaintance who is unfamiliar with your feelings, introduces you to the senator. When the senator extends her hand in greeting, you shake it and say, "I'm pleased to meet you."

Your utterance is an example of what grammarians call a declarative sentence. Although informative language often takes this grammatical form, a declarative sentence is not always intended to communicate information. In this instance, you may not at all be pleased to meet the senator. Is your utterance, then, untrue? No, because it is not intended to impart information — it has no truth value; rather, "I'm pleased to meet you" has here a ceremonial function. It might even be expressive, showing your attitude of friendliness and civility despite your political differences with the senator.

IN BRIEF   There is no strict relationship between the grammatical structure of a passage and its intended function. Declarative sentences are not necessarily, or only, informative; interrogatives (questions) are not necessarily, or only, directive; and exclamations are not necessarily, or only, expressive.

Evaluating Discourse

A related point concerns the criteria for evaluating the respective function of discourse. An informative sentence, such as "AIDS is a sexually transmitted disease," has truth value — it is either true or false. In contrast, the directive use, as in "Practice safe sex," is subject to the criteria appropriate to such counsel, for example, "proper" or "improper." Thus, it is appropriate to describe "Practice safe sex" as "proper" or improper" advice, but not as "true" or "false." Similarly, considered as expressive, the utterance "I'm happy to know you practice safe sex" may be evaluated as a "sincere" or "insincere" expression of feeling, but not as true or false. The same applies to your greeting to the senator: "I'm pleased to meet you." That you felt otherwise makes the utterance an insincere expression of your feelings, but not an *untrue* statement because it was not intended informatively. In short, the various functions of language are subject to their own evaluative criteria.

Even these elementary illustrations underscore that language is an extraordinarily rich medium of communication that requires *active* participation on the part of the receiver of a message. If you said to the waiter in a restaurant, "I'm ready to order," and the waiter ignored you, you would probably grow irritated. "Waiter," you might shout when he next passed your table, "will you *please* take my order?" The scene might quickly grow ugly if the waiter replied: "Oh, you want to place your order. I thought that when you said 'I'm ready to order' you were merely reporting a psychological fact about yourself." Fortunately, no waiter would be so obtuse as to interpret your "I'm ready to order" as anything but a *request* to place an order. But the illustration does point up what is commonly termed "a breakdown in communication."

Communication is a process that involves the *sharing* of meaning between the source and receiver of a message. The waiter's response clearly showed that he did not share your intended meaning. Whether there has been successful communication is indicated by the verbal and nonverbal responses of the receiver. The response, called feedback, indicates whether or not the receiver understood what was intended. Obviously, fundamental to appropriate feedback is understanding what was intended. And this, in part, hinges on one's ability to recognize and distinguish among the different uses of language. If the waiter was not merely being impertinent in this instance, he lacked this ability.

In this case, you were able to summon the waiter and resend the message; but frequently, the source of the message is unavailable — as in written discourse. If you read an editorial, for example, you do not have the writer at your elbow to question about intended meaning. You must use your best interpretive powers to do that. This requires, but is not limited to, a keen sensitivity to the flexibility of language and its many uses.

IN BRIEF   The diversity of language use precludes the formulating of any mechanical way to recognize arguments. Whether or not a passage is argumentative ultimately depends on its intended function, and, as receivers of a message, we need to exercise considerable care in determining this. Writers and speakers also need to strive for clarity in this regard. Awareness of the intended uses of language serves the interests of both transmitters and receivers of messages.

MODULE 3.2

CATEGORIES OF ARGUMENT LANGUAGE

A well-honed sense of the myriad little words that play a big part in extended arguments is as important as an understanding of the intended functions of language. As we implied at the outset, extended arguments usually employ a variety of words and phrases that variously indicate logical relationships among assertions and the relative strength of evidence and force of statements. Familiarity with such language helps you in both identifying and understanding arguments. Though far from exhaustive, the following compilation does identify the major categories of language regularly used in extended arguments. Some of these you will recognize from Chapter 1. Nevertheless, given their key roles in argument, they are worth revisiting.

Premise and Conclusion Indicators

Often arguments contain specific words or phrases that indicate premise or conclusion. Take, for example, the word "because" in the following simple argument:

> **Capital punishment should be legalized** *because* it deters crime.

In this example, "because" shows a logical connection between the first proposition, "Capital punishment should be legalized," and the second, "it deters crime," such that the second is offered as grounds for the first. Stripped of all language but its logical operators, the sentence reads:

> _____ **because** _____ , **where the first blank represents the conclusion and the second the premise.**

Similarly, in the argument:

> **Capital punishment deters crime.** *Therefore,* it should be legalized,

the word "therefore" is intended to show that the second statement, "it should be legalized," logically follows from the first, "Capital punishment deters crime." Thus:

> <u>(premise)</u>. **Therefore,** <u>(conclusion)</u>.

Recall from Chapter 1 that certain words typically introduce conclusions, such as: *therefore, thus, so, it follows that, hence, we may infer,* and *consequently.* Also, the words *must, should, ought,* and *necessarily* frequently appear in conclusions.

By the same token, certain words signal premises. Some of these words are *because, since, as, for, inasmuch as, for the reason that.*

Spotting these connectives will help you to identify the premises and conclusions of more involved arguments, such as this one:

> **We need to continue to drill in U.S. waters for oil. Otherwise, we're going to add to our trade imbalance, for every dollar we spend to buy oil overseas is a dollar added to the trade deficit. Furthermore, by buying oil overseas instead of producing as much as we can domestically, we are, in effect, exporting jobs and profits and forgoing the revenue we would gain by taxing profits that would be earned here. Beyond this, the $2 billion-a-year royalty currently paid to the federal Treasury from offshore oil production will shrink, for production must fall off since exploration will decline.**

The connectives in this passage enable you to follow the author's reasoning and structure the argument. Stripped of all words but its connectives, the passage reads: (Statement 1). *Otherwise,* (Statement 2), *for* (Statement 3). *Furthermore,* (Statement 4). *Beyond this,* (Statement 5), *for* (Statement 6), *since* (Statement 7).

Notice how the indicator "since" signals that statement 7 is being given as backing for statement 6, which in turn is being given as support for statement 5, as the word "for" indicates. Similarly, the word "for" that precedes statement 3 indicates that the statement is being offered as support for statement 2. The words "otherwise," "furthermore," and "beyond this" indicate that statements 2, 4, and 5, respectively, are being given as support for statement 1. Thus, we can portray the argument as follows:

(D) We're going to add to our trade imbalance.

(B) Every dollar we spend to buy oil
overseas is a dollar added
to the trade deficit.

(D) By buying oil overseas instead of
producing as much as we can domestically,
we are, in effect, exporting jobs and
profits and forgoing the revenue we would gain
by taxing profits that would be earned here.   → **(C)** We need to continue
to drill in U.S.

(D) The $2 billion-a-year royalty currently   waters for oil.
paid to the federal Treasury from
offshore oil production will shrink.

(B) Production must fall off.

(B) Exploration will decline.

Nonlogical Use of Standard Premise and Conclusion Indicators   *When used in arguments,* premise and conclusion indicators help locate the basic parts of the argument. Recall that sometimes these words appear in *non*arguments. For example, "Since the restaurant opened, downtown traffic has increased," is *not* an argument. "Since" in this instance has temporal, not logical significance; it is being used to show a time relationship between the restaurant's opening and an increase in downtown traffic.

Because and *for* also can have nonlogical importance in assertions. For example, let's say that you just arrived at the stadium for a ball game, only to find the spectators leaving. When you ask why, someone replies:

The game was postponed because the weather is bad.

or

The game was postponed, for the weather is bad.

The statement "the weather is bad" is not offered as grounds for believing or demonstrating that the game was postponed. That the game was postponed is not in question; that has already been determined. The speaker is not intending to convince you that the game was postponed, but to *explain why* it was postponed. It is true that the speaker is asserting a casual relationship between the postponement and the weather, but he is not interested in establishing the truth of statement 1, merely to explain it.

In contrast, suppose you enter the ballpark and, like everyone else, you are sitting in the stands waiting for the weather to clear and the game to commence. The sky grows darker, the rain falls harder. The field is quickly becoming a quagmire. Finally, the fellow next to you says: "The game should be postponed because (or for) the weather is so bad." Here the speaker is interested in convincing you that the game should be postponed. He is expressing an argument.

IN BRIEF   Premise and conclusion indicators are enormously useful in pinpointing the location of premises and conclusions in arguments. But the presence of a standard premise or conclusion indicator does not make a passage an argument. A nonargument can contain a standard premise or conclusion signal. To determine whether the indicator is truly signaling a premise or conclusion, make sure the passage has the third feature of any argument — it contains an internal relationship among the statements such that one is being claimed to follow logically from the others. If it does, then the key words are functioning to show logical relationships.

EXERCISES ON PREMISE AND CONCLUSION INDICATORS

1. Underline and explain the function of the indicators in the following arguments. Then portray the structure of each argument, using D (for data), B (for backing) and C (for conclusion).
   A. It's fair to say that historians themselves disagree even about what happened in the past. After all, they are hopelessly confused about why historical trends occur. Moreover, philosophers have been and are still in muddled confusion, as a reading of philosophy shows. Beyond this, educators themselves can't agree in their choice of which experts we should listen to. So, we can't turn to history and philosophy in order to solve the problems of our time.
   B. A person educated in modern science believes that reality consists of the operations of immutable natural laws on the material substance of the universe. But shamans in many tribes are known to have defied so-called natural laws. What's more, the languages of some tribes don't have tenses to distinguish past from future. It follows that these tribes interpret the world far different from the way we do. Furthermore, some anthropologists now believe that different cultures hold different world views and that these views are all relative with no one necessarily being true or false. What people think is reality, then, depends

entirely on the kind of culture they are reared in and the experiences they have had.

2. Using the indicators as a guide to the relationship between the sentences, fill in the blanks of the following two arguments, choosing from among the choices given.

   A. The criminal law punishes a person more severely for having successfully committed a crime than it does a person who fails in his attempt to commit the same crime — even though both had the same evil intention. Under the civil law, a person who attempts to defraud his victim, but is unsuccessful, is not required to pay damages. But ____1____. Therefore, it seems that ____2____.

     1. A. the person committed a crime
       B. a person who successfully defrauds is punished
       C. a person who successfully defrauds is required to pay damages
       D. the law isn't supposed to discriminate between successful and unsuccessful criminals

     2. A. people who fail in their attempts to defraud go unpunished
       B. the law is blind to evil intentions
       C. the law is tougher on successful criminals than on unsuccessful ones
       D. there seems to be something irrational about our system of laws

   B. It's commonplace for us to praise the person who sacrifices his or her own life in order to save the life of a loved one under assault. But there's a contradiction in this appraisal, albeit an understandable one. After all, ____3____. For, in the eye of God, ____4____. Likewise, from the viewpoint of society, ____5____. And it doesn't make sense from the rescued loved one's viewpoint, for ____6____.

     3. A. the rescuer freely chose to sacrifice his or her own life
       B. people love heroes
       C. people wouldn't blame the rescuer for not acting heroically
       D. the rescuer's life is as important as the rescued loved one's

     4. A. the rescuer's life is the more valuable
       B. the rescued loved one's life is the more valuable
       C. both lives are equally valuable
       D. there's no praise attached to the act

     5. A. the rescuer's life is the more valuable
       B. heroic acts should be encouraged
       C. assaults are socially disruptive
       D. nothing is gained in the transaction

     6. A. the rescued loved one probably wouldn't have been killed
       B. the rescued loved one would willingly have exchanged places
       C. the rescued loved one will probably feel guilty
       D. the rescued loved one didn't explicitly ask for the rescuer to make the ultimate sacrifice

3. Using indicators as your guide, construct an argument by filling in the blanks of this argument skeleton.

   _____, since _____ and _____. Therefore, because _____, for the reason _____, _____.

Qualifiers

Besides premise and conclusion indicators, longer arguments often contain **qualifiers, which are terms that specify the degree of force or probability.** Qualification plays an important role in formulating and considering generalizations, which are statements that cover many specific instances of something. Consider, for example, these two generalizations:

All Americans are highly materialistic.

Some Americans are highly materialistic.

We should not form the first generalization until we have evidence that every single American has been highly materialistic—an impossible condition. In contrast, the word "some" in the second generalization so restricts the statement that we need evidence of only a single "highly materialistic" American. Similarly, qualifiers like *many, a lot,* or *quite a few* would restrict the generalization to some unspecified number between *all* and *some. It seems, apparently, evidently* and *perhaps* also restrict the force of a generalization. A restricted generalization is easier to defend than an unrestricted one. In argument, then, qualifiers can serve as defensive perimeters around premises.

It is worth noting, however, that although qualifiers have the effect of limiting or restricting generalizations by implying exceptions, their inclusion does not of itself make a statement acceptable. For example, the qualifier "perhaps" in the assertion "*Perhaps* women are more emotional than men" does very little if anything to limit the generalization "Women are more emotional than men." Even with "perhaps" (or *possibly* or "Women *may be. . . .*") the statement remains quite broad and in need of considerable supporting evidence.

Qualifiers have basically two purposes in argument. First, by limiting the scope of a generalization, they make it more defensible. Second, qualifiers can function to anticipate objections. This second purpose is served when arguers express reservations that take account of exceptional or special circumstances. Compare, for example, these two arguments:

Argument 1: Frank did not pass remedial composition. A student who is required to take remedial composition must pass it before taking English 1. Therefore, Frank will not be permitted to take Professor Shakespeare's English 1.

Argument 2: Frank did not pass remedial composition. A student who is required to take remedial composition must pass it before taking English 1. Therefore, Frank will not be permitted to take Professor Shakespeare's English 1, *unless he gets Professor Shakespeare's permission.*

The italicized portion of argument 2 expresses a special circumstance under which Frank may enroll in English 1, even though he flunked remedial composition.

By expressing this reservation, the arguer has qualified his conclusion and, thus, foreclosed the objection that the conclusion of argument 1 invites.

IN BRIEF   The function of a qualifier is to reflect the degree of force or likelihood that the evidence suggests. It does not permit asserting something that a careful examination of experience, observation, and research simply will not support. So, although qualifiers can make statements more defensible and anticipate objections to them, their logical purpose is to help us make statements that more precisely accord with evidence.

Intensifiers

Sometimes we make claims that we feel are beyond reasonable doubt, for example: "Rape should never be condoned," "The ozone layer is eroding," or "The Nazis conducted a pogrom against the Jews." These statements report what are believed to be unquestionable facts. **Intensifiers are words or phrases used to signal what is believed to be an incontrovertible fact.** Thus, "*Surely* rape should never be condoned," "*There's no question* that the ozone layer is eroding," or "*Undoubtedly,* the Nazis conducted a pogrom against the Jews." Intensifiers function to present a claim that, on grounds of reason or overwhelming evidence, is effectively self-evident.

Considered within the activity of argument, intensifiers function to signal a belief that our audience shares (or reasonably should share). Establishing such shared beliefs is important from both a logical and practical point of view. Logically, the acceptability of an argument depends on asserting claims that cannot or will not be reasonably challenged. On the practical side, we need to be able to make, and have accepted, uncontroversial claims. Otherwise, we are doomed to provide backing for every assertion we make — rendering even the simplest argument infinitely long. So, when properly used, expressed, or implied, intensifiers such as *clearly, obviously, indeed,* or *to be sure* are an essential part of the activity of arguing or presenting proofs.

Arguing also involves a measure of trust and good faith. If arguers use intensifiers, they are implicitly guaranteeing that the claims they are making are so uncontroversial and universally accepted as to require no argument or evidence. However, our desire to view complex questions in the simplest terms sometimes invites oversimplification. This is especially true in matters of human conduct or social policies. There is nothing simple about abortion, capital punishment, gun control, commercial nuclear power plants, affirmative action, or a myriad of other contemporary issues. Yet, we sometimes hear people claiming that "Abortion is *clearly* wrong" (or "*Certainly*, women should be permitted to have an abortion on demand") or "There can be *no doubt* that capital punishment should be legalized" (or "*Surely,* capital punishment should not be legalized"). That intense feelings fuel such claims is obvious, but irrelevant. Controversial claims require argument and evidence. To expect a thinking person to accept them on the intensity of the underlying feeling is unreasonable and unfair.

IN BRIEF   Used in argument, intensifiers function to carve out areas of shared belief, to make claims for which evidence need not be made explicit. Thus, used honestly, intensifiers save time and simplify discussion. Sometimes, however, intensifiers are used illicitly to gloss over highly complex and controversial issues. So, in encountering or using intensifiers, always inspect the statement in which they are used to ensure that their use is justified.

Discounts

Let's suppose you are wondering whether to take "Advanced Logic" next term from Professor Einstein, about whom you know nothing. So you consult three acquaintances who recently completed Einstein's course. Here is what they say:

AL: Einstein's tough and fair.
BETH: Einstein's tough, but fair.
CAROL: Einstein's fair, but tough.

These responses are similar and different. Each reports the same facts, that Einstein is tough and Einstein is fair. But these facts operate in the same way only for Al. For Beth, the professor's fairness overrides his toughness; and for Carol, his toughness overrides his fairness. These emphases are communicated by the word "but," which is a discount.

   A discount is a word used to disregard an assertion. Beth used the word "but" to disregard or downplay the assertion "Einstein's tough," and Carol used it to downplay the assertion "Einstein's fair."

   Another common discount is the word *although,* which functions to disregard the assertion that immediately follows it in favor of the connected statement. "*Although* Einstein's tough, he's fair," Beth could have said; and Carol could have said, "*Although* Einstein's fair, he's tough." There is an array of words and phrases used to discount: *yet, nevertheless, despite, in spite of, even though, still, however, no matter, be that as it may, this notwithstanding,* and the like. In the example we have just seen, "but" and "although" function to contrast facts and give them an order of priority. In other words, they are often used to connect facts that point in different directions.

   Discounts have other uses besides downplaying facts contrary to a preferred position. They are frequently used in argument to anticipate criticism. Consider, for example, this passage from the writings of the eighteenth-century German philosopher Immanuel Kant:

> Nothing can possibly be conceived in the world, or even out of it, which can be called good without qualification except a *good will*. Intelligence, wit, judgment, and the other talents of the mind . . . or courage, resolution, perseverance, or qualities of temperament are undoubtedly good and desirable in many respects; but the gifts of nature may also become extremely bad and mischievous if the ill which is to make use of them and which, therefore, constitutes *character* is not good.

Kant realizes that his claim that only a good will has intrinsic worth is controversial. After all, common sense points to other goods — intelligence and courage, for example. Anticipating objections from his audience, he identifies these and other qualities as often desirable. Then he proceeds to discount them ("*but* these gifts. . .) because they can be misused. These qualities are only good if the will which makes use of them is good. It is worth noting that anticipating objections serves several very useful purposes in argument. First, it forces us to critically inspect our own position from the view of its detractors. Second, it allows us to rebut criticisms before they are raised by detractors. Third, it can strengthen our own argument by defusing criticism of it. And fourth, it shows we are thoughtful and fair-minded, qualities that any audience finds appealing.

Still another use of discounts is to block conversational implications of what we have said. Suppose, for example, you are discussing with a friend a mutual acquaintance named Ted. At one point, you say, "Ted's very ambitious." Immediately sensing the dim light in which you may have cast Ted, you quickly add, "But he's not ruthless." Your discount precludes the implication that Ted is self-centered and hard-hearted. "Yes," your friend agrees, "I've also found him to be a hard worker, though well rounded." The *though* phrase effectively blocks out the suggestion that Ted is a boring workaholic.

Of course, the use of discounts to control conversational implications can be far more subtle than these simple examples suggest. Take, as an example, this passage from Daniel Boorstin's *The Discoverers,* an extraordinary saga of human discovery:

> Water, that wonderful, flowing medium, the luck of the planet — which would serve humankind in so many ways, and which gives our planet a special character — made possible man's first small successes in measuring the dark hours. Water, which could be captured in any small bowl, was more manageable than the sun's shadow. When mankind began to use water to serve him for a timepiece, he took another small step forward in making the planet into his household. Man could make the captive water flow fast or slow, day and night. He could be sure of its flow in regular, constant units, which would be the same at the equator or on the tundra, winter or summer. *But perfecting this device was long and difficult.* By the time the water clock was elaborated into a more or less precision instrument, it had already begun to be supplanted by something far more convenient, more precise, and more interesting.
>
> *Yet, for most of history, water provided the measure of time when the sun was not shining.* And until the perfection of the pendulum clock about 1700, the most accurate timepiece was probably the water clock. . . .[2]

---

[2]Daniel Boorstin, *The Discoverers* (New York: Vintage Books, 1983), p. 29.

Notice how the *but* sentence (italicized) cancels the suggestion that inventing the water clock was as easy collecting water in a barrel, and the *yet* sentence (italicized) blocks the implication that the water clock did not find much use in the ancient world.

IN BRIEF Discount words and phrases make mighty contributions to effective communication and argument. They enable us to connect facts that point in opposed directions, anticipate criticism, and cancel false implications. A well-honed regard for their subtle uses is especially vital to understanding the language of longer arguments, of which they are a key part.

Asides

Not everything included in an extended argument may be exactly relevant. Some arguments contain asides, which are departures or digressions from the main point. Often these are signaled by words such as *incidentally, by the way,* or *parenthetically,* as in:

> **Jones is a good choice to build your cabinets. He's an expert carpenter, and, *by the way,* he's also a crack electrician.**

The speaker clearly realizes that Jones' electrical skills have nothing to do with his carpentry skills, which is the point at hand. The phrase "by the way" permits the inclusion of the aside, while at the same time identifying it as such.

If asides are not exactly relevant to an argument, why are they included? What is their function? For one thing, asides can be persuasive. That Jones is an electrician as well as a carpenter speaks well of his breadth of skills and general competence. By the same token, had the speaker said: "Jones is an expert carpenter and, by the way, quite a drinker," you would likely draw a different picture of Jones, even though he is an expert carpenter. (You can see how, in the hands of professional persuaders, asides can be used to shape opinion.)

Asides can also be used to accomplish the same goals of some other categories of language. For example, an aside can function to qualify, as in: "The merger, *as well as I can determine,* will occur within the next ninety days." An aside can intensify, as in "The problem of the homeless, *I'm sure you'll agree,* is a most serious social issue."

In longer arguments, writers sometimes indicate how they became interested in an issue or controversy. They tell their audience what prompted them to address the topic, what their central concerns are, or who the participants are. While such information conceptualizes the argument, it is not exactly relevant to the argument and, therefore, can be viewed as an aside. For example, only the italicized portion of the following passage constitutes the argument; the rest is background/aside:

The most fundamental question involved in the long history of thought on abortion is: When is the unborn a human? To phrase the question that way is to put in comprehensive humanistic terms what theologians question under the heading of "ensoulment" or deal with implicitly in their treatment of abortion. *The answer to the question of when the unborn is a human is simple: at conception. The reason is that at conception the being receives the genetic code.*

Stripped of its background aside, the argument may be structured:

(D) At conception, the new being ⟶ **(C)** The unborn is a
receives the genetic code.   human at conception.

Notice how being familiar with asides helped us to structure this argument, to home-in on the central claim and its support. Paying scrupulous attention to asides is vital in understanding the structure of longer arguments, which often contain an array of incidental material that can divert the unwary from the main issue. For example, here is an excerpt from a long essay that argues in favor of reverse discrimination in hiring policies. Notice how the author is making the *opposite* point — that, in fact, there are good reasons to *oppose* giving women and minorities preferential treatment in the work place:

In recent years government policies intended to ensure fairer employment and educational opportunities for women and minority groups have engendered alarm. Although I shall in this paper argue in support of enlightened versions of these policies, I nevertheless think there is much to be said for the opposition arguments. In general I would agree that the world of business is now overregulated by federal government, and I therefore hesitate to support an extension of the regulative arm of government into the arena of hiring and firing. Moreover, policies that would eventuate in reverse discrimination in present North American society have a heavy presumption against them, for both justice-regarding and utilitarian reasons. (Tom Beauchamp, "The Justification of Reverse Discrimination.")

Having raised this aside, the author proceeds to discount it in the remainder of the essay. Why did he include it? To show the audience that he, like some of them, philosophically opposes further governmental interventionism and to acknowledge that weighty arguments need to be made to justify such interventionism.

Examples Often, writers will signal examples and illustrations with phrases such as *for example, as an illustration, for instance,* or *take the case of.* Sometimes they will merely introduce the example without a signal phrase. Either way it is useful to remember that an example may function as either (1) a mere clarification or illumination of a point, in which case, it would not be part of the supporting details and thus can be handled as an aside, or (2) an attempt to demonstrate a point, in which case it would be considered part of the support material.

Consider, first, the italicized example in the following paragraph, excerpted from an essay in which the author inveighs against the charge that philosopher Bertrand Russell is morally unfit to teach in an American university:

Judge Mcgeehan condemned Russell as an immoral person because of his divorce record in England. This record was known to the authorities of many colleges including those for women and co-educational ones, where Russell was invited to teach and gave a course of lectures. In a country where many leaders of our public life have been divorced, can it be said as a matter of law that teachers who have gone through such marital difficulties must be dismissed? *Many, perhaps a majority, of our people regard George Eliot as one of the noblest women of the nineteenth century, though she lived in what was legally an adulterous relation with George Henry Lewis. . . .* (Morris Cohen, "The Bertrand Russell Case: A Scandalous Denial of Justice.")

In this case, the author is probably using the example as an outstanding familiar illustration of a person who was highly respected though, by conventional standards, could have been thought to be immoral. The example helps to crystallize his incontestable point that many esteemed people go through marital difficulties. But it is probably not being offered to prove that point.

In contrast, consider the extended example that French novelist Albert Camus (1913–1960) uses to open his celebrated essay, "Reflection on the Guillotine":

Shortly before World War I, a murderer whose crime was particularly shocking (he had killed a family of farmers, children and all) was condemned to death in Algiers. He was an agricultural worker who had slaughtered in a bloody delirium, and had rendered his offense still more serious by robbing his victims. The case was widely publicized and it was generally agreed that decapitation was altogether too mild a punishment for such a monster. I have been told this was the opinion of my father, who was particularly outraged by the murder of the children. One of the few things I know about this is that this was the first time in his life he wanted to attend an execution. He got up while it was still dark, for the place where the guillotine was set up was at the other end of the city, and once there, found himself among a great crowd of spectators. He never told what he saw that morning. My mother could only report that he rushed wildly into the house, refused to speak, threw himself on the bed, and suddenly began to vomit. He had just discovered the reality concealed beneath the great formulas that ordinarily serve to mask it. Instead of thinking of the murdered children, he could recall only the trembling body he had seen thrown on a board to have its head chopped off.

This ritual act must indeed be horrible if it can subvert the indignation of a simple, upright man; if the punishment in which he regarded as deserved a hundred times over had no other effect on him than to turn his stomach. When the supreme act of justice merely nauseated the honest citizen it is supposed to protect, it seems difficult to maintain that this act is intended—as its proper functioning *should* intend it—to confer a greater degree of peace and order upon the city.

Far more than merely illuminating a point, this illustration *makes* Camus' point that capital punishment by decapitation is more repulsive than restorative.

It is worth noting that the fact that an example or illustration is not a formal part of an extended argument does not always mean it should not appear in the argument. When well chosen, as with the George Eliot reference, such examples both elucidate and enliven an argument. They provide a common ground of understanding between author and audience and, thus, are most effective rhetorical devices. (Do you think the example given in the second sentence of this paragraph is being used to illustrate or to demonstrate a point?)

Speaking of . . .

Categories of Language

Internal Coherence

The class of devices called *relationship signals* can offer readers guidance. . . through the crystalline patterns of (the writer's) thought. These are expressions which announce first of all whether (the writer) is continuing in the same direction of thought or shifting direction — and second, what kind of continuity or shift to expect.

The following, for example, are signals to show continuation in the same direction:

To show that the same topic continues: this, these, that, such, the same

To introduce another item in the same series: another, again, a second (a third, etc.), further, furthermore, moreover, similarly, likewise, too, finally, also

To introduce another item in a time series: next, then, later on, afterwards, finally

To introduce an example or particularization of what had just been said: for instance, for example

To introduce a concluding item or a summary: finally, altogether, all in all, the point is, in conclusion, to summarize

There are signals to show a shift of direction:

To introduce material which opposes what has just been said: but, however, on the other hand, on the contrary

To introduce a concession to an opposing view: to be sure, granted, of course

To show that the original line is about to resume after a concession: still, nevertheless, nonetheless, all the same

Such signals need not always come first in a sentence; they are often delayed to allow initial emphasis to something else.

(Richard M. Eastman, *Style.*)

EXERCISES ON CATEGORIES OF ARGUMENT LANGUAGE*

In the following arguments, discuss the function of the italicized expressions in terms of premise and conclusion indicators, qualifiers, intensifiers, discounts, and asides. Where examples are given, determine whether they are making a point or merely clarifying one — that is, functioning as evidence or strictly clarification.

1. Laws making suicide a criminal act are absurd. *For one thing,* there's no penalty that the law can assess which inflicts greater injury than suicide itself. *In the second,* it's no business of the state to prevent suicide, *for* a person has an inherent right to inflict fatal injury on himself if he so chooses.

2. *Some* philosophers claim that human beings, simply because they're human beings, have natural rights. *But* rights accorded persons vary from society to society, *as* a review of the law of various societies *well* demonstrates, and social anthropology has anecdotally observed for decades. *Therefore, since* there is no right that is universally accepted, there are no natural rights.

3. This piece of pottery, *it can be concluded, must* belong to the late Minoan period, *inasmuch as* the dress of the female figures accords with the fashion of that period. The activities of the people depicted all suggest that period, as does the centrality of the bull. *Beyond this,* the black, semigloss glaze is the result of a firing process widespread during the Minoan era.

4. A declining growth rate only postpones, not precludes, long-range energy shortages. *For* conservation, say by a factor of two together with a maintenance of five percent growth rate, delays fuel shortage problems by only fourteen years. *And* reduction of the growth rate to four percent postpones the problem for only a quarter century. *Furthermore, if the energy is available,* inequities in standards of living will have the effect of increasing the growth rate. Socio-religious factors, *incidentally,* will have the same effect. *Hence,* advance planning is crucial to avoid drastic shortages in world energy.

5. The process out of which the self arises is a social process, which implies interaction of individuals in the group, implies the pre-existence of the group. It implies *also* certain cooperative activities in which the different members of the group are involved. It implies, *further,* that out of this process there may in turn develop a more elaborate organization than that out of which the self has arisen, *and* that the selves *may be* the organs, the essential parts at least, of this more elaborate social organization within which these selves arise and exist. *Thus* there is a social process out of which selves arise and within which further differentiation, further evolution, further organization, takes place.
(George Herbert Mead, *The Social Origins of the Self.*)

6. It is *quite* possible to study the visible, audible, smellable effulgences of human bodies, and much study of human behavior has been in those terms. One can lump together very large numbers of units of behavior and regard them as a statistical population, in no way different from the multiplicity constituting a system of nonhuman objects. *But* one will not be studying persons. In a science of persons . . . behavior is a function of experience; *and* both experience and

behavior are always in relation to someone or something other than self.
(R. D. Laing, *The Politics of Experience.*)

7. Political economy conceals the estrangement inherent in the nature of labor by not considering the direct relationship between the worker (labor) and production. It is true that labor produces for the rich wonderful things — *but* for the worker, deformity. It replaces labor by machines — *but* some of the workers it throws back to a barbarous type of labor, and the other workers it turns into machines. It produces intelligence — *but* for the worker idiocy and cretinism.
(Karl Marx, *The Economic and Philosophic Manuscripts of 1844.*)

8. Our encounters with others tend increasingly to be competitive as a result of the search for privacy. We less and less often meet our fellow man to share and exchange, and more and more often encounter him as an impediment or a nuisance: making the highway crowded when we are rushing somewhere, cluttering and littering the beach or park or wood, pushing in front of us at the supermarket, taking the last parking place, polluting our air and water, building a highway through our house, blocking our view, and so on. *Because* we have cut off so much communication with each other we keep bumping into each other, and *thus* a higher and higher percentage of our interpersonal contacts are abrasive.
(Philip Slater, *The Pursuit of Loneliness.*)

9. I can not live with a person without my art. *And yet* I have never set that art above everything else. It is essential to me, *on the contrary,* because it excludes no one and allows me to live, just as I am, on a footing with all. To me art is not a solitary delight. It is a means of stirring the greatest number of men by providing them with a privileged image of our common joys and woes. *Hence* it forces the artist to isolate himself; it subjects him to the humblest and most universal truth.
(Albert Camus, Nobel Prize Acceptance Speech.)

10. That logic should have been thus successful [in devising formal rules of all thought] is an advantage which it owes entirely to its limitations, whereby it is justified in abstracting — *indeed,* it is under obligation to do so — from all objects of knowledge and their differences, leaving to the understanding nothing to deal with save itself and its form. *But* for reason to enter on the sure path of science, is, of course, much more difficult, *since* it has to deal not with itself alone but also with objects. Logic, *therefore,* . . . forms, as it were, only the vestibule of the sciences; and when we are concerned with specific modes of knowledge, while logic is indeed presupposed in any critical estimate of them, *yet* for the actual acquiring of them we have to look to the sciences properly and objectively so called.
(Immanuel Kant, *Critique of Pure Reason.*)

11. Let no one when young delay to study philosophy, nor when he is old grow weary of this study. *For* no one can come too early or too late to secure the health of his soul. *And* the man who says that the age of philosophy has either not yet come or has gone by is like the man who says that the age of happiness is not yet come to him, or has passed away. *Wherefore* both when young and old a man must study philosophy, that as he grows old he may be young in blessings through the grateful

recollection of what has been, and that in youth he may be old as well, since he will know no fear of what is to come.
(Epicurus, "Letter of Monoeceus.")

When we observe a young American middle-class girl playing dumb for the benefit of her boy friend, we are ready to point to items of guile and contrivance in her behavior. *But* like herself and her boy friend, we accept as an unperformed fact that this performer *is* (sic) a young American middle-class girl. But *surely* here we neglect the greater part of the performance. It is commonplace to say that different social groups express in different ways such attributes as age, sex, territory, and class status, and that in each case these bare attributes are elaborated by means of a distinctive complex cultural configuration of proper ways of conducting oneself. To be a given kind of person, *then,* is not merely to possess the required attributes, but also to sustain the standards of conduct and appearance that one's social group attaches there to. The unthinking ease with which performers consistently carry off such standard-maintaining routines does not deny that a performance has occurred, merely that the participants have been aware of it.
(Erving Goffman, *The Presentation of Self.*)

MODULE 3.3

WRITING WITH REASON: ACHIEVING ARGUMENT COHERENCE

Verbal expressions like the ones we have discussed in this chapter make several important contributions to writing effective argumentative essays. Clearly **premise and conclusion indicators** are crucial in enabling your audience to follow your line of reasoning and argument. They explicitly show the relationships among sentences and paragraphs and signal premises and conclusions. **Qualifiers** build defensive perimeters around arguments by limiting the scope of statements. As a result, the presence of qualifiers preclude criticisms that might otherwise arise. Used properly, **intensifiers** are good, economical ways of asserting what is incontrovertible. They also lend emphasis to points on which you may wish to focus. While having the effect of conceding facts and at the same time downplaying them, **discounts** allow you to anticipate and perhaps refute opposing viewpoints. Acknowledging opposing viewpoints assures your audience that you are even-handed and thoughtful, that you have given the matter due consideration. Finally, **asides** allow you to include necessary background and clarification or even informative digressions and illuminating anecdotes.

Taken together, these little verbal devices provide your essay necessary coherence, which is a basic element in rhetoric. **Coherence literally means "sticking"** or "clinging," which in writing means sticking together of paragraphs and

Speaking of . . .

The Basic Elements in Rhetoric

Unity, Coherence, Emphasis, Style

Unity in composition means that all the elements in the composition are related to the central theme (i.e., thesis). Thus a good beginning introduces or leads up to the central theme; a good middle develops it; a good ending recapitulates, summarizes, or reaffirms it. The root principles of unity are a clearly defined purpose (i.e., a logical progression of main points). . . .

    Coherence in composition means that the individual elements are also related to one another. Thus, a coherent composition will be marked by its continuity, or the logical *flow* of ideas. Moreover, this continuity will be made apparent to the reader by some expression that signifies the logical relation of one part to another (i.e., by logical operators and other verbal expressions).

    One aspect of coherence is the interrelation of beginning, middle, and end. Each part stems from the other, not in a mechanical but in a logical and organic way. . . .

    Emphasis in composition means that the various elements are arranged in an order best calculated to make the reader aware of and sympathetic to the writer's purpose. The means of creating emphasis are as many as the ingenuity of the writer can command. In general, however, they are:

1. Strong declarative statement
2. Placing the principal ideas in the most prominent places in a discourse, usually at the beginning or at the end
3. Developing the more important ideas at greater length
4. Repetition of the main ideas. . .

    Style, the fourth element in rhetoric, is in general the right combination of words, sentences, and paragraphs. By "right" we mean that it achieves the writer's purpose in the light of his subject and occasion, and in doing so, it reflects acceptable standards of logic and language.

(Francis Connolly and Gerald Levin, *A Rhetoric Case Book.*)

sentences. Appropriate verbal expressions make your essay integrated, consistent, and intelligible.

    The words and phrases we have examined in this chapter—and innumerable others like them—give verbal expression to the actual relationships between the sentences and paragraphs in your essays. When these relationships are not clear, confusion results. Writers must avoid confusion. For in writing, nothing is or should be worse than not being understood. This is why good writers make judicious use of verbal expressions to effect coherence.

Of course, a real relationship between sentences and between paragraphs must exist if coherence is to be achieved. But a fact of language is that, even when a relationship exists, coherence can be lacking. Consider, for example, these three sentences:

> **The Strategic Defense Initiative, popularly known as "Star Wars," can provide the United States a large measure of protection from nuclear attack. If I were president, I would de-emphasize this project. Crime, inadequate health care, mediocre education, and deteriorating infrastructure pose just as serious threats to national security.**

Now, if readers try hard, they can perceive the real relationship that exists between these sentences. But they should not have to *try hard* to see it. They should not experience the momentary hesitation and feel the kind of disjointedness that these sentences cause. The real relationship that exists between these sentences needs to be *expressed*. When it is, the hesitation and disjointedness will vanish because the sentences will then "stick together." Note the improved intelligibility of the sentences when a verbal means of transition is added to the sentences:

> **The Strategic Defense Initiative, popularly known as "Star Wars," can provide the United States a large measure of protection from nuclear attack. *But,* if I were president, I would de-emphasize this project, *for* crime, inadequate health care, mediocre education, and deteriorating infrastructure pose just as serious threats to national security.**

In this example, the discount "but" and the premise signal "for" express the relationship between the sentences and, thus, effect coherence.

This chapter has emphasized the simplest and most recognizable method of achieving coherence: the use of transitional words and phrases (for example, *therefore, so, thus, and, moreover, also; first . . . second . . . third; but, however, yet*). **Coherence may also be effected through the repetition of a key word in a sentence, usually a noun, that appears in the preceding sentence.** The repetition of the word signals to the reader the continuation of a line of thought. As a result, the reader can progress smoothly with the reading.

To understand how repetition of important words can provide coherence, first note the disjointedness between these two sentences:

> **Law is a suitable profession only for those with agile minds. Since problems can shift abruptly, lawyers must be able to alter their modes of thinking quickly to meet unexpected turns of events.**

Even with the inclusion of "since," the absence of an appropriate signal in the second sentence to connect it with the first leaves readers vague or indefinite in their understanding. Notice how the inclusion of a key word helps the reader's mind respond with rapid comprehension:

> **Law is a suitable profession only for those with agile minds. Since problems in *law* can shift abruptly, lawyers must be able to alter their modes of thinking quickly to meet unexpected turns of events.**

Another way of achieving coherence is through **pronoun reference.** When the pronoun of one sentence refers to a noun in the preceding sentence, it functions just as a word repetition or other transitional device to effect immediate comprehension in the reader's mind. To understand the usefulness of pronoun reference, note the disjointedness of these two sentences:

> **The plant manager rejected the union's proposal for improving plant safety. Cost and impracticality were cited.**

There is no specific signal to help the reader follow the line of thought here. Coherence is lacking. Now, notice how the inclusion of the pronouns "she" and "it" provide the needed coherence:

> **The plant manager rejected the union's proposal for improving plant safety. *She* cited the cost and impracticality of *it*.**

Finally, **coherence can be achieved without any specific verbal expression when the movement of ideas is clear.** Consider, for example, this paragraph:

> **Money isn't the root of *all* evil. Driven by ruthless ambition, politicians have committed villainous acts. Sexual psychotics rape and murder. Drunk drivers maim and kill. Disturbed parents abuse their children. No, money is the root of *some* evil.**

In this instance, none of the other three methods for achieving coherence is present. Nevertheless, the paragraph "hangs together" because of a clear pattern of thought and sentence structure.

IN BRIEF   Good argumentative essays have coherence. Their sentences and paragraphs "stick together." Essays are coherent when there is clear linkage between paragraphs, and paragraphs are coherent when their sentences are clearly joined to each other. Coherence can be achieved through a variety of verbal expressions, repetition of key words, pronoun reference, or, in a somewhat more sophisticated way, through a clear movement of ideas. Each of these methods is used by good writers.

EXERCISES ON ACHIEVING COHERENCE

The following paragraphs make sense but they are not as smooth as they could be. With the categories of language in mind—indicators, qualifiers, intensifiers, discounts, asides—fill in the blanks with words or phrases that provide the necessary coherence between sentences and make the most contextual sense. (The first is provided with the appropriate categories from which to select words.)

1. **(Intensifier)** one of the most important qualities for politicians to possess is imagination. **(Discount)** most politicians are singularly unimaginative. **(Intensifier)** some have single-track minds—they never stray from a set line of thought and procedure. Our current mayor **(illustration)** still spends hours a week on arithmetical checkup on employees even though the city now owns a computer. **(Indicator)** he fails to make use of modern technology. **(Indicator)** he's likely soon to be out of a job. **(Qualifying reservation)** he applies more imagination to his work.

2. _____ people have three misconceptions about the nature of rules of grammar. _____ they feel that an arbitrary rule makes an expression correct or incorrect, _____ it is custom only that makes correctness. _____ they think that only whole words are involved in grammatical constructions, _____ parts of words play an important grammatical role. _____ verb parts *ing, en, ed, s,* and so forth are important grammatical entities. _____ they seem to assume that all languages have similar grammatical systems, _____ that isn't true. Estonian, _____, has twelve cases, _____ Latin has only five. _____ there are innumerable differences between grammatical systems. _____ we see that the general public is misinformed about grammar.

3. _____ political liberals condemn the "go slow" tactics of conservatives on the grounds that the liberal ideas of the past have become the conservative ideas of today. _____ these liberals feel that they represent the advanced thought that leads to progress and that the conservatives represent the stagnant thought that prevents progress. _____ it's useful to remember that not every liberal idea of the past has proved to be of value. _____ , conservatives should not be viewed as necessarily antiprogress.

4. _____ space enthusiasts urge that billions of dollars be spent on moon travel on the assumption that valuable minerals might be mined there and transported to earth. _____ these enthusiasts are grossly ignorant of the costs that would be involved in such mineral extraction and transportation. _____ , there is not a single mineral known that could ever be profitably mined on the moon and shipped to earth, which, _____ , has plenty of minerals yet untapped. _____ we can someday learn to manufacture rocket fuel cheaply, we will always have to pay hundreds of dollars a pound to get any substance from the moon to the earth. _____ the cost of outfitting and shipping miners to work on the airless and alternately boiling and freezing surface of the moon will always be thousands of dollars an hour. Yes, mining the moon is an intriguing idea.

_____ we can be pretty sure that no known substance can ever be profitably brought from the moon in commercial quantities.

IMPROVING PERFORMANCE

SUMMARY-TEST QUESTIONS FOR CHAPTER 3*

1. What is the connection between sensitivity to the function of language and argument analysis?
2. Fill in the blanks by choosing one from among: A. informative, B. directive, C. expressive, D. ceremonial, E. performative
   A. Language used to communicate facts and reasons is _____ .
   B. The greeting, "What's new?" is an example of the _____ function of language.
   C. Generally speaking, the language of science is _____ .
   D. The language of legal documents is a good example of _____ language.
   E. Premises and conclusions always serve the _____ function of language.
3. A question can only function directively. True or False?
4. Language used primarily to transmit information may also serve other functions. Give an example.
5. Which of the following statements, if any, would you agree with? Explain.
   A. There's no strict relationship between the grammatical structure of a sentence and its intended function.
   B. It's improper to call the sentence "Don't drink and drive" true.
   C. Premises and conclusions are always true statements.
   D. For an assertion to have truth value, its language must be informative.
6. Which of the following words, if any, does not belong with the others?
   A. thus
   B. therefore
   C. for
   D. consequently
   E. There are no exceptions; each signals a conclusion.
7. What do the words *certainly, surely,* and *obviously* have in common?
8. A statement that contains an intensifier—for example, "*No doubt* AIDS can be transmitted through an exchange of bodily fluids"—is always true. True or False?
9. Choose from among P (for premise), B (for backing), and C (for conclusion) in filling in the blanks of the following argument skeletons:
   A. Because _____ , therefore _____ , for _____ .
   B. _____ , since _____ because _____ .
   C. Inasmuch as _____ and _____ , as _____ , _____ follows.
   D. _____ , for _____ but _____ because _____ .
   E. In the first place _____ , otherwise _____ . Second, because _____ , _____ . Therefore, insofar as _____ , _____ .

10. Which of the following passages, if any, is *not* an argument?
    A. Francis must be guilty since he had motive, means, and opportunity.
    B. Since Francis is guilty, he should be punished.
    C. Francis has been well behaved since he was punished.
    D. Francis, since he has been punished, should be forgiven.
    E. Each of the preceding is an argument.
11. "Harry probably won't qualify, because he missed the application deadline." It may be correctly inferred that
    A. applicants who miss the application deadline definitely will not qualify.
    B. applicants who miss the application deadline occasionally will not qualify.
    C. applicants who miss the application deadline usually will not qualify.
    D. applicants who meet the application deadline probably qualify.
    E. C and D because they logically mean the same thing.
12. If a friend tells you, "The movie was long, yet absorbing," you may rightly infer that your friend
    A. was significantly annoyed by the length of the film.
    B. found the film's length comparatively insignificant.
    C. considers the film's length and execution of equal value.
    D. A and B
    E. None of the above.
13. Under which category of language do the terms *incidentally, by the way,* and *parenthetically* fall?
14. Examples are
    A. always irrelevant to an argument and therefore never function as premises.
    B. sometimes relevant to an argument and therefore may function as premises.
    C. only used in an argument if they are essential to the main point or conclusion.
    D. A and C
15. Coherence in writing can be achieved in what four ways.

CRITICAL THINKING APPLICATIONS

1. Usually when the temperature exceeds eighty degrees for two or more days, weekly sales at Jastrow's Ice Cream Emporium increase by at least ten percent. Upon returning to his shop after a week's absence, Mr. Jastrow observes that the week's sales did not increase by at least ten percent. **Jastrow may correctly infer**
    A. the temperature did not exceed eighty any day that week.
    B. the temperature probably did not exceed eighty any day that week.
    C. the temperature did not exceed eighty for two or more days that week.
    D. the temperature probably did not exceed eighty for two or more days that week.
2. "Bored by monotonous daily exercise? Frustrated by starvation diets? Now a study conducted by a leading university shows it's possible to lose weight quickly and painlessly! Don't miss this rare opportunity to discover whether you can have that lean, svelte body you once had. Try Wanda's Once-A-Week Workout and judge for yourself!" **Which of the following statements, if any, is completely justified, assuming that the preceding statements are true?**

A. Only "Wanda's Once-A-Week Workout" offers a quick and painless way to lose weight.

B. Wanda's workout program is based on the findings of a study conducted by a leading university.

C. You will probably lose weight on Wanda's program.

D. Daily exercise bores most people.

E. None is completely justified, assuming that the statements are true.

3. **Read the following news item carefully, then say whether the statements that follow it are true or false. Explain.**

Risk for Daily Drinkers

Japanese males who drink beer daily are twelve times more likely to develop cancer of the sigmoid colon (at the end of the intestines) than those who do not drink alcohol at all.

A. Males who drink beer daily are twelve times more likely to develop sigmoid colon cancer than men who do not drink alcohol at all.

B. Japanese males who drink beer daily are twelve times more likely to develop sigmoid colon cancer than their fellow countrymen who do not drink beer at all.

C. Japanese males who drink beer daily probably will develop colon cancer.

D. Japanese males who do not drink beer daily have one-twelfth the chance of getting sigmoid colon cancer compared to Japanese males who do drink daily.

E. Drinking beer daily causes Japanese men to develop sigmoid colon cancer at a rate twelve times greater than Japanese men who do not drink alcohol at all.

F. Compared to Japanese males who rarely drink alcohol, Japanese males who drink beer daily are twelve times more likely to develop sigmoid colon cancer.

G. Japanese males who drink beer are twelve times more likely to get sigmoid colon cancer than those who never drink alcohol.

H. The title of this news item is misleading.

4. "Most pediatricians recommend the active ingredient in *Jelly Belly* as one of the most effective medications for the temporary relief of symptoms associated with upset stomach more than any other available in a nonprescription medication." If the preceding statements are true, which of the following statements, if any, must also be true?

A. *Jelly Belly* is the most effective over-the-counter medication for upset stomach.

B. More pediatricians recommend *Jelly Belly* than any other nonprescription medication for the treatment of upset stomach.

C. More doctors recommend the active ingredient in *Jelly Belly* for the treatment of upset stomach than any other ingredient.

D. *Jelly Belly* is at least as effective for treating a person's upset stomach as any other such nonprescription product.

E. None of the above.

5. As the operations officer of a corporation, you receive at year's end the following summary of expenses incurred by each of the corporation's departments. **Which**

of the five entries is the least likely to be weakened by the discovery of additional expenses for the same year? (Pay careful attention to qualifiers.)

DEPARTMENT	NUMBER OF EMPLOYEES	EXPENSES
A. Accounting	only 10	at least $400
B. Marketing	at least 18	at least $28,000
C. Legal	at least 3	no more than $30,000
D. Public Relations	no more than 2	no more than $1200
E. Production	no more than 325	not quite $2000

6. Here are two versions of an ad for a book entitled *Flatten Your Stomach: For Women Over 35*. **Read version 1 and answer the question that follows it before reading version 2.**

> Version 1: "It's never too late to flatten your stomach and narrow your waistline. This book shows you how to flatten your stomach by exercising your stomach muscles."

Make a list of significant questions, objections, or concerns that this version of the ad does not address but which would influence your decision to purchase the book. For example, "Won't dieting have the same effect—flatten my stomach and narrow my waistline?" and "Exactly how is this book geared for women over 35?" Now continue.

> Version 2: "It's never too late to flatten your stomach and narrow your waistline. *But* as you have *probably* noticed, diets alone are not enough. This is *especially* true as you get older. *Even if* you keep your weight down and get some exercise, your stomach *may* bulge and sag because your abdominal muscles are not properly toned. Try sit-ups. *Sit ups alone work only some of these muscles. Sit-ups alone are not enough. But unless* you exercise all major abdominal muscles, your stomach may be hard, *but* it won't be flat. This book shows you how to flatten your stomach by exercising all—not just some—of your stomach muscles. And it is *especially* designed for women over 35. Strenuous exercises are avoided. So, you need not be in shape to get started. *(We recommend you check with your doctor before beginning this or any other exercise program.)*" (The actual ad for *Flatten Your Stomach: For Women Over 35*, Ann Dugan and the Editors of *Consumer Guide*.)

A. Thoroughly explain what functions are served by the italicized words in this version of the ad (keep in mind the categories of language).
B. Which of the significant questions that you (and I) raised does this version satisfactorily address and which does it not?
C. Did this version anticipate any questions or concerns that you did not ask?
D. Which of the two versions is more effective? Why?
E. Does this ad have the effect of raising additional questions and concerns for you?

7. **Read the following passage, then answer the two groups of questions that follow it. Pay careful attention to the italicized language of the argument.**

"Does poetry have educational value for the student who is incapable of a complete experience of poetry *but* who can acquire a limited appreciation which may not seem to survive his years in school or college?" This last question, *which the reader may be inclined to answer with an immediate "No"* is, *in practice,* not so easy to answer. *For* students who may never completely understand a poem can often understand other things through the discussion of poetry. *Those who prefer discussing poetry to reading poems* look to poetry for an illumination of *some* of the problems of living. One cannot afford to dismiss this as irrelevant when one is taking into consideration the whole picture of the education of an individual. *Many* people look to poetry today as an illumination of religious and philosophic problems. *Although* poetry is not and cannot be a substitute for religion and philosophy, *nevertheless,* it *may* lead people to think seriously about such things. It *may* lead them through poetry and out of it into their real interest or vocation.... (Stephen Spender, "On Teaching Modern Poetry.")

GROUP 1: **Without referring to the passage, say whether the following statements are true or false. If false, provide what you think is the correct answer. After answering the questions, reread the passage and change whatever answers you wish and explain your changes by reference to the language of the argument.**

A. The author is concerned primarily with the value of poetry for students with a deep appreciation for it.
B. The author believes that the reader in all likelihood thinks that poetry does not have much educational value for students without much appreciation for it.
C. Poetry is, and can be, a substitute for religion and philosophy.
D. The author believes that poetry leads people to think about religion and philosophy.
E. According to the author, it is possible that poetry helps people discover their interests and vocations.

GROUP 2 (Refer to the passage to answer):
A. What is the function of "for" in sentence 3?
B. Can you find an example of directive language in the passage?
C. Which of the following statements most closely approximates the author's main idea or conclusion?
   1. Discussing poetry often helps students, even if they cannot understand it.
   2. For many people, poetry clarifies religious and philosophical problems.
   3. Poetry may have value for students who do not fully understand it.
   4. Poetry may help people discover their interests and vocations.
   5. Students should be required to take poetry.

8. George Orwell's (1903–1950) "Politics and the English Language" is one of the most celebrated essays dealing with the debasement of language. The opening of that essay is reprinted here. **Read it carefully and refer to it in answering the questions that follow.**

Most people who bother with the matter at all would admit that the English language is in a bad way, but it is generally assumed that we cannot by conscious action do anything about it. Our civilization is decadent and our language — (so the argument runs) — must inevitably share in the general collapse. It follows that any struggle against the use of language is a sentimental archaism, (like preferring candles to electric light or hansom cabs to airplanes). Underneath this lies the half-conscious belief that language is a natural growth and not an instrument which we shape for our own purposes.

Now, it is clear that the decline of a language must ultimately have political and economic causes; it is not due simply to the bad influence of this or that individual writer. But an effect can become a cause, reinforcing the original cause and producing the same effect in an intensified form, and so on indefinitely. A man may take to drink because he feels himself to be a failure, and then fail all the more completely because he drinks. It is rather the same thing that is happening to the English language. It becomes ugly and inaccurate because our thoughts are foolish, but the slovenliness of our language makes it easier for us to have foolish thoughts. The point is that the process is reversible. Modern English, especially written English, is full of bad habits which spread by imitation and which can be avoided if one is willing to take the necessary trouble. If one gets rid of the habits one can think more clearly, and to think clearly is a necessary first step towards political regeneration; so that the fight against bad English is not frivolous and is not the exclusive concern of professional writers. (Excerpt from "Politics and the English Language" by George Orwell, copyright 1946 by Sonia Brownell Orwell and renewed 1974 by Sonia Orwell, reprinted from *Shooting an Elephant and Other Essays* by George Orwell, by permission of Harcourt Brace Jovanovich, Inc.)

A. Closely inspecting Orwell's use of intensifiers, indicate which of these statements, if any, Orwell would consider incontrovertible?
    1. The English language is in a bad way.
    2. The decline of language must have political and economic causes.
    3. One cannot merely blame individual writers for the decline of a language.
B. Based on this selection, with which of the following statements do you think Orwell would agree?
    1. We do not shape language for our own ends.
    2. Effects can also be causes.
    3. We really cannot do a lot to improve language usage.
    4. Our civilization and our language are decadent.
    5. Bad language usage reinforces sloppy habits of mind.
C. Mindful of Orwell's use of discounts, indicate to which of the statements in each of the following pairs (1 and 2) Orwell gives priority.
    A-1: The English language becomes ugly and inaccurate because our thoughts are foolish.
    A-2: The slovenliness of the English language makes it easier for us to have foolish thoughts.
    B-1: The decline of a language must ultimately have political and economic causes.
    B-2: An effect can become a cause.
D. Explain why the second paragraph can be considered as a discount of the first.
E. Cite five instances of qualifiers.

F. What function is served by the drinking example in paragraph 2? Do you think the example makes or merely illuminates Orwell's point?

G. Which of the following statements most closely approximates Orwell's main idea or conclusion?

A. Most people are misinformed about why English is in a bad way.

B. The decline of a language must ultimately have political and economic causes.

C. Political reform requires clear thinking.

D. The struggle to improve language is not trivial or merely of interest to professional writers.

9. Some years ago, Norman Cousins, editor emeritus of *Saturday Review,* overcame a serious collagen disease. His own personal struggle with the disease, and the unorthodox methods he used to fight it, left him with an abiding interest in health matters. Indeed, until his death in 1990, he served on the faculty of UCLA medical school. In the following essay excerpt, Cousins explores the connection between personal attitudes and health. **Read it carefully, then answer the questions that follow.**

Is it possible to *summon* positive attitudes or emotions as an act of will to create a desired physiological effect? Researchers at UCLA have worked with professional actors in an effort to throw light on this question. The actors are hooked up to a wide variety of gauges in an attempt to measure the physiological changes that come in response to contrast in feelings.

For example, an actress was told to imagine that she was in her first Broadway play and that all her work and hopes over the years now connected to the success or failure of the play. In one scenario, she is told that *The New York Times* critic not only has pronounced the play a smash hit but also has singled her out for special praise. The researchers took measurements as the actress "felt" the emotions she could experience as the result of her simulated success. A couple of hours later, the same measurements were applied to the reverse situation—the *Times* critic derided the play, and it closed as a result. The actress' response showed a measurable downturn in vital signs.

This research project is still in progress. A significant number of actors have to be tested before any definitive findings can be announced. Nonetheless, it may be significant that, even on a limited basis, the evidence indicates that "directed" emotions may make a difference in our health.

Obviously, actors have an advantage in summoning contrasting emotions. But the very fact that imagined situations can result in changes in blood pressure, cardiac function, galvanic skin response and immune-system capability should cause us to regard our emotions—positive and negative—as factors affecting the interaction of the body's various organs. Emotions are not the only forces, of course, that can cause a disease or combat it, but they are an important part of the totality.

The ability of the human body to turn back illness is one of the wonders of the world. Indeed, the more we know about the connection between mind and body, the greater the prospect that we can put it to work for out greater good.
(Norman Cousins, "Hope Can Make You Well," *Parade,* October 29, 1989, p. 13)

A. Do you think this essay is primarily argumentative or persuasive? Explain.
B. What is Cousins' thesis or main idea?
C. Is the example of the actress essential or nonessential to Cousins' thesis?
D. Cite specific language that shows how Cousins in paragraph 3 cautiously qualifies the results of the UCLA experiment.
E. Cousins discounts one of the points in each of the following pairs in favor of the other. Using his discounting language as a guide, determine which of the points in each pair is given priority.

From paragraph 3:

1. "Directed" emotions may make a difference in our health.
2. More actors need to be tested before significant findings related to the UCLA experiment can be announced.

From paragraph 4:

1. Emotions play an important role in causing and combating disease.
2. Emotions are not the only influence on disease.

F. Do you think this essay is organized deductively or inductively?
G. Show how Cousins uses the classic form of argument development: Introduction, Body, Conclusion.
H. The following are criticisms that readers of this essay might raise. Does a careful reading of the essay provide any grounds for the criticisms? Explain by reference to the text.

1. Cousins claims on the basis of one scant example that attitudes and emotions can significantly affect health. This is a gross oversimplification.
2. It is not good science to draw conclusions based on a research project that is still in progress. Cousins does precisely that. He should wait until all the evidence is in or provide additional evidence.
3. Cousins fails to acknowledge that professional actors are not typical of people as a whole. By training, they have the ability to call up intense emotions that the average person cannot.
4. The title of the essay, "Hope Can Make You Well," is misleading. It implies that there is an irrefutable connection between hope and good health. But Cousins' evidence does not support that claim. In fact, several times he deliberately pulls back from making it. The best example is the sentence in paragraph 3 that reads:

    . . . it may be significant that, even on a limited basis, the evidence indicates (that is, only suggests but doesn't prove) that "directed" emotions may make a difference in our health. . . .

The title simply does not reflect the guarded nature of Cousins' central point.

POINT/COUNTERPOINT: ESSAYS FOR ANALYSIS

Issue: *Human Nature and Violence*

Resolved: Humans are by nature aggressive and violent.

Background: Even a cursory reading or viewing of the daily news leads to an inescapable conclusion: We humans are very violent creatures. Indeed, our penchant for violence, as both individuals and groups, seems to be intractable. Why is this so? Are humans by nature aggressive and violent and, consequently, can do little but attempt to moderate these tendencies through social controls? On the other hand, do we acquire aggressive tendencies from our social environments and, thus, can we eliminate at least the most horrific kinds of violence by systematically nurturing more cooperative behavior? Perhaps human violence is best explained in terms of both genes and environment, nature and nurture.

From: **Humans Are Born Violent**[3]

Sigmund Freud

The following excerpt is from Civilization and Its Discontents, *a monumental work by Sigmund Freud (1856–1939). Very early in his career as a psychiatrist, Freud, who spent a lifetime studying human behavior, became convinced that humans have certain innate behavioral traits, some of which are destructive to themselves and society. Aggressiveness, Freud held, was one of these traits.*

Men are not gentle creatures who want to be loved, and who at the most can defend themselves if they are attacked; they are, *on the contrary,* creatures among whose instinctual endowments is to be reckoned a powerful share of aggressiveness. *As a result,* their neighbour is for them not only a potential helper or sexual object, but also someone who tempts them to satisfy their aggressiveness on him, to exploit his capacity for work without compensation, to use him sexually without his consent, to seize his possessions, to humiliate him, to cause him pain, to torture and to kill him. Who, in the face of all his experience of life and history, will have the courage to dispute this assertion? *As a rule* this cruel aggressiveness waits for some provocation or puts itself at the service of some other purpose, whose goal might also have been reached by milder measures. In circumstances that are favourable to it, when the mental counter-forces which ordinarily inhibit it are out of action, it also manifests itself spontaneously and reveals man as a savage beast to whom consideration towards his own kind is something alien. Anyone who calls to mind the atrocities committed during the racial migrations or the invasions of the Huns, or by the people known as Mongols under Jenghiz Khan and Tamerlane, or at the capture of Jerusalem by the pious Crusaders, or even, *indeed,* the horrors of the recent World War—anyone who calls these things to mind will have to bow humbly before the truth of this view.

The existence of this inclination to aggression, which we can detect in ourselves and justly assume to be present in others, is the factor which disturbs our relations with our neighbour and which forces civilization into

---

[3]Reprinted from *Civilization and Its Discontents* by Sigmund Freud, translated and edited by James Strachey, by permission of W. W. Norton & Company, Inc. Copyright © 1961 by James Strachey. Copyright renewed 1989. Sigmund Freud Copyrights Ltd., The Institute of Psycho-Analysis and The Hogarth Press. Permission to quote from the *Standard Edition of the Complete Psychological Works of Sigmund Freud,* translated and edited by James Strachey. (Italics added.)

such a high expenditure [of energy]. *In consequence of* this primary mutual hostility of human beings, civilized society is perpetually threatened with disintegration. The interest of work in common would not hold it together; instinctual passions are stronger than reasonable interests. Civilization has to use its utmost efforts in order to set limits to man's aggressive instincts and to hold the manifestations of them in check by psychical reaction-formations. *Hence,* therefore, the use of methods intended to incite people into identifications and aim-inhibited relationships of love, hence the restriction upon sexual life, and hence too the ideal's commandment to love one's neighbour as oneself—a commandment which is really justified by the fact that nothing else runs so strongly counter to the original nature of man. In spite of every effort these endeavours of civilization have not so far achieved very much. It hopes to prevent the crudest excess of brutal violence by itself assuming the right to use violence against criminals, but the law is not able to lay hold of the more cautious and refined manifestations of human aggressiveness. The time comes when each one of us has to give up as illusions the expectations which, in his youth, he pinned upon his fellow-men, and when he may learn how much difficulty and pain has been added to his life by their ill-will. At the same time, it would be unfair to reproach civilization with trying to eliminate strife and competition from human activity. These things are *undoubtedly* indispensable. But opposition is not necessarily enmity; it is merely misused and made an *occasion* for enmity.

The communists believe that they have found the path to deliverance from our evils. According to them, man is wholly good and is well-disposed to his neighbour; but the institution of private property has corrupted his nature. The ownership of private wealth gives the individual power, and with it the temptation to ill-treat his neighbour; while the man who is excluded from possession is bound to rebel in hostility against his oppressor. If private property were abolished, all wealth held in common, and everyone allowed to share in the enjoyment of it, ill-will and hostility would disappear among men. Since everyone's needs would be satisfied, no one would have any reason to regard another as his enemy; all would willingly undertake the work that was necessary. I have no concern with any economic criticisms of the communist system; I cannot enquire into whether the abolition of private property is expedient or advantageous. *But* I am able to recognize that the psychological premises on which the system is based are an untenable illusion. In abolishing private property we deprive the human love of aggression of one of its instruments, certainly a strong one, *though certainly* not the strongest; *but* we have in no way altered the differences in power and influence which are misused by aggressiveness, nor have we altered anything in its nature. Aggressiveness was not created by property. It reigned almost without limit in primitive times, when property was still very scanty, and it already shows itself in the nursery almost before property has given up its primal, anal form; it forms the basis of every relation of affection and love among people. If we do away with personal rights over material wealth, there still remains prerogative in the field of sexual relationships, which is bound to become the source of the strongest dislike and the most violent hostility among men who in other respects are on an equal footing. If we were to remove this factor, too, by allowing complete freedom of sexual life and thus abolishing the family, the germ-cell of civilization, we cannot, it is true, easily foresee what new paths the development of civilization could take; but one thing we can expect, and that is that this indestructible feature of human nature will follow it there.

It is clearly not easy for men to give up the satisfaction of this inclination to aggression. They do not feel comfortable without it. The advantage which a comparatively small cultural group offers of allowing this instinct an outlet in the form of hostility against intruders is not to be be despised. It is always possible to bind together a considerable number of people in love, *so long as* there are other people left over to receive the manifestations of their aggressiveness.

From: **Humans Learn Violence**[4]

René Dubos

The following selection was written by French-born American bacteriologist Rene Dubos (1901–1982), whose studies in the biological sciences led him to conclude that social institutions, not genes, instigate human violence.

The events of recent years seem *indeed* to prove that one of mankind's chief occupations is destructive warfare and other forms of violence — deliberately practiced. Men have consciously tortured and killed their fellowmen in Algeria, Vietnam, Biafra, the Middle East, in city streets all over the world and even on college campuses. Destructive violence is as much a part of life today as it was in Homer's time.

Revulsion against violence, *however,* is also one of the hallmarks of human history. The soul-searching and protests generated by the tragedies of the past few years are almost as impressive as the tragedies themselves. In every part of the world, *furthermore,* there are countless normal human beings who would find it extremely painful, if not emotionally impossible, to kill another human being or even to exhibit aggressive behavior. It takes a great deal of conditioning to prepare a nation for war, and to train soldiers to kill by hand-to-hand combat. While it is obvious that many men are killers, it is equally true that many are not. And *for this reason* it seems *hardly* justified to state that Man — with a capital M — is by nature a killer.

One need not be an anthropologist or a historian to know that violence and conflict have existed in all human societies under many

---

[4]Reprinted from *The American Scholar,* Volume 40, Number 4, Autumn 1971. Copyright © 1971 by the author. Reprinted by permission of the publisher. (Italics added.)

different forms, but opinions differ about the origins of human aggression. *Some* regard it as purely the consequence of cultural or social conditioning. Others believe that it is the direct and inevitable expression of instincts that are indelibly inscribed in man's genetic code. This polarization of views constitutes in reality a pseudo problem, analogous in all respects to the now worn-out nurture *versus* nature controversy. The potentiality for aggressiveness is indeed part of man's genetic constitution, just as it is part of the genetic constitution of all animal species. *But* the manifestation of all genetic potentialities are shaped by past experiences and present circumstances. There is no genetic coding that inevitably results in aggressiveness, only a set of genetic attributes for self-defense that can become expressed as aggressiveness under particular sets of conditions.

Certain men act as killers under certain conditions because social life often distorts the instinctive responses that are essential for self-defense. The instinct for preservation exists in all animals and can generate violent behavior even in the most timid species. Rabbits and mice are readily frightened under ordinary circumstances, but they can fight just as viciously as tigers, wolves, baboons and men whenever any of their fundamental "values" are involved. I have seen a rabbit repeatedly and ferociously assault a huge black snake threatening its nest. Time and time again in the laboratory, I have observed tame white mice — so gentle that a child could handle them — engage in fierce fighting against mice of the same breed and age introduced into their cage from the outside. Violent conflict among these mice occurred *even though* food and water were abundant, the animals were not crowded, and they did not have occasion to fight for females. It would be silly to say that Rabbit or Mouse is a killer because rabbits and mice will fight to defend their young or their territory, or against a stranger introduced from the outside. In animals as well as in men, *many* manifestations of the instinct for self-defense result in aberrant forms of behavior that are destructive rather than biologically useful.

In animal life the instinct of self-preservation evolved to deal through short-term responses with situations apprehended by the senses. In man, the expressions of the same fundamental instinct have *usually* been translated from the plane of nature to the plane of society, from sensual perceptions to symbolic conceptions, from short-term responses to long-range effects. If man behaves more commonly as a killer than do animals, it is because his ways of life, his social history, and his mental processes often place him in situations that differ radically from those under which he evolved and in which he acquired the instinct for self-defense. Comparative observations of animals living in zoos or in their natural habitats help to explain how social forces can make man behave as a killer through aberrations of his instinctive defense responses.

In captivity as well as in the wild, males compete for territory and for the available females especially during the rut season. The savage fights among stags, walrus bulls and seals are part of the wildlife lore. The combat between males, *however,* is *rarely* to the death. The weaker combatant turns aside and retreats; the victor lets the vanquished go unmolested. Among animals under natural conditions and often in captivity, fighting presents some analogy to German student duels; certain types of wounds are permissible but most battles are limited to bluffing contests and to confrontations of wits. Furthermore, fighting between animals of the same species is often symbolic rather than real. Animals tend to ritualize their aggression by such attitudes as rearing up, roaring, showing their teeth, or erecting their ruffs, hackles or neck hair. Ritualization of behavior is widespread among higher apes, and also, of course, among men. . . .

When man emerged from his animal background, he created ways of life and environments in which the social restraints achieved during the early phases of his evolution were no longer effective or suitable. Biological adaptation has not prepared him for the competitive attitudes that prevail in most societies. Man becomes a killer of his own species because he has failed to develop social restraints capable of substituting for the biological wisdom evolved under natural conditions. Violence and internecine conflict are most common in highly competitive societies, particularly during periods of rapid change that upset social order. Man has not yet learned to live in the zoos he has created for himself. . . .

To minimize the destructive effects of violence, we *might* find it profitable humbly to take a lesson from the animal world and try systematically to ritualize our conflicts. War games among primitive people, the jousts of medieval knights, and some of the later gentlemanly conventions of military behavior had in fact some similarities to the sham fights so common among animals, not only in the wild but also in tame populations. If modern societies could develop effective techniques for the ritualization of conflicts—by global Olympic games, for example, or by space exploration—they might achieve something like what William James called the moral equivalent of war. Battles of bravado might go far toward averting the destructive effects of violence.

Man's propensity for violence is not a racial or species attribute woven in his genetic fabric. It is culturally conditioned by history and the ways of life. The instinct for self-defense exists throughout the animal kingdom and can exhibit aberrant manifestations in animals as well as in man—more frequently in man only because he always lives under conditions that differ profoundly from the ones under which he evolved. We cannot escape from the zoos we have created for ourselves and return to wilderness, but we can improve our societies and make them better suited to our unchangeable biological nature.

SOME QUESTIONS CONCERNING LANGUAGE, LOGIC, AND CONTENT

The Categories and Function of Language in the Arguments

1. Identify and explain the function of all italicized words and phrases.
2. Midway through paragraph 1, Freud asks: "Who, in the face of all his experience of life and history, will have the courage to dispute this assertion?" Explain how this sentence is an example of the mixed functions of language.
3. Cite from each essay a statement of fact and a statement of value.
4. Do Dubos' examples in paragraphs 4 and 6 make a point or merely clarify?
5. Would you consider any passages to be mere asides?

The Logical Structure of the Arguments*

1. Outline the Dubos essay following the format presented in Chapter 2.
2. Using D (for data), B (for backing), and C (for conclusion), cast Freud's argument opposing the abolition of private property (paragraph 3).
3. Does Dubos' essay roughly accord with the classical structure of extended argument?
4. Refutation often plays a key role in logical structure of extended argument. Does Freud at any point explicitly engage in refutation? Explain.

The Content of the Arguments

For each of the following statements, determine whether the arguments are in basic agreement or disagreement.
1. Violence and conflict have always existed among human beings.
2. Humans need harmless outlets for their propensities for violence.
3. The human inclination to aggression is indestructible.
4. The institution of private property has corrupted humans who otherwise are good and altruistic.
5. Social institutions make humans violent.
6. Restructuring social institutions can greatly minimize, if not eliminate, violence.
7. Instinct plays a role in aggression.

From: **Basic Humanity vs. Base Behavior**[5]

Roderic Gorney

> *In the following essay, UCLA professor of psychiatry Roderic Gorney moves the violence debate into the area of entertainment. In so doing, he effectively shows that, far from being just an airy theoretical matter, the nature versus nurture controversy has serious social implications.*

Is killing an animal as part of an onstage performance art or abomination? Should it be allowed or abolished?

---

[5]By permission of Roderic Gorney, Professor of Psychiatry, UCLA; Director of the Program on Psychosocial Adaptation and the Future; author of *The Human Agenda*.

This sort of question inevitably raises older questions about human nature: Are people genetically scripted for kindness or cruelty, or is our behavior determined by experience?

News of performance artist Rick Gibson's plan to crush a live rat onstage in Vancouver, B.C., was put in an interesting context by what else was in the news. In the same issue of the Los Angeles Times there was a debate on whether military women should be sent into combat. That week, there also were reports on the people by whom you are most likely to be murdered, on a humor magazine that featured a photograph of a man just after he has gnawed the head off a live chicken, on ritual murders by cultists, on murder by "poison umbrella," on Charles Stuart's murder/suicide in Boston, and so on in grim procession.

Our response to questions about the nature of such behavior determines how we might try to prevent it.

Despite certain inherited behavioral propensities, some of which we share with other primates, for the most part anthropologist Ashley Montagu's axiom is correct: "Human Nature is what humans learn." For example, the capacity for speech is genetic, but the ability to speak any particular language is learned, as is the choice of what to say in that language.

One of our inherited propensities is a craving for intense experience, which in different circumstances might result in avid pursuit of marathon-running or hang-gliding or bear-baiting—or military combat. Which forms of excitement we choose to teach and learn determines our character, not to mention our behavior.

Another unmistakable fact is that people tend to replicate their experiences. Those who have been thrilled by the arts tend to become serious supporters of the arts. Those who were abused as children tend to become child-abusers. And those who consume vast quantities of violent entertainment are less distressed by violence and more inclined toward hurtful behaviors than those who haven't.

The secret guard of Ceausescu, like so many throughout history, apparently was taught to seek and enjoy pain as well as to inflict it. The monstrous Nazi concentration camp guards were carefully taught their hideous tasks—and to relish their own resultant excitement. In Imperial Rome, torture and death were choreographed for the public's amusement.

Note that in this sequence we have subtly moved from killing as a political expedient to killing as entertainment. Though at first glance they may seem unrelated, given the unity of a person, there is a profound connection between the two. It is no accident that among the crowds witnessing the spectacles at the Colosseum were the legions Rome would send off to conquer other peoples at enormous cost in their own and their victims' suffering. There are thoughtful people today who wonder if one of the consequences of decades of horrific motion-picture and television entertainment is that young Americans have been conditioned to be willing and able to die and kill in far-off Vietnam, or Grenada or Panama.

Society already acknowledges that experience, particularly entertainment, shapes people and behavior. This is why we outlaw such spectacles as gladiatorial contests, cock-fighting and cat-roasting. If rat-crushing joins them, it will be on similar grounds.

Some comments in response to Gibson's "act" were illuminating for the abysmal irrelevence that our world inculcates. The issue is not, as another artist said, a matter of degree: that killing a moth onstage is acceptable but killing a rat is not, because it's "big" and has "a lot more blood." Society's concern lies in the motivation for the killing and its likely human consequence.

A primary purpose of any theatrical presentation is to stimulate emotion. One of the outcomes of a successfully titillating performance is to encourage its repetition. And that is the crux. When is a killing titillating? Just consider the difference in motivation and consequence between a performer swatting a distracting moth onstage so as to continue a performance, compared to another who, as part of the performance, slowly and delightedly tears off a moth's wings as it struggles.

To avert civil-liberties infringements, what we must attempt here, as always, is not compulsion but education and voluntary renunciation. Ultimately, our concern must be not only freedom of expression, but freedom from extinction.

ADDITIONAL QUESTIONS

1. Do you think it would be accurate to say that both Freud and Dubos are interested in establishing a view of human nature, but that Gorney is not—that is, Gorney assumes a view and applies it? If you agree that this is an accurate distinction, explain the difference in terms of deductive and inductive organization.
2. With whom is the author in basic agreement—Freud or Dubos? Explain.
3. How do you think Freud would respond to a performer's killing a live rat on stage?
4. How do you think Dubos would view spectacles such as gladiatorial contests and cock-fighting? Explain.
5. Which of the following statements comes closest to expressing the author's thesis or main idea?
   A. We need to teach people to renounce violence.
   B. Artists can be socially irresponsible.
   C. Some art is revulsive.
   D. Killing animals on stage as part of a performance is an abomination.
   E. Violent entertainment breeds violent behavior.
   F. People crave intense experience and tend to replicate their experiences.
6. Based on both what is expressed and implied in the essay, which of the following statements would you consider accurate.
   A. The author favors outlawing the killing of animals as part of an onstage performance.
   B. The author would not consider killing a live rat on stage "art."

C. The author believes that we are what we teach and learn.
D. The author contends that watching a lot of violent entertainment desensitizes one to violence.
E. The author thinks that people can learn to renounce violence.
F. In art, the author values free expression more than nonviolence.
G. The author would agree with the adage: "Art for art's sake."
H. The author believes that cinematic violence conditioned Americans to fight in Vietnam, Grenada, and Panama.
I. The author does not consider the life form killed on stage during a performance morally significant.
J. The author believes that everyone craves excitement.

RELATED THEME TOPICS

1. In his next-to-last paragraph, Dubos writes of the need to "ritualize our conflicts." He says, "Battles of bravado might go far toward averting the destructive effects of violence." Write an essay entitled "Battles of Bravado," in which you argue that many of the games and sports we play (for example, football, hockey, boxing, and so on) serve to minimize the destructive effects of violence. (Alternatively, write an essay in which you argue that such activities actually encourage violence.)

2. One of the goals of education is to instill in students a spirit of cooperation. Write an essay in which you argue that schooling, in fact, can have the opposite effect—encouraging aggressive competition between individuals and between groups.

3. Some people claim that more and more sex is being depicted on the screen as an act of violence directed mainly against women. They say that many of the videos presented on MTV fall into this category and that even female performers, such as Madonna, fuse sex and violence. Write an essay for or against this assessment. (Keep in mind that you will be largely assembling examples to make your general point and, thus, arguing inductively). Alternatively, write an essay in which you start with the assumption that cinematic sex frequently is depicted in the context of violence. Add to this assumption Gorney's two "unmistakable facts" about human nature, then draw out some social implications (for example, the incidence of sex crimes or the practice of sexism). (In this essay, you will be arguing deductively.)

4

Meaning and Definition

INTRODUCTION

We have seen that language can be used for different purposes — to provide information, to express emotions, to give orders and ask questions, to perform certain acts, and to embellish ceremony. Language can also be used to show logical connections; to qualify, intensify, or discount messages; and to express parentheticals or asides. Sensitivity to this array of language usage is fundamental to understanding the logical structure of extended arguments.

Many times, failure in communications, especially in argument, results from simply not understanding or misinterpreting what is said. In Chapters 5 and 6, we will see how such confusion arises when language is abused. In order to maximize the benefit of those chapters, we first need to say something about word meaning and definition and the nature of disputes, which are the concerns of the present chapter.

MODULE 4.1

WORD MEANING

Unless we know the meaning of the words that propositions contain, we cannot understand or evaluate the proposition. Although much can be said of word meaning, we will confine our remarks to the many general terms applicable to familiar objects, words such as *house, tree, automobile, spoon,* and so on.

It is common to view the meaning of general terms as falling into two broad categories, denotation and connotation. The **denotative or extensional meaning of a word is each individual to which the word applies.** For example, we use the word *tree* to denote this tree, that tree, and so on through all trees in the world. The denotation of *human being* is any individual to whom the term *human being* refers — Rob Smith, Marisa Brown, Jorge Sanchez, Rafer Austin, and so on.

Of course, no two trees nor two human beings are identical. Nevertheless, we can apply the words *tree* and *human being* to the individuals because all trees share common features, as do all human beings. It is these features that make a tree a tree, and not, say, a house or a spoon or anything else — and it is what all human beings share that distinguish them from all other things. What exactly are the features that make a tree a tree and a human being a human being and not something else? When we isolate and identify these features we provide a different kind of word meaning, an objective connotation.

The objective connotation of a word is the collection of properties shared by all and by only those objects in a term's extension. In other words, the properties — A, B, C, and so on — that all trees have constitute the objective connotation of the word *tree.* Whatever properties — A, B, C, and so on — all human beings share make up the objective connotation of the word *human being.*

As a simple example, consider the objective connotation of chair: *a piece of furniture used to sit on;* or the objective connotation of snake: *a legless reptilian;* or, the objective connotation of circle: *a closed plane curve, all parts of which are equidistant from some point called the center.*

Your understanding of the word *connotation* probably is not the same as the one just described. Probably you associate *connotation* with the *feelings* some word calls up in the mind of those who use and hear it. This represents still another kind of word meaning. **The subjective connotation of a word consists of the association that a word has in the minds of those who use it.** For many people, the word *snake* not only means a legless reptilian (objective connotation) and all the snakes there are (denotation), but also something slimy and revolting (subjective connotation). Although the word *egghead* is an approximate synonym for *intellectual,* it has different associations, being used as a term of contempt or derision in some circles. The emotive meaning of words is one of their most powerful persuasive aspects, as we will see shortly. But first, let's relate word meaning to definition.

IN BRIEF   The denotative meaning of a general term is the group of things to which the term refers. Its objective connotative meaning consists of the properties that all and only these things share. Its subjective connotative meaning consists of meaning the associations it arouses.

DEFINITIONS

When we define a word we say what it means. **So, a definition is an explanation of the meaning of a term.**

Denotative Definitions

One obvious way to define a word is to explain it in terms of its denotation, that is, by citing examples of an object to which the word extends. A denotative definition of *snake* would be an example of a snake: rattler, python, mamba, and so forth. Thus, **defining denotatively is defining through example,** and a term is said to denote the objects to which it can be applied.

Although denotation seems straightforward enough, we can denote improperly by applying a term to something to which it cannot or should not be applied. To apply *Republican* to Senator Edward Kennedy, a Democrat, or to apply *university* to George Washington Junior High School would be obvious examples of faulty denotations. However, faulty denotation is rarely so transparent. In the hands of skillful persuaders, faulty denotation can go unnoticed, as when a political candidate refers to her opponent as a "radical," "obstructionist," or "big spender." Without establishing exactly how the term applies to her opponent, the candidate is asking the voters to accept the term's extension unexamined.

Sometimes a denotative issue takes on great momentum. Today, for example, a body of law is developing that deals with surrogate parents, as in the case of a woman who bears a child for an infertile couple. To whom does the term *mother* apply—the surrogate or adopter? The courts have always tried to preserve the "family unit," which traditionally has been defined in reference to the biological parents, ultimately the mother. But where surrogates are involved, whom do the terms *mother* and *family unit* denote? Unless the application of these terms is specified, the legal and moral problems could be staggering.

Lexical or Logical Definitions

A second way to define a term is to explain it in terms of its objective connotation. **A logical or lexical definition of a term is one that identifies the properties shared by all and only those objects in a term's extension.** Thus, an acceptable lexical definition of *snake* would be *a legless reptilian.* In defining lexically, we generally place the term being defined in a class of similar terms (for example, "reptilian"), then show how it is different (for example, "legless") from other objects in the class.

A lexical definition is a precise, economical way of identifying something. It is the kind of definition we generally get from a dictionary, which reports what meanings are actually attached to different words by speakers of the language. In extended argument, the lexical definition serves to ease communication and ensure understanding.

Persuasive Definitions

Just as denotative and objective connotative meaning give rise to ways of defining words, so does subjective connotation. When a word has associations in our minds, we sometimes will use it in a way to convey a logical meaning different from its ordinary one in order to make use of the word's favorable or unfavorable association. For example, suppose the word *American* literally means "a native, inhabitant, or citizen of the United States." Because the word has positive associations for most Americans, it is susceptible to attempts at redefinition in order to exploit its favorable associations. Thus, you may be involved in a heated debate with a friend about a particular aspect of foreign policy. Your friend supports the administration's policy; you do not. At some point, your friend says, "Well, if you were a *true* American you'd support our president." Notice how your friend is assuming that words have true and false meanings. They do not. Words have common or uncommon meanings, exact or inexact meanings, but not true or false meanings. What your friend is attempting to do is to use the favorable associations of the word *American* in order to make you respond favorably to the president's position. He is, in effect, adding another essential feature to *American*. Thus, "an American is a native, inhabitant, or citizen of the United States, *who always supports his or her president.*" In short, your friend has given a persuasive definition of *American*. **A persuasive definition is one that attaches a different logical meaning to a word while preserving its emotive associations.**

Not all persuasive definitions involve words with positive associations. For example, suppose the word *socialism* literally means "a social system in which the producers possess both political power and the means of producing and distributing goods." For many Americans the words *socialism, socialist,* and *socialistic* have unfavorable associations. It is tempting to take advantage of these unfavorable associations to give the term a new and different logical meaning, for example, by calling a program guaranteeing national health insurance "really socialistic" or its advocate "an obvious socialist." In altering the literal meaning of the word, while preserving its unfavorable associations, the speaker attempts to persuade the audience to respond unfavorably to a national health insurance program. Controversial subjects in politics, religion, and morality are especially susceptible to persuasive definition.

Persuasive definition is not necessarily a bad thing that should always be avoided. However, we need to be alert to its use, for the writer may be trying to put one over on us by claiming falsely that "x" is part of the meaning of the word or phrase. Be especially watchful of words that often signal persuasive definition, for example, *real, true* (as in "A *true* patriot would never say that"), or *good* (as in, "*Good* citizens always vote"). Authors and speakers do not always telegraph a persuasive definition. "Patriots stand by their country, right or wrong" and "Love is never having to say you're sorry," for example, are persuasive definitions, even though they contain no signal word.

Stipulative Definitions

Sometimes, when authors feel a word is ambiguous or vague, they attempt to give it a more precise meaning. For example, in the beginning of an essay dealing with fairness, a writer may stipulate what he is going to mean by the term. He thus offers a stipulative definition. In contrast to a lexical definition, which reports what people who use the language mean by a word, **a stipulative definition states what the writer or speaker is going to mean by it.**

Suppose you are writing an essay on the subject of the fairest way to allocate scarce medical resources—for example, dialysis machines or transplant organs such as corneas and kidneys. At some point, you must stipulate precisely what you mean by fairness in these matters. Perhaps you want to identify fairness with equality, in which case everyone in need of a kidney machine should have an equal chance of getting one. On the other hand, maybe you intend to identify fairness with social contribution, in which case the patient whose life is more valuable to society should be given preferred consideration. Since the concept of *fairness,* as well as the word itself, is open to multiple interpretations and since your argument hinges on one particular interpretation of it, you must stipulate to your audience exactly which meaning you have in mind. If you do not, you will probably confuse your readers. (Indeed, we court confusion whenever we employ abstract terms such as *loyalty, love,* and *freedom.*) Notice that, in stipulating, you are not only setting boundaries for yourself but, in effect, you are recommending your particular usage to the audience.

Stipulative definitions are also employed when an existing word has strong associations that may intrude on desired sense—and thus mislead—or when there is no existing word for some new object or concept. Confronted with a new phenomenon, we often invent a new word. For example, when very bright and distant celestial objects were discovered in the early 1960s, astronomers named them *quasars.* Similarly, economists invented the word *stagflation* to describe a period of rising costs, low productivity, and high unemployment.

Stipulative definitions typically are used for the purpose of discussion or investigation. Thus, they can be viewed as provisional or temporary definitions, in contrast, for example, to a lexical definition, which has a fixed meaning.

IN BRIEF   Persuasive and stipulative definitions have different purposes. In a persuasive definition, someone is trying to shift the literal meaning of a word, while preserving its associations. In a stipulative definition, someone is trying to ensure common understanding by explaining how a term will be used.

Theoretical Definitions

As used in science and other formal disciplines, a theory is a system of assumptions, or principles, used to analyze, predict, or explain the nature or behavior of a set of specific phenomena. For example, throughout recorded history people have been curious about the changes they have observed in physical objects. What accounts for the countless changes that we experience in ourselves and all things in the world? The earliest philosophers proposed *theories* in an attempt to answer this question. The Greek philosopher Democritus (late fifth century B.C.), to cite just one Greek theorist,

Speaking of . . .

Definitions

What Language Is

Let us agree to use *language* to mean "the system of speech sounds by which human beings communicate with one another." This is not the only possible definition, not the only correct one. The term is used in many other senses. It is customary, for example, to speak of "the language of the eyes," and these imply other and quite different definitions of language. We shall find it convenient, however, to exclude these other meanings.

Notice that the definition specifies *speech sounds.* This means that writing gestures, Morse code, and other such communication systems are excluded. The exclusion does not imply that these systems are unimportant. Indeed, we shall ultimately be more interested here in writing than in speech. But it is most important not to get speech and writing mixed up. We shall try to guard against this by using *language* to refer to speech sounds only. When we want to refer to writing, we shall simply call it writing.

Notice that our definition restricts *language* to the communication system of human beings. We may suppose that lower forms of life have communication systems also. The bees and the ants communicate, and moose calls to moose and perhaps mouse whispers to mouse. All these goings-on we ignore, confining the word *language* to the speech communication of people.

A question less easily brushed off is whether some animals cannot be taught human speech. Parrots repeat what seems to be human sounds, and some apes can learn both words and meanings. Chimpanzees are particularly bright in this respect, and some have acquired a considerable vocabulary. You pronounce the word *cup*, and the chimp ambles off and gets a cup and brings it to you and actually says the word *cup* when he hands it over. Is this not a case of an animal using human language? Well, no, not really, for there is one thing the chimp can't do. He can't learn the system.

Suppose we had an exceedingly brainy ape, and suppose that we succeeded in teaching him these five sentences:

The cup is here.
The bread is here.
The table is here.
I see the cup.
I see the bread.

continued

continued

A human being, having learned these five sentences, could easily produce a sixth: "I see the table." But this is the step the ape cannot take. He can learn random utterances and their meanings, but he never learns the system so he can never use the materials of the language to create new utterances. Until the apes become smart enough to do this, human beings will have a monopoly on language and can continue to mismanage the world as they please.

(Excerpt from **Understanding English** by Paul Roberts. Copyright © by Paul Roberts. Reprinted by permission of HarperCollins Publishers.)

Do you think the author is using both a lexical and stipulative definition of *language***? According to the author's definition, what does the word** *language* **not denote?**

believed that all matter could be reduced to infinitesimally small pieces called atoms. He believed that these atoms were hard, indivisible, invisible, and eternal. According to this *theory,* atoms have been drifting through space since the beginning of time, with no ultimate purpose. Variously shaped—some round, some square, some with knobs on their surface—these atoms occasionally cling together, forming the shapes of the physical objects we see, then drift apart. It is this coming together and drifting apart, said Democritus, that accounts for all the changes we observe in physical objects.

Though primitive by today's standards, this first atomic *theory* was in principle no different from modern theories, for it was proposed to account for what is observable. Today, atomic theory explains numerous phenomena about elements—why they do or do not combine, why they have the properties they have, why they evaporate or ignite at certain temperatures, and so on. Indeed, the facts of modern chemistry almost without exception can be accounted for in terms of atomic theory. The atomic theory is just that—a theory, not an observed fact. Electrons, neutrons, neutrinos, and other minute particles are unobservable. *Thus, the propositions that there are such particles is a theory.* If the particles could be observed, statements about them would be facts. What can be observed, of course, are things that are presumed to be the effects of these unobservable particles. That is why atomic theory—from the ancients to the moderns—arose in the first place, to explain these observable phenomena. This is true of all theories—they are attempts to account for the observable in terms of the unobservable.

A formal theory always contains a term that denotes something that is unobservable. When the *theory*-word—for example, *electron, neutron, neutrino*—is part of a statement, that statement is said to be a theory. An attempt to define the *theory*-word results in a theoretical definition. **A theoretical definition, then, attempts to provide an adequate, comprehensive explanation of the objects to which it is applied.**

As the name suggests, to propose a theoretical definition is to propose the acceptance of a theory. When scientists define *force* as "the product of mass and acceleration," embedded in that definition is an aspect of Newtonian mechanics, a theory. Similarly, embodied in the definition of *quark* — the fundamental unit of matter that refers to any of three hypothetical subatomic particles having electric charges of magnitude one-third or two-thirds that of the electron — is atomic theory.

Just as theories can change as more is learned, so can the theoretical definitions that embody them. Physicists previously defined heat in terms of "subtle imponderable fluid." As their theoretical understanding grew, their theoretical definition of heat changed, so that *now* heat is defined as a form of energy that a body has owing to its irregular molecular motion.[1]

Theoretical definitions are not confined to the physical sciences. All formal disciplines of study have them. Philosophy is a prime example. One example of philosophy that often befuddles students is how philosophers might agree on the application of a term but vehemently dispute each other's proposed theoretical definitions.

For example, one of the perennial questions in the study of moral philosophy is, "What makes a moral act right?" If, for instance, a particular act of truth telling is right, why so? Now, it is entirely possible for philosophers to agree that the truth-telling act in question is the right thing to do but disagree about why. For some, it may be right because it promotes the best long-term interests of the person telling the truth. For others, the truth-telling act may be right because it promotes the greatest happiness for the greatest number of people. For still others, it may be right because, if the positions were reversed, the person would want the truth told to him. Each of these implied definitions of a "right act" embodies a theory of value and obligation. In the first case, the value is probably happiness and the obligation is to promote *one's own* happiness. In the second case, the value might still be happiness, but the obligation is to promote happiness for *the greatest number*. And in the third case, the value might be "a good will" and the obligation is always *to act from a good will,* that is, always to intend to treat people as you yourself would want to be treated.

In our example, the choice of theoretical definition makes no practical difference because we assumed there was agreement that the particular act under discussion was "right" from each party's viewpoint; but adopting one of these theories, rather than some other, can have enormous significance in how we frame and ultimately resolve a whole spectrum of moral issues. Thus, approaching a moral question with *my own* interests uppermost in mind is quite different from approaching it with the interests of *all* parties involved, both of which are different from approaching it with some version of the "Golden Rule" in mind. The difference is not only theoretical, but it can be practical as well. Different theories can and often do yield opposed answers.

---

[1]Morris Cohen and Irving Copi, *Introduction to Logic,* 9th edition (New York: MacMillan, 1986), p. 137.

IN BRIEF   Unlike stipulative definition, theoretical definitions propose comprehensive explanations, not merely provisional or tentative descriptions. At the same time, theoretical definitions, like all others, are subject to revision based on new information and understanding.

Speaking of . . .

Definition

A Definition Poses Difficult Questions

What is creativity?

Volumes have been written on the subject, but a precise and satisfactory definition seems to have eluded experts and novices alike.

Is someone who is very bright — a genius — necessarily creative? Is a creative person necessarily a genius? Is an individual creative just because he or she does something original? What if no one appreciates the work or even notices it? Is the person still creative, or merely crazy, possessed by an *idee fixe*?

And what of the creative act itself? Does creativity mean discovering, inventing, producing something new? Can it be a simple matter of solving a problem, a process of finding a new solution to an old dilemma?

There are no easy answers to these questions, but most scholars now accept a working definition of creativity. It must be original *and* it must be either useful or in some way valued by society. Nonetheless, a debate over the nuances and subtleties of creativity continues.

Recently that debate took a sharp and unexpected twist. This latest furor over creativity was caused by a computer in Pittsburgh.

At a meeting of the American Psychological Assn. in 1985, Herbert Simon, the Nobel prize–winning psychologist and economist at Carnegie Mellon University in Pittsburgh, announced that he and his colleagues had programmed a computer to "rediscover" scientific breakthroughs.

Fed all the relevant data that the scientists had at their disposal, the computer can in a matter of seconds inductively re-create the original discovery, Simon said. Give a computer what Johannes Kepler knew in the 17th Century about astronomy and you will get the laws of planetary motion. Give a computer all that Charles Darwin knew in the 19th Century about animals and you presumably will get the theory of evolution.

Essentially, Simon said, creativity is nothing more than simple problem solving. And if that is true, then a computer can be creative.

Not surprisingly, this conclusion has caused considerable consternation among social scientists who have been studying creativity and who think it involves such complex issues as human emotion and motivation.

continued

continued

One scholar has likened the computer's efforts to forgers who can make flawless copies of great masterpieces but cannot create original works of their own.

Another scholar evoked the words of Albert Einstein. "The *formulation* of a problem," Einstein wrote, "is often more essential than its solution, which may be merely a matter of mathematical or experimental skills. To raise new questions, new problems, to regard old problems from a new angle, requires creative imagination and makes real advances. . . . "

Mihaly Csikszentmihalyi, a psychologist at the University of Chicago, has been studying creativity for more than two decades and is one researcher who has yet to be persuaded of the creative potential of the modern-day computer.

Whatever else the cognitive scientists and computer specialists have done, Csikszentmihalyi wrote in an article last year in the journal *New Ideas in Psychology*, "They are helping to sharpen some of the conceptual issues in a field that has long languished for lack of stimulating controversy."

(Anne C. Roark, Copyright, 1989, **Los Angeles Times.** Reprinted by permission.)

What are the two essential features that most scholars agree define creativity? Would you agree? Does Professor Simon offer a persuasive definition of creativity? Do you agree with it? Does Einstein's formulation of creativity support the claim that computers are creative?

EXERCISES ON DEFINITION*

What kind of definition — denotative, lexical, persuasive, stipulative, theoretical — is each of the following?

1. The word *unicorn* means a horselike animal having a single, straight horn projecting from its head.
2. Philosophy concerns the nature and extent of human knowledge; the relation of the knowing mind to the outside world; the problem of determinism and human freedom; the validation of statements about cause, about God, about the good, the beautiful, and many other things.
3. Abortion is simply the murdering of defenseless human beings.
   Abortion is the deliberate termination of a pregnancy.
   Abortion is what the doctor just performed on that woman.
4. Life is no more or no less than a series of negotiations, and I take "negotiation" to mean "the art of getting what you want through mutual agreement."
5. A literary work is obscene if, to the average person, applying community standards, the dominant theme of the material taken as a whole appeals to the prurient interest.
6. According to Sigmund Freud, the libido is the life force, the instinctual drive to satisfy one's biological urges.
7. For psychologists who see the human animal as primarily a biological creature, human motivation refers to a human being's attempt to satisfy bodily needs.

8. In testifying before a Congressional committee investigating political corruption, former Secretary of the Interior James Watt defined *influence peddling* as "strictly a political term," "when one of the Republican or Democratic party accuses someone else of using his credibility for gaining an objective." When asked if he so acted, would he consider himself guilty of influence peddling, Watt said, "Yes, from the Democratic view. No, from the Republican."

9. Once more we confront a big word—*rationalism.* Like most words, this one can be defined in a variety of ways. We shall here define it very broadly as a cluster of ideas that add up to the belief that the universe works the way a man's mind works when he thinks logically and objectively that therefore man can ultimately understand everything in his experience as he understands, for instance, a simple arithmetical or mechanical problem. The same wisdom that showed him how to make, use, and keep in repair any household contrivance will, ultimately, the rationalist hopes, show him all about everything.
    (Crane Brinton, *Ideas and Men.*)

10. Pornography, like rape, is a male invention, designed to dehumanize women, to reduce the female to an object of sexual access, not to free sensuality from moralistic or parental inhibition. . . . Pornography is the undiluted essence of anti-female propaganda.
    (Susan Brownmiller, *Against Our Will: Men, Women, and Rape.*)

11. If Jesse Jackson were a true black leader, he would be trying to do more to solve the problem of young black men in this country rather than flying to Iraq to try to resolve the Persian Gulf crisis.
    (Letter to the editor.)

12. All well-meaning people want two things in Nicaragua between now and February (1990): An end to the fighting and the holding of democratic elections. In spite of everything he has done, President Bush may mean well. He can demonstrate this by supporting prompt demobilization of the Contras. This might expose him to cries of betrayal from right-wing extremists. But the alternative is to continue to condemn the Nicaraguan people to listen to the daily cries of grief from those whose loved ones are slaughtered by the U.S.-created and financed Contras. A truly "big man" would have no difficulty making the right choice.
    (Nicaraguan Former President Daniel Ortega Saavedra.)

AMBIGUITY AND VAGUENESS

If you look through a dictionary, you will notice that words usually have more than one meaning. In a popular sense, then, most words are ambiguous. But **in logic, a word is considered ambiguous only when it has more than one possible meaning in a given context.** Thus, words themselves are not ambiguous; how they are used may be.

For example, if someone says, "I'm going to see the *painting,*" she may mean that she is going to look at (1) someone in the process of painting something, or (2) the thing that has been painted. Suppose that in assigning a research paper, a teacher cautions the class: "I want at least 3,000 words." When Harry is marked down for not having enough words, he points out that his paper contains 3,200 words. The teacher, however, maintains that many of the words are tokens of the same type of word, for instance, "the" and "a" and "an." "If you use the word 'the' a hundred times," he explains, "in a sense that counts as one-hundred words. But each of these words are instances of the same *kind* of word. So, no matter how many times you use 'the' or 'a' or 'an,' it counts as only one word. In fact, your paper is only 2,600 words long."

It is important to see that it is not the word *word* that is ambiguous here, but how it is used. From the aspect of *types* of words used, Harry used fewer than the prescribed 3,000 words. From the aspect of *tokens* of types, he used more than 3,000. The next time the teacher gives this assignment he will probably explain in no uncertain terms what he means by "words."

As another example, consider the word *store,* which can mean

1. a place where merchandise is offered for sale.
2. a supply reserved for future use.
3. a supply of food, clothing, or arms.
4. a place where commodities are housed.
5. a great quantity or number.
6. to regard with esteem or value (as in "set *store* by").

That *store* has multiple meanings does not thereby make any use of that word ambiguous. In fact, ordinarily the context makes clear the intended meaning, as in: "Go to the *store* for some milk," or "*Store* these records in the attic," or "No one knows what the future holds in *store.*" When writers get careless, however, they can use a word that has multiple meanings in such a way that the context does not make clear exactly which meaning is intended. When this occurs, the term is being used ambiguously.

Many words are also vague. **Vagueness means lacking in precision. When a term is vague, its extensional meaning is unclear.** For example, suppose a teacher tells a student, "Go stand in the back of the room." The obedient child follows, only to hear that teacher bark, "Not there! Over there, under the picture of Abraham Lincoln." The child is not to blame for not positioning herself precisely where the teacher had in mind. She, in fact, went to the back of the room. The problem is that "back of the room" is vague—it can refer to a number of locations along a continuum denoted by "back of the room." The teacher should have been precise: "Go stand in the back of the room under the picture of Abraham Lincoln."

The simplest kind of vagueness occurs when there is no precise cutoff point for the applicability and nonapplicability of the word. Sometimes the word may apply, other times it may not. For example, if you are driving fifty-five mph in a fifty-five mph zone, you are probably not driving "fast." But if you are driving the same speed on a foggy day, you could well be driving "fast," even *too* fast, and get a ticket. At what point does driving "slowly" become driving "fast"? When does "fast" become "too fast"? So-called *polar words* are obvious instances of vagueness—*fast/slow, hard/soft, light/dark, hot/cold, large/small,* and so on.

Words can also be vague when there is no single set of criteria for determining their use. Take, for example, the word *game*. Must an activity be amusing to be a game? Must a game always involve winning and losing or competition between players? In some games, such as baseball and football, there is competition and winners and losers. When a solitary child is playing a game of hop-scotch on a sidewalk, competition is not involved, at least not in the sense that football and baseball are competitive.

Not knowing precisely to what a term applies does not of itself undermine argument. In fact, sometimes vagueness is unavoidable, perhaps even desirable. Problems arise when a term is so imprecise that it precludes understanding the premise, for example, that contains it. As a result, we cannot evaluate the statement because we do not know what it means.

IN BRIEF   A term is ambiguous when it is used in a way that gives it more than one possible meaning. When a term is vague, it has only one meaning, but that meaning is not specific.

EXERCISES ON AMBIGUITY AND VAGUENESS

Determine whether the following sentences contain ambiguous or vague language.

1. Sally is a bright child.
2. Your research must be completed by next Monday.
3. Let's have dinner sometime.
4. I hope you get everything you deserve.
5. Only you could write a paper like this.
6. Milk has something for every body.
7. At Avis we try harder.
8. Irish Spring Soap has an effective double deodorant system.
9. Merrill Lynch is bullish on America.
10. Your argument is nothing if not sound.
11. Announcement: Professor Smith's provocative lecture was entitled "Obsessive Shoppers." Over three-hundred attended.
12. Citrus Hill Plus Calcium orange juice promotes a special delivery system for calcium.
13. News item: Wrapped in nothing but foil to create suspense, a beaming Mrs. Alice McManners carried her prize-winning cake to the judges' stand.
14. AGREE: the Creme Rinse and Conditioner that helps the greasies.
15. Road sign: Slow Children At Play.

MODULE 4.2

✳ DISPUTES

Everything we have said so far points to the importance of using clear and precise language in argument. When people do not share a common understanding of a term, disputes can result.

Verbal Disputes

A dispute is a disagreement or controversy over some topic or issue. **A verbal dispute is one that can be settled by clarifying the words used.**

A classic example of a verbal dispute is the question: "If a tree falls in the forest and nobody is there to hear it, is there a sound?" Yes and no, depending on the intended meaning of "sound." If "sound" is taken to mean sound waves, which can be recorded by instruments, then there is a sound. But if "sound" is meant in the psychological sense of sound *sensations,* then there is no sound, since no one is present to experience the sensations.

As another example of a verbal dispute, recall the "Speaking of . . . " box concerning the meaning of language. When a chimp not only gets you the cup you asked for, but pronounces the word *cup* when he hands it over, it appears that he is using human language. The author claims, however, that the chimp is not really using human language at all. Is he or is he not? In order to answer this question, it is necessary to define "human language," which the author does with reference to the creation of new utterances. If the creation of new utterance is a defining feature of human language and if chimps cannot create new utterances, then they cannot be said to use human language—end of dispute.

Not all disputes are verbal. Some are *genuine disputes,* that is, *disagreements that cannot be settled by clarifying language.* Significant disputes are mostly of this kind—they are not merely matters of semantics but disagreements in belief or attitude. Four common categories of genuine disputes that arise in extended arguments are factual, evaluative, interpretive, and theoretical.

Factual Disputes

A factual dispute is one that can only be settled by an investigation of the facts. Suppose, for example, that you and I disagree on what percentage of American workers use drugs on the job; or whether Andrew Johnson, who succeeded Abraham Lincoln to the presidency, ever ran for the presidency; or whether man first walked on the moon in 1968 or 1969. To settle these disagreements, we must investigate the facts surrounding them. No amount of verbal clarification will help.

Sometimes a dispute may be both verbal and factual. For example, if we disagree on the percentage of the U.S. adult population that is "functionally illiterate," not only must we investigate the facts, but we must also agree on the meaning of "functionally illiterate" as well as who is to count as a "U.S. adult" (persons over eighteen? twenty-one? noncitizens as well as citizens?).

Evaluative Disputes

Evaluative disputes are disagreements that involve values and value judgments. Evaluative disputes arise over issues that invite opposed viewpoints about matters of value. "Should handguns be banned?" "Should sex education be an integral part of public education?" "Should abortions be prohibited, no matter the reason?" "Should the United States set up import restrictions on foreign cars?" "Should the United States have attacked Iraq?" Questions like these elicit conflicting responses that inevitably reflect what people consider to be of worth.

The opinionated nature of evaluative disputes might suggest that one position in such a dispute is as good as another. This is not so if by "good" we mean "logically convincing." The evaluative criteria governing argument apply with equal force to any genuine dispute, including evaluative ones.

Interpretive Disputes

An interpretive dispute concerns how a matter is to be understood. Courts not only interpret laws, but often rule in ways that invite interpretive disputes. For example, in January 1989, the United States Supreme Court overruled Richmond, Virginia's plan for allocating 30 percent of its contracts to minority firms. Some analysts interpreted this ruling as sounding the death knell for affirmative action; others found nothing in the ruling to prohibit employers from continuing to recruit and promote minorities or women.

As another example of an interpretative dispute, consider the November 1989 election of Democrats as mayor of New York and governors of Virginia and New Jersey. Each of the winners had taken a "pro-choice" position on abortion while campaigning. Some analysts interpreted these victories as establishing abortion as a significant issue in the 1990 midterm elections and a boding well and ill for "pro-choice and "pro-life" candidates, respectively. Others, such as then Republican National Committee Chairman Lee Atwater, read the results as confirming the adage that "All politics is local." What was the "correct" interpretation? In complex and multidimensional events, there is no correct interpretation, only interpretations that are better than others. What makes one interpretation better or more convincing than another depends on the kinds of information that are relevant to interpretations.

Theoretical Disputes

A theoretical dispute is a disagreement about which set of assumptions or principles best explains some phenomenon. For example, the basic premise of Freudian psychology is that there is a vast reservoir of forces attributable to the id, superego, and ego—most, if not all, of which are beyond conscious awareness. Since none of these entities of the human psyche can be observed, their proposal is a theory. Through a comprehensive theory involving these concepts, Freudian psychology attempts to explain an array of psychological phenomena from neuroses and psychoses, to dreams and slips of the tongue. Not all students of psychology accept this theory, however. Carl Jung and Alfred Adler, Erik Erickson and Abraham Maslow, Carl Rogers and B. F. Skinner, all offer different personality theories. One reason there are so many theories is the awesome explanatory burden imposed on any one personality theory. Just think about it—a good theory of human personality must explain human sensations, perceptions, values, motivations, ability to learn and change, and the tendency of humans to relate to other humans—and it must do all this in terms that fit with what we know of the human nervous system and the culture we inhabit. No one theory has yet done this.

The potency of any theory is in direct proportion to the range of facts it explains, especially those unknown when the theory was devised. (This is what makes the atomic theory and the theory of the unconscious such potent theories.) When a theory cannot account for new information, it loses credibility.

For example, there is little question that acupuncture works as a painkiller. This ancient Chinese practice of inserting needles into specific points on the human body and then twirling them or passing an electric current through them, does stop pain, but how? This question baffles Western medicine because its traditional theory of pain cannot account for it. The West's specificity theory of pain contends that specific bodily pain receptors relay messages to the brain. Thus, people feel pain where the receptors are stimulated. In acupuncture, the tissues stimulated are often far away from where the person feels the pain. As traditionally formulated, the specificity theory cannot explain this observed phenomenon.

The inadequacy of the theory has led some in the West to propose a so-called "gate-control theory," which argues against the fixed and immutable nature of the transmission of pain signals from points in the body to the brain. In this view, there are neurological links between different body sites, and a gate-like mechanism exists in the pain-signaling system. The gate may be open, partially open, or closed; thus, in some instances signals from injured tissues may never reach the brain. Furthermore, modulation of pain signals can occur in a variety of ways. If the gate-theory can account for everything that the specificity theory does, as well as account for the phenomenon of acupuncture, then it clearly has a wider range of application and is thus a better theory of pain.

Ideally, facts should shape theory, theory should not shape facts. Unfortunately, even scientific minds can become so attached to their theories—their intellectual children, as it were—that they interpret facts to fit their theories. A good example can be found in a correspondence between renowned scientist Karl Popper and noted psychoanalyst Alfred Adler, whose theory of personality relies heavily on the notion of the inferiority complex. In 1919, Popper reported to Adler a case that did not seem to him particularly Adlerian. Adler, however, found little difficulty in analyzing it in terms of his theory. "Slightly shocked," Popper writes, "I asked him how he could be so sure. 'Because of my thousand-fold experience,' he replied; whereupon I could not help saying, 'And with this new case, I suppose, your experience has become

Speaking of . . .

Theoretical Disputes

The Great Attractor

At the winter 1990 meeting of the American Astronomical society, a group of scientists claimed they had proved that a mysterious gravitational field is forcing our galaxy, as well as 139 additional ones, to streak toward a distant point in the southern sky at nearly 400 miles per second. The existence of the "Great Attractor" was first postulated in 1987 by astronomers Alan Dressler and Sandra Faber, along with five colleagues, who were instantly dubbed the "Seven Samurai" because of their slashing attack on conventional theory, which holds that the universe is expanding smoothly.

According to the "Seven Samurai," the center of the Great Attractor is about 150 million light-years away. (A light-year is the distance light travels in a year, nearly six trillion miles.) Even at that enormous distance, they say, the Great Attractor's gravitational field is so powerful that it is tugging on galaxies that are hundreds of millions of light-years away. Therein lies the mystery which continues to divide astronomers.

Conventional theory holds that the universe is smooth and reasonably homogeneous. Therefore, there should be no giant "lumps" of concentrated matter. That is precisely what the Great Attractor would be — a giant region of dense mass pulling other galaxies toward it over a vast region of space. That galaxies are being so attracted clashes with the smoothness of the universe's background radiation. If the Great Attractor does not exist, then how can the observed movement of the galaxies toward this focus in the southern sky be explained?

The Great Attractor theory offers an explanation for the observed perturbation in the otherwise smooth expansion of the universe. But like almost all other scientific theories, it raises as many questions as it answers. What gives the Great Attractor its powerful pull? Why should there be such a thing in the first place? If the universe begins to contract, as some astronomers believe it eventually will, will galaxies captured by the Great Attractor start "banging" into each other? Will there be a "traffic problem" in space? One thing is for sure — at least for the "Seven Samurai": The Great Attractor is real, and, as a result, astronomers must rethink their conventional theory of the universe.

thousand-and-one-fold.' "[2] In this case, Adler seems to have the attitude of the kind of person we are all familiar with, the one who, in effect, says, "Don't confuse me with the facts, my mind's already made up."

---

[2]Bryan Magee, *Karl Popper* (New York: Viking, 1973), p. 39.

IN BRIEF   A theory contains more than the observed facts that it explains. It is not just a summary of the facts. It involves concepts from which new and previously unknown facts can be inferred. This is why a good way to try to resolve a theoretical dispute is to ask, "Which of the competing theories not only best explains the known facts, but allows the most previously unknown facts to be inferred from it?" Or simply, "Which has the greatest predictive capacity?"

EXERCISES ON DISPUTES

Identify the kinds of disputes exhibited by the following pairs (1–13). Choose from verbal, factual, evaluative, interpretive, theoretical.

1. A. Harry is low-keyed.
   B. Harry's a bore.
2. A. Cristi is quick-witted.
   B. Cristi always has to have the last word.
3. A. Betty's stubborn.
   B. Betty has a mind of her own.
4. A. The Coxes served a refreshing snack.
   B. The Coxes served a sumptuous meal.
5. A. Bert generously contributed $10.
   B. Bert gave only $10.
6. A. The child has a rich imagination.
   B. The child plays fast and loose with facts.
7. A. I know of no pursuit in which more real and important services can be rendered to any country than by improving its agriculture, its breed of useful animals, and other branches of a husbandman's cares.
   (George Washington)
   B. With the introduction of agriculture mankind entered upon a long period of meanness, misery, and madness, from which they are only now being freed by the beneficent operation of the machine.
   (Bertrand Russell)
8. A. History is simply a piece of paper covered with print; the main thing is still to make history, not to write it.
   (Otto Von Bismarck)
   B. Anybody can make history. Only a great man can write it.
   (Oscar Wilde)
9. A. Our country: in her intercourse with foreign nations may she always be in the right; but our country right or wrong!
   (Stephen Decatur)
   B. Our country, right or wrong. When right, to be kept right; when wrong, to be put right.
   (Carl Schurz)

10. A. All knowledge about the world comes from and is based on the senses.
    B. Knowledge is based on reason alone, not on sense perception.
11. A. A statement is true if it corresponds with a fact.
    B. A statement is true if it fits in with all other statements already accepted as true.
12. A. A bad peace is even worse than war.
       (Tacitus)
    B. The most disadvantageous peace is better than the most just war.
       (Desiderius Erasmus)
13. A. Gravity once held all matter in the universe together in a massive molten ball.
       Intense gravitational forces so condensed the ball that pressure and
       temperature built up to incredible levels. The matter finally collapsed on itself.
       In this implosion, the outermost layers of the molten ball fell inward until they
       reached a critical point. The molten ball then exploded—a big bang. This big
       bang explains why the universe is "expanding," that is, moving away from the
       earth at constant speeds.
    B. Matter in intergalactic space is constantly created out of nothing. Even if only
       one hydrogen atom is being created every century, it's enough to displace
       existing matter. This process of displacement, this steady state, explains why
       the universe appears to be expanding.
14. Jim promises his girlfriend Tammy to meet her at the beach. Just before he's about
    to join her, Jim's friend Jerry convinces him to play tennis instead of joining
    Tammy. Much to their disappointment, the boys find all the neighborhood courts
    occupied. So, Jim joins Tammy at the beach. Did Jim keep his promise to Tammy,
    or didn't he?
15. Blaine and Jocelyn have just read a survey of 12,000 single men and women
    conducted by research psychologist Srully Blotnick that shows a decline in the
    approval of "recreational sex" since the 1960s. Blotnick's findings also included
    that a majority of young Americans are still very "open-minded" about sex and
    don't oppose premarital sexual intercourse. Blaine says that the study shows that,
    although most younger Americans are concerned about the spread of AIDS and
    other sexually transmitted diseases, they clearly aren't willing to give up casual sex.
    Jocelyn disagrees: "How can you say that?" she asks Blaine. "Clearly today's youth
    are becoming increasingly more discriminating about their sexual conduct." What
    is the basis of their dispute?
16. What kind of disagreement is exhibited in the following pair of statements?
    A. Pornography constitutes a direct attack on significant relationships because it
       helps create a mind-set that eventually treats all people as sexual objects.
       Modern pornography is an education system. It teaches. Its message is: Human
       beings are animals; the highest value is immediate pleasure; other people may
       be used and abused and then discarded. It teaches that sex is divorced from
       love, commitment, morality, and responsibility, that perversion is to be
       preferred to morality and responsibility, that perversion is to be preferred to
       normality, that women are fair game for anyone who cares to exploit them.
       (The Arthur S. DeMoss Foundation, *The Rebirth of America.*)
    B. Most pornography has a limited scope; it contains little else besides sex. This
       is partly because sexual activity has been excluded from socially respectable

portrayals of human experience; it has been driven out into a realm by itself. But almost all events, from sports to concerts, are specialized in their content. They all portray a limited view of human life. There are magazines that specialize in sports, food, music, hobbies, fashion, etc. Do these publications portray people as whole human beings? Do movies or novels that do *not* have sex scenes deny our completeness?: No. Human wholeness in no way precludes focusing on one aspect of ourselves at a time.

(Canadian philosopher F. M. Christensen, *Playboy,* January 1988.)

MODULE 4.3

WRITING WITH REASON: DEVELOPING EXTENDED DEFINITIONS

Sometimes in argument, a definition can be handled simply in a sentence or two. Other times, a simple definition is inadequate to reveal a term's meaning. A paragraph or more—even an entire essay—may be needed. Such lengthy, well-developed definitions are termed extended definitions.

In general, the extended definition is used when the writer's main concern is clarification, or making sure that the writer and audience agree on a definition. In some instances, clarification may involve carefully limiting, in a paragraph or two of an essay, an abstraction or key term. For example, say your purpose is to define the word *Democrat* and break it down into various kinds of Democrats. First, you would have to define *democratic,* which can refer to: (1) a form of government, (2) when capitalized, a political party or its workers, (3) a set of political beliefs, ideals, or values, or (4) a particular social outlook. Clearly, before you can talk about various kinds of Democrats (for example, liberal, moderate, conservative), you must pinpoint your definition of *democratic,* sorting out the meanings you intend from the other possible meanings.

In another instance, you may want to, or may *have to,* devote an entire essay to the definition of a single important, controversial, or abstract term. Abstract terms—words that are extremely general—especially need to be defined because they can be interpreted in so many ways. For example, unless writers ensure understanding with the audience, words such as *honesty, truth, happiness,* and *justice* encourage multiple interpretations and erroneous conclusions.

The thesis of an argumentative essay developed through extended definition is an assertion about meaning. (Of course, in developing the essay the writer may make additional assertions about consequences, value, policy, and fact.) In assembling their main points, writers call on all four sources of support material: personal experience, informed opinion, observation, and organized research. Although the many strategies for developing any essay can be used to write an extended definition, four methods predominate: (1) providing historical background, (2) listing specific qualities and characteristics, (3) isolating a common element, and (4) distinguishing a term from a more familiar term.

Providing Historical Background

Sometimes, the most effective way to clarify the meaning of a term is to trace major stages in its history. **Developing an extended definition through historical background, then, is explaining a word by tracing its development.**

Suppose you want to convince an audience that capitalism no longer exists in the United States (thesis). In order to establish your thesis, you might trace the meaning of the word *capitalism* as follows:

Fact 1:   As classically formulated, capitalism relies primarily on the market system to determine the distribution of goods and services in society. In other words, under classical capitalism, the economic factors working in society were considered free to interplay with one another and establish a stability that would provide the best resources in meeting human needs. This theoretical assumption is evident in the works of classical capitalistic economists such as Adam Smith (1723–1790). . . .

Fact 2:   Although the free market can be said to have operated in the United States in the decades before World War II, since then it has failed. For one thing, high costs, complex machinery, increasing demands, and intense competition have worked against individual productiveness. For another, whereas the earlier economy of the Industrial Revolution was characterized by relatively free and open competition, the hallmark of classical capitalism, the later economy of our time is made up of a relatively few enormous companies that can fix prices, eliminate competition, and monopolize an industry. . . .

Fact 3:   Modern facts of economic life belie the easy assumption that we are a capitalistic economy. If we are, we certainly are not capitalistic in the sense of people like Adam Smith. . . .

Keying on One Element

A second way to develop an extended definition in argument is by keying on some element of a subject, then enumerating specific qualities or characteristics to support the focus. For example, suppose you concluded that the key element in the makeup of a cynic was frustrated idealism. In your view, cynics once perceived people and things as they should be, rather than as they are. When things did not square with their lofty expectations, these people's idealism turned to cynicism. You could develop this argumentative essay by listing the special qualities or characteristics that support this key element. Here is how:

Example 1:   Perhaps the most obvious illustration can be found in the adolescent. Many adolescents have a highly romantic concept of love and the opposite sex, which they may even carry into adulthood. But too often, when people and relationships turn out less than perfect, these would-be romantics turn sour on love and the opposite sex. For example, how many times have we heard a man say, "You can't trust women" or a woman say, "All men are bums"?. . . .

Example 2:   The most striking example of the idealist-turned-cynic is the "nay-sayer," the person who insists that the world is going straight to the dogs and that there is nothing anyone can do to prevent it. Probe a little and you will probably find that these defeatists once cherished lofty notions about themselves and the world. . . .

Example 3:   Beyond these obvious examples, even a cursory look at contemporary films shows the line between cynicism and failed idealism. The character Harry Callahan played by Clint Eastwood in several of his films is a good example. . . .

Finding the Common Element

A variation of the preceding pattern is to take the position of an impartial observer. Thus, **rather than advancing some key element at the outset, you approach the subject with an open mind, inviting your audience to participate in the search to find a common denominator in the application of a term. You then offer a series of test cases, each raising an issue relevant to the term or concept under discussion.** Here is how a paper about punishment might be developed by searching for the common element. Notice that the thesis is not stated until the end.

Statement of issue: Punishment means different things to different people. . . .
First test case: Parents often punish disobedient children. . . .
Second test case: People are fined, imprisoned, even executed for breaking laws. . . .
Third test case: Students consider it unfair for a teacher to punish everyone in a class for the behavior of a few. . . .
Common element: Central to the idea of punishment seems to be some action that is administered for breaking a law or rule. . . .

Distinguishing Terms

A fourth way to develop an extended definition in argument is by distinguishing a term from a more familiar one to which it is closely related. This procedure involves systematic comparison and contrast with a familiar synonym or near synonym. Setting a term off from a related, familiar term is a useful way to clarify a word that may be fuzzy in the reader's mind. It can also be effective when your larger purpose is to win audience assent or consent.

For example, suppose you want to advance the thesis that assertiveness is a good characteristic to have. In order to make your point you decide to distinguish *assertiveness* from *aggressiveness.* You might proceed as follows:

Definition of first term:	To be assertive is to state your feelings, beliefs, or values in a way that, although positive, respects the rights of others. . . .
First example:	If you are assertive, you stand up for your rights. When the waiter brings you a steak that is not cooked to your specification, you politely ask that it be taken back and prepared properly. When the boss continually insists that you work overtime without pay, you tactfully express your resentment. . . .
Second example:	If you are assertive, you express your emotions in personal relations. When you feel that a friend is taking advantage of you, you say so. When you feel that a boyfriend or girlfriend is treating you indifferently, you speak up. . . .
Third example:	If you are assertive, you are civil. When you know that what you say or do will seriously hurt someone else, you think twice before acting in a trivial matter. . . .
Definition of second term:	To be aggressive is to protect yourself in a way that is offensive and hostile and is unmindful of the rights of others. . . .
First example:	If you are aggressive, you try to win through intimidation. For example, in eating out you probably make it clear to the waiter that nothing short of a pound of flesh will placate you, should some dolt foul up your order. . . .
Second example:	If you are aggressive, you try to exploit others. Thus, knowing that your best friend is an easy-going, good hearted sort, you dump all sorts of problems on the person. . . .
Third example:	To be aggressive is to be reckless and impulsive. Regardless of the feelings and rights of others, no matter how trivial the matter, you tell people exactly what you think and let the chips fall where they may. . . .

Following one or the other of these four formats provides a handy way to develop an argumentative essay through definition. Keep in mind, of course, that your purpose is to win the audience's assent or consent, not just to define a term. So, you need to make a compelling case for your definition.

IMPROVING PERFORMANCE

SUMMARY-TEST QUESTIONS FOR CHAPTER 4*

1. Water is a clear, colorless, nearly odorless and tasteless liquid. H_2O, essential for most plant and animal life and the most widely used of all solvents. What kind of definition is this?

    A. denotative

    B. persuasive

    C. logical

    D. stipulative

2. What kinds of feelings, if any, do the following words tend to arouse? Choose from positive, negative, both, neutral.

automobile	mortgage
feminist	permissive
rat	flavor
apple pie	brick
I.R.S.	bureaucrat

3. Give an example of how two terms with different emotive value can refer to the same thing, that is, have the same denotation.

4. Which of the following terms does not belong with the others?

    A. Defining by example

    B. Defining by giving essential features

    C. A lexical definition

    D. A logical definition

5. If you were truly sophisticated, you'd realize that political candidates are sold the same way soap is. The person who said this was

    A. defining by example.

    B. offering a lexical definition.

    C. offering a persuasive definition.

    D. defining by stipulation.

6. Which of the following definitions is different in kind from the others?

    A. Good children never answer back.

    B. Happiness is being a grandparent.

    C. A glitch is a brief, unwanted surge of electrical power.

    D. No American, in the true sense, would question Vice-President Quayle's intelligence.

7. When an author gives a stipulative definition, she is

    A. trying to shift the literal meaning of a word while preserving its favorable or unfavorable connotations.

    B. trying to ensure common understanding with her audience.

    C. indicating exactly how she intends to use a term.

    D. B and C

    E. A, B, and C

8. Which of the following definitions is stipulative, which is persuasive?

    A. I take fairness to mean giving to each his due.

    B. Fairness is nothing more than giving people what they need.

    C. In the context of employment, fairness means giving all applicants equal consideration.

    D. Properly considered, fairness is doing what's expedient.

9. *Dominant* means producing the same genetic effect whether paired with an identical or a dissimilar gene. The definition of "dominant" is a _____ definition.

10. "Defense mechanisms are techniques used by the ego to defend itself against impulses or commands from the id and super-ego." This is a _____ definition.

11. Theoretical definitions
    A. attempt to explain the known in terms of the observable.
    B. contain *theory* words.
    C. are tantamount to proposing the acceptance of a theory.
    D. A, B, and C
    E. B and C

12. True or false?
    A. Theories can influence interpretation of facts. For example, cite and explain the illustration that Karl Popper gives of Alfred Adler.
    B. Theoretical definitions turn up only in the physical sciences. If false, cite an example of a theoretical definition outside the area of physical science.
    C. Words are ambiguous.

13. The word *house* has multiple meanings. Therefore, any use of that word is ambiguous. Do you agree with the conclusion of this argument?

14. Are the following words vague? If so, in what respect?
    sad
    below
    south
    jog
    laugh
    patience (as in, "Patience is a virtue.")

15. In the sentence, "Larry went downtown to see the construction," the word "construction" is ambiguous, but not vague. True or false? Explain.

16. SAM: You can't swim in the same river twice.
    ROY: That's ridiculous. You know very well that you and I have swum in this very same river dozens of times.
    SAM: But it wasn't the same river because the water that was there each previous time had already flowed downstream.
    Is this a dispute? If so, is it verbal or not?

17. You and a friend disagree about the number of American households that are headed by a female. Is this disagreement verbal, factual, or possibly both? Explain.

18. After you and your friend resolve the disagreement in question 17, you fall into another. You believe the increasing number of female-headed households is socially undesirable. Your friend views it as a positive trend. What kind of dispute is this?

19. JEAN: The election of George Bush in 1988 was a vindication of the Reagan presidency.
    JACK: No way! Governor Dukakis couldn't clearly and forcefully articulate the failings of the Reagan administration.
    What is the nature of Jean and Jack's dispute?

20. Explain the kind of dispute represented by these opposing viewpoints: ". . . [I]n man, as in other animals, there exists a physiological mechanism which, when stimulated, gives rise both to subjective feelings of anger and also to physical

changes which prepare the body for fighting. This mechanism is easily set off, and like other emotional responses, it is stereotyped and, in this sense, 'instinctive'. . . ."
(Anthony Storr, *Human Aggression.*)
"Since 'spontaneous' animal aggression is a relatively rare occurrence in nature (and there is the possibility that even these infrequent cases may be accounted for by frustrations or prior learning of the utility of hostile behavior), many ecologists and experimental biologists rule out the possibility of a self-stimulating aggressive system in animals. One important lesson to be derived from these studies is that there is no instinctive drive toward war within man. . . . [I]t is possible to lessen the likelihood of interpersonal conflict by decreasing the occurrence of frustrations and minimizing the gains to be won through aggression."
(Leonard Berkowitz)

CRITICAL THINKING APPLICATIONS

1. In the following diagram, A and B are end points in a straight line. **In your opinion, which of points C, D, E, F, and G are "between" A and B? Explain by clarifying "between."**

   ```
           .D
   .A----------.C----------.B
           .E
           .F
           .G
   ```

2. Scientists can tell whether viruses have powers of locomotion and reproduction. But they cannot always decide whether certain viruses are "living" or "nonliving"? **Why do you think this is so?**

3. Over the years, the FBI has zealously kept files on many of America's greatest writers and artists who were suspected by the agency of being "un-American." Here are a few:
   —Sinclair Lewis, author of such classics as *Babbitt* and *Elmer Gantry* was the subject of a 150-page FBI file. His "un-American" activities included not living with his wife and writing a novel, *Kingsblood Royal,* which the FBI called "propaganda for the white man's acceptance of the Negro as a social equal."
   —Pearl S. Buck, author of *The Good Earth,* was the subject of a 280-page file. Her "un-American" activities included expressed opposition to racism, adopting a half-black–half-Japanese child, and membership in the American Civil Liberties Union, which the FBI called a "Communist-Front Organization."
   —Dorothy Parker, as well known for her wit as her writing, inspired a 1,000-page file. Her "un-American" activities record shows that she belonged to the Consumers Union and the League of Women Shoppers.
   —Tennessee Williams, considered by some to be America's greatest playwright, was considered "un-American" because his play *A Streetcar Named Desire* was

praised by the *Daily Worker,* a Communist newspaper, and because, in the FBI's words, he "has the reputation of being a homosexual."

—Archibald MacLeish, a three-time Pulitzer Prize winner, major poet, and one time librarian of Congress, attracted FBI director J. Edgar Hoover's attention for being "prematurely antifascist" and "a liberal of the New Deal type." In cataloguing MacLeish's "un-American" activities, the FBI also noted that he had been arrested for illegally fishing on private property and fined ten dollars.

What do you think of the FBI's use of the term "un-American"? How would you define "un-American," if you had to? Who, if anyone, do you believe could be currently denoted by the term? Why? Are there any activities that you have ever engaged in which by the FBI's standards could qualify you as "un-American"? Do you think it would be easy to defend yourself against being so labeled?

4. The American philosopher William James recounts a dispute that arose during a camping trip:

> The corpus of the dispute was a squirrel—a live squirrel supposed to be clinging to one side of a tree-trunk; while over against the tree's opposite side a human being was imagined to stand. This human witness tries to get sight of the squirrel by moving rapidly round the tree, but no matter how fast he goes, the squirrel moves just as fast in the opposite direction (that is, away from the man), and always keeps the tree between himself and the man, so that never a glimpse of him is caught. The resultant problem now is this: "Does the man go round the squirrel or not?" He goes round the tree, sure enough, and the squirrel is on the tree; but does he go round the squirrel?

   How would you resolve this dispute?

5. While in Manila, in June 1981, Vice-President George Bush toasted Ferdinand Marcos, president of the Philippines with the words: "We love your adherence to democratic principles and to the democratic processes." Many people, including Filipinos, regarded this statement as patent nonsense, since Marcos had kept the Philippines under martial law for years. **Why is it so difficult to decide whether a country is a "democracy"? What do you consider some of the essential characteristics or features of a democracy? What's the international significance for the United States of determining whether a country has "democratic" governments?**

6. The Veterans Administration gives "disabled veterans" an extension for filing application for college benefits. Two veterans, who happened to be alcoholics, were denied benefits when they missed the deadline. The veterans subsequently sued the VA, arguing that alcoholism made them "disabled veterans" and thus eligible for the extended deadline. **Suppose that you had to rule in this case. Would you honor or deny the veterans' appeal? Justify your ruling by appeal to a definition of "disabled veteran."**

7. "A *New York Post's* lead story, headlined 'AIDS MONSTER,' stereotyped the classic diseased and depraved homosexual, hunted by police for molesting what seemed like countless boys. It is easy to see through the *Post's* bigotry, but the story plays on the same assumptions that support mandatory testing and disclosure: that

people with AIDS remain selfishly ignorant, and deliberately infect—murder—others, so desperate and devoid of social responsibility are they. When they are so unlike "us," Draconian measures like tattooing or quarantine seem necessary "for the greater good." In reality, the greater good demands reaching deep to find our human similarities and also respecting our sexual differences. . . ."
(Judith Levine, "Thinking about Sex. *Tijjun,* March/April, 1988.)

A. **Explain the *Post's* exploitation of subjective connotation.**
B. **What term does the author define persuasively?**
C. **This passage can be viewed as a deductively organized argument. The author offers a principle, cites an application that violates it, and implies a conclusion. What is the principle? What is the violation? What is the implied conclusion? (Hint: The principle is contained in the persuasive definition.)**

8. News Item: Georgetown University students refused to publish an edition of their newspaper Friday, because officials of the Roman Catholic institution had forbidden them to fund an advertisement on an abortion rights rally.

"The ad was not promoting any specific service," said Karl Hente, a senior who serves as the paper's managing editor. "The ad was for a pro-choice rally and was basically expressing a political viewpoint. The newspaper's foundation is freedom of expression. . . ."

"I'm kind of horrified that a university would deny free speech," said National Organization for Women president Molly Yard.

"We are a Catholic, Jesuit institution, and we don't allow advertisements of condoms, abortion, or things like that," said Georgetown spokesman Gary Krull.

A. **Is an "ad" a "promotion"?**
B. **Would you consider this an example of an interpretive dispute? Explain.**
C. **Do you agree with Molly Yard that "free speech" necessarily extends to publishing an ad?**

POINT/COUNTERPOINT: ESSAYS FOR ANALYSIS

Issue: *The Proper Limits of Individual Freedom*

Resolved: Burning the flag as a political protest is a form of free speech protected by the Constitution.

Background: One of the perennial concerns of social and political philosophy is the relationship between the individual and the state. How free should individuals in a society be? What are the justifiable limits of government intervention in individual freedom? Where should the line be drawn between individual freedom and societal interests?

Recently these questions arose in a celebrated case involving the burning of an American flag, which we will take up presently. But first, let's briefly frame the issue in a broader, theoretical context by considering, in general, what the proper limits of individual freedom should be.

Freedom finds what may be its classic description in John Stuart Mill's essay "On Liberty" (1859), in which the British social and political philosopher presents a powerful case for political individualism. In the excerpt that follows, Mill is specifically concerned with what actions individuals in society may perform. In essence, he claims that society may interfere with the individual in matters involving other people, but not in matters involving only the individual. In effect, he distinguishes between two spheres of interest, the outer and the inner. A matter belongs to the outer sphere if it involves more than "just a few" individuals and to the inner if it involves only the self or a few others.

From: **"On Liberty"**

John Stuart Mill

What, then, is the rightful limit to the sovereignty of the individual over himself: Where does the authority of society begin? How much of human life should be assigned to individuality, and how much to society?

Each will receive its proper share, if each has that which more particularly concerns it. To individuality should belong the part of life in which it is chiefly the individual that is interested; to society, the part which chiefly interests society.

Though society is not founded on a contract, and though no good purpose is answered by inventing a contract in order to deduct social obligations from it, everyone who receives the protection of society owes a return for the benefit, and the fact of living in society renders it indispensable that each should be bound to observe a certain line of conduct towards the rest. This conduct consists, *first,* in not injuring the interests of one another; or rather certain interests, which either by express legal provision or by tacit understanding, ought to be considered as rights; and *secondly,* in each person's bearing his share (to be fixed on some equitable principle) of the labors and sacrifice incurred for defending the society or its members from injury and molestation. These conditions society is justified in enforcing, at all costs to those who endeavor to withhold fulfillment. Nor is that all society may do. The acts of an individual may be unhurtful to others, or wanting in due consideration for their welfare, without going to the length of violating any of their constitutional rights. The offender may then be justly punished by opinion, though not by law. As soon as any part of a person's conduct affects prejudicially the interests of others, society has jurisdiction over it, and the question whether the general welfare will or will not be promoted by interfering with it, becomes open to discussion. But there is no room for entertaining any such question when a person's conduct affects the interests of no persons besides himself, or need not affect them unless they like (all persons concerned being of full age, and the ordinary amounts of understanding). In all such cases, there should be perfect freedom, legal and social, to do the action and stand the consequences.

1. What kind of definition of liberty do you think Mill is offering?
2. Do you think Mill succeeds in drawing a clear, sharp line of demarcation between society and individual, or is it vague? If vague, must it necessarily be so?

3. Do you think "few others" is precise or vague?
4. Mill argues that since the individual and not society is the best judge of what advances self-interest, the individual should be free from interference in such pursuits. Do you find anything vague about this assertion? Give an example of conduct that although falling within the "inner sphere" might not be in the person's best interests?
5. Cite some contemporary examples of where the issue of identifying the proper limits of individual freedom and government interference arise.
6. Of the four ways to develop an extended definition, which do you think Mill's most closely parallels?

From: **The Supreme Court's Decision Barring Prosecution in Flag Protest**

Is an individual free to burn the flag as a political protest? Or is the state justified in prohibiting such an action? Following are excerpts from the 1989 Supreme Court decision in Texas v. Johnson, holding that a person may not be prosecuted for burning the American flag as a peaceful political protest. Justice William J. Brennan Jr. wrote the opinion for the 5-to-4 majority. Dissents were filed by Chief Justice William H. Rehnquist and Justice John Paul Stevens. For purposes of this exercise, treat the two dissents as a single extended argument.

From: **The Opinion**

Justice Brennan

After publicly burning an American flag as a means of political protest, Gregory Lee Johnson was convicted of desecrating a flag in violation of Texas law. This case presents the question whether his conviction is consistent with the First Amendment. We hold that it is not.

While the Republican National Convention was taking place in Dallas in 1984, respondent Johnson participated in a political demonstration dubbed the "Republican War Chest Tour."

The demonstration ended in front of Dallas City Hall, where Johnson unfurled the American flag, doused it with kerosene and set it on fire. While the flag burned, the protestors chanted, "America, the red, white, and blue, we spit on you." After the demonstrators dispersed, a witness to the flag-burning collected the flag's remains and buried them in his backyard. No one was physically injured or threatened with injury, though several witnesses testified that they had been seriously offended by the flag burning.

Of the approximately 100 demonstrators, Johnson alone was charged with a crime. The only criminal offense with which he was charged was the desecration of a venerated object in violation of Texas Penal Code Ann. Sec. 42.09 (a)(3) (1989). ["Desecration of a Venerated Object"]. After a trial, he was convicted, sentenced to one year in prison and fined $2,000. The Court of Appeals for the Fifth District of Texas at Dallas affirmed Johnson's conviction, but the Texas Court of Criminal Appeals reversed, holding that the State could not, consistent with the First Amendment, punish Johnson for burning the flag in these circumstances. . . .

To justify Johnson's conviction for engaging in symbolic speech, the State asserted two interests: preserving the flag as a symbol of national unity and preventing breaches of the peace. The Court of Criminal Appeals held that neither interest supported his conviction.

Acknowledging that this Court had not yet decided whether the Government may criminally sanction flag desecration in order to preserve the flag's symbolic value, the Texas court nevertheless concluded that our decision in West Virginia Board of Education v. Barnette, 319 U.S. 624 (1943), suggested that furthering this interest by curtailing speech was impermissible.

•   •   •

The First Amendment literally forbids the abridgement only of "speech," but we have long recognized that its protection does not end at the spoken or written word.

•   •   •

Especially pertinent to this case are our decisions recognizing the communicative nature of conduct relating to flags. Attaching a peace sign to the flag, Spence v. Washington, 1974; saluting the flag, Barnette, and displaying a red flag, Stromberg v. California (1931), we have held, all may find shelter under the First Amendment. That we have had little difficulty identifying an expressive element in conduct relating to flags should not be surprising. The very purpose of a national flag is to serve as a symbol of our country; it is, one might say, "the one visible manifestation of two hundred years of nationhood."

Pregnant with expressive content, the flag as readily signifies this nation as does the combination of letters found in "America."

•   •   •

The Government generally has a freer hand in restricting expressive conduct than it has in restricting the written or spoken word. It may not, however, proscribe particular conduct *because* it has expressive elements. It is, in short, not simply the verbal or nonverbal nature of the expression, but the governmental interest at stake, that helps to determine whether a restriction on that expression is valid.

•   •   •

The State offers two separate interests to justify this conviction: preventing breaches of the peace, and preserving the flag as a symbol of nationhood and national unity. We hold that the first interest is not implicated on this record and that the second is related to the suppression of expression. . . .

We thus conclude that the State's interest in maintaining order is not implicated on these facts. The State need not worry that our holding will disable it from preserving the peace. We do not suggest that the First Amendment forbids a state to prevent "imminent lawless action." And, in fact, Texas already has a statute specifically prohibiting breaches of the peace, Texas Penal Code Ann. Sec. 42.01 (1989), which tends to confirm that Texas need not punish this flag desecration in order to keep the peace.

• • •

If there is a bedrock principle underlying the First Amendment, it is that the Government may not prohibit the expression of an idea simply because society finds the idea itself offensive or disagreeable.

We have not recognized an exception to this principle even where our flag has been involved. In Street v. New York, 394 U.S. 576 (1969), we held that a state may not criminally punish a person for uttering words critical of the flag. . . .

• • •

Nor may the Government, we have held, compel conduct that would evince respect for the flag. . . .

• • •

We never before have held that the Government may insure that a symbol be used to express only one view of that symbol or its referents. To conclude that the Government may permit designated symbols to be used to communicate only a limited set of messages would be to enter territory having no discernible or defensible boundaries.

Could the Government, on this theory, prohibit the burning of state flags? Of copies of the Presidential seal? Of the Constitution? In evaluating these choices under the First Amendment, how would we decide which symbols were sufficiently special to warrant this unique status? To do so, we would be forced to consult our own political preferences, and impose them on the citizenry, in the very way that the First Amendment forbids us to do.

There is, moreover, no indication—either in the text of the Constitution or in our cases interpreting—that a separate juridical category exists for the American flag alone. Indeed, we would not be surprised to learn that the persons who framed our Constitution and wrote the Amendment that we now construe were not known for their reverence for the Union Jack.

The First Amendment does not guarantee that other concepts virtually sacred to our nation as a whole—such as the principle that discrimination on the basis of race is odious and destructive—will go unquestioned in the marketplace of ideas. We decline, therefore, to create for the flag an exception to the joust of principles protected by the First Amendment.

• • •

We are fortified in today's conclusion by our conviction that forbidding criminal punishment for conduct such as Johnson's will not endanger the special role played by our flag or the feelings it inspires. . . .

We are tempted to say, in fact, that the flag's deservedly cherished place in our community will be strengthened, not weakened, by our holding today. Our decision is a reaffirmation of the principles of freedom and inclusiveness that the flag best reflects, and of the conviction that our toleration of criticism such as Johnson's is a sign and source of our strength.

•   •   •

The way to preserve the flag's special role is not to punish those who feel differently about these matters. It is to persuade them that they are wrong. . . .

We can imagine no more appropriate response to burning a flag than waving one's own, no better way to counter a flag-burner's message than by saluting the flag that burns, no surer means of preserving the dignity even of the flag that burned than by—as one witness here did—according its remains a respectful burial. We do not consecrate the flag by punishing its desecration, for in doing so we dilute the freedom that this cherished emblem represents.

From: **Dissenting Opinions**

Chief Justice Rehnquist

In holding this Texas statute unconstitutional, the Court ignores Justice Holmes's familiar aphorism that "a page of history is worth of volume of logic." For more than 200 years, the American flag has occupied a unique position as the symbol of our nation, a uniqueness that justifies a governmental prohibition against flag burning in the way respondent Johnson did here.

At the time of the American Revolution, the flag served to unify the 13 colonies at home while obtaining recognition of national sovereignty abroad. Ralph Waldo Emerson's Concord Hymn describes the first skirmishes of the Revolutionary War in these lines:

> *"By the rude bridge that arched the flood,*
> *Their flag to April's breeze unfurled,*
> *Here once the embattled farmers stood,*
> *And fired the shot heard round the world."*

•   •   •

In the First and Second World Wars, thousands of our countrymen died on foreign soil fighting for the American cause. At Iwo Jima in the Second World War, United States Marines fought hand to hand against thousands of Japanese. By the time the marines reached the top of Mount Suribachi, they raised a piece of pipe upright and from one end fluttered a flag. That ascent had cost nearly 6,000 American lives.

•   •   •

The flag symbolizes the nation in peace as well as in war. It signifies our national presence on battleships, airplanes, military installations and public buildings from the United States Capitol to the thousands of county courthouses and city halls throughout the country.

No other American symbol has been as universally honored as the flag. In 1931 Congress declared "The Star Spangled Banner" to be our national anthem. In 1949 Congress declared June 14th to be Flag Day. In 1987 John Philip Sousa's "The Stars and Stripes Forever" was designated as the national march. Congress has also established "The Pledge of Allegiance to the Flag" and the manner of its deliverance.

• • •

With the exception of Alaska and Wyoming, all of the states now have statutes prohibiting the burning of the flag.

• • •

The result of the Texas statute is obviously to deny one in Johnson's frame of mind one of many means of "symbolic speech." Far from being a case of "one picture being worth a thousand words," flag burning is the equivalent of an inarticulate grunt or roar that, it seems fair to say, is most likely to be indulged in not to express any particular idea, but to antagonize others.

The Texas statute deprived Johnson of only one rather inarticulate symbolic form of protest — a form of protest that was profoundly offensive to many — and left him with a full panoply of other symbols and every conceivable form of verbal expression to express his deep disapproval of national policy. . . .

But the Court today will have none of this. The uniquely deep awe and respect for our flag felt by virtually all of us are bundled off under the rubric of "designated symbols" that the First Amendment prohibits the Government from "establishing." But the Government has not "established" this feeling; 200 years of history have done that. The Government is simply recognizing as a fact the profound regard for the American flag created by that history when it enacts statutes prohibiting the disrespectful public burning of the flag.

The Court concludes its opinion with a regrettably patronizing civics lecture, presumably addressed to the members of both houses of Congress, the members of the 48 state legislatures that enacted prohibitions against flag burning, and the troops fighting under that flag in Vietnam who objected to its being burned: "The way to preserve the flag's special role is not to punish those who feel differently about these matters. It is to persuade them that they are wrong."

The Court's role as the final expositor of the Constitution is well established, but its role as a platonic guardian admonishing those responsible to public opinion as if they were truant school children has no similar place in our system of government.

Justice Stevens

Even if flag burning could be considered just another species of symbolic speech under the logical application of the rules that the Court has developed in its interpretation of the First Amendment in other contexts, this case has an intangible dimension that makes those rules inapplicable.

A country's flag is a symbol of more than "nationhood and national unity." It also signifies the ideas that characterize the society that has chose that emblem, as well as the special history that has animated the growth and power of those ideas.

So it is with the American flag. It is more than a proud symbol of the courage, the determination and the gifts of nature that transformed 13 fledgling colonies into a world power. It is a symbol of freedom, of equal opportunity, of religious tolerance and of good will for other peoples who share our aspirations.

The value of the flag as a symbol cannot be measured. Even so, I have no doubt that the interest in preserving that value for the future is both significant and legitimate. The creation of a Federal right to post bulletin boards and graffiti on the Washington Monument might enlarge the market for free expression, but at a cost I would not pay.

Similarly, in my considered judgment, sanctioning the public desecration of the flag will tarnish its value — both for those who cherish the ideas for which it waves and for those who desire to don the robes of martyrdom by burning it. That tarnish is not justified by the trivial burden on free expression occasioned by requiring that an available, alternative mode of expression — including uttering words critical of the flag — be employed.

•   •   •

The ideas of liberty and equality have been an irresistible force in motivating leaders like Patrick Henry, Susan B. Anthony, and Abraham Lincoln, schoolteachers like Nathan Hale and Booker T. Washington, the Philippine Scouts who fought at Bataan, and the soldiers who scaled the bluff at Omaha Beach. If those ideas are worth fighting for — and our history demonstrates that they are — it cannot be true that the flag that uniquely symbolizes their power is not itself worthy of protection from unnecessary desecration.

SOME QUESTIONS CONCERNING ORGANIZATION, LANGUAGE, AND MEANING

The Organization and Development of the Arguments*

1. Outline both opinions, following the format presented in Chapter 2.
2. Show how the opinion follows the classic form of developing an extended argument, as sketched in Chapter 2.

The Categories and Function of Language in the Arguments

1. Cite as many examples as you can of premise and conclusion indicators, qualifiers, intensifiers, discounts, and asides.

2. Do you think the examples cited by Chief Justice Rehnquist in paragraphs 2 and 3 serve an argumentative or nonargumentative purpose? In other words, do they help make his point, or merely illustrate what he means?

3. What language function(s) did Emerson probably intend in writing the "Concord Hymn"? What function(s) does it serve for Rehnquist?

4. Explain why Justice Stevens' dissent is a good example of the mixed functions of discourse — informative, expressive, and by implication directive.

Meaning and Definition in the Arguments

1. Make a list of terms that you find vague or ambiguous.

2. On which of the following do the opinion and the dissent agree or disagree? Defend your answers by citing the texts.
   A. The symbolic value of the flag
   B. What activities the right to free speech extends to
   C. Flag burning as "speech"
   D. The effects of flag burning on the symbolic value of the flag.

3. Where you indicated disagreement in question 2, what would you say is the nature of the dispute — verbal, factual, evaluative, interpretive, theoretical? Explain. Who presents the more convincing arguments in each dispute?

4. Justice Brennan says that punishing Johnson would be tantamount to establishing "designated symbols." What does he mean by "designated symbols"? Stevens disagrees with Brennan. What kind of dispute is involved? With whom do you agree, and why?

5. Is the dissent more emotive in tone than the opinion? Explain. Do you think the inclusion of emotive language helps, hurts, or has no effect on the strength of the dissent?

6. The Court concludes its opinion by saying: "The way to preserve the flag's special role is not to punish those who feel differently about these matters. It is to persuade them that they are wrong." Chief Justice Rehnquist calls this advice "a regrettably patronizing civics lecture." Do you agree with Rehnquist's evaluation?

RELATED THEME TOPICS

1. *Write an essay in which you argue that Mill's view of individual or political freedom extends or does not extend to flag burning.*

2. *Write an essay in which you argue that individuals need to keep in mind the difference between "freedom" and "license" in their conduct. Make your point through a series of well-chosen examples that distinguish between freedom and license.*

3. *Write an essay that supports or attacks Chief Justice Rehnquist's evaluation that "flag burning is the equivalent of an inarticulate grunt or roar, it seems fair to say, is most likely to be indulged in not to express any particular idea, but to antagonize others." (You might begin by asking yourself whether antagonizing others may be essential to the expression of some ideas.)*

4. Pretend you are the editor of a college newspaper. In an upcoming issue, you want to address the issue of date-rapes involving students at your college. You intend to use as your primary source a number of student rape victims whose anonymity you will preserve but whose graphic accounts you intend to publish. You also intend to conceal the identity of the alleged student-rapists. According to the victims, the incidents were reported to school authorities, who promised to take action but, in the end, did little. The women believe that the college took no action because the alleged rapists were key athletes, or students with "friends in high places," or because the school did not want to "air its dirty laundry in public." You confront the Dean of Students with these charges, hoping to include her opinion in the article, as well. The Dean not only pleads confidentiality but takes measures to stop publication of the article. You are outraged. You consider her intervention as an unjustifiable violation of free speech. *Write an essay for the newspaper in which you argue your case.*

PART 2

Argument Evaluation

5

Linguistic Confusion I: Rhetorical Fallacies

INTRODUCTION

In Chapter 1, we noted that acceptable arguments have premises that are acceptable and relevant and provide adequate support for their conclusion. These three basic criteria of acceptable arguments, we saw, suggest three solid questions that we can use to test the soundness of any argument:

1. Are the premises acceptable?
2. Are the premises relevant?
3. Do the premises provide adequate support for the conclusion?

This part of our study deals with these criteria of an acceptable argument. It is intended to help you spot and avoid violations of these basic criteria, which are termed fallacies. In particular, this chapter and the next one engage the test of acceptability, and Chapter 7 considers relevancy. Since the adequacy or sufficiency of premises raises questions about the quantity and quality of evidence, which can only be addressed by examining different types of argument, we will leave that criterion for the last part of our study.

You may be wondering: "If this chapter deals with the acceptability of premises, then why is it called 'Linguistic Confusion'?" That is a good question, because we tend to think of acceptability simply in terms of the truth value of a statement. Thus, "Lincoln died a natural death" would be an unacceptable premise in an argument because it is false, but "Lincoln was assassinated" would be an acceptable premise in an argument because it is true. Although untrue statements are, indeed, unacceptable as premises, they generally are not the kinds of statements that give us the most trouble. Far more elusive are statements whose unacceptability can be traced directly to some improper use of language. And it is precisely these kinds of statements that we need to detect and avoid in extended arguments, where they find an uncommonly rich soil in which to take root. Thus, the sheer number of words and syntactical arrangements of extended arguments provides a most hospitable culture for ambiguous, vague, or meaningless language; for premises that are as questionable as the conclusions they are attempting to support; and for statements that contradict or are inconsistent with other statements in the argument.

In learning how to spot and avoid fallacies of linguistic confusion, therefore, you are really learning how to apply a basic test of argument acceptability. You are learning to test the acceptability of its premises at their foundational level. For although a premise that is not linguistically confusing may be unacceptable for some other reason (for example, it is simply not true), one that is linguistically confusing is never acceptable.

We begin our examination of linguistic confusion with what we call rhetorical fallacies. Earlier in our study, we distinguished between persuasion and argument and indicated that much contemporary rhetoric employs elements of both. In attempting to win over an audience, arguers can exploit the persuasive effects of language properly or improperly. *Rhetorical fallacies, then, can be viewed as improper applications of the persuasive capacities of language.*

IN BRIEF   Rhetorical fallacies are used in place of good reasons.

MODULE 5.1

SEMANTIC AMBIGUITY

As we saw in the preceding chapter, a word is ambiguous when it has two or more distinct meanings in a given context. **The fallacy of semantic ambiguity consists in presenting an argument that uses a term that can be interpreted in two or more ways without clarifying which meaning is intended.** Usually, semantic ambiguity arises in the presentation of premises. If a premise is open to multiple interpretations, its meaning is not clear or known and is therefore unacceptable.

Stated another way, the conclusion drawn from an ambiguous premise cannot be verified because it depends on how the premise is understood. For example, suppose a friend says, "I just bought a new car." Unless the context makes it clear whether "new" means "different" or "right out of the showroom," you have no logical basis for drawing a conclusion about the kind of car your friend has purchased.

Newspaper headlines often contain semantic ambiguity. For example: PRESI-DENT SEES PROSPECTS FOR LABOR. Without reading the accompanying story, it is impossible to know whether this statement means (1) the president is hopeful about improved work conditions, (2) the president anticipates job opportunities, (3) the president is considering candidates for positions in the Labor Department, or something else (we can safely assume, though, that an addition to the family is not imminent). In such cases, the headline writer ordinarily is not presenting an argument and so commits no fallacy. But readers are set up to draw erroneous conclusions from the ambiguous headline.

Ads glitter with semantic ambiguities. Consider, for example, these three statements that we can view as offering "reasons" for buying products, and thus as arguments:

> "It's natural for fresh breath" (Wrigley's Doublemint gum).

> "It's only natural" (Winston cigarettes).

> "Welcome to the pure and natural world of feminine care" (FDS Pure and Natural).

What is "natural" supposed to mean—that the product contains only natural ingredients?—that the use of the product has become commonplace?—that using the product is as natural, say, as eating or sleeping? *Natural* is a word that makes the health-conscious feel good about a product. Advertisers deliberately draft the ambiguous message to exploit the positive connotations of *natural,* thereby inviting us to draw a flattering, though perhaps untrue, conclusion about a product. Sometimes this tack boomerangs. In 1976, Tree Sweet Products Company was sued by a consumer for $250,000 in punitive damages and an estimated 75 cents refund for everybody who had purchased the company's grape drink since October 3, 1967. The plaintiff argued that the company had misled her by advertising "natural color," when in fact the product contained "artificial color." In this case, semantic ambiguity proved costly.

Since politicians are sold like any other product, it is not surprising that the fallacy of semantic ambiguity turns up in political as well as commercial pitches. During the 1980 presidential campaign, the Republicans devised an ingenious (notorious?) TV ad that made deliberate use of ambiguity. You may recall that at the time many people viewed Ronald Reagan as dangerously militaristic. To the candidate's rescue charged the image-builders, led by pollster Richard Wirthlin brandishing a 30-second TV ad that featured a large, black bear prowling in the woods.

"There's a bear in the woods," a voice intoned. "Some say it's tame, some say it's vicious and dangerous. Since no one knows for sure, doesn't it make sense that we be as safe as possible?. . . If there is a bear . . . " (Fade out bear, fade in the words): "RONALD REAGAN—PREPARED FOR PEACE."

Wirthlin called this ad "a message by parable." "The viewer had to read into it something that was not clearly articulated." He credits this intentional ambiguity with changing the public's perception of Reagan from "trigger happy" to "prudent." Had the candidate changed? No, but the audience inferred that he had, which was exactly what his managers had intended.

ABUSE OF VAGUENESS

In the preceding chapter, we developed the notion of *vagueness,* a lack of precision or clarity in the extensional meaning of an expression. It is worth repeating that vagueness is not always an unfortunate feature of language. There are times, in fact, when vague language is indispensable. For example, if you know exactly what the temperature is outside, you do not need to use words such as *hot* or *cold.* You can simply state the temperature. But if you do not know exactly, you might say, somewhat vaguely, "around 85 degrees," or more vaguely still, "pretty hot." There are numerous vague words for expressing temperature—*cool, chilly, warm, close,* and so on—which we use in the absence of precise information. Sometimes imprecise information is better than none.

Vague expressions, however, can pose a problem in argument when they are used in support of some particular claim. When vague language is used where clarity may legitimately be expected, the persuasive capacity of language is being improperly exploited. When may an audience properly expect clarity? Basically, when clarity is needed in order to understand and evaluate the statement in which the vague term appears. If a statement cannot be evaluated, it is not acceptable.

For example, during every election, candidates inevitably proclaim something about "taking measures" to address one problem or other—drugs, illiteracy, crime. The phrase "taking measures" is hopelessly imprecise. Unless we know to which *specific* policies or strategies the candidates are referring, we can neither understand nor evaluate their boasts as legitimate support for their solicitations.

Again, advertisers commonly try to sell products by making statements that appear to be forthright but, in fact, are vacuous. They accomplish this by using "weasel words," terms that evacuate the substance from what appears to be a substantial claim. "Up to" is a weasel, as in "This aspirin will give you *up to* eight hours pain relief." So is "helps," as in "This toothpaste *helps* fight plaque and tartar." And let's not forget "as much as"—"The secret ingredient in our gasoline can give you *as much as* four miles per gallon more than the competition's." These "reasons" for using the products defy evaluation because of the vagueness of the expressions.

In serious argument, authors who use vague language risk not only being misunderstood, but writing gibberish. Consider this paragraph penned by two historians in support of the presidential candidacy of Senator Eugene McCarthy in the 1968 election. At the time, Democrat McCarthy was contesting with Senator Robert F. Kennedy for their party's nomination. Notice the vagueness of the italicized words.

> The responsibility of *American Intellectuals* is to tell the truth. Always. The truth is: The movement that has made Senator McCarthy its symbol exemplifies *rationality,*

courage, morality. The movement Senator Kennedy commands exemplifies *irrationality, opportunism, amorality.* The truth is: To be *moral* and remain *moral,* a movement must always choose *moral* men and *moral* means. The truth is: The end never justifies the means. Never. If *American Intellectuals* do not know that, they have learned nothing from history. The truth is: In March 1968, history has caught up with *American Intellectuals.* They must choose between *morality* and *amorality,* between McCarthy or Kennedy. And to act on their own choice. Publicly. Unequivocally. Immediately.

In commenting on this passage, which appeared as an ad in the *New York Times,* historian David Hackett Fischer writes:

> The confusion in this extraordinary statement consists not merely in the fact that politicians do not behave according to these Manichaean expectations, but that language doesn't behave this way either. "McCarthy" and "Kennedy" are words of one sort: "Moral" and "amoral" are of quite another. The latter are vague words, like hot and cold, which are qualities which exist in various degrees, and in various respects. If an arbitrary distinction is drawn between "moral" and "amoral," then it must be drawn clearly and explicitly, and its arbitrariness must be borne in mind. If it is not, two shades of gray are converted by semantical mumbo jumbo into black and white. When words are used like this, they become meaningless.[1]

Fisher is right—the use of a word can be so vague as to render a sentence meaningless. Applied to argument, this means that, although a sentence may appear to be a proposition, it is not if it contains language that defies clarification in any ordinary sense. In short, it is unacceptable as a premise; thus, no conclusion should be drawn from it.

EXERCISES ON SEMANTIC AMBIGUITY AND ABUSE OF VAGUENESS*

Would you draw any inferences from the following statements? If not, explain why not in terms of semantic ambiguity and abuse of vagueness.

1. Senator Lloyd Bentsen is not a typical liberal.
2. The average American spends more time per day watching television than sleeping.
3. For America to be great, it must rediscover its traditional values.
4. Secretary of State James Baker reacting to the opening of the Berlin Wall: "It's the most significant event in forty years. It's a heck of a deal."
5. "At General Electric, progress is our most important product."
6. "A woman in Distinction Foundations is so beautiful that all other women want to kill her."
7. "Those on the frontier of sexual choice keep alive options which might otherwise be buried under a reactionary avalanche. What seems experimental and marginal at one time may become an important option—for all women at another time . . .

---

[1]David Hackett Fischer, *Historians' Fallacies* (New York: Harper & Row Publishers, Inc., 1970), pp. 277–278.

Women have come too far to surrender the range of possibilities opened up by a sexual revolution."
(Barbara Ehrenreich, Elizabeth Hess, Gloria Jacobs. *Ms.,* July 1986.)

8. "Pongo Peach color from Revlon comes from east of the sun, west of the moon where each tomorrow dawns. It is succulent on your lips, sizzling on your fingertips, and on your toes, goodness knows. Let it be your adventure in paradise."

9. "Increase the value of your holdings. Old Charter Bourbon Whiskey—The Final Set Up."

MODULE 5.2

SLANTING THROUGH THE USE OF EMOTIVE LANGUAGE

Suppose that a group of Hollywood celebrities sponsors a fund-raising event for a politician. It is possible to report this event in a sentence with strictly literal meaning—"A fund-raiser, sponsored by some Hollywood celebrities for Governor Alexis Brewster, took place at the home of film-producer Steven Spellbound last night." The event can also be reported in a sentence with emotive meaning: "A *sumptuous* fund-raising *bash* was *thrown* for Governor Alexis Brewster by some of Hollywood's *beautiful people* last night at the *sprawling stone-and-glass estate* of *movie mogul* Steven Spellbound." Because of the emotive charge (the subjective connotations) of the italicized words, this sentence not only reports a fact, but editorializes as well. It calls up feelings, gives impressions, that the first sentence does not. In the preceding chapter, we noted the emotive impact that many words carry.

The fallacy of slanting through the use of emotive language consists of illicitly exploiting the emotive aspect of language in order to bias evaluation of evidence. Such rhetorical slanting has the effect of masking literal meaning while advancing one's own evaluation or interpretation of the facts. Where needed evidence for the opinions is not provided, the premise containing the emotive language is unacceptable.

Consider, for example, how the aforementioned second sentence might function in a longer passage to elicit suspicions about the event reported.

Reactionary Politics in the Film Colony

The continued involvement of the Hollywood entertainment industry in radical politics is understandably deplorable to the American people. Americans are outraged because so many stars who have grown rich on box office receipts exhibit such fierce hostility to and contempt for traditional American values and institutions.

Hollywood's anti-Americanism was flaunted last night at a fund-raising bash thrown for Governor Alexis Brewster by some of Hollywood's beautiful people at the sprawling stone-and-glass estate of movie mogul Steven Spellbound. On hand, in addition to movieland types, was a popular televangelist infamous for wanting to replace democracy with theocracy and a handful of multimillionaires widely known to support conservative causes.

After several hours of mingling with the movers-and-shakers, the governor, who openly lusts after her party's nomination for presidency, was treated to Spellbound's archly-conservative political philosophy.

Given the colorful language of this passage, a reader must make a heroic effort to maintain objectivity in evaluating the significance of the event. The writer's clear intention is not merely to report the event, but to get readers to share his view that the event is an example of an anti-American cabal.

When used indiscriminately in argument, emotionally loaded words can function as substitutes for good reasons. They can derail rational discussion and induce blind acceptance of a thesis.

It is unlikely that you would buy a car simply because it is called a "Rabbit" or an "Excalibur," or a toothpaste merely because it is called "Gleem," or a soap simply because it is called "Zest." The reason is that you do not harbor strong emotional attachments to the association these works make. But where emotions run high, and feelings deep, a skilled rhetorician can use words of high emotional content to great persuasive effect.

For example, in September 1988, President Reagan took the ceremonial occasion of the seventieth American Legion convention to deliver a partisan political attack on unnamed "liberals." He accused them of favoring a "Disneyland defense policy" with "Mickey Mouse" treatment of the armed forces and a "Goofy" nuclear strategy. The President also pleaded with the conventioneers, and by implication the rest of the public, to reject the "liberal ideology of decline and retreat." He concluded the twenty-minute ripsnorter, which was repeatedly interrupted with applause, by saying:

> It comes down to this: After eight hard years of rebuilding America's strength, do we really want to return to a Disneyland defense policy—with Mickey Mouse treatment of our men and women in uniform, Goofy strategic plans, and Donald Duck-like lectures telling us that whatever goes wrong is our own blankety-blank fault?

The prolonged standing ovation that ensued convinced some reporters present that the speech was still another example of why the President is termed "The Great Communicator."

But what exactly did the President communicate? His speech was short on information and high on emotion. He never explained why the defense policies he ridiculed were so absurd. He never showed how they would undermine national defense, jeopardize U.S.-Soviet relations, and threaten world peace. Nor did he explain why opposition to a space-based missile defense system ("Star Wars") and reluctance to deploy the MX missile was tantamount to "decline and retreat." And exactly which "liberals" did the President have in mind? Were all "liberals" a threat to American security interests? Did opposition to the President's conception of adequate defense

Speaking of . . .

Slanting Through the Use of Emotive Language

Sticks, Stones, and Words

Someone makes comments that criticize implicitly or explicitly a group of people. The comments and their source are labeled anti-Semitic, racist or sexist. Next come "clarifications," if not retractions or denials. If the remarks were actually made, it is claimed that they were misconstrued, misquoted or taken out of context. The person to whom they are attributed is not anti-Semite, racist or sexist—so goes the defense.

Yet people are hurt and damage is done. Such exchanges breed suspicion that can spin a vicious circle of mistrust. . . .

But when is a remark, a person or group anti-Semitic, racist or sexist? How can we tell the difference between this and legitimate criticism?

An answer, or at least some insight, comes from two important historians.

Stanford University's Gavin I. Langmuir, a leading scholar on the subject, defines anti-Semitism as "the hostility aroused by irrational thinking about 'Jews'." A detailed look at this definition also clarifies racism and sexism.

There are three key components. Anti-Semitism (or racism or sexism) involves (1) irrational thinking (2) about Jews, (or blacks or Asians or women) and the combination (3) arouses hostility.

Irrational thinking is fueled by unsupported, pernicious generalization. Take, for instance, an allegation such as: the Jewish "amen corner" has too much control over American foreign policy in the Middle East.

What does "too much" mean? Who or what comprises the Jewish "amen corner"? What is the evidence, if any, for such a charge and what about evidence to the contrary? Insisting on testable answers to such questions provides a start for differentiating statements that are anti-Semitic, racist, or sexist from legitimate criticism.

Of course, irrational thinking takes many forms, and it alone is not sufficient to constitute anti-Semitism, racism, or sexism. But it does contribute insofar as it targets people sterotypically—for example, "blacks are lazy" or "women are weak." Anti-Semitism, racism, and sexism thrive on the implicit or explicit denial of individual differences among the members of such groups. Blindness to such diversity is a marker for illegitimate criticism.

The arousal of hostility toward Jews is Langmuir's third and most telling mark of anti-Semitism. Insofar as irrational thinking—characterized by pernicious generalization and stereotypical falsification—encourages hostility against its target, anti-Semitism, racism, sexism, or some other cousin can be found at work. One need not consciously intend anti-Semitism, racism or sexism to do or say things outside legitimate criticism. "You will know them by their fruits," as the Christian New Testament wisely puts it.

continued

---

continued

Heinrich von Treitschke, an influential 19th-Century German, is the other historian worth noting here. *"Die Juden sind unser Unglück,"* he generalized irrationally, perniciously, and stereotypically: "The Jews are our misfortune." Treitschke died in 1896, but a generation later his claim became an omnipresent Nazi slogan. It helped to arouse hostility to such an extreme that millions of Jews were put to death at Auschwitz, Treblinka and Adolf Hitler's other killing centers.

Cruel, even deadly — that's what words can be. Had there been no slogans like Treitschke's, hostility toward Jews would never have been aroused to the genocidal form it took in the Holocaust.

Words bear watching. Words can kill. Using them with greater care could diminish the ethnic and racial tensions that do violence to the bond that holds us Americans together: respect for the basic equality and rights of diverse persons.

(John K. Roth, "Sticks, Stones and Words," *Los Angeles Times,* September 21, 1990, p. B7. Reprinted by permission of the author.)

---

qualify one as a "liberal"? The President did not address any of these questions, nor felt obliged to. Knowing the mindset of his audience, understanding and sharing their fears and suspicions, he used an array of expressive language to discredit Democratic presidential candidate Michael Dukakis, whose name he never once mentioned. What he got, predictably enough, was a psychological, not a logical, response. And it is a safe bet that the next day when reports of the speech made front-page news across the country, it triggered a similar response among a large segment of the population.

During the Persian Gulf crisis of 1990, President Saddam Hussein of Iraq evoked one of the most emotionally loaded of Mideast buzzwords when he called on fellow Arabs to wage *jihad* against the multinational force in Saudi Arabia. To many in the West, *jihad* calls up images of fanatical crowds in the streets of Tehran, Iran, chanting, "God is great!" and "Death to America!" It also brings fears of hijackings, airport massacres, hostage-taking, and wild-eyed soldiers joyously rushing to their deaths with keys of heaven hanging from their necks. But the word is no less evocative for the Arab masses. It speaks of Arabs united against the foreign invader; of the many injustices the Arabs believe they have suffered during two-thousand years of foreign rule; of holy war against the infidel according to the teachings of Allah.

IN BRIEF   There is a positive correlation between emotional attachment and susceptibility to manipulation through emotive language. The more emotionally attached we are to some outcome, the more likely we will use or permit to be used highly expressive language as a substitute for good reasons. Becoming sensitive to our own deepest emotional attachments, then, is fundamental to guarding against the *illicit* use of emotive language in argument.

MODULE 5.3

MISUSE OF JARGON

Jargon is the technical language of a trade, profession, or group. Used enough in and outside a field, technical words can turn flaccid, even incomprehensible. For example, here is a sampling of popular jargon words spawned by the social sciences: *thrust, accountability, nitty-gritty, commitment, relate to, identify with, interface with, sensitive, paranoid, viable, existential, meaningful, awareness, options, relevant.* Doubtless, these words once were vital and occasionally continue to be. But indiscriminate use can reduce them to gobbledygook.

The fallacy of misuse of jargon consists in using technical terms for purposes of impressing without clarifying, or masking literal meaning. So used, the jargon word and the premise that contains it are unintelligible. Since the premise defies evaluation, it is unacceptable as support for the conclusion.

The historian Arthur Schlesinger, Jr., in his book *A Thousand Days* rails against the U.S. State Department's use of jargon, much of which is contained in the following fictitious memo:

> With respect to your inquiry about our position vis-a-vis the Arabs, we exhort you to zero in on our official stance in response to their oil embargo: to crank in more bargaining leverage, to phase out economic aid and gin up Israel's defensive reaction posture. It's vital that you pinpoint a viable policy and, to keep open our options, a fallback position that we can assume if the flak from the nit-picking opposition intensifies. Once you are seized of the problem in as hardnose a manner as possible, which is the objective incumbent on us in future cables, you should review with defense echelons overall objectives, seek breakthroughs, consider crash programs, and staff out policies in meaningful depth until we here are ready to finalize our deliberations and implement our decisions.[2]

Why do people use such language? A former Commerce Secretary surmised: "The only reason I could see for talking that kind of talk (is) a subconscious urge to cover one's self. There is a kind of protection in (such) statements and a recommendation so vague that it can be interpreted two or three ways on a single issue. That's not communicating, that's covering one's flanks."[3]

In the early years of the Reagan presidency, Alexander M. Haig, Jr., arrived on the State Department scene articulating foreign policy in bewildering language. For example, in his first press conference after becoming Secretary of State, the retired general and former commander of the North Atlantic Treaty Organization explored the "risk-taking mode of the Soviet Union." He spoke of the State Department as people

---

[2]See Arthur Schlesinger, Jr., *A Thousand Days* (Boston: Houghton Mifflin, 1965), pp. 417–420.
[3]Malcolm Baldridge quoted in "Commerce Chief Lets the Word Go Forth — Don't," *Los Angeles Times,* July 24, 1981, p. 13.

with "in-place pros" as contrasted with the "augmentees" that he had brought with him to his new assignment. At one point, he wanted to "caveat" a remark with a qualification. "Does the new secretary think he would soon travel to the Middle East?" one reporter wanted to know. The secretary said he had "no finite plans." Turning to "global hotspots," Haig saw a need to "clarify the air" regarding South Korea; and he "cautioned" that the United States had a "number of watchpots" in Europe, such as Poland. But he saved his most colorful language for last, when he spoke of international terrorism as not only rampant but "hemorrhaging."

So taken with Haig's unique language of diplomacy was one London newspaper that it lampooned "Haiguition" in an editorial. Here is a snippet:

> Gene Alexander Haig has contexted the Polish watchpot somewhat nuancely. How, though, if the situation decontrols, can he stoppage it mountingly conflagrating? Haig, in congressional hearings before his confirmatory, paradoxed his autitioners by ab-normalling this response so that verbs were nounded, nouns verbed and adjectives adverbised. He techniques a new way to vocabulary his thoughts so as to information-ally uncertain anybody listening about what he had actually implicationed. At first it seemed that the general was impenetrabling what at basic was clear. This, it was sup-positioned, was a new linguistic harbingered by NATO during the time he bellweth-ered it. But close observers have alternatived that idea. What Haig is doing, they con-cept, is to decouple the Russians from everything that they are moded to. (*The Guardian*, February 2, 1981.)

Parody makes a point, and the point here is that sloppy use of language produces gibberish.

ABUSE OF EUPHEMISM

Every language has words that allow its users to talk about things they would prefer not to talk about. Such words are called **euphemisms, which are polite ways of saying something that we find offensive, harsh, or blunt.**

Instead of "lying," we "fib," or "cover up." Rather than "having sexual inter-course," we "make love." Students do not "fail," they merely "don't make the grade." Nations do not always fight a "war," they engage in a "conflict" (as in the "Vietnam conflict") or a "police action" (as in the "Korea police action"). The Central Intelli-gence Agency does not "assassinate" people, it merely "terminates them with ex-treme prejudice." Government officials eschew the word "surrender" in favor of "crisis resolution" or "conflict termination." Bureaucrats dislike "firing" anyone— they prefer to "select him out." They do not "ration" gasoline, they "end-use allo-cate." And politicians who talk about "raising taxes" when the euphemism "enhanc-ing revenue" is available are probably "certifiable."

The use of euphemism is not always objectionable. Indeed, it can serve as an emotional insulator to allow someone the necessary time to absorb and process a harsh reality. That is why we have so many euphemisms for death and dying. Euphe-mism can also escort us into areas that, for one reason or another, we find discomfiting or difficult to talk about—sex, for example. But like jargon, euphemism can be abused.

The fallacy of abuse of euphemism consists in misrepresenting or misleading by using polite or inoffensive words to mask the meaning or character of something. Arguers who abuse euphemism are attempting to sell a position or conclusion by glossing over significant and relevant aspects of an issue, which, if addressed, would point to an opposed evaluation or interpretation of the facts. Sometimes this verbal sleight of hand is obvious, as when Iraq's Saddam Hussein referred to foreigners he was holding hostage as his "guests." With less clearly defined issues, however, euphemism can be used with considerable manipulative effect.

For example, during the Iran-Contra hearings, Colonel Oliver North never called any of his actions "lying." In referring to a false chronology of events that he admittedly helped construct, North said he "was provided with additional input that was radically different from the truth." This "national hero," as President Reagan anointed him, also preferred to use "residuals" as an airy substitute for "money," and insisted that documents were not "destroyed" but were "non-logged" or "kept out of the system so that outside knowledge would not necessarily be derived from having the documents themselves." For his part, National Security Council chief John Poindexter preferred the innocuous "misleads" or "withhold information" to "lying." And he chose to characterize the transfer of millions of dollars of government money as a "technical implementation," rather than a substantive decision. As for sending subordinates to lie to Congressional committees, well, that is acceptable, said the admiral, so long as one does not "micromanage them."

The most sinister aspect of euphemism is its potential for permitting an audience to confront in silence complex moral issues, including abuses that need to be reformed and miseries that can be relieved. Writing in an essay to which we earlier alluded, Albert Camus makes exactly this point in describing the euphemisms shrouding capital punishment:

> ... [N]o one dares speak openly of the ritual act itself. The officials and the journalists whose responsibility it is to speak of it, as if conscious of the simultaneously provocative and shameful aspects of such justice, have devised a kind of ceremonial language for dealing with it, a language reduced to the most stereotyped formulas. Over breakfast we may read, on some back page of our newspaper, that the condemned man "paid his debt to society," that he "expiated his crime," or that "at five o'clock this morning justice was done." Officials deal with that man as the "the accused," "the patient," formerly refer to him as the C.A.M. *(Condamne a mort).* Capital punishment, one might say, is written about only in whispers. In a highly organized society such as ours we acknowledge a disease is serious by the fact that we do not dare speak of it openly. In middle-class families, it was long the rule to say that the oldest daughter had a "weak chest," or that Papa suffered from a "growth": to have tuberculosis or cancer was regarded as something of a disgrace. This is even more certainly true in the case of capital punishment: everyone does his best to speak of it only in euphemisms. The death penalty is to the body politic what cancer is to the individual body, with perhaps the single difference that no one has ever spoken of the necessity of cancer. Yet we do not usually hesitate to describe the death penalty as a "regrettable necessity," justifying the fact that we are killing some-

one because it is "necessary," and then not speaking of what we are doing because it is regrettable."

This excerpt is not offered as a plea for the abolition of capital punishment, but to emphasize that basic to rational, justified belief—a goal of critical thinking—is the moral courage and intellectual honesty to confront issues as they are, not as we would like them to be. This often requires facing disquieting, even horrific, facts; but better we do that than risk forming opinions on illusions, not realities.

Speaking of . . .

Jargon and Euphemism

Doublespeak

Professor William Lutz, who teaches English at Rutgers University, is one of this country's foremost authorities on "doublespeak," an academic hybrid based on the combination of "doublethink" and "newspeak" from George Orwell's novel *1984*. If you have or come across an example of doublespeak in print, Professor Lutz would like to hear about it. You can write him at the following address:

> William Lutz
> National Council of Teachers of English
> Department P, 1111 Kenyon Road
> Urbana, IL 61801

In the meantime, try your hand at this "Doublespeak Quiz," which consists of matching letters on the right with the numbers on the left.*

1. a portable hand-held communications inscriber	A. to smell something
2. a frame-supported tension structure	B. used car
3. an aerodynamic personnel decelerator	C. pencil
4. a wood interdental stimulator	D. pig pens and chicken coops
5. a therapeutic misadventure	E. thermometer
6. terminal episode	F. tent
7. activity boosters	G. repairman
8. safety-related occurrence	H. newspaper delivery person
9. incomplete success	I. parachute
10. fiscal underachievers	J. accident
11. service technician	K. failure
12. non–goal-oriented member of society	L. the poor
13. single-purpose agricultural structures	M. bum, street person
	N. toothpick
	O. malpractice

continued

continued

14. downsizing personnel
15. advanced downward adjustments
16. collateral damage
17. experienced automobile
18. media courier
19. unauthorized withdrawal
20. digital fever computer
21. organoleptic analysis
22. nail technician
23. philosophically disillusioned
24. kinetic kill vehicle
25. ultimate high-intensity warfare
26. social-expression procuts
27. career associate scanning professional

P. firing employees
Q. budget cuts
R. bank robbery
S. civilian casualties during war
T. death
U. amphetamines
V. grocery-store checkout clerk
W. antisatellite weapon
X. scared
Y. greeting cards
Z. manicurist
AA. nuclear war

MODULE 5.4

ASSUMPTION-LOADED LABELS

Life would be impossible if we had to memorize the properties of the countless things we observe. For simplicity we place like things into the same category. That way all we must do is remember the properties of the category to identify the key properties of things. For example, ants fall into the category of "insects," and insects in turn are small, invertebrate animals. Any member of the insect class has these properties; whatever does not have these properties is not an insect. So, the label "insect" facilitates communication by enabling us to bring into a single unit the many kinds of things that the label denotes. So it is with any label.

The more observant we are, the more adept we get at recognizing a category into which like things can be placed. We get skillful at applying labels. But we also get better at spotting differences among like things. For example, cars, airplanes, trains, and bicycles can be labeled "vehicles" or "conveyances." But one of these items lacks at least one property that the others possess: A bicycle is *not* self-propelled. So, considered from the aspect of propulsion, bicycles do not share a property with cars, airplanes, and trains; but they do with roller skates and skateboards, that is, with "non–self-propelled conveyances," which is a subcategory of "conveyances."

Being able to formulate subcategories and correctly apply labels obviously requires a sensitivity to the shared properties that make things that are generally similar also specifically similar. The capacity to formulate and use subcategories helps us to recognize and think intelligently about our experience and to communicate with one another. Without this ability, life would be, in the words of philosopher William James, "an empirical sand-heap."

As necessary and useful as labels are, they invariably overlook individual differences among the things they denote. No two insects — or two ants, two fleas, or two flies for that matter — are ever exactly identical. Nor are two vehicles, cars, bicycles, or skateboards. Nevertheless, we ordinarily do not have trouble communicating by means of "insects," "ants," "bicycles" and so on because the objects these words extend to are sufficiently similar to preclude confusion. But this is not true of all labels.

Sometimes a label can have the effect of getting us to overlook features and properties of something that, in fact, may provide a more accurate representation than the one suggested by the label. Linguist Irving Lee provides a pointed example of this telescopic effect of labels:

> I knew a man who had lost the use of both eyes. He was called a "blind man." He could also be called an expert typist, a conscientious worker, a good student, a careful listener, a man who wanted a job. But he couldn't get a job in the department store order room where employees sat and typed orders which came over the telephone. The personnel man was impatient to get the interview over. "But you're a blind man," he kept saying, and one could almost feel his silent assumption that somehow the incapacity in one aspect made the man incapable in every other. So blinded by the label was the interviewer that he could not be persuaded to look beyond it."[4]

Lee's point is that the label "blind man" does more than merely denote a person who has lost the use of both eyes. It also encourages us to overlook other categories, more relevant ones in his example, into which the applicant without sight could be placed. Embedded in "blind man" is a knot of questionable assumptions about the person's competencies. Thus, if we reduce the personnel man's reaction to an argument, it would go something like this: "Blind people can't do this job. The applicant is a blind man. Therefore, he can't do the job."

Obviously, if the applicant were applying for a job for which eyesight was a demonstrable requisite, the interviewer's reasoning and argument would be impeccable. The label "blind man" would be identifying a relevant piece of evidence for judging the candidate unqualified; its use would be legitimate. But, in fact, the label "blind man" was hiding dubious assumptions about the applicant that the interview was using to disqualify him. **The fallacy of assumption-loaded labels, then, consists in using a label to advance a position or support a conclusion on the basis of questionable assumptions embedded in that label.**

Labels such as "blind man" can be powerfully persuasive because they tend to prevent alternative classification or cross-classification. So are other terms for people with disabilities — *crippled, wheel chair–bound, handicapped, spastic, deformed, deaf and dumb.* They encourage stereotypes, which are fixed, unvarying ideas about something or somebody. Ethnic labels — *blacks, Oriental, Mexican* — often function the same way. So do labels signifying religions such as *Catholic, Baptist, Jew, Muslim*

---

[4]Reported in Gordon Allport, *The Nature of Prejudice* (Reading, Mass.: Addison-Wesley, 1954).

Speaking of . . .

Labels

What's in a Name? Sometimes More than Meets the Eye

A number of years ago, the following experiment was conducted. Thirty photographs of college girls were shown on a screen to 150 students. The subjects rated the girls on a scale from one to five for "beauty," "intelligence," "character," "ambition," "general likeability." Two months later, the same subjects were asked to rate the same photographs (and fifteen additional ones introduced to complicate the memory factor). This time five of the original photographs were given Jewish surnames (Cohen, Kantor, and so on), five Italian (Valenti, and so on), and five Irish (O'Brien, and so on), and the remaining girls were given names chosen from the signers of the Declaration of Independence and from the Social Register (Davis, Adams, Clark, and so on).

When Jewish names were attached to photographs, there occurred the following changes in rating: decrease in liking, decrease in character, decrease in beauty, increase in intelligence, increase in ambition. To those photographs given Italian names there occurred: decrease in liking, decrease in character, decrease in beauty, decrease in intelligence. While the Irish names also brought about depreciated judgment, the depreciation was not as great as in the case of Jews and Italians. The falling likeability of the "Jewish girls" was twice as great as for "Italians" and five times as great as for "Irish."

What tentative conclusions would you draw from this experiment, which was conducted over thirty-five years ago? Do you think that what it points up applies today? It is not uncommon for show business personalities to change their names. Mick Jagger's original name was Michael Phillip, Raquel Welch's was Raquel Tejeda, James Garner's was James Bumgarner, Bob Dylan's was Robert Zimmerman, Anne Bancroft's was Annemarie Italiano, Michael Caine's was Maurice J. Mickelwhite, Ringo Starr's was Richard Starkey. Discuss the significance of these changes.

and socio-political philosophies such as *feminist, pro-life, pro-choice, Communist, liberal, conservative.* Such labels can be so "noisy" that they deafen us to additional discriminations we might otherwise perceive. Labeling a politician "pro-life" or "pro-choice" may be useful for identifying the person's *general* position on abortion, but it says nothing about the person's views on a host of other important issues; indeed, it may overlook substantive discriminations within the person's abortion philosophy. The same applies to "pro" or "anti" gun control, the Equal Rights Amendment (ERA), or prayer in public school. The so-called single issue campaigning that has become popular in contemporary politics is intended to do precisely this — to set off in the voter's mind a siren that drowns out all other considerations. A well-chosen label can accomplish this — *big spender, soft on crime, pro-business, anti-labor, free enterprise, leftist-leaning, reactionary, Kennedy liberal, Reagan Republican, protectionist, women's libber, fundamentalist Christian, Washington establishment.*

The label "welfare recipient," to emphasize the point, can come to signify not only one who legally receives welfare benefits, but also laziness, illiteracy, malingerer, a cheat and a crook. Certainly an individual "welfare recipient," like anyone else, may fall into any of these alternative categories, but our cognitive processes are not always cautious enough not to separate the defining attributes included in the label category (that is, "someone who legally receives welfare benefit") from the probable, improbable, or wildly imagined attributes. Rhetoricians skilled in the art of persuasion capitalize on this by using assumption-loaded labels to persuade illicitly — to substitute questionable assumptions for demonstrable reasons.

FALSE DILEMMA

We have seen that labels get us to ignore individual differences. They can also invite oversimplification of complex issues by representing them as "all-or-nothing," "black-or-white," "either-or" situations. Thus, one is either "pro-choice" or "pro-life" on abortion; "pro- or anti-gun control," "a liberal or a conservative," "persons who are born-again Christians and ones who aren't."

Sometimes, the either-or formula does pose mutually exclusive categories. For example, in the last presidential election, you either voted or you did not; and if you did vote, you voted by absentee ballot or you did not, and you voted for George Bush or you did not. These options cover all possibilities — there is no middle ground because the expressed categories exhaust all possibilities.

Suppose, however, that upon learning you *did* vote for president, I ask: "For whom did you vote, Bush or Dukakis?" I would be creating an "either-or" situation when, in fact, that is not necessarily the case. You could have voted for another candidate on the ballot, for example, the Libertarian Party candidate. The choice I gave you — Bush or Dukakis — did not exhaust all the possibilities.

The fallacy of false dilemma occurs when a situation is misrepresented as *either-or*, or *all-or-nothing*. When an argument erroneously reduces the number of possible alternatives to an issue, it is employing a false dilemma. Like labels themselves, the lure of either-or, black-and-white conceptualizations lies in its reductive nature. By reducing the otherwise complex to simple, comprehensible terms, the false dilemma makes it easier to grasp and manage. Again, like labels, the danger is that, in our desire for simplicity, we may end up mischaracterizing, and therefore misunderstanding, an issue or situation.

Public opinion polls notoriously erect false dilemmas. They then use the responses based on them as a measure of public opinion, which in turn can influence social policy. This typically occurs when a situation, issue, or position is incorrectly reduced to two options which are signified by labels that the respondents are asked to slap on themselves. Thus: "Do you consider yourself *liberal* or *conservative?*" "Are you *pro-life* or *pro-choice?*" "Are you *for or against capital punishment?*" "Do you *favor or oppose sex education* in public schools?" Each of these questions poses a false dilemma. After all, you might be "liberal" on some issues, "conservative" on others; for abortion, capital punishment, and sex education in some cases, but not in others. On the other hand, the following questions pose genuine dilemmas, because they truly exhaust all possibilities in the matter: "Do you ever practice some form of birth control or not?" "Are there any circumstances under which abortion should be permitted or not?" "Should capital punishment never or sometimes be permitted?" "Are you unalterably opposed to sex education in public schools, or do you favor it under certain conditions?" The use of assumption-loaded labels to set up the false dilemma further confuses matters by inviting respondents to choose on the basis of unexamined assumptions. Thus, "Do you think government should do more or less to encourage *free enterprise?*" "Do *fundamentalist televangelists* aid or retard the interests of institutional religion?" "Do you think the United States Supreme Court is promoting or undercutting *democratic freedoms?*" "Should the United States actively support *freedom fighters* trying to overthrow *totalitarian regimes,* or shouldn't it?"

Of course, the false dilemma is not restricted to poll questions. In formal, extended argument, it often functions to frame a complex issue in polarized categories, thereby making the arguer's position seem more plausible than it might otherwise be. For example, in the following passage, syndicated political columnist David Broder raises the issue of nonsubstantive media coverage of presidential elections (italics added to identify the false dilemma):

> There is a reluctance to undertake serious appraisals of (presidential candidates') work—*either because news organizations think viewers and readers would be bored or because journalists are nervous about saying what the people who know them best* (presumably the candidates) *and have worked most closely with them think of the contenders. Either way,* it's a cop-out. . . .

The author then went on to defend his "cop-out" appraisal; but maybe many journalists are themselves ill-informed, lazy, naïve, or unperceptive. Maybe the media excessively emphasizes "sound bites" and visuals. Maybe both of Broder's explanations operate. The point is that without spotting the false dilemma we can blindly follow the author's argument and perhaps accept his conclusions. On the other hand, having spotted the false dilemma, we can intelligently respond to the argument.

As another example of the use of the false dilemma, columnist John Reston argued for the need for European nations to develop their economies on a continental scale. In one article, he so framed the issue as to leave the choice obvious. Thus:

> The question is *whether,* in the upcoming century, *Europe really wants to regain a paramount position in the world, or whether it will become economically what is geographically, a small peninsula on the tip of the Euroasian land mass, dependent, comfortable and complacent.*

Another example is an excerpt from a newspaper editorial which argued that a proposed state budget be adopted:

> Sacramento's annual indulgence in the politics of clenched teeth and budget deadlock is all too familiar. But this is no ordinary deadlock. This time it bears directly on the kind of place California is and will be. This time Sacramento is about to decide *whether to keep California's beacon of excellence shining, or to start turning out the light that marks the path to the future.* . . .

Here we're asked to choose between "progress" or "stagnation." Is it not at least possible to delete or amend some aspects of the budget without inviting catastrophe? The framing of the question in stark either-or categories, seasoned with a dash of emotive language, forecloses this possibility and invites the reader to endorse the editor's position.

The same tactics are used in the following excerpt. The author, Ben Wattenberger of the American Enterprise Institute, advanced the thesis that America should assert itself, militarily if necessary, in Nicaragua:

> The President believes that the Nicaraguan situation may be the most important international issue facing America today. He is right. It will likely set the course of American foreign policy. We are *either going to be an assertive power, an American eagle, that defends our interest and values, or we are going to be an American lame duck, waddling indecisively from crisis to crisis, hamstrung by a Congress with isolationist tropism.*

Here Wattenberger reduces a multilayered, complex issue into two opposed categories: the figurative "American eagle" versus the "American lameduck."

IN BRIEF   Using assumption-loaded labels to frame issues in black-or-white, all-or-nothing terms is a very effective persuasive device. Before being drawn into a writer's bifurcated view of things, make sure all possibilities have been covered. Setting up a false dilemma is fallacious, and any inference drawn from one is unwarranted.

EXERCISES ON ASSUMPTION-LOADED LABELS AND FALSE DILEMMA

Identify and explain the use of labels and false dilemmas in the following passages.

1. When asked by ABC News to describe Oliver North as a "villain" or a "victim," 64 percent said "victim." ABC subsequently used the results to argue that Americans were mainly sympathetic to North.
2. On voting against the Supreme Court nomination of Judge Robert H. Bork, Senator Howell Heflin (D-Ala.) allowed that he was in a "quandary as to whether this nominee would be a conservative justice who would safeguard the living

Constitution and prevent judicial activism or an extremist who would use his position on the court to advance a far-right, radical judicial agenda."

3. Editorial: "The Soviet Union confirms that it is deploying SS-24 missiles, weapons of intercontinental range that can be mounted on railroad cars and trundled about on the 63,000-mile Soviet railway system. . . . Thus, to maintain a nuclear balance, the United States must either develop its own mobile ICBM system or turn to the President's vision of missile defense. Because the "Star Wars" idea is hopelessly flawed by sheer technological and economic impracticality, only the timely development of a mobile ICBM system makes sense. . . ."

4. Senator Daniel K. Inouye (D-Haw.), chairman of the Iran-Contra committee, summed up the debate by asking if "this unseemly chapter in our history is the result of well-intentioned, patriotic zealots . . . or are we here today because of the inadequacy of our laws and our Constitution?"

5. "Lawmakers have been writing too many legalisms into the (foreign) policy process. By substituting these for human judgment, they time and again impale makers of difficult foreign-policy decisions on the horns of a cruel dilemma: whether to keep faith with their responsibility for the nation's safety or to follow blindly the minute dictates of statutes written in other circumstances by legislators who bear no responsibility for the consequences of present actions. . . ." (Columnist Raymond Price then went on to argue in favor of the obvious choice.)

6. Columnist James Kirkpatrick arguing against statehood for Washington, D.C.: "The sole argument in favor of statehood rests on the right to vote. . . . To those residents who regard a right to vote for congressmen as the be-all and end-all, a suggestion is in order that they move to Maryland or to Virginia, where they could vote to their hearts' content. No one compels anyone to live in the District of Columbia. Local residents are here because they voluntarily have swapped the right of franchise for the privilege of enjoying the district's amenities. Washington boasts a magnificent concert hall, beautiful parks, and a superlative subway system — paid for not by the citizens of 'New Columbia' (which is the proposed name for the new state) but by the taxpayers of the nation as a whole."

7. Letter to the editor: "Lt. Col. Ollie North scored yet another victory for the 'squares' of America over the 'best and the brightest.' The squares include military types and small town patriots, people who believe in obedience, loyalty, fidelity and the defense of America against enemies, foreign and domestic — even when that defense takes messy work. Ollie North — God bless him! — is a reproach to everything the 'best and the brightest' stand for!"

8. Advertising executive Malcolm MacDougall defending his company's sexually explicit ad campaign for Revlon's 'Intimate' perfume: "We can't create commercials that will only be approved by the Parent Teachers Association. . . . When you're selling a fragrance by the name of 'Intimate,' you sure as heck better say what it's for."

9. Letter to the editor: "I was so pleased to read that our governor chose in his budget to spend so much money on our prisons. With his cuts in education, we'll definitely need more prison space in the future. We have a choice: Spend the money now on educating our kids or spend it later for their imprisonment."

10. Oliver North attempting to justify the administration's use of the notorious and unsavory Iranian arms broker Manucher Ghorbanifar as a go-between in arms-for-hostages deals with Iran: "I knew, and so did the rest of us who were dealing with him, exactly what Mr. Ghorbanifar was . . . a liar . . . a cheat . . . a man asking enormous sums of money. He was widely suspected to be, within the people I dealt with at the Central Intelligence Agency, an agent of the Israeli government. . . . We knew what the man was, but it was difficult to get other people involved in these kinds of activities. I mean, one can't go to (Nobel Prize winner) Mother Teresa and ask her to go to Tehran. . . . And the good fairy wasn't there."

11. "There are two ways of viewing the U.S. invasion of Panama (December 1989). The first could be called resigned optimism: The invasion is simply a last American hurrah, an anachronistic but final throwback to the days of gunboat diplomacy at a time when the rest of the world has moved beyond petty shows of force. The second viewpoint is more frustrating and stereotypical but perhaps less accurate: The Panama adventure shows that as far as U.S. policy in its sphere of influence (an elegant euphemism for 'back yard') is concerned, there is nothing new under the sun. . . ." The author then went on to defend the first option. (Jorge G. Castaneda, "Blunder Like a Lummox," *Los Angeles Times,* December 27, 1989, p. B7.)

MODULE 5.5

BEGGING THE QUESTION

The premises of an argument must offer independent evidence in support of the conclusion. This means the evidence cannot presuppose the conclusion. Suppose, for example, a person argues, "God must exist because it says so in the Bible and *the Bible is the inspired word of God."* The italicized premise would not be offering independent evidence for the claim that God must exist, because it presupposes that very conclusion. Such an argument is said to *beg the question.*

The fallacy of begging the question consists in presuming as true key assumptions that must be verified to establish the conclusion. One way to beg the question is to offer as evidence what is, in fact, a restatement of the conclusion. For example, in the argument "Miracles are impossible, because they can't happen," "can't happen" means the same as "impossible." Similarly, in the argument, "Pornography is objectionable, for it's *immoral,"* "immoral" implies "objectionable." In the argument, "Users' fees should be tacked onto the purchases of certain goods and services, because that would generate tax revenue," a user's fee is a tax. In this last argument, the arguer is saying no more than: "Taxes should be tacked onto the purchase of certain goods and services, because that would generate a tax revenue."

Of course, no one would present the argument in this form because it would be transparently circular, but we do often include in premises words and phrases that are logically equivalent to ones used in the conclusion. When we do, we merely assert what the conclusion asserts.

A somewhat more subtle version of question begging occurs when a premise is offered that is merely a more generalized version of the conclusion. For example, criticized for employing long-term consultants rather than relying solely on the expertise of regular employees, a school superintendent defends his action by arguing: "It's part of my managerial style." The superintendent, in effect, is arguing:

(D) Hiring long-term consultants
rather than expert regular employees   ⟶   **(C)** My hiring long-term
is part of my managerial style.   consultants rather than
    (W) (Whatever is part of my managerial   expert regular
          style is proper to do.)   employees is proper.

Notice the warrant which in effect asserts that any decision the superintendent makes or any policy he formulates is proper because it is part of his "managerial style." Critics of his decision clearly would be questioning that managerial style. Rather than defending his decision, then, the superintendent is merely asserting a more generalized version of his conclusion. In a word, he is "begging" the critics to accept his managerial style without providing reasons for the acceptance.

Perhaps the most subtle form of question begging occurs when the evidence offered is even more suspect or controversial than the conclusion it purports to advance. Consider as an example this argument:

> **The protesters demonstrating outside this health clinic are anti-American because they oppose abortion and opposition to abortion is anti-American.**

Here the arguer is expecting us to accept the premise that opposition to abortion is anti-American, which is even more dubious than the conclusion that protesting anti-abortionists are anti-American. Again,

> **The student loan program should be expanded because the right to a higher education should not be denied a person for financial reasons.**

Is "higher education" a right? The arguer "begs" us to accept this controversial value judgment without proof. Until she makes a compelling case for that right, we should not accept her conclusion.

As a final example, after the United States Supreme Court ruled (in *Edwards v. Agullard,* 1987) that states may not require public schools to teach "creation science," Beverly LaHave, president of Concerned Women of America, condemned the ruling by arguing:

Now these children will not be exposed to the academic freedom of being taught a variety of scientific theories on the origin of the Earth, but will have their learning experiences limited to the teaching of just one idea.

Underlying the premise (italicized) is the court-discredited assumption that creation theory is a science. Another confusion is that "academic freedom" refers to learning when, in fact, it refers to teaching.

In each of these examples, the conclusion was not supported by the premises. The arguer, in effect, "begged" that the conclusion be accepted anyway.

IN BRIEF   The tricky thing about spotting question-begging is that there is the *appearance* of evidential support, when, in fact, at least a portion of the evidence is a revision of the conclusion. Arguments that beg the question violate a basic criterion of a good argument—that the premises be acceptable. A premise is never acceptable if it's as suspect as the conclusion it allegedly supports.

EXERCISES ON BEGGING THE QUESTION*

Try to explain exactly how the question is begged in each of the following passages.

1. Abortion is immoral because it's wrong.
2. Lola : I think pot smoking is wrong.
   Todd : How come?
   Lola : Because it's a drug.
   Todd : And taking drugs is wrong?
   Lola : Exactly.
3. A defense of the U.S. military intervention in the Mideast after the Iraqi invasion of Kuwait: "Our soldiers and those of other nations are tangible evidence of the international community's concern over this vitally important region of the world."
4. Rich people are obviously superior to poor people. If they weren't, how could they make so much money?
5. Even though we may not understand why tragedies happen, they must have a purpose. After all, God has a purpose for everything that occurs.
6. Sebrina : Meryl Streep's obviously a better actress than Madonna.
   Sally : Are you kidding? Did you see Madonna in *Dick Tracy?* She was awesome!
   Sebrina : Nevertheless, people with good taste prefer Streep.
   Sally : Oh yeah? How do you know they have good taste?
   Sebrina : They prefer Meryl Streep, naturally.
7. Kathy-Ann said she loves me and I know she must be telling the truth because no one would lie to someone she loves.

8. Asked why he had killed hundreds of officers and men of the Iraqi army, Iraq's president Saddam Hussein explained that they had questioned his invasion of Kuwait, that such opposition was traitorous, and that all traitors deserved death.
9. "It's not that I'm jealous," said the husband about his beautiful wife, "I just don't like her talking with other men."
10. It's always in the best interest of the state to allow its citizens unbounded freedom of speech, for the state always benefits when individuals enjoy a perfectly unlimited liberty in expressing their sentiments.

QUESTION-BEGGING DEFINITION

It is worth noting that sometimes arguers will try to foreclose discussion of an issue or establish their points on the basis of a controversial definition. **The fallacy of question-begging definition consists in attempting to establish an irrefutable position in an argument by means of a questionable definition.** Persuasive definitions are especially susceptible to this kind of question-begging because they are often used in an effort to settle an empirical question by appeal to definition alone. (An empirical question is one that can be proved or disproved by observation or experiment.)

For example, suppose a friend uses a persuasive definition to make this controversial claim: "*Genuine* patriots support their country, right or wrong." In response, you marshal historical examples of individuals who did not support their country, but are considered patriots. When presented with such examples, your friend says, "Ah, but they were not *genuine* patriots because they didn't always support their country." That these individuals did not always support their country establishes that they were not patriots *only if* you accept by definition that "genuine patriot" excludes such people. Although that definition of "genuine patriot" is disputable, the arguer "begs" you to accept it.

Notice a similar use of question-begging definition in this exchange:

DON: President Reagan isn't a *true* Republican.
DONNA: Why's that?
DON: Because he was once a Democrat.
DONNA: So what?
DON: Well, a *real* Republican is one who has never been anything but a Republican.
DONNA: That's absurd. Plenty of prominent Republicans once were Democrats— Strom Thurmond and John Connolly, just to name two.
DON: That's precisely why they aren't any more *true* Republicans than Reagan.

Don attempts to establish that Reagan, Thurmond, and Connolly are not "true Republicans" by means of a definition that renders any counterevidence inadmissible.

But question-begging definitions need not exploit only persuasive definitions. Here is one that uses the denotation of the word "deniability," a term used repeatedly during the Iran-Contra hearings. At one point during his testimony, Rear Admiral John

Speaking of . . .

Question-Begging Definition

"Type-A" Personality and Heart Disease

More than two decades after Type-A behavior was first linked to coronary heart disease and heart attacks, some scientists report that the uptight Type-A people — typically aggressive, inwardly hostile workaholics — may survive a heart attack better than their laid-back Type-B counterparts. The original Type-A and Type-B behavior, began in the mid-1960s, found that the middle-aged men who were highly ambitious, competitive and who worked as though there wasn't enough time to get everything done were as much as 4.5 times more likely to develop coronary heart disease than those who were easy-going. Now, researchers have taken a longer-term look at what happened to the men in the initial study. They found that among the men who eventually developed heart disease, Type-A subjects were more likely to survive a heart attack and live longer than the more placid Type-Bs. . . . The latest findings are disputed, however, by one of the radiologists who conducted the original study, Meyer Friedman of Mt. Zion Hospital in San Francisco. Dr. Friedman says the new study is inaccurate because it is based on mistaken diagnoses made in the initial research. Dr. Friedman says he and his colleague Ray H. Rosenmann were inexperienced in identifying Type-A behavior in the 1960s and misdiagnosed a large number of the men as Type-B. Now he says that every one of the men who developed premature heart disease was actually Type-A. "You can't get a heart attack before age 60 if you're Type-B," he says. "At the hospital I offer a bottle of expensive wine to any doctor who can bring me a Type-B patient who's had a coronary, and so far no one has." But David H. Gagland, one of the authors of the new report, says Dr. Friedman's explanation is changing the rules after the act. "He is saying that because all these men developed heart disease, that proves they were really Type-As. That's a fundamental error in logic. . . ."

(Jerry E. Bishop, "Prognosis of the Type-A Personality Improves in a New Heart Disease Study." Reprinted by permission of **The Wall Street Journal** © 1988, Dow Jones & Company, Inc. All Rights Reserved Worldwide.)

Do you agree with Gagland that Friedman's committing a "fundamental error in logic?" Explain.*

M. Poindexter testified that, although he had not told President Reagan about the diversion of profits from Iranian arms sales to the Nicaraguan Contras, he had every reason to believe that Reagan would have approved. When White House officials said that Reagan would *not* have approved, Poindexter stuck to his defense. According to the admiral, by issuing this statement the President was only taking advantage of the "deniability" that Poindexter intended him to have when he chose not to inform Reagan about the diversion in February, 1986. Said Poindexter, "I would have expected him (Reagan) to say that. That's the whole idea of deniability." So, by definition, "deniability" precludes any counterevidence to Poindexter's insistence that he was sure Reagan would approve the deal. In effect, the more Reagan protests, the more Poindexter insists: "See, I told you." Or, to frame the ploy technically: Any counterevidence is, by definition, an example — a denotation — of "deniability."

IN BRIEF   A question-begging definition begs the question at issue by attempting to settle an empirical issue solely by means of definition. A definition that poses an empirical claim is an unacceptable premise because it disallows relevant evidence in settling the empirical issue. It is confusing a definitional claim with an empirical one and counts on the audience not to spot the confusion.[5]

COMPLEX OR LOADED QUESTIONS

The fallacy of the complex or loaded question consists in so framing a question that it falsely presupposes that the answer to some other unasked question has already been established. The classic and still clearest example of a complex question is the old saw, "Have you stopped beating your wife yet?" The question cannot be answered without the husband granting that he, in fact, has been beating his wife. If it has already been established that he is, indeed, a wife-beater, then no fallacy is committed.

Suppose that during a trial the prosecutor asks a defendant, "After you murdered the victim, what did you do then?" The defendant cannot answer this question without granting that he, in fact, murdered the victim. If that has already been established, the assumption built into the question is not questionable; but if that fact is unknown, the prosecutor is forcing the defendant to grant the dubious assumption. In argument, the complex question can be viewed as an unacceptable premise because it either assumes the issue at stake or something related to it. In this sense, it can be considered another form of question-begging. (It is also an example of the mixed functions of language. It is directive, since it asks a question. But it is also informative — it implies a factual assumption.)

Sometimes, a complex or loaded question can treat a series of questions as if it involved only one question. "After you murdered the victim, why did you ransack the house before stealing the car?" This question involves at least three different questions. It asks (1) if the defendant murdered the victim, (2) if the defendant ransacked the house, and (3) if the defendant stole the car. Although it is possible that the defendant would not answer affirmatively to each of these questions, the question is so posed as to allow only a single response.

---

[5]See T. Edward Damer, *Attacking Faulty Reasoning,* 2nd ed. (Belmont, CA: Wadsworth, 1987), p. 44.

It is not uncommon in extended argument for a writer to weave an entire argument around a complex question, as she might with a false dilemma. Consider, for example, this letter to the editor that deals with the tragic case of Paul Gann, self-proclaimed California antitax crusader, who died from AIDS that he contracted from a blood transfusion:

> *Whatever in the world did the fates intend by infecting Paul Gann with AIDS? Was it to show us all that this terrible disease may strike anyone, even a model of decency such as he?* Perhaps. But if so, it's a lesson that most of us did not heed. Few doubt anymore that AIDS is a threat to everyone. But there could have been another purpose involved. By infecting this man of popular causes, who is neither a homosexual nor a drug user, the fates have given him a moral authority over this issue that no lesser-known person could ever achieve. In other words, this 74-year-old man with the air of sexual innocence still about him has nevertheless paid the terrible dues, contracting the disease from blood transfusions. Whether we heed him or not, he has a special right now to tell us what to think of AIDS.

Having assumed a metaphysical cause of Gann's affliction, the writer not only speculates about it, but uses it to give Gann unique credentials for telling us what to think of the scourge that eventually killed him.

IN BRIEF   Nearly all questions make some assumptions. If an arguer has adequate reason to believe that the audience would willingly grant the assumption, the question posed is not a complex one; but when the question begs the audience to concede a dubious assumption, it is a complex question and renders the argument fallacious.

RHETORICAL QUESTIONS

Recall the traffic-jam example from Chapter 2. The longer you and your friend sat in traffic, the more anxious you became until finally you said, "Would you believe we're going to be late?" Although you framed your utterance as a question, you were not seeking information. You were really saying, "We are going to be late." Your question contained an answer within it. It is a rhetorical question.

A rhetorical question is a question with a built-in answer. Embedded in the following questions is the answer "Yes": "Shouldn't we be preparing for the trip?" "Does the United States not have an obligation to honor its commitments?" "Don't children mimic adult behavior?" And embedded in these two questions is a "No" answer: "We shouldn't abandon our allies, should we?" "Would you dare suggest that cheating on an exam is okay?"

Sometimes, in argument, a proposition can be expressed as a rhetorical question, as in:

> **The prohibition against suicide is absurd.** *What penalty can frighten a person who isn't afraid of death itself?*

Here, the conclusion is that prohibitions against suicide are absurd. The expressed premise is that no penalty can frighten a person who is unafraid of death.

Notice the premise (italicized) that is expressed as a rhetorical question in the following arguments:

> *Doesn't everyone want to live in society?* **Then they must give up some of their privacy for the common good.**

> **Logic surely promotes the achievement of desirable social ends,** *for isn't logic one of the principal means which assures discipline and integrity?*

> *Doesn't poetry express the universal? And isn't it true that history expresses only the particular?* **It follows that poetry is finer and more philosophical than history.**

Rhetorical questions are used properly in argument when evidence has been provided in support of its built-in answer. In such a case, the rhetorical question effectively dramatizes a demonstrated point. Consider, for example, this *legitimate* use of the rhetorical question (italicized):

> Today Japan is assuming technological leadership and global financial dominance in the world. These two functions that Japan has assumed directly threaten U.S. economic interests, making the current tensions (between the U.S. and Japan) inevitable.
>
> *But aren't these tensions beneficial for each side and the long-term relationship?* First, it is clear that Japan needs to change and cannot without *gaiatsu* — external pressure from the United States. So rapid has been Japan's advance from ashes to affluence that virtually every institutional dimension in its way of life desperately needs reform, or risk ending up an anachronistic victim of Japan's economic success. . . . Adversarial pressure from the United States is the only way to interrupt this circularity and help the Japanese bring about the reforms that they need. . . . (Alan M. Webber, "Our Cold Peace with Japan," *Los Angeles Times,* June 19, 1989, Part II, p. 5.)

Notice that after the author sets up the rhetorical question, he proceeds to support it.

Another *legitimate* use of the rhetorical question is when the built-in answer is clearly demonstrable, as in:

> *Isn't every American entitled to a speedy trial?* Then the long delays evident in our judicial process strike at a fundamental constitutional right. ("Speedy" and "long" are admittedly vague, but the assumption built into the rhetorical question is fair.)

However, rhetorical questions can be used to cover up the lack of good arguments. In these instances, the author hopes that the audience will unquestioningly accept the controversial built-in answer. **The fallacy of rhetorical question, then, consists in asking a question with a built-in, unsupported answer.**

The illicit use of the rhetorical question can be viewed as a form of question-begging since it is intended to coax the audience to give the preferred answer without adequate justification for so doing. It also can be considered as a case of an unacceptable premise. The arguer is expecting the audience to accept the debatable assumption without support.

Here are two arguments for and against abortion. Each commits the fallacy of rhetorical question:

> Surely a woman has a right to privacy. *And doesn't that right include the disposition of her own body?* When the state forbids her to have an abortion, it undercuts a fundamental right by dictating to a woman how to behave in a matter that's most personal and private.

In this instance, the audience is expected to accept the author's assumption, built into the question, that the right to privacy applies to an abortion decision, and that the right is absolute — it cannot be overridden by competing rights; but whether the privacy right should apply to abortion without qualification is a basic issue in the abortion dispute.

> *Isn't human life sacred? Aren't we expressly prohibited by both the dictates of morality and law from murdering, that is, taking innocent human life?* There can be no doubt, then, that abortion for any reason, at any stage of gestation, is a heinous offense.

In this instance, the audience is expected to endorse the writer's controversial assumptions that (1) the unborn is a "human life," (2) that the unborn is always properly characterized as "innocent," and that (3) an act of abortion is always murder.

IN BRIEF   Unlike a complex question, a rhetorical question usually asks a single question. However, like the complex question, embedded in the rhetorical question is an unsupported assumption that the arguer wants the audience to grant. The arguer who poses a rhetorical question, in effect, is asking the audience to accept the assumption as evidence without providing any adequate reason for the audience to do so.

MODULE 5.6

RHETORICAL INCONSISTENCY

The fallacy of rhetorical inconsistency consists of using contradictory terms or phrases in an argument. If premises contradict each other, one must be false, and therefore, the argument is fallacious.

The following example is taken from a financial newsletter soliciting investments. After acknowledging that his advice is "unconventional," the writer attempts to defend it by saying:

> Economists with sound, but new or unproven, ideas always seem to be in the minority and are called "extremists" and "fanatics" and shunned by the establishment. In the world of finance they are known as "contrarians."

Although the writer's cautions about label-slapping are commendable, his argument seems to lack rhetorical consistency. An unproven idea may turn out to be correct, but how can it be termed "sound" *before* it is proven. Yet, the writer would have us accept his advice as "sound."

The following news item deals with the cancellation of the lowest-rated prime-time TV program of 1987, "Our World." The cancellation produced considerable protest mail.

> Dorothy Swanson, director of Viewers for Quality Television, a grass-roots organization that is hoping to repeat history by convincing the network (ABC) to change its mind and renew the series, said she believes the figure will climb dramatically. Her Fairfax Station, VA–based group, which has been urging a letter-writing campaign on behalf of "Our World" had received copies of 4,000 letters, she said . . . "I have never seen such a spontaneous outpouring of support."

In what sense can the results of an "organized campaign to solicit letters" be termed a "spontaneous outpouring"?

Saying he wished to "get the juices flowing" in the Republican presidential campaign of 1988, candidate Alexander M. Haig attacked his former boss, President Reagan, blaming him for the giant federal deficits, for declining U.S. esteem abroad, and for a host of other "government-maladies." "I am taking a distancing position from the Reagan presidency," Haig said. "I don't think a business-as-usual Republican candidate who goes around the country telling the American people how good they have it provides any solutions to the nation's problems." A reporter who was present said to Haig: "That's a pretty damning analysis of the Reagan administration's policies, don't you think?" "Yes, it is," the former Secretary of State agreed, "and let me suggest to you, so we get the record straight, I support Ronald Reagan. . . . I think history is going to view the Reagan presidency with considerable understanding."

If all inconsistencies were as transparent as Haig's, the inconsistency would lose its rhetorical force to persuade. Unfortunately, many are subtle enough to escape the casual reader and inattentive audience. Spotting the inexact or inexplicit rhetorical inconsistency calls for close reading and listening—a keen eye and ear for language—as in the following example.

> On June 6, 1987, P. W. Botha, president of South Africa, attempted to defend extending police powers to crack-down on people protesting apartheid in that country: "Considering the safety of the public and the maintenance of public order, I have decided to declare a state of emergency once more in the whole of the republic, including the self-governing national states" (that is, black tribal homelands).

The president did not explain how states that have a state of emergency *imposed* on them can at the same time be termed *self-governing*.

DISTINCTION WITHOUT A DIFFERENCE

All that we have said so far about language certainly points up the importance of clarity and precision in argument. To that end, it is often crucial to make distinctions in order to avoid confusion. Sometimes, these distinctions can be very subtle, but extremely useful. On the other hand, arguers occasionally attempt to draw a difference by carefully defining terms where no real difference exists, as when, during the Mideast crisis of 1990, the Iraqi ambassador to the United States insisted that Americans being held in Iraq and Kuwait were not being "detained" — they simply could not travel about.

➥ **The distinction without a difference fallacy (also known as "hairsplitting") consists in attempting to defend or advance a position by linguistically distinguishing it from some other one with which it is supposedly confused, when in fact there is no substantive difference between the two.** Common examples of this fallacy arise when we are trying to defend a rather shaky position. For example, a student who is accused by her parents of not being "a very good student" might voice a distinction without a difference fallacy. It is unlikely that two people will agree exactly on all the features that define "a good student," but all of us probably would include at least the standard of passing courses. Our hypothetical student, Karen, regularly drops or fails her courses. When her parents accuse her of not being a very good student, Karen protests, "I don't think you're being fair. I'm just not interested in school." The problem with Karen's response is that she has made a distinction that exhibits no real difference. Good students *are* interested in school — at least interested enough to complete the courses they take. By offering a phantom distinction between being a good student and being interested in school, Karen does not really blunt the force of her parents' accusation. This is precisely the logical problem with a distinction without a difference — it offers a pseudo-defense for a position.

Suppose someone who opposes the appointment of women as corporate executive officers at the same time protests, "I'm no sexist." However, opposition to the appointment of women to powerful corporate positions is a form of sexism. Basically, it is no different from saying, "I don't want women in charge of things, but I'm no sexist."

The distinction without a difference fallacy seems to play an integral part in the reasoning of so-called radical antiabortionists who blow up abortion clinics, but insist: "We didn't really destroy property — we destroyed an abortuary." Is an abortion clinic, by any other name, not property? The same kind of twisted thinking is expressed by a bank embezzler who insists that he did not really steal any money but that he merely *borrowed* it for awhile with the full intention of repayment.

You are probably beginning to suspect that the fallacy of distinction without a difference sometimes is combined with euphemism in order to mislead or confuse the point at hand. You are right; it is. For example, suppose that answering the charge that her company regularly offers bribes to officials in foreign countries, an executive says: "We're not bribing anyone. We're merely oiling the bureaucratic machinery in order to expedite our business interests abroad."

None of this is meant to preclude the legitimacy of stipulative definition. We are free to stipulate the meaning of any term we use; but if the new meaning functions basically in the same way in the argument, the distinction does not identify any real difference. In addition, if there is not any substantive difference between the meaning of the terms, a premise which asserts that there is, is dubious and thus unacceptable.

EXERCISES ON DISTINCTION WITHOUT A DIFFERENCE

1. The Virginia Military Institute (VMI) is one of the last two all-male public colleges in the United States. Recently, the Justice Department has charged VMI with sex discrimination. The publicly financed institution, say Justice Department officials, cannot deny admission to a female. Faced with the unmistakable facts of quality female military performance at West Point, in the U.S. invasion of Panama, and in the war against Iraq, General John Knapp, VMI superintendent, has taken a novel tack to defend the institute's all-male policy. Knapp says that VMI does not discriminate against women, but is merely protecting them from the institution-alized hazing of new cadets known at VMI as the "rat line." Knapp insists that men are made from such humiliation and women are not. **Do you think that Knapp's distinction is genuine or not?**

IMPROVING PERFORMANCE

SUMMARY-TEST QUESTIONS FOR CHAPTER 5*

1. The use of emotive language, jargon, or euphemism in argument is always fallacious. True or False?
2. "Fifty-thousand illegal aliens are living in the deserted buildings situated along Telegraph Avenue."
   "Fifty-thousand illegal aliens are holed up in the warrens situated along Telegraph Avenue."
   State the fact that both of these sentences report. Which sentence communicates more than this fact? Explain. How did the writer transmit this additional message?
3. When the Massachusetts State Department of Public Works refers to road signs as "ground-mounted confirmatory route markers," it is using
   A. emotive language.
   B. euphemism.
   C. jargon.
   D. a persuasive definition.
4. Why is it wise to avoid using emotive language, euphemism, and jargon in argument?
5. What is meant by the "telescopic effect of labels," as illustrated in the example of the blind man?
6. What, in addition to someone who legally receives welfare benefits, has the term "welfare recipient" come to signify for many people?

7. "Are you pro– or anti–labor unions?" This question
   A. uses labels.
   B. sets up a false dilemma.
   C. encourages the respondent to think in mutually exclusive categories.
   D. A and B
   E. A, B, and C
8. If it has not been established that you voted for a presidential candidate in the 1988 election, then the question "Did you vote for Bush or Dukakis?" is
   A. a false dilemma.
   B. a rhetorical question.
   C. a complex question.
   D. A and C
   E. A, B, and C
9. What kind of questions are the following? Choose from (A) rhetorical, (B) complex, (C) both A and B, (D) neither A nor B.
   A. Should capital punishment be legalized?
   B. What's the most effective way to convince people that capital punishment works?
   C. Isn't capital punishment the best way to deter potential murderers from killing?
   D. Doesn't everyone who has given the matter serious consideration favor capital punishment?
10. Which of the preceding four questions contains a persuasive definition? Explain.
11. The fallacy of _____ consists in presupposing the conclusion in an argument.
12. "The Pentagon is best qualified to draw up the defense budget because it best knows what the nation's military needs are." Does this argument beg the question? Explain.
13. "How much and what kind of support should be given to Eastern European nations that have rejected Communism?" Use this question to explain the connection between a complex question and question-begging.
14. Suppose a friend claims that true love never ends in divorce. You provide examples of what you believe was true love that ended in divorce. Your friend insists that these were not genuine cases of true love because they ended in divorce. What fallacy is your friend using to fend off your counterexamples?
15. Precisely what do question-begging, a question-begging definition, and a complex question have in common?
16. "Hairsplitting" is another name for the fallacy termed _____ .
17. Defending his company's paying bribes to officials overseas, a corporate executive says: "Bribes are absolutely essential to doing international business." What fallacy does the person commit?
18. "The reason that moral values are deteriorating is that people can't distinguish what's right from what's wrong." What is wrong with this explanation?
19. "Opponents of pornography should not be permitted to picket in front of stores selling explicitly erotic materials since that's an attack on freedom of expression." Fallacy?
20. What is a rhetorical inconsistency?

CRITICAL THINKING APPLICATIONS

1. "In her latest speech, my opponent has accused me of playing fast and loose with facts, of distorting her position, and deliberately misleading the American people. In response, I'll simply say this. . . ."

    Which of the following is a clear, unambiguous, direct response to the opponents charges? Explain why the others aren't, by reference to rhetorical fallacies.

    A. "On occasion, I may have misspoken myself or perhaps taken poetic license with a detail or two."

    B. "My record in politics demonstrates my commitment to clean, honest, and accurate campaigning."

    C. "I don't apologize for my campaign style, which, admittedly, may offend the faint of heart and the wishy-washy."

    D. "The positions that my opponent claims I've misrepresented are, in fact, detailed in her own campaign literature, which I'll now share with you."

    E. "What in heaven's name would a candidate who's leading in the polls by fifteen points have to gain by engaging in the tactics my opponent accuses me of?

2. "Is your business going to continue to discriminate against women and minorities in its hiring and promotion practices?"

    Can this question be considered unfair?

    A. Yes, because its construction seeks a "yes" or "no" answer where both may be appropriate.

    B. Yes, because it's internally inconsistent.

    C. Yes, because it contains a hidden presupposition which the respondent might wish to contest.

    D. No, because lots of businesses do discriminate against women and minorities.

3. French social and political philosopher Jean-Jacques Rousseau (1712–1778) assumed that human beings in the state of nature are characterized by a feeling of sympathy toward each other and toward other living creatures. If this is the case, how do we account for the myriad social ills that beset us, for example, the innumerable cases of humans exploiting other humans? In response, Rousseau said that our natural feelings are crushed under the weight of unsympathetic social institutions. **Criticize Rousseau's response in terms of linguistic confusion.**

4. A student was having a difficult time understanding the works of James Joyce. So he asked his professor why Joyce's writings lack "perspicuity," that is, clarity. His professor replied that he preferred to view the lack of perspicuity in Joyce in terms of a lack of perspicacity in some students. (If you do not know the meaning of "perspicacity," consult a dictionary.) **Do you think the student's question was a fair one? Which of the following best describes the tack taken by the professor in answering the student's question?**

    A. He begged the question.

    B. He set up an either/or situation.

    C. He targeted a hidden assumption.

    D. He abused vagueness.

E. He used jargon ("perspicacity"), but legitimately, because he could fairly assume that any student who knew the meaning of "perspicuity" probably would know the meaning of "perspicacity."

5. A newspaper reporter fails to mention that the central figure of her series on teenage runaways is really a composite of many teenage runaways and not just a single, real person. When critics find out, they lambaste her for not disclosing this information when the series was first published. Three years earlier, however, the same critics voted the same reporter a prize for her magazine series *Senator,* which was a dramatized and fictionalized account of a U.S. Senator whose life, looks, and liaisons were obviously patterned closely on that of John F. Kennedy. **In which of the following ways, if any, could the critics claim that they were *not* inconsistent in their treatment of the reporter's works?**
    A. Times change, and with them so do journalistic standards.
    B. The standards that hold for newspaper articles are not necessarily the same ones that hold for magazine articles.
    C. Fictionalization is an accepted journalistic technique for reporting on sensitive subjects, such as runaway teens.
    D. Dramatizing events in fiction is different from presenting distortions of truth as actual fact.
    E. *Senator* was written better than the series on teenage runaways.

6. "All true general statements are based solely on observed phenomena. But even though a true general statement has held true up to a certain point, that doesn't guarantee that it will remain unexceptionless. Therefore, no true general statement can be considered free from possible exception." **The logic of this argument can best be described as**
    A. self-defeating, that is, internally inconsistent.
    B. circular, that is, question-begging.
    C. ill-defined, that is, ambiguous or vague.
    D. valid, that is, the conclusion necessarily follows from the premises.
    E. a strong induction.

7. "We in the United States like to boast about the freedoms we enjoy. But how much freedom do we really have? The cost of health care is soaring. Housing costs in desirable areas of the country are prohibitive. Legal fees are out of sight. People living in nations where such needs and services are met regardless of one's ability to pay obviously are freer than most Americans." **The persuasive effect of this argument depends on the ambiguous use of which of the following pairs of words?**
    A. *we* and *Americans*
    B. *soaring* and *prohibitive*
    C. *needs* and *services*
    D. *freedom* and *freer*
    E. *enjoy* and *have*

8. "You cannot buy a more powerful pain-reliever than OMNIPOTENT without a prescription."
    A. Which of the following statements, if any, is inconsistent with this ad's claim?

1. OMNIPOTENT isn't the cheapest over-the-counter pain reliever available.
2. PAIN-OUT, another nonprescription analgesic, is just as powerful as OMNIPOTENT.
3. Several prescription pain-relievers are not as powerful as OMNIPOTENT.
4. All pain-relievers of the same strength as OMNIPOTENT relieve pain equally.

B. Does the ad's persuasive appeal depend on vague and ambiguous use of terms? Explain.

9. "If you're looking for a new car to buy, look no farther than the new IMPRESS by National Motors, Inc. Recently, we randomly selected 250 motorists to drive the new IMPRESS and the three leading luxury cars. One-hundred and ten drivers ranked the IMPRESS first in handling. And 130 ranked it first in styling. From the responses of these 250 drivers, we can tell you that they ranked IMPRESS first in our composite category of handling, styling, comfort, performance, and drivability. But don't take the word of these drivers—come in today and IMPRESS yourself!" **Which undefined word most weakens the persuasive effect of this ad?**
   A. randomly
   B. styling
   C. handling
   D. responses
   E. composite

10. You have a very lucrative concession for snack food at a local university. One day, the student union, which oversees the vending machines, informs you that you must either freeze the prices of your snacks or remove the machines. At first, you think the union has placed you in a no-win situation: If you raise your prices, you lose the concession; but if you freeze your prices, your profits will start shrinking owing to ever rising production and overhead costs. Then it hits you—a way that will allow you to increase your profits without, strictly speaking, raising your prices. In other words, you see that the dilemma posed by the student union is a false one. **What is your solution?**

11. **Read the following news item, then answer the questions that follow it.** *(Paragraphs are numbered for later reference).*
    1. *(Baltimore)* Taking a more aggressive stand, the nation's Roman Catholic bishops yesterday called the fight against abortion the "fundamental human rights issue" facing the church, and declared that "no Catholic can responsibly take a 'pro-choice' stand."
    2. Their toughened posture, contained in a resolution adopted by the nearly 300 prelates meeting in Baltimore this week, recommends no penalty for Catholics who dissent from church teachings against abortion.
    3. However, several leading bishops said the church should consider excommunicating Catholics who take "an aggressive pro-choice stand."
    4. "When dealing with the taking of a human life, it is not correct to speak of 'pro-choice.' There is no choice to take a human life," said Cardinal Joseph Bernardin, chairman of the bishops' Committee for Pro-Life Activities.
    5. Archbishop John Quinn, in a plea reflecting the tone of the new church

offensive, yesterday compared doctors who perform abortions to physicians who collaborated with the Nazi holocaust.

6. "Physicians at the Nuremberg trials said they saw nothing wrong with illegal experimentation on other human beings," said Quinn, who called abortion "the ax at the root of human rights."

7. "This is about the control by some over the human life of others," Quinn told his fellow bishops.

8. While unanimous in their firm opposition to abortion, some bishops expressed concerns about the increasingly harsh tone of the "pro-life" crusade.

9. Bishop Joseph Sullivan of New York urged his colleagues to remove language from their resolution implying the so-called "pro-choice" proponents are really "pro-abortion."

10. Sullivan called the language "polemical and judgmental" but was rejected in his attempts to change the wording.

11. The resolution calls on the church to expand its public awareness program on abortion, provide better care for pregnant women and their children and to lobby for laws "in defense of human life in all its stages, especially the unborn."

12. "Let us make sure, as we rightfully engage in this debate, that we hear, really hear, the issues, the struggles and the anguish of women who face issues in a way that we never will," Bernardin said. . . . (Don Lattin, "U.S. Bishops Say No Catholic Can Take Pro-Choice Stand," *San Francisco Chronicle.* Reprinted by permission.)

A. **Identify the persuasive definition in paragraph 1.**

B. **Is there any vagueness in paragraph 3?**

C. **Do you see any question-begging in paragraphs 4 and 11?**

D. **Do paragraphs 5 and 6 contain any inflammatory language?**

E. **With reference to the unfair use of emotive language, explain Bishop Sullivan's concerns as detailed in paragraphs 8, 9, and 10.**

F. **Do you find Cardinal Bernardin's plea in paragraph 12 inconsistent with his earlier reported comments? Explain.**

G. **Precisely what is the persuasive effect of using the labels "pro-life" and "pro-choice" as substitutes for "pro-abortion" and "anti-abortion"?**

H. Bishop Sullivan finds the language of the resolution "polemical and judgmental." By implication, his colleagues disagreed. **What kind of dispute is this?**

12. We humans are beset by all kinds of problems: sickness, poverty, suffering, war, death. Yet, the doctrine of theism insists that there is an all-good, all-powerful Creator. This is at least paradoxical. How is evil compatible with an all-good Creator? If God is all-powerful, surely He could destroy all evil. If He does not, why not? Is He really not all-powerful? Or is it that he is unwilling? But if God is unwilling, then He seems to have evil intentions, which certainly are not consistent with the nature of an all-good God.

In his *Dialogues Concerning Natural Religion,* a three-person discussion of the chief arguments for God's existence, Scottish philosopher David Hume (1711–1776) considers this question of evil. His conclusion, in the words of one of his characters, Philo, is that one's experience in the world argues against the existence of an all-good, all-powerful being. What follows is Philo's argument. **Read it carefully, then answer the question that follows it:**

> My sentiments, replied Philo, are not worth being made a mystery of; and, therefore, without any ceremony, I shall deliver what occurs to me with regard to the present subject. It must, I think, be allowed that, if a very limited intelligence whom we shall suppose utterly unacquainted with the universe were assured that it were the production of a very good, wise, and powerful being, however finite, he would, from his conjectures, form *beforehand* a different notion of it from what we find it to be by experience; nor would he ever imagine, merely from these attributes of the cause of which he is informed, that the effect could be so full of vice and misery and disorder, as it appears in this life. Supposing now that this person were brought into the world, still assured that it was the workmanship of such a sublime and benevolent being, he might, perhaps, be surprised at the disappointment, but would never retract his former belief if founded on any very solid argument, since such a limited intelligence must be sensible of his own blindness and ignorance, and must allow that there may be many solutions of those phenomena which will forever escape his comprehension. But supposing, which is the real case with regard to man, that this creature is not antecedently convinced of a supreme intelligence, benevolent, and powerful, but is left to gather such a belief from the appearance of things — this entirely alters the case, nor will he ever find any reason for such a conclusion. He may be fully convinced of the narrow limits of his understanding, but this will not help him in forming an inference concerning the goodness of superior powers, since he must form that inference from what he knows, not from what he is ignorant of. The more you exaggerate his weakness and ignorance, the more difficult you render him, and give him the greater suspicion that such subjects are beyond the reach of his faculties. You are obliged, therefore, to reason with him merely from the known phenomena, and to drop every arbitrary supposition or conjecture.

Explain how this argument can be read as a caution against forming a question-begging definition regarding the existence of an all-good, all-powerful God.

13. **Read these two opposed viewpoints concerning U.S. aid to Nicaragua, then answer the questions that follow.**

Should the United States Help Rebuild Nicaragua?

PRO: With the fair election defeat of Eduardo Ortega's Sandinista rule in Nicaragua, the democratic and capitalistic revolution sweeping the world continues. The United States should financially support all those revolutions, including Nicaragua's, because it's in our best interests to.

CON: The United States can take righteous pride in having helped foment the successful revolution against the Stalinist dictatorship of Eduardo Ortega. The Sandinistas were a Soviet puppet bent on destabilizing freedom-loving governments throughout Latin America.

But now the United States must

But U.S. policy of supporting the Nicaraguan freedom fighters, called the *Contras,* against the totalitarian Ortega regime has left the United States with a special responsibility toward the new, democratically elected government of Violeta Chamorro. After all, don't we owe something to those whose revolution we underwrote? Moreover, during her campaign Chamorro emphasized that her victory would result in massive U.S. aid to rebuild Nicaragua. We either provide that aid, or we invite a resurgence of the Communist-sponsored, oppressive Sandinista rule.

Finally, only serious aid can truly atone for the blunders and cruelties of the Contra war, in which the United States was a central player.

deal with its general role in Latin America. Isn't it time the United States gave up its addiction to domination of the countries south of the Rio Grande? We're not the financial savior of every country in the world that suddenly embraces "our" political ideology. Besides, a healthy free-market economy can no more be built on the basis of international welfare than on domestic welfare. Massive financial aid will only result in making Nicaragua dependent on the United States. In contrast, leaving this budding democracy to its own devices will produce a vital and self-sufficient economy in Nicaragua that will be the envy of all Latin America. The best thing the United States can do for Nicaragua, therefore, is to take a hands-off policy that is long overdue.

A. **What are the main points offered in support of each thesis?**
B. **What kind of dispute do you think is involved?**
C. **On which of the following points are the arguments in basic agreement; on which are they in disagreement?**
   1. The United States helped overthrow the Sandinistas.
   2. The United States was justified in helping overthrow the Sandinistas.
   3. Ortega is a Communist.
   4. The Contras support democracy, the Sandinistas don't.
   5. A nation has an obligation to support a regime that it has helped put in power.
   6. Not giving financial support to the new government will ultimately hurt the United States.
   7. The new government can survive without U.S. aid.
   8. The course that the United States should take with respect to Nicaragua is clear-cut.
D. **Identify and discuss the use of the following rhetorical devices in the arguments: slanting through the use of emotive language; persuasive definition, begging the question, abuse of vagueness, rhetorical question, false dilemma, and rhetorical inconsistency.**

POINT/COUNTERPOINT: ESSAYS FOR ANALYSIS

Issue: *The Death Penalty*

Resolved: The death penalty is justified on grounds of retribution.

Background: What is a suitable punishment for murder? Death, say many Americans; but a large number consider the enforcement of capital punishment no less heinous than the crime for which the murderer pays with his life. These polarized views reflect some basic disagreements about the aim of punishment.

The purpose of punishment can be divided into two categories: (1) in terms of giving people what they deserve, or (2) in terms of the punishment's desirable consequences. The first category includes so-called retributive theories of punishment; the second includes theories of prevention, deterrence, and reform.

It is the first category—punishment as retribution—that is emerging as the core argument for the retention of capital punishment in America. The term "retributive" refers to punishment given in return for wrong done. Thus, the retributivist view of punishment holds that the people who do wrong should pay for it—that is, they deserve to be punished. By this logic, punishment is a principle of justice, whereby those who cause the innocent harm ought to be harmed in return. Arguments advancing capital punishment often make precisely this point, thereby associating retributivist punishment with revenge.

But there is another view of retribution, which associates punishment with respect for persons, both noncriminals and criminals. Proponents of this version of retribution argue that you and I and all other members of society should live under the same limitations of freedom. If I steal a car, I am disrupting this balance of equal limitations by unfairly taking advantage of you. When the state subsequently punishes me—for example, by imprisonment—it is attempting to restore the balance that I have disrupted; it is affirming society's commitment to the fair treatment of all its members. It is as if the state, through its judicial processes, were saying to me: "We must punish you, who have flouted society's limitations, out of respect for those parties who abide by those limitations."

Often overlooked, however, is the flip side of the respect-retribution view: respect for the offender. Respect-retributionists (as opposed to what we might call "revenge-retributionists") argue that not punishing offenders treats them with disrespect by not giving them what they deserve. Only by giving people what they deserve—be it punishment or reward—do we show individuals the full respect and dignity of their humanity. When a deserving person is denied praise, for example, the person is treated with disrespect. By the same token, when someone deserving of punishment is denied punishment, the person is treated with equal disrespect. Thus, according to the respect-retribution view of punishment, when society punishes me for stealing your car, it is effectively saying: "We are punishing you because we respect you as a human being. Respecting human beings means giving them what they deserve. In this matter, you deserve to be punished. Therefore, we will punish you, for if we did not we'd be treating you with disrespect."

From: **Deserved Retribution**[6]

Ernest van den Haag

Ernest van den Haag, professor of Jurisprudence and Public Policy at Fordham University, has long been a prominent advocate of capital punishment. In the following selection, van den Haag presents the retributivist view.

Read the essay carefully, outline it, then answer the questions that follow it.*

1 It has frequently been argued that capital punishment is imposed merely to gratify an unworthy desire for revenge — unchristian, uncharitable, and futile. Is it? And is revenge the reason for capital punishment? Obviously capital punishment is imposed not only for revenge or retribution, but also for the sake of deterrence — to spare future victims of murder by carrying out the threat of execution upon convicted murderers. But let me leave this aside for the moment.

2 Retribution certainly does play a role. It differs from revenge in some respects, though not in all. Revenge is a private matter, a wish to "get even" with a person one feels has injured one, whether or not what the person did was legal. Unlike revenge, retribution is legally threatened beforehand for an act prohibited by law. It is imposed by due process and only for a crime, as threatened by law. Retribution is also limited by law. Retribution may be exacted when there is no personal injury and no wish for revenge; conversely, revenge may be carried out when there was neither a crime nor a real injury. The desire for revenge is a personal feeling. Retribution is a legally imposed social institution.

3 Nonetheless, the motives socialized by punishment, including the death penalty, may well include the motive of revenge. But motives should not be confused with purposes, and least of all with effects. The motive for, say, capital punishment may well be revenge, at least on the part of the father bereaved by the murder of his daughter. The intention of the law, however, may be to deter other murderers or to strengthen social solidarity by retributive punishment. Either or both or neither of these effects may be achieved.

4 Consider now the motive of revenge. Is it so contemptible after all? Perhaps forgiveness is better. It does not follow that revenge is bad. It can be, after all, a compensatory and psychologically reparative act. I cannot see wherein revenge must be morally blameworthy if the injury for which vengeance is exacted is. However, revenge may be socially disruptive: Only the avenger determines what to avenge, on whom, to what degree, when, and for what. This leaves far too much room for the arbitrary infliction of

---

[6]From Ernest van den Haag and John P. Conrad in *The Death Penalty: A Debate* (1983), Plenum Publishing Corporation. Reprinted by permission of publisher and author.

harm. Therefore, societies always have tried to limit and regulate revenge by transforming it into legal retribution, by doing justice according to what is deserved in place of the injured party.

5 Retribution is hard to define. It is harder still to determine the punishments that should be exacted by "just deserts" once the *lex talionis* is abandoned. Yet retribution does give the feeling of justice that is indispensable if the law is to be socially supported. In the case of murder, there is not much doubt about the penalty demanded by our sense of justice. It is hard to see why the law should promise a murderer that what he did to his victim will never be done to him, that he will be supported and protected in prison as long as he lives, at taxpayers' expense.

6 Although trendy churchmen recently have tended to deny it, historically the main Christian churches, Roman Catholic and Protestant, have staunchly supported the death penalty, often on the basis of numerous biblical passages advocating it for murder and sometimes for transgressions that today we regard as minor. The oft-quoted "vengeance is mine, I will repay, saith the Lord" (Rom. 12:19) is not as opposed to vengeance as it is made to appear. Paul does not quote the Lord as rejecting vengeance but as reserving it to himself: You must not seek vengeance, you must leave it to the Lord. According to Christian tradition, the punishments the Lord will inflict upon those whom he does not forgive are far more terrible and lasting than what any vengeful mortal could inflict on another. What could be worse than hell, the punishment inflicted for violating God's law? God recognizes and does not deprecate the desire for vengeance. He tells us to leave the fulfillment of this desire to Him.

7 If we return to earth and read on after Romans 12, we find in the next chapter, 13, what the Apostle Paul actually had in mind. "The Ruler," he says in 13:4, "beareth not the sword in vain: for he is the minister of God, a revenger to execute wrath upon him that doeth evil." The meaning is clear. The Ruler, not the injured individual, should "execute wrath." Disruptive private vengeance should be institutionalized and replaced by social retribution, retribution by the ruler.

8 If offenders are to suffer the punishments deserved by their crimes, if punishments are to proclaim the blame the community attaches to their crimes, capital punishment certainly accomplishes as much. It expresses the extreme disapproval of the community by imposing its most extreme punishment. Of the four ends punishment may accomplish — retribution, rehabilitation, incapacitation, and deterrence — capital punishment accomplishes three, more thoroughly than any other punishment can, while making rehabilitation irrelevant. . . .

9 Morally, I do not believe that having done something wrong entitles an adult to rehabilitation. It entitles him to punishment. Murder entitles him to execution.

10 If rehabilitation were our aim, most murderers could be released. Quite often they are "rehabilitated" by the very murder they committed. They

are unlikely to commit other crimes. We punish them not for what they may or may not do in the future but for what they have done. . . .

11 The Romans thought that *"homo homini res sacra"* — every human being should be sacred to every other human being. To enforce the sacredness of human life, the Romans unflinchingly executed murderers.

12 One may well argue that human life is cheapened when murderers, instead of being executed, are imprisoned as pickpockets are. It is not enough to proclaim human life inviolable. Innocent life is best secured by telling those who would take it that they will forfeit their own life. A society that allows those who took the innocent life of others to live on — albeit in prison for a time — does not protect the lives of its members or hold them sacred. The discontinuity between murder and other crimes should be underlined by the death penalty, not blurred by punishing murderers as one punishes thieves. Murder is not quite so trifling an offense.

13 To insist that the murderer has the same right to live as his victim pushes egalitarianism too far. It blurs moral distinctions and seems to recognize only physical equalities. His crime morally sets the murderer apart from his victim. The victim did, and therefore the murderer does not, deserve to live. His life cannot be sacred if that of his victim was.

1. The two questions in paragraph one are
   A. rhetorical.
   B. complex.
   C. both rhetorical and complex.
   D. neither rhetorical nor complex.
2. Paragraph 1 functions to
   A. set up the issue.
   B. state the thesis.
   C. establish that capital punishment is a deterrent.
   D. refute the notion that revenge is un-Christian, uncharitable, and futile.
3. The definition of "retribution" offered in paragraph 2 is
   A. persuasive.
   B. theoretical.
   C. stipulative.
   D. lexical.
4. Do you think that the distinction the author draws between revenge and retribution (paragraph 2) is a real or phantom distinction?
5. In paragraph 3, do you think the author clearly distinguishes between "motives," "purpose," and "effects"? If not, would his meaning be clearer if he did?
6. According to what the author says in paragraph 3, capital punishment
   A. deters other murderers.
   B. strengthens social solidarity.
   C. may neither deter murder nor strengthen social stability.
   D. A and B
7. Throughout paragraph 3, the author uses the words "may" and "may be." The

terms "may" and "may be" could indicate possibility (as in "Laura may be at the concert") or permissibility (as in "Laura may be admitted to the concert because she has a ticket.") Which of the meanings do you think the author intends? Does it make any difference?

8. After reading paragraph 4, Lowell says: "The author, in effect, is saying that 'legal retribution' is society's way of giving expression to its members' desire for revenge. So, the distinction he draws between revenge and retribution in the preceding paragraph is simply an attempt to avoid the fact that retribution is a form of revenge." Do you think this is a good criticism?

9. Do you think that the meaning of the phrase "compensatory and psychological reparative act" is clear enough (paragraph 4)? Do you think some examples (that is, denotations) would be useful?

10. Paragraph 4 suggests that the author believes that revenge is
    A. contemptible.
    B. not as good as forgiveness.
    C. can lead to harm.
    D. is always psychologically healthy.
    E. None of the above.

11. In paragraph 4, the question "Is it (revenge) so contemptible after all?" is
    A. rhetorical.
    B. complex.
    C. neither rhetorical nor complex.
    D. both rhetorical and complex.

12. The author says that *retribution* is hard to define (paragraph 5). Do you think that what he said earlier supports this evaluation?

13. Which of the following arguments most closely parallels the author's assertion "I cannot see wherein revenge must be morally blameworthy if the injury for which vengeance is exacted is" (paragraph 4)?
    A. "You hurt me. So, it's okay for me to hurt you."
    B. "You hurt me. So, it's not necessarily wrong for me to hurt you."
    C. "You hurt me. So, I should hurt you."
    D. "You hurt me. So, you deserve to be hurt in return."

14. Do you think that the logical relationship between the last two sentences of paragraph 5 is clear? In other words, if we assume that these sentences comprise an argument, which is the premise, and which is the conclusion?

15. Do you think the phrase "our sense of justice" is clear enough (paragraph 5)?

16. Do you think the last sentence of paragraph 5 slants through the use of bias?

17. The first sentence of paragraph 6 states a fact and expresses a judgment. Explain.

18. The word "trendy," in the aforementioned sentence,
    A. confuses through the use of jargon.
    B. confuses through the use of euphemism.
    C. discredits through word bias.
    D. fairly characterizes clerics who oppose capital punishment.

19. After reading paragraphs 6 and 7, Ronna says: "I agree that we should leave revenge to the Lord. And that's exactly why I'm opposed to capital punishment. It's also why I feel the author's being inconsistent. On the one hand, he approves

of revenge through what he calls state-sponsored retribution. On the other hand, he clearly accepts the Biblical warning against our seeking revenge. He can't have it both ways." Do you agree or disagree with Ronna's analysis?

20. After reading paragraph 7, Milt says: "Even if the author's interpretation of Paul is accurate, that only makes a Biblical case for institutionalized punishment. It doesn't demonstrate that the Bible supports capital punishment." Do you agree with Milt's implication—that at this point in the essay the author should be providing support for capital punishment and not for institutionalized revenge?

21. Paragraphs 6 and 7 will be persuasive only to those who
    A. believe that the Bible is the inspired word of God.
    B. accept the author's interpretation of the passages he cites.
    C. agree that churchmen who oppose capital punishment are "trendy."
    D. A and B
    E. A, B, and C

22. After reading paragraph 7, Wanda says: "What 'Ruler' means in the Bible is hardly what it means in a democratic society such as ours. We have no 'ruler,' but a tripartite system of governance whereby one branch makes the laws, another executes them, and the third rules on their legality. Furthermore, the lawmakers themselves represent the popular will. The author would have us overlook these important differences in the way 'rule' functions in a democracy, compared with, say, how it operates in a tribe or a totalitarian state." Do you think that Wanda is making a distinction without a difference?

23. Which of the following statements, if true, would *most* weaken the point made in paragraph 8?
    A. Studies show that capital punishment does not deter crime.
    B. More than one-hundred persons that we know of have been executed in the United States for crimes that they did not commit.
    C. Males and members of minority groups are executed more often than females and Caucasians who committed identical crimes.

24. To be *entitled* means to have a right to do or to have something. The first use of "entitle" in paragraph 9 coincides with this meaning. Do you think that the author preserves or shifts the meaning of *entitle* in his next two usages of it? Does it make any difference?

25. Do you think it is accurate to say that paragraph 10 demonstrates that society should not attempt to rehabilitate murderers?

26. Do you regard the Roman belief that every human being should be sacred to every other human being consistent with executing murderers (paragraph 11)?

27. In paragraph 12, the author sets up roughly the following dilemma: "Either society executes murderers, and thereby demonstrates that it holds life sacred. Or it does not execute murderers, and thereby cheapens life." Do you think this is a genuine or false dilemma?

28. Which of the following arguments most closely parallels the reasoning of the last paragraph?
    A. "You stole his car. Therefore, you should go to prison."
    B. "You stole his car. Therefore, you must make amends."
    C. "You stole his car. Therefore, you don't deserve to drive."

D. "You stole his car. Therefore, you don't deserve to own a car."

E. "You stole his car. Therefore, you are immoral but I am not."

 From: **All-Embracing Affect of the Death Penalty**[7]

John Cole Vodicka

> *John Cole Vodicka is a long-time death penalty abolitionist who currently is a member of Loinonia Farms Community of the Christian Peace and Justice International Community, located near Americas, Georgia. In the following selection, Vodicka responds to the retributivist defense of capital punishment.*

Read the essay carefully, outline it, then answer the questions that follow it.

1 No matter how one feels about the death penalty, no matter what arguments one uses to bolster his or her position, one thing seems absolutely certain to me: State-sanctioned executions expose more of the violence and injustice that are in us all. It is a dehumanizing ritual, one that brings more injury to each of us.

2 I have been a lifelong opponent of the death penalty. My opposition stems from a variety of reasons: Capital punishment does not deter; it is applied arbitrarily and in a discriminatory fashion; it is cruel and unusual punishment; it is irreversible; and it mocks the commandment, "Thou shalt not kill."

3 I also oppose the death penalty because in my work I have come to know the issue in human terms, in the names and faces of those involved or caught up in this grisly business. Some of these faces are of prisoners who have been executed; in the last 12 months I have lost six friends to the electric chair. Other faces are of the condemned prisoners' families, the families of their victims, of prison officials and guards, of chaplains, lawyers, judges, elected officials and witnesses to executions. And there are the angry faces of those who, out of frustration and fear, have told me they believe the death penalty, whether it "works" or not, is "just desert" for anyone convicted of murder. Countless faces and names, each in his or her own way, a victim of a degrading process that prohibits us from recognizing each other's humanity.

4 On May 25, 1979, I stood with several hundred people in front of the Starke, Florida penitentiary, where John Spenkelink was about to be executed. We were there to pray and to stand in opposition to the impending execution. Standing nearby, though, were several dozen people, a coffin perched atop their Winnebago, chanting "Go, Sparky, Go!" Some were wearing T-shirts that depicted an electric chair with the words, "1 down, 131 to go!"

5 On December 7, 1982, hundreds of college students gathered and gawked outside the Texas Penitentiary at Huntsville and celebrated the impending

[7]From *The California Prisoner*, January, 1985. Reprinted by permission of the publisher and author.

lethal-injection execution of Charlie Brooks, Jr. They ate popcorn and drank beer, taunting those of us gathered there standing in silent opposition. Some of the students held up handmade signs that read, "Kill Him in Vein" and "Put the Animal to Sleep."

6 On October 12, 1984, across the street from the Virginia Prison in Richmond, rowdy, beer-drinking death-penalty proponents gathered to cheer on the execution of Linwood Briley. They too displayed signs that conveyed a lynchmob mentality. "Fry, nigger, fry!" read one poster. "Burn Briley, Burn," encouraged another. The demonstrators set off firecrackers when word finally came from the prison that Briley was dead.

7 And here in California earlier this year condemned prisoner Robert Harris lost another round of appeals, thereby temporarily clearing the way for his execution date to be set. The next day, I am told, the switchboard at San Quentin lit up, as dozens of people, including a Los Angeles County district attorney, phoned the warden's office requesting to be an official "witness" to the gassing of Robert Harris.

8 One of the callers was Steven Baker, the father of the child Robert Harris is accused of killing. Baker believes the death penalty will ease his pain, ease his anger. But listen: "Every time Harris files an appeal and his name gets in the papers, myself and the families have to go through it all over again," Baker says. "The longer this has dragged on the more my rage has been directed at the criminal justice system."

9 It is clear to me that the ritual of capital punishment brutalizes us all; it extends the violence, provokes anger, and hinders, rather than encourages, healing. The death penalty exposes a system which is based on revenge and retaliation. To the detriment of us all, it justifies lethal vengeance.

10 Virginia Governor Charles Robb, when asked about the pro-death penalty demonstration in Richmond on the night Linwood Briley was executed, called it "inappropriate behavior." But my colleague and friend Marie Deans, who worked to halt Briley's electrocution and who is herself a family member of a murder victim, remarked that the crowd's behavior was "no different than Governor Robb's allowing Briley to be executed, no more inappropriate than what occurred behind those prison walls."

11 "The ultimate result of this and every execution," Deans said, "is nothing less than a total disregard for life."

12 I am convinced that as we deny a death row prisoner his or her humanity, so do we lose a little more of our own.

13 Several years ago my friend Tim Baldwin faced imminent execution in Louisiana. Then, at the last hour, we were successful in obtaining a stay order from a panel of federal judges. A frustrated, vengeful public expressed its outrage. "Killer Cheats Chair" screamed one daily newspaper headline. And on one popular New Orleans radio talk show, the host suggested that not only should Baldwin have been electrocuted but that I should have been forced to sit in Baldwin's lap! (Tim Baldwin is one of those faces; he was ultimately executed on September 10, 1984.)

14 The death penalty doesn't end the suffering, it prolongs it. It doesn't limit the tragedy, it widens it. It doesn't abate the anger, it keeps the wounds open. Each execution draws dozens and dozens more people into its web. The circle of tragedy is always expanding and ultimately, all of us are affected.

15 During the periods of publicity and ritual surrounding executions in several Southern states, I have watched with sadness as victims' families and friends often become public spectacles. They are subjected to infrequent indignities and damaging publicity at the time of trial. Healing is retarded as they are dragged through the experience again, usually years later, at the time of appeal and execution. "For many," says Howard Zehr, director of the Mennonite Central Committee's Office of Criminal Justice, "the ritual of the death penalty takes precedence over the ritual of mourning and remembrance."

16 I know of at least one Southern prison warden who, when asked how an execution affected him personally, tearfully explained: "This society makes me do its dirty work. I have to take care of these prisoners — one year, two years, maybe even 10 years. And then I have to kill them."

17 The death penalty creates more victims.

18 Former San Quentin warden Lawrence Wilson, who participated in a number of executions, told Oakland freelance journalist Michael Kroll: "You never get used to seeing [an execution]. You get sort of a sinking, sick feeling. After all, there's a guy in front of you, and he struggles to stay alive, but his life support system fails him. He expires before your eyes."

19 The death penalty dehumanizes.

20 When Robert Wayne Williams was executed in Louisiana last December, Governor David Treen, who refused to grant clemency to Williams, broke down and cried. He called his decision not to spare Williams' life "the most agonizing I've ever had to face." Sam Dalton, Williams' attorney, said, "I felt like I had been amputated when I heard he had been executed. It was a loss that I just couldn't believe."

21 The circle of tragedy grows.

22 And Howard Brodie, an artist for CBS News who witnessed the 1967 execution of Aaron Mitchell in California and the 1979 execution of John Spenkelink in Florida, called those experiences "the most dehumanizing of my entire life."

23 "The death penalty only allows us to extend the pain," says Virginia activist Marie Deans. "It allows us to continue to blame one another, to turn against one another, to learn to hate better."

24 Yes, I have seen the full effects of capital punishment. It is measurable in the strain and stress of broken families, ill health, alcoholism, mental breakdown, hospitalization, and for those who survive these ills, in a brutalization born of desperation. It is a brutalization that mars not only the lives of prisoners but of all those touched by the death penalty.

25 Colin Turnbull, the noted anthropologist, has undertaken a study of the death penalty and its effect on society. And he concludes:

"Until we face the harsh facts of what happens on death row and in the execution room, in the witness room and in the offices and homes of the prison officials, lawyers and judges, we are not entitled to have an opinion on capital punishment and call it just. If we were really concerned with the well-being of society, there would be little or no need for the death penalty in the first place."

26 There's the rub. Are we really concerned with society's welfare or are we content in merely providing ourselves with the illusion that something is being done? Do we really believe we will be able to get rid of evil by defining it out of the human species? Or is it no more than revenge, the need to strike back, to get even?

27 "If it is vengeance, that's bad for society," says New York Governor Mario Cuomo, one of four current U.S. governors opposed to the death penalty. "We don't have the right to get even. It reduces the value of life, and we've done that enough in past years."

28 But will we ever learn? Will we ever admit to our past mistakes and begin to explore more constructive alternatives to the death penalty, alternatives that still convey firmly and clearly that murder is wrong? I hope so.

29 I know it is not easy for any of us to ward off bitterness and the desire for retaliation. But I also believe that for too long we have treated violence with violence and that's why it never seems to end.

30 Coretta Scott King has lost both a husband and mother-in-law to murder. Still, she speaks out powerfully against the death penalty, against killing people who kill people. Hers, too, is a face I cannot forget. Nor can I forget her words:

31 "The truth is, we all pay for the death penalty because every time the state kills somebody, our society loses its humanity and compassion and we sow the seeds of violence. We legitimize retaliation as the way to deal with conflict. Yes, we all pay. And in this sense the death penalty means cruel and unusual punishment for not only the condemned prisoner but for the innocent as well, for all of us."

1. The first paragraph
    A. sets up the issue.
    B. provides needed background.
    C. states the thesis.
    D. refutes the opposition.
2. Van den Haag and Vodicka disagree on which of the following points?
    A. The deterrent value of capital punishment
    B. The religious basis of capital punishment
    C. The cruelty of capital punishment
    D. A and B
    E. A, B, and C
3. What would you say is the nature of the dispute between the authors on the points you identified in the preceding question?

4. Van den Haag believes that the Bible sanctions the death penalty but Vodicka disagrees. Their disagreement is basically
   A. verbal.
   B. factual.
   C. evaluative.
   D. interpretive.
   E. theoretical.
5. With which of the following statements would both authors agree?
   A. There is often an element of revenge connected with the death penalty.
   B. Some individuals appear to derive satisfaction from the execution of a murderer.
   C. Deriving satisfaction from the execution of a murderer is degrading.
   D. A and B
   E. A, B, and C
6. Do you think the series of examples offered in paragraphs 4–8 serve an argumentative purpose? Explain.
7. Which of the following statements are implied by paragraph 9?
   A. The incidents cited earlier (paragraphs 4–8) prove that capital punishment brutalizes us.
   B. A legal system should not be based on revenge.
   C. Capital punishment is institutionalized revenge.
   D. A and B
   E. A, B, and C
8. Neville and Nancy are talking about paragraph 9:

   NEVILLE : The author claims that capital punishment "brutalizes us all." I don't feel good about the death penalty. In fact, I find the whole idea of killing someone repulsive. And I have plenty of friends who feel the same way. But, like me, they still favor capital punishment.

   NANCY : You miss Vodicka's point. When he says that capital punishment "brutalizes us all," he means "all" collectively, not individually. It dehumanizes us as a people, as a civilized society.

   NEVILLE : Then why didn't he say that?

   NANCY : He did.

   NEVILLE : I don't think he did.

   What kind of dispute is this? Exactly how has the author's language given rise to it?

9. NEVILLE : The author claims that the ritual of capital punishment "extends the violence, provokes anger, and hinders, rather than encourages, healing" (paragraph 9). To me, the example the author gives of Steven Baker (paragraph 8) indicates the opposite. If Harris were executed, Baker would experience a catharsis. But if Harris could never be executed, Baker, likely as not, would forever stew in the juices of rage. So, for some people the impossibility of capital punishment could be as "degrading" as its enforcement.

   NANCY : Again, you miss Vodicka's point. He's saying that capital punishment, not its absence, degrades.

   NEVILLE : Yes, it degrades because in his view it provokes anger and hinders healing. What I'm saying is that the *absence* of capital punishment can have the same effect. And in that sense, not having the possibility of execution can be just as degrading.

Do you think Neville raises a good point? How might the author respond?

10. In paragraph 9, the author uses the emotive words "brutalizes," "revenge," "retaliation," and "lethal vengeance." Do you think he uses them legitimately, or do they have the effect of slanting the argument through word bias?

11. After reading paragraphs 4–8, Lester says: "The author's making too much of the events he describes. To me, they just show a bunch of people letting off steam. In fact, it's probably healthy for them to unload some of their pent-up anger and frustration." The author obviously would not agree with Lester's
   A. evaluation.
   B. interpretation.
   C. facts.
   D. A and B
   E. A, B, and C

12. LESTER: A sign that reads "Put the Animal to Sleep" or "Burn, Briley, Burn" isn't really a call for revenge. It's simply saying that people should get what they deserve. And who can seriously claim that a monstrous murderer doesn't deserve to die?

   Which of the following statements do you think is the *best* criticism of this passage?
   A. It draws a distinction without a difference.
   B. It assumes without demonstration that murderers "deserve" the death penalty.
   C. It slants through word bias.
   D. It employs a persuasive definition.

13. Governor Robb's description of the Richmond demonstration as "inappropriate behavior" (paragraph 10) is
   A. vague.
   B. ambiguous.
   C. euphemistic.
   D. meaningless.
   E. clear and precise.

14. In response to paragraph 10, Betty says, "Marie Deans confuses the meanings of the word *inappropriate*. When Robb called the demonstration 'inappropriate behavior,' he probably meant it was 'out of place' or 'in bad taste' or something like that. But Robb's decision to allow Briley to be executed wasn't inappropriate in this sense. As governor, Robb is empowered to stay the execution or not. Either decision would be *appropriate* for him to make as governor. When Deans says that Robb's behavior was inappropriate, she really means that it was immoral and that she disagrees with it, as she would with any decision to permit an execution. Robb's not guilty of any inconsistency, as Deans implies. Deans is guilty of shifting the meaning of the term *appropriate*." Do you agree with Betty or do you think she has made a distinction without a difference?

15. In paragraph 11, the words "ultimate," "nothing less than," and "total" function to

    A. qualify.
    B. quantify.
    C. intensify.
    D. signal a premise.

16. The headline "Killer Cheats Chair" (paragraph 13) is an example of
    A. emotive language.
    B. slanting through word bias.
    C. subjective connotation.
    D. A and B
    E. A, B, and C

17. The main point of paragraph 15 is that
    A. the death penalty is unjust.
    B. the media turn capital punishment cases into spectacles.
    C. the friends and relatives of victims are injured by the existence of capital punishment.
    D. mourning and remembrance should take precedence over the death penalty.

18. Hillary responds to paragraph 15 as follows: "There's no question that a death sentence sets off an almost interminable round of appeals. And, as a result, a lot of innocent people suffer. But that only shows there's something wrong with the appeals process, not with the death penalty. Let's reduce the harm to the innocent by limiting the appeals process, not abolishing the death penalty." Do you think that Hillary's attempt to clarify the issue is relevant and effective?

19. Which of the following statements, if true, would be the most effective rebuttal to Hillary's point?
    A. The appeals process costs taxpayers hundreds of thousands of dollars.
    B. Limiting the appeals process would encourage more death sentences.
    C. Trial attorneys oppose any limitation of the appeals process in capital punishment cases.
    D. Abridging or expediting the appeals process would deny the defendant due process and thus be unconstitutional.

20. What evidence does the author offer for asserting: "The death penalty creates more victims" (paragraph 17), "The death penalty dehumanizes" (paragraph 19), and "The circle of tragedy grows" (paragraph 21)?

21. In paragraph 25, Turnbull is quoted as saying: "If we were really concerned with the well-being of society, there would be little or no need for the death penalty in the first place." This statement seems to imply that anyone who favors the death penalty is not really concerned with the well-being of society. If it does imply this, what kind of definition is Turnbull offering for what it means to be "concerned with society's welfare"?
    A. stipulative
    B. lexical
    C. persuasive
    D. theoretical

22. Tom expresses a strong opinion about Turnbull's conclusion: "Turnbull is saying that only people with first-hand experience with the death penalty—lawyers, judges, prison officials, and people like that—are in a position to fairly evaluate

it. Couldn't it be that these people are *too* close to the so-called 'harsh facts' Turnbull alludes to? In fact, Vodicka cites plenty of cases of the emotional trauma the death penalty produced in people with a first-hand experience of the death penalty. Emotion and passion don't provide a good basis for formulating laws and punishments. What we need are clear, dispassionate minds making laws and deciding punishment — not ones clouded by passion. I'm not saying that the input of the people Turnbull has in mind isn't important — it is. But to say that only their opinions on the death penalty are legitimate is an open invitation to the substitution of passion for reason. And ironically, this is the very thing that abolitionists accuse capital punishment advocates of doing — surrendering to base emotion in demanding that the murderer be executed." What do you think of Tom's rebuttal to Turnbull?

23. Which of the following responses to Cuomo, King, and Vodicka (paragraphs 27–31) would be consistent with van den Haag's sentiments?
    A. They are confusing revenge and retaliation with retribution.
    B. One important function of the death penalty is to give social expression to our intrinsic appetite for revenge and to discourage disruptive private acts of revenge.
    C. In not executing murderers, society in fact loses its humanity by refusing to enforce the sacredness of human life.
    D. A and B
    E. A, B, and C

RELATED THEME TOPICS

In *Gregg v. George* (1976), the United States Supreme Court ruled that the death penalty does not violate the Eighth Amendment's prohibition against cruel and unusual punishment. Writing for the majority view, Justices Stewart, Powell, and Stevens explained:

> The instinct for retribution is part of the nature of man, and channeling that instinct in the administration of criminal justice serves an important purpose in promoting the stability of a society governed by law. When people begin to believe that organized society is unwilling or unable to impose upon criminal offenders the punishment they "deserve," then there are sown the seeds of anarchy — of self help, vigilante justice, and lynch law. . . . The decision that capital punishment may be the appropriate sanction in extreme cases is an expression of the community's belief that certain crimes are themselves so grievous an affront to humanity that the only adequate response may be the penalty of death. . . . The truth is that some crimes are so outrageous that society insists on adequate punishment, because the wrong-doer deserves it, irrespective of whether it is a deterrent or not.

In dissenting, Justice Marshall called the majority statement "wholly inadequate to justify the death penalty." Addressing the preceding argument, he wrote:

> Some of the language of the plurality's opinion appears positively to embrace this notion of retribution for its own sake as a justification of capital punishment.

The mere fact that the community demands the murderer's life in return for the evil he has done cannot sustain the death penalty, for as the plurality reminds us, "the Eighth Amendment demands more than that a challenged punishment be acceptable to contemporary society." To be sustained under the Eighth Amendment, the death penalty must "(comport) with the basic concept of human dignity at the core of the amendment"; the objective in imposing it must be "(consistent) with our respect for the dignity of other men." Under these standards, the taking of life "because the wrongdoer deserves it" surely must fall, for such a punishment has as its very basis the total denial of the wrongdoer's dignity and worth.

The death penalty, unnecessary to promote . . . any legitimate notion of retribution, is an excessive penalty forbidden by the Eighth and Fourteenth Amendments.

Write an essay in favor of the majority or dissenting opinion.

6

Linguistic Confusion II: Fallacies of Ambiguity

INTRODUCTION

In the last chapter, we looked at fallacies of linguistic confusion related to the capacities of language to persuade. Confusion can also arise when a word, phrase, or sentence of an argument is not clear and precise. **Fallacies of ambiguity are errors in reasoning or argument that arise when language is used that can be understood in more than one way.** Because language that invites multiple interpretations is not understandable, premises that contain ambiguous language are not acceptable and thus violate a basic criterion for a sound argument.

MODULE 6.1

EQUIVOCATION

The fallacy of equivocation consists in drawing (or leading someone to) an unwarranted conclusion by using a word or phrase in two different ways in the same argument.

For example, suppose someone argues:

Logic is the study of argument. But there's altogether too much argument in the world as it is. So, this world would be better off if people didn't study logic.

This argument is fallacious because two different senses of "argument" are confused in it. An argument, as used in logic, is a group of propositions, one of which is claimed to follow logically from the others. The word *argument* may also mean a bitter disagreement between individuals.

Although both meanings are legitimate, they should not be confused in the same argument. The premises of this argument are only plausible when "argument" is interpreted differently in each of them. Thus, "Logic is the study of groups of propositions, one of which is claimed to follow logically from the others," and "There's altogether too much bitter disagreement among individuals in the world as it is." When we state the premises this way, it is easy to see that the conclusion does not even appear to follow, although it appeared to in the original version. Of course, "argument" could carry the same meaning in both premises; however, the argument would lose its plausibility because it would have either the false premise "Logic is the study of bitter disagreements among individuals" or the mind-bending premise "There's already too much disagreement in the world as it is, too many groups of propositions, one of which is claimed to follow logically from the others."

As another example of the fallacy of equivocation:

People object to sexism and racism on grounds of discrimination. But what is objectionable about discrimination? We discriminate all the time — in the cars we buy, the foods we eat, the books we read, the friends we choose. The fact is that there's nothing wrong with discrimination. So, there's nothing wrong with discriminating against people on the basis of color or sex.

When applied to racism or sexism, *discrimination* means making a distinction in favor of or against a person on the basis of color or sex alone. As such, racial and sexual discrimination raise questions of social justice. When people object to racism and sexism on grounds of discrimination, then discrimination is understood to mean unfair selection. When applied to cars, foods, books, and friends, *discrimination* means to distinguish items on the basis of some standard, but not a moral one.

Notice how equivocation differs from semantical ambiguity. In equivocation, the meaning of a word has actually shifted in the argument — two separate meanings of a term are being used to produce the conclusion. Close inspection is enough to reveal those meanings. In semantic ambiguity, however, it is not clear which of several meanings a term is supposed to carry.

For example, having heard the testimony of Oliver North at the Iran-Contra hearings, someone says, "Based on all the testimony that was given, it's *fair* to say North was lying." "Fair" here is used ambiguously. It could mean "reasonable," "just," both, or possibly something else.

Contrast the *shift* in the meaning of the word "fair" in this argument:

A *fair* performance is a mediocre one.

In his treatment of subordinates, Oliver North was always *fair.* Therefore, Oliver North is a mediocre officer.

In this example, there is no question about the two separate meanings of *fair.* For the first premise to be plausible, "fair" must mean "moderately good." In the second, it means "impartial" or "showing no prejudice."

Equivocation gives two words the appearance of having the same meaning, when they do not. In longer arguments, deception of this kind can be subtle and difficult to spot. A word or phrase may function in one way in one part of the argument and function quite differently elsewhere in the argument. By shifting the word's meaning, the author may appear to be giving support for a conclusion or thesis simply because the words look or sound the same.

IN BRIEF   In good arguments, words or phrases employed or implied must retain the same meaning throughout the argument unless a shift in meaning is understood or stipulated. Absent this, the argument is deceptive. Whether or not the arguer intends the deception, the argument is fallacious.

EXERCISES ON EQUIVOCATION*

Can you spot the equivocation in these arguments?

1. Having first alerted local TV stations, some animal lovers are turning up on public land where hunting is permitted. They then proceed to ring cowbells or shout through bullhorns in order to frighten off game. They've even needled and badgered hunters. Asked to defend their behavior, one protester says: "We have as much right as the hunters to do what we please on public lands." (Hint: Is the hunter's "right" and protester's "right" identical in this matter?)
2. Letter to the editor: "I recently read that the Senate and House voted to extend the expiring Fairness Doctrine. This is proof again that our representatives can't help but preserve what's dead and useless."
3. Politics is an avenue to right public wrongs. The Democrats are holding the President's nominee to the Supreme Court hostage to politics. Therefore, the Democrats are only acting to right public wrongs.
4. "All issues are political issues, and politics itself is a mass of lies, evasion, folly, hatred, and schizophrenia" (George Orwell). (From which it presumably follows that all issues are lies, evasion, and so on.)
5. Minutes of a White House meeting on November 10, 1986, show that President Reagan led a White House effort to conceal facts about the secret arms deal with

Iran, when reports of the arms shipments to Iran had become public. Despite warnings by Secretary of State George Shultz, that the scheme had left U.S. antiterrorism efforts in a "state of total disintegration," Reagan fought to keep his arms-for-hostage deal going forward: "The rumors have endangered what we're doing (and) endangered our contacts (with Iran). When an American citizen is taken hostage a purpose of government is to go to his or her support," to which Secretary of State Shultz replied: "I agree that a purpose of government is to protect citizens, but the whole purpose is to protect them by discouraging terrorism." (Did Shultz shift the meaning of any of Reagan's terms?)

6. Don Hewitt, creator of "60 Minutes," has argued that if broadcasters are required by the "Fairness Doctrine" to broadcast opposing views, then newspapers should, too. Before the FCC abolished the Fairness Doctrine in August 1987, television and radio broadcasts were distinguished from print media on grounds of the former's use of the public airwaves. Arguing his case, Hewitt said, "Newspapers have the airwaves. . . . They have satellites. . . . There should be a fairness doctrine for any newspaper that moves its news over satellites." (Has Hewitt shifted the meaning "airwaves"?)

7. Well before they summoned Admiral Poindexter for questioning, the Iran-Contra congressional committee had established that the CIA was not involved in the affair. When Poindexter was asked whether as head of the NSC he was "complying with the letter and spirit of the Boland Amendment," he said he was. When it was later established that the NSC was in fact not in compliance, Poindexter was asked to explain his answer. He said that he took "complying with the letter and spirit of the Boland Amendment" to mean that the CIA was not involved. (Do you think Poindexter altered the meaning of Congress's question to avoid a forthright reply?)

AMPHIBOLY

The fallacy of amphiboly consists in drawing (or leading one to) an unwarranted conclusion by making an assertion the meaning of which is not clear because of its grammatical construction. Suppose, for example, you come across this item in your college newspaper: "The noted author and lecturer, Dr. Isaac X. Weatherspoon, will talk to graduating seniors about job opportunities in the theatre tonight." Will the good doctor speak in the theatre, or will he speak of job opportunities in the field of drama? The sentence is unclear because it is poorly constructed and thus invites an unwarranted conclusion. Probably, the writer meant, "Tonight in the theatre, Weatherspoon will talk to graduating seniors about job opportunities." But the reader cannot know this for sure and could very well infer that Weatherspoon will speak about job opportunities in the theatrical profession.

The difference between amphibolous ambiguity and semantic ambiguity is that the former deals with misleading or unclear syntax (that is, sentence structure), and the latter with misleading or unclear words or phrases. Thus, amphibolies are corrected by reconstructing the sentences; semantic ambiguity is corrected by clarifying the ambiguous words or phrases.

The following are among the typical grammatical errors that make a sentence ambiguous:

1. Unclear pronoun reference, as in "Alice would never talk to Pamela when she is on a date." (Who is on the date, Pamela or Alice?)
2. Elliptical construction (that is, the omission of one or more words that are supposed to be understood but must be supplied), as in "Ethel likes bridge better than her husband." (Does she like bridge better than she likes her husband or better than her husband likes bridge?)
3. Unclear modifiers, as in "I have to take the final exam in two hours." (Will you take the final two hours from now, or will you be limited to two hours to complete it?)
4. Missing or misplaced punctuation, as in "Anthropology is the science of man embracing woman." Without a comma after "man," this course may be X-rated.

The problem with syntactical ambiguity in general is that it invites multiple interpretations. Consider, for example, this passage from a newspaper account of a proposed Richard Nixon Library to be housed at Duke University:

> On the face of it the proposal by Duke University President Terry Sanford seems innocuous enough. By donating land where an estimated 36 million pages of documents and 880 reels of tape from Nixon's six-year presidency could be housed, university scholars would gain access to a great wealth of research material.

The second sentence, which supports the first, is amphibolous. Who is donating the land? The sentence says that university scholars are, a most unlikely possibility given the modest means of the typical university scholar.

Here are two other examples taken from newspapers:

> —Some 50,000 undocumented immigrants have gotten a preliminary OK to live legally in America during the first month of the government's unprecedented amnesty offer.

> —Tammy Faye Bakker, wife of PTL leader, Jim Bakker, speaking of her life since the couple's topple from position and power: "I wake up every morning wishing they had killed me, and Jim does, too."

Although we might be initially confused by sentences like these, the confusion is short-lived because one interpretation typically is more plausible. Thus, Tammy surely means that both she and Jim share the same wish, that the vaunted "they" had killed them both. It is less likely, though possible, that she means Jim also wishes "they" had killed her.

Sometimes, syntactical ambiguities defy easy resolution. Take, for example, this item:

> *Moscow* Aides to Mikhail Gorbachev, the Soviet leader, say their boss wants to sign an arms pact with George Bush this year. Because it threatens their plans, the Kremlin brass recoils from the recent pounding Bush has suffered at the hands of conservatives. Yet Russian big shots sense that a reserve of goodwill toward Bush on his home turf will pull him through. . . .

Given the ambiguous syntax of the second sentence, we do not know whether the arms pact or the pounding Bush has suffered at the hands of conservatives threatens the plans of Soviet brass.

Finally, Oliver North made the following statement, commenting to the Iran-Contra committee on traveller's checks he kept in his office to help finance contra supply operations and other activities:

> You gentlemen may not agree that we should have been pursuing covert operations at the NSC, but we were. We had an operational account, and we used the money for legitimate purposes within that covert operation.

Does this statement mean that the purposes were legitimate when viewed within the context of covert operations or that the purposes were in and of themselves legitimate? It makes a difference.

EXERCISES ON AMPHIBOLY

Explain why each of the following sentence constructions is amphibolous. Then suggest a clarifying revision.

1. Ad for a fitness program: "Sign up for our new fitness program and learn how to have a trim, svelte figure in only 3 weeks!"
2. Headline: "Zsa Zsa Gabor loses appeal"
3. News item: "Justice William Brennan, the Supreme Court's senior member and leading liberal, is following the advice of two justices with prostate cancer by being tested at the Mayo Clinic for prostate trouble."
4. "Governments must move to dismantle trade destroying subsidies and labor laws that promote unemployment."
5. "Judge Bork's nomination to the Supreme Court is being opposed by some because he practices judicial restraint. That means he won't put their opinions ahead of the law; he won't put his own opinions ahead of the law. And that's the way it should be." (Ronald Reagan)
6. "A U.S. Chamber of Commerce study suggests that up to 75 percent of all employees steal at least once, and half of these steal at least twice. . . ."
   (William A. McGurn, "Spotting the Thieves Who Work Among Us," *Wall Street Journal,* March 7, 1988, p. 18.)
7. I am very grateful that we have education up where it's high on the education agenda of this country.
   (Secretary of Education, T. H. Bell)
8. Message on bathroom stall doors of New York's Hard Rock Cafe: "No drugs or nuclear weapons."
9. In a May 1982 press conference, President Reagan tried to answer a question about arms control negotiations by observing that land-based nuclear missiles could not be recalled once dispatched. He then tried to contrast the danger from such missiles with those launched elsewhere: "Those that are carried in bombers, those that are carried in ships of one kind or another, or submersibles, you are dealing

there with a conventional type of weapon or instrument, and those instruments can be intercepted. They can be recalled if there has been a miscalculation.''

MODULE 6.2

ACCENT

Unintended meaning can arise not only from syntactical ambiguity, but also from confusion regarding emphasis or accent. **The fallacy of accent consists in drawing an unintended conclusion (or directing one to it) by the use of improper emphasis.** The improper emphasis, in turn, can result when: 1. Certain words are wrongly stressed; 2. when words, phrases, sentences, or even whole paragraphs are taken out of context and thus given a significance they were not intended to have; or 3. when a statement is spoken in a tone of voice not intended for it.

Consider, for example, this exchange:

BETH: Why do you dislike Joe so much when the *Bible* says, "Love thy neighbor."
JACK: But Joe's not my neighbor. He doesn't live anywhere near me.

The Biblical injunction quoted means that we should honor and respect *all* persons. But by improperly stressing the word "neighbor," Jack draws the unintended conclusion that the injunction applies only to people who live near him.

Confusion arising from accent is rarely this simple. For example, all of us are familiar with the sentiment expressed in the Declaration of Independence, "All men are created equal." One can wonder whether Thomas Jefferson meant that all men are *created* equal, or that all men are created *equal*. If the former, we might infer a narrow ideal of equality that focuses on the differences that distinguish, even separate, people after their birth. But if the emphasis belongs on "equal," we might infer a more extended ideal of equality. (An emphasis on "men," moreover, would impose gender limitations on the extension of equality.)

A common form of the accent fallacy involves the out-of-context quote. For example, suppose that Professor Johnson says to her class, "Executing convicted murderers is certainly the best form of punishment from a strictly economic view. After all, it's cheaper than housing a criminal for life." A student leaves class and tells a friend, "Professor Johnson said today that executing convicted murderers is certainly the best form of punishment." Yes, Johnson did say that, but she qualified her judgment.

Here is another example of out-of-context misrepresentation:

When asked whether he thought excommunicating Catholics who take a public stand in favor of abortion would rally antiabortion sentiment in the United States, a Catholic bishop replied, "I don't think it would help one bit to change American's thinking on abortion."

In context, this statement meant that, in the bishop's view, excommunicating Catholics who publicly express a pro-choice position on abortion would not be an effective way to increase antiabortion; in fact, it would probably retard it, given the abortion sentiment in the United States and belief in Church/State separation. In the following example, notice how the writer of this letter to the editor draws an unintended conclusion by taking the statement out of context:

> I was shocked to hear an American cleric — a bishop at that — say he didn't think it would help to change America's thinking on abortion. Doesn't he understand the Church's position on abortion? If abortion is evil, as the Church teaches, then we all should avoid it. With all due respect, Your Eminence, outlawing abortion certainly *would* help America regain its spirituality!

There is nothing wrong with quoting out of context so long as the quote fairly represents the speaker or writer's intended meaning. But it is fallacious to draw an unintended inference on the basis of an out-of-context quote. In this regard, be alert to the abuse of ellipsis points, which are used to indicate the omission of words. Used fairly, the ellipsis helps us write economically. Used unfairly, it warps meaning. For example, suppose a film critic wrote of a movie: "Despite an occasional and usually contrived warm, humorous moment, this film is the worst piece of film making that it's been my misfortune to see all year!" In the hands of the film's promoters, this devastating review might become: ". . . warm, humorous. . . !"

IN BRIEF   The accent fallacy can be quite difficult to detect when it results from the subtle change in a speaker's voice inflection. A sentence can easily take on different meanings depending on the stress or accent given to a word or phrase. When accenting from sarcasm or mocking intonation, for example, leads an audience to an unwarranted conclusion, the speaker is misleading the audience, even though the words themselves might not be expressing an untrue statement.

INNUENDO

Innuendo consists of implying a judgment, usually derogatory, on the basis of words that suggest, but do not assert, a conclusion. Suppose, for example, that someone asks you whether a couple you know is still married. You may reply directly, "Yes," or you may say, "Yes, *as of today*." The first response carries no implication, the second does. Later that day, your friend meets the couple in question and says, "I hear your marriage is on the rocks." They are outraged. "Where did you hear that?" they ask her. She tells them you told her. The next day the couple pay you a visit and dress you down for spreading malicious gossip. "But I never said your marriage was through," you protest, but they are not appeased.

Now you cannot blame your friend for inferring from what you said that the couple's marriage was tenuous. Your choice of words, "as of today," implied that. You set her up to infer that the couple's marriage was in imminent danger. Nevertheless, your friend had no *logical* grounds for drawing the inference she did. Similarly, without providing evidence for your implication, you had no *logical* grounds for suggesting it through innuendo.

Sometimes innuendo can have far-reaching effects. For example, during a meeting of the House Foreign Affairs subcommittee on Europe and the Middle East, Chairperson Lee H. Hamilton (D-IN) asked John H. Kelly, assistant secretary of state for the Middle East, if the United States would come to Kuwait's defense if it were invaded by Iraq. Kelly responded that the United States had no defense treaty with Kuwait. That sounded as if the United States would not come to Kuwait's aid, which of course it did just days later when that nation was invaded. Hamilton subsequently scolded Kelly publicly for sending mixed signals to Iraqi President Saddam Hussein. "Your response left the impression with me that if Kuwait was attacked we would not respond," Hamilton told Kelly. Representative Tom Lanton (D-CA) agreed, "Obviously . . . the impression that was left with our chairman was the same impression that was left with Saddam Hussein." Then Lanton added, lest there be any doubt about what he was implying, "This obsequious treatment of him [Saddam] by a large variety of high-ranking officials encouraged him to take this action."

As with most fallacies, the presence of innuendo in longer arguments can be rather furtive. Through implication, authors may be conveying an impression that goes beyond the literal meaning of their words. Consider, for example, how in this paragraph, the author uses one carefully chosen illustration to imply, but never assert, that President Reagan is an autocrat:

> "Can't we do something unilaterally?" (President Reagan) asks after Congress
> passes the Boland Amendment. The question, which Poindexter claims to have
> taken as his commission to use the profits from trading arms for hostages to subsi-
> dize secret attacks on Nicaragua, is in the great tradition of autocratic rulers. In
> olden days, kings merely had to make their wishes known for some loyal servant to
> turn royal passion into policy. Henry II of England, for example, just had to ask,
> "Who will free me of this tumultuous priest?" and Thomas Becket was promptly mar-
> tyred in the cathedral. . . . (Richard J. Bafnet, senior fellow of the Institute for Policy
> Studies.)

Consider this passage:

> The reason I have considered myself a conservative for twenty-five years is that it ap-
> peared to me that conservatives are people who believe in universal and objective
> principles of morality. (Jim Warner, White House senior policy analyst)

Innuendo: Liberals do not believe in universal and objective principles of morality.

Sometimes, by putting words or phrases in quotation marks, writers imply negative judgments. For example:

Speaking of . . .

Innuendo

A Sobering Word

In his book, *The Old Shipmasters of Salem*, Charlie E. Trow recounts this exquisite example of innuendo:

> Captain L. had a first mate who was at times addicted to the use of strong drink, and occasionally, as the slang has it, "got full." The ship was lying in port in China, and the mate had "beenfull" on shore and had there indulged rather freely in some of the vile compounds common in Chinese ports. He came on board, "drunk as a lord," as though he had a mortgage on the whole world. The captain, who rarely ever touched liquor himself, was greatly disturbed by the disgraceful conduct of his officer, particularly as the crew had all observed his condition. One of the duties of the first officer is to write up the "log" each day but as that worthy was not able to do it, the captain made the proper entry, but added: "The mate was drunk all day." The ship left port the next day and the mate got "sobered off." He attended to his writing at the proper time, but was appalled when he saw what the captain had done. He went on deck, and soon after the following colloquy took place:
>
> "Capt'n, why did you write in the log yesterday that I was drunk all day?"
> "It was true, wasn't it?"
> "Yes, but what will the owners say if they see it? It will hurt me with them."
>
> But the mate could get nothing more from the captain than "It was true, wasn't it?" The next day, when the captain was examining the book, he found at the bottom of the mate's entry of observation, course, winds, and tides: "The captain was sober all day."

(Charlie E. Trow. *The Old Shipmasters of Salem.* New York: Macmillan, 1905, pp. 14–15.)

If you were the ship's owners, what would you infer?

> Senator Foggyhead, the "economist" that he is, thinks that we can eliminate our deficits simply by raising taxes.

If the writer really believed that the senator was a reputable economist, he would not have put "economist" in quotes. By doing so, he implies that Foggyhead's economics are worthy of his name. The same innuendo occurs by using a term such as "so-called," as in "Foggyhead, the so-called economist."

IN BRIEF   In confronting innuendo, always try to make the conclusion explicit. Require a defense for the implied conclusion. Veiled meanings are acceptable so long as they are aligned not only with purpose but reasons and evidence as well. The fallacy of innuendo, like accent, does not consist in the use of emphasis but in its *unfair* or *inaccurate* use.

EXERCISES ON ACCENT AND INNUENDO

Explain how accent or innuendo is used in the following passages to imply or infer an erroneous, or at least questionable, conclusion.

1. Campaign pitch: "Vote for me and restore honesty to government."
2. It is said that when one-time heavyweight boxing champion, Max Baer, suffered a heart attack in a Hollywood hotel room, he phoned to the front desk for emergency help. "Do you want the house doctor?" the clerk asked. "No silly," Max responded, "a people doctor."
3. When asked why he robbed banks, notorious bank robber Willy Sutton replied: "Because that's where the money is."
4. Sam Donaldson (ABC News): "Mr. President, Senator Jesse Helms has been saying on the Senate floor that Martin Luther King, Jr., had communist associations, was a communist sympathizer. Do you agree?" President Reagan: "We'll know in about thirty-five years, won't we?" (At that time records that might throw light on that subject will be unsealed.)
5. On the day that the Nixon "enemies list" was revealed in testimony to the Watergate Committee, a reporter asked columnist Mary McGrory, "It says here that you write daily 'Hate Nixon' articles." "That's not true," replied McGrory, "I only write three days a week."
6. Nonplussed dad trying to assemble a Christmas toy: "It says here on the box that a child of five can put this thing together. Send somebody to fetch a five-year-old, will you?"
7. "The meek shall inherit the earth, but not its mineral rights."
   (J. Paul Getty)
8. President Reagan, campaigning against the Democratic budget proposal: "The so-called budget process . . . that's why I have come to you, the American people, asking for your support to put pressure on Congress to bring reliability and credibility to the federal budget process."
9. ". . . [I]f the (Supreme) Court (in deciding that the theory of biological evolution could be taught in public schools without having to give creation theory equal time) was saying that only the theory of evolution may be taught in public schools, we are in deep trouble. (Justice William) Brennan (who wrote the majority opinion) walked to the very brink of such a disaster. The majority offered but a single sentence of reassurance: '. . . teaching a variety of scientific theories about the origins of human kind to school children might be validly done with a clear secular intent of enhancing the effectivenes of science instruction.' Note the heavy verb: This might be done. Brennan's doubt is as palpable as a stone." (James Kilpatrick, syndicated columnist) [Hint: What terms did Kilpatrick accent to draw his inference? Do you think that accenting "validly done" in the Brennan quote would suggest a different conclusion?]
10. In his essay, "Self Reliance," Ralph Waldo Emerson wrote: "A foolish consistency is the hobgoblin of little minds, adored by little statesmen and philosophers and divines. With consistency a great soul has simply nothing to do. He may as well concern himself with his shadow on the wall. Speak what you think now in hard words and tomorrow speak what tomorrow thinks in hard words again, though

it contradict everything you said today." Suppose that in a discussion with a friend you take a stand which is inconsistent with a position you previously took. When asked to explain your change of mind, you reply: "There's no need to explain it, for as Emerson once said, 'consistency is the hobgoblin of little minds.' " Would you be quoting Emerson out of context fairly or unfairly? Explain.

MODULE 6.3

COMPOSITION

The fallacy of composition consists in reasoning improperly from a property of a member of a group to a property of the group itself. For example, a man observes that every member of a local club is wealthy and therefore infers the club itself must be wealthy. It may not be.

What the man fails to realize is that a whole represents something different from simply the sum or the combination of its parts. The whole either takes on a new character because of its composition or at least does not maintain the particular character of its parts. Thus, each chapter of a book, considered individually, may be a masterpiece, but the book, considered as a whole, may not be. Each member of an orchestra may be an outstanding musician, but that does not mean that the orchestra as a whole is outstanding. People who commit the composition fallacy ignore or forget that integration of the parts often alters the character of the whole. "Should we not assume that just as the eye, the hand, the foot, and in general each part of the body clearly has its own proper function, so man too has some function over and above the function of his part?" asks Aristotle in his *Nicomachean Ethics*. No, we should not. That the parts of a human have a function does not necessarily mean that the integration of the parts (that is, the human being) has a function.

The composition fallacy also results when the collective and distributive meanings of a term are confused. Consider, for example, this argument against urban mass transit as a way to control pollution:

> Air pollution in Los Angeles, or any great metropolitan area for that matter, won't be helped by making people forsake their cars for public buses. Buses obviously are worse polluters than automobiles.

Considered *distributively*, an *individual* bus does emit more pollutants than an *individual* car. But considered *collectively*, automobiles produce more pollution because there are far more of them than buses.

Similarly, more people die in plane crashes than in car accidents when each is considered individually. But thousands more die in auto accidents every year than in plane crashes, when the two are compared collectively.

DIVISION

The fallacy of division consists in reasoning improperly from a property of the group to a property of a member of the group. Division is the reverse of composition. Thus, observing that a club is rich, a man infers that each club member must also be wealthy or that member, Stone Broke, must be. However, just as a property of the part does not imply a property of the whole, so a property of the whole does not imply a property of the part. That a book is a masterpiece does not mean that each chapter is; that an orchestra is outstanding does not imply that each member is a virtuoso.

According to historian David Fischer, fellow historian Vernon Parrington committed the division fallacy more than once in his monumental *Main Currents of American Thoughts,* as a result of framing problems in group stereotypes and transferring the stereotypes to individual members. Fischer illustrates:

> Most Calvinists were theological determinists. Most New England Puritans were Calvinists. Therefore, most New England Puritans were theological determinists. The fortunes of the Federalists decayed after 1880. Joseph Dennie was a Federalist. Therefore, the fortunes of Joseph Dennie decayed after 1800.[1]

Like composition, another form of division fallacy arises from a confusion of the collective and distributive uses of a term. For example, to argue that because college students study philosophy, therefore each, or even any particular, college student studies philosophy would be to commit this form of the division fallacy. Taken collectively, as a whole, college students do study philosophy, but each individual college student does not. Again, collectively considered, automobiles use more fuel than buses, but an individual automobile uses less fuel than an individual bus.

IN BRIEF   The implicit premise employed in the fallacy of composition is unacceptable. It is false that what is true of the parts is necessarily true of the whole. The implicit premise employed in the fallacy of division is unacceptable, because it is false that what is true of the whole must necessarily be true of the parts.

EXERCISES ON COMPOSITION AND DIVISION*

Explain the fallacy of composition or division present in each of the following arguments.

1. ". . . [S]pace is nothing but a relation. For, in the first place, any space must consist of parts; and if the parts are not spaces, the whole is not space."
   (F. H. Bradley, *Appearance and Reality.*)

---

[1]David Fischer. *Historians' Fallacies.* (New York: Harper Row, 1970), p. 222.

2. In selecting an all-time National Football League (NFL) team, members of the Pro Football Writers' Association did not select a single member of the Pittsburgh Steelers. Steelers' President Dan Rooney thought this an indefensible oversight. ". . . [E]verybody has players that they think should be on there," he said, "but we did happen to play the best football that was ever played in the NFL for at least six years, if not more."

3. Letter to the editor: "You report that your readers, by a margin of 2 to 1, disapprove of President Bush's invading Panama, capturing Manuel Noriega, and returning him to the U.S. for trial. Yet, national reports indicate an approval rating of Bush's tactics, by over 50 to 1. Obviously, your survey has about as much credibility as the Panamanian gangster Noriega."

4. "Once again, in the Iran-Contra hearings, as in those of Watergate, we are witnessing the power of television to turn important current events into an enthralling immediate experience for scores of millions of Americans. We see the medium's power to inform in vividly impactive ways the individual minds that become, collectively, the American public mind, and to arouse strong emotions pro and con [about] the actors in public affairs. But surely this demonstration is also a test of the capacity of individual American minds, hence of the general public mind, to deal in rationally judgmental ways with information obtained in this way—obtained, that is, through dramatic audio-visual experience. . . ."
(Historian Kenneth Davis)

5. Early in 1988, Transportation Secretary James Burnley IV proposed rules to test a half-million pilots and aviation industry employees for drugs. "Every day millions of Americans put their trust and confidence in the aviation system and its workers," the secretary explained. "The abuse of drugs by airline employees is a life-threatening violation of that trust." Asked to cite evidence of the widespread use of drugs in the aviation industry, Burnley admitted he could not. Nevertheless, "I think there's compelling evidence that we've got a pervasive drug problem in America today and (therefore) aviation is not exempt."

6. During the 1988 presidential campaign, Democratic candidate Michael Dukakis argued that he could do for America what he had done as governor of Massachusetts. Dukakis boasted that in Massachusetts 300,000 jobs had been created since 1984, that unemployment had been kept under 3 percent, and taxes and spending had been kept in check. If he could do it there, asked Dukakis and his supporters, why not in the whole nation?

7. "No reason can be given why the general happiness is desirable, except that each person, so far as he believes it to be attainable, desires his own happiness. This, however, being a fact, we have not only all the proof which the case admits of, but all which it is possible to require, that happiness is a good, that each person's happiness is good to that person, and that the general happiness, therefore, a good to the aggregate of persons."
(John Stuart Mill, *Utilitarianism*)

8. "The pawnbroker thrives on the irregularities of youth; the merchant on a scarcity of goods; the architect and contractor on the destruction of buildings; lawyers and judges on disputes and illegalities; the military on war; physicians on sickness; and morticians on death. If, then, we have more profligacy, destruction, lawlessness,

war, disease, and death, we shall have unparalleled prosperity."
(Michael de Montaigne, "That One Man's Profit is Another's Loss")

MODULE 6.4

HYPOSTATIZATION

The fallacy of hypostatization consists in creating confusion by personifying ideas, concepts, or inanimate objects. To personify is to attribute to things and animals qualities that, strictly speaking, are attributable only to human beings. For example, a headline that reads "Drugs Aim Damaging Blow to American Worker's Productivity" implies that drugs are purposive, that is, they can have goals and purposes. When we hypostatize, we treat ideas, concepts, or inanimate things in this manner. Thus, "Big business lacks a soul," "The hand of government reaches deep into everyone's pockets," and "Democracy cries out for citizens' participation in the electoral process."

Perhaps the most dangerous aspect of hypostatization in argument is that it can mask responsibility and serve as pseudojustification for questionable activity. The highly emotive phrases *national security* and *national interests,* for example, have been hypostatized to account for all kinds of dubious conduct, from lying to violating constitutional rights, to supporting notorious regimes, to overthrowing foreign governments. Thus, we have had wiretaps, burglaries, and illicit payoffs that supposedly were conducted because national security or national interests "demanded" such actions. In the late 1960s and early 1970s, U.S. pilots were bombing Cambodia, although U.S. Government representatives were telling the people and Congress that no such bombing was occurring. Later, when the truth came out, government officials said that national security "demanded" the bombing.

In marketing, advertisers have elevated hypostatization to a new level of consumer manipulation with the introduction of "brand personality," which refers to how a brand makes people feel about it. Some ad agencies and their clients believe that brand personality is what separates exceptional advertising from the ordinary. By their account, Marlboro has brand personality, and Pall Mall does not. Charmin toilet paper does, but Scott Tissue does not.

Before it can be shaped, we are told, a brand personality must be defined. So, some agencies are trying to describe their products as people. Jell-O, for example, "is the very nice lady who lives next door," says Joseph Plummer, research director at Young & Rubicam, the product's agency. "She's not too old-fashioned, loves children and dogs, and has a little streak of creativity, but isn't avant-garde."[2] Once a personality

---

[2]Bill Abrams, "Ad Men Say Brand Personality Is As Critical As The Product," *The Wall Street Journal,* August 13, 1981, p. 25.

is defined, it can be used to determine such features as the advertisement's tone, participants, and locale. Thus, in keeping with Oil of Olay's "character," which is described as "a little sophisticated, foreign, mysterious, and slightly exotic," Young & Rubicam executives design exotic settings and focus most skin care products on a model.

By developing brand personality, advertisers treat their products as people that consumers can look on as buddies or pals. Thus, when properly developed, says Plummer, brand personality results not just in purchase motivation, but in a friendship between product and consumer. Right. Next time you need five bucks, try asking a bowl of Jell-O for it.

EXERCISES ON HYPOSTATIZATION

Explain and discuss the use of hypostatization in the following passages.

1. Bumper sticker: "Stand up to authority."
2. Letter to the editor: "The government was right in capturing General Noriega for trial in the U.S. Noriega broke the law. And justice demands that lawbreakers be punished."
3. Editorial: "The hue and cry resounding in the land over the fires ravaging Yellowstone National Park miss the point. Nature caused these fires, and what nature destroys she also restores. In time, nature shall replenish Yellowstone. So, rather than deploring the destruction, we should view it in the context of Nature's wondrous plan of death and rebirth."
4. "THE SYSTEM IS THE SOLUTION — AT&T
   THE SYSTEM IS THE PROBLEM — *The Progressive*
   If you are one of the growing number of Americans who realize that AT&T's slogan means, 'What's good for big business is good for America,' then . . . welcome to *The Progressive,* the monthly magazine that knows it's long past time to make fundamental change. More and more of us see that:
   —The System squanders our nation's wealth.
   —The System rapes our natural and human environments.
   —The System pours hundreds of billions of dollars down a rat hole called 'national security.'
   —The System puts profit ahead of people.
   The System works, all right — it works for AT&T and Lockheed, for IBM and Exxon — but it doesn't work for us, the American people."
   (Ad for *The Progressive;* reported in S. Morris Engel, *Analyzing Informal Fallacies.*)
5. "Our sensitive child. Among all our children the Pinot Chardonnay grapes are perhaps the most delicate. Shy and temperamental, they do poorly in most climates. Yet, here in the Almaden Vineyards in Northern California, warmed by the sun and cooled by the night breezes of the Pacific, they ripen to an abundant perfection. Pinot Chardonnay grapes — we coddle them, nurture them, encourage them along. The result is a most distinguished white wine. Golden in color,

full-bodied, fragrant and smooth. A wine reminiscent of the great still champagnes. Yes, we are proud parents."
(Ad for Almaden Vineyards)

IMPROVING PERFORMANCE

SUMMARY-TEST QUESTIONS FOR CHAPTER 6*

1. Drawing or leading someone to an unwarranted conclusion by using a word in two different ways in an argument is termed_____.
   For example:_____

   _____.

2. What is the difference between semantical ambiguity and equivocation? Between amphiboly and equivocation?
3. The only way to clear up an amphiboly is to rewrite the sentence. True or False? For example:

   _____

   _____.

4. Mom tells little Greta: "Don't eat any cookies before dinner. You'll spoil your appetite." When Mom leaves the kitchen, Greta helps herself to a big piece of chocolate cake and, as a result, does not want any dinner. Mom is furious. "Didn't I tell you not to eat before dinner?" she asks the child. "No," says the precocious tyke, "You said not to eat any *cookies* before dinner." What is the fallacy in Greta's reasoning?
5. What inference does each of the following sentences invite you to make?
   A. Smith has not been fired, yet.
   B. I'm running for governor in order to restore honesty and integrity to that office.
   C. Today's "liberated" woman considers the "right" to abortion as basic as the right to vote and views anyone who thinks otherwise a "sexist."
6. In the _____ fallacy, one erroneously assumes that a property of a member of a group must be a property of the group itself. But in the _____ fallacy, one assumes that a property of the group must necessarily be shared by the members of the group.
7. Identify and explain the fallacy, if any, in each of the following arguments.
   A. I see plenty of kids, but none who are playing. So I needn't slow down for the little dears because the road sign only told me to be cautious of children playing.
   B. You cannot condemn my rather unorthodox strategies. National security dictated my every action.
   C. All men are created equal. So, since you're a woman, your opinion isn't worth anything.
   D. Diamonds are rarely found in this part of the world. So, be careful not to misplace your wedding ring.
   E. You have the right to have an abortion. What's right for you to do, you ought to do. Therefore, you ought to have an abortion.
   F. It's ridiculous to say that America has poor people. Isn't America the richest nation on earth?

G. Atoms are so small they can't be seen. Since all matter consists of atoms, it follows that all matter is invisible. From which it further follows that you never saw what you just read!

H. I don't see how you can consider my boy a troublemaker. Our family is known for their upright and honorable behavior.

I. Why aren't you applying to any of the Ivy League Colleges to study engineering? Don't you know that they are among the best universities in the world?

J. Unexpected events happen almost every day. But what happens almost every day is to be expected. Therefore, unexpected events are expected events.

K. It's perfectly all right for businesspeople to set their own prices. So, I don't see what's wrong with all businesspeople getting together to set the prices of the items they all make.

L. Dizzy: I feel great!
Daffy: Why's that?
Dizzy: I was mugged last night.
Daffy: What are you—some kind of nut?
Dizzy: Listen and learn, pal. According to the latest figures, a person is mugged once a year in this city.
Daffy: So what's your point?
Dizzy: It's only January. I'm looking at eleven mug-free months, dummy!
Daffy: You lucky stiff—I've never been mugged.

CRITICAL THINKING APPLICATIONS

1. In her book, *The Gift of Tongues,* Margaret Schlauch recounts the illuminating story of a little girl who, having recently learned to read, was spelling out a political article in the newspaper. "Father," she asked, "what is Tammany Hall?" And her father replied in the voice usually reserved for the taboos of social communication, "You'll understand that when you grow up, my dear." According to this adult whim of evasion, she desisted from her inquiries; but something in Daddy's tone had convinced her that Tammany Hall must be connected with illicit *amour,* and for many years she could not hear this political institution mentioned without experiencing a secret non-political thrill. (Reported in Irving Copi, *Introduction to Logic.*) (Tammany Hall was an organization of the Democratic party in New York City, founded as a fraternal society and later associated with considerable political corruption.) **What did "Tammany Hall" suggest to the little girl? What led the girl to this erroneous inference? Can you recall ever having formed a false belief based on someone's tone of voice?**

   The questions in this group of exercises (2–7) ask you to analyze and evaluate the reasoning in the passages. **Read the passages carefully, keeping in mind what you have learned about ambiguity. Then answer the question asked. In each case, explain your answer.**

2. EVERLAST GUM offers you twice as much flavor for the money as DOUBLE BUBBLE. Here's why. A stick of EVERLAST is twice as large as a stick of DOUBLE

BUBBLE. And the more gum, the more flavor. It's that simple. So, if you want more flavor in your gum, try EVERLAST.

Which of the following propositions, if true, would undercut the persuasive appeal of this ad? (More than one answer is possible.)

A. For the same price, a package of EVERLAST has twice as many sticks as a package of DOUBLE BUBBLE.

B. The flavor in DOUBLE BUBBLE is more concentrated than in EVERLAST.

C. A stick of DOUBLE BUBBLE weighs twice as much as a stick of EVERLAST.

3. It's impossible to foretell the future, as this example will prove. Let's suppose that a woman could foresee that she would be killed in a plane crash on her way to a business meeting the next day. She'd obviously cancel the trip, or at least not travel by plane. Therefore, since she wouldn't be killed in a plane crash the next day, it cannot in any way be said that she foretold the future.

Which of the following criticisms of this argument best explains its weakness?

A. The author never explains how the woman could alter the future.

B. The author never explains how this woman, or anyone for that matter, could foretell the future.

C. The argument is inconsistent.

D. The argument begs the question.

E. The author uses the word "future" in two different ways.

4. When you enroll with Computech Professional Training School, you're guaranteed the services of our placement center. Last year, over 90 percent of our graduates who asked us to help them find jobs found them! So, if you want a promising career in the exciting world of computers, enroll with COMPUTECH.

Which of the following questions would be appropriate to ask in evaluating COMPUTECH's claim? (More than one answer is possible.)

A. How many COMPUTECH graduates asked for assistance?

B. How many students did COMPUTECH graduate last year?

C. Of those who asked for assistance, how many found jobs in the areas for which they were trained?

D. Did COMPUTECH find the jobs or did the graduates find them on their own?

5. "Whom did you pass on the road?" the King went on, holding his hand out to the messenger for some hay.

"Nobody," said the messenger.

"Quite right," said the King. "This young lady saw him, too; so of course, nobody walks slower than you."

It may be inferred that the King believes:

A. The messenger is good at his job.

B. "Nobody" is a person that might be seen.

C. The messenger is lying.

D. The messenger did not actually see anyone on the road.

E. The young lady is a more reliable witness than the messenger.

6. Women typically are several inches shorter than men. They also weigh, on the average, 20 to 50 pounds less than a man of the same height. And, in general, women aren't physically as strong as men. Therefore, a woman would be a less effective firefighter than a man would be.

Which of the following propositions, if true, would most weaken this argument?

A. Potential firefighters go through intensive training before being certified.
B. There are plenty of desk jobs in fire departments which women could fill.
C. Some female applicants for firefighting jobs are taller, weigh more, and are stronger than some currently employed male firefighters.
D. Women handle stress better than men do.

7.   JACK: We should reduce the amount of money we spend on space programs. All that money should be spent right here on Earth instead of on space stations and interstellar problems.

JAN: In fact, all that money you speak of *is* spent here on Earth, creating countless jobs and yielding useful consumer products.

Which of the following best describes Jan's response to Jack?

A. It shows that Jack is contradicting himself.
B. It tries to refute Jack's position by pointing out a hypostatization in his argument.
C. It illuminates an amphiboly in Jack's argument.
D. It exploits an ambiguity in a key phrase in Jack's argument.

8. **Carefully read the following argument, then answer the questions that follow it.**

The welfare state, in its fervor to bring about utopia, is engaged in a whole network of programs, operating with the heavy hand of the tyrant to enforce what the government, in its limited wisdom, has proclaimed to be the principles of justice. Some time ago, a young man stopped by to see me. He works as a field agent for a national church group calling upon student organizations affiliated with his church that operate on both public and private campuses. It seems that some of the civil rights legislation has been interpreted to require every campus organization to file an affidavit that its membership is open to all students. The student organization served by my visitor is only open to members of his church and has as its purpose, to help its members grow in their knowledge and commitment to their faith. Since these groups could not sign the affidavit of open membership, the field representative had called on presidents, deans, and ombudspersons on the various campuses to seek advice on what to do about this dilemma. The answer he received was virtually the same on all campuses: Tell your student groups to lie about it. . . . Here is bureaucracy gone berserk, forcing dishonesty upon the officers of the institutions whose purpose it is to train our youth, and teaching deceit to the students. The welfare state by nature is a tyranny which in order to carry out its judgments must impose its will on the people trampling on the most sacred tenet of liberty.

(From a speech by John A. Woard delivered to the American Farm Bureau Tax and Spending Limitation Conference, Chicago, September 18, 1978.)

Discuss the speaker's use of hypostatization. Do you think that the hypostatization has the effect of clarifying or obscuring blameworthiness in the episode the speaker cites? Try to find some examples of a similar use of hypostatization in contemporary rhetoric.

9. **Before reading this passage, consult a dictionary for the various meanings of the word *victim*, which plays a crucial role in the argument.**

... [T]he government along with the clinics/hospitals/public health groups and religious leaders—from the Pope to Jerry Falwell—have blamed homosexual promiscuity for AIDS. They have more or less echoed President Reagan's speech writer: "Call it nature's retribution, God's will, the wages of sin, paying the piper, ecological kickback, whatever phraseology you prefer. The facts demonstrate that promiscuous homosexual conduct is utterly destructive of human health." Calling AIDS a "natural sanction," the Vatican Office of Social Communication said, "Some diseases or physical conditions are the direct result of personal actions, like a hangover or venereal disease." Like Daniel Defoe in *A Journal of the Plague Year* (1721) they have blamed the victims: "There was a seeming propensity or a wicked inclination in those that were infected to infect others. . . ."

Displacement of responsibility for illness and mortality is quite common. Thus, it is argued that failure to seek medical care explains the high infant and mother mortality rates among the poor, when the real problems are malnutrition, poor housing, and inadequate living standards. During the Bubonic Plague, Jews, because they kept cats, were accused of bewitching Christians, who then killed both the cats and the Jews in order to counter the disease. During the auto heyday of the '50s, automobile deaths were *defined* as "accidents," and blamed on those killed. Consumer activists have only partially corrected this "accident" construct. Highway deaths are seldom blamed on faulty automobiles, lousy engineering, poor roadways or inadequate public transportation. If not completely "accidental," then casualties are blamed on the driver—particularly the drunk or drugged driver. Mothers Against Drunk Drivers (MADD) don't call for free public transportation; instead they blame drunk drivers, who bring sorrow to mother, children and other innocent victims. (Charley Shively, "AIDS and Genes: AIDS as Psychological Warfare," *Gay Community News,* Oct. 11–17, 1987. Reprinted by permission of Charley Shively, *Fag Rag* collective member.)

Your dictionary research should have revealed two meanings of the word *victim* that are relevant to analyzing this passage. A victim may be:

A. one who is harmed by or made to suffer from an act or circumstances over which the person exercises little if any control. Thus, "victims of war," "earthquake victims," "innocent victims," and the like. In this sense, victims are not blameworthy.

B. a person who suffers injury, loss or death as a result of a *voluntary* undertaking, as in "a victim of his own greed" or "a victim of her own recklessness." In this sense, victims are blameworthy.

Can persons who contract AIDS be called "victims"? If yes, in which sense or senses? (Give examples to clarify.) Do you think the author has used the word *victim* equivocally? Explain.

10. One of the most important Supreme Court decisions in modern times produced what is termed the "Miranda ruling." According to Miranda, if the police propose to question a person, they must first inform him that he is entitled to a lawyer and that "if he cannot afford one, a lawyer will be provided for him prior to any interrogation."

In the summer of 1989, the high court announced an opinion invoking the Miranda ruling in the case of *Duckworth v. Eagan*. The case involved a man named Gary Eagan, who agreed to go to police headquarters in Hammond, Indiana, for questioning about his possible involvement in a murder. The police told Eagan that he had the right to the presence of a lawyer even if he could not afford one. Then the police added: "We have no way of giving you a lawyer but one will be appointed for you, if you wish, if and when you go to court." Eagan later argued that he was not properly informed of his rights under the Miranda ruling.

However, a majority of the Supreme Court decided that the Hammond police warnings "touched all of the bases required by Miranda." Writing for the majority, Chief Justice William Rehnquist saw nothing sinister about the "if and when you go to court" language. That information, he said, "simply anticipates" a question a suspect might ask, for example: "When will I actually get a lawyer?"

Commenting on this case, Yale Kamisar, professor of law at the University of Michigan, has written:

> To be sure, Eagan was told at the very outset that he had a right to talk to a law-yer before the police asked him any questions. But taking into account what he was told in the next breath, Eagan might plausibly have concluded that since indigent persons like him have no way of getting a lawyer at this stage, there was no point in asking for one. . . . Now if Eagan were a smart, sophisticated fellow, he might have dissected the Hammond police warning the way Rehnquist did and figured out that he could stop the questioning—indeed, prevent the police from ever questioning him again unless he initiated further communication with them—simply by asking for a lawyer, regardless of when he actually obtained one. But not-so-smart people need help understanding that asserting one's right to a lawyer is the significant act, not the actual availability of a lawyer. The warnings in this case did not provide that help. . . . The Hammond police sent Eagan the wrong message (or at least an unnecessarily confused and misleading one). (Yale Kamisar, "Miranda Now Misses One Base," *Los Angeles Times,* July 27, 1989, Part II, p. 7)

What would you say is the nature of the dispute between the court's and Kamisar's opinions? Do you agree with Kamisar that Hammond police used innuendo to mislead Eagan? Or do you agree with the court that they "touched all the bases required by Miranda"?

POINT/COUNTERPOINT: ESSAYS FOR ANALYSIS

Issue: *Pornography*

Resolved: In general, pornography should not be controlled.

Background: The problem of pornography continues to ignite heated social debate among civil libertarians, religionists, feminists, film makers, and book publishers; and among parents and the general public. The central issue concerns the regulation of pornography. Should pornography be controlled? If so, how and to what extent?

In pornography case law, United States *v.* Roth *(1957) stands as a landmark deci-sion. The case involved a New York City businessman named Roth who used sexually explicit circulars and advertising material to solicit sales. Roth was charged with and convicted of mailing obscene circulars and ads and of mailing an obscene book, all in violation of a federal obscenity statute. His conviction at the District Court level was sub-sequently upheld by a Court of Appeals and by the United States Supreme Court. The Supreme Court's ruling is best remembered for the definition of pornography that it laid down and continues to be applied in cases of alleged pornography. By the Court's account, a work is pornography if, considered in terms of its appeal to the* average per-son, *it offends* community standards, *because its theme, taken as a whole, appeals to* pru-rient interests *and is* without social value.

From: **The Dangers of Antipornography Legislation**[3]

Jerome Frank

What follows is a portion of the dissenting opinion in the Court of Appeals ruling, written by Judge Jerome Frank. Although written prior to the high court's decision, Frank's comprehensive opinion still provides a focal point around which those opposed to censorship of pornography gather.

1 For a time, American courts adopted the test of obscenity contrived in 1868 by L. J. Cockburn, in *Queen v. Hicklin,* L.R. 3 Q.B. 360: "I think the test of obscenity is this, whether the tendency of the matter charged as obscenity is to deprave and corrupt those whose minds are open to such immoral influences, and into whose hands a publication of this sort might fall." He added that the book there in question "would suggest . . . thoughts of a most impure and libidinous character."

2 The test in most federal courts has changed: They do not now speak of the thoughts of "those whose minds are open to . . . immoral influences" but, instead, of the thoughts of average adult normal men and women, determining what these thoughts are, not by proof at the trial, but by the standard of "the average conscience of the time," the current "social sense of what is right."

3 Yet the courts still define obscenity in terms of the assumed average normal adult reader's sexual thoughts or desires or impulses, without reference to any relation between those "subjective" reactions and his subsequent conduct. The judicial opinions use such key phrases as this: "suggesting lewd thoughts and exciting sensual desires," "arouse the salacity of the reader," "allowing or implanting . . . obscene, lewd, or lascivious thoughts or desires," "arouse sexual desires." The judge's charge in the instant case reads accordingly: "It must tend to stir sexual impulses and lead to sexually impure thoughts." Thus the statute, as the courts construe it, appears to provide criminal punishment for inducing no more than thoughts, feelings, desires.

---

[3]*United States* v. *Roth* (354 U.S. 476, 1957)

4 Suppose we assume, *arguendo,* that sexual thoughts or feelings, stirred by the "obscene," probably will often issue into overt conduct. Still it does not at all follow that that conduct will be antisocial. For no sane person can believe it socially harmful if sexual desires lead to normal, and not antisocial, sexual behavior since, without such behavior, the human race would soon disappear.

5 Doubtless, Congress could validly provide punishment for mailing any publications if there were some moderately substantial reliable data showing that reading or seeing those publications probably conduces to seriously harmful sexual conduct on the part of normal adult human beings. But we have no such data.

6 Suppose it argued that whatever excites sexual longings might *possibly* produce sexual misconduct. That cannot suffice: Notoriously, perfumes sometimes act as aphrodisiacs, yet no one will suggest that therefore Congress may constitutionally legislate punishment for mailing perfumes. It may be that among the stimuli to irregular sexual conduct, by normal men and women, may be almost anything—the odor of carnations or cheese, the sight of a cane or a candle or a shoe, the touch of silk or a gunnysack. For all anyone now knows, stimuli of that sort may be far more provocative of such misconduct than reading obscene books or seeing obscene pictures. Said John Milton, "Evil manners are as perfectly learnt, without books, a thousand other ways that cannot be stopped."

7 To date there exist, I think, no thoroughgoing studies by competent persons which justify the conclusion that normal adults' reading or seeing of the "obscene" probably induces antisocial conduct. Such competent studies as have been made do conclude that so complex and numerous are the causes of sexual vice that it is impossible to assert with any assurance that "obscenity" represents a ponderable causal factor in sexually deviant adult behavior." Although the whole subject of obscenity censorship hinges upon the unproved assumption that 'obscene' literature is a significant factor in causing sexual deviation from the community standard, no report can be found of a single effort at genuine research to test this assumption by singling out as a factor for study the effect of sex literature upon sexual behavior." What little competent research has been done points definitely in a direction precisely opposite to that assumption.

8 Alpert reports that, when, in the 1920s, 409 women college graduates were asked to state in writing what things stimulated them sexually, they answered thus: 218 said men; 95 said books; 40 said drama; 29 said dancing; 18 said pictures; 9 said music. Of those who replied "that the source of their sex information came from books, not one specified a 'dirty' book as the source. Instead, the books listed were: The Bible, the dictionary, the encyclopedia, novels from Dickens to Henry James, circulars about venereal diseases, medical books, and Motley's *Rise of the Dutch Republic*." Macaulay, replying to advocates of the suppression of obscene books, said: "We find it difficult to believe that in a world so full of temptations as this, any gentleman whose life would have been virtuous

if he had not read Aristophanes or Juvenal, will be vicious by reading them." Echoing Macaulay, Jimmy Walker, former mayor of New York City, remarked that he had never heard of a woman seduced by a book. New Mexico has never had an obscenity statute; there is no evidence that, in that state, sexual misconduct is proportionately greater than elsewhere.

9   . . . Judge Clark speaks of "the strongly held views of those with competence in the premises as to the very direct connection" of obscenity "with the development of juvenile delinquency." . . . One of the cited writings is a report, by Dr. [Marie] Jahoda and associates, entitled "The Impact of Literature: A Psychological Discussion of Some Assumptions in the Censorship Debate" (1954). I have read this report (which is a careful survey of all available studies and psychological theories). I think it expresses an attitude quite contrary to that indicated by Judge Clark.

10   Maybe someday we will have enough reliable data to show that obscene books and pictures do tend to influence children's sexual conduct adversely. Then a federal statute could be enacted which would avoid constitutional defects by authorizing punishment for using the mails or interstate shipments in the sale of such books and pictures to children.

11   Let it be assumed, for the sake of the argument, that contemplation of published matter dealing with sex has a significant impact on children's conduct. On that assumption, we cannot overlook the fact that our most reputable newspapers and periodicals carry advertisements and photographs displaying women in what decidedly are sexually alluring postures, and at times emphasizing the importance of "sex appeal." That women are there shown scantily clad increases "the mystery and allure of the bodies that are hidden," writes an eminent psychiatrist. "A leg covered by a silk stocking is much more attractive than a naked one; a bosom pushed into shape by a brassiere is more alluring than the pendant realities." Either, then, the statute must be sternly applied to prevent the mailing of many reputable newspapers and periodicals containing such ads and photographs, or else we must acknowledge that they have created a cultural atmosphere for children in which, at a maximum, only the most trifling additional effect can be imputed to children's perusal of the kind of matter mailed by the defendant. . . .

12   I have no doubt the jury could reasonably find, beyond a reasonable doubt, that many of the publications mailed by defendant were obscene within the current judicial definition of the term as explained by the trial judge in his charge to the jury. But so, too, are a multitude of recognized works of art found in public libraries. Compare, for instance, the books which are exhibits in this case with Montaigne's *Essay on Some Lines of Virgil* or with Chaucer. Or consider the many nude pictures which the defendant transmitted through the mails, and then turn to the reproductions in the articles on paintings and sculptures in the *Encyclopaedia Britannica* (14th edition). Some of the latter are no less "obscene" than those which led to the defendant's conviction. Yet these Encyclopedia volumes are readily accessible to everyone, young or old, and, without let or hindrance,

are frequently mailed to all parts of the country. Catalogues of famous art museums, almost equally accessible and also often mailed, contain reproductions of paintings and sculpture, by great masters, no less "obscene."

13 To the argument that such books (and such reproductions of famous paintings and works of sculpture) fall within the statutory ban, the courts have answered that they are "classics"—books of "literary distinction" or works which have "an accepted place in the arts," including, so this court has held, Ovid's *Art of Love* and Boccaccio's *Decameron*. There is a "curious dilemma" involved in this answer that the statute condemns "only books which are dull and without merit," that in no event will the statute be applied to the "classics," that is, books "of literary distinction." The courts have not explained how they escape that dilemma, but instead seem to have gone to sleep (although rather uncomfortably) on its horns.

14 *Prosecutors, as censors, actually exercise prior restraint.* Fear of punishment serves as a powerful restraint on publication, and fear of punishment often means, practically, fear of prosecution. For most men dread indictment and prosecution; the publicity alone terrifies, and to defend a criminal action is expensive. If the definition of obscenity had a limited and fairly well-known scope, that fear might deter restricted sorts of publications only. But on account of the extremely vague judicial definition of the obscene, a person threatened with prosecution if he mails (or otherwise sends in interstate commerce) almost any book which deals in an unconventional, unorthodox manner with sex may well apprehend that, should the threat be carried out, he will be punished. As a result, each prosecutor becomes a literary censor (dictator) with immense unbridled power, a virtually uncontrolled discretion. A statute would be invalid which gave the Postmaster General the power, without reference to any standard, to close the mails to any publication he happened to dislike. Yet a federal prosecutor, under the federal obscenity statute, approximates that position: Within wide limits, he can (on the advice of the Postmaster General or on no one's advice) exercise such a censorship by threat without a trial, without any judicial supervision, capriciously and arbitrarily. Having no special qualifications for that task, nevertheless, he can, in large measure, determine at his will what those within his district may not read on sexual subjects.

15 Governmental control of ideas or personal preferences is alien to a democracy. And the yearning to use governmental censorship of any kind is infectious. It may spread insidiously. Commencing with suppression of books as obscene, it is not unlikely to develop into official lust for the power of thought-control in the areas of religion, politics, and elsewhere. Milton observed that "licensing of books . . . necessarily pulls along with it so many other kinds of licensing." Mill noted that the "bounds of what may be called moral police" may easily extend "until it encroaches on the most unquestionably legitimate liberty of the individual." We should beware of a recrudescence of the undemocratic doctrine uttered in the seventeenth

century by Berkeley, Governor of Virginia: "Thank God there are no free schools or preaching, for learning has brought disobedience into the world, and printing has divulged them. God keep us from both."

16 Plato, who detested democracy, proposed to banish all poets; and his rulers were to serve as guardians of the people, telling lies for the people's good, vigorously suppressing writings these guardians thought dangerous. Governmental guardianship is repugnant to the basic tenet of our democracy: According to our ideals, our adult citizens are self-guardians, to act as their own fathers, and thus become self-dependent. When our governmental officials act towards our citizens on the thesis that "Papa knows best what's good for you," they enervate the spirit of the citizens: To treat grown men like infants is to make them infantile, dependent, immature.

1. The first three paragraphs
   A. state the thesis.
   B. refute the opposition.
   C. offer a main point for the thesis.
   D. provide useful background.
2. Do you think that the phrases "the average conscience of the time" and "social sense of what is right" (paragraph 2) are clear and precise? (What about "contemporary community standards," "prurience," and "social value" as used in the current definition of pornography?)
3. After reading paragraphs 2 and 3, Willy concludes that the author is accusing the courts of making a distinction without a difference? Do you agree with Willy?
4. Which of the following inferences do you think is best supported by paragraphs 1–3?
   A. The author opposes antipornography legislation.
   B. The author thinks the antipornography statute, in effect, censors thought and feeling.
   C. The author believes the language of the test for obscenity is vague.
   D. The author is convinced the traditional test of obscenity is absurd.
   E. The author thinks the contemporary tests of obscenity are more valid than the traditional one.
5. Which of the following best expresses the warrant needed to complete the argument expressed in paragraph 4?
   A. People sometimes act on sexual feelings and thoughts.
   B. Sexual thoughts can often result in antisocial conduct.
   C. Sexual thoughts sometimes lead to normal sexual behavior.
   D. Sexual thoughts always precede sexual conduct.
6. Cast the argument presented in paragraph 4 in terms of "C" (conclusion), "P" (premise), "B" (back-up or premise support), and "W" (warrant).
7. Assuming their truth, which of the following statements, if any, would weaken the logic of the author's argument in paragraph 5?
   A. A study of prisoners serving time for rape finds that the overwhelming majority regularly used pornography prior to their crimes.

    B. The use of pornographic materials has increased substantially in the past five years.

    C. The author was himself once charged with a sex crime, but not convicted.

    D. Most adult American males admit to using pornography occasionally.

    E. The President's Commission on Obscenity and Pornography reports that erotic dreams, sexual fantasies, and conversations about sexual matters tend to increase after exposure to erotic materials.

8. Explain exactly how in paragraph 6 the author attempts to refute an argument for censorship on grounds that it might possibly produce sexual misconduct.

9. In paragraph 7, quotations around the word "obscene" have the effect of
    A. giving the word emphasis.
    B. introducing ambiguity.
    C. creating vagueness.
    D. communicating innuendo.
    E. None of the above.

10. Laura thinks that the author is using a persuasive definition in the first sentence of paragraph 7. "It's just like saying 'Truly competent persons don't believe that reading or seeing obscene materials induce antisocial conduct.'" Do you think that the author is in effect saying this?

11. Enrique believes that the author is defining "sexual deviation from the community standards" too narrowly (paragraph 7). "Frank obviously is associating 'sexual deviation from the community standard' with sexual conduct. And because no studies show that sexual literature leads to antisocial or deviant sexual conduct Frank believes there's no basis for restricting pornography under the statute. But there are plenty of liberty-limiting statutes based on community standards concerning matters of 'public morals.' For example, it's against the law to walk down a street naked or make love in public. And if you want to sunbathe in the 'altogether,' you better do it where nude sunbathing is permitted. Why are these things illegal? Not because they will lead to antisocial behavior. Presumably they're illegal merely because they violate some standard of the community. I think Frank misses this point when he demands proof that a community standard regarding obscenity is preventing antisocial conduct. And if he insists that these examples are irrelevant because they have nothing to do with free speech, then what about the liberty-limiting restrictions communities impose when they dictate to shopkeepers the size, nature, and even content of store signs, for example?" Evaluate Enrique's criticism.

12. Harriet is troubled by paragraphs 7 and 8. "Judge Frank," she says, "is taking the absence of proof that 'dirty' books can lead to antisocial conduct as proof that they can't. Isn't that like saying because we can't prove that TV violence contributes to real life violence that it musn't? Or, because we can't disprove that TV violence contributes to real life violence, it must? It seems to me that something can be the case even if we can't prove it." What do you think of Harriet's point?

13. Paragraph 9 implies a/an _____ dispute between Judges Frank and Clark:
    A. evaluative
    B. interpretive

C. verbal

D. theoretical

E. factual

14. Eli suspects the author of "pulling a fast one" in paragraph 11. He explains: "When Frank refers to stuff 'dealing with sex' (sentence 1), I think of magazines like *Playboy* and *Penthouse*. I mean they make no bones about it: They're peddling beautiful bods; they're trying to turn you on. And if they don't, well see you later—they're out of business. But I don't think bra and panty ads in newspapers are doing that. Sure, these ads may be 'alluring' to some people, like he says. But they don't deal with sex like, say, *Dude.*" Do you agree that Frank, by implication, has shifted the meaning of "dealing with sex" in order to discredit the censorship position?

15. Do you think that the last sentence of paragraph 11 is or is not a false dilemma?

16. In paragraphs 12 and 13, is the author accusing the courts of drawing a distinction without a difference? Explain.

17. As noted in Chapter 5, vague language undermines argument because such language is open to multiple interpretations. Do you think this fact is relevant to the author's point in paragraph 14?

18. Carol senses a paradox in paragraphs 15 and 16. "Let's suppose," she explains, "that the majority of people want to restrict pornography. In other words, public opinion is squarely behind censorship of so-called sexual literature. Judge Frank apparently would still oppose enforcing public opinion in this case because it limited freedom of expression that doesn't lead to antisocial conduct. But since democracy is rule by the people, shouldn't censorship be enforced in this case? In other words, is censorship always and unavoidably incompatible with democracy?" Evaluate Carol's claim that censorship and democracy are not always at odds.

19. Which of the following propositions, if any, would be inconsistent with what the author says?

    A. Given the opportunity, government tends to restrict rather than expand individual freedom.

    B. A film that portrays Jesus and Mary Magdalene as lovers should be censored.

    C. Child pornography should be prohibited.

    D. So-called classics that contain sexual material clearly are not obscene in the way that smutty magazines are.

20. What is the logical function of the author's citing studies (or the absence of them) on the supposed link between pornography and antisocial conduct?

    A. They prove beyond a reasonable doubt that there is no connection between pornography and sex crimes.

    B. They help refute a key argument of those supporting antipornography legislation.

    C. They indicate how when once permitted government censorship spreads like a cancer.

    D. A and B.

    E. B and C.

Traditionally, responses to the question of the regulation of pornography have divided along political lines, with liberals generally opposing regulation as a violation of the First Amendment and conservatives supporting regulation as a justifiable limit on the First Amendment's protection of free speech. Recently, a curious and powerful coalition has formed between conservatives and some traditionally liberal feminists, both of whom believe that pornography must be regulated to ensure the civil rights of those they view as victims of pornography, mainly women and children.

This novel focus—on the civil rights of the alleged victims of pornography rather than on those who trade in what is considered pornographic—found expression in an antipornography law that was drafted in 1983 by feminist author Andrea Dworkin and professor of law Catharine MacKinnon, at the request of the City Council of Minneapolis, Minnesota. Dubbed the "Minneapolis ordinance," the proposal defines pornography as "the sexually explicit subordination of women, graphically depicted, whether in pictures or in words" that also includes one or more of the following nine characteristics:

1. presenting women "dehumanized as sexual objects, things, or commodities"
2. presenting women as "sexual objects who enjoy pain or humiliation"
3. presenting women as "sexual objects who experience sexual pleasure in being raped"
4. presenting women as "sexual objects tied up or cut up or mutilated or bruised or physically hurt"
5. presenting women "in postures or positions of sexual submission, servility, or display"
6. exhibiting "women's body parts—including but not limited to vaginas, breasts, or buttocks" in such a way that "women are reduced to those parts"
7. presenting women as "whores by nature"
8. presenting women "being penetrated by objects or animals"
9. presenting women in "scenarios of degradation, injury, torture, shown as filthy or inferior, bleeding, bruised, or hurt in a context that makes these conditions sexual."

To be considered pornography, material must meet each part of the definition—it must be graphic and sexually explicit and subordinate women—and meet at least one of the nine preceding characteristics. Most important, anyone who traffics in such material is guilty of sex discrimination and is subject to an action that can be brought by any woman, man, or child who alleges injury by that material in the way women, as a whole, are injured by it through subordination. In other words, any person may claim to be a victim of pornography and thus sue the pornographer for violating his or her civil rights.

So controversial was the proposal that the mayor of Minneapolis vetoed it, but that has not diminished its impact. Indeed, similar propositions in New York, Los Angeles, and other communities have generated acrimonious debate.

From: **The Need for Antipornography Legislation**[4]

Janella Miller

Janella Miller, an attorney, was with the Legislature Action Committee of the Pornography Resource Center in Minneapolis, Minnesota, when she wrote this response to the "Minneapolis ordinance." **Read it carefully, outline it, and answer the questions that follow it.**

1   The latest movie in the stream of Hollywood offerings in which women are brutally murdered has arrived—*Body Double.* Director Brian De Palma's attitude toward the violence and toward the encroachment of pornography into the mainstream media demands a response. De Palma told interviewer Pally that he opposes pornography legislation because he has a right as an individual to take pictures of anything he pleases, including pictures of a woman being violently murdered with a drill. He says that he does not believe viewing pornography has any effect upon male viewers or their likelihood of committing acts of aggression against women.

2   De Palma has obviously not been paying any attention to the victims of pornography, the *women* who are hurt by and through pornography, who have courageously spoken out about the abuse they have experienced because of pornography. Nor has he studied the most recent research linking pornography to increased aggression against women. If he had, he would know that pornography is not just ideas or words or pictures on a page; it is a *practice* that harms women and children.

3   Recent legislation passed in Minneapolis and in Indianapolis addresses, for the first time, the harm done by pornography. Feminist writer and activist Andrea Dworkin and University of Minnesota law professor Catharine MacKinnon, at the request of the Minneapolis city council, wrote a civil rights ordinance on pornography that defines pornography as a form of sex discrimination and as a violation of women's civil rights. The ordinance defines pornography as "the sexually explicit subordination of women, graphically depicted, whether in pictures or in words," that also includes one or more of nine listed characteristics which range from "women are presented as sexual objects who enjoy pain or humiliation" to "women are presented in postures of sexual submission or sexual servility, including by inviting penetration" to "women are presented being penetrated by objects or animals."

4   There have been many, however, who claim that the civil rights ordinance on pornography is censorship. They misunderstand what the ordinance does and also what censorship means in a society that values freedom of speech. The word *censorship* implies official examination of pictures,

---

[4]This article first appeared in the December 1984 edition of *Film Comment.* Reprinted by permission of Janella Miller, J.D. Harvard Law School, 1984.

plays, television, etc., for the purpose of suppressing parts deemed objectionable on moral, political, military, or other grounds. The ordinance works on an entirely different principle. There are no prior restraints, no criminal penalties, and no increase in police powers. A particular work could be removed only after an adversarial hearing before a judge. Both sides could present evidence, as in any legal case. The ordinance provides no mechanism for telling people that they *cannot* publish what they want. What it *does* do is tell pornographers that if they print material in which women and children are harmed, or material that *leads* to harm or discrimination, they must be responsible for the harm that they cause. In that regard, the ordinance works much like libel laws which hold the media accountable for false information that harms an individual if the individual can prove that he or she was injured.

5 If the ordinance were effectively applied, pornographers would undoubtedly choose not to publish certain materials because it would be too costly for them. There *would* be fewer pornographic pictures, movies, and books. Supporters of the ordinance intend that result. For the first time, people are challenging the idea that the First Amendment should shield pornography from any legal challenge. The harm done to women in this legal system is great enough to justify limitations on the pornographers' right to "freedom of speech" under which they have committed atrocities against women for centuries.

6 Those who cry censorship whenever someone mentions the ordinance act as though the right to freedom of speech were absolute and that it exists in a vacuum apart from any other social concern. But no lawyer who has ever studied the First Amendment would ever claim that we have an absolute right to freedom of speech.

7 We have libel laws, slander laws, and court decisions which limit words that create a "clear and present danger" or that constitute "fighting words." Obscenity is not protected speech under the First Amendment, nor is child pornography. In *New York v. Ferber,* 458 U.S. 747 (1982), the Supreme Court said that the *harm done* to children in pornography justified restricting the pornographers' right to print what they please. There is thus a precedent for weighing the harm done to *women* against the pornographers' right to "freedom of speech." That harm was well documented in the hearings before the Minneapolis city council in December 1983 and the Senate Sub-committee on Juvenile Justice in September 1984.

8 Social scientists, researchers on pornography, people who work in the field of sexual assault, and victims of pornography have all testified about the effects of pornography. Using this documentation to support legislation and legal decisions would not be a new idea. The Supreme Court has used sociological data in the past, most notably in *Brown v. Board of Education,* to support their finding that the harm done to black children in segregated schools was so great that integration was required to alleviate it.

9 Opponents of the ordinance are also fond of claiming that we are on a slippery slope that will end in the suppression of the Bible or of Shakespeare. The concern about the Bible and Shakespeare is very interesting, since they are not sexually explicit and would not be covered under the ordinance as it is written. But opponents also seem to be arguing that *any* limitation on freedom of speech will lead to the institution of a repressive regime. These arguments are based not upon facts about the ordinance or upon a reasoned analysis of the First Amendment, but rather upon the manipulation of people's fears. Forecasting the worst possible outcome for any piece of legislation is an old legal strategy that is particularly powerful when the predicted outcome is the suppression of ideas. However, it does not necessarily follow that the worst possible outcome will occur *because* we are in the area of the First Amendment. In fact, the opposite outcome is more likely. Americans guard their right to freedom of speech with a tenacity that would surprise people in other countries which also value their freedom of speech. A judge would likely interpret the ordinance narrowly, finding that material falls under the ordinance only if it clearly degrades and subordinates women.

10 We always trust the courts to make decisions which clarify and illuminate the law. To say that the task is difficult begs the question. Asking the courts to decide which works subordinate women and which works fall within the definition of pornography, when a woman claims to be harmed, will be far less onerous than asking them to decide which works are "obscene" under obscenity laws or what constitutes "discrimination" under civil rights laws. There is actually much less potential for abuse under the ordinance than there is under obscenity laws, under which we allow judges to make moral decisions about what we should view. Under the ordinance, as written, morality plays no role. The ordinance speaks only to the subordination of women and the harm done to women in pornography. I fear more the continuation and legitimation of a system which treats women as less than human, as objects to be consumed, than I do allowing our judges to decide what is covered under a specific and narrow definition of pornography.

11 An amendment to the ordinance further prevents frivolous abuses of the trafficking provision by precluding legal actions based upon isolated passages or isolated parts. The ordinance does not specify a certain percentage of the work that must be pornographic to be actionable, but the authors clearly intend to require more than a *de minimum* amount.

12 Finally, the ordinance avoids any interpretation leading to the suppression of *ideas* by defining pornography as "the sexually explicit subordination of women, graphically depicted, whether in pictures or in words." Pornography does not present the "idea" of subordination or of any other idea. It is an active *practice* of subordination. Only pictures and words that *do* subordinate women are pornography and fall within the scope of the ordinance.

13 We cannot wait for a solution any longer. Pornography has grown into an $8 billion-a-year industry that has spread into every form of media and

advertising. America's culture has become pornographic. It is time to look at the harm done by pornography and weigh it against the pornographers' claimed right to freedom of speech. We legislate for the good of society—to establish justice, equality, and freedom for all Americans. But women still do not have justice, equality, or freedom. The pornographers tell lies about women which lead to terrorism and intimidation. Men rape and torture women with the use of pornography. Men force women to perform in pornography. A beaten and tortured woman is not free, nor is she an equal member of our society. She is a second-class citizen with no way to improve the daily condition of her life, because no one hears her screams.

1. The first paragraph of the essay functions to
   A. refute De Palma.
   B. state the thesis.
   C. provide background.
   D. present a main point in support of the thesis.
   E. offer an aside.
2. There is always a danger of misrepresentation in quoting someone out of context. One simple way to check the believability of a quote is to see if it is consistent with other things you know about the party quoted. Ask yourself: "Does this sound like something that person would say?" Apply this test to the quotation attributed to De Palma in paragraph 1. Does it sound like the kind of thing someone who makes films such as *Body Double* and *Taxi Driver* would say?
3. The main idea of paragraph 2 is that
   A. De Palma is a sexist.
   B. De Palma is not informed about the effects of pornography.
   C. pornography harms people.
   D. pornography should be banned.
   E. De Palma's *Body Double* should be censored.
4. Opponents of antipornography legislation say that proponents assume without convincing evidence that pornography harms women. Do you think that it is (A) *very important,* (B) *somewhat important, or* (C) *not really important to their case* that antipornographers establish a causal link between pornography and harm to women? Does the author make an attempt to do this? Do you think she succeeds?
5. It is reasonable to infer from paragraph 4 that the author probably
   A. objects to censorship.
   B. favors censorship.
   C. has no clear position on censorship.
   D. objects to censorship, but considers it justified in cases of pornography.
   E. favors the censorship implicit in libel laws.
6. Which of the following statements best describes the disagreement that Miller and Frank have about censorship?
   A. They disagree about the conditions under which censorship is permissible.
   B. They disagree that the First Amendment effectively prohibits censorship.

C. They disagree about the meaning of censorship.

D. A and C.

E. A, B, and C.

7. The author attempts to refute the charge that antipornography legislation is censorship

   A. by agreeing that it is, but arguing that it is justified in order to save women and children from harm.

   B. by clarifying the meaning of censorship.

   C. by citing similar cases of permissible censorship.

   D. A and B.

   E. A, B, and C.

8. If after reading paragraph 5, Mike says, "Obviously, the ordinance doesn't apply to film, because film isn't print material," he

   A. draws a valid conclusion.

   B. gives unintended emphasis to the word "print."

   C. shifts the meaning of the term "print material."

   D. hypostatizes "ordinance."

   E. begs the question.

9. According to paragraph 4, which of the following is *not* a necessary feature of censorship?

   A. Official scrutiny

   B. The intention of suppressing what's thought to be objectionable

   C. Military or political content

   D. Criminal penalties

   E. Prior restraints

10. Do you agree with the author that the "Minneapolis ordinance" is not censorship or do you think that there's no substantive difference between it and censorship?

11. In paragraph 4, do you think that the reference to like laws makes the author's point or merely clarifies what she means?

12. Which of the following, if true, would *most* undermine the author's comparing the "Minneapolis ordinance" with libel laws *(paragraph 4)?*

   A. One can, at least in theory, prove factually that libel causes injury, but that is impossible with pornography.

   B. Most cases of libel are dropped because it is difficult to prove injury.

   C. It is rather easy to get around libel laws by fictionalizing the target of an attack.

   D. Libel laws, in fact, impose self-censorship on newspapers.

   E. Pornography does not libel people; it dehumanizes them.

13. Do you find any inconsistency between the definition and provision of the "Minneapolis ordinance" and the author's interpretation in paragraph 4 that a person would have to prove that she was harmed by pornographic material in order to prevail in a legal case?

14. The disagreement between Miller and Frank over whether such an ordinance would be censorship would be mainly a/an _____ dispute.

   A. factual

   B. verbal

   C. evaluative

D. interpretive

E. theoretical

15. Using "D" for data, "B" for backing, and "C" for conclusion, portray the logical structure of paragraph 7.

16. Which of the following statements best expresses the warrant of the argument in paragraph 7?

    A. A Supreme Court decision is always unimpeachable.

    B. There are clear limits to the right to free speech.

    C. If children can be harmed by pornography, so can women.

    D. The Minneapolis city council agreed that pornography harms children.

    E. Opponents of antipornography legislation view children differently from women.

17. Does the author mention *Brown* v. *Board of Education* (paragraph 8) to make or merely clarify a point?

18. Read paragraph 8 again. What does it assert by innuendo?

19. Do you agree with the author that opponents of antipornography legislation, in effect, commit faulty denotation when they suggest that the ordinance could be applied to the *Bible* or *Shakespeare*?

20. Paragraphs 4, 6, 7, 8, and 9 function mainly to

    A. explain.

    B. refute.

    C. summarize.

    D. compare and contrast.

    E. assert the thesis emphatically.

21. In paragraph 9, the sentence "... it does not necessarily follow that the worst possible outcome will occur *because* we are in the area of the First Amendment,"

    A. is inconsistent with what the author says elsewhere.

    B. is an example of hypostatization.

    C. is amphibolous.

    D. would be amphibolous if the author had not italicized "because."

    E. would be amphibolous if the context did not clarify it.

22. The phrase *"in fact"* that follows the aforementioned sentence functions as

    A. a discount.

    B. a quantifier.

    C. a qualifier.

    D. an intensifier.

    E. a premise signal.

23. In paragraph 10, the author says, "We always trust the courts to make decisions which clarify and illuminate the law. To say that the task is difficult begs the question." **Do you think it does?**

24. Which of the following statements would be the best counterpoint to the point the author tries to make in paragraph 10?

    A. A legal judgment about subordination and harm done to women by pornographic material calls for a moral judgment.

    B. There is no proof that pornography causes harm to women.

C. The author is exaggerating the unfair treatment that women currently receive in the legal system.

D. Any law can be misapplied.

E. The basis of all law is morality.

25. In paragraph 12, the author attempts to distinguish between "idea" and "practice." **Do you think she succeeds?**

26. The last paragraph

    A. uses some assumption-loaded labels.

    B. is intended to persuade.

    C. slants through the use of biased language.

    D. A and B.

    E. A, B, and C.

27. Robin sees a two-hour film which contains a two-minute scene that qualifies as "pornographic" under the "Minneapolis ordinance." She concludes that the film therefore must be considered pornographic. Her date, Rick, disagrees. "Maybe, considered by itself, the scene is pornographic," he says, "but taken as whole the film is not pornographic. So that scene couldn't have been pornographic." **Evaluate Robin and Rick's reasoning.**

RELATED THEME TOPICS

1. Write an essay in which you defend or oppose the "Minneapolis ordinance."

2. Write an essay in which you argue for or against the thesis that a college bookstore should not carry for sale magazines with erotic content, such as *Playboy, Hustler,* and *Penthouse.*

3. Write an essay in which you defend or oppose the proposition that a community is justified in imposing on its members its moral standards relating to the depiction or representation of sexual material in films, magazines, and books.

4. One of the most intriguing arguments against pornography was advanced about twenty years ago by political scientist Walter Berns, who claimed that pornography has the effect of undermining democracy. Pruned to its essentials, the argument develops as follows:

> Pornography can have political consequences, intended or not. The chief political consequence is that it makes us "shameless." Indeed, one of the purposes of pornography seems to be to convince us that shame is unnatural. But shame is not only natural but necessary for the proper functioning and stability of society. Without shame individuals are "unruly and unrulable." Once having lost all measure of self-restraint, individuals will have to be ruled by tyrants. Thus, tyranny, not democracy is the proper government for the shameless and self-indulgent. Therefore, since pornography induces shamelessness and self-indulgence, it undercuts democracy.

Write an essay defending or opposing Berns' viewpoint.

7

Fallacies of
Irrelevance

INTRODUCTION

Earlier, we established that the premises of a good argument must be relevant to the truth of the conclusion. This means that the premises must provide some reason to believe or to disbelieve the conclusion. An irrelevant premise, on the other hand, is one that provides no reason to believe or disbelieve the conclusion. In other words, it makes no difference to the truth or falsity of the conclusion.

Fallacies of irrelevance are arguments in which premises, despite appearance, do not support the conclusion drawn from them. In this chapter, we will examine three categories of fallacies of irrelevance: *ad hominem,* emotional, and diversionary arguments. The particular fallacies that we will study, though far from exhaustive, represent those most frequently met in argument. Each owes its persuasive capacity to the audience's inattention to the subject matter of an argument. Familiarity with these fallacies, therefore, will make you a keener analyst of arguments. It will also help you ensure logically relevant bases for your own arguments.

MODULE 7.1

AD HOMINEM APPEALS

Ad hominem is a Latin phrase meaning *to the man.* When we argue *ad hominem,* we target the person who is making an assertion or voicing an opinion, rather than the assertion or opinion itself. The irrelevancy of *ad hominem* appeals in argument derives from the fact that the merits of an argument or claim are independent of the character, behavior, beliefs, or other aspects of the individuals who hold them. While such personal considerations may be relevant to suspending judgment or seeking confirmation in other sources, they do not of themselves discredit an argument. This point will become clearer as we consider six specific fallacies that can be considered *ad hominems:* **the abusive ad hominem, the circumstantial ad hominem, well poisoning, and two wrongs make a right which includes tu quoque and common practice.**

Abusive Ad Hominem

The abusive ad hominem fallacy consists in attacking one's opponent in a personal way in order to discredit what the person is saying. Those employing *ad hominems* attempt to discredit ideas by discrediting the persons who hold them. It is as if they were saying: "Since so-and-so is *(an abusive term),* anything so-and-so says is without merit."

Abusive *ad hominems* take three principal forms:

1. Raising Suspicions about a Person.   "Since Richard Nixon was forced to resign the presidency, his advice regarding U.S.-Sino relations isn't worth heeding."
2. Showing Contempt for a Person.   "We should reject Rothchild's views on educational reform, because, as a banker, he can't be expected to know much about anything but making money."
3. Attacking the Source of an Idea.   "Daycare centers are a bad idea because they're socialistic in origin." This kind of attack is sometimes called the *genetic fallacy* because it attacks the origin or genesis of an idea or assertion.

Of course, where ideas originate or who holds them is irrelevant to the merits of the ideas themselves. To argue that viewpoints are false because of the character flaws of their exponents or because they are asserted by certain groups of people — atheists, fundamentalist Christians, socialists, feminists, libertarians, pro-lifers, the medical establishment, radicals, and so on — is to argue fallaciously by abusive *ad hominem* appeal.

Abusive *ad hominems* function to persuade by tapping into the audience's attitudes of disapproval. When I use an *ad hominem,* it is as if I am saying to you, "I want you to share my disapproval of this person and to transfer this disapproval to this person's ideas." The invitation is, of course, logically irrelevant; ideas should be judged on their own merits. However, it might work, if you share my bias. Even if you do not, I stand a good chance of planting a logically irrelevant seed of suspicion in your mind.

Here are some further examples of the abusive *ad hominem* fallacies with comments:

Example 1:   In announcing his resolute opposition to the nomination of Judge Robert Bork for Supreme Court Justice, Senator Edward Kennedy (D-Mass.) declared that "the man who fired (Watergate special prosecutor) Archibald Cox (when both of Bork's Justice Department superiors resigned rather than obey Nixon's order to fire Cox) should not be rewarded with a place on our highest court."

Yes, Bork did do Nixon's bidding when Attorney General Elliot Richardson and Deputy Attorney General William Ruckelshaus refused and resigned. But exactly how is that relevant to Bork's nomination for the Supreme Court? Kennedy was attempting to raise *suspicions* about Bork by implicating him in the Watergate affair and thereby discredit his nomination. If Bork's Watergate conduct did, in fact, exhibit a *relevant* character flaw, Kennedy should have spelled it out. But he never did.

Example 2:   During a speech in which they advocated AIDS (Acquired Immune Deficiency Syndrome) testing for immigrants, federal prisoners, and people getting marriage licenses, President Reagan and Vice-President Bush were noisily jeered by some of the 7,000 scientists and doctors comprising the audience. "What was that, some gay groups out there?" Bush asked over a microphone he did not realize was live.

Even if the jeers did emanate from some gays, so what? *Why* were they booing? Perhaps they felt the president's proposal insufficiently dealt with AIDS. Whatever the reasons, Bush chose to ignore them by attacking their *source*. An audience that shared the Vice President's apparent bias — for example, some viewers watching the episode on the nightly news — might well transfer the bias to the reasons behind the booing. Thus: "Those booing are gay. Therefore, what they have to say can't be worth listening to."

Example 3:   Letter to the editor: "President Reagan is Hollywood-formed. He mistakes the symbolic spectacular for actual power. He thinks sounding the charge and flying the flag is what combat is all about. Such muddle-headed theatrics got 241 Marines killed in Beirut. They were a fat target with no mission other than to be visible, and never mind that's the way Ronnie did it in *Hellcats of the Navy*."

The unmistakable *contempt* of the letter writer for Reagan "the actor" substitutes for a well-reasoned argument against Reagan's strategy in Beirut. In fact, the attack seemingly aims to discredit any Reagan foreign policy initiative.

Speaking of . . .

Ad Hominem

Getting Personal

A story is told about Lincoln as a young lawyer. In one of his first jury cases, he showed his political shrewdness by an adroit and quite non-malicious use of *ad hominem*. His opponent was an experienced trial lawyer, who also had most of the fine legal points on his side. The day was warm and Lincoln slumped in his chair as the case went against him. When the orator took off his coat and vest, however, Lincoln sat up with a gleam in his eye. His opponent was wearing one of the new city-slicker shirts of the 1840's, which buttoned up the back.

Lincoln knew the reactions of frontiersmen, who made up the jury. When his turn came, his plea was brief: "Gentlemen of the jury, because I have justice on my side, I am sure you will not be influenced by this gentleman's pretended knowledge of the law. Why, he doesn't even know which side of his shirt ought to be in front!"

Lincoln's *ad hominem* is said to have won the case. . . .

Not every personal attack, however, can be classed faulty logic. When the scandal of Grover Cleveland's illegitimate son was used against him in the presidential campaign, the argument had some point. Did Americans want a President of such a character? (The sovereign voters decided that his virtues overrode his defects.) If, however, Cleveland's enemies had introduced the natural son as an argument against his tariff policy, then a true *ad hominem* would appear. In the first case, Cleveland himself was the issue; in the second the tariff was the issue. When a man is running for office, or being chosen for any position in government or elsewhere, his personal behavior is always relevant.

(Stuart Chase, *Guides to Straight Thinking*)

Do you think that Stuart Chase would consider Senator Gary Hart's extramarital affair a relevant or irrelevant personal aspect of the senator's life during Hart's bid for the 1988 Democratic presidential nomination? Would you agree with Chase?

Example 4: "Such firebrands as columnist Charles Krauthammer . . . wonder whether a democracy can defend itself, given the constraint laws and opinion placed on a president's whim for making war. That's the nonsense of armchair Napoleons who've never heard shots fired in anger." (Syndicated columnist Jim Fain)

The issue here—whether the nature of democracy handicaps a president's capacity to respond militarily—is doubtless important. One *relevant* way to support the writer's clear implication that democracy does not unduly restrict a president would be to show through historical examples how presidents have made effective use of military might. Another way might be to illustrate that democratic constraints are, in the end, more beneficial than not. Instead, the author attacks Krauthammer's legitimate query as "nonsense" and accuses him of being incapable of understanding war ("armchair Napoleons"). When used in argument, name-calling and related abusive epithets, as well as character attacks, express contempt for the position-holder, but do nothing to discredit the position.

Circumstantial Ad Hominem

Another argument directed at the person rather than the person's position is termed the circumstantial *ad hominem.* **The circumstantial ad hominem fallacy consists of trying to persuade someone to accept a position based upon the special facts or circumstances of that person's life, rather than on the merits of the position itself.**

It is not uncommon, when two people are arguing, for one to ignore whether or not his own position is true or false and instead try to show that his opponent should accept the position owing to the special circumstances of the person's life. For example, rather than showing why a proposed tax bill is a bad idea and Jane, therefore, should not support it, Jim reminds her: "You're a businesswoman, and the U.S. Chamber of Commerce opposes this tax bill." Similarly, Dr. Henry cannot understand how a fellow doctor can support national health insurance. "Don't you realize that such a program could drastically reduce your income?" Dr. Henry asks her colleague. Notice that Jim and Dr. Henry do not try to prove that the tax bill and national health insurance are bad proposals; they simply assert that their opponent cannot consistently support these proposals because of the opponent's special circumstances. Although likely to place one's opponent on the defensive, such arguments are beside the point. Consider these three additional illustrations of the circumstantial *ad hominem.*

Example 1: Letter to the editor: "During the Pope's visit, I was shocked to hear and read a number of Roman Catholic priests disputing the Holy Father's view of birth control and *in vitro* fertilization. I also saw interviewed a Catholic couple who had conceived a baby that way. They said they saw nothing wrong with what they had done. It's beyond me how these people can hold positions fundamentally at odds with their church's teaching."

Notice how the writer never attempts to show what is wrong with *in vitro* fertilization. Instead, he argues that a Catholic cannot consistently endorse the procedure of conception outside the body. (Of course, if the conclusion is simply that these people are imperfect Catholics, then the evidence cited would be relevant and not a circumstantial *ad hominem.* But the context seems strongly to suggest that the Catholics mentioned should oppose *in vitro* fertilization because their church does.)

Example 2:   "I find it ironic that Senator Joseph Biden (D-Del.) would take issue with Judge Bork's judicial philosophy. That philosophy is one of judicial restraint, and what that means above all else is that Congress should make the laws, not the court."
(Vice President George Bush)

Bush is arguing, in effect:

> Bork will increase the power of the legislature. As a member of the legislature, Biden should be interested in having his power increased. Therefore, Biden should not oppose Bork's nomination.

But what is to be said for Bork's judicial philosophy? How will such a philosophy improve the Supreme Court? Bush needed to address these questions in order to make a *relevant* argument on behalf of Bork's philosophy. Instead, he accuses Biden of not understanding his own best interest.

Example 3:   Letter to the editor: "I was profoundly dismayed by the badgering of witnesses during the Iran-Contra hearings by Senator Rudman (R-NH). Doesn't he realize that such criticism reflects negatively on the president, a member of his own Republican party? If we can't expect Republicans to support the president in a time of crisis, just who can we turn to?"

Rather than showing why Rudman's questioning was irrelevant, ill-considered, or misinformed, the writer charges him with betraying his fellow Republican president. That Rudman is himself a Republican has no bearing on the nature of his questions.

Well Poisoning

The preceding examples show how the *circumstantial ad hominem* is generally used to force an opponent to accept one's own position. When the intent is to *reject* the opponent's position, then well poisoning often comes into play.

The fallacy of well poisoning consists in rejecting an opponent's position because of that person's special circumstances or self-serving motives. Figuratively speaking, the idea is to "poison the well" before anyone can drink from it; that is, to avoid opposition by foreclosing any discussion or reply. There are basically two ways to poison the well:

1. *Discrediting in advance the key or sole source of significantly relevant evidence for or against a position.*   For example, during Oliver North's testimony at the Iran-Contra hearings, it was not uncommon for some critics to argue as follows: "We must assume that North is lying, because he says he's not, which is exactly what a well-versed intelligence agent is expected to say." By this logic, anything North says

is untrue because he is a professional liar. North's testimony is so effectively polluted as to have no credibility. Here is another example:

PROFESSOR : Students are always offering lame excuses for having missed class.

   STUDENT : I disagree. I think I have a very good reason for missing class yesterday.

PROFESSOR : Look, any attempt to show me that you had a good reason to miss class is itself a lame excuse that does nothing more than confirm my thesis.

2. Discrediting an assertion or position by charging one's opponents with serving their own interests or having ulterior motives. For example, "Of course Jones would favor higher salaries for school teachers. He's a teacher himself" or, "As an EXXON executive, Johnson naturally would be expected to support offshore drilling for oil," or, "The nominee's seemingly innocuous replies to our queries mask the conservative agenda that he will attempt to implement once in office." That each of these parties has a vested interest in the outcome of a decision or policy is irrelevant to the merits of their positions. This does not mean that we should be oblivious to a person's motives of self-interest in advancing a position. Indeed, such knowledge should make us sufficiently skeptical to consult more impartial sources—but being skeptical is not the same as rejecting outright. That EXXON executive, Johnson, for example, stands to profit from offshore oil drilling gives reasonable grounds for wondering whether Johnson may be conveniently overlooking significant opposing facts and viewpoints, but it does not give reasonable grounds for summarily rejecting Johnson's viewpoint.

Can you spot the well poisoning in this argument?

The most vigorous and persistent criticism (of the Strategic Defense Initiative, better known as "Star Wars") has come from the groups of "concerned" Soviet scientists who claim that their analysis has already shown the futility of the SDI, its potential for escalation of the arms race and its debilitating effect on the U. S. economy. We might believe that these Soviet scientists are truly concerned for the health and wealth of the U. S. society and that the new-found altruism is just another manifestation of *glasnost* (i.e., the policy of "openness" initiated by Soviet Premier Gorbachev). A more likely possibility, however, is that they are rather happy with the status quo and rather uncomfortable about change—particularly change that might be spurred on by American advances in technology . . . SDI deserves a determined effort. It is the only logical thing to do.

> (Gerold Yonas, former chief scientist and acting deputy director of the SDI Organization and president of Titan Technologies)

There may be good reasons for Star Wars, but the ulterior motives of Russian scientists are not among them. Yonas should address the scientists' objections, not their presumed motives. He needs to show that SDI will not escalate the arms race and sap the U. S. economy, which are charges, incidentally, made by Americans as well as Russian scientists.

Speaking of . . .

Well Poisoning

Jack's Paranoiac Love for Jill

Jack persistently refuses to infer from Jill's behavior towards him, however loving, that she "really" loves him, but believes, despite evidence from Jill's manifest behavior . . . that she loves Tom, Dick or Harry. A curious feature of Jack's tendency to attribute to Jill a lack of love for him and a love for Tom, Dick or Harry . . . often seems to be that she tends to make this attribution in inverse proportion to Jill's testimony and actions to the contrary.

Jack may reason: "Look at all the things that Jill is doing to try to prove to me that she loves me. If she really loved me she would not have to be so obvious about it and try so hard. The fact that she is trying so hard proves she is pretending. She must be trying to cover up her feelings—she must be trying to cover up her feelings. She probably loves Tom."

At this point Jill is in a double-bind. . . . If she tries to act even more loving, she further activates Jack's assumption that she is pretending. If, on the other hand, she pretends to act less loving and more aloof then she certainly will activate his view that she does not love him. He then can say: "See, I told you so, she really doesn't love me. Look at how aloof she has become."

Now, Jack may decide to resolve his mistrust by various moves that one generally regards as part of the paranoid strategy. He may pretend to Jill that he does think she loves him, so that, in his view of her, she will think she has fooled him. He will then mount evidence (she has exchanged glances with a man, she smiled at a man, her walk gives her away because it is the way a prostitute walks, etc.), that seems to him to substantiate his secretly held view that she does not love him. But as his suspicion mounts, he may discover that the evidence he has accumulated suddenly looks very thin. This does not prove, however, that his attribution is correct; it proves that he has not taken into account how clever she is. . . . Thus he reasons: "I have not been smart enough. She realizes that I am suspicious so she is not giving anything away. I had better bluff her by pretending to some suspicions that I do not feel, so that she will think I'm on the wrong track." So he pretends to her that he thinks she is having an affair with Tom, when he "knows" that she is having an affair with Dick.

(R. D. Laing, H. Phillipson, A. R. Lee. *Interpersonal Perception: A Theory and a Method of Research*; 1966; Springer Publishing Co., Inc., New York 10012. Reprinted by permission.)

Two Wrongs Make a Right

The fallacy of two wrongs make a right consists in attempting to justify what is considered objectionable by appealing to instances of similar wrongdoing. For example, a student caught cheating on an exam pleads that he was not the only one cheating — at least one other student was as well. The student is trying to justify or defend his own misconduct by introducing the same misconduct of another. That someone else was cheating is irrelevant to the charge that the student himself was cheating. Two *wrongs* do not make a right.

The two-wrongs fallacy takes two general forms:

1. **Tu Quoque.** *Tu quoque* is a Latin phrase meaning "You also" or "You, too." A more colloquial translation would be "Look who's talking!" **In its** *tu quoque* **form, the two-wrongs fallacy consists in charging one's accuser with acting in a way that contradicts or is inconsistent with the very position that he or she is advancing.**

For example, Jack advises Jill to get more exercise. Jill reminds Jack that, being the world's greatest couch potato, he is in no position to give such advice. Again, a mother cautions her teenage son about drugs. "That's really something coming from you!" he replies. "Why, you smoke, drink, and use caffeine." Even if Jack is sedentary and mom is addicted to alcohol, nicotine, and caffeine, that does not make their advice any less wise. And it is the advice that is at issue, not whether or not those who preach it practice it.

2. **Common Practice.** A second version of the two-wrongs fallacy, **the fallacy of common practice, consists in appealing to a widespread practice to defend a questionable activity.** For example, trying to justify using company stationery and postage stamps for personal correspondence, a worker says: "Why everybody does it," or "Workers have always helped themselves to things like that." Simply because the practice is widespread does not make the behavior right.

Years ago, Regimen, manufacturer of weight-reducing tablets, was charged by the Justice Department with deliberate misrepresentation and falsehood in advertising its product. In fact, the U.S. Attorney General described Regimen's tactics as one of the most brazen frauds ever perpetrated on the public, mostly women. In response, Regimen spokespersons pointed out that other advertisers and agencies were doing the same kind of thing. But no matter how pervasive the practice, misrepresentation is misrepresentation — hence, the irrelevancy of Regimen's defense.

It is worth noting that the two-wrongs fallacy can be considered a personal attack, because it is a way of impugning others rather than addressing the accusations made against us. When the other person is our accuser, this tack can be especially effective, shattering as it may the glass house from which she casts the stone at us. For all of that, a two-wrongs argument, including *tu quoque* and common practice, is logically irrelevant and thus fallacious.

Consider these further examples of two-wrongs and its variants:

Example 1: "Sure, plenty of things are wrong in the United States today. . . . But . . . none of our contemporary failings approaches the offenses that have strained the American past. . . . Yes, there is some empirical evidence of changes in some moral values. . . . Chastity and fidelity seem no longer to be widely revered. But it is a fair inquiry to ask if adultery is more prevalent today than it was in the time of Grover Cleveland. . . . '' (James Kilpatrick, syndicated columnist)

The immoralities of the past are no reason to temper a critical inspection of today's morality. Even if marital infidelity was more prevalent in the nineteenth century, that does not make it of any less moral and social concern today.

Example 2:   Letter to the editor: "I was greatly disturbed to learn that a U.S. Congressman has threatened to cut the funding for Orbiter 105 if NASA (National Aeronautics and Space Administration) decides to build it at Vandenberg AFB (which is located in Lompoc, California) rather than in his hometown. It is alleged that it will cost $150 million more to build Orbiter 105 at Vandenberg than at Palmdale, California. That figure is slightly more than twice what it cost the taxpayers for the half-day shutdown of the government when Congress failed to meet an appropriate deadline in 1986. Does the congressman feel any guilt for that debacle?"

The writer seems to think that it is all right to spend an additional $150 million to locate the project at Vandenberg than in Palmdale, because Congress wasted about half that sum shutting down the government for half a day in 1986. But waste is waste. One wasteful episode does not justify another. The writer should be showing how and why the Vandenberg location is worth the extra cost. Instead he enlists a *tu quoque*.

Example 3:   At one point during France's trial of former Gestapo chief of Lyon, Klaus Barbie, defense attorney Jacques Vergas argued: "Does crime against humanity provoke emotion and merit commemoration only when it strikes down Europeans? We share the grief over the children of Izieu (where, in 1944, Barbie was accused of ordering the roundup of forty-four Jewish children and their deportation to the Auschwitz death camp), but we do not ignore the deaths of Algerian children (who were killed during the French action in the Algerian civil war)."

Vergas would have the French judges think better of Barbie's atrocities for the irrelevant reason that the French themselves have blood on their hands. But this *tu quoque* cuts no ice — Barbie was convicted.

Example 4:   Here is Chrysler Corporation Chairman Lee A. Iacocca acknowledging that for forty years Chrysler:

1. disconnected the odometers on new cars being test-driven by company managers prior to sale, and
2. sold as new, cars that had been damaged during tests and later repaired.

"Did we screw up? You bet we did. We're human, and sometimes people do some pretty dumb things. . . . Going back through my forty years in the business, a lot of test cars have been driven with the odometers unhooked."

Iacocca is using a **common practice** argument to mitigate Chrysler's culpability. Even if this practice had been industry wide, that should not have made it acceptable; nor is it any more acceptable because humans do "some pretty dumb things." Here we have a situation where common practice was used initially to condone a wrong and then used years later in an attempt to excuse it.

Example 5: Syndicated columnist and former Nixon speech writer, Raymond Price, argues for the necessity of keeping covert actions covert: ". . . That's the way both our allies and our adversaries do it. That's the way any country serious about the harsh requirements of dealing effectively with troublesome nations in a dangerous world do it. . . ."

What Price should be detailing are the *reasons* that other nations do it—that is what is relevant, not *that* they do it. Other nations do all sorts of things. So what? Rather than trying to demonstrate the wisdom of "keeping covert activities covert," Price attempts to persuade his audience by appealing to a most human rationalization of questionable conduct: "Everybody does it," from which it is supposed to follow, "It must be all right." Maybe it is, maybe it is not. At best, common practice only suggests the possibility of good reasons; it is, of itself, never a good reason.

IN BRIEF *Ad hominem* attacks result from a failure to distinguish between what is being said and who is saying it. The personal character, motives, associations, and conduct of a person, at best, provide grounds for withholding endorsement of what the person says before consulting perhaps more impartial, reliable, and trustworthy sources. But they never of themselves justify rejecting the person's claim, position, or idea.

EXERCISES ON AD HOMINEM APPEALS*

Identify the kind of ad hominem argument present in each of the following passages: abusive, circumstantial, well poisoning, two-wrongs (*tu quoque,* common practice).

1. Letter to the editor: "Those who object to the media's poking into the background of Dan Quayle have no basis for yelling, 'Foul!' I don't remember any cries of media persecution when the same press went after Senators Joe Biden and Gary Hart,

who had reporters from the *Miami Herald* stationed outside his door until the wee hours of the morning."

2. "... The new role of government also brings into sharp focus a wasteful self-contradiction of bureaucracy. If people are employed to attend to a problem the last thing they want to do is solve that problem and put themselves out of work. One can only regard with awe and admiration the great skill of bureaucrats in nourishing a problem into something of gigantic proportions, generating research, undertaking surveys, holding conferences, traveling to the far corners of the earth to learn if the residents of Oz and Shangri-La have the same problem. . . . The bureaucracy has a fairly consistent record of not solving the problem it tackles, thus assuring that the jobs of the problem-solvers will be safeguarded and multiplied. . . ."

(John A. Hoared, speech delivered to the American Farm Bureau Tax and Spending Limitation Conference, September 18, 1978.)

3. "Criticism of the (the *Los Angeles*) *Times* coverage of the McMartin (child molestation) case is particularly widespread among journalists who covered the case and among supporters of the defense. In interviews conducted before the (not-guilty) verdicts were returned last week, three basic charges emerged:

   —*The Times* published a number of stories, especially early in the case, that seemed to assume the charges were true.
   —*The Times* published many stories that were biased against the defense.
   —*The Times* never published major investigative stories examining the prosecution's case.

   Noel Greenwood, deputy managing editor of *The Times,* vigorously denies that *The Times* was biased or unfair and attributes these charges to a 'mean, malevolent campaign conducted by people . . . whose motives are highly suspect and who have behaved in a basically dishonest . . . and dishonorable way.'

   Greenwood . . . declined to specify who these people are, but he says their 'Monday morning quarterbacking' could be applied to the coverage of any major running story. . . ."

   (David Shaw, "*Times* McMartin Coverage Was Biased, Critics Claim," *Los Angeles Times,* Jan. 22, 1990, p. 16.)

4. ". . . (Businessmen believe) that they are defending free enterprises when they declaim that business is not concerned 'merely' with profit but also with promoting 'social ends'; that business has a 'social conscience' and takes seriously responsibility for providing employment, eliminating discrimination, avoiding pollution and whatever else may be the catchwords of the contemporary crop of reformers. In fact, they are—or would be if they or anyone else took them seriously—preaching pure and unadulterated socialism. Businessmen who talk this way are unwitting puppets of the intellectual forces that have been undermining the basis of a free society these past decades."
   (Milton Friedman)

5. "Socialism has come down in the world and top people have deserted it. It now belongs, if anywhere, to a world of semi-literate and the semi-educated; to South American priests dedicated to new-fangled liberation theology; to tribal oligar-

chies in black Africa, and in Europe to the dropouts of higher education — a sort of Lumpenpolytechnik of bitter Trotskyites to whom mid-Victorian concepts of class and consciousness still look like the latest thing."
(George Watson)

6. When a convicted cocaine trafficker told Congress that he had helped the Nicaraguan Contras smuggle drugs into the United States and ship automatic weapons and explosives to Central America, a Contra spokesman replied: "We've heard this gentleman's accusations before. He is a convicted drug dealer."

7. Letter to the editor: "Something happens to my stomach every time New York Yankees owner George Steinbrenner or Philadelphia 76ers' owner Harold Katz or any of the other sports franchisers opens his mouth to complain about the 'character' of the players they employ. If character counted, half of those who own professional teams wouldn't own their own shoes."

8. News item: *(Bloomington, Ind.)* "Bobby Knight received a standing ovation from Indiana University basketball boosters Wednesday after saying he was wrong to pull his team off the floor in an exhibition game against the Soviets. 'I made a mistake and no one can regret that mistake more than I do,' said Knight. 'It was a mistake in judgment. I would appreciate each of those of you who has not made a mistake or two in the past 17 years to drop me a note in the morning.' "

9. Editorial: "What's this? Convert our beloved District of Columbia into the 51st state, named New Columbia? Are they serious? Yes, they are. Many of the Democratic leaders in Congress today are quite serious because in recent presidential elections, D. C. residents have shown themselves to be overwhelmingly Democratic voters and statehood could increase D. C.'s number of electoral votes from three prescribed in the 23rd Amendment of the constitution, passed in 1961. The idea for New Columbia has been introduced in the House by the district's non-voting delegate to the House, Democrat Walter E. Fauntroy. Its chief sponsor on the other side of the capital is Democratic Senator Edward Kennedy, an old vote-counter from way back. The House District of Columbia Committee has approved it, by a vote of 6 to 5. All six approval votes were by Democrats."

10. After a newspaper ran an article about charges leveled against a local police officer, one irate reader wrote: "Consider your newspaper's source of the story. The police union will pick on anything managers of the department do and try to stir up a problem."

11. Letter to the editor opposing California Governor George Deukmejian's returning the state's surplus monies to taxpayers rather than spending it on education: "The governor was educated in public schools of New York at a time when the per capita expenditure of monies in that state was the highest in the nation. The quality of his education was enhanced by that outstanding support. Even though Deukmejian enjoyed as a pupil a school that was financially well supported, he is unwilling to provide the same for young Californians."

12. Editorial regarding the *Piaget* hunt for the sunken oceanliner *Titanic:* "Once again, the affluent dilettantes have conspired to destroy a priceless historical resource for purposes of commercialism and profit. The resulting 'exhibition' will be a commercialized carnival of curious and morbid mementos no doubt highlighted by the patent-leather shoe of a drowned child. . . ."

13. "Not surprisingly the studies gathered by the National Beer Wholesalers Association conclude that distribution monopolies do not increase the price of beer. One study the beer wholesalers have in mind is described in the association's 'Washington Update.' In fact, the association paid for this study."

14. Editorial: "The results of a recent poll on bilingual education among Los Angeles teachers were predictable and distorted. They can safely be ignored in shaping the problem's future. The poll showed that substantial numbers of teachers favor plunging students from foreign countries directly into substantive courses taught in English rather than letting them learn substance in their native language until they are up to speed in English. It is safe to say the poll represented teachers whose alternative to teaching in English is learning a second language themselves. The answers were also so predictable as what one would expect if one asked police officers whether they would rather chase robbers who were armed or robbers who were not. . . ."

15. Letter to the editor: "In her vice-presidential debate, Geraldine Ferraro (the 1984 Democratic candidate for vice president) acted affirmatively to assure Americans that she has no qualms about sending men off to wars; in fact, she was even so magnanimous as to offer her sons for the draft. Strangely enough there was no mention of including herself or other women in the deal, let alone the offer of her daughters for conscription. Just why is it that female leaders should be able to order males off to fates that they themselves have held lifelong exemption from?"

16. Editorial: "When Congress raises the curtain next week on Act II of the Iran-Contra show trial, there are two contextual points of departure to keep in mind. The first point is that for the past two-hundred years there has been a constant struggle for supremacy between the executive and legislative branches of government. . . . This intensity increases dramatically when the two branches are controlled by opposing political parties. . . . And it reaches fever pitch when a presidential election approaches and half the members of the majority in Congress (Democrats) are running for President against the incumbent's party (Republican). The second point concerns the selective way in which these congressional show trials are scheduled and stated. They expose only dereliction in the executive branch, and only in the Republican administrations. The reasons are simple: Congress never investigates itself because Democrats control Congress."

17. "It is clear now that charges that (Supreme Court nominee) Robert Bork is too ideological are themselves ideologically inspired and that criticism of him as outside the mainstream can only be held by those themselves so far outside the mainstream that they long ago lost sight of the moderate center."
(President Reagan)

18. "Judge Bork reminds me of those dogmatic, right-wing eccentrics encountered on college campuses who like to tease and provoke, and make stimulating teachers and affable colleagues. But there is something basically frivolous about his approach to constitutional interpretation. He loftily rebukes other justices for succumbing to their 'moral predilections'; then identifies his own predilections with the intent of the Framers."
(Arthur Schlesinger)

19. "Literally millions of Americans older and younger than (Supreme Court nominee) Douglas Ginsburg have smoked marijuana often or occasionally. Literally millions still do, and aim to keep on. . . . It seems unfair to suggest that behavior so widespread and so widely accepted should prevent someone from holding high office — even a Supreme Court seat." (Note: Ginsburg admitted to having used marijuana socially while a law professor at Harvard in 1979.)
   (Tom Wicker)

20. "Nietzsche was personally more philosophical than his philosophy. His talk about power, harshness, and superb immorality was the hobby of a harmless young scholar and constitutional invalid."
   (George Santayana, *The German Mind: A Philosophical Diagnosis*)

21. "When we had got to this point in the argument, and everyone saw that the definition of justice had been completely upset, Thrasymachus, instead of replying to me, said:

    'Tell me, Socrates, have you got a nurse?'

    'Why do you ask such a question,' I said, 'when you ought rather to be answering?'

    'Because she leaves you to snivel, and never wipes your nose: she has not even taught you to know the shepherd from the sheep."
    (Plato, *Republic*)

22. "Once again Jesus addressed the people: 'I am the light of the world. No follower of mine shall wander in the dark; he shall have the light of life.' The Pharisees said to him, 'You are witness in your own cause; your testimony is not valid.' "
   (John 8:12–14)

MODULE 7.2

EMOTIONAL APPEALS

During the 1936 U.S. presidential elections, psychologist G. W. Hartmann conducted an interesting experiment on the relative value of emotional versus logical appeals to voters. Hartmann prepared two different leaflets urging people to vote for the Socialist party. One leaflet expressed the wisdom of voting Socialistic in highly sentimental and romantic language. The other presented the case for Socialism in rational, unemotional terms, citing facts and figures about the goals of the Socialist party. Hartmann had the leaflets distributed to different parts of an "average" U.S. city. A third part of the city, served as a control or comparison, received no leaflets at all.

You may know that in 1936 the United States was mired in the Great Depression, and that, probably as a direct result, many people voted Socialist. Thus, that part of the city that did not receive any Socialist party leaflets showed a twenty-four percent increase in Socialist preference as compared with the 1932 election. Those parts of the city that received the so-called rational or logical leaflets showed a thirty-five percent increase. Those areas that received the highly emotional leaflets showed a whopping fifty percent rise in support for the Socialist candidate.[1]

In the last half-century, nothing has occurred to shake the implication of the Hartmann study's strong suggestion that emotional messages do influence people's behavior and attitudes that rational appeals fail to produce. Indeed, today's intensely emotional campaigns in advertising and politics testify to the highly persuasive capacity of the emotional message.

When we distinguished earlier between persuasion and argument we noted that some of our most enduring literature, including argumentative discourse, crackles with passion. It is not the presence of emotion in argument, then, that should give us pause; but the substitution of emotion for reasons. No doubt, in the game of persuasion, emotion often pinchhits successfully for reason—the audience does conform to the author's will. But the goal of argument is *demonstration,* and the only way to demonstrate the truth of a proposition is on the basis of other statements' known truth or acceptability. An emotion such as fear or pity is not a truth. It may be true or false that we are experiencing a given emotion, but the emotion itself is an intrapsychic feeling.

The point is that I might well succeed in persuading you of my claim or position by getting you to feel fear or pity, or some other emotion, without actually offering you a shred of demonstrable evidence. In fact, there is a good chance that I do not have any evidence, otherwise I would present it. Instead, I choose to manipulate you psychologically instead of convincing you logically. I induce you to confuse a feeling with a reason.

Years ago, Dale Carnegie, author of *How To Win Friends and Influence People,* wrote, "When dealing with people we're dealing with creatures of emotion, creatures bristling with prejudice and motivated by vanity and passion." Today's advertising executive and political campaign manager, in tandem with opinion pollsters, live by this credo. The pollster zeros in on what we feel—what we fear and love and hope for; what we are anxious and feel guilty about—then, the hucksters press the appropriate emotional buttons to sell us everything from toothpaste to presidents. Their real accomplishment is leaving us *feeling* that we made an "informed decision."

As you might imagine, many informal fallacies fall within the category of emotional appeals. In our limited space, we will focus on three of the most common: mob, fear, and pity.

Mob Appeal

The fallacy of mob appeal consists in trying to persuade others by appealing to their deepest emotions and popular sentiments instead of evidence. The mob appeal can be exploited in basically two ways: 1) by playing to the audience's

---

[1]See James V. McConnell. *Understanding Human Behavior,* 2nd edition. (New York: Holt, Rinehart and Winston, 1977), p. 665.

deepest human needs, or 2) by inciting an audience's feelings and enthusiasms owing to its culturally conditioned prejudices.

1. *Human Needs*   Each of us shares a repertoire of basic human needs and drives — for survival, emotional security, sexual gratification, peer approval, status and success, and so on. What we perceive as satisfying those needs and related wants, we generally approve of, accept, or are sympathetic to. And whatever presents itself as satisfying those needs inevitably elicits a powerful emotional response, which at once can impede rational thought and substitute for relevant evidence.

For example, in addressing an audience of potential voters, a political candidate says, "As intelligent, hardworking, God-fearing people, you, better than anyone, know that this country needs someone like me...." By *flattering* the audience, the candidate plays to the human need for *self-esteem.*

Again, an ad that portrays an automobile as being for "the discriminating buyer, for whom only the best will do" feeds the audience's appetite for *status;* and certainly we are all familiar with the ubiquitous pitch to *sexual gratification,* as in the ad for Black Velvet Smooth; "Just the thought of it can give you a good feeling. Black Velvet. Canadian Whiskey. The smooth Canadian."

2. *Culturally Conditioned Prejudices*   Besides basic human needs, each of us harbors many unexamined assumptions transmitted by our culture through what is termed cultural conditioning, the process by which society's attitudes and values and role expectations are passed on to its members. Although we do not completely understand how cultural conditioning works — or what its lasting effects are — we do know that cultures subtly condition their members. You and I are largely the products of the particular places and times in which we were raised. We have been significantly shaped by the customs, social forms, and material traits of those settings. So embedded in our outlooks are culturally conditioned assumptions about self, other, and the world, that we are not conscious of most of them. Indeed, one of the goals of higher education in general, and of critical thinking in particular, is to help us confront and examine these presuppositions.

For example, most Americans *believe in* "individuality." Individuality is a value toward which we have a favorable attitude. Similarly, many of us *believe in* "the American dream": Through sheer hard work, we can become just about anything we want to become. And many of us firmly *believe in* "progress" as measured by such things as an increasing Gross National Product and a higher standard of living. The list of cultural assumptions that Americans have inherited could be extended to include the following:

"Socialistic" means "communistic."

Socialism and communism are inherently evil.

There exists a single God Who is all good and all powerful, and Who intervenes in the
     lives of *His* creation.

Democracy is the best form of government.

The two-party system is the best way to structure our political system.

Capitalism is the best economic system.

We should never intentionally put to death the old and infirm, or even deprive them
     of scarce medical resources.

Anybody can grow up to be president of the United States.
People should marry for love, not money.
Money is the root of all evil. Money cannot buy happiness.
Rich people are not really happy.
People should be physically punished for crimes.
Women are passive, men aggressive.
It is acceptable, even normal, for males to be sexually promiscuous, but not females.
Women make better nurses and elementary school teachers than men do.

The list goes on and on, expanded according to our own subcultural assumptions. Some of these assumptions are today being openly reassessed, as with gender roles. Others—our beliefs in democracy, capitalism, monotheism—are so deeply ingrained as to resist almost entirely any impartial, public re-examination. In each case, it is not so much observed specifics that lead us to a cultural assumption but accepted beliefs regarding a particular aspect of culture—social behavior, gender roles, politics, religion, economics, and so on.

Speaking of . . .

Mob Appeal

In the Gulf War on Whose Side Was God?

Have you ever noticed how adversaries in war inevitably claim that God is on their side? Little wonder—it is not easy to get people to fight and die and make the sacrifices that war requires. Believing that the cause is sanctioned by God helps. That is why both Saddam Hussein and George Bush relentlessly proclaimed divine support for bombing, burning, poisoning, pillaging, raping, maiming, killing, and thus breathed new life into moribund talk shows. (Historians can sort out who did what to whom.) From Saddam, whom fundamentalist Muslims used to consider an infidel, we heard:

> We are convinced that God is on our side.
> *From an interview with Peter Arnett of CNN, Jan. 30, 1991)*

> The world needs to tell the one with the big stick [*presumably President Bush*] that the stick in your hand cannot destroy the house of God or the humanity of man.
> *(From a domestic speech, January 29, 1991)*

> We are being faithful to the value that God Almighty has inspired in us, for we have no fears of the forces of Satan, the devil that rides your shoulder.
> *(In a letter to President Bush, January 17, 1991)*

> In the coming period, the response of Iraq will be on a larger scale, using all the means and potential God has given us.
> *(From some domestic comments, January 20, 1991)*

> Iraq is not ready to relinquish the role given to it by God.
> *(From a domestic speech, February 10, 1991)*

continued

continued
Bush responded in kind:

> Saddam tried to cast this conflict as a religious war, but it is nothing to do with religion per se. It has, on the other hand, everything to do with what religion embodies—good versus evil, right versus wrong, human dignity and freedom versus tyranny and oppression.
> *(From a speech to National Religious Broadcasters Association, January 28, 1991)*
>
> May God bless each and every one of them, and the coalition forces at our side in the Gulf, and may He continue to bless our nation, the United States of America.
> *(From a speech, January 16, 1991)*
>
> God willing we will win this war.
> *(January 27, 1991)*
>
> During the darkest days of the Civil War, a man we revere—not merely for what he did but for what he was—was asked whether he thought the Lord was on his side. And said Abraham Lincoln, "My concern is not whether God is on our side, but whether we are on God's side." My fellow Americans, I firmly believe in my heart of hearts that times will soon be on the side of peace, because the world is overwhelmingly on the side of God.
> *(From a speech to National Religious Broadcasters Association, January 28, 1991)*
>
> I believe the Lord does hear our prayers.
> *(From a speech at National Prayer Breakfast sponsored by members of the House and Senate)*

Amen.

Blindly accepting such presuppositions leads us to selective perception—to seeing only what we want to see—but thinking logically requires objectivity, a dispassionate and disinterested evaluation of the evidence that confirms or refutes a claim. When we think rationally, we must try to put aside our preconceptions and biases about an issue; we must attempt to keep an open mind. Although none of us can ever be completely impartial, we can be objective enough to allow our views to conform to the evidence, rather than making the evidence conform to our views.

IN BRIEF   *There may be good reasons for holding any cultural assumption.* But when we leave the assumption unexamined and allow it to color our thinking, we violate a prerequisite of logical thought: objectivity.

Mob appeals that tap into our cultural presuppositions use those preconceptions, rather than evidence, as support for assertions. Typically, they employ highly inflamed rhetoric that triggers those presuppositions and the strong emotional attachments we have to them. For example, when domestic car manufacturers implore

Speaking of . . .

Mob Appeal

The 1988 Presidential Election

Certainly the 1988 presidential campaign offers one of the most egregious examples of mob appeal. With such severe problems facing the nation — deteriorating environment, soaring deficits, decaying infrastructure, widespread drug abuse, epidemic venereal disease, government corruption, the slumping posture of American business in the global economy, shameful illiteracy — we had every reason to expect in the spring of '88 that the fall would offer a feast of substantive issues over which Bush and Dukakis would contest. What we got instead was a gruel consisting of flags, furloughs, and family. Which candidate was the more patriotic, as determined by his support of, or opposition to, mandatory flag saluting in public schools? Which was tougher on crime, as measured by his support for, or opposition to, furloughs for convicts? Which of the two family men was the more family man? These became the "burning" questions of the campaign.

Thus, the endless photo opportunities, slavishly recorded by the media, featuring flags; merciless renderings of the impossible-to-sing "Star Spangled Banner"; and candidates' spouses, children, grandchildren, nephews, nieces, cousins, *ad infinitum*. "Flag sales are doing well and America is doing well," the future president assured a New Jersey audience and a nightly news audience in the tens of millions. Lest anyone think that his blood was no less red-white-and-blue than his opponent's, the Massachusetts governor delivered more than one stemwinder enveloped in a sea of Old Glorys. And to dispel any doubt of his humble-as-apple-pie origins, Governor Dukakis unforgivingly droned on about his immigrant grandparents, reminded us that the Democrats were "the party of the American Dream," and vowed that he would bash on "with the winds at our back and courage in our hearts." Not to be outdone, the Bush campaign countered with the stirring message: "The President — the heart, the soul, the conscience of the Nation," superimposed over their baby-nuzzling candidate. And let's not forget Bush's "thousand points of light," which was adapted from Reagan's 1984 contagious "sparks of genius"; the pictures of Dukakis atop a tank or power-walking; and pictures of Bush fishing and jogging — each candidate with a phalanx of police officers, presumably living embodiments of the candidates' tough-on-crime philosophies.

All these visuals and "power phrases" had one function, and it was not to inform. It was to arouse feeling intense enough to wring out a vote. If you think otherwise, ask yourself how much you have heard lately about flags and furloughs. Naturally little, because they were contrived controversies, *ad hoc* nonissues, that provided the ongoing appeal to emotion that all persuasion requires.

(Adapted from PBS' *The Public Mind* with Bill Moyers.)

us to "Buy American" they want us to substitute strong feelings of group loyalty for evidence in deciding which car to buy. They use the mob appeal. So do politicians who solicit our votes by metaphorically wrapping themselves in the flag, demagogues who seek to pollute our thinking with their own prejudices, and propagandists who systematically propagate doctrines and allegations reflective of their own views and interests.

Appeal to Pity

The fallacy of pity consists in trying to persuade by exploiting the single emotion of sympathy. For example, the student who deserves a "C" in history might try to persuade his teacher to raise his grade for a variety of lamentable reasons: It is the first "C" he has ever received, it spoils his 4.0 GPA, he needs a higher grade to get into law school, and so forth. Similarly, a local pound might run an ad of a pitiable looking puppy asking, "Won't you please adopt me?" AT&T (the "telephone company") suggests that it is time to "reach out and touch someone," perhaps a neglected grandparent or an old friend.

It is important to realize that the relevance of an appeal to pity depends upon what is being argued. Sometimes, invoking sympathy is altogether justified, as when an attorney asks a sentencing judge to consider the squalid upbringing of a client. Although such an appeal would be irrelevant and fallacious in arguing the person's guilt, it may be germane to the severity of the sentence. Recall the German youth who, in the summer of 1987, flew a small plane into the middle of Red Square in Moscow. That he may have been the victim of youthful exuberance is irrelevant to whether he acted illegally, but quite relevant to the sentence he would get. (A Soviet court sentenced him to four years in a labor camp.)

Emotions are a doubtless important part of our make-up. The capacity to sympathize frequently is the first step toward correcting social injustice. Still, emotions in general, and pity in particular, can impede rational assessment and thereby block resolution of the very problems that provoked them. In the end, we must assess the relevancy of the appeal to pity precisely as we would any other premise, by asking: Does it support, provide a reason to believe, or affect the truth or falsity of the conclusion? If not, the appeal is irrelevant and therefore fallacious.

The following is an additional example of fallacious appeal to pity:

> Just before Mother's Day 1987, an editorial appeared in a major U.S. newspaper in support of two bills to help underserved areas provide prenatal care to working, poor, and unsecured pregnant women. The editorial said that "the bills would be a fitting tribute to motherhood if they received favorable reception by lawmakers. . . . Today's burdened mothers need and deserve all the breaks they can get. They are expected to be a superwoman on the job and at home, but today, let her just be mom. Give her a break."

Instead of showing exactly how these bills would ease the plight of these women and why these bills were the best alternative, the writer tried to invoke the reader's sympathy. Maybe these women are deserving of our sympathy and of legislative attention. But that is not the point. We want to enact sound legislation. Noble intentions may inspire but they do not guarantee good laws.

Appeal to Fear

The fallacy of fear consists in employing a threat of harm to compel acceptance of a position. Also known as "swinging the big stick" or "the scare tactic," this fallacy is summed up in the adage, "Might makes right." Of course, it does not, but by substituting the emotion of fear for calm, cool reflection, rhetoricians can convince their audience that might does make right.

Just as not every appeal that induces pity is fallacious, neither is every argument that induces fear. For example, concerned for the welfare of a friend who smokes, you say to the person: "You know, you really ought to quit smoking. Every scientific study done indicates that smoking carries a high morbidity rate. And, increasingly, nonsmokers find smoking in their presence offensive because they suffer from inhaling the smoke." Quite possibly, your sage advice might scare your friend. But you are not attempting to get your friend to quit smoking by threatening the person with harm; rather, you are offering facts—frightening ones, perhaps, but facts nonetheless. The picture you draw is, or should be, disquieting to any rational, considerate person. But reasons like the ones you give are significantly relevant to your advice, your conclusion. That smoking has been proven to be harmful to one's own and other's health supports or provides reasons to believe your claim that your friend should quit smoking.

Suppose your recalcitrant friend replies, "Look, I enjoy smoking. It's fun. It calms me. It gives me something to do with my hands and helps me control my weight. So why should I quit?" Exasperated, you fire back, "Look, if you don't quit, we're through. I don't ever want to see you again."

In this instance, you are attempting to force the person to stop smoking by threatening to end your friendship. Perhaps you will prevail and your friend may be persuaded to quit. However, you probably will not have convinced the person of the rightness of your position, And *that,* from the viewpoint of logic, is the issue, which your threat does not address.

As another example, suppose a case is made based upon significant data that the U.S. military defense is inadequate and needs to be improved. Given the gloomy facts offered in support of the claim, one easily might become alarmed. The facts, after all, are disquieting. Those so arguing would not be using a threat of harm to get us to accept their conclusions; rather, they would be offering relevant and important data to demonstrate the inadequacy of our defenses and the need for improvement.

In contrast, suppose a politician argued, "We need to spend more on defense. Otherwise, we are inviting our destruction at the hands of our implacable foes." In this instance, the person offers no proof for the need to increase defense spending. Exactly why are our defenses inadequate? Precisely how will increased military spending remedy these shortcomings? Answers to these questions would help provide demonstrable evidence for the assertion that we need to spend more on defense. Instead of answering these questions—that is, providing relevant reasons—the politician tries to scare the audience into agreement with him.

Speaking of . . .

Emotional Appeals

Tears and Theatrics in the Courtroom

. . .White-collar defendants often make heart-rending pleas at sentencing in a teary-eyed attempt to stay out of prison. Their lawyers gather moving testimonial letters about the client. Privileged people who have stolen millions of dollars are suddenly portrayed as kind and generous souls with a special fondness for children and small animals. . . .

The defense bar has formulated certain rules to maximize the chance of softening a judge's heart. For example, letters from congressmen, priests and rabbis are out, because judges assume they will say nice things about the worst scoundrels; letters from "little people" . . . are in.

"It's amazing how often you can put together some acts of kindness and you can humanize your client," says Gerald Feffer, a Washington lawyer. "You try to find as many of those anecdotes as you can. . . ."

Most attorneys say a convincing showing of remorse is crucial. If the defendant is appealing the conviction, however, the trick is to atone for mistakes or misjudgments without actually breaking down and confessing to the crime.

Failure to show remorse can be "catastrophic," says Feffer. "The guy has to sit there and just sort of seep with remorse."

But even the most heartfelt plea can backfire. E. Robert Wallach, the longtime friend of former Attorney General Edwin Meese, gave a rambling talk at his recent sentencing for fraud and racketeering.

"I, a bright and gifted individual, gifts given by God, to have made such a blunder with my life. . . . Of course I feel remorse," Wallach said.

But Wallach's plea seemed to anger Judge Richard Owen, who rebutted each point with a blistering lecture, scoffing even at the claim that the San Francisco lawyer had done lots of *pro bono* work. "That's the way to get notoriety and get clients and get known by the bar. . . . It helps to get business. We all know that," Owen said. He gave Wallach six years in prison.

Another rule of thumb is to have loved ones on hand. "It's important for family to attend, to show it's a close family," says (attorney) Frederick Hafetz. "If someone's going to go away, and he's the only breadwinner and going to leave a wife and three kids, that's a factor you want to play on."

But this too can boomerang, as former Representative Mario Biaggi, D-N.Y., found out. When the septuagenarian congressman was being sentenced for obstructing justice and accepting a free vacation from a Brooklyn Democratic boss, he erred by invoking the failing health of his wife.

continued

continued

The prosecutor inconveniently noted that the "aging Romeo," as he put it, had been visiting a Florida spa with a 45-year-old model while his wife was suffering from Hodgkin's disease. The judge gave Biaggi 2 and a half years.

Former Deputy Defense Secretary Paul Thayer seemed to have all the elements in place at the 1985 sentencing for his role in an insider-trading scheme. His wife of 38 years was at his side. He had letters of support from such luminaries as President Gerald Ford and the chairman of the Joint Chiefs of Staff. He apologized to the judge. And his lawyer said Thayer "did not receive a penny" from the scheme.

But that allowed prosecutors to emphasize that Thayer had used $150,000 from the illegal trading to support his girlfriend. Thayer received a four-year prison term. . . .

(Howard Kurtz, "Tears, Theatrics Seldom Sway Judges," Copyright 1990, *The Washington Post*, reprinted with permission.)

Two additional examples of the appeal to fear, with comment, follow.

President Reagan during a radio address: "When you hear talk about a tough trade bill, remember that being tough on trade and commerce, the lifeblood of the economy, will have the worst possible consequences for the consumer and American worker."

Exactly how will a tough trade bill ruin U.S. consumers and workers, as the President argues? He does not say. Instead, he uses the threat of harm as a substitute for the evidence and reasons needed to establish his claim. If Reagan's audience is not alert, they may accept his claim unexamined, trembling all the way.

Premier Andreas Panandreous of Greece, reacting to U.S. charges that Greece negotiated with terrorist Abu Nidal: "There will be no talks (about U.S. military bases in Greece) and the base will close in 1988 (when U.S.-Greek accord expires) if the United States doesn't withdraw fully, officially, and publicly these accusations against our country."

Are the charges true? If not, then Panandreous should offer some evidence, although admittedly it's tough to prove a negative. (Try proving that you are *not* attempting to subvert the government.) At the very least, he could show that the charges are baseless; unsupported by evidence; erected on half-truths, innuendo, or unfounded suspicion — in other words, cite some reasons and evidence that would effectively discredit the charge. He instead threatens the United States with the loss of strategic military bases, which of course has nothing to do with the charge to which he is reacting.

EXERCISES ON EMOTIONAL APPEAL

Identify and explain the emotional appeals—mob, fear, pity—present in the following situations and arguments.

1. Asking American business leaders not to pull out of South Africa, South African Zulu leader Magosuthu Buthelezi, an influential black moderate, told them: "If American firms completely pull out of South Africa, South Africa will be thrust into a cauldron of revolution and be reduced to Third World chaos."
2. Letter to the editor opposing a bill requiring motorcyclists and their passengers to wear helmets: "If I am injured wearing a state-approved helmet, I will litigate the state, the dealer, and the manufacturer of the same helmet and let's see what that will cost the state and the public."
3. President Reagan, speaking to employees at the Dictaphone Corporation company picnic, one week before the Democratic-controlled Congress approved a $1 trillion federal budget resolution calling for $65 billion in higher taxes over the following three years, 1988–1991: "Some in Congress are reverting to their old habits of tax and tax, spend and spend. They're squandering your hard-earned money on politically motivated spending projects and special interest payoffs. Well, I say no way. No way are the American people going to be made to foot the bill for the tax-and-spend crew on Capitol Hill."
4. Reagan again: "Make no mistake—we face a clear and present danger in Congress. The momentum of big government, which we've managed to hold back the past few years has only been gathering steam, getting ready to burst through all the restraints we've imposed upon it. . . . If a tax hike makes it to my desk, I'll veto it in less time than it takes Vanna White to turn the letters V-E-T-O."
5. Embarrassed by several well-publicized cases in which children's savings were seized to pay their parents' overdue taxes, the IRS announced new procedures designed to make sure that practice didn't recur. In an interview discussing the new regulations, IRS commissioner Lawrence B. Gibbs said: "(The new procedure) is in keeping with our initiative of trying to treat taxpayers like customers, making it easier for us to do a difficult job. . . . Some of the stories indicate we are a large, un-caring, insensitive agency, but believe it or not . . . we haven't done this intentionally."
6. News item: *(Washington)* "(National Football League Players') union chief Gene Upshaw, while calling for talks to resume, said that negotiations between the union and management were turning into a 'black versus white' issue. 'I didn't want to say this, but I think (management) is having a lot of trouble with me,' Upshaw said at a news conference. 'I was wondering when it would ever get to me, and it has. It's gotten to the point now where they look at me as being black, I'm militant, I'm going to stop (games) at the stadiums. When all else fails, that's the next avenue that they'll take, to try and divide us along the lines of black versus white.' Upshaw cut off the news conference before he could elaborate."
7. "One cannot think of punishment without considering the causes of crime. Take the case of the English teenagers who, after their favorite side loses a football match, wreck trains, throw bottles, and kick referees. . . . Born in a mean street,

in a home without culture, with no books, no good conversation, no music except pop, born into a home with perhaps a stupid drunken father and a screaming ignorant mother, what chance has a lad of turning out to be socially minded and pro-life?" (A. S. Neill, "Punishment Never Cures Anything")

8. News item: "*(Washington)* Senate Majority Leader Robert C. Byrd (D-WV) threatened to hold President Reagan's nomination to the Supreme Court hostage unless Republicans stop obstructing legislation important to Democrats. . . ."

9. President Reagan, assuring the nation that he was not ready to draw the curtain with eighteen months left in his presidency: "We've come this far together, but the journey isn't over. We've won many battles and our brows are covered with sweat and our bodies have wounds, but let our hearts remain full and strong. . . . For our nation and for the cause of freedom and democracy America must stand by the freedom fighters in Nicaragua. . . . All those who must talk about the lame duck and the post-Reagan era are dead wrong. There will be no post-Reagan era because there's been no Reagan era in the way these people mean it. This has been the era of the American people. . . ."

10. Letter to the editor: "When the U.S. moves forward into space again, here is a compelling reason why NASA should include ordinary citizens on every endeavor, large or small, mundane or wonderful: Because the nation trusts in the wisdom, courage, and integrity of 'We the People.' "

11. Oliver North, responding to testimony that he had used money raised to finance *Contra* resupply operations for personal items: "I want to make it very clear that when you put up things *[on the wall, as exhibits]* like 'Parklane Hosiery' and you all snicker at it, and you know that I've got a beautiful secretary, and the good Lord gave her the gift of beauty and the people snicker that Ollie North might have been doing a little hanky-panky with his secretary, Ollie North has been loyal to his wife since the day he married her. And the fact is I went to my best friend *[that is, his wife]* and I asked her, 'Did I ever go to Parklane Hosiery?' And you know what she told me? 'Of course you did, you old buffoon, you went there to buy leotards for our two little girls. . . .' "

12. Letter to the editor: "The highest paid cross-examiner from New York, (Iran-Contra committee's chief counsel) Arthur L. Liman tried to win Ollie North's sympathy by praising Ollie North's medals, his valor and his values. Liman wanted to win Ollie's sympathies in order to turn Ollie against 'higher ups' who, he insinuated, had betrayed Ollie. To make Ollie North denounce his commander-in-chief would have left Ollie North in moral ruin, a Marine who had violated his honor. In this vein, Arthur Liman was shameless. . . ."
(Michael Novak)
(Note: North's attorneys subsequently defended the colonel on grounds that he was following orders from "higher ups.")

13. President Reagan, commenting on his involvement in the arms for hostages deal: "I let my preoccupation with the hostages intrude into areas where it didn't belong. The image—the reality—of Americans in chains, deprived of their freedom and families so far from home, burdened my thought. . . ."

14. Senator Orin G. Hatch (R-UT) to North at the end of North's testimony: "I don't

want you prosecuted. I don't. I don't think many people in America do. And I think there's going to be one lot of hell raised if you are.''

15. Benjamin Hook, executive director of the NAACP, opposing the nomination of Judge Robert Bork to the Supreme Court: ''Bork will in effect wipe out all our gains of the past thirty years.''

16. Letter to the editor: ''I know what it's like to be in a free country and have communists take it over. I am from Ethiopia. When my father refused to give the Communists there our land, they killed him and took it. I hate Communists. And, America, you had better wake up and inform yourselves. The next enemy to freedom is at your back door in Central America.''

17. Shortly after her husband's election to his first Senate term in 1972, the wife of Senator Joe Biden (D-DE) was killed in an auto accident and his two young sons seriously injured. Biden, who remarried and fathered a daughter, has maintained his home in Wilmington, and, it is said, commutes there almost every night to be with his family. In introducing Biden on the occasion Biden would announce what turned out to be his short-lived candidacy for president, fellow Democrat Sen. Daniel Inouye (D-HI) referred to that tragedy and Biden's lifestyle: ''That's fatherhood, that's family. This nation needs a president with a family.''

18. In May 1983, Vice President George Bush posed dramatically with several hundred pounds of cocaine and stacks of greenbacks confiscated from dope smugglers. Proof positive, said Bush, that Fidel Castro was trying to destabilize the United States by smuggling drugs into Florida and other points of entry. Other administration officials staged similar displays, designed to associate leaders of the Sandinista government in Nicaragua with dope trafficking into the United States. Richard Kerr, deputy director of the CIA, subsequently testified before a cabinet-level board, the National Drug Enforcement Policy Board, that American Cubans in Florida and Nicaraguan *Contras* probably are involved to a greater degree in drug smuggling into the United States than anti-U.S. forces. Testified Kerr: ''. . . [I]t was hard to identify Cuban government link to trafficking. There is no solid evidence to support this. The Nicaraguan Sandinista role appears to have been episodic.''

19. Interviewing seven Democratic presidential candidates in 1988, host William F. Buckley began by noting that President Reagan had five portraits in one room and then asked each candidate which portraits he would replace. Richard Gephardt said no portrait could be as pretty as a framed copy of the U.S. Constitution, and Paul Simon said he would have portraits of just plain folks — steelworkers, coal miners, family farmers, working mothers, teachers, inner-city school children.

20. From an editorial opposing the nomination of Judge Robert Bork to the U. S. Supreme Court: ''The last time the Supreme Court considered abortion, in 1986, it ruled 5 to 4 against restrictions imposed by a state. Justice Lewis F. Powell, Jr., the moderate whom Bork would replace, was the fifth vote. Bork seems sure to vote the other way, moving the country back to the scandalous state of affairs that existed before 1973 *[when* Roe *v.* Wade *gave pregnant women abortion rights].*''

21. During the Iran-Contra hearings, Oliver North was asked about several thousand dollars spent from the profits of arms sales to Iran on a security system installed at his residence after threats were made by Palestinian terrorist Abu Nidal. North

explained: "I'll be glad to meet Abu Nidal on equal terms anywhere in the world. OK? There's an even deal for him. But I am not willing to have my wife and four children meet Abu Nidal or his organization on his terms. . . . Gentlemen, I have an 11-year-old daughter, not perhaps a whole lot different than Natasha Simpson *[the American killed by a Nidal terrorist in Rome]*, and so, when *[former CIA technical expert]* Mr. Robinette told me . . . that he could immediately install a security system, I said, 'Please try to keep it to $8,000 and $8,500. I am, after all, a Marine lieutenant colonel, and I live on my salary.' And he installed the system. . . ."

MODULE 7.3

DIVERSION

So far we have seen two categories of irrelevant premises. By introducing logically irrelevant issues into arguments, *ad hominem* and emotional appeals turn an audience's attention to secondary matters before it has adequately analyzed logically prior or more significant considerations. Thus, in a sense, these fallacies can be considered diversionary tactics. But there are some fallacies that more directly invoke diversion and distraction. Two of the more prominent are called red herring and straw argument.

Red Herring

A form of psychological persuasion, **the red herring fallacy consists in drawing attention away from the real issue to a side or logically separate one, in order to conceal the weakness of the arguer's position.** Arguers usually will employ red herrings when trying to conceal the weakness of their positions. Sometimes, they simply do not realize, until it is pointed out to them, that they have, in fact, introduced a peripheral concern—that is, one that is not relevant to the point at issue. In such a case, it would seem no fallacy has been committed. They have simply become sidetracked.

The graphic name of this fallacy evidently derives from the sport of fox hunting, in which dog trainers used to teach hunting hounds to follow a trail by dragging the fresh carcass of a rabbit, bird, or squirral through a field. This track was allowed to grow cold overnight. The next morning, a smoked, "red" herring, which had been allowed to "ripen," was dragged over the original trail, and the young dog was set off. When the dog came to the scent of the red herring, he naturally would be distracted by the fresher, stronger odor—and his trainer would coax him back on the scent of his original prey. In this way, the dog learned to stay on the trail of the prey and not be sidetracked by competing smells. So, too, in argument arguers must stick to the point and not wander afield, chasing a red herring.

An argument that attempts to demonstrate a conclusion or thesis on the basis of the truth or falsity of a side issue is relying on an irrelevant premise. Perhaps even worse, the red herring can effectively turn a discussion or debate in an unfruitful direction, thereby leaving the real issue unaddressed.

You have probably had the experience of complaining about something, only to be reminded that things could be a lot worse. Maybe they could, but the real issue concerns your specific complaint, not the sorrier state of the alternative. The writer of the following letter to the editor uses precisely this kind of red herring in responding to tourists' criticisms of San Francisco:

> Apparently these tourists to our city have never been to any other city in the nation. As a former East Coast resident, I have been to New York, I have been to Philadelphia. To truly appreciate the decadence of cities, visit either of these towns. I have been afraid to enter Philadelphia neighborhoods in broad daylight. Residents and tourists of our city should be grateful these problems do not match those of other locations.

Similarly, the writer of the following letter may think he is addressing the issue at hand — in this case, a policy of making condoms available in public schools and other institutions — but he is really introducing a red herring.

> Instead of passing out condoms in schools, churches, and to homosexuals, how about trying this first? There's nothing wrong with making a morally sound decision to be faithful to one's marriage partner before marriage, as well as afterward. Just think how much taxpayer money and heartache would be saved if the programs and "education" being initiated weren't needed because couples were being faithful to their future partners.

The writer misses the point: For whatever reasons, lots of people are sexually active outside marriage. Is making condoms available to them in order to minimize the spread of venereal diseases and AIDS a desirable social and institutional policy? That is the issue. Instead of addressing this issue, the writer addresses the issue of marital fidelity. It is easy to imagine how such a reply could unhinge the discussion from the real issue by inciting a debate over the morality of marital infidelity.

Finally, Reverend Jerry Falwell defends his view that no criminal charges for financial wrongdoing should be filed against defrocked television evangelist Jim Bakker:

> I was glad when Gerald Ford pardoned President Nixon. I think there was enough punishment already, and it would have hurt the country for the president to be charged criminally. (Imprisoning) a major minister of the Gospel in this country would hurt the entire cause of Christ across the world. . . . Most of the people I know in the Christian family have long since forgiven Jim and Tammy.

What Ford did with Nixon and what Falwell's acquaintances in "the Christian family" feel are red herrings — they are totally irrelevant to whether Bakker should have been charged with, tried, and, if found guilty, punished for fraud and tax evasion. As for the potential effects of criminal action against Bakker, they are relevant only insofar as the effects of taking action against anyone suspected of breaking the law are relevant (for example, the expense to the state of prosecuting, the likelihood of prevailing in a trial, the deterrent value of prosecuting, and so on). The potential effects on a particular religion, however, are no more relevant than would be the potential effects of prosecuting a banker or a politician, for example, on the banking profession or a political party. (Of course, in this case, Falwell not only exaggerates, if not miscasts, the effects of punishing Bakker, but also overlooks the potential positive effects.)

Straw Argument

The straw argument fallacy consists in so altering an opponent's position that the altered version is easier to attack than the original. It is a "straw" argument because (a) it is deliberately fabricated, and (b) it does not have the force of the real argument, just as a straw version does not have the force of the real thing. Putting words into someone's mouth is another way to describe a common form of straw argument.

There are various ways of altering and distorting an opponent's position, such as utilizing only a part of it, exaggerating it, or oversimplifying it. For example, suppose a legislator proposes a spending bill that would raise the tax on gasoline by one cent to be spent *only* on repairing interstate highways. In opposition, an opponent charges the legislator with wanting to repave perfectly good roads in the nation. Of course, the legislator wants to do neither — she wants work done only on interstate highways in disrepair. Her opponent sets up a straw argument by exaggerating her proposal.

A widespread form of straw argument consists in distorting an arguer's position by drawing from it unintended inferences. Suppose, for example, you argue that, given the overcrowded conditions of our prisons, we need to investigate other forms of punishment besides incarceration. "So," says your opponent, "if you had your way you'd simply open the jailhouse door and let loose murderers, rapists, and drug pushers." Of course, you never intended what your opponent inferred. In fact, criminals such as the ones he mentioned might stand a greater chance of being incarcerated longer if alternative forms of punishment were utilized. In any event, your opponent has distorted your position by extending it beyond your intended limits and has effectively portrayed you as being "soft on crime."

Not all straw argument fallacies are obvious, however. For example, the dean of a prestigious graduate school of business once objected to the inclusion of business ethics in his school's graduate program. "Much can be said about the moral and ethical nature of an economic system," he admitted, "but by the time students get to graduate schools, their moral and ethical standards have long been set. And I think it's quite presumptuous of us to tell them what's right and what's wrong."

This argument is psychologically persuasive because it associates courses in business ethics with dictating morality to students. Since we probably do not want moral dogma taught in public classrooms, we should not want business ethics. Is it accurate to infer, as the dean did, that business ethics courses are designed to indoctrinate moral dogma? In fact, such courses typically investigate numerous possible bases for a just economic system; explore the relationships between business and various claimants, such as employees, stockholders, consumers, and government; and consider a host of business issues within the framework of diverse and often competing ethical principles. The real issue, then, is whether such topics warrant a place in the business curriculum. If not, why? The dean misrepresented business ethics courses by erroneously inferring that their purpose is to tell students what is right and what is wrong.

IN BRIEF   A straw argument is a distortion of a single issue. A red herring is a logically separate issue. Both divert attention from the point at hand and thus result in the introduction of irrelevant premises into an argument.

EXERCISES ON DIVERSION

Identify and explain the use of red herring or straw argument in each of the following passages.

1. Letter to the editor: "Everybody complains about the U.S. mail these days — prices going up and service down. But our Postal Service seems like a winner compared with the Canadian one. In fact, our neighbors to the north have elevated post-official bashing into the national sport." (The writer proceeded to catalogue deficiencies in the Canadian postal system.)

2. "My opponent says that women have a right to decide what happens inside their own bodies. That the state has no right to interfere. What my opponent means is that teenagers should be encouraged to use abortion as a morning-after birth control device. Well, I'm opposed to that, and I think you are, too!"

3. TOM: The theory of creationism should be taught in public schools right along with biological evolution.
   TRISH: Why do you say that?
   TOM: Well, prohibiting the teaching of creationism is precisely what is done in Communist countries.
   TRISH: Well, I certainly don't want our public schools acting like Communist schools.
   TOM: That's my point.
   TRISH: You know, I never thought of it that way. I'm going to write my legislators right away and have them look into this.

4. Justice Lynn Compton of the California Court of Appeals, defending her decision to overturn the conviction of a salesman in the rape of a waitress who was hitchhiking: "A woman who enters a stranger's car 'advertises' that she has less concern for the consequences than the average female."

5. A letter to the editor attacking Darwinian evolution: "Didn't evolution have to take place day by day, month by month, and year by year? You never hear of anything about what happened on a year-to-year basis. I submit to you this: No evolution per year, multiplied by however many millions of years you wish, still equals no evolution." (Evaluate the writer's argument in the context of this excerpt from Charles Darwin's *Origin of Species:* "It may be said that natural selection is daily and hourly scrutinizing throughout the world every variation, even the slightest;

rejecting that which is bad, preserving and adding up all that is good. . . . We see nothing of these slow changes or progress, until the hand of time has marked the long lapses of the ages, and then so imperfect is our view into the long past geological ages, that we only see that the forms of life are now different from what they formerly were.'')

6. The California Coastal Commission is a voter-created body established to protect the California coast from wanton commercial development. In a memo dated May 29, 1987, Interior Secretary Donald Hodel urged Commerce Secretary Malcolm Baldridge to weaken the commission because ''if we countenance an agency usurping power, we are failing in our responsibility to the president and our commitment to America's form of government.''

7. When fire and flood destroyed a church's campground and buildings, local officials declared the area a flood plain and banned, at least temporarily, any new construction there. Claiming denial of the use of its land, the church went to court seeking monetary damages. On June 9, 1987, the U.S. Supreme Court ruled in favor of the church (six to three), declaring that the Fifth Amendment prohibits government taking of property without just compensation. Of this ruling, Neil R. Peirce of the *National Journal* wrote, ''It was Black Tuesday at the U.S. Supreme Court for the natural environment, the mountains, the wetlands and open space of America that lie in the path of developers' juggernauts. . . . The justices, in short, have declared open season for property owners and land speculators to shower lawsuits on cities and counties that try to control or guide growth.''

8. Benjamin Linder was a 27-year-old volunteer helping a small village in northern Nicaragua. On April 28, 1987, while planning a dam to generate electricity for the village, Linder was shot in the legs by Nicaraguan Contras, then killed with a shot to the head from less than two feet away, as gunpowder burns on his face indicated. Three weeks later, Linder's parents appeared before a congressional hearing investigating their son's death, and charged that it was a murder effectively perpetrated by the U.S. government and ''its effectors, the Contras.'' In reply, Representative Connie Mack (R-FL) told the parents that they had not allowed an appropriate time to grieve for their son before trying to alter U.S. policy in Nicaragua. ''I can't understand how you can use the grief I know you feel to politicize this situation,'' said Mack. ''I really feel that you have asked for it. . . . It is less than three weeks since your son died.''

IMPROVING PERFORMANCE

SUMMARY-TEST QUESTIONS FOR CHAPTER 7*

1. The argument, ''The proposed tax bill cannot serve the general welfare, because it has been drafted by some of the wealthiest interests in the country,'' contains an abusive *ad hominem* fallacy since it
   A. raises suspicions about a person.
   B. shows contempt for a person.
   C. attacks the source or genesis of an idea.

    D. A and C.

    E. A, B, and C.

2. A fallacy like the preceding one is sometimes termed

    A. circumstantial.

    B. *tu quoque.*

    C. genetic.

    D. well poisoning.

    E. none of the preceding

3. Which of the following fallacies does not belong with the others? Explain.

    A. Abusive *ad hominem*

    B. Circumstantial *ad hominem*

    C. Well poisoning

    D. Two-wrongs

    E. Mob

4. Which of the following arguments illustrate(s) an abusive *ad hominem* arising from raising suspicions about person?

    A. Since the social security reform plan has been proposed by Pat Robertson, an ordained minister and televangelist, it cannot be worth considering.

    B. There is no point in considering the social security reform plan proposed by Senator Moynihan. He simply does not have a head for numbers.

    C. We can trace the modern roots of daycare centers to the writings of Karl Marx. Therefore, daycare centers have no place in a capitalist society like ours.

    D. A and C.

    E. A and B.

5. If I tell you that, as a student, you cannot consistently support an increase in college tuition, I would be arguing by

    A. fear.

    B. abusive *ad hominem.*

    C. *tu quoque.*

    D. well poisoning.

    E. circumstantial *ad hominem.*

6. _____ consists of rejecting someone's claim because of that person's special circumstances or self-serving motives.

    A. pity

    B. abusive *ad hominem*

    C. common practice

    D. well poisoning

    E. circumstantial *ad hominem*

7. Give an example of the fallacy defined in question 6.

8. " Yond Cassius has a lean and hungry look. . . . Such men are dangerous." This quotation from Shakespeare's *Julius Caesar* illustrates the fallacy of

    A. abusive *ad hominem.*

    B. mob appeal.

    C. well poisoning.

    D. fear.

E. circumstantial *ad hominem.*

9. Suppose you argued that the federal government should be more lenient in collecting student loans. I reply: "Of course you would think that. After all, you're a student." I would be

    A. trying to discredit your position by attributing to you motives of self-interest.
    B. attempting to taint anything further you might say on the issue.
    C. well poisoning.
    D. A and C.
    E. A, B, and C.

10. "If you reject my solution you obviously don't grasp the seriousness of the situation." The rhetorical device used here is the same as the one used in _____ above.

    A. 5
    B. 6
    C. 8
    D. 9
    E. 6 and 9

11. Which of the following fallacies does not belong with the others? Explain.

    A. Two wrongs
    B. *Tu Quoque*
    C. Common practice
    D. Well poisoning

12. Explain how inconsistency plays a part in both the circumstantial *ad hominem* and *tu quoque* fallacies. Then, give an original illustration of each.

13. Which of the following fallacies does not belong with the others? Explain.

    A. Mob appeal
    B. Appeal to pity
    C. Abusive *ad hominem*
    D. Appeal to fear

14. The mob appeal can play to

    A. sex.
    B. status.
    C. security.
    D. peer approval.
    E. A, B, C, or D.

15. "Emotional messages seldom influence people's behavior." True or false? Explain.

16. "Passion has no place in argument." True or false? Explain.

17. Mob appeals persuade by _____ and _____ (fill in the blanks).

18. A dermatologist informs a patient that sun exposure is not good for the skin, because it can prematurely age it and cause skin cancer. This information frightens the patient into using a sun block. Did the dermatologist commit the fallacy of fear?

19. "Like Socrates, 2,000 years before, Galileo too was threatened with execution if he did not repudiate his own teachings. Galileo gave in and was spared. Does Galileo merit moral censure? Since only those can criticize Galileo who have chosen as Socrates, we may dispense with moral appraisals of Galileo's choice."

What fallacy, if any, does this argument commit? (Note: Socrates chose death rather than recant his teachings.)

20. An ad for Boeing Company: Superimposed over a picture of an elderly couple standing on their front porch with dog: "Swing by home on your next business trip." What emotion is this ad appealing to?

21. A teacher refuses to give a student a make-up test because the student did not have a good enough reason for missing the test. The student subsequently tells a friend that the teacher is not a very understanding person because he never allows make-ups. The student commits the fallacy of _____ .

22. In arguing for more U.S. foreign aid to eastern European countries such as Romania and Czechoslovakia, a speaker points out that Israel, Egypt, and the Philippines are getting most of our current foreign aid. Does the speaker commit any fallacy?

Logic Jeopardy—Like the popular television show "Jeopardy," numbers 23 through 33 are answers to questions. Based on the information in this chapter, devise a precisely suitable question for each answer. SAMPLE: Confusing the arguer and the argument. *Question: What is an* ad hominem *argument?*

23. mob, fear, pity
24. "Capitalism is the best economic system," "Rich people aren't really happy," "Women make better nurses than men"
25. a side issue
26. a distortion of an opponent's position
27. exaggeration
28. facts that do not support a conclusion
29. the 1988 presidential election
30. "Carrying the big stick," "Might makes right"
31. the sport of fox hunting
32. evoking sympathy to advance an argument
33. Latin phrase for "You, also"

CRITICAL THINKING APPLICATIONS

1. The following is a newspaper account of an anticrime speech delivered by President Bush on January 23, 1990. Read the account very carefully, then make a list of, and explain, all the fallacies of irrelevancy that Bush seems to have used in his speech. Compare your analysis with other class members.

Bush Takes a Shot At the Democrats' Bill to Fight Crime[2]

By Andrew Rosenthal
New York Times
Kansas City, Mo.

Evoking the legends of Bat Masterson and Wild Bill Hickok to bolster his anti-crime message, President Bush urged Congress yesterday to adopt his proposal for new

---

[2]Copyright © 1990 by the *New York Times* Company. Reprinted by permission.

laws on drug abuse and violent crime and attacked a Democratic alternative as a "Trojan Horse" that would bind the hands of police and prosecutors.

Bush traveled to Kansas City on the opening day of the 1990 congressional session to meet with a local citizens' anti-drug group, visit a former crack house and address state and local law enforcement officers.

Most of Bush's speech to the police group was devoted to an anti-crime message that darted from homespun references to Normal Rockwell paintings to Old West metaphors and the kind of tough-on-crime lines that Bush used in his 1988 presidential campaign.

In a passage more reminiscent of his predecessor, Ronald Reagan, than his own oratorical style, Bush recounted a scene from the novel "Lonesome Dove" in which two former Texas Rangers hang an old partner after catching him with an outlaw gang.

Bush said that passage revealed the "simple truth" that "each of us faces the innate temptation to succumb to evil and yet always has the freedom to instead choose to do good."

Later in his speech, Bush said: "As in the days of legendary U.S. marshals like Bat Masterson and Wild Bill Hickok, places like Kansas City again need the support of top-notch federal lawmen."

Bush, who started the day saying he would not attack Congress on the opening of its new session, thanked lawmakers for approving a measure last year providing funds for new federal law enforcement agents and increasing prison space.

But then he said, "It's time for Congress to finish the job. Because it does no good to send the troops into battle wearing handcuffs."

Bush noted that the portion of his anti-crime legislation that allows for stricter sentencing laws and anti-crime statutes was not acted on by Congress before it recessed.

"Today, there's another bill—a Trojan Horse—standing at the gates of Congress," Bush said. "It's called S-1970. It looks like a real crime bill. It sounds like a real crime bill. But in actuality, it will be tougher on law enforcement than on criminals."

He was referring to a bill introduced by Senator Joseph Biden, the Delaware Democrat who is chairman of the Senate Judiciary Committee.

Biden actually introduced two measures. One of them would, among other things, increase Bush's request for aid to state and local police, from $350 million to $600 million, and more than triple Bush's request for new agents for the FBI, from 300 to 1,000.

Bush's legislation would expand the death penalty for crimes involving drugs beyond current provisions applying to drug kingpins. Biden's bill would exclude juveniles and the mentally retarded and seek to outlaw "racial patterns" of death sentences.

Alixe Glen, a White House spokeswoman, said these and other exclusions would be "like having no death penalty at all."

Bush's crime legislation would allow the use of evidence gathered by police officers who acted "in good faith" but did not have a search warrant. Biden's bill would require a search warrant but allow introduction of evidence if the warrant was invalid.

Although Bush's bill would provide stricter penalties for using semiautomatic weapons in crimes, Biden's adds a provision that the president opposes, a ban on the six most commonly used kinds of semiautomatic weapons.

2. A woman who signed her letter "Practically Untouched" complained to Abigail Van Buren ("Dear Abby") that her husband of two years had made love to her only five times in the preceding six months. On one occasion, the woman said, she had even gift-wrapped herself in Saran Wrap and greeted him at the door with a martini, but all that raised from her inattentive spouse was a limp, "Hi. What's for supper?" The woman wanted to know if his behavior was "normal." In response, Abby said that the couple obviously was not operating on the same frequency, and that if they could not "fix" their marriage by seeing a doctor, they should see a lawyer. Objecting to Abby's advice, a reader wrote:

> Why do you perpetuate the idea that frequent sex is "normal"? You seem to believe that any other arrangement is so bizarre that people ought to see doctors or lawyers for a cure or a divorce.
>
> Millions of couples have infrequent sex — or none at all — and they are happy. For you to suggest that sex should be at the top of the list with air and water is a peculiar blind spot of yours.
>
> A street-wise punk uses the "sex-is-normal" for argument to persuade his virginal girlfriend to give in by implying that she is weird if she doesn't.
>
> Let people off the hook, Abby. Tell them that sexual frequency is a private arrangement that each couple must decide for themselves. Who cares if it's once a decade, or never again, if they're content with their lives?
>
> Wise people stay married — sex or not sex. Apparently that's news to you, as you advise 'Practically Untouched in Tulsa' that if her husband didn't see a doctor, she should see a lawyer.[3]

Evaluate this letter in terms of relevancy.

3. "Last night my opponent, Senator Ragsdale, accused me of taking money from special interest groups, contradicting my own previous stands, and having a political slush fund."

Which if any of the following possible responses to Senator Ragsdale's charge would be at least relevant?

A. **"Senator Ragsdale evidently misunderstood my previous positions. So, I'll explain them again to clear up any confusion."**

B. **"Special interest groups! Why, Senator Ragsdale has been on the payroll of big business for the past ten years."**

C. **"What Senator Ragsdale terms a 'slush fund,' in fact, is legally acquired monies that I've raised for this campaign. Not a penny has been spent for any other purpose. And if you give me a few minutes, I think I can prove that."**

D. **"If Senator Ragsdale didn't sense that her own campaign was in trouble, she wouldn't have begun to smear me as she has."**

E. **"The whole process of political campaigning needs reform. And, if elected, I intend to cleanse political campaigning of its corrupt practices."**

---

[3] "Dear Abby," *Los Angeles Times,* January 22, 1990, p. E4.

4. As Chrysler Corporation struggled for survival in the 1970s, government leaders debated whether to offer the company federal assistance. Those opposed to a bail-out asked: "Are we supposed to bail out Chrysler every time it gets into financial difficulties?"

This question can be criticized because it
A. appeals to emotion rather than to logic.
B. impugns Chrysler's motives as self-serving.
C. assumes Chrysler is in financial trouble.
D. exaggerates the issue, thereby setting up a straw argument.
E. introduces a side issue.

5. "Some philosophers have argued that there is a body of natural or moral rights that belong to human beings by virtue of their humanity. But cross-cultural legal studies show clearly that different societies acknowledge different rights. In fact, the rights accorded individuals often vary within a society over time. So, since there is no right that is universally protected, there are no natural or moral rights."

Which of the following responses, if any, would be a relevant response to this argument?
A. Some societies are more primitive than others.
B. To deny natural rights will have the effect of bringing about all manner of injustices and inhumanities.
C. Amnesty International has collected overwhelming evidence that natural rights are violated in dozens of countries, including so-called democracies.
D. Even though a body of natural rights is not agreed to or protected by all nations, natural rights may still exist.

6. "The money and time a person invests in acquiring a professional degree is a waste. For example, I know several people who spent a lot of money and time getting a law degree but who have never practiced law. Some have become homemakers, others are earning a living in a completely unrelated field. In none of the cases is the person practicing law."

It would be reasonable to infer that the speaker believes
A. legal studies are a waste of time.
B. professional training should not cost so much or consume so much time.
C. wealth is more important than learning.
D. professional education is useful only in pursuing activities in that profession.
E. homemaking is not as good a use of time as practicing law.

7. "Programs on American television give children a warped view of reality. Sit-coms, for example, inevitably raise complex problems that are neatly resolved in about twenty-three minutes. Police shows typically depict a loaded gun as an effective tool in problem resolution. And cartoons portray violence as having no harmful effects on its victims. Thus, children are erroneously taught that all problems are easily resolved, usually by violence."

Which of the following, if true, would weaken the author's conclusion?
A. The author has no children.
B. It is not the intention of TV producers to misinform children about the nature of problems.
C. Television is primarily an entertainment, not an educational medium.

D. TV shows in Japan are far more violent than ones in the United States.

E. Some shows teach cooperation and compromise.

8. Letter to the editor regarding the Lincoln Savings & Loan scandal and the alleged preferential treatment Senator Alan Cranston, (D-CA) showed the financial institution as a result of Lincoln's contributing to his campaign:

> The right wing is certainly out to get Senator Cranston.
>
> Sure *[Lincoln Savings and Loan President Charles]* Keating contributed to Cranston's election campaign. Keating gave to both parties. He gave to Republican *[California]* Governor George Deukmejian. Wasn't there a state official to check on savings and loans? If so, where was he?
>
> What about M. Danny Wall, appointed by President Reagan to keep an eye on federal savings and loans? Obviously he didn't. And he didn't need campaign money. He was appointed.
>
> Senators need campaign money. It's the American way—the way senators and presidents get elected.
>
> Wall probably knew that President Reagan was against government checking up on business.

How many fallacies of irrelevance can you detect in this letter?

9. The following viewpoint glitters with *ad hominems,* assumption-loaded labels, and biased language—but that is not the central problem with its logic. Even if stripped of its personal attacks and inflammatory rhetoric, the argument would still be seriously flawed because it sets up a straw argument through equivocation, that is, shifting the meaning of a key term. **Can you explain exactly how this occurs?**

> The Bard of Avon must be stirring in his grave. His fans—as dwindling a group as William Shakespeare partisans might be—should also find reason for woe.
>
> This time it was Hollywood that shunned him, that chose the neurotic musings of the likes of Woody Allen, for heaven's sake, over the timeless poetics of Mr. Shakespeare. The city of glitz, glamor, and gargantuan egos proves once again it doesn't know quality when it's right in front of its face.
>
> Mr. Allen and four other writers all gained Academy Award nominations this year (1990) for original movie scripts. Yet for the new production of *Henry V,* Mr. Shakespeare didn't even get a nod. . . .
>
> Hollywood would thus have us believe that Mr. Allen's *Crimes and Misdemeanors,* Tom Schulman's *Dead Poets Society,* Spike Lee's *Do the Right Thing,* Steven Soderbergh's *sex, lies and videotape,* and Nora Ephron's *When Harry Met Sally*—all of which received nominations—are better than the Bard? . . .
> ("Hollywood Thumbs Nose at the Bard," from *The Anchorage Daily News*)

10. "And so, a new political era begins right now, friends," Representative Les AuCoin (D-Ore.) intoned during a debate on a motion by Representative Robert K. Dornan (R-Ca.) to again deny the District of Columbia the right to spend money on abortions for poor victims of rape and incest. "Those of us who defend a woman's freedom of choice are drawing a line in the sand today,

a line of decency, a line of fair play — and a line of serious politics. . . . If you vote for those amendments, you will be held accountable in ways you have never dreamed possible at ballot boxes all over this county. The pro-choice movement is mobilized. And from this day forward, it is going to take names and kick *[pause]* ankles."

An hour-and-a-half later, no one appeared more surprised than AuCoin and his allies that the House, for the first time in ten years, voted down an antiabortion amendment, 219 to 206. Confirming that vote, three months later, the House voted 216 to 206 to not restrict Medicaid funding of abortion cases of rape and incest.

Of the votes, AuCoin said: "I was astounded. I don't think anyone dreamed we were going to win."

Which fallacy of irrelevancy did AuCoin use, apparently with great effect? Embedded in AuCoin's pre-vote speech is another fallacy, one that we covered in the last chapter under linguistic confusion resulting from the ambiguous use of language. Can you spot it?

11. In the winter of 1989, TV commercials introduced the *Infiniti,* a $38,000 car imported by Nissan. The commercials showed everything from wind-blown trees to flying geese, but never showed a clear look at the car itself. The West Coast firm that created the ads — Holliday, Connors, Cosmopulos, Inc. — admitted purposely placing executives on the *Infiniti* account who had no experience whatever creating car ads. **Precisely what do you think the commercials were appealing to?**

POINT/COUNTERPOINT: ESSAYS FOR ANALYSIS

Issue: *Abortion*

Resolved: Extreme tactics are justified to stop abortions.

Background: Bombings, arson, threats to individuals — we have become all too familiar with such acts performed by those espousing one cause or another. Indeed, we are no longer shocked by the act of violence that occurs in Beirut or Belfast or some other far-away place — we almost expect it. What about when such acts occur at home? What do we think about fellow Americans who feel so strongly about the rightness of their cause that they will do whatever is necessary to achieve it? Increasingly, the tactics adopted by antia-bortionists are pressing this question.

On November 19, 1984, a family-planning clinical in Maryland was bombed. In the same year, twenty-four abortion clinics were damaged by fires. Other clinics have suf-fered the same fate since then, and hundreds of cases of vandalism to abortion clinics and harassment of abortion counselors have been reported. There is no conclusive proof that pro-life groups were behind any of these acts of violence, but one thing is certain: Such acts are increasing and occurring in an atmosphere of general frustration of esca-lating hostility and mounting pressure for action among antiabortion activists. Another thing we know is that an influential number of antiabortionists regard these acts as mor-ally justifiable means of stopping what they believe is the wholesale slaughter of human beings by women who have abortions and those who assist them.

The two essays that follow engage the issue of the tactics employed by anti-abortionists to shut down abortion clinics and stop women from having abortions.

As you read these essays, bear in mind that the issue under debate is not the morality of abortion, but the legitimacy of the tactics employed to halt it. In framing the resolution, we are using the word "extreme" to denote acts beyond the conventional ways of working for social change, for example by picketing, boycotting, or similarly operating within the political process. Since antiabortionists have themselves characterized some of their tactics as "extreme," the term as it is used here seems free of bias.

From: **Closed: 99 Ways To Stop Abortion**

Joseph M. Scheidler

Joseph Scheidler, head of the Pro-Life League in Chicago, has received national attention for the tactics he regularly recommends to put a halt to abortions, such as accosting and harassing patrons of abortion clinics, and using gory photos to shock and disgust people. The following excerpt is from his book Closed: 99 Ways To Stop Abortion. **Read and outline the selection, then answer the questions that follow it.**

1   Even though some of the things pro-life activists do to stop abortion may seem hostile, we must never lose sight of the fact that what we are trying to do is save lives, while helping preserve women's mental, physical, and spiritual health. We can do these things only if we love the people we confront.

2   Our concern is manifest in what Fr. John Powell, S.J. calls "tough love." It is not soft saccharine love, but a love that says, "We want you to do the right thing. But since you don't know what is right, we will make you look at abortion in its ugly reality. If you can't learn through persuasion, we will use pressure." That doesn't mean we don't love the abortionists. The parent who never punishes an unruly child doesn't love his child. A weak parent is concerned about being liked and fails to do the loving thing. What we are doing has to be done, like punishing an unruly child. What the abortionists are doing is evil. Out of love, we do what we must to change their minds.

3   Franky Schaeffer told pro-lifers that the most loving thing he had done in the past year was to spank his son, who had run into the street and nearly got hit by a truck. To prevent future tragedy, punishment had to be administered. Punishment might save his son's life. It was given because Franky Schaeffer loves his son and wants him around for a few more years.

4   Those of us who confront the abortionists and debate them on radio and television, do not like them very much. They are selfish and humorless. But occasionally one is likeable, and you feel a genuine concern for him. Sometimes it is hard to realize that to make a living, he kills children and ruins women's lives.

5   But whatever natural revulsion or even attraction they elicit, the fact remains that everything we do in relation to the abortionists is done because we love them. We do not want anyone to lose his soul. We do not

want the abortionists to be punished in hell for eternity. Yet we believe there is reward and punishment after this life, that good will be rewarded and evil punished. Our determination to get the abortionists out of their grizzly [*sic*] business is a greater act of love than they are shown by their colleagues.

6 To talk a person out of doing abortions or to put him out of business shows greater love than excusing what he does. We tell abortionists that what they do is wrong. Who loved Herod? John the Baptist, who pointed out his evil and told him to repent, or Herodias, who asked for the head of John? John tried to convert Herod. Herodias merely wanted the Baptist silenced. Throughout history, it has been those who really love who try to convert people from evil to good.

7 We know in advance that love for our enemy will be misconstrued and that we will be made fun of for mentioning it. Many cannot understand what we are talking about. Most of them will not believe us. But some suspect that we may be right. One abortion clinic operator told us she realized what she was doing would send her to hell, but that was her decision to make and not ours. She was right. But we had to try.

8 We don't expect most abortionists to understand that what we are trying to do is for their own good. It is not important that they understand.

9 We must be careful not to do any of these things out of hatred. We cannot fight the battle for the unborn with hatred. We do it selflessly for someone who will never know we did it. We do it knowing that the person we save at the clinic door may never realize he was in mortal danger. We do it to bear witness to society, and to the abortionists, that there is a better way to solve problems than by killing children.

10 Pro-life is a movement based on the highest form of altruism, so there is no room for hatred. We can hate abortion, but we cannot hate the abortionists or we betray our cause. We do everything for the love of God and the children. We are trying to save the parents who, under different circumstances, would not consider abortion. We do it even out of love for the abortion providers, some of whom have been deceived into thinking they are solving a problem. Some may believe that abortion is the lesser of two evils. It is difficult to understand such a deception, but we are not in a position to judge their guilt.

11 We can base our activities on our hatred of abortion, but not on hatred of the abortionists. Scripture admonishes us to love our enemies and do good to those who hate us. We are told that charity is the greatest virtue and that God loves each of us. If God loves the abortionists, we must love them, too.

12 The ultimate hatred is that which sends a soul to hell. In *Hamlet*, the prince in planning to murder his step-father, catches him in prayer and decides not to kill him then, because he might send him to heaven. Hamlet wants his step-father to go to hell and decides to murder him in the midst of some debauchery. It is true hatred to wish to see a person eternally lost.

13 This is not what we want. We want the abortionists to be converted, returned to God, and be saved. We bring them to God by loving them, not by hating them.

14 Many women who have had abortions have repented and are now pro-lifers. Many former supporters of abortion now defend the unborn. A young Chicago couple, Darryl and Debbie Trulson, go to clinics, appear on radio and television to discuss abortion, and fight tirelessly for the unborn. At one time they supported abortion and defended it. Seeing them totally committed to pro-life, it is hard to realize that they were once the enemy. I frequently encounter pro-life people who confess, "Last year at this time I was fighting you." People are fighting us today who will be pro-life tomorrow. We love them when they join us. We should love them before they join us.

15 As Christians, we must love everyone. We want to change society so that it is not so difficult to love, and someday that may happen. In the meantime, we must love what we've got, pray for the abortionists and, through "tough love", help them realize that what they are doing offends God. Never stop believing that your prayers and efforts to close their clinics will turn them from the evil of killing children.

16 No matter what anyone says about our activities, and our attitudes, whether it is evident or not, we know that pro-life nonviolent direct action is based on love.

1. In paragraph 1, the word/phrase _____ functions as a discount.
   A. "while"
   B. "only if"
   C. "even though"
2. Which of the following sentences best describes the sentiments of paragraph 1?
   A. Love your neighbor.
   B. Love conquers all.
   C. What is done out of love is right and proper.
   D. Only love can help save lives and preserve health.
   E. All pro-life activists are loving.
3. Which of the following adjectives best describes the author's attitude toward abortionists, as expressed in paragraph 2?
   A. contemptuous
   B. condescending
   C. hostile
   D. indulgent
   E. indifferent
4. The definition of "tough love" offered in paragraph 2 is most probably
   A. denotative.
   B. persuasive.
   C. stipulative.
   D. theoretical.
   E. connotative.

5. Underlying the definition of "tough love" is the assumption that those who practice it
   A. are loving.
   B. are favored by God.
   C. are always antiabortion.
   D. know for sure what is right.
   E. act like responsible parents.
6. Throughout the essay, the author refers to his position as "pro-life," rather than "antiabortion," and to those who perform abortions as "abortionists" rather than, say, "physicians" or "abortion practitioners." What is the persuasive effect of these label choices?
7. In paragraph 4, the author employs
   A. well poisoning.
   B. abusive *ad hominem*.
   C. two wrongs.
   D. circumstantial *ad hominem*.
   E. fear.
8. It would be fair to say that, in paragraph 5, the author implies through innuendo that
   A. pro-lifers love abortionists.
   B. pro-lifers want everyone to be saved.
   C. abortionists are on the road to hell.
   D. the good will be rewarded and the evil punished.
   E. the colleagues of pro-abortionists do not love them as much as pro-lifers do.
9. After reading paragraph 6, Kay says, "I'm a Christian who loves her neighbor. But I don't think it's loving to destroy people's property and force them to conform to my beliefs." In response, a pro-lifer says, "Then you don't know what real love is. If you had real love for abortionists, you would do everything possible to stop them from committing abortions." Evaluate the pro-lifer's response to Kay.
10. In the last sentence of paragraph 6, the author makes use of
    A. a persuasive definition.
    B. a faulty denotation.
    C. a circumstantial *ad hominem*.
    D. a red herring.
    E. a straw argument.
11. What function does the Biblical reference in paragraph 6 serve?
    A. It shows that John the Baptist was a messenger of God.
    B. It shows that the author believes in the Bible.
    C. It shows that Herodias was evil.
    D. It shows that John the Baptist was trying to get Herod to do good, but that Herodias was trying to get him to do evil.
    E. It shows that the Bible provides evidence for the antiabortion position.
12. Paragraph 6 is basically irrelevant to the argument because the issue at hand
    A. is whether abortion is moral.
    B. concerns the tactics used by pro-lifers.
    C. is whether the Bible is the inspired word of God.

D. is whether abortionists are evil.

E. is the true nature of love.

13. Underlying the first sentence of paragraph 6 is the assumption that
    A. abortionists are evil.
    B. Christians have an obligation to talk a person out of doing abortions or put them out of business.
    C. driving abortionists out of business is a loving act.
    D. not trying to talk persons out of performing abortions or to put them out of business is the same as excusing what they're doing.
    E. abortionists will continue performing abortions unless they are stopped.

14. Are paragraphs 5, 7, and 10, when taken as a whole, consistent?

15. In paragraph 5, the author employs
    A. straw argument.
    B. red herring.
    C. two wrongs.
    D. pity.
    E. fear.

16. Paragraph 7 is irrelevant to the argument because
    A. the abortionist cited probably is not typical.
    B. the author has no way of knowing what abortionists believe.
    C. it deals with the motives of pro-lifers, not their tactics.
    D. it abuses abortionists.
    E. it sets up a straw argument.

17. In response to paragraph 9, Jeff says, "But as noble as your intentions may be, that's not the issue. The question is whether the *means* you're taking are lawful and moral, not what your motives are." Do you think this would be a legitimate charge of irrelevancy?

18. After she has finished her essay, Cheryl says, "Why, the author's position comes right out of the writing of Christian fundamentalism. So, we needn't take it seriously." Which specific form of *ad hominem* is Cheryl using to discredit the argument?

19. Cheryl's friend Chad agrees and adds, "Why, if the author had his way, he'd kill abortionists if that's what it took to stop them." Chad's criticism is
    A. a mob appeal.
    B. a common practice appeal.
    C. a straw argument.
    D. a red herring.
    E. a fair characterization of the author's position.

20. A friend of Cheryl's and Chad's, Mona chips in, "It's beyond me how the author, a Christian, can justify acts of violence on the basis of getting people to do what he thinks is right. Doesn't he realize that in the past Christians were persecuted and even killed at the hands of those who believed they were right?" Mona's criticism employs
    A. an abusive *ad hominem.*
    B. two wrongs.

C. red herring.

D. well poisoning.

E. circumstantial *ad hominem.*

21. Which of the following undemonstrated assumptions does the author make at various points in the essay?

    A. The unborn are children.

    B. Hell exists.

    C. Everyone has an immortal soul.

    D. A and B.

    E. A, B, and C.

22. Paragraph 10 is basically

    A. emotional.

    B. diversionary.

    C. *ad hominem.*

    D. a relevant point.

23. The key implication of paragraph 12 and 13 is:

    A. Hamlet wanted his father to go to hell.

    B. Hatred is ungodly.

    C. Abortionists are hateful.

    D. Anyone not actively trying to shut down abortion clinics is wishing to see abortionists eternally lost.

    E. Persons who do not try to shut down abortion clinics will be eternally lost.

24. In response to paragraph 14, Kay says, "The example of the Chicago couple only shows that in some cases people change their minds after having an abortion. But so what? There are probably plenty of women who were happy they had abortions. How anyone feels after an abortion is beside the point. The issue is whether the tactics the antiabortionists are using are justifiable. So, introducing postabortion remorse is a side issue, a red herring." *Do you agree?*

25. The author uses the following words and phrases in arguing his case. Do you find them clear and precise enough, or open to multiple interpretations? "Love," "soul," "hell," "evil," "good," "pro-life nonviolent direct action" (last paragraph).

From: **Antiabortion Violence on the Rise: How Far Will It Go?**

Lisa Cronin Wohl

Lisa Cronin Wohl is a poet and writer, currently working on a novel. She and like-minded pro-choice activists, as well as some antiabortion activists, find extreme tactics used to halt abortions morally repugnant, if not illegal. **Read her essay, outline it, then answer the questions that follow it.**

1 Picture yourself as a women who has made the difficult decision to terminate a pregnancy. Like most people facing a medical procedure, you are somewhat apprehensive.

2 As you approach the clinic or doctor's office, you are accosted. A stranger, a self-designated "sidewalk counselor," thrusts an antichoice pamphlet at

you and mutters a demand that you change your mind. If you're lucky, that's all you encounter. If your "counselors" are more extreme, you may be confronted with garbage cans full of red paint-splattered dolls representing fetuses. A full line of picketers may bar the entrance to the clinic door, screaming "murderer" at you as you try to go in.

3   You could be confronted with a baby doll nailed to a cross, or yelled at by someone with a megaphone. Someone may pray the rosary loudly or someone may throw "holy" water at you or follow you to the clinic door with a tape recording of a crying baby. Someone may photograph you or conspicuously take down the license number of your car. Someone will almost surely thrust pictures of bloody, mangled fetuses in your face.

4   If your "counselor" is truly aggressive, he or she may try to physically block your path. This stranger may ask intrusive, intimate questions. "Are you pregnant? Are you married? Have you had an abortion before? Do you profess any particular religion?" Then, as quickly as possible, for you are probably trying to get away by now, your "counselor" will assault you with lies and distortions about the abortion procedure, all intended to terrify you.

5   Who are these people? Why are they attacking you and other women who seek to exercise their right to abortion? They are the antichoice radicals who are attacking at the street level because they are losing the fight against abortion on almost every other front. Some fanatics go even further, moving secretly to destroy abortion facilities. As Alice Wolfson of the Committee To Defend Reproductive Rights, puts it, "If they can't make abortion illegal, they're going to try to make it impossible."

6   [On] July 4, [1983] while Washington, D.C., was still celebrating the nation's independence with fireworks, someone pumped propane gas into the kitchen area of the town house headquarters of the National Abortion Federation (NAF), a national organization of abortion providers. Around midnight, the gas, ignited by a stove's pilot light, caused an explosion that blew out windows and left the building structurally damaged.

7   A half hour later, not long after some NAF staffers returned to the building, they were hurriedly evacuated by police. A bomb had been found, a pipe bomb capable of flattening the town house and damaging its adjoining neighbors, had it been detonated by the propane explosion. If it had gone off with the NAF staffers and police in the building, 8 people could have been killed, and some 40 or 50 July 4 celebrants at a nearby park might have been injured. "They're going to hurt somebody," says NAF executive director Barbara Radford. "It's bound to happen."

8   It almost happened three days later on July 7 when someone bombed a Planned Parenthood clinic in Annapolis, Maryland, at 1:35 A.M. The clinic shares a building with several other companies, and two Air Cargo employees were working through the night when the bomb went off. They were not injured, but police say they could have been. And anyone walking near the clinic could also have been hurt. The force of the blast was strong enough to drive shrapnel through the steel sides of a pickup truck parked 150 yards away.

9 Of course, there has always been some picketing against abortion clinics and occasionally violent action. More than three dozen abortion facilities across the country have been hit with arson attacks since abortion was legalized in 1973, and some abortion providers have been subject to vicious, ongoing harassment. But these latest attacks represent a new level of danger. It was only by chance that the bombers and arsonists did not become murderers. . . .

10 Elasah Drogin, president of the antichoice activist group Catholics United for Life (CUL), says that "People with the stick-to-itiveness to be involved with a movement like this for ten years are getting a little impatient with the National Right to Life. They want to see more happen. They want more activity . . . more radical thinking. . . ."

11 The basic strategy of most of these groups is twofold. First through what they call "sidewalk counseling," they try to convince women—who are literally on their way into the doctor's office—to change their minds about abortion decisions. Second, they intimidate those who provide abortion services in order to force them out of the field.

12 "Some of them are profoundly fanatical people," charges Uta Landy, former executive director of NAF. But how far will they go? The right-to-life movement, whether mainstream or more radical, insists it is nonviolent. "If you are truly prolife you are nonviolent," says Michael Gaworski of PEACE [People Expressing Concern for Everyone]. "But I'm not a pacifist. I'm a nonviolent activist."

13 But violence happens. The fire bombings, vandalized clinics, slashed tires, crosses on an abortion staffer's front lawn, midnight phone calls that threaten injury and death—these too-common events in the antichoice war are disclaimed by movement groups. They are presented by the groups discussed here as isolated acts by unknown individuals who have no connection to the right-to-life movement as a whole.

14 But the meaning of nonviolent activism varies from group to group. For some the limit is nonviolent picketing, an action that the prochoice movement recognizes as a legitimate First Amendment right. Other more aggressive groups say they are nonviolent, but claim a civil disobedience right to law-breaking activities such as trespassing. Their justification is the inventive legal "doctrine of necessity," the notion that you can break one law in order to obey a higher law.

15 "I'll sit in a clinic, there's no question about that," says Joseph Scheidler. "I'll bar the entrance. It's illegal. It's a form of trespass. But I feel exactly the way a fireman [feels] if he saw a burning building and saw people screaming upstairs. . . . You have a higher law and that is the law of necessity. . . ."

16 Compounding this tendency to justify lawbreaking is the antichoice extremists' characterization of the prochoice movement as the very essence of evil. Joseph Scheidler and the extremists claim that abortion is the American Holocaust, the equivalent of the Nazi Holocaust. The irony is that Hitler was antichoice: he outlawed abortion in Nazi Germany and

one of the key goals of the Third Reich was to force Aryan women to have as many children as possible.

17 But, ignoring historical accuracy, the antichoice extremists label abortion clinics as "abortuaries" and "death chambers." Scheidler calls abortion clinic workers "S.S. guards."

18 This, obviously, is inflammatory language. Anyone who seriously believes that abortion is mass murder—the mass murder of children—might well feel compelled to take more direct, possibly even violent, action against a clinic to stop it.

19 Certainly, Scheidler is left talking out of both sides of his mouth. On the one hand, he says he's against violence; on the other, he says, "violence is permissible as a last resort when it must be used to prevent or stop a greater violence." The Chicago *Sun-Times* has quoted him as telling followers, "You can try for fifty years to do it the nice polite way, or you can do it next week the nasty way. . . ."

20 He tells the story of a father who had beaten his own children to death, using "a hammer and an ax and a baseball bat and whatever it took. They couldn't tell if they were boys or girls he beat them up so badly." Then he adds that he sees "no difference between that sort of murder and abortion.

21 Can the antichoice leaders really claim no responsibility for violence when they fail to condemn it and when their rhetoric can be seen to subtly encourage it? Or must we see the current wave of violence as part of a continuum that begins with simple picketing and goes on to catastrophe? Certainly that pattern of escalating attack is the experience of many clinics. The Everett, Washington, Feminist Health Center, for example, was picketed regularly beginning two days before it opened on August 9, 1983. The picketing started weekly and then became daily. On opening day, picketers had placed huge signs depicting bloody fetuses in the clinic windows. One woman carried a tape recording of what she said was fetal heartbeat and played it loudly as she trailed the patients into the clinic. . . .

22 Usually vandalism and arson occur at night and the perpetrators are rarely caught. But the other kind of violence, violence to the truth in order to undermine the psychological health of abortion clients, is easy to document. The "facts" that Scheidler uses to "counsel" women entering abortion facilities include: "About ten percent of women become sterile after one legal abortion. Tubal pregnancies, miscarriages, and premature births of your future babies are greatly increased because of an abortion. Also there is an increase in deformed babies after a woman has had an abortion. . . ."

23 As we all know, one of the great boons of legalized abortion has been a dramatic reduction in the complications and death rates among women terminating their pregnancies. A review of more than 150 studies worldwide on the effects of abortion on subsequent reproduction, published in 1982 and sponsored in part by the U.S. government's Centers for Disease Control, found no evidence that abortion increases the risk of sterility, complications of subsequent pregnancies, or infant morbidity or

mortality. As for the risk to the woman, a study published in the July 9, 1982, *Journal of the American Medical Association,* found that "between 1972 and 1978, women were about seven times more likely to die from childbirth than from legal abortion. . . ."

24 If Scheidler and his allies really believe that stopping abortion is the same as stopping child murders, the question arises, why aren't they *more* violent? It is this question that could tilt the movement toward violence no matter how loudly its leaders proclaim their commitment to nonviolent action. Surely, they share some responsibility for those antichoice true believers who choose vigilante action in the night. . . .

1. Paragraphs 1–4 rely heavily on
   A. *ad hominems.*
   B. emotion.
   C. diversion.
2. By placing the terms "sidewalk counselor," "murder," and "holy" in quotation marks (pars. 2 and 3), the author
   A. draws the reader's attention to those terms.
   B. suggests through innuendo that they are misapplied.
   C. slants through the use of biased language.
   D. quotes someone.
3. In the paragraphs 2 and 3, the author uses "may," "could be," and "almost surely" in order to
   A. quantify.
   B. signal a premise.
   C. signal a conclusion.
   D. qualify.
   E. intensify.
4. In paragraph 3, the author accuses the hypothetical "counselor" of using _____ and in paragraph 4 of using _____ .
   A. pity, mob
   B. mob, pity
   C. fear, mob
   D. pity, fear
   E. fear, pity
5. Do you think that the scenario reported in paragraphs 1–4 is consistent with Scheidler's philosophy, or do you think the author might have set up a straw argument through exaggeration?
6. In paragraph 5, the author asks: "Why are they attacking you and other women who seek to exercise their right to abortion?" This question is
   A. complex.
   B. rhetorical.
   C. both rhetorical and complex.
   D. neither rhetorical nor complex.
7. If you think that the aforementioned question is complex, then what is the key assumption embedded in it?

    A. Some women want abortions.

    B. Antiabortionists violate a woman's right to an abortion.

    C. A woman has a right to an abortion.

    D. Antiabortionists attack women in front of clinics.

    E. None of the preceding

8. Again, if you think the question is complex, would you regard its use as fallacious or not?

9. The term "antichoice radicals" in paragraph 5 is an example of

    A. an irrelevancy.

    B. an assumption-loaded label.

    C. jargon.

    D. vagueness.

    E. ambiguity.

10. In citing the alleged motives of the "antichoice radicals," the author attempts to discredit their position through

    A. circumstantial *ad hominem.*

    B. abusive *ad hominem.*

    C. well poisoning.

    D. genetic appeal.

    E. fear.

11. A pro-choice group that calls itself "Committee to Defend Reproductive Rights" suggests through the innuendo embedded in its name that

    A. abortion is a right.

    B. an abortion decision is pretty much the same as a decision a young married couple might make to start a family.

    C. abortion rights are under attack.

    D. A and C.

    E. A, B, and C.

12. Do you think that the extended example in paragraphs 6–8 makes or merely clarifies a point?

13. Indicate which of the following propositions is

    A. a fact,

    B. a judgment, or

    C. a mix of fact and judgment.

    1. (On) July 4 (1983), while Washington, D.C. was still celebrating the nation's independence, someone pumped propane gas into the kitchen area of the town house headquarters of the National Abortion Federation, a national organization of abortion providers. (paragraph 6)

    2. If it (the pipe bomb) had gone off with NAF staffers and police in the building, 8 people could have been killed and some 40 or 50 July 4th celebrants in a nearby park might have been injured. (paragraph 7)

    3. More than three dozen abortion facilities across the country have been hit with arson attacks since abortion was legalized in 1973, and some abortion providers have been subject to vicious, ongoing harassment. (paragraph 9)

    4. But these latest attacks represent a new level of danger. (paragraph 9)

14. Do you think that paragraphs 6–9 illustrate (A) how facts can scare people or (B) the deliberate use of fear to persuade an audience illicitly?

15. The following conversation occurs between two people, Rhonda and Rick, who are discussing paragraph 10:

    RHONDA : The author is trying to raise suspicions about the National Right to Life organization — to discredit it through abusive *ad hominem*.

    RICK : I don't agree. The organization is deserving of suspicion.

    RHONDA : But don't you think that the Drogin quote implies that the NRL is dangerous?

    RICK : Sure, but I think the author has made a case for that through the examples she's given.

    RHONDA : But she's still raising suspicions about the organization — trying to get the audience to distrust it. And that's not kosher in argument.

    RICK : But she's backed up those suspicions — she hasn't just smeared the NRL.

16. The dispute here is basically
    A. verbal.
    B. theoretical.
    C. evaluative.
    D. interpretive.

17. With whom would you tend to side — Rhonda or Rick? Explain.

18. In paragraph 10, the phrase "more radical thinking" is
    A. ambiguous.
    B. vague.
    C. meaningless.
    D. precise enough.

19. On which of the following points, if any, are the two authors in basic agreement?
    A. The basic strategy of antiabortionists (see paragraph 11)
    B. The tactics are morally legitimate.
    C. The antiabortionists act out of love.
    D. The motives of the antiabortionists are relevant to a discussion of the acceptability of the tactics.
    E. They do not agree on any of the preceding points.

20. Michael Gaworski of PEACE is quoted as saying, "But I'm not a pacifist. I'm a nonviolent activist." Do you think there's a substantive difference between a "pacifist" and a "nonviolent activist"? Or is this a distinction without a difference?

21. The author's main point in paragraph 14 is that
    A. some antiabortionists break the law.
    B. not all antiabortionists are nonviolent.
    C. "nonviolent activism" is open to multiple interpretations.
    D. the pro-choice movement, in fact, recognizes the legitimacy of some of the antiabortionists' tactics.
    E. the legal "doctrine of necessity" masks illegal activities.

22. After reading paragraph 14, Melissa observes, "The history of civil disobedience is full of examples of individuals who broke one law in order to obey a higher law of consciousness. And today we admire many of these actions and the people who performed them. Dr. Martin Luther King and his struggle for racial equality is one obvious example." Would this be a relevant or irrelevant response to paragraph 14? How do you think the author would reply?

23. In paragraphs 15 and 16 the author quotes Scheidler. Does this sound like something Scheidler would say? In other words, is it consistent or inconsistent with the sentiments Scheidler expressed in his essay? (Remember, this strategy is a good, quick test of accuracy in quoting out of context.)

24. If Scheidler did make the comparison attributed to him in paragraph 16, then he engaged in
    A. slanting through word bias.
    B. abusive *ad hominem.*
    C. fear.
    D. A and B.
    E. A, B, and C.

25. When the author points out that Hitler outlawed abortion, she seems to be saying to Scheidler, "How can you compare the pro-choice movement with the Nazi holocaust when, in fact, Hitler outlawed abortions, which is the very thing you want to happen in the U.S.? Why, if anything, Hitler should be one of your social heroes." So characterized, her retort could be considered
    A. an abusive *ad hominem.*
    B. a genetic fallacy.
    C. a straw argument.
    D. a circumstantial *ad hominem.*
    E. well poisoning.

26. In response to the essay, Bob says, "It's clear to me the author considers abortion an unlimited right. Thus, a woman five or six months pregnant who decides, say, that she really doesn't like what the pregnancy is doing to her figure, should be permitted to have an abortion. I can't buy that." Bob has
    A. legitimately extended the author's argument.
    B. presented an impossible hypothetical situation.
    C. introduced a red herring.
    D. set up a straw argument by extending the argument beyond its intended limits.
    E. attempted to discredit the author by raising suspicions about her.

27. In paragraphs 17 and 18, the author
    A. suggests that inflammatory language can lead to violence.
    B. suggests that those who use inflammatory language are contributing to violent action, even though they claim to be nonviolent.
    C. is setting up a straw argument through exaggeration and distortion.
    D. A and B.
    E. A, B, and C.

28. In paragraph 19, the author accuses Scheidler of
    A. being inconsistent.
    B. effectively encouraging violence.

C. actually participating in the violent actions she previously cited.

D. A and B.

E. A, B, and C.

29. Do you think the author uses rhetorical questions legitimately in paragraph 21?

30. In paragraph 22, the author puts the word *counsel* in quotation marks. By so doing, she suggests through innuendo that, as used by antiabortionists, the term is

A. jargon intended to confuse.

B. vague.

C. part of a longer quote by Scheidler that she has excerpted.

D. a euphemism for "intimidation."

31. By placing the word *facts* in quotation marks (paragraph 22), the author suggests through innuendo that these are not really facts. Does she back up this innuendo?

RELATED THEME TOPICS

1. *Write an essay in which you argue for or against the proposition that abortion is so evil that extreme measures are justified to stop it.*

2. Shortly after returning home, a 27-year-old mother was gagged, tied up, and raped by a 220-pound guard from a nearby Air Force base who had forced his way into her home. The woman received medical treatment at a hospital and from her own physician. Nevertheless, the episode left her pregnant.

    Not wanting the child, the woman sought an abortion. Although the state's abortion law was at that time (1955) one of the least restrictive, no hospital in her state would permit her to have an abortion.

    Unable to afford to travel abroad for a legal abortion, the woman and her husband were left with two choices: a clandestine illegal abortion or having the baby. Deeply religious and law abiding, the couple chose to carry the baby to term.

    During her pregnancy, the woman admitted to hating the fetus she was carrying and to eagerly awaiting the time she would be rid of it. Thus, the child, conceived in violence and born in hatred, came into the world. (Reported in Burton M. Leiser, *Liberty, Justice and Morals.* New York: Macmillan, 1973, p. 96)

    Write an essay in which you argue that abortion should or should not be permitted in cases such as this one.

PART 3

Types of Argument

8

Generalizations I: Formulation and Extension

INTRODUCTION

The conclusion or thesis of many argumentative essays is derived inductively. This means that the writer basically attempts to demonstrate the logical *probability* of the thesis from a body of evidence. Sometimes, the thesis is derived deductively, that is, as a logically *necessary* or *inevitable extension* of a body of evidence. In either case, what is called a general statement frequently plays a key role; for the conclusion of an induction may be a general statement, and the conclusion of a deduction may be an extension of a general statement. Furthermore, the general statement forms the core of a most common type of argument, termed *generalization.* This chapter focuses on how generalizations are formulated and extended. Chapter 9 deals with some basic criteria for evaluating generalizations.

MODULE 8.1

GENERAL STATEMENTS

The general statement is probably the most common kind of statement found in argument, especially in extended arguments. **A general statement can be viewed**

as a statement that refers to more than one member of a class or population of things, but not necessarily to all members of that class.

Some general statements are *universal,* which means they refer to every member of the class. The following are some examples of universal general statements.

All humans are mammals.
Men can't conceive children.
No human can remain underwater long without air.
An object will maintain its line of direction until acted upon by some outside force.

Notice that all it would take is a single exception to disprove any of these statements. One human who was not a mammal, one man who could bear a child, and so on. That, in fact, is the hallmark of a universal statement: One exception would falsify it. **Nonuniversal general statements, by contrast, cannot be falsified by a single exception because they refer only to a portion of the entire class.** Typically, the portion referred to is rather large, as in:

Most members of Congress are lawyers
Many people support *Roe* v. *Wade*
Sixty-three percent of adult Americans favor capital punishment
Almost all students must take logic before graduating from this institution.

Certainly, we could find students who *do not* have to take logic to graduate or people who *oppose Roe* v. *Wade.* But that would not falsify these statements, for there is nothing about them that discounts exceptions.

IN BRIEF   Universal and nonuniversal general statements are distinguished by the breadth of their claims. Universal statements are intended to apply to every instance or member of a class, whereas nonuniversal statements are intended to apply to a number less than all. Answering the following question is a surefire test for telling the difference between general statements: Will a single exception falsify the general statement? If yes, then the statement is a universal. If no, then it is a nonuniversal. (Notice that you are not asking if there actually is an exception, rather, *if there were one.*)

In Chapter 2, we noted that words that quantify or qualify might not be expressed but implied. This is important to emphasize in connection with general statements. Often universal quantifiers such as *all, every,* or *no* may not be stated but implied in a universal statement. Thus, "Humans are vertebrates" and "Voters are citizens." Similarly unexpressed but implied can be nonuniversal indicators. For example, "Germans rejoiced in October 1990 when East and West Germany were united" most probably is intended to mean that *most* Germans, but not necessarily all, rejoiced at

German reunification. When exact numerical designation is not expressed, context must determine whether the general statement is intended as a universal or a nonuniversal.

Finally, it is worth remembering that general statements make claims that are intended to be true all or most of the time. Thus, "Basketball players are tall" means that *in most cases* basketball players are tall people. Similarly, "Infants can't speak" means that in no cases can infants speak, and "Robert E. Lee was a brilliant general" presumably is intended to mean that *in most cases* (Gettysburg excepted, for example) Lee exhibited brilliant generalship.

GENERALIZATIONS

Arguments that are offered in support of general statements are termed generalizations. One of the most common kinds of generalization is termed inductive generalization. *Inductive generalization* can refer to either (1) the method of arriving at general statements from particular facts of experience, or (2) the conclusion of an argument in support of a general statement. In what follows, the context should make it clear whether inductive generalization refers to the method of inference or the inference itself.

Inductive Generalizations

Like any other argument, an inductive generalization has premises and a conclusion. Its premises attribute some characteristic to a portion or sample of a class or population of things. Its conclusion then asserts the same characteristic of either the entire class (a universal statement) or to a portion, usually *most* of the class (a nonuniversal statement).

For example, from premises that assert that three particular pieces of blue fabric lost their blue color when soaked in bleach, we might conclude that any blue fabric soaked in bleach will lose its blue color. Thus, the premises report a number of instances in which two circumstances or phenomena occurred together. By inductive generalization, we infer that all instances of one of the circumstances or phenomena will also be instances of the other. An inductive generalization of this form —

> **Instance 1 of phenomenon X (soaking blue fabric in bleach) is accompanied by circumstance A (loss of blue color).**
> **Instance 2 of phenomenon X (soaking blue fabric in bleach) is accompanied by circumstance A (loss of blue color).**
> **Instance 3 of phenomenon X (soaking blue fabric in bleach) is accompanied by circumstance A (loss of blue color).**
>
> **Therefore, all instances of phenomenon X (soaking blue fabric in bleach) is accompanied by circumstance A (loss of blue color).**

is termed an induction by *simple enumeration*.

In Chapter 9, we will look at the conditions under which a truth about a portion or sample of a population of things provides adequate support for an inductive generalization about an entire class or most of the class. It is worth mentioning here, however, that only evidence that is representative of the class can provide adequate support for a general statement about a class.

If, for example, in the earlier illustration, three different kinds of fabrics (for example, cotton, silk, rayon) were involved, that sample would be more representative of the entire class of fabrics than if only one kind of fabric was involved. Again, let's say that 60 percent of the married Catholic women you interview say they practice some form of artificial birth control. From this, you form the inductive generalization that 60 percent of all married Catholic women practice some form of artificial birth control. The strength of your inductive generalization depends on how representative your sample is of the entire population of married Catholic women. Thus, if, say, 50 percent of all married Catholic women are between twenty-five and forty-five, and 15 percent are over fifty-five, your sample needs to reflect that distribution in order to be representative of the entire class.

Basing inductive generalizations on unrepresentative data is not only illogical but unwise and potentially harmful. For example, suppose that you find a course in Elizabethan drama boring. From this single specific instance, you decide that Elizabethan drama *in general* is boring. So, you vow never again to read Shakespeare or any Elizabethan play. Although this is obviously a false inductive generalization, you might well use it to foreclose any future exposure to Elizabethan drama, for example, a riveting production of *Hamlet* that you might thoroughly enjoy. As an actual case in point consider the following letter to "Dear Abby":

> I'm glad I'm not the only person in the world who finds vulgar language offensive. Thirteen years ago, I went to a movie, and in the opening scene a little girl (about 6 years old) was talking to her doll. She used a gross four-letter word! I was so shocked, I walked out, and I haven't seen a movie since.

Besides individuals, groups of people can misinterpret evidence and form a false inductive generalization. Anthropology yields a classic and amazing illustration. Anthropologists studying a South Seas tribe found that its members believed that body lice advanced good health. The reason for this belief was that every healthy person was *observed* to have body lice, but very few sick people did. Although there was a correlation between having body lice and being healthy, the lice did not promote health. Rather, a healthy body offered a most appetizing meal for lice. In this case, a *group's* misinterpretation of evidence led to a false generalization.

Noninductive Generalizations

The statements "When seat belts are used, traffic fatalities decrease," "If detected early enough, most cancers can be cured," "Apple trees grow better in the state of Washington than in Florida," and "Curdled milk tastes sour" are, we have seen, general statements. They also happen to be inductive generalizations. They were reached only after a number of specific instances ended with the same result. From this, observers were led to conclude that, in the future, similar occurrences or

Speaking of . . .

Inductive Generalizations

Indispensable Guides

Generalizations are dangerous, but we must generalize. To quote Justice Holmes (who was an associate justice of the U.S. Supreme Court from 1902 to 1932): he said that he welcomed "anything that will discourage men from believing general propositions." But, he added, he welcomed that "only less than he welcomed anything that would encourage men to make such propositions!" For generalizations are indispensable guides. One of the values of knowledge lies in its predictive power—its power to predict the future. Such knowledge is stated in generalizations. It is of little help to me to know that water froze at 32° F yesterday unless this information serves as a warning to put antifreeze in my car radiator before winter comes. History, in the "pure" sense of this term, merely tells us what has happened in the past, but science furnishes us with general laws (i.e., strong generalizations), and general laws tell us what *always* happens under certain specified conditions.

Science is interested in the general, rather than in the particular or individual. When Newton saw an apple fall from a tree in his orchard . . . he was not interested in the size and shape of the apple. Its fall suggested an abstract law to him, the law of gravity. He framed this law in general terms: Every particle of matter attracts every other particle of matter with a force directly proportional to the product of their masses and inversely proportional to the square of their distances. Chemists seek general laws concerning the behavior of matter. The physician wants to know the general characteristics of the disease called myxedema, so that when he has a case he will recognize it and know exactly how to treat it. The finding of general laws, then, is the aim of all science—including history insofar as it is a science.

The problem of the scientist is one of achieving sound generalizations. The scientist is careful not to make assertions which outrun his evidence, and he refuses to out-talk his information. He generalizes but recognizes that no generalizations can be more than probable, for we can never be certain that *all* the evidence is in, nor can the future be guaranteed absolutely—not even future eclipses of the sun and moon. But the scientist knows that certain laws have a very high degree of probability.

(Lionel Ruby, *The Art of Making Sense.*)

circumstances will yield the same results (for example, many early detected cancers will continue to be cured, or curdled milk will continue to taste sour).

Of course, we ourselves need not have gone through the process of inductive reasoning that led to these generalizations. We do not need to have tasted curdled milk once, twice, three times to learn that curdled milk generally tastes sour. We have learned this, as we have thousands of other inductive generalizations, from the experience of others. If they are good generalizations, they have been, and can be, adequately supported, although we rarely give their support much attention because these statements have become, as it were, part of our intellectual background.

Not every general statement that we accept and that gives meaning and shape to our lives has an inductive basis in simple enumeration, which the foregoing do. In fact, there is a huge body of general statements — both universal and nonuniversal — that we seem to form (and sometimes passionately defend) without direct, clearly discernible reference to any observed specifics. Many core assumptions about religion, politics, economics, and social behavior fall into this category, which might be termed *noninductive generalizations*. We absorb hundreds of these general assumptions as part of our socialization or accultural process. In homogeneous societies, these beliefs are held by all members of the group. An enduring example is the following general statement accepted by Eskimos who have had little contact with cultures other than their own: "A man should share his wife with any overnight male guest." In more heterogeneous cultures, many *conflicting* general statements compete for their members' loyalties. The following are some examples of statements that are both held and rejected by some Americans:

Social drinking is acceptable.
Premarital sex is wrong.
A college education is a right.
A woman should be a homemaker.
Americans should always support their president.
Vegetarianism is virtuous.
Material wealth is a measure of success.
Capital punishment is evil.

Arguments could be made for or against any of these general statements — in which case, they would be considered generalizations. None of these statements, however, have any solid inductive base, at least not one that is obvious, as in the case of induction by simple enumeration. Generalizations that derive from what might be called *inner conviction* also seem to fall into this category of noninductive generalization. A possible example would be the statement "Women and minority members are entitled to preferential treatment in the workplace." Furthermore, within as diverse a society as ours, numerous general statements of political beliefs cannot be traced directly to observed specifics, such as the following:

Libertarianism is a form of government most consistent with democratic capitalism.
The government should guarantee a minimum income for its citizens.
The two-party system is the best way to structure a political system.
There should be no restrictions on how long an individual can hold an elective office.
Government has no business restricting the sexual freedoms of consenting adults.

In short, many of the general statements we ardently accept do not have a readily discernible inductive basis. They are not provable in the same way inductions by simple enumeration, for example, are. If we forget this, we can gullibly accept in argument premises that we should be questioning. Similarly, we can interject premises in our own arguments that we blithely assume cannot, will not, or should not be questioned. This does not mean that noninductive generalizations are not worth believing or that there are no good reasons to believe them. It simply means that, like any other argument, noninductive generalizations must be based on *acceptable* and *relevant* evidence and reasons which, taken collectively, offer *adequate* support for them.

IN BRIEF   Not all the general statements that exist in an individual's mind, or in the "public mind," have been inductively concluded—literally thousands have been formed without direct reference to any observed specifics. These derive from cultural value systems, religion, inner conviction, politics, and other areas too numerous to mention. A powerful case can be made for many of these statements—they might be acceptable generalizations. Nevertheless, we need to guard against blindly accepting or glibly using them as premises in arguments.

EXERCISES ON INDUCTIVE AND NONINDUCTIVE GENERALIZATIONS

Decide which of the following generalizations you think came into being because of inductive reasoning—that is, because some individuals noted specific instances before they thought of the general statement. The others will be noninductive generalizations.

1. Like mother, like daughter.
2. College graduates make more money in their lifetimes than do people who do not graduate from college.
3. Smoking cigarettes leads to cancer.
4. Azaleas and camelias need acidic soil to grow well.
5. It takes longer to stop a car going sixty mph than one going fifty mph.
6. Democracy is the best form of government.
7. Men make better scientists than do women.
8. Women are better with children than are men.
9. People with addictions lack willpower.
10. Teenage marriages have less than a fifty-fifty chance of success.
11. Polygamy and polyandry are immoral.
12. Communists are atheists.
13. One can be saved by faith alone.
14. Blondes have more fun than do brunettes.
15. Rich people are not really happy.
16. Eclipses of the sun can be predicted.

17. If you try hard enough, you can be anything you want to be.
18. Anyone can grow up to be president.
19. Freedom is having nothing else to lose.
20. Honesty is the best policy.

MODULE 8.2

FORMING AND APPLYING GENERALIZATIONS

Quite often, we use general statements that we form inductively and noninductively—that is, inductive and noninductive generalizations—as premises in an attempt to provide conclusive support for the conclusion of an argument. Suppose that, wanting something to eat, you open the refrigerator and find a bag of apples. You pick one up, bite into it, and find it is sour. You notice, too, that it is hard and green. You pick out another apple and find that it, too, is hard and green—and sour. You rummage through the bag and find that all the remaining apples are hard and green. On the basis of these observed specifics, you form the inductive generalization by simple enumeration that all the apples in the bag are sour. (Let's ignore for now whether your generalization is justified.)

Now, suppose that a little while later, someone else opens the refrigerator and offers you one of the apples. You instantly refuse. If we made explicit the reasoning process that led to your refusal, it would go something like this:

All apples in the bag are sour.
The apple I'm being offered has come from the bag.

Therefore, the apple is sour.

Not liking sour apples, you turn down the offer. In this case, you applied or extended the universal generalization—"All apples in the bag are sour"—to an instance covered by it and ended with a specific conclusion—"This apple is sour." Granting the truth of the premises, they do provide *conclusive* support for your conclusion. Your argument is a valid deduction (but not necessarily sound).

Although we are rarely conscious of the logical processes involved, each of us daily reaches or acts on hundreds of specific conclusions—probably, deductions—whose origins and bases are the generalizations stored in our minds. The reasoning process whereby we decide what courses to take, films to see, books to read, foods to eat, people to associate with, places to visit, causes to support, and viewpoints to hold usually can be traced back to the generalizations, faulty or not, that we consciously or unconsciously have deposited in our minds and draw upon when the need arises. Some of these generalizations we have formed based on our own direct experience. Many are generalizations that we have inherited based on the formulations of others. Some are inductive, some noninductive; but, whatever their sources, these generalizations function as rudders for steering our lives. To put it in terms of logic: We frequently employ generalizations in deductive arguments, whose premises are intended to provide conclusive support for our conclusions.

A good many of our deductions help us get through life safely and successfully. For instance, knowing that driving on wet pavement can be dangerous, you act on the deduction that you need to drive slowly when the road is wet. Acting on the inductive generalization that caffeine keeps you awake, you deduce that, if you want to sleep tonight you must not have an inviting cup of coffee before retiring, unless it is decaffeinated.

On the other hand, our deductions can be harmful. For example, perhaps a girl has in mind the generalization that if she appears too intelligent, boys will not like her. Not wanting to intimidate a boy she likes, she acts ignorant around him.

We can hurt not only ourselves through faulty generalizations but others as well. A personnel director, for example, may hold the faulty inductive generalization, formed on the basis of two experiences with unmarried female employees, that unmarried females quit work to get married within two years of being hired. On the basis of this inductive generalization, he refuses to consider seriously the job application of an unmarried female, despite her impeccable qualifications. A dyed-in-the-wool Democrat (or Republican) harbors the generalization that only Democrats (or Republicans) are competent to hold office. From this generalization, based on some instances of incompetent or corrupt Democratic (or Republican) office holders, she infers that a specific candidate of the opposing party cannot even be worth considering.

The point is that we need to be careful about the breadth of the generalizations that we form or store in our minds and later use. Generalizations that are improperly qualified end up being improperly extended or applied. That is the problem with the reasoning of the aforementioned personnel director. If he is using only his scant experience with unmarried female employees, it does not support either a universal inductive generalization about *all* female employees or a nonuniversal one about *most* female employees. The best his evidence supports is that "*Some* unmarried women quit work to get married within two years of being hired," in which case, all he may validly conclude is that "Ms. Brown *might or might not* get married within two years of being hired."

EXERCISES ON FORMING AND APPLYING GENERALIZATIONS*

Determine whether the writers of the following arguments are, in all likelihood, forming or applying a generalization. In each case, identify the generalization in question and indicate whether you think it is inductive or noninductive.

1. Most chain smokers run a considerable risk of getting lung cancer. So, I must admit that, since I'm a chain smoker, I stand a good chance of getting lung cancer.
2. Children should be seen, not heard. That's why, Joey, I don't want you to say anything this evening when the adults are present.

3. Inasmuch as more than half of all automobile accidents involve drivers under twenty-five, it follows that such drivers are probably a greater driving risk than those over twenty-five.
4. As Maine goes, so goes the nation. The election results from the state of Maine are in, and they show a clear victory for the incumbent. So, the incumbent will be re-elected.
5. Every class I've taken this year has had far more females than males in it. I'd say, then, that females probably outnumber males at this college.
6. Only Christians will be saved. Since Goldstein is a Jew, he won't attain salvation.
7. It's foolish to say that Sam is normal. There's nothing normal about being a homosexual, and Sam's a homosexual.
8. "Statistics show a harrowing increase in urban crime. Crimes are up in every American city. Therefore, you should vote for my anticrime bill."
9. Extraterrestrial life probably exists, since there's a high probability that atmospheric conditions similar to Earth's exist elsewhere in the universe.
10. Given the fact that the number of homeless is higher in this town than in other comparable towns, it can be reasonably concluded that the median price of a house is probably higher here as well.

MODULE 8.3

GENERAL STATEMENTS IN SYLLOGISMS

The application of general statements and generalizations can be seen in some basic argument patterns commonly used in the development of essays. These patterns involve what logicians term *syllogisms.*

A syllogism is a deductive argument that contains two premises and a conclusion. Ancient and medieval thinkers explored in detail the various forms of *categorical* syllogisms, that is, syllogisms considered from the viewpoint of the relationships between the expressed classes or categories. Their treatments of categorical syllogisms and other logical structures are full of technicalities that need not concern us here. What does interest us, however, is the correct application of a general statement, because that is an important part of argument evaluation and formulation.

Categorical Syllogisms

Let's begin with this simple categorical syllogism:

Premise 1: All students are members of the debate team.
Premise 2: Annie is a student.

Conclusion: Annie is a member of the debate team.

Premise 1 of this syllogism happens to be a universal statement that covers all members of the category "students." It connects every member of that category to a second category "members of the debate team." This universal statement is asserting that every single case of a student is also a case of a member of the debate team. (Notice that it is *not* asserting that every member of the debate team is necessarily a student.)

Premise 2 identifies a specific, "Annie," as a member of the category "students" covered by the first premise. The conclusion — "Annie is a member of the debate team" — follows from the application of the universal statement expressed in premise 1 to the specific of premise 2. Since the premises provide conclusive support for the conclusion, the argument is *valid*.

> **Premise 1:** **All voters are citizens.**
> **Premise 2:** **All the jurors are voters.**
> _____
> **Therefore:** **All the jurors are citizens.**

Here again, premise 1 is a universal that covers all members of the category "voters." Premise 2 identifies a specific type of voter, "jurors." The conclusion is the deduction that results from the extension of what is asserted as universally true of all voters — that they are citizens — to a specific type of voter, "jurors." Like the first argument, this one offers a very strong connection between its conclusion and premises — so strong, in fact, it is logically impossible to affirm the premises while at the same time deny the conclusion. To do so would be self-contradictory. Therefore, this argument is also valid.

The extension of premise 1, "All voters are citizens," can be illustrated by a diagram of concentric circles representing the expressed relationships between the argument's class terms. Thus, where "V" stands for "voters," and "C" stands for "citizens," premise 1 can be diagrammed as follows:

Premise 1: All voters are citizens.

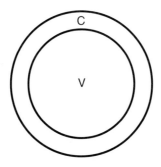

Notice that the diagram shows that every case of a voter is a case of a citizen — all of "V" is included within "C."

Similarly, allowing "J" to stand for "jurors," we can diagram premise 2 as follows:

Premise 2: All jurors are voters.

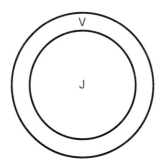

This diagram shows that every juror is also a voter. All "J" is included within "V."

Now, combine these diagrams to show the relationship between "J," "V," and "C."

Premise 1: All voters are citizens.
Premise 2: All the jurors are voters.
———————
Conclusion: All the jurors are citizens.

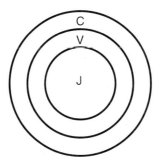

Notice that by the conditions expressed in the premises every juror "J" is also a citizen, "C," which is, of course, the conclusion of this syllogism. Notice also that in relation to the premises, the conclusion, "All the jurors are citizens," is the "narrowest" of the three general statements, even though its grammatical form is identical to the premises'. In the logic of the argument, then, it is a specific application of the argument's broader general statement.

Now consider a third argument:

Premise 1: Some parents are males.
Premise 2: All males are mortals.
———————
Conclusion: Some mortals are parents.

In this syllogism, premise 2 is a universal statement that covers all members of the category "males" and connects it to a second category "mortals." It is asserting that every single instance of a male is also an instance of a mortal (it is *not* asserting, that every single instance of a mortal is a male).

Premise 1 identifies the specific, "parents," as a member of the category "males" which is covered by premise 2. The conclusion, "Some mortals are parents," follows from the application of the universal generalization, premise 2 in this case, to the specific of premise 1. Again, the premises provide conclusive support for the conclusion. The argument is valid. (It also happens to be acceptable. Can you tell why?)

EXERCISES ON CATEGORICAL SYLLOGISMS

1. Treat each of the following statements as the conclusion of a valid syllogism. Make up two premises for each of the conclusions and thereby create a syllogism for each. (Three examples are given to get you started.)
   A. Class will not be held today.
      Syllogism: **Any time professor Jones is ill, class is not held.**
      Professor Jones is ill today.

      Therefore, *class will not be held today*.
   B. The United States should oppose German reunification.
      Syllogism: **Anything that threatens world peace, the United States should oppose.**
      German reunification threatens world peace.

      Therefore, *the United States should oppose German reunification*.
   C. A college education is worth getting.
      Syllogism: **Whatever increases one's earning potential is worth getting.**
      A college education increases one's earning potential.

      Therefore, *a college education is worth getting*.
   D. Senator Smith is a corrupt politician.
   E. Nelson Mandela qualifies as a hero.
   F. The "F" grade should be abolished.
   G. All schools should have an honor code.
   H. Critical thinking is vital to one's survival and prosperity.
   I. Personality tests used as pre-employment screens are unfair.
   J. Harry is going to be punished by God.
   K. Mary Beth will not make a good dentist.
   L. There should be laws restricting the sale of handguns.
   M. The Olympic games are an exercise in political posturing.
   N. The United States has the best political system.
2. Consider the general statements that you just formulated to be generalizations. Determine whether they are likely to be inductive or noninductive generalizations. For example:

A. "Any time Professor Jones is ill, class is not held" is an inductive generalization formed on the basis of observed specific instances of Jones' being ill and his class not being held.

B. "Anything that threatens world peace the United States should oppose" is probably a noninductive generalization that springs from value and political orientations.

"German reunification threatens world peace" might be considered an inductive generalization based on specific observed effects of a unified Germany during the nineteenth and twentieth centuries.

C. "Anything that increases one's earning potential is worth getting" is a noninductive evaluative generalization. "A college education increases one's earning potential" could be considered an inductive generalization based on observing college graduates' earnings compared to the earnings of people who did not graduate from college.

Invalidity and Misapplied General Statements

Whenever we apply a general statement syllogistically, we believe we are reasoning validly—that our premises provide conclusive support for our conclusion. Sometimes, however, we are mistaken—what we believe to be a valid deduction is, in fact, invalid. Of course, this does not necessarily mean our argument is unacceptable. But it does not suggest that we are confused about the strength of our premises.

We have seen that an invalid deduction is one in which the premises, even if true, do not provide conclusive evidence for the conclusion. At this point, we want to connect this notion of invalidity to the misapplication of general statements.

Let's begin with this example of a misapplication expressed symbolically as follows:

All C are B.
All A are B.
_____
Therefore, all A are C.

Now, even if "All A are B," and "All C are B," it does not necessarily follow that "All A are C." After all, there is nothing in the premises that precludes the possibility of an A that is a non-C. Since the premises do not rule out that possibility, it is invalid to conclude that they do, which is what "All A are C," in effect, does.

Notice that we did not even need to know what "A," "B," and "C" represented in order to determine the invalidity of this argument. That is because validity is a function of argument's form, not its content. Since validity is a function of form, we can demonstrate the invalidity of the preceding argument very easily by setting up an analogous argument. **An analogous argument is an argument of the same form, but one in which the premises are actually true and the conclusion is actually false.** Since no valid deduction can ever have two actually true premises and a false conclusion, a single example of such an argument has the effect of proving the form of the argument invalid. We can illustrate this very simply as follows:

All apples are fruits. (True Premise)
All oranges are fruits. (True Premise)
_____
All oranges are apples. (False Conclusion)

or

All mothers are parents. (True Premise)
All fathers are parents. (True Premise)
_____
All fathers are mothers. (False Conclusion)

What these examples prove is that an argument of the form

All A are B.
All C are B.
_____
Therefore, all A are C.

may have true premises and a false conclusion. Since no such argument is ever valid, no argument *of this form* is ever valid.

Some incorrect procedures in deductive reasoning are called *formal fallacies.* A proper consideration of these fallacies is rather complex and is therefore best left to a full-scale study of logic. For our purposes it is enough to emphasize the importance of inspecting the scope of the general statement that is being applied because it is a misapplication of a general statement that is often at the root of invalid deductive reasoning.

For example, there is a big difference in *scope* between the following two general statements:

All seniors study Shakespeare.

Only seniors study Shakespeare.

The first statement is nonexclusive, which means that it is including *all* seniors but it does not exclude anybody else. Thus, if you learned that your friend Brenda is studying Shakespeare, you can merely infer: Brenda might or might not be a senior. If, on the other hand, you inferred that Brenda *is* or *must be* a senior, your deduction would be *invalid.* If you did draw this invalid conclusion, it would be because you did not pay enough attention to the scope of the statement "All seniors study Shakespeare."

The second general statement — "Only seniors study Shakespeare" — is far more restrictive. It limits students of Shakespeare to seniors. In other words, any student who is studying Shakespeare is a senior. So, if you learn that Brenda is studying Shakespeare, then you may correctly infer that "Brenda *must be* a senior." In fact, you have logical grounds to infer that any student studying Shakespeare — Tim, Blanche, Preston, and so on — is a senior.

IN BRIEF   General statements may refer to all members of a group. They may apply to all members of a group and to no one else, or they may apply to all members of a group and to others also.

Following are some additional examples of general statements that are applied properly and improperly. The improper ones represent some of the most common errors in deductive reasoning:

1. Some (or "most" or "many" or any other limiting quantifier) students are intelligent.
   Brenda is a student.

   Therefore, Brenda *is* intelligent. (Invalid Conclusion)
   Therefore, Brenda may or may not be intelligent. (Valid Conclusion)

Since the first premise speaks only of *some* students, we have no way of knowing whether Brenda is one of those students who is intelligent. Therefore, we have no basis for drawing an unqualified conclusion.[1]

2. No one but students are intelligent.
   Brenda is a student.

   Therefore, Brenda *is* intelligent. (Invalid Conclusion)
   Therefore, Brenda may or may not be intelligent. (Valid Conclusion)

The first premise asserts that anyone who is intelligent is a student — *not* that all students are intelligent. So, even if Brenda is a student, she is not *necessarily* intelligent — she *may or may not be.*[2]

In each of these arguments, the invalidity has resulted from a misreading of the scope of one of the premises. More precisely, from thinking that the general statements (the first premise of each argument) are covering *every* case of a student when that is not necessarily so.

Sometimes a general statement is misapplied as a result of applying two negative premises. For example:

---

[1]In the study of deductive logic, this particular error is called the *fallacy of the undistributed middle term.* The fallacy takes its name from the fact that, in at least one of the premises, some claim must be made about every member of the class designated by the middle term, which is the term that appears in both premises.
[2]This error is termed the *fallacy of drawing an affirmative conclusion from a negative premise,* which means that an affirmative conclusion can never be validly drawn from a negative premise.

3. No students are intelligent.
   Some athletes aren't students.
   _____

   Therefore, some athletes are intelligent. (Invalid Conclusion)
   Therefore, some athletes *may* or may not be intelligent. (Valid Conclusion)

Although the first premise denies that any student is intelligent, it says nothing of nonstudents. So, even if some athletes are not students, that does not necessarily mean that some athletes are intelligent — these particular athletes could be nonstudents who are unintelligent.[3]

Sometimes, we simply draw a conclusion that overextends the evidence expressed in the premises. Let's illustrate this with an obviously invalid argument:

4. Some females are college graduates.
   Some mothers aren't college graduates.
   _____

   Therefore, some mothers aren't females.

This argument obviously is invalid because it contains two true premises and a false conclusion. But the misapplication of the general statement "Some females are college graduates" is not obvious.

A good way to understand how the conclusion illicitly goes beyond the evidence expressed is to note that the first premise covers only *some* females, not all. The conclusion, however, is really covering *all* females. It is excluding some mothers from the *entire* class of females. It is, in effect, making the *unqualified* assertion that *no* female is an instance of the mothers denoted by "some mothers." In this case, the conclusion has no valid basis for universalizing females because its premise covers only *some* females.[4]

The preceding example of an overextended general statement was easy to spot because both premises were true and the conclusion false. But when the premises *and* the conclusion are true, the error is more difficult to detect, as in this example:

Some students are voters.
Some men aren't voters.
_____

Therefore, some men aren't students.

Here again, the conclusion covers *all* students. It is saying that *no* student is an instance of the men denoted by "some men." But the first premise covers only *some* students. Thus, the conclusion overstates the evidence. So, even though the conclusion happens to be true, it does not validly follow from the premises or

_____

[3]This error is termed the *fallacy of exclusive premises,* which means that no unqualified conclusion can be validly drawn from two negative premises.
[4]This fallacy is sometimes termed the *illicit end term,* which consists in drawing a conclusion that universalizes a term that has not been universalized in one of the premises.

evidence. In other words, the premises do not provide *indubitable* support for it. If, on the other hand, the argument had read

> *All* students are voters.
> Some men aren't voters.
> _____
> Therefore, some men aren't students.

the conclusion would be valid. Notice that, in this form, the first premise covers *all* students and, therefore, provides a solid base for covering all students in the conclusion.

EXERCISES ON INVALIDITY AND MISAPPLIED GENERAL STATEMENTS

Determine whether the following syllogisms are valid or invalid. Remember that you are trying to determine whether the general statements are being applied correctly. In each case, explain your answer.

1. All eighteen-year-old males must register for the draft.
   Jess is an eighteen-year-old male.
   _____
   Therefore, Jess must register for the draft.

2. All eighteen-year-old males must register for the draft.
   Jess must register for the draft.
   _____
   Therefore, Jess is an eighteen-year-old male.

3. Some Republican administrations cause inflation.
   The Bush administration is Republican.
   _____
   The Bush administration will cause inflation.

4. Some Republican administrations cause inflation.
   The Bush administration is Republican.
   _____
   The Bush administration may or may not cause inflation.

5. Smoking pot always leads to drug addiction.
   Harry doesn't smoke pot.
   _____
   Harry won't become a drug addict.

6. No man can be a mother.
   Fran is not a mother.
   _____
   It follows that Fran must be man.

7. Killing a human being is never justifiable.
   Self-defense sometimes involves killing a human being.
   _____
   Clearly, then, self-defense sometimes isn't justifiable.

8. Thousands of young couples today are living together before marrying. Ted and June are living together and they aren't married.
   _____
   So, Ted and June must be a young couple.

9. The brighter a person is, the better grades she'll probably make in this class.
   Jane is brighter than anyone else in this class.
   _____
   So, Jane undoubtedly will make higher grades in this class than anyone else.

10. Most athletes are in super shape.
    Some members of the gym class are athletes.
    _____
    Some members of the gym class are in super shape.

11. No triangle has four sides.
    Some of these geometric figures don't have four sides.
    _____
    It follows that some of these geometric figures are triangles.

12. A good deal of our problems are self-created.
    I'm having a problem with my marriage.
    _____
    I have created the problem I'm having with my marriage.

13. Some Y are not Z.
    Some X are Y.
    _____
    Therefore, some X are not Z.

14. All X are Y.
    Some Y are Z.
    _____
    Some Z are X.

15. All X are Y.
    No Z is Y.
    _____
    So, no Z is X.

MODULE 8.4

CONDITIONAL SYLLOGISMS

Categorical syllogisms are based on the connections of the class terms that comprise them. Other syllogisms are based on the connections of the statements of which they are composed. Conditional and disjunctive syllogisms fall into this latter family of syllogisms, and they, too, play a prominent role in extended argument. Let's first consider conditional syllogisms.

"All students are members of the debate team" can be expressed as "*If* a person is a student, *then* the person is a member of the debate team." And "No students are members of the debate team" can be expressed as "*If* a person is a student, *then* the person is not a member of the debate team." Certain "if . . . then . . ." statements are called *logical conditionals,* or simply *conditionals.*

A conditional statement is one consisting of two assertions, the first of which implies the second. Conditional statements are expressed in the form of "If (or some equivalent conditional word such as *when, whenever, where, wherever,* and so on) . . . then (which may not be expressed, but merely implied). . . ." The translations of the universal statements we just offered are conditional statements because they follow this form. Each consists of two assertions (for example, "A person is a student" and "the person is a member of the debate team") that are so connected that the truth of the first assertion implies the truth of the second. The portion of the conditional that does the implying is the assertion that appears between the "if" and the "then." It is called the *antecedent.* The portion that is implied, which follows the "then," is called the *consequent.* " Thus, we can symbolically represent any conditional statement as follows, where "A" stands for any antecedent assertion and "C" for any consequent assertion:

If A, then C.

Quite often, conditional statements appear as premises in syllogisms. When this occurs, the syllogism is called a *conditional syllogism.* Here is an example of a conditional syllogism with its conditional premise italicized:

If a person is a student, then the person is a member of the debate team.
Annie is a student.
_____
Therefore, Annie is a member of the debate team.

or

If a person is a voter, the person is a citizen.
The jurors are voters.
_____
Therefore, the jurors are citizens.

You probably recognize these syllogisms as similar to two we examined earlier. The only difference is that these syllogisms are expressed in conditional form. Rather than the first premise of the first argument asserting "All students are members of the debate team," it expresses the idea in conditional form; and rather than the first premise of the second argument asserting "All voters are citizens," it expresses the idea in conditional form.

As in any other kind of syllogism, the validity of a conditional syllogism depends on whether its premises provide indubitable support for its conclusion. For conditional syllogisms such as these, there are two, and only two valid forms.

Valid Form 1: Affirming the Antecedent **One way that we can reason validly in a conditional syllogism is to provide a premise that affirms the antecedent of the conditional and then draw a conclusion that affirms its consequent.** In other words, we can assert that its antecedent is true, then assert that its consequent is, too. Thus, it would be valid to argue:

If a person is a student, then the person is a member of the debate team.
Annie is a student. *(Affirmation of antecedent)*
_____
Therefore, Annie *is* a member of the debate team. *(Affirmation of consequent)*

or

If a person is a voter, the person is a citizen.
The jurors *are* voters. *(Affirmation of antecedent)*
_____
Therefore, the jurors *are* citizens. *(Affirmation of consequent)*

Since the validity of any deduction is dependent only on its form, any conditional syllogism that has this form is valid. Thus, we can express this valid form symbolically, again following "A" to represent any antecedent assertion and "C" to represent any consequent assertion:

If A, then C.
A.
Valid Procedure: Affirming the Antecedent[5]
_____
Therefore, C.

Valid Form 2: Denying the Consequent **The second valid form of a conditional argument consists in providing a premise that denies the consequent of the conditional, then drawing a conclusion that denies the antecedent.** In other words, we can assert that the consequent is false, then assert that the antecedent is false. The following two arguments illustrate this valid procedure:

If a person is a student, then the person is a member of the debate team.
Annie is *not* a member of the debate team. *(Denial of consequent)*
_____
Therefore, Annie is *not* a student. *(Denial of antecedent)*

or

If a person is a voter, the person is a citizen.
The jurors are *not* citizens. *(Denial of consequent)*
_____
Therefore, the jurors are *not* voters. *(Denial of antecedent)*

_____
[5]The Latin term for the valid process of affirming the antecedent, then affirming the consequent is *modus ponens.*

Since the validity of a deduction is dependent only upon its form, any conditional syllogism in the following form is valid.

> If A, then C.
> *Not* C.
>
>   Valid Procedure: Denying the Consequent[6]
> _____
> Therefore, *not* A.

These two valid forms — affirming the antecedent and denying the consequent — must not be confused with two superficially similar but invalid forms.

Invalid Form 1: Denying the Antecedent   It is not uncommon for people to think that denying the antecedent of a conditional logically guarantees a denial of the consequent. It does not. Consider, for example, this argument:

> **If a person is a student, then the person is a member of the debate team.**
> **Annie is *not* a student.**
> _____
> **Therefore, Annie is not a member of the debate team.**

On first look, this argument might seem valid. But the conditional premise, as we have seen, is tantamount to the universal statement "All students are members of the debate team." That universal, as we previously noted, covers every specific instance of a student. It asserts that any instance of a student is an instance of a member of the debate team. But the statement in no way excludes nonstudents from the debate team. The same can be said of the conditional "If a person is a student, then the person is a member of the debate team." It asserts that being a student implies being a member of the debate team, but it does not assert that nonstudent status implies nondebate-team status. Therefore, when the argument denies that Annie is a student, it does not *guarantee* that she is not a member of the debate team. Annie might be a nonstudent member of the debate team.

> **We can symbolically represent this invalid conditional form as follows:**
> **If A, then C.**
> **Not A.**
>
>   Invalid: Fallacy of Denying the Antecedent
> _____
> **Therefore, not C.**

Invalid Form 2: Affirming the Consequent   Perhaps an even more common fallacy of conditional reasoning is the one that results when the consequent of the conditional is affirmed, and then the antecedent is affirmed in the conclusion, as in:

_____
[6]The Latin term for this procedure is *modus tollens.*

If a person is a student, then the person is a member of the debate team.
Annie is a member of the debate team.

Therefore, Annie is a student.

We can pinpoint the invalidity in this form as we did with its companion fallacy. Thus, the conditional premise means "All students are members of the debate team." Notice again that this universal statement covers all *students,* but not necessarily all members of the debate team. Yes, every case of a student is an instance of a debate team member, but not every case of a debate team member is necessarily an instance of a student. In other words, "All students are members of the debate team" no more implies that "All members of the debate team are students" than "All mothers are females" implies that "All females are mothers."

The same analysis applies to the conditional "If a person is a student, then the person is a member of the debate team." This means that any instance of a student implies an instance of a debate team member. But the conditional *is not* asserting that membership in the debate team implies that one is a student. An arguer who attempts to affirm an antecedent by affirming a consequent misses this point entirely. In short, even if Annie is a member of the debate team, she is not necessarily a student. She could be a nonstudent member of the debate team.

We can represent this invalid conditional form symbolically as follows:

If A, then C.
C.
Invalid: Fallacy of Affirming the Consequent

Therefore, A.

It is worth noting that some conditional syllogisms contain only conditional statements, as in this one:

If Annie is a student, then she's a member of the debate team.
If she's a member of the debate team, then she's on the dean's list.

Therefore, if Annie is a student, then she's on the dean's list.

There are three things about this conditional syllogism that make it, and any argument of this form, valid: (1) The consequent of the first premise is the same as the antecedent of the second premise; (2) the antecedent of the first premise is the same as the antecedent of the conclusion; and (3) the consequent of the second premise is the same as the consequent of the conclusion. If we allow "C-1" to represent the consequent of the first premise, and "C-2" to represent the consequent of the second premise, we can represent this valid form symbolically as follows:

If A, then C-1.
If C-1, then C-2.

Therefore, if A, then C-2.

Regardless of the number of conditional statements that comprise a conditional argument such as this, the argument is valid so long as the aforementioned relationships among the statements hold. Thus, an argument of this form is valid:

> If A, then C-1.
> If C-1, then C-2.
> If C-2, then C-3.
> If C-3, then C-4.
> _____
> Therefore, If A, then C-4.

EXERCISES ON CONDITIONAL SYLLOGISMS

Identify and explain the validity or invalidity of each of the following conditional arguments.

1. If the first suspect is honest, then she denied being at the crime scene. The first suspect didn't deny being at the crime scene. Therefore, she's not honest.
2. If the candidate is elected, he will increase taxes. The candidate will increase taxes. Therefore, the candidate will be elected.
3. If the student knew the answer, he volunteered. The student didn't know the answer. Thus, he didn't volunteer.
4. Whenever the president is asked a question, he dodges the issue. The president is asked a question. So, he'll dodge the issue.
5. Where there's smoke there's fire. There's no fire in the building. So, there must not be any smoke in it.
6. If Bob told the truth, then his buddy lied. If Bob's buddy lied, then Bob's wife is guilty. It follows that if Bob told the truth, his wife is guilty.
7. If I pass this exam, I'll graduate and if I pass this course I'll graduate. So, if I pass this exam, I'll pass this course.
8. "Mankind, judging by their neglect of him, have never at all understood the power of Love. For if they had understood him they would surely have built noble temples and altars, and offered solemn sacrifices in his honor; but this is not done. . . ."
   (Plato, *Symposium*)
9. If Pluto, according to Halliday's calculations, had a diameter of more than 4,200 miles, then an occultation would have occurred at McDonald Observatory, and the records clearly indicate that it did not. Thus, Pluto must be that size or smaller; it cannot be larger.
10. "There is no case known in which a thing is found to be the efficient cause of itself; for so it would be prior to itself, which is impossible."
    (Thomas Aquinas, *Summa Theologica*)
11. "I do know that this pencil exists; but I could not know this, if Hume's principles were true; therefore, Hume's principles, one or both of them, are false."
    (George Edward Moore, *Some Main Problems of Philosophy*)

12. "When we regard a man as morally responsible for an act, we regard him as a legitimate object of moral praise or blame in respect of it. But it seems plain that a man cannot be a legitimate object of moral praise or blame for an act unless in willing the act he is in some important sense a 'free' agent. Evidently free will in some sense, therefore, is a pre-condition of moral responsibility."
    (C. Arthur Campbell, *In Defense of Free Will*)

13. "Syllogism is not the great instrument of reason. If syllogisms must be taken for the only proper instrument and means of knowledge, it will follow, that before Aristotle, there was not one man that did or could know anything by reason; and that since the invention of syllogisms there is not one of ten thousand that do. But God has not been so sparing to men to make them barely two-legged creatures, and left it to Aristotle to make them rational."
    (John Locke, *An Essay Concerning Human Understanding*)

MODULE 8.5

DISJUNCTIVE SYLLOGISMS

We have just seen that a conditional statement is a compound statement in that it consists of two statements. Sometimes, a compound statement takes the form of an "either . . . or . . . " construction, as in: "Annie is either a student or she's a member of the debate team." A statement such as this is called a *disjunctive* because it presents at least two alternatives, each of which is termed a disjunct. In this example the two disjuncts are "Annie is a student" and "Annie is a member of the debate team."

The word *or* is ambiguous — it has two separate meanings. Sometimes, *or* may be used in a strong or exclusive sense to mean "at least one and at most one." For example, when an airline ticket agent informs you that "You can fly either first class or coach," the agent means that you can fly one or the other, but obviously not both — at least not at the same time! When a mother tells a child who is insistent on having both ice cream and cake for dessert, "You will have either ice cream or cake," she clearly means one and only one of these choices.

But *or* can also be used in a weak or inclusive sense to mean "either, but possibly both." For example, the disjunctive statement "Benefits will be paid in the event of disability or unemployment" clearly does not mean that those who are both disabled and unemployed will not receive benefits. Thus, benefits will be paid for disabled persons and for unemployed persons, but also for persons who are *both* disabled *and* unemployed. An inclusive disjunction is true if one or the other, or both adjuncts are true. Only if both disjuncts are false is the inclusive disjunction false. Where precision is crucial, as in legal documents, this sense is made explicit by use of the phrase *and/or.*

IN BRIEF   The weak or inclusive disjunction of two statements is interpreted as asserting that at least one of the statements is true, but both may be true. The strong or exclusive disjunction of two statements is interpreted as asserting that at least one of the statements is true, but *not* both are true.

Now, what about a disjunction such as:

"Annie is either a student or she's a member of the debate team"?

In this instance, it is possible that "or" is intended in either sense, strong or weak. If the strong sense is intended, the statement is interpreted as asserting that Annie is one or the other, but not both a student *and* a member of the debate team. On the other hand, if the weak sense is intended, the statement is interpreted as asserting that Annie is at least one, but possibly both. In other words, if "or" is intended in the weak or inclusive sense, this disjunctive statement carries three possible meanings, not merely two:

1. Annie is a student, but not a member of the debate team.
2. Annie is a member of the debate team, but not a student.
3. Annie is both a student and a member of the debate team.

Often we can tell the intended meaning of *or* from context, as in the situations described earlier involving your airline ticket, the child's dessert, and the insurance benefits. This is why we must pay close attention to linguistic and environmental contexts, which provide clues to intended meaning. **But after due consideration, if the word *or* remains ambiguous in a disjunction, we interpret it in its weak or inclusive sense to mean "either, but possibly both."** In this way, we preserve the partial common meaning of both uses of *or*—namely, that at least one of the disjuncts is true.

IN BRIEF   Unless the context clearly indicates that *or* is intended in its strong or exclusive sense *("at least one and at most one"),* we take it in its weak or inclusive sense *("either, possibly both").*

When a disjunctive statement appears as a premise of a deduction, that deductive argument is termed a disjunctive syllogism.

Here are two disjunctive syllogisms:

Annie is either *a student* or *a member of the debate team.*
Annie is *not* a student.

Therefore, Annie *is* a member of the debate team.

Annie is either *a student* or *a member of the debate team.*
Annie is *not* a member of the debate team.

Therefore, Annie *is* a student.

Notice that the second premise of each syllogism *denies* one of the disjuncts or options offered by the disjunctive premise. Since one of the disjuncts is taken to be true, the denial or elimination of one establishes logical grounds for affirming the other, which is precisely what the conclusion of each argument does. Thus, where "D-1" and "D-2" represent any two disjuncts or alternatives, we can symbolically represent this valid form of disjunctive reasoning as follows:

Either D-1 or D-2.
Not D-1.

Therefore, D-2.

or

Either D-1 or D-2.
Not D-2.

Therefore, D-1.

A common fallacy in disjunctive reasoning occurs when we *assume without good reason* the strong or exclusive sense of *or* in a disjunction, then attempt to deny one of the disjuncts on the basis of affirming the other. Thus:

Annie is either a student or a member of the debate team.
Annie *is* a student.

Therefore, Annie is *not* a member of the debate team.

or

Annie is either a student or a member of the debate team.
Annie *is* a member of the debate team.

Therefore, Annie is *not* a student.

If it has not been previously determined that Annie can be only one or the other, then she may be both a student and a member of the debate team. Therefore, since she may be both, affirming one of the disjunctives does not provide conclusive support for denying the other. Thus, any disjunctive argument in which *or* is ambiguous is invalid when it attempts to deny one of the disjuncts on the basis of affirming the other. This fallacy can be expressed symbolically as follows:

> Either D-1 or D-2.
> D-1.
> ──────────
> Therefore, not D-2.

or

> Either D-1 or D-2.
> D-2.
> ──────────
> Therefore, not D-1.

Of course, if it has been previously established that one and only one of the disjuncts is true, then such a procedure would be valid. Thus, if Annie cannot be both a student and a member of the debate team, then affirming one of these disjuncts would provide sufficient grounds for denying the other.

IN BRIEF   Whenever the word *or* in a disjunction is ambiguous, it is taken to mean "either, possibly both."

EXERCISES ON DISJUNCTIVE SYLLOGISMS*

Identify and explain the validity or invalidity of each of the following disjunctive arguments. In all cases, assume the weak or inclusive sense of *or*.

1. Millie is either secretary or president. She's not the secretary. Therefore, she is the president.
2. The stranger is either a friend or an impostor. The stranger must not be an impostor, because she's a friend.
3. Mr. Steinberg is the physician's next-door neighbor, because Ms. Crosby is the physician's next-door neighbor, or Mr. Steinberg is, and Ms. Crosby isn't.
4. Money isn't the root of all evil, for it's sometimes the source of good, and it's either the root of all evil or at times the source of good.
5. The car must be out of gas. After all, the battery is okay, and the car's either out of gas or the battery is dead.
6. **Either non-X or non-Y.**
   Not non-Y.
   ──────────
   Therefore, X.

7. Either not non-X or non-Y.
   X is the case.
   _____
   Therefore, non-Y is the case.
8. Either not non-X or not non-Y.
   Non-Y is the case.
   _____
   Therefore, not non-X.
9. Either X or Y or A and B.
   Not A.
   _____
   Therefore, either X or Y.
10. Either X or Y, or A or B.
    A is not the case.
    _____
    Therefore, X or Y.
11. Either Jennifer will work and Liz will be off; or Sue will be sick or the supervisor will be angry. Liz won't be off. It follows that either Sue will be sick or the supervisor will be angry.
12. Mr. Quayle is either slow or clever, and we know he's not clever. Moreover, Mr. Bush is either insecure or brilliant. But we know Bush isn't brilliant. It follows that Mr. Quayle is slow and Mr. Bush is insecure; or maybe this entire analysis is biased. In fact, there's a good reason to suspect that this entire analysis is biased. So, we can conclude that Mr. Quayle isn't slow and Mr. Bush isn't insecure. (Hint: Make the miniconclusions of this argument explicit and you will find it quite manageable. One implied miniconclusion follows from the first sentence. A second miniconclusion is implied by the second and third sentences.)

MODULE 8.6

GENERAL STATEMENTS AS WARRANTS

All of the syllogisms that we just studied made their general statements explicit so it was rather easy to see how the statement was being applied. Often, however, arguments do not express but imply general statements. This fact is perhaps the biggest obstacle to effective argument analysis.

In Chapter 1, we agreed to use the term *warrant* to refer to an unexpressed premise that states a general, law-like relationship between an argument's data and conclusion. For example, suppose you took your car to a garage for a tune-up. The mechanic asks why you believe your car needs a tune-up. "Because it's been missing at low speeds," you tell him. "It's also stalling at lights, using more gas than usual, and simply lacks pep." The mechanic nods and agrees that a tune-up is in order.

Now, using "D" for data, "C" for conclusion and "W" for warrant, we could represent your reasoning as follows:

(D) My car's missing at low speeds,
getting poor gas mileage, and
lacks pep.   → (C) My car needs a tune-up.

(W) (A car with these signs
needs a tune-up)

Like many arguments, this one left a key premise unexpressed, its warrant. In this case, the warrant is an inductive generalization that was formed many years ago based on countless observed specifics such as the ones you described. So consistently indicative of the need for a tune-up are the signs you have observed, that all of us who know anything about cars automatically apply that generalization, law-like, to determine that in a specific case our car needs a tune-up. That is precisely what you did and what the mechanic did, as well. (In fact, it explains why the mechanic did not say to you after you described your car's feeble performance: "But I still don't understand why you think your car needs a tune-up." Like you and the rest of us, he has in his mind the generalization that a car with the signs you described needs a tune-up.)

The ideal in reconstructing warrants is to fill in a premise that validates the conclusion — to devise a statement which, when combined with the expressed premise, provides conclusive support for the conclusion. This is easier said than done.

In practice, filling in warrants is always tricky because it poses a danger of misrepresenting the arguer's intended meaning. If a reconstruction warps intended meaning, it sets up a straw argument, a distortion of the original argument. Obviously, we want to avoid doing this. Unfortunately, there is no easy formula which, when followed, will always guarantee a legitimate reconstruction. Indeed, the ability to reconstruct faithfully is both an analytic and interpretive skill that can only be mastered through practice. Still, there are things we can *avoid* doing in filling in warrants, which will maximize our chances of devising premises that are faithful to the author's intended meaning.

IN BRIEF   The object of filling in a missing warrant is to complete the argument — that is, to make it explicitly valid.

Things to Avoid When Reconstructing Warrants

1. Disconnectedness   Before continuing, try to fill in the blank of the following argument with a premise you think provides *conclusive* support for the conclusion.

A is greater than B + ___?___ . Therefore, A is greater than C.

You probably filled in the blank with "B is greater than C" because you saw that that premise provides the missing link, as it were, in the argument chain. It conclusively connects "A is greater than B" and "A is greater than C."

What about "C is greater than B"? Would that complete the argument by providing *conclusive* support for the conclusion? No, because even if

> A is greater than B, and
> C is greater than B,
> we cannot say for sure that
> A is greater than C.

In short, "C is greater than B" would leave the stated premise and conclusion deductively disconnected.

The best way to ensure connectedness in reconstructions is to pay careful attention to an argument's content, because it reveals intended meaning. That is why sensitivity to language is so important to effective argument analysis. Consider, for example, this simple argument:

> **Cigarettes cause disease. Therefore, they should be banned.**

We can represent this argument as follows:

> **(D)** Cigarettes cause disease. → **(C)** They should be banned.

Clearly something has been omitted from this argument, for the conclusion talks about what should be banned, but the expressed premise does not. The arguer has left unexpressed a warrant that provides a logical link between datum and conclusion.

Now, suppose you surmise that the missing general statement, the warrant, is "Cigarettes have been linked to cancer" or "Cigarettes are a drug." Even though these statements are true and may provide a reason for believing the conclusion, they do not form a logical bridge between datum and conclusion. In the language of valid reasoning, they do not provide *conclusive* support for the conclusion.

What is needed is a warrant that expresses exactly how "cigarettes should be banned" logically follows from "cigarettes cause disease." A statement such as "Anything that causes disease should be banned" would express the general, law-like relationship between datum and conclusion that the arguer seems to have in mind. In filling in the warrant with a general statement such as this, we, in effect, complete the arguer's fragment argument. Thus,

> ***Whatever causes disease should be banned.***
> **Cigarettes cause disease.**
> _____
> **Therefore, cigarettes should be banned.**

Let's examine another example:

> Young people should do whatever maximizes their earning potential.
> ────────────
> So, they should complete college.

This argument can be represented as follows:

(D) Young people should do → **(C)** They should
whatever maximizes their   complete college.
earning potential.

Again, this argument requires a general statement of the relationship between datum and conclusion, between maximizing earning potential, on the one hand, and completing college, on the other. For example, "Completing college maximizes earning potential." The addition of this general statement makes the argument explicit. Thus:

> *Completing college maximizes earning potential.*
> **Young people should do whatever maximizes their earning potential.**
> ────────────
> **So, they should complete college.**

2. Overstatement or Understatement Ensuring connectedness in reconstructing warrants does not of itself guarantee a proper reconstruction. To see why, consider this argument:

> **Since Mrs. Patterson is a working mother, she probably supports daycare centers.**

We know that this argument requires an additional premise because the conclusion covers supporters of daycare centers but the stated premise does not. Some warrant is needed to make explicit the connection between datum and conclusion. Three possibilities are:

1. *All working mothers favor daycare centers.*
2. *Most working mothers favor daycare centers.*
3. *Some working mothers favor daycare centers.*

Each of these general statements connects working mothers, on the one hand, and supporters of daycare centers, on the other. What distinguishes them, however, is their scope. Candidate 1 speaks of *all* working mothers—it is a universal statement. Candidate 2 is nonuniversal, covering as it does a consensus of ("most") working mothers, that is, some unspecified number above a majority. Candidate 3 is the narrowest of the three statements, covering at least one but not necessarily all or most mothers.

In deciding which of these three possible statements best expresses the relationship between datum and conclusion, we want to choose the one that is strong enough to entail the conclusion, but is no stronger. *Strong enough, but not too strong*—there are good reasons for this advice.

If the reconstructed warrant is not strong or general enough, then it will not help provide conclusive support for the conclusion. On the other hand, if it is too strong, it will misrepresent the argument by overstatement.

Apply these cautions to the three warrant candidates that we have isolated. Unqualified warrant 1, "All working mothers favor daycare centers," is so strong that it entails the conclusion "Mrs. Patterson *must* (or certainly does) support daycare centers." But the argument's conclusion is a qualified statement—"Mrs. Patterson *probably* supports daycare centers." So this argument does not need a universal statement as a warrant, and if we insisted on such an unqualified warrant, we would unfairly make the argument an easy target for criticism. After all, a single example of a working mother opposed to daycare centers would prove the warrant false and the argument unacceptable. (Of course, since we have erected a straw argument, our criticism would be fallacious, not the argument.)

Consider candidate 3: "Some working mothers favor daycare centers." This general statement is so narrow as to overlook the *high likelihood* expressed in the conclusion by the word "probably." It does not capture the "good chance" that Mrs. Patterson is a supporter of daycare centers. So, whereas candidate 1 is too strong a warrant, candidate 3 is too weak.

Candidate 2 refers to "most" working mothers. It is, therefore, a stronger statement than candidate 3 but weaker than candidate 1. It thus avoids the understatement of candidate 3 and the overstatement of candidate 1. It exactly reflects the sentiment of the conclusion and thus gives conclusive support for the inference that Mrs. Patterson *probably* supports daycare centers. By expressing the warrant with this general statement we complete the arguer's syllogism. Thus:

> *Most working mothers support daycare centers.*
> **Mrs. Patterson is a working mother.**
> _____
> **Therefore, she probably supports daycare centers.**

3. Repetition   There is a tendency in reconstruction merely to repeat data in other words. The result is that the reconstruction does nothing to cast light on, expose, or pinpoint the missing premise. To see how this can happen, consider the following argument:

> **Because TV violence is portrayed in graphic detail, it contributes to real-life violence.**

This argument can be represented as follows:

(D) TV violence is portrayed → **(C)** It contributes
in graphic detail.   to real-life
                                       violence.

Notice that the conclusion covers real-life violence, while the datum says nothing about this topic. Clearly, then, this argument is incomplete. A warrant is needed to show how the conclusion logically follows from the datum. Here are two candidates:

1. *Whatever portrays violence in graphic detail contributes to real-life violence.*
2. *If TV violence is portrayed in graphic detail, it contributes to real-life violence.*

Both of these reconstructions provide conclusive support for the conclusion. Is one preferable to the other?

If you look carefully at these two general statements you will notice that they differ in the scope of their claims. Candidate 1, in effect, asserts that *anything* that portrays violence in graphic detail contributes to real-life violence, but candidate 2 covers only the connection between TV violence and real-life violence. Although candidate 2 does stick more closely to the topics covered in the argument—that is, TV violence and real-life violence—it merely repeats what is already implicit in the logic of the argument. In other words, anyone who argues "Because TV violence is portrayed in graphic detail, it contributes to real-life violence" obviously believes that the datum she offers leads to the conclusion she draws.

That is how arguments and reasoning work: premise supports conclusion. All candidate 2 does, then, is to make the assumption about the nature of arguments and the reasoning process explicit. It is tantamount to an expression of the general principle that leads an arguer from data to conclusion, namely: "If you accept my data, then you must logically accept my conclusion." Candidate 2, however, does not tell us anything about the reasoning *behind* the argument; it does not show how, on what grounds, the arguer moved from datum to conclusion. Candidate 2, in effect, leaves the argument begging the question, since it can still be asked: "But *why* does TV violence contribute to real-life violence?"

Candidate 1, on the other hand, does not repeat what is already implicit in the argument. It illuminates exactly how the arguer moved from datum to conclusion. It forecloses the very question that candidate 2 begged. We may no longer ask "But why does TV violence contribute to real-life violence," because candidate 1 provides an answer: "Whatever portrays violence in graphic detail contributes to real-life violence."

Following these guidelines will not guarantee perfect reconstructions of missing premises. But they will help you avoid implausible reconstructions, that is, reconstructions with little or no contextual credibility. Remember, when filling in missing elements, always give the arguer the benefit of the doubt. The idea is not to make the person's argument look bad, but to have it make sense. When, despite more plausible alternatives, we fill in warrants that are disconnected, too weak or too strong, or repetitious, we do not play fair.

IN BRIEF   A bad reconstruction of a warrant is itself an example of poor reasoning because it (1) introduces what is irrelevant by not focusing on the relationship between conclusion and stated premise; (2) sets up a straw argument, by not being of appropriate strength; or (3) begs the question, by merely repeating what is implicit in the argument.

Speaking of . . .

General Statements as Warrants

Sherlock Holmes and "The Case of the Norwood Builder"

The almost universal human habit of reducing things to the simplest possible terms is the weakness on which the unscrupulous writer thrives. Clever persuaders deliberately omit such words as *always, never, only, every, all* . . . because if they appear, they signal the reader to take a second, more critical, look at what is being said. Without them, a statement is more likely to be accepted at its face value. If we keep always in mind the fact that a statement can be positive and sweeping only to the degree to which its implied premises are positive and sweeping, we are well equipped to expose the unjustified dogmatism of writers and speakers.

When we first read the adventures of Sherlock Holmes, we are impressed by the uncanny accuracy of his split-second deductions. But our admiration is somewhat tempered when we realize that much of it is due to the unwarranted positiveness with which the deductions are phrased. In "The Case of the Norwood Builder," for example, Holmes welcomes John Hector McFarlane to his Baker Street rooms with these words: "I assure you that, beyond the obvious facts that you are a bachelor, a solicitor, a Freemason, and an asthmatic, I know nothing whatever about you."

"Familiar as I was with my friend's method," writes Dr. Watson, "it was not difficult for me to follow his deductions, and to observe the untidiness of attire, the sheaf of legal papers, the watch-charm, and the breathing which had prompted them."

The implication is that Holmes reasoned in this fashion:

Men who dress untidily are bachelors.
This man is dressed untidily.
This man is a bachelor.

and so on with the other three deductions. On that basis, we are prone to assume that there could be no question whatsoever that McFarlane was everything Holmes deduced he was. But let us phrase the syllogism more strictly . . . :

All men who dress untidily are bachelors.
This man is dressed untidily.
This man *must* be a bachelor.

Or:

A man who dresses untidily *can only* be a bachelor.
This man is one who dresses untidily.
This man *can only* be a bachelor.

Now we have brought the vital idea of *all* or *only* (which was hidden in the syllogism as previously stated) into the open, and the weakness of the (first) premise is exposed. Obviously it is untrue that *all* men who

continued

continued

dress untidily are bachelors; there must be some untidy men who have loving wives at home. Therefore the conclusion—that this man *must* be a bachelor—is (valid but unsound). Maybe he is a bachelor, but the proof does not lie in the syllogism.

Actually, of course, what Holmes did, though his manner concealed the fact, was to count on the probabilities:

> *Most* men who dress untidily are bachelors.
> This man is dressed untidily.
> This man *probably* is a bachelor.

Thus it appears that even though the odds may have been in favor of McFarlane's being a bachelor, it was quite possible that Holmes could have been mistaken. The degree of probability in the conclusion depended, as always in such reasoning, on the degree expressed in the (generalized) premise.

(Richard D. Altick, *Preface to Critical Reading*)

EXERCISES ON FILLING IN WARRANTS*

1. For each of the following incomplete syllogisms, choose the warrant that will complete it from the alternatives given. Remember, you are selecting the statement that will validate the argument.

   A. Some books are westerns. So some westerns must be novels.
      1. Some books are novels.
      2. All books are novels.
      3. All novels are books.
      4. Some novels are books.
   B. Thomas Jefferson must have been a male because he was a U.S. president.
      1. U.S. presidents typically have been males.
      2. If Jefferson was a U.S. president, he must have been a male.
      3. Males have been U.S. presidents.
      4. U.S. presidents have been males.
      5. 2 and 4 are equally good reconstructions.
   C. Bill wasn't present for the roll call on Tuesday. So, he was marked absent.
      1. Anyone who misses roll call is marked absent.
      2. If Bill wasn't present for the roll call on Tuesday, he was marked absent.
      3. Bill is not always present for roll call.
      4. Whoever missed Tuesday's roll call was marked absent.
      5. 2 and 4 are equally good reconstructions.
   D. I'll probably get sick today because we're having a logic test.
      1. I always get sick on days we have logic tests.
      2. Logic makes me sick.

3. Most students get sick on days there's a logic test.

4. Any time there's a logic test I generally get sick.

E. Any belligerent country is a threat to world peace. Therefore, no member of the United Nations is a belligerent country.

1. U.N. members usually aren't threats to world peace.

2. Some U.N. members aren't threats to world peace.

3. U.N. members are never threats to world peace.

4. If a country is a threat to world peace, it's no member of the U.N.

F. Jones should not be volunteering for hazardous duty, because he's not brave.

1. No one who isn't brave should be volunteering for hazardous duty.

2. If Jones isn't brave, he shouldn't be volunteering for hazardous duty.

3. Anyone volunteering for hazardous duty should be brave.

4. 1 and 3 are equally good reconstructions.

5. 1, 2, and 3 are equally good reconstructions.

G. Whatever invades privacy threatens justice. That's why subjecting job applicants to polygraph tests threatens justice.

1. Subjecting job applicants to polygraph tests invades privacy.

2. Sometimes subjecting job applicants to polygraph tests invades privacy.

3. Privacy can be invaded by subjecting job applicants to polygraph tests.

4. 2 and 3 are equally good reconstructions.

5. None of the preceding is a good reconstruction, because each would make the argument invalid.

2. Provide the warrant that will complete each of the following fragment syllogisms.

A. We should pray regularly so our souls will be pure.

B. U.S. companies need to modernize their management techniques because other nations are out-competing them.

C. Students should study computer science because computer literacy is fundamental to survival today.

D. Drinking liquor harms your liver. Reason enough not to drink liquor.

E. Many politicians obviously are honest, for the majority of them have never been convicted of taking bribes.

F. A nation without a soul cannot live long. That's why a nation without a conscience can't live long.

G. Mrs. Bronson attended the football game; so her husband must have attended, too.

H. Man tends to increase at a greater rate than his means of subsistence; consequently, he is occasionally subject to a severe struggle for existence.

I. We can have no freedom at all in a philosophical sense, for we act not only under external compulsion but also by inner necessity.

J. We have no experience of divine attributes and operations. It follows that we cannot know the divine.

MODULE 8.7

WRITING WITH REASON: SUPPORTING AND EXTENDING GENERAL STATEMENTS

In the essays you write, there will be paragraphs that are intended to support general statements and ones intended to extend them. In the former, you will typically attempt to establish the generalization with specifics in the form of facts, illustrations, statistics, and so on. The following is an example of such a paragraph, with the generalization italicized.

> Many people thought that with the passage of the Endangered Species Act of 1973, the waterways of North America would be made safe for the approximately 1,100 species and subspecies of freshwater fish in North America. *Unfortunately, this has not occurred.* Today one in three species or subspecies of native freshwater fish in North America is or may be threatened by the degradation of lakes, rivers, and streams. Of the approximately 1,000 species and subspecies of freshwater fish in the United States, Canada, and Mexico, 364 fit into one of three categories: "endangered," which means facing extinction in all or in a significant portion of their ranges; "threatened," meaning soon to become endangered; and of "special concern," that is, even minor environmental disturbances could endanger them. Of special concern is that 113 more species fall into the categories than did just ten years ago. What's more, of the many kinds of game fish that are endangered or threatened—including sunfish, perch, catfish, and thirty-four kinds of trout—only three percent of them are threatened by recreational or commercial fishing. The rest are being affected by a mix of urban, agricultural and industrial development; pollution; and the introduction of competitive or predatory fish.

The paragraph opens with what the writer believes is a widespread assumption, which he immediately *discounts* ("unfortunately") with a general statement (italicized) that he then attempts to establish with specifics. One possible schematic of the inductive line of reasoning in the argument is:

(D) Today one in three species or subspecies of native freshwater fish in North America is or may be threatened by degradation of lakes, rivers, and streams.

    (B) Of the approximately 1,000 species and subspecies of freshwater fish in the United States, Canada, and Mexico, 364 fit into one of three categories: "endangered," "threatened," or "special concern." → (C) The Endangered Species Act of 1973 has not ensured the safety of freshwater fish.

(D) 113 more species fall into these
categories than did ten years ago.

(D) Most fish are threatened by urban,
agricultural, and industrial development;
pollution; and the introduction of
competitive or predatory fish.

The following passage is another illustration of a paragraph developed by first making a general statement, then marshalling specifics to support it.

> *All of us should be concerned with the imminent loss of freshwater fish in North America.* First, fish are an important food source. As more and more of us are avoiding beef for health reasons, freshwater fish pose an increasingly valuable source of needed protein. Second, freshwater fishing provides significant recreational activity for millions of people. As urban centers continue to grow, we need all the recreational outlets we can get. Beyond this, the deplorable condition of freshwater fish reflects the tenuous state of an element necessary to all life on earth—water.

The conclusion here could be considered a noninductive generalization. As we saw, specific observable instances do not lead to noninductive generalizations, as they do to inductive generalizations such as the one in our first example ("The Endangered Species Act of 1973 has not ensured the safety of freshwater fish.") Nevertheless, similar kinds of data—facts, illustrations, statistics, and so on—are as much needed to support noninductive generalizations as inductive ones. In this paragraph, the writer has assembled three key facts in support of the generalization. The argument, then, could be represented as follows:

(D) Fish is an important food source.
    (B) It's a valuable source
        of protein, as we   →   **(C)** All of us should be
        consume less beef.   concerned with the
(D) Freshwater fishing provides   imminent loss of
    a popular recreational   freshwater fish in
    activity.   North America.
(D) The growth of urban
    centers calls for the
    preservation of recreational
    outlets.
(D) The deplorable condition
    of freshwater fish reflects
    the deplorable state of
    our water.

In a paragraph that *extends* a general statement, the main idea will usually be one that would be the conclusion of a syllogism if a syllogism were actually constructed. The following is an example, with general statement italicized and the main idea or conclusion in bold print:

A static concept is one that doesn't change with time. The concept expressed in the Eighth Amendment is that "cruel and unusual" punishment is unconstitutional. But the Court has been ambivalent about whether capital punishment always qualifies as "cruel and unusual" punishment. For example, in *Furman v. Georgia* (1972), four justices would have held that capital punishment is not constitutional. Two justices would have reached the opposite conclusion. And three justices, while agreeing that the statutes then before the Court were suspect as applied, left open the question whether such punishment may ever be imposed. At present, the Court holds that the punishment of death does not invariably violate the Constitution. **It is clear from the foregoing precedent that the Eighth Amendment has not been regarded as a static concept.**

In this paragraph, the writer applies a general statement about the meaning of a static concept to the Eighth Amendment in order to establish that the Eighth Amendment is not a static concept. The argument could be cast as follows:

(D) A static concept is one that doesn't change with time.

(D) The concept of "cruel and unusual" expressed in the Eighth Amendment has changed.   →   **(C)** The Eighth Amendment is not a static concept.

(B) *Furman* v. *Georgia.*

If we ignore the backing (B), we can readily see the syllogism that comprises the paragraph. Thus:

> **All static concepts are ones that don't change with time.**
> **The concept of "cruel and unusual" punishment expressed in the Eighth Amendment has changed with time.**
> ___
> **Therefore, the concept expressed in the Eighth Amendment is not a static concept. (Valid)**

> or, alternatively, as a *conditional*

> **If a concept is static, it does not change with time.**
> **The concept of "cruel and unusual" punishment expressed in the Eighth Amendment has changed with time.**
> ___
> **Therefore, the concept expressed in the Eighth Amendment is not a static concept. (Valid—*Denying the Consequent*)**

In this argument, the general statement applied was expressed. But as we have learned, when the general statement is not expressed, but implied, it functions as a warrant that needs to be reconstructed in order to make explicit the logical movement from the data to the conclusion. The following is an example of such an argument, with conclusion in bold print:

Death is an unusually severe punishment. It's unusual in its pain, in its finality, and in its enormity. Furthermore, death serves no penal purpose more effectively than a less severe punishment. **Therefore, capital punishment violates the Eighth and Fourteenth Amendments.**

The conclusion of this argument addresses the Eighth and Fourteenth Amendments, neither of which is mentioned in the premises. So, something is missing, a warrant that will provide indubitable support for the conclusion. The warrant could be stated as a universal to the effect, "The Eighth and Fourteenth Amendments prohibit excessive punishment when less severe punishment can adequately achieve the same purpose." This, or some equivalent statement, is the general statement that the argument is applying to a specific instance, the death penalty, to reach the conclusion that the death penalty violates the Eighth and Fourteenth Amendments. The argument can be represented as follows:

(D) Death is an unusually severe punishment.
(B) It's unusual in its pain,
    finality and enormity.   →   **(C)** Capital punishment
                                     violates the Eighth
                                     and Fourteenth
                                     Amendments.
(W) (The Eighth and Fourteenth Amendments prohibit
    excessive punishment when less severe punishment can
    adequately achieve the same purposes.)

Notice that the original argument can be viewed as a fragment syllogism which we can complete, making minor language changes to accommodate the syllogistic forms we have learned.

All cases of excessive punishment when less severe punishment can adequately achieve the same purposes are violations of the Eighth and Fourteenth Amendments.
Death (capital punishment) is a case of an excessive punishment.
_____
Therefore, death (capital punishment) is a violation of the Eighth and Fourteenth Amendments. (Valid)

or alternatively, as a *conditional:*

If a punishment is excessive compared to a less severe punishment that can adequately achieve the same purposes, then it violates the Eighth and Fourteenth Amendments.
Death (capital punishment) is a punishment that's excessive compared to a less severe punishment that can adequately achieve the same purposes.
_____
Therefore, death (capital punishment) violates the Eighth and Fourteenth Amendments. (Valid—*Affirming the Antecedent*)

Notice that, in both of these general statement-extension passages, the relationship of the sentences is different from the relationship of the sentences in the general statement-development examples. In the latter, the writers probably selected details in the number and appropriateness they chose and ordered them in an arbitrary way, since the details were strictly related to the conclusion and not to each other. Thus, in the example dealing with freshwater fish, the data could have been presented other than they were. Some of the details could have been deleted and other relevant facts substituted to establish the probability of the conclusion. The data, then, amount to a *series of independent reasons* that are offered to establish the likelihood of the conclusion. They are connected not to each other but by their common interest in establishing the main idea or conclusion.

In contrast, where the general statements were extended — the key statements were closely related to, or grew out of, previous statements, not just the main idea. This tight, step-by-step progression of logic is always necessary in deductive development, although not every step need be expressed. A kind of dove-tailing occurs between the statements, as illustrated by the syllogisms that we set up for the last two arguments considered. The data, or premises, of such arguments are *interdependent* (as opposed to independent). Taken together they form a *chain of reasons* (as opposed to a series), each link of which is vital to every other link.

Although one of these two processes — developing or extending — usually will predominate in an essay, quite often both will appear. For example, the core of the following argument is a syllogism (in bold print) in which one of the premises (first bold assertion) is an inductive generalization.

In setting up a plant, a comany intends simply to manufacture and distribute its product. But *the operation of the plant results in unintended side effects,* what economists term "externalities." These are pertinent to the issue of plant relocation.

When a person agrees to work for a company, her pay is a return for effort expended to produce the product. But these wages don't account for the many relationships she builds up as a result of accepting the job. Not only does the work provide labor for the company, she adopts a lifestyle that contributes to the job. She may move her place of residence, enroll children in schools, join churches and clubs, get involved in civic affairs — in a word, she makes a total commitment of her life and her family's to the community and the company. She builds a whole network of relationships as a direct result of her association with the company.

The company's presence also affects the local community. City engineers adjust traffic patterns to accommodate traffic generated by the flow of employees and freight associated with the plant. The municipality may have to plan, build, and maintain water, sewerage, and other facilities on a much larger scale to accommodate the company's needs. Police and fire departments may need to be beefed up because of the plant.

Clearly, then, the presence of a plant in a community creates all sorts of unintended side effects. And **when a plant shuts down, significant potential injury can occur** when a company doesn't take into account the impact of its move on workers and community. A basic ethical principle of fairness and justice is that **we must attempt to repair the injury that we cause. It's a company's moral obligation, therefore, to mitigate significantly the injury it causes in closing down a plant.**

If asked to identify the thesis of this essay, some readers might erroneously point to the italicized sentence of the first paragraph: "The operation of a plant results in unintended side effects." This misinterpretation of the thesis probably stems from the fact that the author takes special pains to develop this inductive generalization. Indeed, if it were not for the final paragraph, this statement *would* be the passage's thesis—an inductive generalization that the author attempts to establish by means of the observed specifics cited in paragraphs 2 and 3.

In fact, the italicized statement is functioning as a premise of a syllogism which establishes the thesis that a company must help ease the injury caused by closing its plant. Focusing on the sentences in bold print in the last paragraph, we can construct the following syllogism:

> **We always have a moral obligation to attempt to repair the damage that we cause.**
>
> **In closing a plant, a company causes damage. (A restatement of the italicized sentence.)**
> _____
> **Therefore, a company has a moral obligation to attempt to repair (that is, to mitigate significantly) the damage it causes in closing down a plant.**

Once we make the syllogism explicit, we can see that the essay is an extension of a noninductive generalization—a moral principle, in this case—to a specific case, plant closing. At its core, the argument is deductive—two premises are offered as interdependent reasons for the conclusion. The inductive aspect of the essay is composed of paragraphs 2 and 3, which are offered as support for the inductive generalization that closing a plant causes injury, the second premise of the syllogism.

IMPROVING PERFORMANCE

SUMMARY-TEST QUESTIONS FOR CHAPTER 8*

1. A general statement refers to more than one member of a class or population of things, but not necessarily to all members of the class. True or False?
2. Which of the following general statements is different in type from the others?
   A. Many students enjoy school.
   B. Summer days are hot.
   C. Seventy percent of the electorate oppose higher taxes.
   D. Humans are created equal.
   E. Kids like to compete.
3. A _____ statement can be falsified by a single exception.
   A. general
   B. universal
   C. nonuniversal
   D. true
   E. false

4. An argument that is offered in support of a general statement is called a/an _____ .

5. From premises that assert that three particular pieces of blue litmus paper turned red when dipped in acid, it is concluded that all blue litmus paper will turn red when dipped in acid. This argument can most accurately be termed
   A. a generalization.
   B. a noninductive generalization.
   C. a valid deduction.
   D. an inductive generalization.
   E. a syllogism.

6. What kind of general statement is the conclusion of the preceding argument?

7. The argument expressed in question 5 is an example of an induction by simple enumeration. True or False?

8. The more representative a sample of the entire population, the stronger the inductive generalization that is based on that sample. True or False?

"Logic Jeopardy": Formulate a precise question for each of the following answers (9–13):

9. A generalization that appears to be based on observed specifics, but is not.

10. An argument that contains conclusive support for a conclusion.

11. Can I logically accept that premises of the syllogism and deny its conclusion without contradicting myself?

12. An incorrect procedure in deductive reasoning.

13. A deductive argument consisting of two premises and a conclusion.

14. Why is a qualified general statement more easily confirmed by observation of specifics than an unqualified general statement?

15. Which of the following statements has a noninductive basis?
   A. A good citizen always votes.
   B. Voter participation in presidential elections has declined over the past thirty years.
   C. Slightly more than half of the eligible voters voted in the last election.
   D. People who express a party preference are more likely to vote than people who don't.
   E. Voters under twenty-five-years-old tend to vote the same as their parents.

16. Give an example of a generalization.

17. Noninductive generalizations cannot be justified. True or False?

18. A _____ argument is one whose premises provide _____ support for its conclusion, whereas an _____ argument is one whose premises offer _____ support but not _____ support for its conclusion.

19. Name three key sources of noninductive generalizations.

20. In deduction, we typically _____ generalizations.
   A. formulate
   B. confirm
   C. validate
   D. avoid
   E. apply

True or False (21–26)

21. Generalizations influence our decisions.
22. Generalizations can play a part in prejudice.
23. Often, the generalization we apply deductively is one that we have formed inductively or noninductively.
24. Most of the generalizations we hold we have formed on the basis of our own observations.
25. Only generalizations based on observed specifics are worth believing.
26. Knowing a little about generalizations helps one understand why inductive and deductive reasoning are incompatible.
27. Which of the following, if any, is *not* true of syllogisms?
    A. two premises
    B. a valid conclusion
    C. a deduction
    D. an argument
    E. Each can be correctly associated with all syllogisms.

Questions 28–34 pertain to the following diagram:

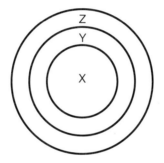

True or False?

28. Every X is a Z.
29. All Z are Y.
30. All X are Y.
31. Any Y is a Z.
32. X is both Y and Z.
33. All Y are Z, but no Y is an X.
34. Which of the following arguments does the diagram represent?
    A. **All Z are Y.**
       All X are Y.
       _____
       Therefore, all X are Z.
    B. **All Y are Z.**
       All Y are X.
       _____
       Therefore, all X are Z.

C. All Z are Y.
All Y are X.

Therefore, all X are Z.

D. All Y are Z.
All X are Y.

Therefore, all X are Z.

35. Validity means all of the following *except*

A. accepting the premises while at the same time denying the conclusion would be self-contradictory.

B. the conclusion of the induction necessarily follows from the premises.

C. the premises cannot be true and the conclusion false.

D. the argument is deductively certain.

36. It is impossible to determine the validity of an argument unless you know for sure that the premises are true. True or False?

37. ROB : Jane's definitely a mother.

PEG : Why's that?

ROB : Because she's a member of Mothers Against Drunk Drivers and all members of M.A.D.D. are mothers.

PEG : Do you know for sure that all members of M.A.D.D. are mothers?

ROB : Well, no not for sure. But if they are —

PEG : Until you verify that all members are mothers, you have no grounds for saying that Jane's a mother. It's that simple.

Explain why the underlying dispute involves the difference between the validity and the acceptability of the argument in question.

38. Are the following syllogisms valid or invalid?

A. **All 3-sided figures are squares.**
All polygons are 3-sided figures.

Therefore, all polygons are squares.

B. **Any student in the class is a business major.**
Every business major is enrolled in Management 101.

Every student in the class is enrolled in Management 101.

C. **Only ticket holders will be admitted.**
Bart is a ticket holder.

Bart will be admitted.

D. **No Supreme Court justice is an elected official.**
Some Supreme Court justices aren't Republicans.

Some Republicans aren't elected officials.

E. **Some U.S. presidents have been Democrats.**
Some women aren't Democrats.

Some women haven't been U.S. presidents.

39. In filling in a missing premise, the basic idea is to:

A. complete the fragment argument.

B. create a valid syllogism.

    C. isolate the error in the argument.

    D. A and B.

    E. A, B, and C.

40. A good reconstruction always avoids:

    A. disconnectedness.

    B. repetition.

    C. overstatement and understatement.

    D. A and B.

    E. A, B, and C.

Select the premise that *best* completes the argument. Explain why the others are not as good. (41–43)

41. Marcia and Brad seldom eat the same thing. Marcia puts ketchup on everything she eats.

    A. If Marcia puts ketchup on everything she eats, Marcia and Brad seldom eat the same thing.

    B. Brad never eats anything with ketchup on it.

    C. Brad realizes that ketchup is not good for him.

    D. Brad usually avoids anything with ketchup on it.

    E. Marcia and Brad frequently dine together.

42. Debbie is trim and muscular. She must be an athlete.

    A. All athletes are trim and muscular.

    B. If Debbie is trim and muscular, she must be an athlete.

    C. Debbie's probably anorexic.

    D. All trim and muscular individuals are athletes.

    E. A or D.

43. Adamson cannot have a license, for his name is not listed in the directory.

    A. If Adamson is not in the directory, he cannot have a license.

    B. Only people with licenses are in the directory.

    C. Only people in the directory have licenses.

    D. Either Adamson is in the directory or he is not.

    E. Adamson is not interested in having a license or being in the directory.

Complete each of the following arguments (44–48) by filling in its missing premise (that is, warrant).

44. Jack must not have gone to work today. He took his briefcase.

45. The defendant has produced an alibi. So, he may not be guilty.

46. You have not paid the late fee, which is why you will probably be detained.

47. The aggressive will not inherit the earth, for only the meek will.

48. Clearly, Kate's dismissal was unjustified since she was not disloyal.

Indicate whether the following syllogisms are valid or invalid. Explain (49–53).

49. The first candidate cannot be qualified because, if she were she would have passed the test, and she did not.

50. It is raining. Games are played unless it rains. Therefore, the game will not be played.

51. If Jones is the president or the vice president, then we should consult him. We should not consult him. Therefore, Jones cannot be the president or the vice president.
52. Whenever the phone rings, the dog barks. The phone must not be ringing, because the dog is not barking.
53. There is smoke where there is fire. Inasmuch as there is smoke, there must be a fire.

CRITICAL THINKING APPLICATIONS*

1. In the seventeenth century, virtually everyone, even the most learned, believed in witches. In Germany alone, a hundred thousand people believed to be witches were burned at the stake. In America, learned and common people also took witchcraft as a matter of fact. **Consult a good encyclopedia in order to find out what kind of evidence was used to convince and hang nineteen witches in Salem, Massachusetts, in 1692.**
2. **Report to the class any experience you have had in a school laboratory in which you used observation of specifics to derive a generalization that presumably holds for all future specifics of the same kind.**
3. Suppose that someone reads in a newspaper the account of a woman who is brutally raped and beaten. As he reads the gory details, he greatly sympathizes with the victim and thinks about how horrible this experience must have been for the woman and how it may haunt her the rest of her life. Then, at the end of the article he learns that the woman was a prostitute, and says to himself, "Oh, well, that doesn't matter much." **Discuss in terms of generalizations the logic that this person has unconsciously used.**
4. If you contribute to an organization that helps mend injured animals, you can write-off the contribution on your income tax form; but if you privately help heal an injured animal, you cannot deduct your expenses. Examine and discuss the logic of this paradoxical policy. **Specifically, what kinds of generalizations underlie this distinction?**

POINT/COUNTERPOINT: ESSAYS FOR ANALYSIS

Issue: *Teenage pregnancies*

Resolved: There should be parental notice laws.

Background: On June 25, 1990, the United States Supreme Court, sharply divided again on an issue that it had confronted seven times in the previous fourteen years, ruled five to four in Hodgson v. Minnesota *that a state may require a minor to notify both parents before obtaining an abortion—provided it gives her the option of seeking permission from a judge instead.*

At issue was a Minnesota law requiring notification of both parents—although not their permission—before an abortion, even if the parents are divorced or if one has long since been estranged from the pregnant girl. Anticipating court challenges, drafters of the Minnesota law inserted a provision permitting a so-called judicial bypass of its parental notification rule. During the five years, 1981–86, that the Minnesota law was in force 3,573 girls in the state sought judicial approval to have an abortion without telling their parents. Only nine were refused. Of these, six withdrew their petitions before the judge decided. At the same time, many teenagers were delayed or prevented from having abortions because of having to meet the law's requirements. (The Allan Guttmacher Institute estimates that approximately 1.5 million legal abortions are performed annually in the United States, about 183,000 or 12 percent on minors under 18.)

On the same day as the Minnesota decision, in a separate six to three decision (Ohio v. Akron Center for Reproductive Health), *the Court upheld an Ohio law that requires notification of one parent or a court procedure. In effect, the Court said a two-parent law must allow for a court procedure to bypass parents. They did not decide whether a one-parent notice law must allow a court bypass. They simply upheld Ohio's law, which does provide for a court procedure. Despite the limited scope of the Minnesota decision, both sides in the highly political debate claimed victory and rallied their faithful for the inevitable next court battle.*

From: **Safeguarding the Welfare of Young Women**[7]*

Louise Cox

Louise Cox, M.S.W., with a specialization in mental health, happens to be pro-choice but also supports parental notice laws. **Read and outline her essay, then answer the questions that follow it.**

1 Probably no event causes more anxiety and stress for an unwed young woman than an unintentional pregnancy. She faces two choices: bear the child or kill it through an abortion. In the first instance, the thought of having to care for the child — to be completely responsible for it, perhaps to mortgage her future for it — can be paralyzing. But the thought of murder can and should strike her as abominable.

2 To expect such a troubled young woman to make a prudent decision is, to say the least, naïve. Indeed, it's a cruel hoax because it invites her to pretend to be something she's not: mature and dispassionate enough to decide on her own to have the baby or an abortion. What she really needs is the advice of those whose love is unqualified, whose support is total, and whose sole concern is her welfare. Her parents and family.

3 Those who work with teens — teachers, counselors, health professionals — typically encourage them to seek out parental advice on all manner of decisions, from buying a car to choosing a college to taking a job. Moreover, today's parents are rightly urged to take a more active role in their children's lives. TV ads needle us with the question: "It's eleven P.M. — do you know where your child is?" Bumper stickers challenge us: "Have you hugged your child today?" Political leaders, sociologists, clergy persons, all remind us of the critical importance of wholesome stable families. The

---

[7]Printed by permission of Louise Cox, all rights reserved.

message is clear: Young people desperately need and deserve the steadying influence of a loving parent in order to negotiate our troubled times. This is precisely why parents are urged to "get involved" in the lives of their children. And yet, when it comes to an unintentional pregnancy, many would send out a counter message: "Don't tell your parents; secretly suffer an abortion and get on with your life." And this often comes from those who insist that schools keep them informed of the academic progress of their children. Isn't a child's decision about an unintentional pregnancy at least as important as the quality of her school work? Can we sensibly urge parents to monitor their children's academics while at the same time forbid schools to notify parents of deficiencies and truancies? Of course not. But this is the very mixed message society transmits when it strikes down parental notice laws. It is in effect exhorting parental involvement while at the same time denying parents access to the information they need to get involved. And just as bad, it's engraving an invitation to young women to shut out their parents precisely when such troubled teens need them most.

4 To be sure, some would claim that the pregnant young woman can make the decision on her own. Perhaps so. But what kind of decision? Is it a truly informed and free decision? Can it be when she's thoroughly confused and frightened? Basic to all informed choice is calm, well-measured reflection. This isn't possible for a young woman carrying an unintended baby.

5 Others point to abortion clinic staff as adequate counselors. This is like saying the salesperson offers the best advice about what car to buy.

6 The indisputable fact is that the young woman is best served when her parents assist her in making the decision. To their credit, some states, such as Minnesota and Indiana, have publicly recognized this fact by enacting laws requiring parental notice prior to the young person's having an abortion. In fact, in 1990 the U.S. Supreme Court in *Hodgson* ruled that such a requirement is constitutional so long as it provides for a "judicial bypass" alternative. Justice Kennedy well expressed the signal importance of the family in a young woman's hour of need when he wrote:

> A free and enlightened society may decide that each of its members should attain a clearer, more tolerant understanding of the profound philosophic choices confronted by a woman who is considering whether to seek an abortion. Her decision will embrace her own destiny and personal dignity, and the origins of the other human life that lie within the embryo. The State is entitled to assume that, for most of its people, the beginnings of that understanding will be within the family, society's most intimate association.

In so ruling, the Court has implicity acknowledged the good, common-sense reasons for parental notice laws cited by Attorney Maura K. Quinlan (see Maura K. Quinlan, *Parental Notice Requirement in Teenage Sexuality.* St. Paul, MN: Greenhaven Press, 1988.)

7 First, parents almost always have the best interests of their children at heart. Unfortunately there are some exceptions, even some rare cases

when a disclosure of a pregnancy might be greeted with violence. But the judicial bypass alternative is available in these instances. And these anomalies shouldn't be permitted to overshadow the fact that the purity of the parental motive, the depth of parental knowledge about the child, and the ongoing parental commitment to the child whatever the decision, make parents not only the girl's best but requisite counselor at this time.

8 Second, contrary to the contentions of opponents, it is the absence, not the presence, of parental notice laws that strain intrafamily relations. This is because, no matter how hard a child tries to conceal an abortion from them, parents find out about it sooner or later. Take, for example, the case of the young teen who developed postabortion complications. Because she lived in a state that didn't have a parental notice law, her parents were not informed prior to the abortion. But their permission to perform the urgent surgery was required before surgeons could operate. When parents find out like this, they feel hurt, left out, diminished, and even betrayed. At the very least they're left wondering why in her time of greatest need — literally in a matter of life and death — their daughter didn't seek their advice. (I'll leave unembellished the curiosity of requiring parental permission to perform the needed surgery on this young adolescent but not requiring that her parents be notified before her abortion.) In contrast, being included in the decision makes parents feel an important part of their children's lives.

9 Third, requiring parental notification has the effect of framing "the problem" as not just the child's but the entire family's. In these matters the social, emotional, and moral considerations are every bit as important as the biological. Increasingly, families appear to be abdicating their responsibilities for the conduct of their children, thereby overburdening social services. Society simply can't afford to function at every turn as parental surrogates. Parental notification laws compel parents in a nonpunitive way to confront their own complicity in the troubles of their children.

10 Fourth, these laws appear to reduce the number of unintentional pregnancies. For example, parental notification laws went into effect in Minnesota in 1981. Between 1981 and 1985, abortions and births for Minnesota teens under eighteen declined by about thirty percent, and the pregnancy rate dropped by about twenty percent. Sheer coincidence? Hardly. All of us think twice before doing something whose consequences we know we will be held accountable for. When a young woman knows that her parents will find out about a pregnancy, it's fair to assume that she will act more cautiously than if she believed they wouldn't find out. This means more responsible sexual behavior and fewer unintentional pregnancies.

11 Finally, parental notification laws indirectly blunt what has always been a spur to adolescent sexual activity: peer pressure. In the past, young women might have defeated sexual advances by expressing fear of pregnancy. *Roe v. Wade* shattered that defense. Absent parental notification laws, she can't invoke the time-honored excuse of parental discovery. Isn't it about time

that we rescued the youngster who might lack the maturity and self-esteem to simply say no?

12 There will be cases where parental notification laws will backfire. Undoubtedly there will be some cases of teens who, so fearful of parental discovery, they will seek out back-alley abortions with perhaps dreadful outcome. But these will be far and few between. No law benefits everyone all the time. The issue here is whether parental notification laws benefit the overwhelming majority of young women. Of that there's no doubt.

1. Is the first sentence of paragraph 1 a qualified or unqualifed generalization?
2. Is the author formulating or extending the generalization?
3. Explain how the author begs the question in expressing the two options facing a young, unintentionally pregnant woman (paragraph 1).
4. Which of the following general statements best captures the innuendo of paragraph 2?
   A. Teenagers can't make decisions for themselves.
   B. If left to decide for themselves, teenagers will usually have an abortion.
   C. A girl who becomes unintentionally pregnant is in no position to decide for herself whether to have the baby or abort it.
   D. Unless carefully monitored, teenage girls stand a good chance of getting pregnant.
5. Which of the following conditional statements most closely reflects the reasoning in paragraph 3?
   A. If those who deal with young people typically advise them to seek parental advice, they should also encourage the pregnant teen to seek her parent's advice.
   B. If young people require the steady influence of their parents, they should be encouraged to seek parental counsel in the matter of unintentional pregnancy.
   C. If parents should be informed of their children's academic progress, they surely should be informed about their children's planned abortions.
   D. If children are typically encouraged to seek parental counsel, it makes no sense to discourage them from so doing in the grave matter of a planned abortion.
6. Which of the following general statements would you say is the key unexpressed assumption that underlies paragraph 3?
   A. Parents do not usually get involved in their children's lives.
   B. Most young people urgently need parental guidance.
   C. Most parents will support their children who are in trouble.
   D. A young woman does not usually want to inform her parents of her pregnancy.
   E. One cannot consistently argue for effective parent/child communication and oppose parental notice laws.
7. Cindy believes that, by misrepresenting the issue in paragraph 3, the author ends up attacking a straw argument. She explains, "The question is whether by law a parent must be notified of a child's planned abortion. It isn't whether notifying a parent is a good idea or whether kids could benefit from it—they probably could. I know my mom and dad would help me a lot if I got pregnant, and I'd want their input. But that doesn't mean I should be required by law to notify them." What do you think of Cindy's criticism?

8. Cindy's friend Joanne agrees and adds, "I don't think that not requiring parental notice is the same as saying "Don't tell your parents," as the author implies. Just because the law doesn't require me, say, to pick up someone who's tripped and fallen in the street, that doesn't mean society is saying, "Don't help." Personally, I think helping someone when you can is a good idea and I do it. But I don't think the law should make me." Do you agree with Cindy or the author? Explain.

9. In paragraph 4, do you think that the rhetorical question — "Is it a truly informed and free decision?" — is used legitimately?

10. Express in the form of a categorical syllogism the core argument expressed in paragraph 4.

11. Do you think the preceding syllogism is valid or invalid? Is the argument acceptable or unacceptable? Explain.

12. What is the author saying by innuendo about abortion clinic personnel (paragraph 5)?

13. Paragraph 5 is an example of
   A. abusive *ad hominem.*
   B. begging the question.
   C. well poisoning.
   D. circumstantial *ad hominem.*
   E. None of the preceding.

14. Is the first sentence of paragraph 6 an inductive or noninductive generalization, or neither?

15. What is the logical function of the Kennedy quotation in paragraph 6?

16. Does the author attempt to refute any of the objections to parental notice laws?

17. In paragraph 7, the author states that judicial bypass is a satisfactory alternative for young women for whom parental notice is not feasible. What problems, if any, might judicial bypass raise?

18. Cast paragraph 8 in terms of D (data), B (back-up), and C (conclusion).

19. Do you think the example cited in paragraph 8 is being used to make a point or merely to clarify? If the former, what is the point? Do you think the example establishes the point?

20. Roberto thinks he detects a false dilemma in paragraph 8: "The author views parental notice laws in black-and-white terms. We either have parental notice laws and strengthen family relations or we don't have them and weaken family relations. But it seems to me that sometimes requiring parents to be notified could actually hurt a family. I know a girl who told her parents she was pregnant and they went nuts. They finally chilled out and she got an abortion. But things have never been the same between her and her parents. Then there's the case of Becky Bell in Indiana. Becky was so scared to have her parents notified that she was planning an abortion that she had one of those back-alley abortions. It was botched and a week later she died. Her family was shattered. Her mother says she no longer supports parental notice laws, and in fact is waging a kind of personal crusade against them. On the other hand, I can see where letting your parents know could actually help family relations, like the author says. To me it all depends on the particular situation. It's not as black-and-white as the author seems to

think." Do you agree with Roberto that the author has set up a false dilemma?

21. With which of the following general statements would the author probably agree?
    A. Parents are partly to blame for the unintentional pregnancies of their daughters.
    B. Not requiring parental notice is tantamount to exonerating parents of any responsibility for the unintentional pregnancies of their daughters.
    C. Parental notice laws would help ease the burden on social services.
    D. A and B.
    E. A, B, and C.

22. Paragraph 10 illustrates both the formulation and application of generalizations. Explain how.

23. Which of the following facts, if true, would weaken the argument expressed in paragraph 10?
    A. During the years cited, Minnesota public schools instituted a sex education program.
    B. Between 1984 and 1988, with parental notice laws still in effect, the number and rate of pregnancies increased.
    C. The number and rate of pregnancies declined during the years cited in states that did not have parental notice laws.
    D. A and B.
    E. A, B, and C.

24. Is paragraph 11 in any way inconsistent with what the author stated earlier in the essay?

From: Shattering the Dreams of Young Women: The Tragic Consequences of Parental Involvement Laws[8]

American Civil Liberties Union

> *The Reproductive Freedom Project of the American Civil Liberties Union Foundation keys on what are perceived to be violations of reproductive civil liberties. The excerpt that follows is from the Project's most recent position paper on parental notice laws.*

Read and outline the selection carefully, then answer the accompanying questions.

1 The tragic consequences of all parental involvement laws are too serious for public policymakers to ignore. Regardless of the Supreme Court's rulings, these laws are dangerous to the lives and health of young women.

2 More than half of the young women seeking abortion voluntarily tell at least one parent about their decision. The younger the teen, the more likely her parents are to know about, and to have even suggested, the abortion. Nonetheless, a significant minority — about 25 percent of teenagers — will

---

[8]From *Shattering the Dreams of Young Women: The Tragic Consequences of Parental Involvement Laws,* 1991, ACLU Reproductive Freedom Project. Reprinted by permission.

not tell their parents nor go to a clinic if parental notification is required. Often coming from severely dysfunctional or single-parent families, most of these teenagers hope to avoid the family crisis that the news of their abortion will cause.

3 It is standard medical practice to explain the abortion procedure and its medical risks to every patient. Physicians have a legal responsibility, independent of parental involvement laws, to ensure that each patient has given voluntary and informed consent to medical procedures. Even in the absence of parental involvement laws, nearly all clinics encourage young women to discuss their abortion choice with a parent. In an emergency, medical ethics require parental notification.

4 Studies show that teenagers, like adults, can understand and reason about health care alternatives and make abortion decisions consistent with their own sense of what is right for them. Studies also note that adolescents are self-observant and able to provide their health histories as accurately as their parents. Certainly if a minor were too immature to decide to have an abortion, she should also not be mature enough to fulfill her duties as a parent. In fact, studies conclude that young women who choose abortion are more able to realize family goals and avoid later unwanted pregnancies than those teenagers who carry their pregnancies to term. Recognizing that minors are fully capable of providing informed consent, all 50 states authorize minors to consent either to treatment for sexually transmitted diseases or to general medical care. Twenty-seven states authorize minors to consent to the treatment of pregnancy—including Caesarian section surgery—without parental involvement, and to consent to medical care for their children. Abortion is the only reproductive health decision singled out for special treatment.

5 Clinic and court personnel who have experience working with teenagers and their families universally agree that young women show an impressive degree of sensitivity and maturity in deciding whether to involve their parents. Both the state court judges assigned to court bypass hearings in Minnesota and the state's witnesses in the *Hodgson* case testified that teenagers accurately assess their family circumstances. Young women in Minnesota gave many reasons for their decision not to notify one or both parents: their parents' psychiatric or physical illness, drug or alcohol abuse; religious or moral views; likelihood of physical or sexual abuse. Several had no previous contact with the parent.

6 Most parents love their children, but conversations about sexuality and reproduction between loving parents and their adolescent children are often extremely uncomfortable for both sides. Not surprisingly, these kinds of discussions are entirely absent from many parent-child relationships. Although family experts believe that families generally benefit from voluntary and open communication, the same experts agree that compelled communication can destroy any existing good will among family members, particularly when parents are unable or unwilling to react supportively to the news of a daughter's abortion.

7 Half of all recent marriages will end in divorce. Close to 60 percent of children born during the 1980s will live in a single-parent family before they reach the age of 18. Many noncustodial parents maintain little, if any, communication with their children. Pregnant adolescents are often perplexed as to why their noncustodial parents should become an important factor in their lives when they previously have offered little or no financial or emotional support. Woman battering has come to be recognized as the most frequently committed violent crime in the nation. Some estimate that at least one in four women will be battered by a spouse or partner during her lifetime, and that at least 55 percent of children in these families also will be battered. In addition, experts estimate that one in five female children are sexually victimized during childhood; many of these young women will become pregnant. Forcing a young woman to notify her abusive parent of a pregnancy can have dangerous or even fatal consequences. Long-term studies of abusive families reveal that the incidence of violence escalates during pregnancy and during adolescence. Dr. Lenore Walker, an eminent expert on the psychological effect of battering, has testified that telling a batterer that his daughter is pregnant is "much like showing a red cape to a bull."

8 There are no abortion providers in 83 percent of all U.S. counties. In most states, providers are located only in major metropolitan areas, and few public and private hospitals will perform the procedure. This scarcity of providers forces rural women to travel hundreds of miles for services. Because only twelve states provide Medicaid funding for medically-necessary abortions, many women who are too poor to obtain care are forced to carry their pregnancies to term. Even for women with slightly higher incomes, the increasing costs of later abortions may prevent them from getting one. Those women who do find a provider and can afford the cost also face obstacles — frequent harassment by anti-abortion activists who blockade clinic entrances. Because young women with irregular menstrual cycles take longer to recognize the signs of pregnancy, and because they have difficulty raising the money for an abortion, they often delay longer than older women when seeking an abortion. As a consequence, teenagers disproportionately need second trimester abortions, which are more complicated and costly to perform. Even after acquiring the money and locating a provider, teenagers have difficulty explaining their absence from school, as well as arranging transportation to the clinic and housing nearby.

9 Although abortion is one of the safest surgical procedures that doctors perform, and significantly safer than childbirth, the later an abortion is performed, the more complicated and costly it is. Nevertheless, where parental involvement laws are in effect, court bypass procedures can routinely delay the abortion procedure from one to three weeks. A panel of the National Research Council, which has specifically recommended against mandatory parental involvement, based their recommendation in

part on the "growing evidence that parental consent statutes cause teenagers to delay their abortions."

10 Public defenders, guardians *ad litem,* and judges all agree that going to court is a frightening experience for young women. Teenagers, most of whom have never been to court before, approach the hearing with apprehension and anxiety—feeling embarrassed, ashamed, or that they have done something wrong. The court bypass process deprives teenagers of the orderly and reassuring experience essential to the provision of quality medical care. The young woman spends her morning under interrogation by strangers in the intimidating and usually chaotic courthouse. She often returns to the clinic tense, angry, or physically ill—in the worst possible condition to undergo surgery. Courts and court houses are public places. Young women who go to court can face as many as 20 or more strangers who know they need an abortion. Many teenagers do not seek hearings in their home counties because they are afraid of being recognized. Instead, they endure added expense, further delay, and the burdens of traveling to a distant city—all to preserve some semblance of confidentiality.

11 Although many laws do not require that "emancipated minors" notify their parents, they do not always define which young women are considered "emancipated." Clinics, which are subject to criminal penalties for violating the law, often require women to obtain a court order rather than risk a misinterpretation of the law. Similarly, the physical or sexual abuse exceptions listed in many state laws do not protect young victims, who often are reluctant to reveal that the abuse exists. Even those young women who want to seek help will stop when they learn that other state laws pertaining to abuse require government authorities to be notified, creating a substantial risk that their confidentiality will be destroyed. Since no consensus among judges on the appropriate criteria has been reached, the determination of whether a teenager is "mature" or whether the abortion is in her "best interest" rests solely on the individual state court judge—not the young woman's actual developmental status or family circumstances. One judge may examine whether the minor has considered all the available options, another may question whether she can understand her situation. When determining a young woman's "best interests," some judges ask whether it would be in her best interest to have an abortion, others ask whether it would be in her best interest to notify her parents. Recently in Ohio, one judge applied Catch-22 reasoning when he denied a young woman's request for an abortion by finding that she was not mature. "If she was mature," he reasoned, "she would have notified her parents."

12 Parental involvement laws cause some minors who would otherwise terminate unwanted pregnancies to carry to term. In Minneapolis, where complete data is available, the statistics are startling: the birthrate for 15–17-year-olds increased 38 percent compared to only a .3 percent rise for 18–19-year-olds who were not covered by the parental notification law.

Prior to the law's enactment, there was no significant difference between the two age groups.

13 Motherhood is often debilitating educationally, economically, and physically to the teenage mother and her children. National studies show that mothers who give birth in their twenties are twice as likely to have graduated from high school, and four times more likely to finish college, than those who become mothers in their teens. With small children to care for, little education, fewer job skills, and no committed partners, teenage mothers are seven times more likely than other mothers to be poor. The younger the mother at childbirth, the lower her family income. Children of teenage mothers are more likely to be born with a low birth weight, which can lead to serious childhood injuries or illnesses; they are also twice as likely to die in infancy as children born to women in their twenties.

14 The real goal of parental involvement laws is to discourage abortion. Drafted by anti-choice groups that seek to end all abortions, these laws are opposed by organizations traditionally concerned with helping teenagers and their families. To those who would outlaw all abortions, parental notification or consent is but one step in a series of legislative strategies intended to criminalize abortion again. Passage of these restrictions will merely intensify debate, not eliminate the abortion issue from the legislative agenda.

15 Since parental involvement laws do not promote family communication, safeguard teen decision-making, or protect teenagers' health, what measures would accomplish these objectives? We should begin by repealing or substantially modifying all parental consent and notification laws—a crucial step in making reproductive health care and education accessible to young women. We should also provide funding for dramatically increased levels of reproductive health services and counseling—including contraception, abortion, and prenatal, labor, and post-partum care. We should work to institute comprehensive policies of sex and health education in communities and schools. The development of educational, job training, and family support services that relieve the burdens on families, promote communication, and prevent teenage pregnancy are also needed. Although expensive to start up, these programs will more than pay for themselves by reducing the long-term state dependency that teenage motherhood can create.

16 Whatever services are provided must be accessible. For teenagers, this means they must be located in or near schools or popular hang-outs, be open after school hours, and be free. Perhaps most important, programs must be strictly confidential. Young women who are ready to communicate with their parents about sexuality and reproductive health—including abortion—do so on their own. Mandated parental involvement will only cause those teens who are unable to communicate with their parents to forego necessary care, risking both their lives and health with tragic and sometimes even deadly consequences.

1. Paragraph 1
   A. provides necessary background.
   B. refutes the opposition.
   C. expresses the thesis.
   D. expresses a main point in support of the thesis.
2. Pick out the discount in paragraph 1.
3. Which of the following generalizations is supported by the data of paragraph 2?
   A. Parental notice laws are not necessary for the majority of teenagers.
   B. Parental notice laws can strain family relations.
   C. Parental notice laws will not insure that teens will tell their parents.
   D. A and C.
   E. A, B, and C.
4. Complete the following critique of paragraphs 2, 3 and 4: "Paragraphs 2, 3, and 4 all attempt to refute points made by the opposition. For example, paragraph 2 _____ . Paragraph 3 tries to refute the claim that _____ . As for paragraph 4, it attempts to refute the charge that _____ .
5. Which of the following conditional statements most closely approximates the reasoning in paragraph 4?
   A. If studies show that teens think as well as adults, they should be allowed to decide for themselves.
   B. If studies show that teens can give accurate health histories, they should be allowed to decide for themselves.
   C. If minors can provide informed consent, they should be permitted to decide for themselves.
   D. If some states authorize minors to consent to the treatment of pregnancy, they should be permitted to decide for themselves.

Questions 6–10 deal with sentences 3 and 4 of paragraph 4.

6. These sentences comprise
   A. a fragment syllogism.
   B. a disjunctive syllogism.
   C. a conditional syllogism.
   D. A and B
   E. A and C.
7. The author
   A. leaves a premise unexpressed.
   B. leaves the conclusion unexpressed.
   C. expresses a complete argument.
8. If the argument is incomplete, state the proposition that would complete it.
9. If this is a syllogism, is it valid or invalid? Explain.
10. What follows these sentences in the paragraph represents the formulation or application of a generalization? Explain.
11. Which of the following generalizations is an underlying assumption of paragraph 5?
   A. A good reason not to notify one or both parents is the parents' psychiatric or physical illness.

    B. A good reason not to notify one or both parents is a lack of previous contact with the parent.

    C. A good reason not to notify one or both parents is the existence of a court bypass procedure.

    D. A and B.

    E. A, B, and C.

12. With which of the following generalizations would the author likely agree, given what is expressed in paragraph 6?

    A. Families cannot benefit from compelled communication between their members.

    B. Most parents find it difficult to discuss sexuality with their children.

    C. Children typically find it easier to discuss sexual matters with their parents than vice versa.

    D. Some families will be damaged if children are forced to tell parents about a pregnancy or abortion.

13. Identify the premise and conclusion of the argument expressed in the final two propositions of paragraph 7. What kind of generalization — inductive or noninductive — is the conclusion?

14. Which of the following generalizations is the one to which the data expressed in paragraph 8 lead?

    A. There should be more abortion providers in the United States.

    B. Rural areas need abortion providers.

    C. Abortion raises a special risk to pregnant teens.

    D. At present, young women face obstacles when obtaining abortions.

15. What argument advanced by supporters of parental notice laws does paragraph 9 attempt to refute?

16. Jan says that the first time she went to court she did not feel especially anxious or intimidated. "In fact, I sailed through the bypass procedure and had my abortion." She concludes from her experience that what the author says about teens in paragraph 10 is unjustified. Evaluate Jan's reasoning.

17. Paragraph 11 illustrates the practical problems involved in defining

    A. ambiguous words.

    B. vague words.

    C. jargon.

    D. theoretical terms.

18. The Ohio judge cited in paragraph 11 seems to have

    A. set up a straw argument.

    B. made a distinction without a difference.

    C. poisoned the well.

    D. begged the question.

19. Do the statistics cited in paragraph 12 necessarily clash with those in paragraph 11 of the previous essay?

20. Does paragraph 12 formulate or apply a generalization?

21. Leticia believes that, in paragraph 14, the author is poisoning the well. Explain Leticia's criticism. Do you agree with it?

22. Mario thinks that he detects a false dilemma in paragraph 14: "The author's saying that you're either for parental notice laws and, therefore, pro-life; or you're against them and, therefore, pro-choice. I don't see why a person couldn't be for such laws and pro-choice, too." Has the author set up a false dilemma, as Mario says, or is the dilemma genuine?
23. What is the function of the final two paragraphs?
24. You may have observed that throughout the essay the author refers to parental *involvement* laws rather than parental *notice* or *notification* laws. Are there any connotative differences between "involvement" on the one hand and "notice" or "notification" on the other? Does the choice of "involvement" in any way help the author's case?

RELATED THEME TOPICS

1. Both sides in the parental consent law debate insist that the concept affects communication between parents and their teenage daughters. *Write an essay in which you argue that parental notice laws enhance or inhibit parent-child communciation.*
2. Advocates of parental notice laws support the concept in the name of protecting young adolescents who are unable to make mature decisions. *Write an essay supporting or questioning this view.*
3. *Write an essay in which you argue that premarital teenage sex is never permissible, or one in which you argue that under certain circumstances it is not objectionable, perhaps even desirable.*

9

Generalizations II: Evaluation

INTRODUCTION

A good generalization is one for which there is enough of the right kind of support. In other words, both the *quantity* and the *quality* of the evidence affect the acceptability of a generalization. Quality refers to the kind or nature of the evidence offered and can be viewed largely in terms of the conditions surrounding premise acceptability and relevancy. Quantity refers to the amount of evidence offered for the generalization. This cuts to the third basic criterion of an acceptable argument—that the premises adequately support the conclusion. For a generalization to be good, it needs to be supported by enough evidence, but how much is enough? How much evidence constitutes adequate support for a generalization?

As we learned in Chapter 8, a single observed specific sometimes is enough to support a generalization. Other times, several are needed. In still other cases, numerous observed specifics are required. In short, there is no single "acid" test for determining whether enough evidence is present for a generalization. But that does not mean we are "at sea" when it comes to testing them. On the contrary, we can enormously simplify our task of evaluating generalizations if we remember that the reliability of generalization hinges largely on *how* it was formed.

To understand what this means, imagine that a friend tells you that she has decided to go to a particular college in order to study engineering. When you ask her why she chose the school, she says she likes the campus, or the school's location in the Sunbelt, or because she wants to be near her boyfriend. Doubtful that these are the best reasons in selecting a college, you might ask her, "But how's the school for engineering?" If she replied that she had not looked into that much, you might suggest that she do so before deciding. In so doing, you are not saying she has made the wrong decision or a poor choice; you are simply questioning the basis for her choice.

On the other hand, suppose that she has looked into the matter—she has carefully examined the engineering program at this institution and found it satisfactory. Although this evidence is clearly relevant to her decision, you might still ask her if she has shopped around. Has she spoken with any students or graduates of the institution? Has she thought about the institution's reputation in the field? These questions are getting at the amount of evidence that supports her decision. You are implying that perhaps she should gather more information before making such an important decision.

How much evidence does she need? She does have some evidence, but you think she needs more. How much more? That is impossible to say because the strength of any generalization is relative, which means that some generalizations are stronger than others. The more relevant factors that go into her decision, the stronger it will be. Conversely, the fewer relevant factors, the weaker it will be. *In evaluating a generalization, then, we are basically judging its relative strength in terms of how many significant factors went into its formulation.* Admittedly, even after such factors are introduced, we may feel vaguely uneasy about a generalization because, owing to the nature of the beast, there is usually room for doubt. Thus, your friend may not rest easily with her decision even after she has marshalled "enough of the right kind of evidence." This psychological phenomenon is worth commenting on.

Psychologically, it is typically hard for us to maintain some intermediate state between belief and disbelief in which we suspend judgment. We tend to move to one of two possibilities, fervently embracing one and denouncing the other. Yet, despite this most-human proclivity, empirical knowledge—the kind we acquire through sense experience—never has absolute certainty. Not even in science, to which we traditionally turn for a firm understanding of what is true or false. We tend to think that exacting scientific experimentation and verification ultimately lead to "proof," that is, one-hundred percent certainty. Scientists, however, would be the first to admit it does not. Understanding well their inductive method, they realize the probabilistic nature of their conclusions. This is why we rarely if ever come across the word *proof* in scientific literature. Most scientists simply do not consider *proof* an appropriate term outside the pure world of mathematics.

Yet, generalize they must, and so must we. Indeed, the paramount goal of science is to formulate generalizations that approximate a one-hundred percent level of certainty—a generalization whose probability or likelihood is so strong that, for all intents and purposes, it can be treated as if it were certain. It is not, of course—tomorrow or the day after may turn up additional confounding evidence. For the present, though, it can be treated as if it were a "firm truth," and integrated within the mass of other assumptions which themselves enjoy a similarly high statistical probability.

Actually, attaining such a high degree of probability is comparatively easy in some fields of science, such as physics. Although an extremely complex discipline, physics nonetheless comes to precise quantitative predictions—extraordinarily reliable

Speaking of . . .

Reliable Generalizations

Scientific Laws

Let us look at the logic involved in forming sound generalizations. The number of cases investigated in the course of formulating a scientific law (which is a form of unqualified generalization) is a factor in establishing the truth of the law, but it is by no means the most important one. Obviously, if we observed one hundred swans, all of which are white, our generalization that "all swans are white" does not have the same probability it would have if we observed one thousand swans. But no matter how great the number of specimens involved in this type of observation, no more than a high degree of probability is ever established. Countless numbers of white swans were observed throughout the ages (without any exceptions) and then in the nineteenth century black swans were observed in Australia.

The weakness of the method of "induction by simple enumeration of cases" is amusingly illustrated by Bertrand Russell's parable in his *A History of Western Philosophy:*

> There was once upon a time a census officer who had to record the names of all householders in a certain Welsh village. The first that he questioned was called William Williams; so were the second, third, and fourth. . . . At last he said to himself: "This is tedious; evidently they are all called William Williams. I shall put them down so and take a holiday." But he was wrong; there was just one whose name was John Jones.

Scientific generalizations based on other types of evidence than simple enumeration often acquire a much higher degree of probability after only a few observations. When a chemist finds that pure sulphur melts at 125 degrees C., in an experiment in which every factor is accurately analyzed and controlled, the law concerning the melting point of sulphur achieves as great a degree of certainty as humanly attainable. Accurate control of every element of one case, then, is more important in establishing probability than is *mere enumeration* of many cases.

Or consider the generalization concerning the mortality of mankind. This law is based not merely on the fact that countless numbers of human beings have died in the past, but also on the fact that all living beings must, by reason of physiological limitations, die; and that all matter wears out in time. So the harmony of a particular generalization with the rest of our knowledge is also a factor in giving it a high degree of probability.

generalizations because it is dealing with relatively few variables. In this sense, then, physics is "simple" compared to multidisciplinary fields involving many variables and great uncertainties. It is this latter category of generalizations that we ordinarily formulate and come across in everyday living. Forming reliable generalizations about which college to attend or what to major in; or ones about values or social policy; or ones in the areas of education, criminology, politics, or economics are difficult because of the many variables and great uncertainties involved.

Still, we *can* isolate some basic ingredients of reliable generalizations. Understanding what these are will enable us to evaluate intelligently the great variety of generalizations that appear in arguments. It will also help us formulate good generalizations of our own. We begin with the basis of all inductive generalizations — observations.

MODULE 9.1

OBSERVATION

When we observe, we become aware of, or obtain information about, something through the use of the senses — we notice it. Sometimes, we "notice" things in a most formal, systematic manner by employing scientific method. Scientific method is a way of investigating things, based on the collection, analysis, and interpretation of evidence in order to determine the most probable inference. When scientists weigh, measure, or take the temperature of something, and when they record their findings, they are making observations. Although most of us do not apply exacting scientific standards of measurement to our observations, we often perform activities roughly analogous to the scientist's before we draw a generalization. For example, before purchasing a new car, you might do some research, sample the experiences of other owners, compare alternative vehicles, drive them, and so on. The more significant observations you can make, the more reliable your conclusion will be. Of course, all of this presupposes that the observations are themselves reliable. If they are not reliable, your generalization will not be reliable either.

Quite often in extended argument, writers will present what seems to be a powerful case for a generalization. On closer examination, though, the observations that supposedly support the generalization simply are not reliable. A good way to avoid being taken in by such arguments is to ask yourself the following questions about the observations substantiating the offered evidence.

1. Under what physical conditions were the observations made? This question cuts to a fundamental criterion of all reliable observations: They must be made under circumstances conducive to an accurate observation. Thus, a visual or audio observation made under conditions in which vision or hearing is impaired is obviously unreliable.

For example, you may have seen on TV a rerun of the film *Twelve Angry Men,* a classic in the individual-versus-group genre. A lone juror, played by Henry Fonda, takes on the formidable task of planting a doubt in the minds of his fellow jurors, who are initially convinced that the accused is indeed guilty of the murder with which he is charged. Further, the prosecution has presented an overwhelming case based upon eyewitness testimony. Fonda argues that the testimony is tainted because of the conditions under which the observations were made. For example, one witness, who swore that he *saw* the murder committed, had to see through the dimly lighted windows of an elevated train that ran between the witness' apartment building and the victim's—not exactly optimum conditions for seeing something accurately.

2. How keen are the observer's senses?   Observations must also be appraised with reference to the observer's ability to make them. Thus, at another point in *Twelve Angry Men,* Fonda impugns the damning testimony of a witness on the grounds that the witness may not have heard exactly what he claimed to hear, because he was hearing-impaired.

In evaluating the observer's senses, it is important to avoid assuming without proof that certain events can only be accurately observed by a particular sense—for example, a basketball game can only accurately be observed visually. Most of us probably would find it difficult to believe that a blind person could accurately observe the fast-paced action of a professional basketball game. Who has the ball and where it is, who is shooting and what kind of shot it is, whether he hits or misses—these and countless other events of the game seem accessible only to the sighted. Are they? Not for one basketball fan, who happens to be blind. So acute is this man's power of hearing, as he demonstrated on television, that he can observe a pro game as well as, if not better than, most sighted spectators.[1]

Today, technology has extended the range of sense observation, sometimes dramatically so. When functioning correctly and used properly, appropriate technology—cameras, recorders, X-rays, and so on—can yield extraordinary data. The telescope poses a classic example. Only with its invention in the fifteenth century could many of the astronomical claims of Copernicus and Kepler be confirmed. Modern astronomy has its share of mechanical marvels, as well. The *Pioneer 11* spacecraft, for example, employed exquisitely sensitive cameras allowing scientists to observe radiation belts girdling the planet Saturn. And the day probably is not far off when a "new and improved" *Hubble,* billed as the most powerful telescope ever made, will allow us to see what before we could only imagine, and yield data that require a revision of some astronomical generalizations.

3. Is the observer qualified to interpret the observation?   Even though an observation is made under hospitable circumstances by someone with reliable senses or instruments, it may still be unreliable if the observer offers an interpretation that

---

[1]See Vincent E. Barry and Joel Rudinow, *Invitation to Critical Thinking,* 2nd ed. (Fort Worth, Texas: Holt, Rinehart and Winston, Inc., 1990), pp. 365–366.

he is not qualified to make. All of us probably have had occasion to note in ourselves or someone else certain physical changes. A gaunt look, a sallow complexion, a sudden weight loss or gain, a bout of insomnia, and so on. What does it mean? Only someone who is qualified by training can say, and sometimes even the "experts" disagree.

Although not obvious, every observation carries an element of interpretation. This can be illustrated by considering the eyes, which are the main sensory route by which most of us observe or acquire information. When light strikes the retina, it sets off a wave of neural-electrical activity that passes along the optic nerve to the brain. These sensory messages, called sensations, have little meaning in themselves. When they reach the brain, they trigger a number of complex activities, one of which involves the brain's scanning or comparing messages of past experience with the recent incoming sensations. If the two are similar enough, the brain "recognizes" what we are looking at (or hearing or touching or tasting or smelling) as something it has encountered in the past. If there is no memory that matches the incoming sensation, the brain "recognizes" that whatever we are experiencing is new or different and lacks an identifiable verbal label. Psychologists call this process of recognition *perception* — the process of matching sensations with memories of past experiences. In everyday parlance, to perceive simply means to recognize.

In a word, all of us make observations with reference to what is already in our minds. Thus, the question, "Is the observer qualified to interpret the observation?" is in effect asking, "Is there good reason to believe that the observer's mind contains the requisite past experience to make this observation?" This question has far-reaching implications for inductions formed on the basis of expert testimony, as we will see.

4. Is the observer objective? Objectivity—also termed *impartiality* or *disinterestedness*—is the quality of viewing ourselves and the world without distortion. Of course, no one can ever be completely objective, not even the scientist. No matter how refined the instruments, or sophisticated the telescope or computer, some individual must still make the observations. Where there is a person, there will be a viewpoint—a perceptual filter, as it were, through which input will pass and emerge not exactly as it entered.

Nevertheless, we can significantly minimize the potential for distortion by becoming aware of our biases and reducing their impact on our observations.

The challenge posed by objectivity is more easily met when the observations are not ours, but belong to someone else, for it is usually easier for us to see the mote in someone else's eye, than the beam in our own. Still, identifying a person's "frame of reference" requires careful deliberation.

The phrase *frame of reference* refers to the organized body of accumulated beliefs that we use to interpret new experience and guide our behavior. Most of the beliefs and assumptions that compose an individual's frame of reference probably fall into the noninductive category — they are generalizations that individuals have put into their minds without conscious deliberation. Furthermore, the vast bulk of an individual's belief structure probably functions below the threshold of an individual's awareness and thus remains unexamined. But the subsurface nature of these beliefs does not mean they are uninfluential. On the contrary, they tremendously affect how

Speaking of . . .

Observation

Perceptual Defense

One of the most interesting sets of studies on perception was the "dirty word" experiments conducted in the 1950s and 1960s. Researchers began by determining the perceptual threshold for ordinary individuals. For example, they showed student-subjects simple words such as *table* and *chair* at faster and faster speeds. With each student, and for each word, they were able to calculate an exposure time so rapid that the subject could perceive the word exactly fifty percent of the time. For a word such as *whale*, this perceptual threshold might be about 10 milliseconds (a millisecond is $\frac{1}{1000}$ of a second). For an emotionally laden word such as *whore*, however, the threshold was typically much higher, about 200 milliseconds or more. Researchers believed that the subjects' internal "censors" were "defending" against such "disturbing" words. They called this act of suppressing or re-pressing threatening stimuli "perceptual defense." Student subjects *defending* themselves perceptually against recognizing "dirty words," in fact, raised their perceptual threshold for perceiving those words.

On the other hand, a few student-subjects had *lower* thresholds for "dirty words" than for "clean" ones. Researchers speculated that, while most people have censors who *defend* against sexual stimuli, a few of us have censors that are vigilantly searching the world for anything that smacks of smut. Researchers refer to the lowered thresholds as "perceptual vigilance." Whether one's censor tends to seek or defend against sexual stimuli seems to be a matter of each individual's own past experience and moral upbringing.

Do you think this research provides any insights into the reliability of personal observations?

we deal with new information. How you and I deal with incoming information is largely influenced by what we already believe.

There are two major implications of this. The first, and more obvious one, relates to what we just pointed out: We must inform ourselves, at least in a general way, of the intellectual and emotional predispositions of the observer in order to determine his degree of objectivity. The second implication relates to ourselves: We must be equally aware of our own biases which may be distorting incoming information. Take, for example, the essays in this text. You probably hold a viewpoint, perhaps a strong one, about some of the issues raised by these essays. Having a strong point of view is a double-edged sword: It can sharpen criticism, but also blunt objectivity. Well-considered opinions should give rise to trenchant criticism, not wall-off or distort opposed input.

The challenge in confronting opposed viewpoints, then, is to suspend or "bracket out," as it were, our own preconceptions—to effect disinterest or impartiality. This does not mean that we jettison what we know to be fact or overlook errors in reasoning. It *does* mean *not* being blinded by emotion, unexamined assumptions, or personal prejudice. This is no easy habit of mind to develop, especially when issues trigger strong feelings, but it is a quality that we must demand as much of ourselves as we do of others.

IN BRIEF Good inductive generalizations are rooted in reliable observations. Reliable observations should meet certain criteria concerning the conditions under which they were made and the abilities of the people who made them. Four key factors to consider in evaluating observations are: (1) the physical conditions under which the observations were made, (2) the sensory acuity of the observer, (3) the background knowledge of the observer, and (4) the objectivity of the observer.

EXERCISES ON OBSERVATION

1. As a general rule, courts will not permit "hearsay" evidence, that is, a testimony that the witness has heard others say. Why do you think experience has shown this kind of evidence to be unreliable?
2. Clip a large picture from a magazine. Write a series of observations about the picture, making sure to avoid all inference (that is, a conclusion drawn from your observations). Show the class the picture and your observations and find out if they think you succeeded in separating your observations from inference or judgment.
3. It is often said that "we see things not as they are, but as we are." Find a picture filled with detail and ask two people you know well, a female and a male, to write a list of observations about the picture. Do the lists tend to confirm the old dictum?
4. Specify two situations in which a single observation is strong enough evidence for an inductive generalization (for example, the temperature of water in a bathtub).

MODULE 9.2

REPRESENTATIVENESS

The reliability of observations is *not* sufficient to establish a generalization. One apple, correctly observed to be hard, green, and sour, does not establish that most or even many of the one-hundred apples in a basket are the same. The sample, or portion selected, may not be representative of the apples as a whole. To ensure that a sample truly represents the population from which it is drawn, we need to consider its quantity and quality in relation to that population. In short, we must inspect both the size and typicality of the sample.

IN BRIEF   Representativeness is a key factor in evaluating inductive generalizations. This means that the observed specifics in both quantity and quality must accurately reflect the make-up of the whole unit.

Sample Size

Ordinarily the more observed specifics the more reliable the generalization because large numbers tend to follow fixed laws. For example, the chances of "4" coming up on the role of a die are one in six, but rolling the die once or twice does not properly ground the generalization. Four could turn up once or twice or not at all. In order to form a reliable generalization, we need to roll the die hundreds, even thousands of times. The more rolls we include in the sample the closer to the one-in-six outcome we will observe.

As a rule of thumb, the larger and more diversified the population, the larger the sample needs to be. A good illustration of this can be found in a public opinion poll, or survey. For example, suppose we want to form generalizations about the drug habits of 18–25-year-olds in (1) U.S. colleges, (2) in one particular U.S. college and (3) in the school of business of one particular U.S. college. The sample required for (1) should be larger than for (2), which in turn should be larger than for (3).

It is important to remember that sample size is directly tied to the number of subgroups within the main group. "U.S. college students between 18 and 25" is an extremely diverse group. Contained within it are a number of subgroups that might be designated in a variety of ways—for example, by age, sex, major, geographical region, and so on. This is another reason that a sample of this population should be larger than for a population of business majors in a particular college, which is a far more homogeneous group.

Nevertheless, *sample size does not always substantively affect the accuracy of a generalization that is based on it.* A properly conducted poll that samples 1,500 registered voters would be large enough to support a reliable generalization about how a voting population of 800,000 or 80,000,000 people are likely to vote in an upcoming election. Statistically the margin of sample error—the numerical designation in percentage of how inaccurate a poll may be—is the same in both cases, about ±3. In other words, in *quantity* the sample is equally representative of each population despite the enormous difference in their sizes. But in *quality* the sample may not be representative if it is not typical of each subgroup within the general population. This brings us to the second factor that bears on the representativeness of a sample, what we will term *typicality.*

Typicality

A tiny sample may be representative if it is typical of the whole, and a large sample may not be representative if it is not typical of the whole. For example, a mere glassful of water drawn from a kitchen tap may be sufficient for drawing a reliable generalization about whether a municipal water supply exceeds the maximum concentration levels of iron or sodium established by the "Federal Safe Drinking Water Act." On the other hand, a poll of 1,500 registered voters who live in large urban centers would be unreliable for predicting how the U.S. voting population as a whole is likely to vote on election day. The problem is not with the sample size but with its focus on only one kind of voter, the urban dweller. Contained within the voting population as a whole are numerous subgroups that the poll needs to account for in order to ensure that the sample is typical of those who will vote.

Moreover, a sample may not be typical of the whole, even when all significant subgroups are accounted for. This occurs when the individuals within the subgroups are not given an equal opportunity to voice an opinion. For example, suppose that all important subgroups within the voting population were identified in the preceding poll, and the pollster then sampled these subgroups by telephone on a Wednesday evening between 6 P.M. and 10 P.M. Excluded from the sample would be anyone who (1) did not have a telephone or (2) was not available at that time. Thus, the opinions sampled would not necessarily be typical of those subgroups. In order to avoid such a procedural misrepresentation, professional pollsters attempt to approximate the idea of randomness.

➤ *To draw a sample randomly means that each member of the group has an equal chance of being sampled.* When the group is especially large, ensuring randomness can be complex and expensive. As a result, pollsters ordinarily employ what is termed a stratified random sample.

In a stratified random sample, relevant strata or subgroups within the main group are identified, and a random sample from each subgroup is selected in direct proportion to its percentage of the main group. Suppose, for example, that in order to determine the popularity of one of its programs, a TV station decides to sample viewers. Within this sample, it could establish relevant groups on the basis of characteristics that could influence viewer preference—for example, age, sex, educational level, and so on. (The selection of subgroups depends on what the pollster is attempting to discover.) If fifty-five percent of its audience is female, and if it considers gender a significant subgroup, the station will make sure that fifty-five percent of its sample will reflect the views of female viewers. It will also ensure that each female has an equal chance of ending up in the sample. In short, the stratified random sample, which is the most reliable method of contact when sampling large, diverse groups, consists basically of three steps: 1) identifying the subgroups within the main group; 2) determining the percentage of each subgroup in relation to the main group; and 3) randomly selecting members of a specified number of the subgroups in direct proportion to their percentage of the main group.

Although we used the example of public opinion polls to illustrate the meaning and importance of representativeness in *establishing* inductive generalizations, writers often use poll and survey results in order to *support* conclusions of arguments.

Therefore, it would be useful for us to have some guidelines for evaluating evidence that consists of the findings of polls and surveys.

Some Basic Questions for Evaluating Polls and Surveys

Unreliable measurements of opinion yield unreliable results. So, in evaluating poll- or survey-based evidence, we need to determine the reliability of the poll or survey. A good way to do this is to ask and answer the following questions:

1. Who conducted the poll or survey?   Recall that one of the criteria for reliable observation is observer *objectivity*. Obviously, it is impossible to determine the objectivity of the persons who conducted the poll or survey without knowing something about them. That the source of a study may have a vested interest in the outcome is important to know. By the same token, it is important to know that the source has no particular interest in the outcome beyond unearthing attitude or opinion. Of course, simply because the source may have a vested interest in the outcome does not of itself discredit the results. If we insist that it does, then we are poisoning the well. However, identifying a source's interest in the outcome does and should alert us to a potential conflict of interest or bias. This in turn leads us to ask a legitimate question in evaluating the poll- or survey-generated data that are offered as support for a thesis, namely, "Why doesn't the essay include a less partial, and more independent, source of data?" In the absence of a disinterested source, we are justified in considering the data offered inadequate by itself to support the thesis.

2. When was the poll or survey conducted?   When a poll or survey was conducted — the date of contact — is important to know because it affects the *interpretation* of the results. For example, a poll may support the inductive generalization that a president is enjoying unprecedented popularity, but this conclusion does not mean much if the poll was taken prior to some major international or domestic blunder.

3. What procedure was used in conducting the poll survey?   The method of contact, as we have just seen, is crucial to both the objectivity and representativeness of the sample. In its method of contact, a poll or survey should approximate the ideal of randomness. A classic violation of this principle is the notorious *Literary Digest* poll of 1936 which predicted victory by the Republican presidential candidate Alf Landon over the Democratic incumbent Franklin Roosevelt. The problem with the poll was that ballots were sent mainly to people listed in the telephone and city directories, thereby restricting the sample to the relatively well-to-do and only to those who returned ballots.

4. How large was the sample?   It is wise never to accept as support for a conclusion the results of a poll or survey without first learning how large the sample and the population are. Without knowing these facts, we cannot determine the margin for error in the inductive generalization drawn from the sample.

     For example, suppose an essay argues that the United States should provide substantial aid to the fledgling democracies of eastern Europe. As part of the evidence in support of this thesis, the essay includes a recent public opinion poll that shows that a majority of Americans, fifty-two percent, support this position while forty-eight percent oppose it. Without knowing what the sample size was, we are justified in questioning this evidence. In fact, in this case, our grounds for skepticism are especially solid since, at best, the margin for error is probably ± 3, which means that a majority of Americans could well oppose substantial aid to eastern European democracies.

5. What questions were asked?   Since the nature of a question can bias the reply, we need to know as much as we can about the questions asked. As we saw in previous chapters, questions can be ambiguous or vague (for example, "Do you think it's a *good practice* for employers to *actively* seek out "women and minority members for jobs?"). They can also be "loaded" (for example, *"Given that the future of the free world depends on U.S. military strength,* do you think it's wise to reduce defense spending by fifteen percent as some members of Congress are suggesting?"). Questions can also be complex (for example, "What action should the government take to ensure the survival of at-risk American industries, such as steel and auto manufacturing?" assumes that the government *should* intervene). Questions can also set up false dilemmas (for example, "Should handguns be outlawed or shouldn't they?" overlooks restrictions that could be imposed on handgun acquisition). In short, when questions are ambiguous, vague, loaded, or complex, or when they mischaracterize through false dilemma, they yield unreliable responses and, thus, unacceptable data in support of inductive generalizations.

6. Are the respondents likely being forthright?   There probably is not an individual who at some time or another has not told someone what he thinks the person wants to hear, rather than what he actually feels. Obvious examples involve our interactions with authority figures. Thus, what children tell their parents often reflects parental expectation more than the children's true feelings. The same applies to student-teacher and employer-employee relations. Even the sodden couch potato is not above reporting to his physician that he takes regular exercise and only an "occasional" drink.

Because, to some degree, we are all concerned with how we appear to others in social and professional interactions, we try to create a favorable image. Generally speaking, the more concerned we are with the *public self,* the more we neglect our *subjective being.* Existentialist philosopher Martin Buber (1878–1965) makes roughly this distinction in contrasting "image man" and "essence man." "Essence man" approaches life from the standpoint of being who he is without undue regard for the way others perceive him. In contrast, "image man" focuses on what he wishes to appear to be. As Buber notes, although all of us are a mix of both these aspects of self-expression, we tend to develop a lifestyle that favors one over the other. This distinction bears directly on the question of respondent reliability.

When individuals are asked their opinions on controversial issues, they may answer in a way that will receive approval, which may not coincide with how they truly feel. For example, a house-to-house survey was once made to find out what magazines people read. The replies indicated that a large percentage read *Harper's,* but only a few regularly read *True Story.* This was odd because publishers' figures indicated that *True Story* sold millions of magazines, while *Harper's* sold less than a million. Eliminating all other possible explanations, the publishers faced the unmistakable conclusion that many of the respondents had lied. Similarly, during the 1970s, *in response to consumer surveys,* companies began to provide so-called generic products in plain, unadorned packaging. Despite the cheaper price and adequate quality of these products, consumers studiously avoided them for the "name brands." Today, surveys conducted by the Gallup organization show that more than ninety percent of consumers are willing to make a special effort to buy products from companies trying to protect the environment; more than ninety percent say they would sacrifice some convenience, such as disposability, in return for environmentally safer products or packaging; and nearly ninety percent are willing to pay more for them. Whether we put our money where our mouths are remains to be seen.

The point is, that on personal subjects, respondents often confuse, intentionally or otherwise, their "ideal" and "actual" selves. This can lead to survey results that are faulty generalizations owing to respondent bias.

IN BRIEF   The reliability of a poll or survey is in question when: (1) the pollster has something to gain by the outcome; (2) the poll was taken prior to events that affect its outcome; (3) the polling procedure lacks randomness; (4) the sample is too small or atypical; (5) the questions bias the answers; or (6) there is good reason to suspect that respondents were not telling the truth. Since such a poll is unreliable, so are its findings. Thus, the findings of an unreliable poll or survey are never acceptable evidence for a conclusion.

MODULE 9.3

HANDLING STATISTICAL EVIDENCE

The pervasiveness of polls and surveys is one indicator of the important role played by statistics in our age. Indeed, today we have an astonishing technological capacity to collect, store, and retrieve tremendous amounts of data. This allows us to generate statistics about anything we choose for whatever reason we desire—from sports enthusiasts' quoting batting averages and point spreads, to securities analysts citing "P. E. ratios" and "yield percentages," to politicians reporting the feeling of the "average voter." It is not surprising, therefore, that statistical evidence often turns up in argumentative essays as support for conclusions, and, given their authoritative air, statistics can be most persuasive.

Most of us probably nurse considerable ambivalence toward statistics. On the one hand, we may find ourselves quoting favorable statistics to make our point, as if their sheer recitation should be enough to convince all but the addle-headed that what we claim is true. On the other hand, and perhaps in the same breath, we may scorn statistics that are unfavorable to our beliefs as little more than sleight-of-hand tricks. We may even remind our opponent of the saying: "There are lies, damn lies, and statistics." In short, we both trust and distrust statistics, depending on our viewpoint.

As a case in point, take the battle of the drug studies. In December 1990, President Bush reported to the nation what he termed "wonderful and welcome news." It seemed that we were beginning to win the "War on Drugs," which the administration had declared in the late 1980s. Buoying the president's optimism was a study conducted in the spring by the administration's National Institute of Drug Abuse, which had called about 10,000 Americans and asked them: "Would you be willing to talk about your use of illegal drugs?" About one-fifth politely declined. Based upon conversations with the others, the NIDA concluded that far fewer Americans were using drugs of any kind than we had suspected.

No sooner had Mr. Bush unveiled this rosy picture than Senate Democrats began chipping away at the paint. They too, as it happens, had employed researchers to answer similar questions about drug use by zeroing in on persons who were arrested and tested for drugs in jail and those being admitted to drug treatment centers. Guess what? Their findings portrayed a strikingly different picture of our drug use, a far bleaker one of 2.4 million regular cocaine users—four times the estimate in the NIDA studies.

The challenge raised by statistical evidence is to determine when it is being used legitimately and when it is not; when it is relevant to a claim and when it is not; when it provides adequate support, and when it does not. Fortunately, we need not be statisticians to throw some light on these questions. As with so many aspects of argument evaluation, we can help ourselves assess statistical evidence by asking some basic questions, such as the ones just raised and the four that follow.

Evaluative Questions

1. How reliable is the source?   Obviously, statistical evidence is the product of someone's observations. So, before accepting the statistical evidence offered for a claim, we should satisfy ourselves about the qualifications and objectivity of the observer. Even more important, we should assure ourselves of the impartiality of the person offering the statistics because, in most cases, arguers cite statistics derived not from their own observations but from those of others.

For example, any stockbroker worth her salt can make a powerful case for investing in the stock market, no matter what the direction of the economic wind is. If, however, a stockbroker's profits come from the volume of securities sold, she can hardly be considered a disinterested party. She might attempt to offset her obvious vested interest by citing other statistics that indicate her successful track record. Still, it is prudent to wonder whether she is presenting her *entire* track record or being statistically selective in order to persuade you to follow her advice. In short, an independent party would be a more reliable source of statistical evidence.

2. Are the statistics complete? Statistics that are incomplete do not adequately support a claim. For example, suppose that, in attempting to justify an increase in its premium rates, an insurance company argues that it has paid out $3 billion more in claims than it collected in premiums over the past eight years. Although perhaps accurate, this statistic does not present a complete profit picture of an insurance company—we need to know how much was made by investing the premiums.

Since a single statistic rarely provides a complete picture, it is tempting to use statistics selectively—employing those that make our point and overlooking those that do not. For example, a national survey of how American adults feel about abortion may indicate that most favor abortion on demand. Broken down, however, the statistics may indicate that the majority of people in a particular state oppose abortion. Presuming both results are derived from reliable samples, they are accurate measures of public opinion. This allows a person to use either, depending on his position, and, whichever he uses, he is telling the truth. The burden falls to the audience to determine whether he is telling the whole truth or a "half-truth."

Consider this news item which appeared under the headline "Poverty Declines":

> *(Washington)* The percentage of Americans living below the poverty line dropped last year (1986) to the lowest level since 1980, the Census Bureau reported Thursday. It shrank from 14% in 1985 to 13.6% in 1986.

In fact, even though it dropped for the third year in a row, the poverty rate still remained well above the levels of the 1970s, and the income of the poor fell further behind the income of the rest of the country, thus widening the gap between the haves and have-nots. Also, the total number of Americans living in poverty increased from 32.4 million in 1985 to 33.1 million in 1986. While the poor made only modest gains in 1986, the average American family enjoyed one of the largest increases in real income in fifteen years, as median family income rose 4.2 percent to $29,460. Notice that all of these Census Bureau statistics were available—the writer simply ignored them, and, as a result, probably misled some readers about the severity of poverty in America.

3. Do the statistics make a difference? Statistics are useful when they tell us something worth knowing, and they tell us something worth knowing when they make a difference. For example, suppose that the U.S. Department of Health and Human Services releases figures showing that diabetes is the nation's third most common disease, behind cancer and heart disease and that its incidence among people under twenty-five has risen five percent in the last ten years. Such figures certainly would alert government, the medical community, and the general public to an alarming health problem and to the need for corrective measure. In brief, the figures would make a difference to anyone concerned about disease control.

Unfortunately, statistics often are bandied about in ways that make no difference at all, although they may appear to. For example, in the past, the U.S. Postal Service sold its used delivery vehicles to the general public. Presumably as support for purchasing these vehicles, pasted on the dashboards were stickers that read: "This vehicle has met all applicable safety standards." Although such an assertion sounds meaningful, it is not, because so few safety standards applied to the vehicles — far fewer than apply to passenger cars and pick-ups. The vehicles, in fact, had some very dangerous features such as high centers of gravity that made it easy for them to roll over; unupholstered dashboards with protruding knobs and switches; and steering columns that could be likened to iron pipes pointing at the drivers' chest. Indeed, the abnormally high incidence of single-vehicle accidents involving these vehicles belied the safety reassurances of the stickers. Thus, the message boasting that the vehicle had met all applicable safety standards was implying a statistic that was useless to an evaluation of the vehicle's safety. In fact, it was worse than useless — it was dangerously misleading.

As another example, consider one of the shop-worn arguments made by makers of some diet aids. It claims that eating a diet candy before meals will raise the blood-sugar level by some percentage, which in turn will have the effect of suppressing appetite. There is, however, no clinical evidence that an increase in blood sugar inhibits appetite. Besides, even if something were inhibited, it would not be appetite, it would be hunger. It is not hunger that leads to obesity, though, it is appetite, which is a learned way of behaving, associated with a complex network of pleasurable physical and psychological feelings. So, although the statistical evidence may sound good to the would-be dieter, it really makes no difference.

4. Are the statistics misleadingly precise?   As we have learned, good arguments require the clear and precise use of language. Because vague and ambiguous premises invite multiple interpretations, they cannot be objectively evaluated, and thus do not express acceptable evidence for a conclusion. Given the importance of precision, a mathematically exact statistic has a certain allure. In some cases, however, statistical precision is impossible to obtain. When the degree of precision is estimated or is unknown — that is, when inexact data are treated as if they were precise — then the *fallacy of false precision* is committed.

The fallacy of false precision consists in using a statistic with a mathematical precision that is impossible to obtain. For example, suppose half the money spent on birth control worldwide is spent for abortions. Opposing abortion on moral grounds, a writer uses this statistic as evidence to oppose U.S. aid to developing countries for birth control programs. For anyone sharing the writer's view on abortion — and perhaps even for some who oppose it — this statistic may be rather persuasive, but the statistic is probably a wild guess. After all, there are widespread taboos concerning birth control and abortion in many parts of the world, and socialist and Third-World countries have very different economies from not only the United States but often from each other. Without reliable data, no one can say precisely how much birth control money goes for abortions.

Similarly, not long ago, an article dealing with the widespread use of drugs in the U.S. workplace appeared in a leading newspaper. The thrust of the essay was that workplace drug use was seriously damaging the U.S. economy. A key piece of evidence was the statistical claim that the United States could raise its GNP by twenty-five percent if drugs could be eliminated at work. The problem with this statistic is that evidence for it simply is not available because it is impossible to determine exactly what impact drug use has on productivity and efficiency. It probably has some, but twenty-five percent? How could that be determined? By citing the statistic, however, the author strengthened, albeit illicitly, the otherwise mundane claim that drug use probably lowers the GNP.

A useful way to criticize what you think is a statement of false precision is to raise some direct questions about it. For example, in response to the aforementioned claim about workplace drug use and the GNP, you could ask: "How did you arrive at such a precise figure?" "Can poor performance among workplace drug users be attributed exclusively or primarily to their drug use?" "Do you have back-up for this assumption?"

IN BRIEF Before accepting statistical evidence as support for a claim, make sure of the objectivity of the source, as well as the completeness, significance, and knowability of the statistics.

Speaking of . . .

Useless Statistics

Nibbling and Cholesterol

Grazing received a much-publicized boost in October (1989) from a study reported in the *New England Journal of Medicine.* Researchers found that men who increase the number of meals they ate (without changing the amount or type of food consumed) lowered their blood cholesterol levels. The likely explanation: when people eat large meals their bodies tend to make more insulin, which has been linked to increased cholesterol production.

This new research is of no practical value. The study had only seven subjects and lasted just two weeks. The men ate 17 meals a day—a snack every waking hour. And the result was an average drop of about 8% in cholesterol, which is not much compared to the results of conventional lowering diets. Most people would find it inconvenient to eat 17 meals a day (an ounce of chicken at noon, another ounce at one o'clock, a slice of bread at two, two cookies at three, etc.), and most would end up eating more food (perhaps high-fat snacks) each day. And if you eat more, your cholesterol level may well head up, not down.

(Berkeley Wellness Letter, February 1990, p. 20.)

EXERCISES ON HANDLING STATISTICAL EVIDENCE*

1. Almost a half-century ago, Alfred C. Kinsey and his staff published a monumental study entitled *Sexual Behavior in the Human Female.* Kinsey's study tabulated and classified data concerning 5,940 white American females, ages two to ninety. At the time, there were about 70 million American females. Most of Kinsey's subjects were from Illinois, Florida, and California. They were more highly educated than the general female population—seventy-five percent of them went to college as compared with a national average of thirteen percent; three percent of them did not go beyond grade school, as compared with the national average of thirty-seven percent. A larger-than-average proportion of the subjects were from middle- and upper-economic groups. Very few were Roman Catholics or orthodox Jews. Discuss the representativeness of the sample used in the study.

2. Suppose that in the most recent presidential election total contributions by individuals to political parties went up fifteen percent, compared to the previous election. It is concluded that people are taking a greater interest in politics than they were. Which of the following additional statistics, if true, would most weaken this argument?

   A. The average contribution per individual actually declined during the same four-year period.

   B. Per-capita income of the population increased by ten percent during the four years in question.

   C. Large corporate contributions to political parties declined during the four-year period.

   D. Fewer people voted in the most recent presidential election than in the one four years earlier.

Evaluate the use of statistics in each of the following instances:

3. Many people ask, "How effective is PAIN-EZ?" To find out, we checked the medicine cabinets of 150 homes in this typical American neighborhood. Guess what? Seven-out-of-ten contained a bottle of PAIN-EZ. Doesn't it stand to reason that you, too, should have the most effective pain reliever on the market?

4. News Item: "The AFL-CIO said today that a total of 2.5 million jobs have been lost because of the trade deficit, including 631,000 in textiles, 475,000 in electronics, 324,000 in steel, 380,000 in shoes and leather, and 171,000 in automotive."

5. News Item: "According to a study conducted for the White House Office of Consumer Affairs, 96% of unhappy customers don't complain about the discourtesy but up to 91% will not buy again from the business that offended them. In addition, the average unhappy customer will tell his or her story to at least nine other people, and 13% of unhappy customers will tell twenty or more people."

6. A solicitation for charity: "Every day more than 8,000 children die of poverty in our hemisphere. Although this appears a hopeless situation, the truth is that most of these deaths are entirely preventable."

7. News Item: "A report says that 31% of the answers given by the IRS to telephone inquiries are incorrect. But the IRS commissioner says that only 20% are wrong."

8. News Item: "So the Postal Service deliberately will antagonize customers while it raises prices. It hopes the consumer outrage will be directed at Congress forcing it to ante up more money. Yet more money is precisely what the U.S. Postal Service has been getting. Since 1968 first-class rates have quadrupled. If rates had been tied to inflation, a first-class stamp would cost 18 cents today (as opposed to 29 cents)."

MODULE 9.4

FALLACIES OF MISSING EVIDENCE

Some argumentative essays fail to offer enough support for a generalization thesis. Although several fallacies fall under the heading of "missing evidence," the most common are the hasty generalization, the misapplied generalization, and neglect of relevant evidence.

Hasty Generalization

The fallacy of hasty generalization consists in drawing a conclusion based on an unrepresentative sample. For example, after reading of a notorious case of securities fraud, a person concludes that *most* securities analysts cannot be trusted or that the stock market is rigged. Clearly, a case or two of such corruption is not enough to justify the generalization.

Just as common as the hasty generalization formed from too few observed specifics is the one based on unusual or atypical cases. For example, someone argues that the United States is not really committed to the principle of one-person–one-vote because inmates of U.S. prisons cannot vote; or someone insists that narcotics are not really habit forming because patients taking them under medical supervision usually do not become addicted. These arguers could cite thousands of cases of prisoners and medically supervised, unaddicted patients in support of their generalizations. Nevertheless, the cases simply are not typical enough to establish that the United States, *in general,* does not respect voting rights or that narcotics, *in general,* are not habit-forming.

Notice that the evidence in these examples is acceptable and relevant, but insufficient to support the conclusion drawn. An argument that contains acceptable and relevant evidence can give the *appearance* of acceptability. But acceptable, relevant premises may not provide adequate support, in which case, any generalization drawn from them is hasty.

In *extended arguments, hasty generalizations often function as premises.* Thus, the writer does not form the generalization, but assumes it as the legitimate inference of an unexpressed argument or line of reasoning. When functioning as premises, hasty generalizations usually take the form of unqualified statements, for example:

Punishment always deters crime.
Consumers choose on the basis of emotion, not reason.
Foreign policy is too complex to be understood by the average voter.
Men make better scientists, engineers, and mathematicians than women do.
Politicians always operate out of self-interest.
Philosophy tests are not clear.
Police officers have an authority complex.
Only specialists can understand modern poetry.

If such generalizations are to be used at all, they need to be qualified with words and phrases such as those given in Chapter 3 — *some, many, a percentage,* and so on. Used as a premise, a generalization that is questionable can be considered a hasty generalization.

    Also worth noting is the connection between labels and hasty generalizations. *Sometimes the basis for a hasty generalization is a mere evaluative or identifying word.* Advertising copy provides numerous examples. Thus, the makers of ULTRA-BRITE toothpaste would like consumers to infer, presumably from nothing more than the name, that using that toothpaste will dramatically brighten their teeth. The makers of GLEEM would have us believe, on the basis of its name alone, that using its product will make our teeth gleam. Similarly, the makers of computers invite us to infer that their computers are easy to master because they are billed as "user friendly." The label lure is hardly confined to advertising. For example, a person forms a hasty generalization when inferring, on the basis of their names alone, that "Americans for Democratic Action" and "The Moral Majority" necessarily represent the will of the people, as these organizational titles imply.

    The flip side of forming a hasty generalization on the basis of a label or evaluative term is to use such a term without sufficient evidence. For example, on learning that his daughter plans to quit school to marry, a father calls her "rebellious." Maybe she is, but quitting school to marry is not enough to prove she is rebellious. Similarly, some of the most egregious corporate polluters have appropriated the term *environmentalist* merely because they have let a species or two escape their bulldozers, nets, and drills. When used honestly — that is, when supported by an adequte body of evidence — a label or identifying term can be an efficient expression of evidence, but without sufficient support, it masks a hasty generalization.

Misapplied Generalization

We may consider the misapplied generalization as a fallacy that consists in erroneously applying a general rule or principle to an exception to it. The error arises from assuming that what is true under some circumstances must be true under all circumstances. Consider, for example, this argument with the operative generalization italicized:

Speaking of . . .

Hasty Generalization

A Popular Vice

Hasty generalization is perhaps the most important of popular vices in thinking. It is interesting to speculate on some of the reasons for this kind of bad thinking. One important factor is prejudice. If we are already prejudiced against unions, or businessmen, or lawyers, or doctors, or Jews or blacks, then one or two instances of bad conduct by members of these groups will give us the unshakeable conviction that "they're all like that." It is very difficult for a prejudiced person to say, "Some are, and some aren't." A prejudice is a judgment formed *before* examining the evidence.

A psychological reason for asserting "wild" generalizations is exhibitionism: The exhibitionist desires to attract attention to himself. No one pays much attention to such undramatic statements such as "Some women are fickle," or that some are liars, or "Some politicians are no better than they ought to be." But when one says that "all women are liars," this immediately attracts notice. Goethe once said that it is easy to appear brilliant if one respects nothing, not even the truth.

Let us avoid careless hasty generalizing. The proverb warns us that one swallow does not make a summer. Unfortunately, we usually forget proverbs on the occasions when we ought to remember them. We ought to emulate "the Reverend" in Faulkner's novel, *The Hamlet*. He was discussing the efficacy of a rural remedy. "Do you know how it will work Reverend?" his friend asked. "I know it worked once," the Reverend answered. "Oh, then you have knowed it to fail?" "I never knowed it to be tried but once." The fault of bad generalizing, however, need not make us take refuge in the opposite error; the refusal to generalize. This error is illustrated in the anecdote concerning the student who wrote an essay on labor relations, in which he argued equal pay for women. Women, he wrote, work hard, they need the money, they are the foundation of the family, and, most important, they are the mothers of most of the human race! There is another old anecdote about the cautious man whose friend pointed to a flock of sheep with the remark, "Those sheep seem to have been sheared recently." "Yes," said the cautious man, "at least on this side."

(Lionel Ruby, *The Art of Making Sense.*)

U.S. citizens have a right to travel where they want. Therefore, prisoners have a right to travel where they want.

Notice that the premise expresses a general principle that we ordinarily accept. The writer is using it as a basis for inferring that prisoners, who are U.S. citizens, have a right to travel where they want. The problem with the preceding argument is not that the arguer has formed a conclusion hastily, but has applied a generalization, which is true under most circumstances, to the exceptive case of prisoners. This argument, therefore, represents a misapplied generalization, not a hasty one.

A common argument against administering powerful painkillers to the terminally ill in excruciating pain is that these patients will become addicted to the drugs. Although it is true that powerful drugs can be addictive, they need not always be. Under proper supervision, they can be used effectively with no addictive effect. The experience of institutions that care for the terminally ill—for example, hospices—indicates that rarely if ever does addiction result from administration of even the most powerful of painkillers. The misapplication of the generalization, then, results from overlooking an exception, namely, the unique case posed by the suffering terminally ill.

EXERCISES ON HASTY AND MISAPPLIED GENERALIZATIONS

Explain whether the generalization (italicized) in each of the following arguments is hastily formed or misapplied.

1. Moscow, Russia, is the only city in the world that is defended by anti-ballistic missiles designed to destroy nuclear warheads. On May 28, 1987, a 19-year-old German man flew a single-engine Cessna-172 from Helsinki to Moscow, crossing the heavily defended Baltic Sea border and landing, unimpeded, next to the Kremlin Wall at the foot of Red Square. It is concluded, on the basis of this incident, that *the Soviet Union, including its capital, is quite vulnerable to air attack.*

2. During the purges and spy-mania of the late 1930s in Russia, Soviet propagandists were hard-pressed to boost Joseph Stalin's image. An opportunity came in 1938, when a young Briton flew his light plane into the Soviet Union in search of his Russian sweetheart. Through Stalin's intervention, the Briton was not only not imprisoned but allowed to marry the young woman. "Love knows no frontiers," Stalin was supposed to have said. In memoirs published by Soviet writer Lev Sheinin in 1959, the incident was used to suggest that, on balance, *Stalin wasn't really such a bad fellow.*

3. On November 25, 1986, Fawn Hall's "dream boss," Oliver North, was fired on national television. Immediately afterward, as she cleaned out her desk, Hall found potentially incriminating duplicates of documents that she and North had destroyed or rewritten days before. She proceeded to stuff the papers into her boots and down the back of her dress, then strolled out of the White House grounds with the highly classified material. When later asked by investigators about her actions, Hall defended herself by saying: *"Sometimes you have to go above the written law."*

4. Letter to the editor: "Watching Fawn Hall and listening to the studied way in which she answered questions made it at once apparent that *she had not only been coached in how to dress for the 'show' but also exactly how to address the august*

body questioning her. For she carefully used the term 'sir' in the super respectful manner of a Marine Corps member."

5. News Item: "At a noon press conference, Los Angeles Distric Attorney Ira Reiner said the daylight theft of his car in front of a busy and exclusive restaurant proves that *'No one's safe anywhere, anytime.'*"

6. Letter to the editor: "I think it is about time that Jesse Jackson got his priorities straightened out and stopped trying to dictate to Americans the terms he will accept regarding equal rights. The very term 'equal rights' has been misrepresented; all people do not have equal rights. *Does a many-times-convicted criminal have the same rights as a law-abiding citizen?*"

7. Letter to the editor: "I'll always remember the late comedian Jackie Gleason fondly because he was 71 when he died, thereby proving that *you can eat all you want, drink all the booze you want, smoke cigars, chase women until your legs start to go, and all it costs you is two years off your life expectancy. That's a terrific trade.*"

8. During the trial of former Gestapo chief of Lyon Klaus Barbie, his attorney, Jean Martin d'Bemba, attempted to counter charges of racism against his client. d'Bemba, a black lawyer from Brazzaville in the Congo, argued: "*Someone who believes in the superiority of the white race over the black race cannot hide this sentiment.* Can you imagine Adolf Hitler, if he were alive today, shaking the hand of a black man? But Klaus Barbie, when he met me, took my hand within his two hands and held it warmly." (From which it presumably follows that Barbie is no racist.)

9. During the Iran-Contra hearing, Oliver North admitted making "blatantly false" representations to the Iranians in order to advance the arms-for-hostages deal. Regarding the misrepresentation, Senate Counsel Arthur L. Liman asked North: "Did you also talk about the fact that there were two million homeless people in Iran? . . . And did you talk about the fact that the United States would supply aid, like the Marshall Plan, for them?" North: "The fact that I exaggerated my connection with the president of the United States . . . I have already admitted. The fact is, *we in this country have always expressed concern for those kinds of matters. . . .*" (From which it presumably follows that North's misrepresentations were justified.)

10. A poll conducted in February 1987 found that Americans opposed aid to the Nicaraguan Contras, fifty-four percent to thirty-one percent, with fifteen percent undecided. Five months later, during North's testimony before the congressional hearings investigating Iran-Contra, a poll finds Americans equally divided on the issue, forty-two percent to forty-two percent, with sixteen percent undecided. It is concluded that *public sentiment has swung back in favor of supporting the Contras.*

11. Asked why President Reagan could not recall signing a "finding" approving an arms-for-hostages deal with the Iranians, presidential spokesperson Marlin Fitzwater defended his boss by pointing out: "*The president deals with hundreds and thousands of pieces of information and documents in a day, in a week, and in a year.*"

12. Letter to the editor: "Probably, if a test were given, the sad news would be that

most school kids today have heard of Ollie North but not of Neil Armstrong. Just as sad, the same would be true of adults. *What is it about a confessed liar that infatuates the American public is beyond me."*

13. During the Watergate investigation of 1973, special prosecutor Archibald Cox subpoenaed presidential tapes he believed were relevant to the investigation of possible "high crimes and misdemeanors" in the executive branch. Robert Bork, who was at that time Solicitor General, told President Nixon that he did not have to surrender the tapes. Some years later, when he had been nominated by President Reagan for the Supreme Court, Bork was asked to defend his advice. Bork responded by saying that *it was his job to defend executive privilege.*

14. Nominee to the Supreme Court Douglas Ginsburg had served on the U.S. Court of Appeals for the Washington D.C. circuit fourteen months before his nomination to the Supreme Court. Previously, he had been an official in the Justice Department and at the Office of Management and Budget. He had written little; so his view on a wide range of constitutional issues, such as abortion, privacy rights, and rights of minorities, were not known. Most of his writing focused on technical, regulatory, and antitrust issues. In welcoming the Ginsburg nomination on the day it was announced, Senate Minority Leader Robert Dole described *Ginsburg as well qualified.*

15. The "Speech and Debate" clause of the Constitution says that "for any Speech or Debate in either House (Senators and Representatives) shall not be questioned in any other Place." *The clause,* intended as a separation-of-powers safeguard, *prohibits prosecutors and judges from accusing or convicting Congress members of crimes while on official business.* After Representative Mario Biaggi (D-N.Y.) was convicted in federal court of accepting an illegal gratuity—a Florida-spa vacation for himself and a woman friend—House Speaker Jim Wright (D-Tex.) had the House's general counsel file a brief with the court, arguing that because Biaggi had also visited a Florida nursing home on official business, he should be immune from prosecution, whatever else went on during the trip. (Biaggi got two years in jail and a $500,000 fine.)

Neglect of Relevant Evidence

The fallacy of neglect of relevant evidence consists in overlooking or downplaying significant evidence unfavorable to one's position. For example, an investment counselor advises a client to invest in municipal funds because they are "tax-free." However, the counselor overlooks the following additional information that is *unfavorable* to the advice: (1) interest from municipal bonds is less than that from treasury or corporate bonds, and (2) many municipal bonds can be heavily discounted, which means their prices often are less than their face value.

Sometimes the evidence neglected relates to the observations on which a generalization is based. For example, as of 1989, according to U.S. government estimates, two-thirds of all American adults have had their blood cholesterol measured, many of them by "finger-stick" tests. In fact, the finger-stick test has become popular at malls and supermarkets. Before accepting the results of such tests, keep in mind the following traits which typically go unmentioned but bear directly on the tests' results: (1) Finger-stick tests must be done properly. Thus, squeezing the finger, rather than having the blood flow freely, can dilute or break down red blood cells and yield a false result; (2) a random selection of seventy-one screening sites monitored by government employees, who had their own cholesterol levels measured, indicated that in more than half the cases observed finger pricks were done improperly; (3) conditions at the screening sites often are frenetic and the staff distracted; (4) the personnel taking the measurements frequently are untrained and inexperienced; (5) reliable cholesterol measurements require fasting for about twelve hours prior to the test. Clearly this additional information makes, or should make, one skeptical about the reliability of the observations that are made during a typical finger-stick test. The unreliability of the observations, in turn, counts as unfavorable evidence to the results of the test.

Other times, neglected evidence is of a statistical nature. Consider, for example, the highly publicized connection between oat bran and blood cholesterol. You may recall headlines and news stories in 1990 that made it sound as if a study of oat bran had single-handedly demolished the billion-dollar oats industry and, along with it, nutritionists' quarter-of-a-century-old claim that a long-term diet high in oat products and/or other foods rich in soluble fiber can lower blood cholesterol levels. The news reports were based on a study reported in the *New England Journal of Medicine* on January 18, 1990. The study involved twenty patients, who were told to add about three ounces of oat bran to their normal diet for six weeks. This led to a 7.5 percent drop in their total blood cholesterol. The same people then ate a similar diet, but with low-fiber wheat products instead of oat bran. Their cholesterol levels fell nearly as much, 7 percent, over the same length of time. Researchers concluded that this small drop occurred because *both* diets made the subjects lower their intake of saturated fat and dietary cholesterol. Presumably, the oat bran, as well as the wheat products, substituted for fatty foods such as bacon and eggs. Most important, the oat bran seemingly had nothing to do with it—any high-carbohydrate food would do, perhaps even white bread. Thus, the news reports began discrediting the belief that oat bran and other types of fiber lower blood cholesterol.

Even if the study was well designed, the sample was too small to justify the researchers' conclusions, let alone the newscasters'. Beyond the inadequate sample, media reports *neglected to reveal* that participants in the study initially had cholesterol levels in what the American Heart Association considers the *desirable* range (averaging 186 milligrams per deciliter). It should not have been surprising, therefore, that oat bran failed to reduce these levels further, because earlier studies had consistently discovered that the greatest cholesterol reductions occur in persons with cholesterol readings well into the *undesirable* range. Also neglected was the fact that all participants began with a healthful diet fairly low in fat and high in fiber, averaging twenty-three grams of fiber a day, about twice as much as most Americans; but, again, most of the earlier studies supporting the efficacy of oat bran in controlling cholesterol studied subjects with dangerously high cholesterol levels and far less healthful diets.

This additional information, which did not appear in the mass media, effectively evacuates the media's interpretations of the study's findings. Still, it is a safe bet that few of their readers and viewers had these facts. So, any of them who made a sudden change in their diets on the basis of these reports acted on a faulty generalization that resulted from the neglect of relevant statistical evidence.

The same problem is represented in recent media stories claiming that coffee raises cholesterol levels. As evidence for this claim, many newspaper accounts simply reported the findings of clinical studies which showed that adults who drink at least four cups of coffee a day significantly raise their "bad" cholesterol levels (LDL). However, the evidence that generally went unreported was that only *boiled* coffee seems to have this effect. There is very little, if any, change in the LDL levels of those who drink the same amount of *filtered* coffee. Is this significant? For Americans it is, because virtually none of us drink boiled coffee, a method used in some parts of Europe.

Of course, the neglected relevant evidence may be nonstatistical. For example, in the late 1970s, the Soviet Union launched a campaign against neutron weapons by announcing that, even though it had the capacity to build such weapons, it would not. This act of self-restraint presumably was intended to demonstrate the Soviet commitment to arms limitation and persuade the United States to end its flirtation with the neutron bomb. What the Soviets neglected to mention, however, was that unlike NATO forces, they had no use for such a weapon, since it is designed primarily for use against overwhelming tank forces. A superior number of tanks was one of the Soviet's military advantages in Europe. When, in 1981, the United States decided to start producing and stockpiling neutron warheads, the Kremlin labeled the weapons "colonial" and "capitalistic," because they are designed to kill people while sparing property. The Kremlin did not mention, however, that the people targeted were Soviet and Warsaw Pact tank crews, and the property was European cities, including their civilian habitants. For its part, the U.S. State Department, in attempting to sell skeptical NATO members on the idea of neutron weapons, emphasized that the weapons would be produced and stored in the United States, while conveniently downplaying the fact that was unsettling to its NATO allies—the weapons were intended for ultimate *deployment*, not in the United States, but in Europe.

IN BRIEF   If you want to determine whether a piece of neglected evidence is significant to an argument, ask yourself this question: Does it make the conclusion less acceptable? If it does, the fallacy of neglect of relevant evidence is present.

Three Guidelines for Uncovering Neglected Evidence

A good argumentative essay—one that is logically persuasive—confronts unfavorable evidence and attempts to refute it, but many essays do not do this. Zealously attempting to win acceptance of their theses, writers often overlook or suppress unfavorable evidence, much like a lawyer omits evidence unfavorable to her case. The courtroom, however, provides the opposing attorney ample opportunity to "set the record straight." As readers, we do not have that luxury—we must function as our own lawyer, as it were, and judge and jury as well. Consequently, we need to be reasonably well informed about the topic under discussion in order to discover neglected relevant evidence. Reason enough, then, to stock our minds with lots of diverse information, for supplementing specialized training with general education courses, and for developing eclectic reading habits.

Even when faced with an essay on a subject about which we know little, we can still help ourselves tease out of it possible neglected evidence as follows.

1. Be suspicious of any essay that fails to acknowledge counterarguments to its position.   Remember that, in its classical form, the argumentative essay includes *refutation.* When the issues are complex, this means more than just token acknowledgement of the other side. It can call for identifying and countering the opposition's key points. An essay that does not even attempt to do this may be flawed not only stylistically but logically as well. Omitting unfavorable evidence detracts from the writers' *persona* of being fair-minded and even-handed and signals to the audience, or should, that opposing points may be so damaging to the writer's argument that he does not want to mention them.

2. Be especially cautious of arguments that advance value or social policy theses.   That we struggle, as individuals and as a society, to formulate clear and convincing positions on questions concerning abortion, capital punishment, gun control, sex education, animal experimentation, and nuclear powerplants, testifies to the multilayered nature of these topics. We should see signs of this complexity and authorial struggle to deal with it in any essay that engages such topics—that is, a clear indication that the author has considered all significant counterevidence. An essay that glibly advances a highly controversial generalization without confronting mainstay counterevidence, likely as not, is neglecting relevant evidence.

On the other hand, an essay that faces up to the opposition not only shows the courage of the writer's conviction and respect for the intelligence of the audience, but establishes a basis for an "on balance" resolution—in other words, a generalization drawn from a consideration of *all* relevant evidence. As an example, consider this passage from an essay that argues for strong affirmative action, that is, definite preference for women and minorities in hiring and promoting. In this excerpt, the author raises and reacts to positions *opposed* to his own:

> . . . *[Strong affirmative action]* is justified, most clearly with respect to blacks. But I also believe that a defender of the practice must acknowledge that there are serious arguments against it, and that it is defensible only because the arguments for it have great weight. Moral opinion in this country is sharply divided over the issue because significant values are involved in both sides. My own view is that while strong affirmative action is intrinsically undesirable, it is a legitimate and perhaps indispensable method of pursuing a goal so important to the national welfare that it can be justified as a temporary, though not short-term, policy for both public and private institutions. In this respect it is like other policies that impose burdens on some for the public good. . . .

There are three *objections* to strong affirmative action: that it is inefficient; that it is unfair; and that it damages self-esteem.

The degree of inefficiency depends on how strong a role racial or sexual preference plays in the process of selection. Among candidates meeting the basic qualification for a position, those better qualified will on the average perform better, whether they are doctors, policemen, teachers, or electricians. There may be some cases, as in preferential college admissions, where the immediate usefulness of making educational resources available to an individual is thought to be greater because of the use to which the education will be put or because of the internal effects on the institution itself. But by and large, policies of strong affirmative action must reckon with the costs of some lowering in performance level: the stronger the preference, the larger the cost to be justified. Since both the costs and the value of the results will vary from case to case, this suggests that no one policy of affirmative action is likely to be correct in all cases, and that the cost in performance level should be taken into account in the design of a legitimate policy.

The charge of unfairness arouses the deepest disagreements. To be passed over because of membership in a group one was born into, where this has nothing to do with one's individual qualifications for a position, can arouse strong feelings of resentment. It is a departure from the ideal—one of the values finally recognized in our society—that people should be judged so far as possible on the basis of individual characteristics rather than involuntary group membership.

This does not mean that strong affirmative action is normally repugnant in the manner of racial or sexual discrimination. It is nothing like those practices, for though like them it employs race and sex as criteria of selection, it does so for entirely different reasons. Racial and sexual discrimination are based on contempt or even loathing for the excluded group, a feeling that certain contacts with them are degrading to members of the dominant group, that they are fit only for subordinate positions or menial work. Strong affirmative action involves none of this: it is simply a means of increasing the social and economic strength of formerly victimized groups and does not stigmatize others.

There is an element of individual unfairness here, but it is more like the unfairness of conscription in wartime, or of property condemnation under the right of eminent domain. Those who benefit or lose out because of their race or sex cannot be said to deserve their good or bad fortune. . . .

The third objection concerns self-esteem, and is particularly serious. While strong affirmative action is in effect, and generally known to be so, no one in an affirmative action category who gets a desirable job or is admitted to a selective university can be sure that he or she has not benefited from the policy. Even those who would have made it anyway fall under suspicion, from themselves and from others: it comes to be widely felt that success does not mean the same thing for women and minorities. This painful damage to esteem cannot be avoided. It should make any defender of strong affirmative action want the practice to end as soon as it has achieved its basic purpose. . . .[2]

---

[2]Thomas Nagel in testimony presented before the Subcommittee on the Constitution of the Senate Judiciary Committee, June 18, 1981.

After examining these three objections and trying to assess their weight, the author then proceeded to present what he considered strong countervailing reasons for accepting a policy of strong affirmative action.

3. Be especially careful of positions that you happen to agree with.   When we are emotionally or intellectually predisposed to a position, we tend to be less critical of the argument that advances it than of one that opposes it. Just as we tend to like people who like us and overlook their flaws, in reading we are inclined to blindly endorse arguments that reflect our own thinking and overlook their weaknesses. This human tendency to agree with what we find agreeable sets us up to overlook or ignore unfavorable evidence that an author may have omitted.

EXERCISES ON NEGLECT OF RELEVANT EVIDENCE*

1. Last year the Duchy of Fenwick received $1 billion in loans from the World Monetary Fund, and its GNP grew by 5 percent. This year, the Duchy has requested $2 billion in loans, and its leaders expect that its GNP will rise by a full 10 percent. Which of the following facts, if any, would represent significant unfavorable evidence that the Duchy's leaders neglected to point out?
   A. The 5 percent GNP increase last year is attributable to extraordinarily large harvests, owing to unusally good weather.
   B. The Duchy of Fenwick's economy is not strong enough to absorb more than $3 billion in outside capital each year.
   C. The Duchy of Fenwick does not have sufficient heavy industry to fuel an increase in its GNP by more than 3 percent.
   D. Tourism, which accounts for a fraction of 1 percent of the Duchy's GNP, was down last year, owing to political unrest.
2. In May of 1987, President Reagan slapped Japanese TV manufacturers with a 100 percent tariff, to remain in effect until Japan agreed to buy semiconductors (chips) from U.S. manufacturers. Six weeks later, Reagan lifted the sanctions, saying that the Japanese had agreed to buy U.S. chips. In the interim, the Administration pointed out, Japanese companies were prohibited from shipping $51 million worth of 20-inch TV sets to the United States. Thus, said Administration officials, the sanctions had effectively cut the U.S. trade deficit by $51 million. Which, if any, of the following facts would constitute relevant unfavorable evidence that the Administration neglected to mention?
   A. Long before the tariff was imposed, the Japanese had all but stopped shipping sets to the United States, opting to sell out of plants in the United States.
   B. Well before the sanctions, the rise of the Japanese yen compared with the falling U.S. dollar had made TV sets exported from Japan very expensive.
   C. TV sets imported from Japan were hard to find in the United States by the end of March, a month before the sanctions were imposed.

3. In the summer of 1987, a House Rules subcommittee was considering bills that would allow refugees from Nicaragua and El Salvador to stay in the United States temporarily while the General Accounting Office assessed whether they would face persecution back home. Speaking in favor of the bill, subcommittee Chairperson Joe Moakley (D-MA) said, "There are violent wars ensuing [*sic*] in both El Salvador and Nicaragua—there can be no denying that basic fact." Would this fact nudge you to vote for the bill? If so, would you be less inclined to vote for the bill if Moakley had also pointed out that, at the time, there were over forty wars of one type or another occurring in the world, although people from those war-torn countries were not extended the same consideration as Nicaraguan and El Salvadoran refugees?

4. Suppose you are a member of a jury that has just convicted a man of murder for which he can receive the death penalty. Before you sentence the defendant, the judge informs you under what is termed the "Briggs instruction," that the governor can commute a sentence of life in prison, thereby clearing the way for parole of a convicted murderer. Do you think this instruction would make you more or less disposed toward giving the death penalty? Would the following fact, which the U.S. Supreme Court has ruled does *not* have to be mentioned, affect the impact of the "Briggs instruction": *The governor can also commute death sentences?*

5. What do you think would be readers' reaction to the following "Question of the Week" posed by a newspaper: "What do you think of a recent Supreme Court ruling that government restrictions can amount to an unconstitutional 'taking' of private property?" In fact, the response was overwhelmingly supportive of the ruling. Do you think it might have been otherwise if the newspaper had mentioned that the Court had emphasized that its ruling involves only cases in which all use of land is blocked and was silent on whether regulating use of property short of total deprivation may constitute a "taking" of private property?

6. Suppose you were present on the House floor when Representative Gerald Solomon (R-NY), pointing to a photograph of Soviet submarines cruising near the coast of Texas, said, "God bless Ollie North for alerting us. We owe him a debt of gratitude." Would you be inclined to be sympathetic toward North? If so, would your sympathy ebb if Solomon also mentioned that it is commonplace for nations to cruise the international waters off the coasts of other nations, and that the United States does it regularly?

7. Los Angeles Mayor Tom Bradley told a news conference that he and aides had held round-the-clock discussions with the Pentagon about potentially danerous rocket fuel being trucked through Los Angeles on route to a local Air Force base. The Pentagon had agreed, Bradley reported happily, not to ship toxic fuel through the city during the next sixty days while considering less congested routing. What impressions of Mayor Bradley and the Pentagon would you likely form on the basis of this announcement? Would your feelings change if you knew that the Pentagon never had any plans to ship the dangerous fuel through Los Angeles during that sixty-day period, and that it made no promise to refrain from doing so after the sixty days had passed?

MODULE 9.5

AUTHORITY AS EVIDENCE

Most of the generalizations we hold are not based on our own observations, but on the observations of others. We take and claim much on the authoritative say-so of somebody else. Quite often in argument, these authoritative sources are cited as support for claim. For example, someone might argue: "Cigarette smoking is unhealthful because the Surgeon General says so." Of course, it is not the Surgeon General's opinion that makes cigarette smoking unhealthful. It is the fact that cigarette smoking has been found unhealthful on the basis of extensive clinical observations, study, and analysis. When the person supports the claim about cigarette smoking by appeal to the Surgeon General, he is, by implication, invoking the enormous body of evidence — the observed specifics — that the Surgeon General is eminently qualified by training and position to be familiar with.

On the other hand, if someone said: "Gold is a good investment, because the Surgeon General says so," you would probably wince. "What does the Surgeon General know about gold as an investment?" you might ask, "He's not qualified to speak as an authority on financial investments." You are right — the Surgeon General is not in a position to have made, or to be intimately familiar with, the observations necessary to support the claim. If, on the other hand, the person said: "Gold's a good investment, according to my financial counselor," you would likely be more impressed because a financial counselor could be in a position to speak with authority on the issue. You would be less impressed with the argument if you had just read an article in *The Wall Street Journal* cautioning against investment in gold, for there is obvious disagreement among the experts.

The opinion and wisdom of others may be the most common means of attempting to support a thesis in an argumentative essay. In fact, it is a rare essay that does not employ some appeal to authority as support for a claim. If you reconsider the essays in this textbook, you will meet the appeal to authority at one turn or another in virtually all the arguments. Thus, the authors variously use individuals, institutions (religious, governmental, educational), books (for example, the Bible), and other sources to give their positions authoritative clout. Whatever its form, the appeal to authority — that is, the testimony of others, informed opinion, expert witness, and so on — makes a thesis credible; that is why authors use it. Our job in evaluating arguments that rely on authority is to determine when expert opinion is used legitimately and when it is not. Most appeals to authority can be evaluated by asking and answering two basic questions.

Two Questions for Evaluating Authority

1. How much does the source know about the specific question at issue?   If the source is not an authority on the issue, his viewpoint is irrelevant. As we learned earlier, the introduction of irrelevancy violates a basic criterion of an acceptable argument — that its premises be relevant to the conclusion. (This is why, incidentally, appeals to authority often are discussed under fallacies of irrelevance. We are considering them here instead in order to emphasize their role as evidence for generalizations.)

Advertising provides the most obvious examples of irrelevant sources of authority. Exploiting our adulation of athletes, movie stars, TV personalities, and the like, advertisers use these figures in the hope that a naïve audience will transfer the celebrity's credibility to an area where there is no logical reason for accepting that credibility. Thus, because actress Lindsay Wagner praises Ford automobiles and TV talk-show sexologist Dr. Ruth Westheimer lauds Signal mouthwash, we are supposed to buy these products. But Wagner's expertise in acting and Westheimer's in sexology does not qualify them to make authoritative statements about cars and mouthwashes.

Of course, the abuse of authority in many ads (and their first cousins, political endorsements) is easy to spot. This is not always the case, certainly not in extended arguments, which often invoke economists, scientists, politicians, religious and educational leaders, and other "heavyweights" to support their claims. Still, the test of genuine authority applies equally in these contexts. Remember that an expert's opinion is good evidence only in the area in which she is an expert. Thus, an economist's view on the subject of atmospheric pollution may or may not be relevant, depending on the point she is trying to make. If the opinion pertains to the economics of pollution, the expertise is relevant; but if the opinion deals with the health hazards of pollution, then it is suspect. This does not mean the person's opinion is incorrect — it could well be on-target. The opinion is not the issue, the qualifications of the person is; for it is the expert's credibility on which the essay is trading to establish the credibility of the opinion. The author is, in effect, asking the audience to accept the opinion on the expert's say-so.

2. What do other authorities say about the matter?   Even though an authority has expertise in the area under discussion, citing that opinion may be irrelevant if it is not supported by a majority of other authorities in that field. So, if a nutritionist claims that Vitamin C can cure the common cold, his opinion is not authoritative if a majority of other qualified people in the field dispute it. After all, if you try hard enough, you can generally find someone who has said something in support of even the most foolish statements in his alleged field of expertise. In fact, this is the problem that haunts trials in which a defendant pleads innocent by reason of insanity. No sooner does the defense usher in a bevy of psychologists testifying to the insanity of the defendant, than the prosecution trots out a string of equally qualified experts who adjudge the defendant sane. (The esteemed John Marshall (1854–1925), who served as Chief Justice of the United States Supreme Court for thirty-five years, once made much the same point about the relative ease of securing authoritative support for a judicial decision. Immediately upon hearing the arguments in a case, Marshall, who was serving with the fastidious Justice Joseph Story, is said to have quipped: "Judgment for the plaintiff. Justice Story will provide the authorities.")

You may feel vaguely uneasy with this consensus test of authority on grounds that it is itself an objectionable appeal to status quo thought. Thus, "Why should an opinion expressed by an expert in the field be judged on the basis of how well it fits in with accepted thought? After all, doesn't the history of science glitter with examples of how inaccurate and incomplete accepted thought can be?" This query is understandable and deserving of a reply.

Compatibility with a body of knowledge already accepted as true is in fact an eminently reasonable criterion for evaluating expert opinion if we keep in mind the following. In trying to encompass additional facts, any field of organized knowledge and beliefs seeks to achieve a system of explanatory hypotheses, which are basically assumptions whose truth is under investigation. But such a system must be self-consistent. A body of self-contradictory statements cannot be intelligible, let alone true. In doing science, to cite just one discipline, scientists hope to perfect such a system by expanding their hypotheses so that they account for more and more facts. But to make any progress, they must attempt to fit new hypotheses to hypotheses that have already been confirmed.

Nevertheless, it is true that many important new hypotheses were not compatible with existing accepted beliefs. For example, in the twentieth century Einstein's theory of relativity unmoored many Newtonian suppositions. Similarly, the phenomenon of radioactivity, first observed in the 1890s, led to the modification of many time-honored theories. One of these was the principle of the conservation of matter, which held that matter could be neither increased nor destroyed. The belief that radium atoms underwent spontaneous disintegration did not fit in with that principle, but it was not summarily dismissed. In fact, the principle was modified and ultimately became the more comprehensive principle of the conservation of mass-energy. Even in these instances, however, a compatibility with expert opinion operated, for each of these hypotheses could account for the same facts as well as, or better than, the other hypotheses could.

An organized body of knowledge does not develop capriciously. Any change in an accepted belief represents an improvement by making an explanation more comprehensive. The criterion of compatibility is a vital part of this organic development. Thus, it is quite correct to say that, if an expert's opinion agrees with established thought, its reliability is thereby strengthened; conversely, if it does not, it is thereby weakened, though admittedly not disproved.

Only if the two aforementioned questions can be answered "yes" may the appeal to authority be considered relevant evidence. If the authority fails either of these question-tests, then it is a false or questionable authority. **The fallacy of false or questionable authority, then, consists in attempting to support a claim by quoting the judgments of someone (1) who is not an authority in the field, or (2) whose opinion is not supported by the majority in the field.**

There are two variations of the questionable authority fallacy that occur frequently enough to be aware of: popularity and tradition.

The Appeal to Popularity

The fallacy of popularity (a.k.a. the bandwagon effect or common opinion) consists in urging acceptance of a position merely because large numbers of people support it. In an appeal to popularity, sheer numbers take on the force of

Speaking of . . .

Evaluating Authority

The Case for Psychic Phenomena

"I hope I never see a flying saucer," a friend of mine once told me. "And I certainly hope I never go for a ride in one."

"Why not?" I wondered.

"Because," he said, "I don't want everybody to think I'm crazy."

This conversation came to mind while reading "Margins of Reality" by Robert G. Jahn and Brenda J. Dunne, a book, to put the matter bluntly, that lays out an experimental case on behalf of psychic phenomena. Telepathy, psychokinesis, precognition, in short, the works.

Where to begin? The authors are neither kooks nor charlatans. They have impressive credentials. One of them (Jahn) is dean emeritus of the School of Engineering and Applied Sciences at Princeton University. His co-author (Dunne) is manager of the Princeton Engineering Anomalies Research laboratory, where the experiments described in this book were conducted over the last decade.

Throughout, they adopt a moderate and reasonable stance, which makes it hard for their opponents not to seem unreasonable. "It could be unwise," they say, "to dismiss categorically the possibility that human consciousness may be capable of more than passive interaction with its microelectronic aids. Can we be quite confident, for example, of the invulnerability of all modern instrumentation, control and operational equipment to inadvertent or intentional disburbance associated in any way with the psyches of its human operators, especially in periods of intense emotional stress or intellectual demand? . . . Or should some direct, systematic study be mounted to assess the possibilities of such interactions?"

Notice how reasonable they are. Anyone who dismisses the possibility of the psychic interaction of people and machines must be unreasonable and closed-minded. What scientist wants to be called that? Who could oppose a "systematic study"? Scientists are supposed to be open to new ideas.

But the authors know full well that their views are heretical. "Seldom do we present a technical seminar, entertain visitors to the laboratory, or engage in discussions with our professional colleagues that some question does not eventually arise concerning our motivation in pursuing these studies," they write.

"Occasionally, such queries are cast in quite direct, even blunt terms, such as 'What are nice folks like you doing in a field like this?' or 'I'm surprised to find someone of your background interested in such topics.' "

I'll leave aside the experimental results that Jahn and Dunne report, which persuade them that more is going on in the world than traditional

continued

continued

science takes account of. Suffice to say that they have conducted experiments under carefully controlled conditions in which, they claim, human thought affects the behavior of machinery.

I am not in a position to decide which of their anomalies are statistically significant and which ones aren't, so I leave it to scientists to decide whether these findings should be pursued further or dismissed outright.

What is really at issue here are the broad questions of how do we know what we know and what makes an argument persuasive? If someone doesn't want to be persuaded of something, he can always say, "Show me more data." How much data is enough?

The answer to that question is not clear, but there is a good rule of thumb: *Extraordinary claims require extraordinary proof.* The experimental findings of Jahn and Dunne fly in the face of virtually every shred of evidence that science has amassed for hundreds of years at least.

It is not merely an article of faith among scientists that psychic phenomena are impossible. It is a view of the world bolstered by experiment after experiment after experiment.

Now, Jahn and Dunne claim that great changes in science are always brought about by experimental anomalies that scientists at first ignore and then try to sweep under the rug. Some results don't fit with the existing theories, and they don't do away.

The arguments are always the same. The established view says, "Oh, but there is so much evidence supporting us." Their opponents respond, "Yes, but what about these anomalies?" That is how Copernicus overthrew the Ptolemaic model of the solar system, and that is how Einstein overthrew Newtonian physics.

The trouble is that not every new theory is right. In fact, most of them are wrong. The Copernicuses and Einsteins are rare indeed.

Have Jahn and Dunne identified anomalies that will wind up overthrowing modern science? Nothing less is at stake here. I don't want to appear closedminded, but my money is on science. (italics added)

(Lee Dembart, "The Case for Psychic Phenomena," Copyright 1989, *Los Angeles Times.* Reprinted by permission.)

authority, as in, "Two million people have seen this film. Isn't it about time you did?" or "Professor Jones must be a good instructor because her classes are always heavily enrolled." Notice how the speakers assume that the numbers of people who have seen the film or enrolled in Professor Jones' class are relevant reasons for accepting their claims. But numbers do not prove the truth or merit of an idea—thus, the fallacy of popularity.

The fallacy of popularity in these two passages was easy to pick out. But popularity can be subtle and elusive when offered as support of social policy positions. For example, faced with a $700 million surplus, the California legislature in 1987 voted to give the money to schools to carry out what the legislature termed desperately needed educational reforms. Governor George Deukmejian, however, vetoed the plan, preferring to return the money to taxpayers. Specifically, the governor proposed a multiple-choice box on the income-tax form, whereby taxpayers could indicate whether they wanted money back or wanted it to go to the schools. Deukmejian subsequently defended his tax rebate plan by pointing out that the vast majority of taxpayers voted to have the money back.

The implication of the Deukmejian defense is that the best and fairest use of the money was rightly determined by a taxpayer head count. But that a majority wants or believes something does not make it fair or wise. To be sure, government officials need to be sensitive to the feelings of their constituencies, but they must also provide leadership, which frequently calls for a course opposed to popular sentiment. Making precisely this point, the *Los Angeles Times* editorialized about the Deukmejian plan as follows:

> Not many pioneers would have reached California if their scouts had wanted to see which direction the wagon train wanted to move and then galloped to the head of the line. That's not what the scouts were for. Yet, Governor George Deukmejian has something like that in mind on the question of whether $700 million should be invested in the state's very future, the education of its children, or handed back to the taxpayers. . . . Legislators exist to gather data, talk out policy differences and set priorities based on something more than whim and the highest priority for California these days is an education system capable of graduating young people who can think their way through problems to a livable future. A scout who waits to see where his wagon train is going so that he knows where to lead is not much help. ("This Is Governing?" *Los Angeles Times,* June 23, 1987, Part II, p. 4.)

The Appeal to Tradition

The fallacy of tradition consists in appealing to an audience's feelings of reverence or respect for some custom or tradition instead of evidence in order to support a viewpoint. For example, Jane's friend tells her: "I don't think you should keep your maiden name after marrying because in this society women customarily take their husband's name. That's what distinguishes a married woman from a single one." Although there may be good reasons for a woman taking her husband's name, the appeal to custom or convention probably is not one of them. Again, Mr. Miller insists that his son Bob go to State U. because "My father and his father before him went to State U." Maybe so, but State U. may not be the best institution for Bob.

As with popularity, tradition takes on the force of authority. Although traditional beliefs, practices, and policies usually carry a presumption of credibility, that credibility cannot be blindly transferred to the present. There could well be good reasons to override a tradition, reasons which effectively make the tradition irrelevant to a current situation. Consider some of the practices and policies that would still be in effect by the benchmark of tradition: Women still would be disenfranchised, blacks still would be sitting in the back of the bus, a college education still would be an elitist privilege, and so on.

As with so many other aspects of logical and critical thought, a sensitivity to language is invaluable in spotting appeals to tradition. Thus, be alert to phrases such as the *founding fathers, the earliest settlers, from time immemorial, tried and true, the lessons of history, look at the record,* and the like. Of course, not every argument that uses such language is employing tradition illicitly. These phrases may be signaling the presence of *relevant* lessons that history, custom, or precedent teach. Still, they may be masking irrelevant appeals to the revered past.

EXERCISES ON AUTHORITY

1. What do the experts say about the following propositions?
   A. Light travels at 186,000 miles per second.
   B. A body probably cannot accelerate to the speed of light.
   C. Capital punishment deters murder.
   D. Marijuana use can cause a loss of sexual desire.
   E. Fluoridated water is a health hazard.
   F. The earth follows an elliptical orbit.
   G. Sugar contributes to tooth decay.
   H. The earth was once visited by astronaut gods.
   I. Democracy is the best form of government.
   J. Smoking contributes to heart disease.
   K. Women are not suited for military combat.
2. We must rely on authority in many situations, and there are countless experts available for our consultation. What or who would you consult if you:
   A. wanted facts about President Bush's life for a biographical sketch?
   B. wanted the best equipment for a car sound system?
   C. wanted to know whether to take a particular college course?
   D. wanted help in choosing your major or your career?
   E. were planning a bicycle tour of Europe next summer?
   F. wanted help deciding whether or not to join the Peace Corps?
   G. wanted advice about how best to invest $5,000?
3. Clip out an ad that quotes a so-called authority to sell its product. Write a paragraph in which you apply the tests of authority and reach a conclusion about the legitimacy of the testimonial. If you are critical of the testimony, suggest a more reliable source that the ad might have used.
4. Identify and discuss the uses of authority in the following passages. Form an opinion about the relevancy of the authority to the point at issue.
   A. News Item: "It was unclear how the president intended to have his administration maintain support for the Contras while remaining within the law but the White House did get a legal opinion from the President's Intelligence Oversight Board that prohibitions didn't apply to the National Security Council."
   B. News Item: "The Pentagon successfully conducted another in a series of Star Wars rocket experiments Thursday aimed at developing a ground-based 'interceptor' that could destroy nuclear missiles, officials said. The Pentagon declined to discuss the test."

C. "... Behind the smile of Mikhail Gorbachev and the sunshine of *glasnost* policy, our intelligence sources say, is the dark fact that the Soviets have been increasing their special forces rapidly over the last 2 years. There are at least 30,000 of these intensively trained experts in behind-the-lines disruption, poised in the Soviet Union and Eastern Europe for rapid deployment into the West." (Syndicated columnist Jack Anderson)

D. A member of the Communist party commenting on Gorbachev's *glasnost* policy: "I feel deep in my bones that it won't work. Russians are such traditionalists, so conservative, the people have no background for taking responsibility. They don't understand." (Before answering, be clear about the speaker's conclusion.)

E. "In (our) legal system the circumstances that will reasonably justify belief in the necessity for the use of deadly force (i.e., killing in self-defense) is largely a question for the jury. The 'reasonableness' criterion (i.e., before a person may kill in self-defense he or she must honestly *and reasonably* believe that deadly force is necessary to protect against an imminent threat of death or serious bodily harm) is vague, but it allows the jury to express what is essentially a moral judgment and to reflect changing social attitudes about when fear of death or threat of bodily harm is appropriate." (Stephen J. Morse, professor of law at the University of Southern California)

F. Pope John Paul II defending his controversial decision to grant alleged Nazi officer and Austrian President Kurt Waldheim a private papal audience: "The meeting is in keeping with the standard practice of the Holy See to receive duly elected political leaders."

G. News Item: "Widespread 'sexual illiteracy' among the people and doctors of the Soviet Union has led to a high rate of abortion and divorce, a leading sociologist, Igor Kon, says in an unusually explicit article on sex. Kon did not supply statistics on abortion and divorce rates in the Soviet Union, and authoritative figures are not released by Soviet officials. But U.S. sources say that the average Soviet woman has 7 abortions in her life. The sources also say 50% of all Soviet marriages end in divorce."

H. New York Yankees owner George Steinbrenner, defending his use of "boy" in describing his chief accountant, a 30-year-old black man, during a TV interview about racism in baseball: "I have been using 'boys and girls' since my parents taught me what it meant on restroom doors in my grammar school. I've always referred to my team as the 'varsity' and to my players and younger members of the front office as my 'boys and girls'—and I ain't about to change for nobody."

I. "Public opinion's always in advance of the law." (John Galsworthy)

J. Brandon Tartikhoff, president of NBC, defending his network's accepting sexy ads it once banned: "Our advertising is changing because the world around us is changing. There are limits, of course, but most viewers not only accept this type of ad, they expect it."

K. Letter to the editor: "We need to draw down federal deficits to promote saving and long-term investment in new plants, in technology, in worker retraining and scientific education and training, and to bring a new view of negotiating realism to our international economic affairs. These suggestions, given time, will work because they've worked before.''

L.   GEORGE VAN CELEVE (the Republicans' deputy counsel on the House Iran-Contra investigating committee): . . . If Congress told the President he couldn't ask foreign countries or private individuals for financial and other official assistance for the Contras, there would be serious doubt about whether Congress had exceeded its constitutional power. Correct?

OLIVER NORTH: It would clearly, in my opinion, be unconstitutional.

VAN CELEVE: And you're basing that at least in part on your conversation with John Morton Moore of the University of Virginia law school. Is that correct?

NORTH: And others. Marines can read.

M.   SENATE COUNSEL ARTHUR L. LIMAN: Didn't you think that *[securing a ship to help transmit a radio broadcast into Libya]* was a decision the president of the United States should make?

NORTH: If the director of the central intelligence asked me to produce a ship, I think that is good and sufficient.

N. A newspaper editorial questioned the appropriateness of calling barely avoided mid-air collisions "near-misses": "Near-hits," opined the editor, seemed more descriptive. A reader disagreed: "According to my dictionary, 'near-miss — N. Hit, nearly.' It has meant thus since the earliest days of aerial bombing when there was not enough aircraft to pose collision dangers. So what is the big deal?"

O. Letter to the editor: "Only the Constitution can compel responsibility. We desperately need the power of a constitutional amendment to help us balance the budget. Over 70% of the American people want such an amendment."

P. Vice President George Bush, responding to fellow Republican and presidential hopeful Senator Robert Dole's assertions that "more needs to be done" to stem the flow of drugs: "Our nation has a longstanding aversion to the military performing civil law-enforcement functions." (Incidentally, as president, Bush did precisely what Dole had suggested.)

MODULE 9.6

ADDITIONAL EVALUATION STRATEGIES: CHECKING FOR CONSISTENCY AND TRACING IMPLICATIONS

We have learned some ways of evaluating the adequacy of certain kinds of evidence. There are two other useful strategies: checking for consistency and tracing implications.

Checking for Consistency

If any part of an argument contradicts or conflicts with another part, it is a sure sign that something is wrong with the argument. After all, if premises contradict each other, one of them must be false. Of course, we may not know which is false, but we do know they cannot all be true. When the facts surrounding an issue are not clear, cannot easily be determined, or are open to multiple interpretations, the audience ultimately must weigh the believability of an argument. Court cases often are like this. In such matters, a check for internal consistency, of how well someone's argument "hangs together," is an especially potent tool for argument evaluation.

For example, in the summer of 1987, during his first day before the Congressional committee investigating the Iran-Contra affair, Oliver North said, "I don't think there is another person in America that wants to tell the (Iran-Contra) story as much as I do. . . . I come here to tell you the truth, to tell you and this committee and the American people." Curiously, however, North said he could not recall several crucial facts—who ordered him to prepare a false history of Iran arms deal, to divert Iran arms sales profits to the Contras, to prepare memoranda seeking President Reagan's approval to divert those profits to the Contras. Perhaps North's memory had failed him, but given the significance of the forgotten details and the array of other inconsistencies in his testimony (see box, p. 422), one has reason to question North's commitment to telling the truth.

You may also recall that during the hearing, President Reagan remained tight-lipped, promising to comment when the session ended. "Then you won't be able to shut me up," Reagan said. On the evening of August 12, 1987, Reagan got his chance. In an eighteen-minute speech billed as a "final comment" on the summer-long Congressional inquiry, the president devoted about four minutes of the speech to the issue; the remainder dealt with his goals for his final eight months in office. When subsequently reminded of his earlier expansive promise, Reagan said that as far as he was concerned the Iran-Contra issue was closed.

This example also illustrates how inconsistencies can result when people contradict themselves at different times without attempting to justify the change of mind. A graphic example involves Senator Edward Kennedy's (D-MA) assessment of Judge Douglas Ginsburg. On October 1, 1986, in introducing Ginsburg to the Judiciary Committee for unanimous approval as an appeals judge, Senator Kennedy said:

> He has an insightful mind to deal with complex and involved facts and situations and to be able to dissect particular legal issues and questions with clarity and with a sense of compassion. . . . I have found him and I know that other members of the Judiciary Committee and the Congress have found him to be open-minded, to be willing to listen, and to be willing to consider views which he has not himself held.
> I think we are fortunate to have this nominee for this extremely important position.

President Reagan could not have agreed more. The following year, he nominated Ginsburg for the Supreme Court. Leading the opposition to the nomination was Senator Kennedy, who declaimed on October 29, 1987, "Ginsburg is one of the least experienced nominees ever submitted by any president to the Supreme Court. *[Ginsburg is]* an ideological clone of Judge Bork *[whose nomination had been previously defeated]*—a Judge Bork without a paper trail." Kennedy never explained his turnaround. Without some explanation, one is left to doubt one or the other of Kennedy's assessments of Ginsburg.

Ralph Waldo Emerson once observed that "A foolish consistency is the hobgoblin of small minds." True enough—stubbornly clinging to an idea or position despite contradictory facts is illogical and foolish. However, when arguers serve up inconsistent premises or draw logically incompatible conclusions, we are entitled to know why. When inconsistencies glitter in a body of beliefs or set of conclusions, we should ask why. Of course, internal consistency is not the only kind of consistency to look for. We should also test what someone says against our own knowledge and well-considered beliefs.

Consistency can also be used as a general strategy in challenging evaluative

---

Speaking of . . .

Consistency

Testing for Truth in Iran-Contra Testimony

Consistency is one of the most powerful tools we have for testing the truth of ideas or statements of alleged facts. For example, suppose that it is a *known fact* that a man was present at a meeting when the participants planned a bank robbery they later carried out. When the man is subsequently asked whether he was aware of the plot, he says indignantly: "Absolutely not." Now this assertion obviously is inconsistent with the *known fact*. Unless the man or somebody else can explain how he could have been present and remain ignorant of the conspiracy, we have good reason to disbelieve the man. **Testing for truth through consistency consists of asking whether the idea or alleged fact squares with known fact.** Sometimes, this simple, though indispensable, test is all we have to decide whether public officials are telling us the truth, but we do not use it.

For example, judging from the polls taken during and after the Iran-Contra hearings, many Americans simply reacted to the "favorable" or "unfavorable" images portrayed on their TV screens. Rather than using the test of consistency to cut through the rhetorical posturing of the witnesses, they allowed those skilled in image-making to shape their impressions that ultimately formed public opinion. Rather than being dazzled by uniformed officers, aroused by pleas to patriotism, and muted by appeals to sacrosanct "national security," they should have been asking questions such as the following:

> —President Reagan was passionately committed to the Contras. *Is it consistent with this known fact that the president would show no curiosity about the source and amount of money going to the Contras?*

> —CIA chief William J. Casey was one of Reagan's closest friends. They had frequent and intimate conversations. *Is it consistent with these known*

continued

continued

> facts that Casey would never have mentioned his Contra-aiding initia-
> tive to the president?

— Rear Admiral John M. Poindexter, head of the National Security Council
(NSC), like Lt. Colonel North, was an unwavering "chain-of-command"
man with a well-honed sense of loyalty to his commander-in-chief. *Is it
consistent with this known fact that Poindexter would follow his own
counsel in diverting Iran sales funds to the Contras?*

— Poindexter's unfailing, photographic memory was legendary in Washington circles. *Is it consistent with this known fact that he would forget
crucial memoranda that North gave him for Reagan's approval?*

— Attorney General Edwin Meese brought to the Iran-Contra hearings volu-
minous notes that he had taken during his investigation. *Is it consistent
with this known fact that it was merely an "accident," as Meese characterized it, that he didn't write down a single word of his conversations
with Reagan, Vice-President Bush, Casey, or Poindexter?*

arguments. In ethics and public policy, for example, often invoked is a general moral principle that like cases should be treated alike. As a result, it is sometimes possible to challenge a policy or position as violating this principle—in other words, as being inconsistent. This is the tack employed in the following passage that challenges those who favor using lie-detector tests to screen prospective workers:

> Suppose that the businesses in a certain industry are trying to get a government contract. The government, however, has had difficulties with other corporations breaking the rules of other contracts. As a result it has lost large sums of money. In order to prevent this in the present case it says that it is going to set up devices to monitor the reactions of board members and to managers when a questionnaire is sent to them which they must answer. A business, of course, need not agree to this procedure but if it does then it will be noted in their file regarding this and future government contracts. The questionnaire will include questions about the corporation's past fulfillment of contracts, competency to fulfill the present contract, loopholes used in past contracts, collusion with other companies, etc. The reactions of the managers and board members, as they respond to these questions, will be monitored and a decision on the worthiness of that corporation to receive the contract will be made in part on this basis.
>
> There can be little doubt, I think, that the management and directors of the affected corporations would object to the proposal even though the right of the government to defend itself from the violation of its contracts and serious financial losses is at stake. It would be said to be an unjustified violation of privacy of the decision-making process in a business and illegitimate encroachment of the government on free enterprise. *But surely if this is the legitimate response for the corporate job applicant, the same kind of response would be legitimate in the case of the individual job applicant* (italics added). . . .
>
> (George Brenkert, "Privacy, Polygraphs and Work," *Business & Professional Ethics Journal.*)

Using consistency this way is tricky—we need to make sure that the things are sufficiently alike to question the arguer's consistency. When properly used, though, consistency is a trenchant tool for analyzing evaluative arguments.

Tracing Implications

Theses or conclusions of argumentative essays ordinarily have implications. Without knowing for sure whether the evidence offered adequately supports the thesis, we can sometimes test the argument by assuming the thesis is true, then asking, "What follows from this conclusion if it is true?" If what follows is false, absurd, or contradicts the conclusion, the argument is unacceptable.

As a simple example of this strategy, suppose your friend Heide has just enough money to cover the $450 rent on an apartment she desperately wants. She is confident, therefore, that she can afford the place. You are not so sure. So, you challenge her reasoning by treating her argument hypothetically. In other words, you accept her conclusion that she can afford the apartment. Then you trace some of the implications of this conclusion, such as:

— She can afford to pay a $25 monthly electric bill
— She can afford a $30 monthly phone bill
— She can afford an $18 monthly water-and-garbage bill, and so on.

Therefore, you conclude, Heide can afford $523 ($450 + $25 + $30 + $18) for the apartment. Obviously this conclusion is false, given the fact that Heide can only cover the rent of $450. Therefore, her original claim, that she can afford the apartment, must be false too. In fact, Heide *cannot* afford the apartment. Notice that you proved her conclusion false by showing that it led a *false* implication. This particular pattern of reasoning goes by the Latin name *reductio ad absurdum,* which means "reduction to absurdity."

Consider a more difficult and interesting example of how tracing the implications of an argument can be used to criticize it. The issue involves the often-drawn distinction between passive and active euthanasia: It is permissible on humanitarian grounds, at least in some cases, to withhold treatment and allow a patient to die; but it is never permissible to take any direct action designed to kill a patient. Notice how, in the following passage, the author implicitly *accepts* this distinction, then attempts to *use its implications to defeat it:*

To begin with a familiar type of situation, a patient who is dying of incurable cancer of the throat is in terrible pain, which can no longer be satisfactorily alleviated. He is certain to die within a few days, even if present treatment is continued, but he does not want to go on living for those days since the pain is unbearable. So he asks the doctor for an end to it, and his family joins in his request.

Suppose the doctor agrees to withhold treatment, as the conventional doctrine says he may. The justification for his doing so is that the patient is in terrible agony, and since he is going to die anyway, it would be wrong to prolong his suffering needlessly. But now notice this. If one simply withholds treatment, it may take the patient longer to die, and so he may suffer more than he would if more direct action were taken and lethal injection given. This fact provides strong reasons for thinking that, once the initial decision not to prolong his agony has been made, active euthanasia is actually preferable to passive euthanasia, rather than the reverse. *To say otherwise is to endorse the option that leads to more suffering rather than less, and is contrary to the humanitarian impulse that prompts the decision not to prolong life in the first place.* (italics added)

(James Rachels, "Active and Passive Euthanasia.")

MODULE 9.7

WRITING WITH REASON: DEVELOPING THE ARGUMENT OF OPINION

Writing argumentative essays requires skillful use of generalizations. Sometimes, you might build to a generalization, for example, when arguing the merits of gun-control legislation. Thus, having offered a series of reasons, you form the *generalization* that there should (or should not) be gun control. Other times, you might begin with a generalization and attempt to apply it to a relevant situation. For example, you might try to apply to cases of euthanasia the generalization that we should save people from pain and ultimately conclude that, in at least some cases, euthanasia is not only permissible but obligatory. Whether you make effective use of generalizations in writing depends very much on their reliability. If the audience is likely to doubt your generalizations, you need to take special pains to establish them. This is crucial when the generalization is controversial. You can employ various ways to support your generalizations: by a solid listing of facts and figures; by using outstanding familiar cases; by citing authentic examples that will strike the audience as typical; by invoking legitimate authority, and so on.

More specifically, one of the most common argumentative essays you are called upon to write in college is the one in which you attempt to convince the audience of your opinion on some subject. Always keep in mind that in such an essay you are really developing a generalization. Your job, then, is to convince the audience that you have enough of the right kind of evidence for your opinion-generalization. There are two very effective strategies for writing the argumentative essay of opinion-generalization: (1) defending the opinion, and (2) adjusting the opinion.

Defending the Opinion-Generalization

If defending an opinion, you can state it early in the essay, then proceed to support it. The defense typically is arranged *inductively* through examples, illustrations, facts, statistics, authority, and other forms of evidence. The strength of this approach is that, from the beginning, your essay rivets your own attention as well as the audience's on the main idea or thesis. As a result, you reduce your chances of straying from the thesis and introducing irrelevant material, and the reader is protected from confusion and drawing erroneous inferences from what you are saying. Here are excerpts from two essays developed by defending an opinion-generalization (italicized):

School Athletics

Opening Paragraph (Opinion-Generalization Thesis)
Probably for as long as interscholastic sports have been around, people have wondered about their merits. As school funds dry up, the debate grows hot. The upshot is that today many athletic programs are at risk. But if school districts are wise, *they will resist the impulse to discontinue athletic programs.*

Facts
Athletic programs serve vital functions in a school. First, they provide students an outlet for pent-up energy. Second, they teach students to compete. . . .

Facts
Furthermore, if athletic programs are discontinued, many extracurricular activities will expire. The reason is that activities such as dramatics, music, forensics, and various clubs depend on the revenue generated by interscholastic athletic programs. . . .

Authority
If skeptics aren't convinced by these considerations, they should ponder the recommendations of the National Education Association and the President's Council on Physical fitness. . . .

Punishing Juvenile Offenders

Opening Paragraph (Opinion-Generalization Thesis)
In recent years, the United States has experienced an alarming increase in juvenile crime—that is, crimes committed by individuals under the age of majority. Whether the category is murder or robbery, mugging or rape, vandalism or arson, the story is the same: Juvenile crime is on the rise. In order to combat this trend, *society needs to rethink its treatment of juvenile offenders that currently distinguishes them from their adult counterparts.*

Statistical Evidence
There's a growing body of evidence that suggests that many youthful offenders have no more or less developed a sense of right and wrong than their adult counterparts. One particular study is especially revealing. . . .

Case Example
Moreover, the motives behind the criminal activities of many youths often parallel those of adult offenders. Take, for example, the case of a gang of youths who raped, beat, and left for dead a young female jogger in Central Park, New York. . . .

Authority
Furthermore, according to some psychologists, when society conveys the youthful offender to a youth authority, it effectively diminishes the gravity of the crime in the youth's mind. Professor Abraham Stern, for example, has written that. . . .

Adjusting the Opinion

A second effective way to develop an opinion-generalization is to withhold your opinion until the end of the essay. In this strategy, you establish common ground with the audience by first presenting a widely accepted view before inspecting it and eventually modifying or adjusting it.

A point-counterpoint format is a most appropriate way for structuring this kind of essay. In such a format, you attempt to reach a balanced conclusion by treating an issue as an open question worth thinking about. The pro-con discussion that ensues serves as a basis for adjusting the widely held opinion. It also involves both you and your audience in the kind of process by which opinion-generalizations are actually formed.

Here are two examples of the adjusted-opinion essay, based on the same topics as before—school athletics and juvenile crime. Notice how the writer makes basically the same support material conform with this strategy and that the generalization-opinion thesis (italicized) comes at the end.

School Athletics

Opening Paragraph (Common View)	Probably for as long as interscholastic sports have been around, people have wondered about their merits. Do they put too much emphasis on winning? Are they overly exclusionary? Today, cutbacks in school funds have sharpened the criticism that school sports are a frill that many school districts can no longer afford.
Point/Counterpoint 1	It is true that any coach worth his or her salt wants to win and attempt to inculcate a winning spirit in student athletes. It's also true that teams limit participation to the best players. But let's not forget that a competitive, winning spirit pays off in life, and that athletic programs involve the entire student body at least indirectly. . . .
Point/Counterpoint 2	Undoubtedly, many athletic programs are very expensive. Big college football is an outstanding example. But such programs also generate considerable revenue that helps finance many extracurricular activities, such as drama, music, forensics, and various clubs. . . .
Point/Counterpoint 3	Recently, a number of well-intentioned individuals and groups have scored interscholastic sports, and their viewpoints deserve an honest airing. In fact, their concerns about exploiting student athletes and violating interscholastic regulations in order to win at all costs are well founded. But so are the opinions of the National Education Association and the President's Council on Physical Fitness. . . .
Adjusted View: Thesis	Although the inclincation to discontinue school sports is understandable in the light of recent scandals, *several factors argue for their retention.*

Punishing Juvenile Offenders

Opening Paragraph (Common View)	In recent years, the United States has experienced an alarming increase in juvenile crime—that is, crime committed by individuals under the age of majority. Whether the category is murder or robbery, mugging or rape, vandalism or arson, the story is the same: Juvenile crime is on the rise. Our society has a long tradition of treating juveniles as special kinds of offenders, ones who warrant punishment different from that given to an adult, even though the crime may be the same. It's a safe bet that a great portion of our population still holds this attitude.
Point/Counterpoint 1	It's understandable for people to think that youths don't have the maturity to understand the full implications of what they do. But age isn't necessarily a measure of maturity. Some minors show more responsible judgment than some adults do. For example. . . .
Point/Counterpoint 2	Certainly, many socially offensive things that young people do can be chalked up to youthful exuberance. But we're not talking about some hell-raising here. These are very serious crimes that the vast majority of people do and can be expected to recognize as such very early in life. . . .
Point/Counterpoint 3	It's sometimes argued that harsh punishment simply hardens youthful offenders and can turn them into career criminals. Obviously, society has an interest in preventing this. But it also must impress on juvenile offenders the seriousness of what they've done. Treating them as if their age somehow reduces the gravity of their crimes might encourage them to continue their criminal ways. Take, for example, the case of. . . .
Adjusted View: Thesis	No one questions that the desire to protect our children springs from the noblest of human instincts and that society has special obligations for teaching, shaping, and protecting youth. But *it's questionable that society does itself or youth any good by treating juvenile offenders differently from adults.*

IMPROVING PERFORMANCE

SUMMARY-TEST QUESTIONS FOR CHAPTER 9*

1. The basis of all inductive generalizations is
   A. personal observation.
   B. authority.
   C. assumptions.
   D. observed specifics.

2. Briefly explain what is meant by *scientific method.*
3. Scientific generalizations or laws rarely acquire a high degree of probability after only a few observations. True or False?
4. Which of the following considerations, if any, bears on the reliability of an observation?
   A. The conditions under which the observation was made
   B. The sensory keenness of the observer
   C. The observer's qualifications to interpret the observation
   D. Observer objectivity
   E. All of the above affect the reliability of an observation.
5. Reliability observations are sufficient to yield reliable generalizations. True or False?
6. Sample _____ and _____ affect sample representativeness.
7. **Which of the following statements is/are true?**
   A. The larger and more diverse the population, the larger the sample should be.
   B. The more subgroups in a population, the larger the sample should be.
   C. Sample size always significantly affects the accuracy of the generalization based on it.
   D. A and B.
   E. A, B, and C.
8. In order to find out what students think about the athletic program at your school, you ask the opinion of all physical educations majors. Exactly why will your survey be unreliable?
9. Why is it important to know the size of a poll sample?
10. Illustrate how, although tiny, a sample still may be representative of the whole.
11. Which of the following questions, if any, is/are unbiased?
    A. Statistics indicate that crimes of violence are on the rise. Given that, do you favor the death penalty?
    B. Should people convicted of murder be given the death penalty or life in prison?
    C. Do you oppose the death penalty or favor it in some circumstances?
    D. How tough should the courts by on convicted drug dealers?
    E. Do you favor capital punishment for convicted drug dealers?
12. Exactly how can Martin Buber's distinction between "essence" and "image" be related to sample bias?
13. **Statistics**
    A. have an authoritative air.
    B. pervade our society.
    C. usually are not reliable.
    D. A and B.
    E. A, B, and C.
14. Explain how objectivity plays a key role in the reliability of observations, polls, statistics, and authority.
15. An independent accounting firm concludes, on the basis of a thorough examination of the books, that the XYZ company's profits from one of its products declined by one percent in the last twelve months. The board of directors uses this as a reason to reduce shareholder dividends by one percent. If you

were an XYZ shareholder would you be persuaded by the board's rationale? If not, which one of the following questions would you especially want answered? Explain your choice.

A. Is the source reliable?
B. Is the statistic complete?
C. Does the statistic make a difference?
D. Is the statistic misleadingly precise?

16. A study of a consumer safety organization estimates that lap-shoulder belts are forty-two percent effective in reducing driver fatalities. Add an air-bag and you gain another six percent. But the air-bag alone, without the belt, reduces driver fatalities only by eighteen percent. These statistics probably

A. are unreliable owing to the source bias.
B. are incomplete.
C. do not make a difference.
D. are misleadingly precise.

17. After learning of the aforementioned safety statistics, Alfred generalizes that the air-bag/seat-belt combination offers drivers better protection than using either by itself. Assuming that the study is reliable, do you think that Alfred's generalization is reliable?

18. Unqualified generalizations are never acceptable. True or False?

19. With great fanfare Daisy Dairies introduces "Extra light" milk, thereby inviting the consumer to

A. be influenced by authority.
B. be impressed with an implied statistic.
C. form a hasty generalization.
D. misapply a generalization.

20. It turns out that "Extra light" means one percent low-fat milk, which Daisy and other dairies already market. Which fallacy, if any, is Daisy intentionally exploiting to market "Extra light"?

21. What we buy today we eat tomorrow. I bought an uncooked steak at the market today. So, I'll be eating an uncooked steak in the near future. What is wrong with this argument?

22. Suppose that you suspect that an argument is overlooking unfavorable evidence, but you are not sure whether the evidence is relevant. What question would you ask to determine the relevancy of the evidence?

23. A good argumentative essay usually presents only evidence favorable to its thesis. Would you agree or disagree?

24. Which of the following propositions, if any, is not a value judgment? Explain.

A. Capital punishment should be legalized.
B. A study shows that capital punishment does not deter crime.
C. Capital punishment is immoral.
D. Capital punishment violates the constitution.
E. None of the above—each is a value judgment.

25. Are we more inclined or less inclined to raise overlooked evidence in essays presenting positions with which we agree or with which we disagree, or do our own feelings not matter much?

26. When it appears in an essay, unfavorble evidence typically is part of the
    A. body.
    B. introduction.
    C. refutation.
    D. conclusion.
    E. B and D.
27. What two basic questions would you ask before accepting any appeal to authority?
28. Which of the following statements is/are true?
    A. Authority often figures in the main points of an essay.
    B. Majority of expert opinion is a test of truth.
    C. A so-called expert whose view clashes with most other experts in the field is considered false authority and his view is thereby proved false.
    D. B and C.
    E. A and C.
29. Which of the following terms, if any, does not belong with the others?
    A. Popularity
    B. Bandwagon
    C. Common opinion
    D. Tradition
30. Jennifer's parents are disturbed to learn that their daughter is dropping out of college. They point out that she will be the first member on either side of the family that has done that. Jennifer's parents are using the appeal to _____ to influence their daughter.

CRITICAL THINKING APPLICATIONS

1. A famous story is told of Abraham Lincoln's first defense at a murder trial. The prosecutor's case rested mainly on the testimony of a witness who swore that he saw the defendant fire the shot and run away. Cross-examining the witness, Lincoln led the man into testifying that he was standing twenty-feet or more from the defendant at the time of the shooting; that the shooting occurred in heavy timber; that he could see how the pistol was pointed; that, although the shooting occurred at night and the nearest lights were candles one-quarter of a mile away, that he saw the shooting by moonlight. In one deft stroke, Lincoln proved that the man was lying.
   How do you think Lincoln discredited the man's claim?
   (Hint: (1) What's the crucial element in the witness' testimony? (2) What fact would shatter it? (3) How might this fact be established?)
2. Suppose that you wish to find out what students at your college think about the college newspaper (or the registration system, cafeteria food, or some other appropriate item). **How would you go about it?** Remember, the idea is to devise a survey that will yield a reliable generalization about student opinion. **Compare your approach with the approach of other students.**
3. Political campaigning is rife with the neglect of relevant evidence. For example, during the presidential campaign of 1988, Massachusetts Governor Michael

Dukakis boasted that 300,000 jobs had been created in his state since 1984, that unemployment was under three percent, and that taxes and spending had been kept in check. Dukakis used this "Massachusetts miracle" as the mainstay of his campaign, arguing that he could do for the country what he had done for Massachusetts. He did not mention, however, that the U.S. Defense Department had awarded Massachusetts 6.4 percent of its prime contracts since 1964 — not bad for a state with only 2.6 percent of the U.S. population. Also neglected by Dukakis was the fact that Dukakis had opposed Proposition 2-1/2, whose passage cut property taxes by 40 percent, or that jobs actually had been lost in the sector where Dukakis' "industrial policies" had been most in evidence — manufacturing. In fact, since mid-1984, 74,000 manufacturing jobs had been lost. A study by the Associated Industries of Massachusetts reported, "Massachusetts — with only 3.1 percent of the nation's industrial employment — lost 41 percent of all manufacturing jobs lost nationally from 1984 to 1987." **Scan the newspapers for examples of political boasts that you believe neglect relevant evidence. In all cases, cite the overlooked evidence and explain why you believe it is significant.**

4. **Report to the class on the concealed evidence in political speech, an editorial, a letter to the editor, or an advertisement.**

5. During Iran-Contra, it was argued that the Reagan Administration, through its appointed National Security Council (NSC), had every reason to believe it was acting legally in giving U.S. military aid to the Nicaraguan Contras, because White House lawyer Bretton G. Sciaroni had said so. Sciaroni was the counsel for the Intelligence Oversight Board, which is appointed by the president and supposed to review the legality of intelligence activities. It was Sciaroni who wrote the 1985 legal opinion saying that the NSC was exempt from the Congressional ban on assistance to the Contras. Sciaroni, who had passed the Bar examination (after four earlier failures) little more than a year before he drafted his opinion, admitted to the Iran-Contra Congressional investigating committee that (1) he had spent no more than five minutes questioning Oliver North of the NSC staff about possible illicit conduct, and that North had misled him; and (2) that he was denied documents directly relevant to his study. **Analyze this episode in the light of this chapter's coverage of observations, missing evidence, and authority.**

6. **Analyze the following news item with respect to statistics and hasty generalization.**

Patients Prefer Female Physicians, Study Says

Farmington, Conn.

Both male and female hospital patients prefer female physicians and consider a physician's technical and interpersonal skills equally important, a professor of medicine has found. Dr. Dale Matthews, an assistant professor of medicine at the University of Connecticut Health Center, asked 381 patients at two hospitals in Connecticut to rate the performance of 26 interns on 14 broad features. These features include common courtesy, bedside manner, and availability. The interns also were rated on 31 specific items of behavior.

7. *Fact:* In less-developed countries, exclusive of China, the world's most populous nation, from 1985 to 1986 the "total fertility" rate fell from 5.0 children per woman to 4.8.

   Fact: In the years immediately prior to 1985, birth limitations were either relaxed or violated in China.

   In the spring of 1986, headlines such as "World Population Growth Accelerating" (from the New Orleans *Times-Picayune*) and "World Birth Rate Said to Be Rising" (from *The Washington Post*) appeared across the United States with accompanying stories about how the "crude birth rate," according to the Population Reference Bureau, had gone up from 27 births per 1,000 population in 1985 to 38 in 1986. **Do you think that the aforementioned two facts, which largely went unreported, are relevant to the media's inferences about increasing world population?**

8. **Write an analysis of this news item in the context of this chapter's coverage. Try to apply as much of the chapter content as you can.**

Study Reports Healthy Living Can Reverse Heart Disease

(London) A low-fat vegetarian diet, clean living, and stress management can reverse heart disease in many patients in as little as a year, according to a study published in this week's edition of *The Lancet*.

Dr. Dean Ornish of the Preventive Medicine Research Institute of Sausalito (CA) who coordinated "The Lifestyle Heart Trial," said it is the first evidence that heart disease can be reversed without surgery or drugs.

"Comprehensive lifestyle changes may be able to bring about regression of even severe coronary atherosclerosis after only one year," the study said.

Researchers stressed the "adherence to this life-style program needs to be very good for overall regression to occur, although more moderate changes have some beneficial effects."

The study noted only two other controlled studies had shown regression of coronary atherosclerosis and both used cholesterol-lowering drugs as the main treatment.

The 10 researchers participating in the study cautioned that important questions remained unanswered.

The study involved only 41 patients and the researchers said it was important to determine whether these results can be sustained in large numbers of patients with coronary heart disease.

Further research is also needed to determine the relative contribution of each component of the life-style program, the researchers said.

Scientists should also study just how the disease regresses and compare the results of changing life-styles vs. using drugs or surgery, they said.

The study of 41 patients from the San Francisco area, ages 37–75, were randomly assigned to an experimental group and a control group.

The 22 patients in the experimental group ate a low-fat, vegetarian diet. Smoking and caffeine were banned and alcohol was limited to two drinks a day, although drinking was not encouraged.

They exercised regularly and attended stress management training classes.

Eighteen of the 22 patients showed a reversal of coronary artery blockages; three showed slight deterioration, and one patient with "poor adherence" to the diet became markedly worse, the study reported.

POINT/COUNTERPOINT: ESSAYS FOR ANALYSIS

Issue: *Euthanasia*

Resolved: Living wills should be used and respected.

Background: On June 25, 1990, the United States Supreme Court denied the family of Nancy Cruzan the right to remove life-support equipment because of a lack of evidence defining the young woman's wishes. The High Court made it clear, however, that it does support the right to terminate life-sustaining care. It denied the Cruzan request because the family could not provide "clear and convincing evidence" that Nancy Cruzan would wish to die. Cruzan, 32, who had been in a vegetative state since an auto accident in 1983, had not stated her wishes in writing.

The High Court's ruling sent the case back to a Missouri probate judge who in November heard former co-workers testify that the young woman would not want to live like a vegetable. On December 14, the judge decided that the Cruzans could order that Nancy's feeding tube be removed. Within two hours it was, and within ten days Nancy Cruzan died, as protesters from antieuthanasia and antiabortion groups kept vigil outside her hospital.

The Cruzan decision revived Americans' interest in living wills or advanced directives, which are documents intended to clarify the wishes of people before they become terminally ill and cannot speak for themselves. There are two basic types of living wills. One specifically states an individual's wishes about life-sustaining care; the other, termed durable power of attorney, assigns the power to make such decisions to a health care agent, such as a relative or close friend. Public opinion polls have long showed overwhelming support of living wills, although only about fifteen percent of Americans have them.

From: **Withhold Treatment[3]***

Judith Areen

Judith Areen is a professor at Georgetown University Law Center. Although the following essay originally appeared in the Journal of the American Medical Association, *its appeal is sufficiently broad to acquaint the general reader with the pro–living will case.* **Read the essay carefully, outline it, then answer the questions that follow it.**

---

[3](Judith Areen, "The Legal Status of Consent Obtained from Families of Adult Patients to WIthhold or Withdraw Treatment," *Journal of the American Medical Association,* vol. 258, July 10, 1987, pp 229–235. Copyright 1987, American Medical Association.)

1 In recent years, a consensus has developed among legal and medical authorities that physicians should be guided in deciding whether to withhold or withdraw treatment by the wishes of patients who are competent and able to communicate their wishes. Recent polls show that three of every four American adults agree. The right to refuse is not absolute, but it is generally overridden only when the life or health of third parties is at stake. One court has even held that a physician may be sued for placing and maintaining a patient on life-support systems without the informed consent of the patient or his guardian.

2 A majority of the states have now extended this principle of respect for individual choice to formerly competent patients. Thirty-eight states and the District of Columbia have passed living will statutes, also known as natural death acts, which enable competent adults to prepare directions for health care to be followed if they become terminally ill and unable to direct their own care.

3 These statutes place limitations on the preparation of binding advance directives. Under most statutes, the directive becomes operative only if and when the patient is determined to be terminally ill by more than one physician. In some states, a directive is legally binding only if, after the onset of terminal illness but before the onset of incompetence, the patient reaffirms the directive. In addition, many of the model directives set forth in the statutes fail to make clear which forms of care may be foregone (e.g., whether artificial hydration and nutrition constitute "extraordinary care" and thus may be foregone). Finally, a living will, no matter how detailed, cannot possibly anticipate the full range of difficult treatment decisions that may have to be made.

4 An increasingly attractive choice for many patients, therefore, is to delegate to a particular person the legal authority to make health care decisions in the event the delegator becomes unconscious or incompetent. Several states have enacted statutes that explicitly authorize such delegation. Others provide for a person to be designated as a proxy to carry out the intent of a living will. The remaining states have general durable power of attorney statutes, which appear to be broad enough in most instances to authorize delegation of authority to make medical treatment decisions.

5 Advance directives are without a doubt a better way to determine the wishes of patients unable to speak for themselves than the traditional route of having a court appoint a guardian, who must attempt to figure out the patient's wishes. Physicians and hospitals could avoid many of the uncertainties now faced in making treatment decisions for patients who cannot speak for themselves if they encouraged greater use of such directives. But even with encouragement, there will still be some patients who will not have advance directives. . . .

6 Family members are likely to be in the best position to know whether the patient expressed views on treatment while competent, and to interpret what the patient probably would want even if no explicit statements were made. Even if the matter went to court, the court's determination would

no doubt turn in large part on testimony from family members. Similarly, if the patient had delegated decision-making authority under a durable power of attorney statute, it is likely that the person selected would have been a family member. More formal legal mechanisms, in short, would probably rely primarily on the family for data about the patient's values and beliefs. Thus, the family is likely to be as skillful as less knowledgeable but theoretically more impartial decision makers in determining what the patient would want, although this claim to expertise decreases when the family has not been in close touch with the patient in the years or months immediately preceding his incapacity, or when the patient has never been competent.

7 Delegation to families of authority to exercise a patient's right to terminate treatment has the additional virtue of avoiding a major shortcoming of judicial resolution of such cases—the almost total lack of legal precedent (at least before the Karen Ann Quinlan case in 1976) for withdrawing treatment even when that treatment is merely prolonging the process of dying rather than contributing to the health or well-being of a patient. The shortage of precedent is, no doubt, one reason judges often express discomfort with being asked to decide treatment controversies.

8 But the trend toward reliance on families is not without problems. The term *family* is not very precise. When relatives disagree as to what the patient would want, therefore, the dispute will probably require judicial resolution, at least in the absence of a statute or court decision that specifies whose decision is to be given priority. The family may also not include the most knowledgeable proxy decision maker. Thus, even if a patient has lived for years with someone who is not a legal relative, the nonrelative will have legal authority to speak for the patient only if he or she is designated as the proxy by the patient in an advance directive.

9 A more serious problem is how to protect patients from families who decide on the basis of ignorance or in bad faith. One alternative is to require all families to justify any decision to terminate or withhold treatment to a hospital ethics committee. Unfortunately, mandatory administrative review of every decision to terminate treatment could well become as burdensome as court review, with little gain in the quality of decisions made.

10 The most prudent course would be a standard that directs health care providers to accept family decisions to withhold or withdraw care unless it appears the family is acting out of ignorance or in bad faith. Only these latter decisions would be referred to a hospital ethicist or ethics committee. There should be, in short, a legal presumption in favor of family consent, but one that can be challenged for good reason in an administrative setting. After consideration by the hospital ethicist or ethics committee, judicial review could be sought, but only if the initial suspicion of ignorance or bad faith turns out to be well founded.

11 Physicians and other health care providers are likely to be uncomfortable at first with the responsibility of assessing whether family members are

acting in good faith. This is yet another reason for health care professionals to encourage more patients to prepare advance directives. For patients without directives, a procedure designed to protect those few patients whose families are not acting in good faith is surely preferable to the alternative of subjecting every family decision to committee or court review. An important aspect of the proposed procedure will be the standard by which a failure to report is judged. Fairness dictates that a failure to report should subject a health care provider to liability only if, on the facts reasonably available in the ordinary practice of medicine, the provider knew, or should have known, as measured by the conduct of other professionals, that the family was not acting in good faith.

12 Although many physicians routinely obtain consent to medical treatment from family members on behalf of adult patients who are incapable of making decisions for themselves, the law until recently has not recognized such consent unless the family member has been appointed by a court to be the patient's legal guardian. A good way to avoid both the legal uncertainty surrounding family consent, and the burden that being a proxy decision maker places on family members, is to having a living will or a durable power of attorney with instructions governing health care. Health care providers should encourage more patients to prepare such advance directives.

1. What questions would you want answered before accepting the results of the "recent polls" cited in paragraph 1?
2. Which of the following generalizations do paragraphs 1 and 2 support?
   A. The patient's right to refuse treatment is absolute.
   B. The patient's right to refuse treatment is virtually absolute.
   C. The patient's right to refuse treatment is widely viewed as being absolute.
   D. The patient's right to refuse treatment is widely viewed as virtually absolute.
3. Identify and explain the author's use of authority in paragraphs 1 and 2.
4. Is the author in a position to speak authoritatively on the subject of a living will?
5. Paragraph 3 functions to
   A. portray living wills as immoral.
   B. show the limitation of living wills.
   C. show the inconsistency of the law.
   D. show that, despite a consensus view to the contrary, patients shouldn't have a right to refuse treatment that physicians think is necessary.
6. Cecilia reacts to paragraph 3 by saying, "I think that the author's being inconsistent. In paragraph 1, she says that a consensus has formed supporting the patient's right to make decisions for themselves. But then she goes on to point out the differences among the statutes that deal with advance directives. If there are so many differences, how can there be a consensus?" Do you agree or disagree with Cecilia's analysis?
7. Which of the following scenarios, if any, could not occur, according to paragraph 3?

    A. A patient who has been certified terminally ill by five physicians slips into a coma after having reaffirmed the directive he signed before getting ill. While still in the coma, the patient contracts pneumonia. His family, sincerely believing that they are implementing the man's wishes, tell his physicians not to treat him. The physicians refuse.

    B. The same scenario as in A, except that the patient did not reaffirm his decision before lapsing into the coma.

    C. The same conditions as in A, except that two, not five, physicians certified the patient as terminally ill.

    D. A and B.

    E. A and C.

    F. B and C.

    G. A, B, and C.

    H. Each of the preceding scenarios could occur.

8. The first sentence of paragraph 4 includes the word "therefore." Exactly what has led up to and accounts for the use of this conclusion signal?

9. Is it clear how the delegation of authority proposed by the author in paragraph 4 meets the problems associated with living wills as sketched in paragraph 3?

10. Identify the intensifier in paragraph 5.

11. What kind of generalization is the first sentence of paragraph 5—inductive or noninductive?

12. Does the author offer any evidence for the two generalizations that begin paragraph 5? Do you think any is needed?

13. Identify every qualifier in paragraph 6.

14. Ellie questions the author's unqualified belief that the courts' decisions would usually parallel the family's representation of their loved one's wishes. She points to celebrated cases, including Cruzan and Quinlan, where this was not the case. She concludes that the author has neglected relevant evidence. Do you agree?

15. What kind of generalization is the first sentence of paragraph 7?

16. "Thus," which begins the last sentence of paragraph 6, implies that the statements in the paragraph that precede it are offered as support for the statement that follows it. Do they? Has the author made a believable case for the claim, "Thus, the family is likely to be as skillful as less knowledgeable but theoretically more impartial decision makers in determining what the patient would want"?

17. Is the sentence quoted in the preceding question consistent with the first sentence of paragraph 6?

Questions 18–20 are based on the following dialogue:

    PHYLLIS: I agree with the author that delegating authority will give judges some basis for making decisions in these tough cases (paragraph 7).

    PHIL: Really? Frankly, I don't quite see how setting up a precedent counts as a reason for delegating decision-making authority to families.

    PHYLLIS: It'll make it easier for judges to decide.

    PHIL: Maybe so. But when did we start passing laws on the basis of making life easier for judges?

PHYLLIS: You miss the point. It's a matter of providing judges some direction or framework for making the decisions.

PHIL: Even so, it sounds to me like the author's saying: "Let's establish delegation of authority because that'll give judges a legal basis for delegating authority."

PHYLLIS: So, you're saying the author's reasoning is circular?

PHIL: I believe it is.

PHYLLIS: I don't agree. I think she's given independent support for legislation that would have the effect of delegating authority.

18. What kind of dispute is this?

19. Do you think that the dispute is significant in assessing the overall strength of the author's argument?

20. Would you be inclined to side with Phyllis or Phil in this dispute? Explain.

21. Does the author identify any counterarguments to her position? If so, identify them.

22. If there are counterarguments, does the author successfully refute them? Explain.

23. If the author does acknowledge counterarguments, do you think it helps, hurts, or has no effect on her own argument?

From: **Living Will or Death Warrant?**

George A. Kendall

George A. Kendall is a pro-life activist. **Read this essay carefully, outline it, then answer the questions that follow it.**

1 If there is anything we have learned to count on in my home state of Michigan (besides rain), it is the emergence, with every legislative session, of "living will" or "durable power of attorney" legislation. "Living will" laws are designed to make it possible for a person, while mentally competent, to provide by some sort of declaration that in the event that he becomes seriously ill and unable to participate in decisions concerning his medical treatment, no extraordinary medical treatment will be given. "Durable power of attorney" is slightly different. It provides that, while one is mentally competent, one may appoint a third party with the authority to make decisions about one's medical treatment should one become unable to participate in such decisions. Presumably, patients would choose people who shared their own views about what kind of treatment is appropriate.

2 Why is such legislation felt to be needed? Because situations do arise where a decision has to be made about what and how much treatment is appropriate for a sick or dying person who is unable to participate in making the decision. Such legislation tries to provide either a precise criterion or a precise procedure in advance for dealing with such situations. But is this either possible or necessary?

3 The answer to both questions is: No.

4 As regards necessity, the law does not now require physicians to use extraordinary measures of treatment. By extraordinary measures, I mean treatment that is so burdensome that its cost (in terms of suffering by patient and family, money, etc.) is in excess of its likely benefit to the patient. This basically requires a kind of cost-benefit analysis.

5 In cancer cases, for example, such treatments as radiation and chemotherapy are often given for palliative rather than curative reasons. They will not significantly prolong the patient's life, but will shrink the tumor and (it is hoped) make the patient more comfortable. At the same time, these therapies may themselves cause much pain and misery, so that in some cases it may be very doubtful that the therapy will provide enough relief to outweigh the costs, to the patient and loved ones, of the treatment.

6 This type of situation requires, first of all, a medical judgment weighing the probable costs and benefits, because it involves predictions about the effects of treatment or nontreatment which cannot be made without medical expertise. When this judgment is made, then, in the ordinary course of things, it is shared and discussed with the patient (if able) and with the family. If the patient is incompetent and there is no family, it may sometimes be necessary for the decision to be made on the physician's judgment alone.

7 Because the decision as to whether the treatment would be of net benefit to the patient and hence whether it is ordinary or extraordinary requires medical judgment, a statement in advance by the patient that he does not want extraordinary treatment will not resolve the issue, which is precisely whether the treatment is ordinary or extraordinary. Most medical decisions involved in the treatment of the dying are of this nature. Similarly, it would not be appropriate to entrust this judgment to a nonmedical person, who would not be competent to make the decision whether, in a particular case a particular treatment is ordinary or extraordinary. As a physician friend of mine likes to say, every case is a law unto itself. Every case is unique just as every person is unique. Thus the effort to establish a precise rule or procedure for making these decisions before the fact is inappropriate. It is also dangerous, for the following reasons (among others):

8 1) Living will and durable power of attorney laws have a tendency to make no distinction between treatment and care (such as food and water). The courts have tended to reject this distinction, as has the AMA [American Medical Association]. This being the case, the legislation would merge with existing legal trends to make it even easier than it is now to put a person to death by starvation and dehydration, as was done to Paul Brophy. Brophy, a Massachusetts fireman, suffered a cerebral aneurysm in 1983 and went into a coma. On the strength of the fact that, when healthy, he had remarked to friends that "if I'm ever like that, just shoot me," his wife was able to convince the Massachusetts Supreme Court to order removal of his feeding tube in September, 1986, a measure which led to his death eight days later. There is little doubt that living will legislation will move us beyond the issue of ordinary versus extraordinary treatment into the

question whether to feed and hydrate, a question we have no business even raising. But there is really no valid difference between starvation and dehydration on the one hand, and the administration of a lethal injection on the other. Since the latter is quicker and probably less painful, it is bound to occur to people that it would probably be a more humane way out for dying patients, and thus we will move from alleged withholding of extraordinary treatment to out and out killing.

9 2) In the case of durable power of attorney laws, there is usually no requirement that the decision-making person be someone with nothing to gain from the person's death. The danger is thus there of, for example, a patient's children wanting to hurry the patient out of this world rather than have him spend all his money on chemotherapy.

10 3) Under any of these laws, decisions may be made over the head of the patient's doctor, his family, friends, etc. The danger of someone being railroaded into any early grave is thus increased.

11 4) The great difficulty of precisely defining such terms as "terminally ill" or "incompetent" is also an issue. How close does death have to be for us to consider the condition terminal? After all, diabetes is a terminal illness. If you have it, it will kill you sooner or later, unless something else gets you first.

12 I have also noted a marked tendency, both in legislation and in court actions, to blur the distinction between the terminally ill person and the merely incurably ill person. By the latter, we usually mean the person in an apparently irreversible coma, the chronically mentally ill person, or the mentally retarded person (it is frightening, in reading pro-euthanasia literature, to note how very quickly its authors leap from talk of compassion for the dying to loose talk about "incurable imbeciles and lunatics" — these people aren't sliding down a slippery slope but going over a cliff, like the demoniac Gadarene swine).

13 The dangers here are obvious. And who decides whether a person is competent or not, and thus whether to invoke the living will or durable power. Who decides whether I am hopelessly insane or just somewhat eccentric (my relatives have been debating that for years)? Here we have a very serious possibility that people could be put to death by dehydration or starvation based solely on someone's subjective judgment about that person's quality of life.

14 The problem with living will and durable power of attorney laws is that they are being introduced into a social, cultural, political, and legal milieu in which respect for the sanctity of human life has almost disappeared. If we look at the values we find in the pages of *Playboy* or *Penthouse* or on our TV screens, we see a society which holds that the world is for the young, the healthy, and the beautful, for those who can give us pleasure or otherwise be useful to use. There is no room in Hugh Hefner's world for the old, the handicapped, and the terminally ill.

15 In this environment, any legislation which will make it easier to put people to death by neglect is quite dangerous. We don't need to make it easier to

withhold treatment or care. If anything, we need to move in the opposite direction. The only real point such legislation has is to move us in the direction of out-and-out assisted suicide laws, something already being pushed by pro-euthanasia groups such as the Hemlock Society which, interestingly enough, also support living wills. People who try to engineer major changes in a society are generally intelligent enough to do it a little at a time, so as not to unduly alarm the intended "beneficiaries" of their benevolence. Living will and durable power of attorney laws, viewed in this perspective, make perfect sense.

16 The old system for making medical treatment decisions, in which doctor, patient, family, friends, and clergy may all be involved in the decision, is cumbersome and confusing in its workings, but at least is open enough to participation by a variety of people so that arguments on behalf of life at least have a chance to be heard. There is no point in abandoning this way of making decisions, whatever its imperfections, for one which has a built-in bias against the sanctity of human life.

1. Paragraphs 1 and 2 serve to
   A. refute objections to the author's view.
   B. establish the authority of the author.
   C. introduce the topic.
   D. express the thesis.
2. Is there any reason to question the author's objectivity?
3. In paragraph 4, the author offers a _____ definition.
   A. persuasive
   B. lexical
   C. denotative
   D. stipulative
   E. theoretical
4. Gary believes that the author has introduced a side issue in paragraph 4. He explains, "The issue is whether directives of authorization are necessary or not. The author says they're not. As proof, he says that present laws don't require physicians to use extraordinary measures of treatment. But even after somebody determines that such-and-such treatment is extraordinary, the law doesn't require the physician *not* to provide extraordinary treatment. So somebody has to decide whether to give such treatment or not. The author misses this point entirely. Or if he doesn't, then he's saying: 'Let the physician decide,' not just what's extraordinary and ordinary, but also whether or not to continue extraordinary treatment. Placing that kind of power in physicians is surely controversial enough to need a defense, which the author doesn't make." Discuss Gary's analysis.
5. Is the example given in paragraph 5 argumentative or strictly illustrative?
6. Which of the following additional pieces of information, if true, would weaken the author's point made in paragraph 6 and constitute neglect of relevant evidence?
   A. A 1984 article in the *New England Journal of Medicine* co-authored by ten physicians at top medical schools suggested that the severely demented be added to the list of comatose and vegetative as candidates for passive

euthaniasia, as well as even the "pleasantly senile," that is, mildly impaired people in nursing homes, be given intensive medical care only "sparingly."

B. A poll finds that, in the absence of a clear expression of feeling and desire from the patient or a family member, physicians are extremely reluctant to discontinue extraordinary treatment.

C. A study finds that most doctors find it very difficult to depart from their curative role in dealing with the terminally ill.

D. A and B.

E. B and C.

F. A and C.

G. A, B, and C.

7. Do cases like Quinlan and Cruzan support or belie paragraph 7?

8. Which of the following generalizations best fills in the premise that is missing in the argument expressed in the first sentence of paragraph 7?

A. Extraordinary treatment is treatment whose costs outweigh its benefits.

B. Only medical professionals can determine what is extraordinary and what is ordinary.

C. A decision about what is ordinary or what is extraordinary is the same as a decision to refuse extraordinary treatment.

D. Extraordinary means should never be used.

9. Identify and evaluate the use of authority in paragraph 7.

10. Do you think the phrase "of this nature" in paragraph 7 is clear enough?

11. Chico believes that the author has set up a straw argument through exaggeration in paragraph 7. He explains why: "The author says that it's 'inappropriate' to set up a precise rule or procedure before the fact. But who's wanting that? All I want is the legal right to select someone to plead my case if I can't. What's so complicated about that? The law already has the notion of 'power of attorney.' Delegating authority in death decisions is just extending power of attorney, which seems to work pretty good. To me, the author's making a mountain out of a molehill—setting up a phony problem." Do you agree with Chico's analysis?

12. The use of the word "appropriate" in paragraph 7 is

A. vague.

B. ambiguous.

C. A and B.

D. clear and precise enough.

13. In response to paragraph 7 Carrie says, "Paragraph 7 is a blatant appeal to the paternalistic authority of the medical profession. The author says that only medical people are qualified to decide what's ordinary and extraordinary. That's ridiculous. They may be qualified to decide what's ordinary and extraordinary from a *medical* viewpoint, but that's all. The author himself defines extraordinary in paragraph 4 in terms of treatment that's so burdensome that its cost (in terms of suffering by patient and family, money, etc.) is in excess of its likely benefit to the patient. What makes doctors so all-knowing and wise that they alone are qualified to tell me what's too expensive and what isn't, what

emotional burden I can and can't bear, what a family is able to endure? Yes, doctors are qualified to speak on medical matters. But that's all." What do you think of Carrie's reaction?

14. State the generalization that paragraphs 8–11 are intended to support. What kind of generalization is this?

15. Why do you think the author uses the phrase "put a person to death" rather than, say, "allow a person to die" (paragraph 8)? Does the choice of phrase make any difference here?

16. The innuendo(s) of the first three sentences of paragraph 8 is(are)
    A. positive or active euthanasia is practiced today.
    B. the AMA makes little if any distinction between active and passive euthanasia.
    C. the courts make little distinction between active and passive euthanasia.
    D. B and C.
    E. A, B, and C.

17. B. J. thinks that the Brophy example undoes most of what the author previously said. "After all," he explains, "this is a case where, presumably, Brophy's physicians considered Brophy's further maintenance 'extraordinary treatment.' The author may consider feeding to be 'care' and not 'treatment,' but that seems to be beside the point. If he wants physicians to decide what's extraordinary treatment, then he should accept the full implications of this. In this case, it means that he should accept the decision of Brophy's physician." Do you agree with B. J. that the author is being inconsistent.

18. Is the word "valid" in paragraph 8 clear and precise?

19. Is the phrase "out and out killing" (paragraph 8) emotive?

20. Which of the following would be a relevant criticism of paragraph 9?
    A. In a sense, one always has "something to gain" from the death of a terminally ill loved one — to see the person's suffering end.
    B. Children generally love their parents.
    C. Outside parties are not necessarily more qualified to evaluate conflicts of interest than the person who designated and reaffirmed the durable power of attorney.
    D. A and B.
    E. B and C.
    F. A and C.
    G. A, B, and C.

21. What is the emotive word in paragraph 10?

22. Paragraphs 9, 10, and 12 exploit the emotions of
    A. anger.
    B. loyalty.
    C. jealousy.
    D. fear.
    E. love.

23. In response to paragraph 10, Neil says, "The laws could override a doctor or relative's desires, thereby 'railroading' someone 'into an early grave.' But by the same token, the override might have the effect of easing someone's suffering,

saving the person from wasting money on futile and exotic medical treatment, saving the family from the emotional ordeal of watching their loved one suffer, and carrying out the person's expressed wishes. So, since the author's evidence really can support opposed conclusions, it's of no value to his argument."

Do you agree with this analysis?

24. GEORGE: I agree with the author that the phrase "terminally ill" [*paragraph 11*] is pretty vague.

GERALDINE: But it's not so vague that we don't understand what it means and can't apply it meaningfully. For example, most of us probably would agree, including doctors, that a person with inoperable stomach cancer has a "terminal" disease, despite our inability to say exactly how much time the person has left. Probably what we mean is that the disease is incurable, uncontrollable, and life threatening within the foreseeable future. Diabetes is not a terminal disease in this sense any more than hypertension is. If the author insists that they are, then he's switching the common meaning of "terminal illness."

GEORGE: But what he means is that, because it's difficult to precisely define when an illness is "terminal," a durable power of attorney is useless because it involves the existence of a terminal disease.

GERALDINE: What I'm saying is that the term is precise enough to be useful. But beyond that, Cruzan and Brophy weren't suffering from a terminal disease. They were in a chronic vegetative state, where, in all likelihood, they would remain. So, the durable power of attorney is applicable to these cases regardless of any problems in defining "terminal illness." But even if the living will and power of attorney are to be confined to terminal illness cases, let me ask you this: Who, according to the author, is to decide what is "extraordinary treatment"?

GEORGE: The doctor.

GERALDINE: And on what basis?

GEORGE: Cost/benefit.

GERALDINE: Right. Now isn't it pretty difficult to decide at exactly what point cost outweighs benefit?

GEORGE: Difficult, but not impossible.

GERALDINE: That's exactly my point about determining terminal illness. In fact, I'd say we have a firmer ground for calling an illness terminal than calling a treatment extraordinary.

GEORGE: Why's that?

GERALDINE: Because we can test diagnoses of terminal illness against actual outcomes. And when we do, we find that in the vast majority of cases, forecasts of life expectancy based on some terminal illness are very accurate. The reason is that we have a mountain of material concerning the morbidity of these diseases. It's on this basis that physicians can call a disease "terminal" in the first place. But it's impossible for us ever to verify a decision about extraordinary versus ordinary treatment, because of the basically subjective nature of the decision.

GEORGE: So what's your point?

GERALDINE: My point is that if the author is going to attack "terminally ill" as hopelessly imprecise, then he should admit that "extraordinary" and "ordinary" are no better.

Discuss Geraldine's analysis.

25. Does the author give any specifics to support his observations about the "marked tendency" (paragraph 12) to blur the distinction between terminally and incurably ill?

26. Is the generalization about pro-euthanasia literature in paragraph 12 qualified or unqualified? If unqualified, do you think it should be qualified? Does the author cite any specifics to support this generalization? Do you think any are in order?

27. Do you agree that a distinction between terminally and incurably ill is relevant to the issue at hand, which concerns the efficacy of durable power of attorney laws?

28. In paragraph 14, is the author drawing or applying a generalization?

29. Do you think the aforementioned generalization is adequately supported?

30. In paragraphs 14 and 16, the author uses the phrase "sanctity of human life." The author believes that those favoring living wills disrespect life. But living will advocates insist that it is precisely out of respect for the "sanctity of life" that living wills are needed. How do you acount for this dispute?

31. In paragraph 15, the author
    A. tries to plant suspicions about the motives of those favoring living wills.
    B. attempts to associate living wills with suicide.
    C. implies that living will advocates do not have the interests of the intended beneficiaries in mind.
    D. A and B.
    E. B and C.
    F. A and C.
    G. A, B, and C.

32. Can you spot and explain the false dilemma in paragraph 16?

RELATED THEME TOPICS

1. *Write an article for the school newspaper in which you try to convince your audience that, as young as some of them are, they should consider drawing up a living will.*

Topics 2 and 3 are based on the following actual case:

Seventy-eight-year-old Earle N. Spring was suffering from end-stage kidney disease, which required him to undergo hemodialysis three days a week, five hours a day. He was also suffering from chronc organic brain syndrome, or senility, which left him completely confined and disoriented, and thus mentally incompetent. Physicians considered both the kidney disease and the senility permanent and irreversible, and saw no prospect of a medical breakthrough that would provide a cure for either disease. Without the dialysis treatment, Spring could die; with it, he might survive for months or years.

Spring's wife and son, who had been appointed temporary guardian of his father, petitioned a probate court for legal authorization to discontinue Spring's life-sustaining medical treatment. The court appointed a guardian for Spring to look into the matter. Although the guardian opposed the cessation of treatment, the judge authorized it. In response, the guardian appealed the judgment to the Massachusetts Appeals Court, which upheld the judgment of the lower court. Undaunted, the court-appointed guardian made other legal moves. But before any final resolution, Earle Spring died.

2. Suppose the appeals court had overturned the lower court's decision, thereby upholding the court-appointed guardian's request that treatment be continued. *Write an essay in which you argue that, if this happened, Spring's family would have been morally justified in discontinuing Spring's hemodialysis treatment, or, alternatively, that they would not have been.*

3. *Write an essay in which you argue (1) that only the court should decide when the use of life-sustaining treatment should be discontinued;* or, alternatively, (2) that other parties should decide — for example, the patient, if competent; the patient's family or physicians, or a hospital ethics committee, when the patient is incompetent or even competent.

Arguments From Comparison and Analogy

INTRODUCTION

A young job applicant is pondering a question on a psychological test administered by a large company: "Which of the following magazines do you read regularly?" Among the magazines listed are *People, Mother Jones, Business Week, Playboy, Fortune, Time, Harper's, Sports Illustrated,* and *Barron's.* The candidate ordinarily reads *Mother Jones, Playboy,* and *Sports Illustrated,* but if he lists *Mother Jones,* he fears he will be considered too liberal for the job; if he lists *Playboy,* he thinks he might be judged a bounder, or worse; and if he cites *Sports Illustrated,* he suspects he might be viewed as a "jock." So, he decides to put down *Barron's, Fortune,* and *Business Week,* none of which he reads on a regular basis.

Owing to a merger, a woman who solicits magazine ads for a living suddenly finds herself unemployed. She is fifty-seven and, despite a good record, stands little chance of landing a job in her field because of its bias in favor of youth. She is vigorous and healthy, and would look much younger if it were not for her grey hair. So, before beginning her job hunt, she dyes her hair black. "Why, you don't look a day over forty-five," her husband beams. Emboldened by her youthful appearance, she begins to state her age as forty-five on job applications.

What do you think of such behavior? A number of years ago, a Harvard professor of business administration attempted to justify such behavior as acceptable lying. The following excerpt is from his controversial essay.

448

Most executives from time to time are almost compelled, in the interests of their companies or themselves, to practice some form of deception when negotiating with customers, dealers, labor unions, government officials, or even other departments of their companies. By conscious misstatements, concealment of pertinent facts, or exaggeration—in short, by bluffing—they seek to persuade others to agree with them. I think it is fair to say that if the individual executive refuses to bluff from time to time—if he feels obligated to tell the truth, the whole truth, and nothing but the truth—he is ignoring opportunities permitted under the rules and is at a heavy disadvantage in his business dealings.

We can learn a good deal about the nature of business by comparing it with poker. While both have a large element of chance, in the long run the winner is the man who plays with steady skill. In both games ultimate victory requires intimate knowledge of the rules, insight into the psychology of the other players, a bold front, a considerable amount of self-discipline, and the ability to respond swiftly and effectively to opportunities provided by chance.

No one expects poker to be played on the ethical principles preached in churches. In poker it is right and proper to bluff a friend out of the rewards of being dealt a good hand. A player feels no more than a slight twinge of sympathy, if that, when—with nothing better than a single ace in his hand—he strips a heavy loser, who holds a pair, of the rest of his chips. It was up to the other fellow to protect himself. In the words of an excellent poker player, former President Harry Truman, "If you can't stand the heat, stay out of the kitchen." If one shows mercy to a loser in poker, it is a personal gesture, divorced from the rules of the game.

Poker has its special ethics, and here I am not referring to rules against cheating. The man who keeps an ace up his sleeve or who marks the cards is more than unethical; he is a crook, and can be punished as such—kicked out of the game or, in the Old West, shot.

In contrast to the cheat, the unethical poker player is one who, while abiding by the letter of the rules, finds ways to put the other players at an unfair disadvantage. Perhaps he unnerves them with loud talk. Or he tries to get them drunk. Or he plays in cahoots with someone else at the table. Ethical poker players frown on such tactics.

Poker's own brand of ethics is different from the ethical ideals of civilized human relationships. The game calls for distrust of the other fellow. It ignores the claim of friendship. Cunning deception and concealment of one's strength and intentions, not kindness and openheartedness, are vital in poker. No one thinks any the worse of poker on that account. And no one should think any the worse of the game of business because its standards of right and wrong differ from the prevailing traditions of morality in our society.[1]

You would probably agree that the author's position is quite provocative. What is of particular interest to us, however, is the way he develops his argument—by drawing a specialized comparison, called an analogy, between poker and business. His analogical form of argument can be represented as follows:

---

[1]Albert Z. Carr, "Is Business Bluffing Ethical?" *Harvard Business Review,* January/February 1968.

Poker has certain characteristics — the element of chance, a bold front, self-discipline.
Business has these same characteristics.
But poker has an additional characteristic — its own brand of ethics, which we accept as different from conventional ethics.
_____

Therefore, business has its own brand of ethics, which we should accept as different from conventional ethics.

Notice how an inferred resemblance is formed on the basis of assumed resemblances. This kind of inductive argument, termed an argument from analogy, turns up in many essays, so it is well worth our study. Before inspecting analogies, however, we need to say something about the general nature of comparisons.

MODULE 10.1

COMPARISON AND CONTRAST

In general, comparison can be considered a basic arrangement of ideas — a pattern of thinking translated into writing. In a strict sense, comparison focuses on likenesses, usually between things we view as different (for example, living at home and living on campus while attending college). The term *comparison* also refers to *contrast,* and an essay developed by comparison typically employs contrast as well. Contrast points up differences, mainly between things that are usually considered similar, such as male and female brain structure. Since comparison and contrast usually function together, what we will say about comparison applies equally to contrast.

We need not go far to spot everyday decisions that involve comparisons. The foods we eat, clothes we wear, television programs we watch, books we read, friends we choose, and recreational activities we enjoy all involve comparisons, although perhaps on an unconscious level. Sometimes, the comparisons we make become explicit. Thus, we seriously weigh the choice of a major, wonder whether to experiment with drugs or casual sex, or we think about where we would like to live. In little and big ways, subtle and overt, our decisions reflect the centrality of comparative thought in our lives.

Regarded as a way of thinking and writing, a comparison establishes similarities between things from the same class. For example, you might compare rock and country, two kinds of music; or you might compare electronic (television and radio) news with print news, two kinds of journalism. Comparisons involve two operations: (1) isolating two categories of the same subject and (2) isolating common features of the two categories. The relationship can be charted as follows:

X is like Y with respect to S.

Category 1	Likeness	Category 2
X	L_1	Y
X	L_2	Y
X	L_3	Y
X	L_4	Y

In this scheme, X represents the first category in the comparison and Y the second. S represents the subject under which the categories fall. L_1, L_2, L_3, and L_4 represent the bases for establishing *likenesses* (or, alternatively, differences, in which case D_1, D_2, and so on could be substituted).

To illustrate the process involved in comparison, suppose you are interested in comparing living at home with living on campus while attending college. You might employ the following sort of arrangement:

Living location while attending college

At home		*On campus*
_____	Cost	_____
_____	Convenience	_____
_____	Independence	_____
_____	Educational	_____
	experience	

Although simple, this comparison points up some important aspects of the logic of comparisons. *First, the items compared should come from roughly similar areas of experience or levels of abstraction.* For example, it would be appropriate to compare one science-fiction film with another, one political philosophy with another, or one form of protein with another. It generally would not be appropriate to compare, say, an automobile with a forest or an economic philosophy with a baseball game. *A second aspect of comparison is that the items must share at least several characteristics;* otherwise there is no basis for the comparison.

Comparisons often serve merely to illustrate or clarify. Consider, for example, this excerpt from a book about the dangerous trek of pioneers across the overland trail in the nineteenth century. Notice how the author contrasts writing styles to illustrate the separate social and cultural worlds of pioneer women and men:

> Differences between the worlds of women and men are reflected in the emigrant diaries. . . . Women usually wrote with a pervasive personal presence most often using the first person. . . . "I am now sitting on a hill side on a stone, a little distant from the camp," Rebecca Ketcham wrote in her diary late one afternoon. "After I commenced writing Mrs. Dix called to me to come to her to see a beautiful bunch of verbena she had found. . . ." Even in less fluently written women's diaries, the subject "I" tended to be the ultimate standard of perception. . . . Men, on the contrary, typically employed the more impersonal "we." . . . Usually the "we" most clearly referred to the men as a group.
>
> (May 4, 1851) We traveled 16 miles this day over a hilly road. . . .

(May 7) This day we gathered up and started after traveling five or six miles it commenced blowing and raining very hard. We all got very wet.

(May 8) This morning some of our women washed. We gathered up afternoon and traveled ten miles and camped on an open prairie, where we had no woods and but little grass.

Men's writing was usually plain, unadorned, and terse. . . . Women, on the other hand, frequently employed a range of stylistic elaboration. . . . Most women used extended description: colorful adjectives, qualifying phrases, long passages of explanation and summary. . . . It was a rare man, however, who regularly employed elaborating devices in diary writing. . . .

In general, men and women were concerned with different orders of meaning. There was an almost inverse relationship in the way most men wrote about objects and things, most women about people. . . . These differences in writing style conform to the differences between the social and cultural worlds of men and women. . . .[2]

But comparison and contrast can also be used to persuade and convince, as when advertisers tout the strengths of their products compared with the competition's or when scientists use a comparison of the effects of an experimental drug on control groups to draw conclusions about the drug.

It is also worth noting that occasionally the comparison is implied. For example, in the following passage the author bases his indictment of the news media on an implied industry-wide comparison of their news coverage, which he finds uniform throughout the industry.

While having an abundance of numbers and giving the appearance of great diversity, the U.S. news media actually offer a remarkably homogenized fare. News services for dailies throughout the entire nation are provided by the Associated Press (AP), United Press International (UPI), the *New York Times* news services, the *Los Angeles Times–Washington Post* news service, and several foreign news services like Reuters. The ideological viewpoint of these news conduits are much the same, standardized and narrow in the kind of information they allow the American public to receive. The same conservative commentators, along with an occasional liberal one, appear in newspapers coast to coast on the same day.

Many newspapers, in the smaller cities, publish editorials and political cartoons supplied by the central news services, and other features that specialize in blandness and in the implicit acceptance of the existing system and existing social conditions. The blandness disappears, however, when law and order, communism, the Soviet "threat," labor strikes, and minority unrest are discussed.

More and more newspaper space is given over to "soft" rather than "hard" news, to trivialized features and gossip items, to stories about movie and television stars, to crime, scandal, and sensationalism. Television, radio and newspaper coverage of national and local affairs is usually scant, superficial, and oriented toward "events" and "personalities," consisting of a few short "headline stories" and a number of conservative or simply banal commentaries and editorials.

---

[2]From John Mack Farragher, *Women and Men on the Overland Trail,* (New Haven, Conn: Yale University Press, 1979). Reprinted by permission of Yale University Press.

Pouring into editorial offices and news rooms across the United States from the centralized news-service syndicates are photographs, news features, women's features, comic strips, sports columns, advice to the lovelorn, horoscopes, book reviews, and film and threater reviews. Whichever newspaper one reads or television stations one views, in whatever part of the United States, one is struck by the indistinguishable and immediately familiar quality of the news and political views presented and of the people presenting them. One confronts a precooked, controlled, centralized, national news industry that is in sharp contrast to the "pluralistic diversity" of opinion and information which is supposed to prevail in the United States. . . .[3]

EXERCISES ON COMPARISON AND CONTRAST

Set up a comparison and contrast between the following pairs. Indicate at least three points of comparison and three points of contrast.

1. Two politicians
2. Two kinds of automobile
3. Two cities
4. The attitudes of the present generation of young people toward work and the attitudes of their parents or a previous generation
5. Solar and nuclear energy
6. Capital punishment and life in prison
7. College education and noncollege education
8. Living in an apartment and living in a house
9. Having children and not having children
10. Having a pet and not having a pet

FAULTY COMPARISONS

Comparisons used in argument can go awry in many ways. Three of the more common ways involve incompleteness, selectivity, and false dilemma.

Incomplete Comparison

The fallacy of incomplete comparison consists in making a comparison on too few points. As indicated, a good comparison must include at least several significant, common points. If it does not, any conclusion based on the comparison will probably be a hasty one. For example, it would be hasty to conclude that living at home is better than living on campus on the basis of just one point of comparison: costs. Similarly, it would be premature to infer that solar energy is preferable to nuclear energy simply because the former may be safer. Although it is one's prerogative to weigh safety more heavily in any comparison, it is not good form to disregard other

---

[3]Micharel Parenti, "Does the U.S. Have a Free Press?" *The Witness*, March 1985. Reprinted with permission from *The Witness*, Box 359, Ambler, Pa. 19002, and from the author.

points of comparison. In not broadening the base of comparison to include at least several significant points, the writer lacks sufficient evidence for drawing a conclusion and thus violates the third criterion of a good argument—that the premises provide adequate support for the conclusion.

Selective Comparison

The fallacy of selective comparison consists in selecting only those points of comparison that advance one's claim, while ignoring or suppressing other significant points. Overzealous to make a point, writers may select only points of comparison that establish the conclusion, while ignoring or suppressing points that detract from it. When they do this, they render the comparison faulty by neglect of relevant evidence. For example, suppose you were comparing the relative merits of two automobiles, A and B. You compare them in terms of safety, style, price, and power. By these criteria, car A excels. But missing from your bases of comparison are such significant categories as fuel efficiency, maintenance costs, performance, and engineering. Should comparison on these points weaken your conclusion, you are arguing erroneously. In fact, since these factors are so significant in assessing a car, any conclusion drawn without considering them probably would be incorrect.

We can also make selective comparisons and argue erroneously when we introduce a point of comparison, then ignore relevant information about it. For example, suppose that car A is cheaper than car B because its basic price does not include a radio and air conditioner, whereas B's basic price does include these items. Omitting this fact in the comparison misleads the audience.

Incomplete and selective comparisons often go in tandem. Not long ago, for example, some fast food chains (for example, McDonald's), reacting to pressure from environmentalists, switched to paper containers from plastic foam (Styrofoam) containers. The decision to switch was based on the perception of paper's recyclability. Because paper is easier to recycle than plastic foam, environmentalists argued, it is better for the environment than Styrofoam. But a more evenhanded comparison suggests otherwise. Accordingly:

1. Starting with raw materials, the manufacture of both the foam cup and the paper cup require the same amount of petroleum products (about four grams of fuel). In the case of paper, however, additional environmental damage occurs from the destruction of forests.
2. To make a paper cup requires about 1.8 grams of environment polluting inorganic chemicals (for example, chlorine, sulfuric acid, calcium hydroxide) compared with 0.5 grams to make a plastic cup.
3. The paper cup consumes about twelve times as much steam, thirty-six times as much electricity, and twice as much cooling water as a Styrofoam cup.
4. The unremovable contaminants in wastewater from pulping and bleaching operations are anywhere from ten to one-hundred times greater than in wastewater from styrofoam processing.
5. When paper degrades in a *moist* landfill, it gives off methane gas, which is believed to contribute to global warming. For its part, plastic foam emits environmental

pollutants from the use of the blowing agent pentane, but overall harmful emissions from paper are greater.

So, are we helping clean up the environment by insisting that our burger and fries come in paper rather than Styrofoam containers? Before deciding, we better compare the two on *all* significant points. (While we are at it, let's make sure that this is not a false dilemma—that there might not be environmentally safer options than either paper or styrofoam.)

False Dilemma

Another fallacy associated with comparisons is one we examined earlier—the false dilemma. This results when the writer assumes that two or more categories exhaust all available options, then proceeds with a comparison that, in effect, argues for one of the options. Advertisers particularly exploit this technique. Thus, an ad for a bank begins: "A logical alternative to the stock market: Madison Savings and Loan." Although a comparison involving the relative merits of investing in the stock market and in a bank is certainly permissible, it is not logical to use that comparison to conclude that one or the other is the best investment of *all* the alternatives. Again, manufacturers of modestly priced cars like to compare their products with luxury cars (for example, Volvo or Subaru with Mercedes or BMW). Based on the points considered (usually price and fuel efficiency), the modestly priced car inevitably comes out the better choice. Not only do such ads usually omit relevant points of comparison on which their product might not fare as well (for example, engineering and maneuverability), they erroneously imply that there are only two alternatives—their modestly priced car or the competition's very expensive car. In drawing comparisons that do not exhaust all the alternatives, then, the fair-minded writer is careful to point this out. Failing to do this, one can write a rather lengthy and otherwise acceptable essay that is predicated on a false generalization—that the two categories cited are exhaustive.

EXERCISES ON FAULTY COMPARISONS*

1. Identify what is being compared in the following passages and the points of resemblance or difference cited. Then evaluate the comparison in terms of their completeness, selectivity of resemblances, and exhaustiveness of alternatives.
   A. Arthritics: Arthritis Strength Bufferin provides more complete help than Anacin, Bayer, and Tylenol. Greater amount of pain reliever than Bayer or even Anacin for hours of relief from minor arthritis pain. Stomach protection ingredient Bayer and other aspirin do not have. More anti-inflammatory and anti-swelling ingredients than Anacin.
   B. For generations textbooks and children's books used in our school have depicted girls as passive observers, boys as bold achievers. Boys have been playing baseball or football while girls watch admiringly, hands clasped behind their backs. Girls were easily frightened; brave boys saved them from danger.

Boys made rockets and peered through microscopes; girls played with their dolls and tea cups. Boys have been portrayed as tousled and dirty from boisterous contact with life; girls as starched and pinafored, made of sugar and spice and everything nice.
(Dan Lacy)

C. Among preliterate peoples adolescence frequently does not cause the amount of trouble it does with us. From an early age the boy is in almost constant association with his father and learns almost all his skills and attitudes from him. With us, however, an adolescent boy is educated more by other associations in the community than by his father. Furthermore, among many primitives, boys and girls at about the time of puberty are inducted into manhood and womanhood or at least take their first step toward that goal. Initiation rites and impressive ceremonies mark a definite change in their status, and they acquire new rights and freedom through new responsibilities as well. In our society, however, there is no social recognition of new status when adolescence comes on. The boy becomes a young man physiologically, but he is still treated as a child and does not attain his majority till he is twenty-one. He is like a child who has outgrown his clothes and toys but is not given any others. This is at the root of his rebellion, when it comes to such a pass. His parents still try to dominate him in all his behavior — in his choice of clothes, work, friends, recreation, and even bedtime. In other words, the parent-child relationship continues long after it should have changed to a parent-adult relationship. The youth resents this, and the fight is on.
(Rab E. Baber)

D. Television . . . is depressing. The shuddering fluorescent jelly of which it's made seems to corrode the eye of the spectator and soften his brain. It's quite different from the movies, which seem to be made of nothing except the images themselves. There are no epiphanies to be had in television. There are none of the sometimes shattering apocalypses that one can get, even with the worst movies, in the dreamy caverns of the cinema. Possibly it's because Telly is so small and stingy. How could one ever hope to get an epiphany from it? Movies start with the advantage of an oceanic form, which can at least engulf the spectator and force him into a delicious surrender. Telly, on the other hand, is a mean, fidgeting irritant, far smaller than one's own field of vision, flickering away in the corner of the eye like a dull, damaged butterfly. . . .
(Jonathan Miller)

E. If I had been asked in my early youth whether I preferred to have dealings only with men or only with books, my answer would certainly have been in favor of books. In later years this has become less and less the case . . . I revere books — those that I really read — too much to be able to love them. But in the most reverable of living men I always find more to love than to revere: I find in him something of this world, that is simply there as the spirit never can be there. . . . Books are pure, men are mixed; books are spirit and word, pure spirit and purified word; men are made up of prattle and silence, and their silence not that of animals but of men. Out of the human silence behind the prattle the spirit whispers to you, the spirit as soul. . . . Here is an infallible test. Imagine yourself in a situation where you are alone, wholly alone on earth, and you are offered one of the two, books or men. I often hear men prizing their solitude, but that is only because there are still men somewhere on earth, even though in the far distance. I knew nothing of books when I came forth from the womb of my mother, and I shall die without books, with another human hand in my own. I do, indeed, close my door at times and surrender myself to a book but only because I can open the door again and see a human being looking at me. (Martin Buber)

2. Try constructing an argument of at least 100 words using comparison and contrast. Use one of the following sentences as a lead or topic sentence, or construct a lead sentence of your own.

   A. Seeing a film at the movies is better than seeing it on television.

   B. We can learn to value "assertiveness" by comparing it with the related notion of "aggressiveness."

   C. More and more women are becoming corporate executives. This probably will lead to some basic changes in the way business operates.

   D. Choosing a major is more difficult today than it was ten years ago.

MODULE 10.2

ANALOGY

Simple comparisons typically show similarities between *like* things, or things drawn from the same general category. Sometimes, however, comparisons are drawn between *unlike* things, as in "Football is war," "The human brain resembles a computer," or "Business is like poker." *Comparisons between unlike things in several respects is what, roughly stated, constitutes an analogy.*

An analogy has been likened to a simile, which involves a comparison between two things in some specified respect, for example, "My love is *like* a red, red rose" or "The expectant father is *as nervous* as a long-tailed cat in a room full of rockers." Things can be compared in basically two different kinds of respects. One comparison is in terms of qualities. For example, two things may be bright, soft, cold, coarse, pungent, shrill, and so on. Thus, when the poet writes "I wandered lonely as a cloud," he compares the properties or qualities he finds in his experience with what we all find in a cloud: isolation, drift, fragility, evanescence. He uses a simile to make some suggestion implicitly. But we can also compare things in terms of *relationships,* which in fact marks the analogy.

All things consist of parts that are arranged or organized in a certain way. What comprises a thing's organization are the relationships that its parts have to each other. Sometimes the relationships among the parts of one thing so closely correspond to the relationships among the parts of another that a comparison between the two things is possible and instructive.

For example, suppose you wanted to compare an actual airplane with a plastic model of it. Since they are made of different materials, you could not compare them in terms of qualities, but you could make comparisons in terms of the relationships between the parts of each. Thus, if the model is a good one, the positions and sizes of its parts will be related to each other exactly as they are in the actual airplane. To the extent that the relationships of the model's parts reflect the relationships of the airplane's parts, the model is a good one. It is this notion of relationship that characterizes the analogy. Thus, an analogy can be considered as an extended simile in which things are compared in terms of relationships.

On exhibit in Queens, New York, is a stunning model of Manhattan Island. What makes the model extraordinary is not just that it contains every building in New York City—about 800,000—but that its structure corresponds with the city itself. In other words, the relative sizes of the actual buildings are like the relative sizes of the miniatures; the relative distance between, say, JFK Airport and the Empire State Building is like the relative distance between their counterparts in the model; the relative lengths of the city's streets are like the relative lengths of the streets in the model, and so on. In a word, the analogy between the city and the model is extremely close—so close, in fact, that city planners have used the model in appraising proposals for new construction.

Analogy Problems

You have probably taken a test which asks you to solve analogies, or problems of the form A is to B as C is to D. This kind of problem is often written:

A:B::C:D.

When given on a test, one of the four terms is missing. In its place there are usually four options. The test-taker must select the option that best fits the analogy.

For example, the following simple analogy might be presented in any of four ways: WHITE:BLACK::LIGHT:DARK

1. WHITE:BLACK::LIGHT:(a. serious b. blue c. dark d. gray)
2. WHITE:BLACK::(a. gray b. light c. obscure d. serious):DARK
3. WHITE:(a. heavy b. color c. black d. somber)::LIGHT:DARK
4. (a. gray b. color c. somber d. white): BLACK::LIGHT:DARK

Implied in such problems is that a *relationship holds between the terms on the left that is like the relationship between the terms on the right.* In order to complete the analogy, you need to see the relationship.

In the above sample, you can conceive of the relationship between the terms in two ways. One way is to look at the two terms on the left (A:B) as one unit and the two terms on the right (C:D) as one unit. The relationship between the terms of each unit is one of *opposites:* WHITE is the opposite of BLACK, and LIGHT is the opposite of DARK. Thus, the correct answers to 1 and 2 are c and b, respectively.

The second way to conceive of the relationship between these terms is to consider the first and third terms as a unit, A:C; and the second and fourth terms as a unit, B:D. Thus, WHITE *is* LIGHT and BLACK *is* DARK. The correct answers to 3 and

4, then, are c and d, respectively. Regardless of the way you conceive of the relationship—which is dictated by the particular problem—the key thing to grasp is that you are trying to discover a *relationship* between the two terms in each unit that is the same. You can look for relationships either (1) between the first and second terms, then between the third and fourth terms; or (2) between the first and third terms, then between the second and fourth terms. *Never* find a relationship between the first and fourth or second and third terms.[4]

EXERCISES ON ANALOGY PROBLEMS*

For each of the following problems, select from the four options the term that best completes the analogy. Before making your choice, state the common relationship between the terms in the two units you are considering.

SAMPLE: GRAY:ELEPHANT::(a. white b. brown c. green d. gray):GRIZZLY BEAR

Relationship: An elephant is gray, a grizzly is brown.

Answer: b

SAMPLE: MALLET:(a. rugby b. hockey c. croquet d. hunting)::BAT: BASEBALL

Relationship: Croquet is played with a mallet, baseball with a bat.

Answer: c

1. CANARY:(a. red b. blue c. brown d. yellow)::POLAR BEAR:WHITE
2. HAT:WEAR::MILK:(a. pour b. spill c. drink d. chill)
3. (a. donkey b. horse c. bulldog d. snake):DEMOCRAT::ELEPHANT:REPUBLICAN
4. RACKETBALL:BADMINTON::TENNIS:(a. lacrosse b. football c. handball d. soccer)
5. YEN:JAPANESE::(a. dollar b. ruble c. doubloon d. France):RUSSIAN
6. TERRESTRIAL:(a. palatial b. partial c. martial d. celestial)::EARTH:HEAVEN
7. (a. velocity b. humidity c. temperature d. pressure):BAROMETER::MILEAGE: ODOMETER
8. ANESTHESIA:FEEL::(a. eyeball b. eyes c. glasses d. blindness):SEE
9. RAIN:(a. tempest b. frost c. hail d. dry ice)::WATER:ICE
10. NATURE:NURTURE::HEREDITY:(a. gene b. progenitor c. evolution d. environment)
11. YELLOW:(a. blue b. white c. green d. red)::COWARDLY:GLOOMY
12. BIOGRAPHY:AUTOBIOGRAPHY::(a. 1st b. 3rd c. 4th d. 5th):1st

---

[4]For further study of, and practice in, solving analogy problems, you can consult any of a number of guides for taking the Miller Analogies Test (MAT). (The MAT, which was developed for use at the University of Minnesota, where it was first administered in 1926, continues to be a popular instrument for testing one's recognition of relationships.) Barron's *How To Prepare for the MAT,* 5th ed., is one such guide.

13. LOBBYIST:LEGISLATOR::(a. lawyer b. judge c. court stenographer d. fore-man):JURY
14. ACTUAL:VIRTUAL::IN FACT:(a. in cause b. in time c. in truth d. in effect)
15. MEGAPHONE:CONE::TORNADO:(a. funnel b. cloud c. hurricane d. dictaphone)
16. (a. chroma b. violet c. rainbow d. black):COLOR::VACCUM:AIR
17. EMERALD:MINE::PEARL:(a. oyster b. clam c. mine d. river)
18. PART:TRAP::(a. farewell b. catch c. tail d. tar):RAT
19. (a. *Hamlet* b. plays c. Elizabethan d. theater):SHAKESPEARE::E = MC^2: EINSTEIN
20. SPRINGS:PALM::(a. Old b. York c. Reed d. Testament):NEW

Uses of Analogy

The ordinary analogy is not as strong as our model plane or city example. Still, analogies can be very useful in helping to illustrate or clarify general principles. Studying the interactions of an anatomically correct model of a human being, for example, can simplify our understanding of some basic principles involved in biochemistry and kinesiology. Analogies can also be used to suggest ideas that lead to important discoveries. Consider, for example, how our knowledge of the atom has developed.

Early scientists wondered how the atom's positive and negative electric charges were arranged so that atoms could exist as stable entities and not simply fly apart. Experiments by English physicist Ernest Rutherford (1871–1937) suggested that the atom's positive charge was highly concentrated. So Rutherford, and later Danish physicist Niels Bohr (1885 1962), suggested that the atom was *analogous* to the solar system. An atom, they theorized, is like a miniature solar system. Just as the sun is in the center of the solar system, so all of the positive charge is in the center of the atom. Similarly, just as the planets orbit the sun, so electrons move around the center of the atom while carrying the negative charge.

In effect, Rutherford and Bohr saw the solar system as a model of the atom, hypothesizing that the structure of the atom is *analogous* to the structure of the solar system. Even today, this model is employed in elementary discussions of atomic physics.

Consider Archimides' (c. 287–c. 212 B.C.) discovery that a body immersed in fluid loses in weight an amount equal to the weight of the fluid it displaces. Supposedly, the discovery occurred while the ancient Greek mathematician was trying to solve a problem for King Hieron, who wanted to know what metals had been used in his crown. An obvious way to find out would be to melt the crown. The downside to that approach, of course, was that Hieron would be left crownless. Archimides solved the problem by using an analogy. Having observed that the water in his bath rose as his body displaced it, he reasoned by analogy that a certain weight of gold would displace less water than silver of the same weight, because gold is smaller in volume. When he so tested the crown, he found that it was, in fact, made of impure gold.

Another example of the power of analogical reasoning is found in Copernicus's (1473–1543) momentus theory of a sun-centered universe. Boating near the bank of a river one day, the brilliant Polish astronomer is said to have been struck by the illusion that the bank, and not his boat, was moving. Could a similar illusion produce

Speaking of . . .

The Uses of Analogy

The Discovery of Penicillin

The discovery of this remarkable weapon against disease dates back to 1929. It was purely accidental. Dr. Alexander Fleming, in St. Mary's Hospital, London, was growing colonies of bacteria on glass plates for certain bacteriological researches. One morning he noticed a spot of mold had germinated on one of the plates. Such contaminations are not unusual, but for some reason, instead of discarding the impurity and starting fresh, Dr. Fleming decided to allow it to remain. He continued to culture the plate, and soon an interesting drama unfolded beneath his eyes. The area occupied by the bacteria was decreasing, that occupied by the mold was increasing, and presently the bacteria had vanished.

Dr. Fleming now took up this fungus for study on its own account. He recognized it as of the penicillin genus, and by deliberately introducing a particle into culture mediums where bacteria were growing, he found that quite a number of species wouldn't grow in its presence. . . . In his laboratory, whenever he wanted to get rid of a growth of gram-positive bacteria, Fleming would implant a little penicillin, and after that the microbes disappeared. . . . So the medical scientist began to speculate. Since the mold destroyed gram-positive organisms on a culture plate, could it be used to destroy gram-positive disease germs in the living body?

(George W. Gray, *Science at War.*)

the common belief that the sun moves around a stationary earth? The thought so intrigued Copernicus that he went on to formulate his principle of heliocentric planetary motion, which, of course, revolutionized our understanding of the universe.

It is important to realize that none of these analogies proved anything — analogies never do. They suggest a possibility, a line of investigation, a hypothesis that, absent the analogy, might be overlooked. Bohr's solar system model of the atom was illustrative, provocative, and illuminating. It even suggested hypotheses. But, of itself, it did not prove a thing. When Benjamin Franklin (1706–1790) drew an analogy between the electric sparks and lightning based on a number of observed resemblances, he did not thereby prove that lightning was a form of electricity. Only a test, an experiment, could establish that. Thus, Franklin's famous kite-and-key experiment.

Models as the basis for analogies often play a crucial role in scientific research, in the creation of new theories; but do they play any role in the *justification* of these new theoretical hypotheses? Philosophers of science continue to debate this matter. The consensus view is that a theoretical hypothesis about a system different from the model cannot be justified by information about the model on which it is based, but only by information about that type of system. Nevertheless, analogies frequently form the basis of ordinary arguments in which someone infers resemblance based upon assumed resemblance.

MODULE 10.3

ARGUMENTS FROM ANALOGY

An argument from analogy is an argument in which the assumed resemblance between two things is used as evidence for inferring additional resemblances between them. For example, suppose that you are thinking about buying a car and that you are leaning toward a Toyota Celica because you are happy wth the one you currently own. You think that you will equally enjoy the new Celica because (1) it is the same model, (2) you will be driving it under the same conditions, and (3) you will maintain it at the same garage. Your analogical reasoning could be represented as follows:

> The old Celica is model GT; it has been driven exclusively by me, mainly on highways; and it has been maintained at the ACME garage.
> The new Celica will be model GT; it will be driven only by me and mainly on the open road, and will be maintained at the ACME garage.
> But the old Celica also has performed very well.
> _____
> Therefore, the new Celica probably will perform very well, too.

The form of any argument from analogy can thus be represented symbolically as follows, where X and Y represent the things compared, and a, b, c, and d the resemblances:

> X has characteristics a, b, c.
> Y has characteristics a, b, c.
> But X also has characteristic d.
> _____
> Therefore, Y probably has characteristic d.

Underlying an argument from analogy is the assumption that the *relationship* between the things compared (X and Y) is strong enough in terms of their assumed resemblances (a, b, c) to infer still another resemblance (d).

Arguments from analogy are inductive in that the known similarities between the two things are intended to provide some, but not indubitable, support for the conclusion that the two things have an additional similarity. Furthermore, an argument from analogy is similar to an induction by simple enumeration, differing only in the *particular* nature of its conclusion. Thus, from the premises in our Celica example, we might conclude by simple enumeration that *all* Celicas probably will perform well, which would be an inductive generalization. To draw a conclusion about a particular Celica, the one about to be purchased, would be an argument from analogy.

You would readily agree that if you could identify further relevant resemblances between the old and new Celicas, you would thereby strengthen your analogy. For example, the engines are identical as are the transmissions. Moreover, the more instances of Celica GTs you could plug into the analogy, the stronger the analogy would be. For example, suppose you had owned not one but two similar GTs with the same good results. In fact, you probably could imagine a *dissimilarity* that would have the effect of strengthening the analogy—for example, a friend who owned a GT and drove it mostly under punishing stop-and-go, urban conditions, but, like you, was completely satisfied with the car's overall performance. In this case, the experience of a different person driving under more trying conditions speaks well of the car. The point is that, like any inductive generalization, the strength of the argument from analogy is relative. The number of instances lying at the base of the analogy (that is, how many GTs are being compared) and how many dissimilarities (that is, *strengthening* differences) that differentiate them all affect the relative strength of the argument from analogy.

IN BRIEF   In evaluating an argument from analogy, we are interested in determining how strong the connection is between the things compared. The stronger the connection, the stronger the conclusion; the weaker the connection, the weaker the conclusion. The stronger the conclusion, the better the analogical argument; the less likely the conclusion, the poorer the analogical argument. Three key factors affect the relative strength of an argument from analogy:
(1) *the number of entities involved in the comparison;*
(2) *the number of relevant resemblances;*
(3) *the number of dissimilarities, that is, strengthening differences.*

It is worth noting that some arguments from analogy employ statistics. For example, assume that you have averaged twenty-five miles-per-gallon with your old Celica. Having satisfied yourself on the aforementioned grounds that the new Celica will probably perform like the old one, you buy the car fully expecting to get: (a) twenty-seven miles-per-gallon, (b) twenty-five miles-per-gallon, (c) twenty-two miles-per-gallon. Which of these conclusions is the safest? If you said (c), twenty-two miles-per-gallon, you are right. The reason is that (c) provides a greater margin for error than either of the other two. So, in some arguments from analogy it is appropriate to evaluate the breadth of the conclusion relative to the premises. This criterion is identical to the one we developed earlier for statistical generalizations: The greater the margin for error—the more "breathing" room the conclusion allows—the stronger the conclusion.

EXERCISES ON ARGUMENTS FROM ANALOGY*

1. Analyze the structure of the following arguments from analogy with reference to:
   (a) what is being compared, (b) their assumed resemblances, and (c) inferred

resemblance. Then try to provide an additional resemblance or dissimilarity which you think would have the effect of strengthening the analogy.

A. Children are very much like puppies. They have to be trained and taught how to behave. And we all know that puppies occasionally need to be swatted to behave properly. So, we shouldn't condemn the parent who on occasion spanks an unruly child.

B. Most women have a penchant for child care. But the sick and infirm are like children in their need for attention, security, and nurturing. It follows that most women are well equipped to care for the ill.

C. Library books and textbooks are alike in many ways. They both contain information, help satisfy curiosity, and in general enrich peoples' lives. Therefore, since we don't charge people to withdraw books from libraries, we shouldn't charge students for textbooks.

D. It's likely that life exists on Venus, because it exists on earth and Venus has roughly the same diameter and approximately the same mass.

Each of the following two analogical arguments is followed by several additional premises. Indicate and explain where the additional premise would (A) strengthen, (B) weaken, or (C) have no effect on the conclusion. Then supply two additional premises for each argument that you believe would strengthen it.

2. On two separate occasions, you have really enjoyed the pepperoni pizzas you bought at Sam's Italian Villa. In the mood for some good lasagna, you decide, on the basis of your previous experiences, to get it at Sam's.
   A. Suppose you had previously also enjoyed a spaghetti dinner at Sam's.
   B. Suppose that on the two previous occasions Sam himself had prepared the food, but this time he is off.
   C. Suppose that Sam now serves beer and wine, which he did not previously.
   D. Suppose that a friend reports having a pizza at Giuseppe's Spaghetti House that makes Sam's pizzas pale by comparison.
   E. Suppose that Sam uses basically the same tomato sauce in his lasagna as in his pizzas.
   F. Suppose that the pizzas were smothered in mozzarella, which Sam does not use in lasagna.
   G. Suppose that you expect the lasagna to be at least edible.
   H. Suppose that Sam has put his business up for sale.
   I. Suppose that Sam has only recently introduced lasagna, whereas pizza has been on his menu since he opened.
   J. Suppose that the lasagna will cost you twice as much as a pizza would.

3. Connie has taken two literature courses and found both interesting and rewarding. She got an "A" in each. So, she signs up for another literature course, fully confident that it too will be rewarding.
   A. Suppose that the previous courses were in American literature, and the next one will be in English literature.
   B. Suppose that one of the courses was in medieval literature, the other in modern American literature.

C. Suppose Professor Chaucer taught the two literature courses Connie took and Professor Thackeray will teach the next one.

D. Suppose a close friend of Connie's equally enjoyed the two courses Connie took and found the one Connie intends to take disappointing.

E. Suppose the first two courses were offered at 9–10 A.M. M-W-F, and the new one is scheduled for 7–10 P.M. on Thursdays.

F. Suppose that Connie was an English major when she took the first two courses and that recently she switched her major to pre-med.

G. Suppose the textbook for the intended course will cost $10 more than either of the books in the previous courses.

H. Suppose she expects to get at least a B.

I. Suppose that the first two courses required term papers and that the next one will not.

J. Suppose that Connie has just taken on a part-time job.

MODULE 10.4

RESPONDING TO ANALOGIES

Since the argument from analogy turns up so often in essays, it is important to know how to respond to one. To begin, always make sure you understand the analogy. What is being compared? What are the assumed resemblances? What are the inferred resemblances? Once you have answered these questions, you are poised to assess the analogy.

Three approaches are available for evaluating the argument from analogy. Each aims to uncover significant weaknesses in the comparison and, thus, in the argument itself. These three strategies can be expressed in the form of the following questions.

1. Are there significant disanalogies between the things compared? Earlier we saw that sometimes differences between the things compared can actually strengthen an analogy. On the other hand, some differences *weaken* an analogy. *Weakening differences are termed disanalogies.* The comparison between your new and old Celica, for example, probably would be weakened if, say, the new one contained pollution control devices that the old one did not, or you intended to do far more intracity driving than with the old one, or you planned to share the car with another party. When arguers overlook disanalogies, they are really neglecting relevant evidence that counters the conclusion.

Since, by their nature, analogies compare unlike things, it is common for an argument from analogy to omit relevant, weakening differences. Thus, inspecting the comparison for disanalogies is usually a fruitful line of approach.

Consider, for example, this argument, the analogical conclusion of which is italicized.

> *Advertisement should no more be regulated than is poetry.* Just as a poem deals in fantasy, hope, and promise, so does the well-crafted ad. In fact, the purpose of the ad, like the poem, is to go beyond reality and offer illusion. But we never hear people clamoring for restrictions on poetry. The same can't be said of advertising. Why, we even have regulatory agencies whose mission it is to monitor and control advertising. And the most ardent advocates of such regulation probably would be among the first to shout "Censorship!" if anybody, let alone the government, attempted to muzzle the poet.

We could portray the analogical reasoning in this passage as follows:

Poetry deals in fantasy, hope, and promise. It goes beyond reality and offers illusion.
Advertising deals in fantasy, hope, and promise. And it, too, goes beyond reality and offers illusion.
But poetry is not regulated.

Therefore, advertising shouldn't be regulated.

Perhaps you feel an almost irresistible urge to dismiss this argument with the retort: "But advertising and poetry are different." Although understandable, such a reaction merely begs the question, for all analogies compare unlike things. The issue is whether the differences so weaken the comparison that the conclusion is not believable. Thus, a good criticism of an argument from analogy is not to point out what is implicit in any analogy—that the two things are different—but to *identify* the differences.

If we allow the arguer's generalizations about advertising and poetry, the argument is a rather intriguing one. It does, after all, pinpoint some key features that both advertising and poetry share. In fact, it would not be difficult to cite specific poems that contain the very features that the arguer associates with advertising. But the arguer overlooks the intention, function, and effects of advertising, which make it significantly different from poetry.

The intention of advertising is to persuade someone to buy something. Thus, advertising partially functions socio-economically to generate a perception of needs, which consumers translate into product demand. This, in turn, increases productivity, sales, profit, and employment. Moreover, advertising arguably has many serious social effects, including a blurring of the distinction between what some have termed "true" and "artificial" needs; a quickening of the impulse for immediate gratification; a heightening of unrealistic expectations and demands; an increase in the frustration that arises from the overselling of a product (as, for example, when an ad promises more than a product can deliver), and so on. Additionally, in advertising the informative and expressive functions of language are so fused—often intentionally, sometimes dangerously—that the consumer may no longer be able to distinguish between fact and non-fact. This, in turn, undercuts the consumer's capacity to make an informed, prudent decision. If this analysis is correct, it would seem that society has a highly legitimate interest in advertising that it does not have in poetry.

2. Is there a questionable generalization underlying the analogy? To understand this question, reconsider the form of an argument from analogy:

> **X has characteristic a.**
> **Y has characteristic a.**
> **But X also has characteristic b.**
> _____
> **Therefore, Y probably has characteristic b.**

There is an unexpressed premise in this argument. It is the generalization that whatever has characteristic "a" probably also has characteristic "b." Only that generalization would justify the inference that Y probably has characteristic "b." If this generalization is not true — if having characteristic "a" does not increase the likelihood of having characteristic "b" — the analogy is weak. Now let's try to apply this to an actual argument.

Suppose that a father is trying to convince his son of the harmful physical effects of alcohol. He points out that the delicate membranes of the stomach are much like the delicate membranes of the eye. "If you want to see what alcohol does to your stomach," he tells his son, "just put some gin into your eye." Now, the father's argument from analogy could be portrayed as follows:

> **The stomach has delicate membranes.**
> **The eye has delicate membranes.**
> **But alcohol can hurt the eye.**
> _____
> **Therefore, alcohol can hurt the stomach.**

It is not necessary to get into the physical differences between the stomach and the eye in order to answer this analogy. A more direct way is to spell out the generalization warrant that underlies it, namely: Anything that hurts the eye will also hurt the stomach. If this generalization were true, then lemonade would not be good to drink because it hurts the eye.[5]

3. Does the analogy boomerang when extended? Perhaps the most rhetorically effective and entertaining way to discover and point out the weakness in an analogy is by extending it. Consider, for example, this dialogue:

BILL : If a dog bites, club him. If a man commits a crime, imprison him.

TESS : Fair enough. But we also feed, shelter, and heal dogs when they're sick and injured. I guess you're in favor of government providing these services for people.

BILL : No way! There's already too much mollycoddling that goes on.

_____

[5]This example is as fine an illustration of answering an analogy by making its generalization explicit as when Professor Monroe Beardsley first presented it over forty years ago.

Notice that Tess seizes Bill's analogy and extends it to the point where Bill objects to it. She has, in effect, used Bill's own analogy to show the weakness in his reasoning and to refute his argument.

The same tack can be demonstrated by using this advertising slogan for a "high-protein" hair dressing:

> Cut out the greasies. Put your hair on a low-calorie diet.

Sounds good; after all, a greasy diet can make us fat, clog up our arteries with cholesterol, and disrupt our metabolism. Okay, let's see what kinds of low-calorie foods we can smear into our hair to keep it looking nice and healthy. Lettuce comes to mind. So does tofu, a rice cake, alfalfa sprouts, and refried beans, without lard of course. That should take care of the greasies![6]

In a more serious vein, consider this rather common analogy used by those opposing government regulation of business:

> Nobody interferes with runners in a race. In fact, the only way to determine who's the best runner is not to interfere with them. The economic race is no different. The only way the most efficient companies can prevail is by not interfering with the participants.

Insofar as this analogy pinpoints the competitive aspect of both a footrace and business, it has some merit. But let's push the analogy by suggesting that the runners should be allowed to jump the gun, or load up on steroids, or elbow a competitor off the track, or break out of their lanes at will. Chances are those advancing the preceding argument would object to these allowances on grounds of unfair competition, or, more to the point, of defeating the purpose of the race, which is to identify the best runner. In effect, then, the argument really implies the need for regulations in a foot race and, by analogy, in the economic race, as well. Indeed, it suggests that in business, as in a foot race, all participants should start at the same point, with equal access to the resources needed to compete equally, relying only on their native or acquired capacities to "run the race." But this would require strict regulation. In short, the analogy boomerangs by suggesting the very thing that it aims to defeat.

EXERCISES ON RESPONDING TO ANALOGIES*

1. Answer the four analogies in Exercise 1 of "Exercises on Arguments from Analogy" by (1) pointing out disanalogies, (2) showing that the analogy is based on an untrue generalization, or (3) extending the analogy to the point it boomerangs.
2. Evaluate each of the following arguments from analogy in terms of the same three strategies.
   A. Colleges should start paying students for getting high grades. After all, business handsomely rewards its top people with bonuses and commissions, and everybody can see the beneficial effects of that practice on worker productivity.
   B. A good reason for avoiding saccharine is that the chemical has produced cancer in experimental rats.

---

[6]See Ray Kytle, *Clear Thinking for Composition,* 4th edition. (New York: Random House), p. 102.

C. The government does not intervene to save a failing small business. So it should not bail out businesses like Chrysler and Pan American.

D. When I first moved into this complex, the ages of the tenants varied from twenty-one to thirty-five. Then the older generation moved in and most of my friends said how the place would go to pot. Well, today would you believe that the place is better because of them? That's why I think it wouldn't be bad to allow children in here.

E. The Congress extended the time in which the Equal Rights Amendment can be passed—it decided to send the struggle, the game into extra innings—a 40-month extension. To anyone in the stands this would be like an umpire on the field saying to a team with a 7-to-0 lead at the end of the last inning: "I am now changing the rules of the game to give the losers another chance to win." How many more chances, oh, umpire? Until the loser becomes the winner? (Cited in Jerry Cederblom and David W. Paulsen, *Critical Reasoning.* Belmont, California: Wadsworth, 1982, p. 140.)

F. "Are interior decorators really necessary? Yes. But not for the accepted reasons. Since one cannot set one's own broken leg one relies on a doctor. Without a formidable knowledge of legal intricacies one depends on a barrister. Likewise, unless the individual is well versed in the home furnishing field the services of an interior decorator are a distinct advantage."
(Helen-Janet Bonellie, *The Status of Merchants: The Trade of Interior Decoration.*)

G. "One ought to be able to hold in one's head simultaneously the two facts that *[surrealist artist Salvador]* Dali is a good draughtsman and a disgusting human being. The one does not invalidate or, in a sense, affect the other. The first thing that we demand of a wall is that it shall stand up. If it stands up, it is a good wall, and the question of what purpose it serves is separable from that. And yet even the best wall in the world deserves to be pulled down if it surrounds a concentration camp. In the same way it should be possible to say, This is a good book or a good picture, and it ought to be burned by the public hangman."
(George Orwell, "Benefit of the Clergy.")

H. "A married woman in her late twenties says she has been going topless for the last four years when the weather is pleasant, when she is working in her yard, driving her car, or riding a motorcycle with her husband. . . . A state highway patrolman, T. L. Hooks, stopped her Sunday while she was riding topless on a motorcycle with her husband. . . . Hooks said he later let her go because there is no law prohibiting her from being topless in public. 'I guess it's not legally indecent to do that,' he said, 'but I still believe it's improper. It could cause accidents.' The woman's husband supports her action. 'You can't have two sets of moral values, one for men and the other for women,' he said. And she said: 'If a man can go without a shirt, then so can I. There's not much difference between the chest of a man and the chest of a woman. A little more fat on the woman, a little more hair on the man. . . .'"
(Reported in Howard Popesel and David Marans, *Argument: Deductive Logic Exercises.*)

I.   Look here, Jim; does a cat talk like we do?

No, a cat don't.

Well, does a cow?

No, a cow don't, nuther.

Does a cat talk like a cow, or a cow talk like a cat?

No, they don't

It's natural and right for 'em to talk different from each other, ain't it?

'Course.

And ain't it natural and right for a cat and a cow to talk different from us?

Why, mos' sholy it is.

Well, then, why ain't it natural and right for a Frenchman to talk different from us? You answer me that.

Is a cat a man, Huck?

No.

Well, den, dey ain't no sense in a cat talkin' like a man. Is a cow a man?—or is a cow a cat?

No, she ain't either of them.

Well, den, dey ain't got no business to talk like either one er the yuther of 'em. Is a Frenchman a man?

Yes.

Well, den! Dad blame it, why doan he talk like a man? You answer me dat! (Mark Twain, *The Adventures of Huckleberry Finn.*)

J.   Letter to the editor criticizing a condominium rule prohibiting tenants from housing pets, in this case a pet cockatiel: "As for the noise, we wonder if the crows, the jay, the mockingbirds are somehow going to be dispossessed also. They are certainly noisier. Furthermore, living on the same street, we can attest to the fact that numerous motorcycles make more noise than a dozen birds, and at worse times, as well. Birds sleep at night. Cyclists don't."

MODULE 10.5

WRITING WITH REASON: DEVELOPING THE ARGUMENT FROM COMPARISON OR ANALOGY

If you are writing an argumentative essay that relies on the development of a simple comparison or analogy, it is crucial to be clear about what you are comparing, the resemblances and, in the case of the argument from analogy, the inferred resemblance. Be sure to include all significant similarities and not to overlook relevant differences. If your essay assumes that the subjects being compared are the only alternatives on which a choice rests, be sure that is actually the case. Otherwise, you will erect a false dilemma.

Regarding analogies, keep in mind that they basically function to illustrate and clarify—they never prove anything. This means that a resemblance inferred from even the strongest analogy should be supported by other means—for example—analysis, facts, reasons, and so on. Never attempt to establish a thesis *solely* on the basis of an analogy. *Use the analogy to reinforce a body of independent evidence that you are offering in support of the thesis.*

Also, remember that there is no perfect analogy. At some level, in some degree, differences will be found between the things compared. Thus, there will always be a tension between the logical limits and rhetorical utility of a constructive analogy. The writer's job is to determine just how far the analogy can be pushed. In determining the limits of your analogy, list beforehand all the relational correspondences, and all the differences. This will help you define the limits of the comparison before your audience does.

There are two basic ways for developing an essay by comparison or analogy: subject by subject or point by point. In both, the thesis is best stated early.

Subject-by-Subject Method

In this format, one of the two or more subjects of comparison or contrast is dealt with fully, point by point, then the other is. The approach is best used when the comparison is to be brief and the points not so elusive that readers forget what was said in the first half of the essay. When using this format, take care that both subjects are being compared according to the *same* points of comparison. Following is a subject-by-subject arrangement for an argumentative essay comparing TV news with print news:

I.   Introduction, including a thesis that makes an argumentative assertion.
II. TV journalism
    A. Nature
    B. Format
    C. Coverage
III. Print journalism
    A. Nature
    B. Format
    C. Coverage
IV. Summary

Such an essay might evolve as follows:

Introduction/Thesis: For most of us today, television is our main source of news. This is unfortunate, because the print media, especially newspapers, are a better source. A look at the nature of television and newspapers, as well as the news format and coverage of each, leads to this assessment.

First Subject

Point 1:   Television is essentially a passive medium. All we have to do is sit in front of the tube and "let it happen." This has sinister implications when it comes to news. . . .

Point 2:   The most noteworthy thing about the format of television news is time. Regardless of the complexity or significance of an event, it somehow must be fitted into a prescribed number of minutes. The problem with such an approach is that. . . .

Point 3:   Regarding coverage, television news excels in bringing into our living rooms dramatic events of singular importance: presidential inaugurations, space launchings, natural disasters, and so on. But because of its time limitations, television news cannot cover important stories in the depth they may deserve. Even more important, it cannot devote much attention to investigative reporting, which as often as not is left to such fine shows as "60 Minutes" and "20/20". . . .

Second Subject

Point 1:   In contrast to television, the print media encourage active involvement in what is being reported. Not only must we make some effort to acquire a newspaper, we must then read it. Reading requires mental involvement, often at a rather high level. It also accommodates individual differences in our capacity to follow and absorb what is being reported. . . .

Point 2:   With respect to format, print news is not restricted by considerations of time. A newspaper can devote as much space to a story as it sees fit and can afford. . . .

Point 3:   Of course, newspapers cannot give the visual coverage to stories that television does. Admittedly this is a distinct disadvantage, for the significance of some events, such as a war, is best communicated by pictures, not words. But newspapers can cover a war, or other stories, in far greater detail. . . .

Summary: What, then, does a consideration of television versus print journalism on the basis of nature, format, and coverage reveal? . . .

Point-by-Point Method

In the point-by-point method, the bases for comparison are discussed one by one within paragraphs of the essay that present each of the points in relation to each subject. Each of the points of comparison could be developed in either a single paragraph or a series of paragraphs, with a roughly equal amount of space given to each of the sides. The advantages of the point-by-point method are that it allows the writer to draw fine connections between subjects and eliminates the possibility that the reader will forget what was said earlier. The essay just discussed might be set up by point-by-point as follows:

I.   Introduction, including a thesis that makes an argumentative assertion.
II. Nature
   A. Television journalism
   B. Print journalism
III. Format
   A. Television journalism
   B. Print journalism
IV. Coverage
   A. Television journalism
   B. Print journalism
V.   Summary

The essay might develop as follows:

Introduction/Thesis: Same as in subject-by-subject method
     First Point: By nature, television is a passive medium. All we have to do is sit in front of the tube and "let it happen." This has sinister implications when it comes to news. . . .

          In contrast, the print media encourage active involvement in what is being reported. Not only must we make some effort to acquire a newspaper, for example, but then we must read it. Reading requires mental involvement. . . .

  Second Point: With respect to format, television news is severely restricted by considerations of time. Regardless of the complexity or significance of the event, . . .

          No such time limitation is imposed on print journalism. A newspaper can devote as much space to a story as it sees fit and can afford. . . .

    Third Point: Regarding coverage, television news excels in bringing into our living rooms dramatic events of singular importance. But because of its time limitations, television news cannot cover important stories in the depth they may deserve. . . .

          While print journalism cannot compete with television visually, it is superior to television news in fleshing out stories, in providing detail and depth. . . .

     Summary: Same as in subject-by-subject method.

IMPROVING PERFORMANCE

SUMMARY-TEST QUESTIONS FOR CHAPTER 10*

1. A comparison
   A. is an arrangement of ideas.
   B. is never useful in argument.
   C. is always an analogy.

    D. focuses only on similarities.
2. State the two operations that all comparisons involve.
3. Comparisons can be used to
    A. illustrate.
    B. clarify.
    C. argue.
    D. A and B.
    E. A, B, and C.
4. A comparison is faulty if it
    A. uses too few resemblances.
    B. erroneously reduces the number of options.
    C. omits relevant points.
    D. A and C.
    E. A, B, and C.
5. Analogies involve
    A. like things.
    B. relationships.
    C. unlike things.
    D. B and C.
    E. A, B, and C.
6. An analogy always implies a comparison, but a comparison does not necessarily imply an analogy. True or false?
7. Analogies
    A. are used to clarify.
    B. never prove anything.
    C. generate hypotheses.
    D. A and C.
    E. A, B, and C.
8. HORSE:DEAR::(a. precious b. dare c. book d. shore)::READ
9. Bohr's model
    A. demonstrated that the structure of the atom is like the structure of the solar system.
    B. suggested hypotheses.
    C. made use of what was known to help conceptualize what was unknown.
    D. A, B, and C.
    E. B and C.
10. Explain and illustrate the difference between an argumentive and a nonargumentive analogy.
11. Arguments from analogy are similar to induction by simple enumeration, differing only in the particular nature of their conclusions. True or False?
12. Express the argument from analogy in symbolic form.
13. Several responses follow this argument from analogy. Indicate which of the reasons is a good one and explain why in terms of its (a) pointing out disanalogies, (b) showing that the analogy is based on an untrue generalization, or (c) extending the analogy to the point it boomerangs.

THE ARGUMENT : A softball is round, and so is a bowling ball. So, since I can throw a softball a distance of one-hundred feet before it touches the ground, I can do the same with a bowling ball.

RESPONSE 1 : Right. And you can bat a bowling ball a hundred feet and drop it on your toe without feeling any pain. Get real!

RESPONSE 2 : Gimme a break. A softball doesn't have holes in it.

RESPONSE 3 : That's ridiculous. A bowling ball is different from a softball.

RESPONSE 4 : But a bowling ball weighs a lot more than a softball.

RESPONSE 5 : You're forgetting that a bowling ball and a softball are used in different kinds of activities.

RESPONSE 6 : So what you're saying is that what's true of one round object is true of all round objects. Interesting, I wonder how far you can throw that huge, round boulder over there.

Match the terms in the right column with those in the left.

14. disanalogy	A. weakening
15. analogy	B. strengthening
16. comparison	C. premise
17. argument from analogy	D. unlike things
18. dissimilarity	E. analogical problem
19. inferred resemblance	F. like things
20. assumed resemblance:_____	G. induction
:: inferred resemblance : conclusion	

21. Iran's Ayatollah Khomeini once defended state executions of adulterers, prostitutes, and homosexuals as follows: "If your finger suffers from gangrene, what do you do? Let the whole hand then the body become filled with gangrene, or cut the finger off? . . . Corruption, corruption. We have to eliminate corruption." Write a brief answer to his argument from analogy.

22. Each of the following passages can be considered an analogy; however, not all of them are *argumentative* analogies. Indicate which is an argument from analogy and which is not.

A. How like a winter hath my absence been from thee
   (Shakespeare)

B. TV programs shouldn't be interrupted by commercials; movies in theaters aren't, are they?

C. It's so hot today you could fry an egg on the sidewalk.

D. Perhaps the most startling discovery made in astronomy this century is that the universe is populated by billions of galaxies and that they are systematically receding from one another, like raisins in an expanding pudding.
   (Carl Sagan)

E. The objections which have been brought against a standing army, and they are many and weighty, and deserve to prevail, may also at last be brought against a standing government. The government itself, which is only the mode which the people have chosen to execute their will, is equally liable to be abused and perverted before the people can act through it.
   (Henry David Thoreau)

F. Thou *[west wind]* from whose unseen presence the leaves dead are driven, like ghosts from an enchanter fleeing
   (Shelly)
G. Sin, like barn fowl, comes home to roost.
H. Suppose that someone tells you that he has had a tooth extracted without an anesthetic, and I express my sympathy, and suppose that I am then asked, "How do you know that it hurt him?" I might reasonably reply, "Well, I know that it would hurt me. I have been to the dentist and know how painful it is to have a tooth stopped without an anesthetic, let alone taken out. And he has the same sort of nervous system as I have."
   (Alfred J. Ayer)
I. By what conceivable standard can the policy of price-fixing be a crime, when practiced by businessmen, but a public benefit, when practiced by the government? There are many industries in peacetime — trucking, for instance — whose prices are fixed by government. If price-fixing is harmful to competition, to industry, to production, to consumers, to the whole economy, and to the "public interest" — as the advocates of the antitrust laws have claimed — then how can the same harmful policy become beneficial in the hands of the government?
   (Ayn Rand)
J. Salesman Willie Loman has stayed at the Grand Illusion Inn every spring for the past five years on his annual swing through Connecticut, and has been quite satisfied with his accommodations. On his visit to Connecticut this spring, he fully expects to enjoy his stay at the Illusion. State whether each of the additional premises would make Willie's expectation more or less probable or have no effect on it. Explain.
A. Suppose that when he stayed at the Illusion before he had occupied a single room twice, a double room twice, and a suite once.
B. Suppose that a new manager now runs the Illusion.
C. Suppose he had occupied a single room on all of his previous trips and is assigned a single room this time, too.
D. Suppose that on his previous trips he had driven to Connecticut, but this time he will fly.
E. Suppose that the Illusion still is not recommended by the American Automobile Association.
F. Suppose that Willie has begun to experience job burn-out.

CRITICAL THINKING APPLICATIONS*

1. **Evaluate the poker/business analogy in the passage that began this chapter.**
2. **Analogies often play an important role in legal thinking and rulings. Here is an example from an important court case. Identify what is being compared, the assumed resemblance, and the inferred resemblance. Do**

you think that the correspondence between the things compared is strong enough to infer the resemblance the courts did?

In *Sweatt v Painter* . . . in finding that a segregated law school for Negroes could not provide them equal educational opportunities, the Court relied in large part on "those qualities which are incapable of objective measurement but which make for greatness in a law school." In *McLaurin v Oklahoma State Regents*, 339 U.S. 637 . . . the Court, in requiring that a Negro admitted to a white graduate school be treated like all other students, again resorted to intangible consideration: "his ability to study, to engage in discussions and exchange views with other students and, in general, to learn his profession." Such considerations apply with added force to children in grade and high schools. To separate them from others of similar age and qualifications solely because of their race generates a feeling of inferiority as to their status in the community that may affect their hearts and minds in a way unlikely ever to be undone. (U.S. Supreme Court. *Brown v Board of Education of Topeka*, 1954.)

3. **Analogies are very useful in investigating problems. The problem can be related to the analogy and then the analogy is pursued along its own lines of development. At each stage the development can be transferred back to the problem, and in this way the problem is carried along with the analogy.**

> **For example:** suppose you wanted to investigate the spread of rumors. You might use the analogy of a snowball rolling down a hill. Thus, as the snowball rolls down the hill, it gathers momentum and gets bigger and bigger. (The more a rumor spreads, the stronger it gets.) While it's rolling, the snowball gets bigger, collecting more and more snow in its course. (The more people who hear the rumor, the more it gets passed on to.) Of course, for a snowball to get bigger, there must be snow. At this point, confusion arises about what's being compared: the size of the snowball with the number of people who know the rumor or with the strength of the rumor itself. Does the snow correspond merely to the people who can be influenced by the rumor or to those inclined to believe this sort of rumor? Notice how the analogy is forcing us to really inspect the problem. A large snowball—perhaps an avalanche—is potentially very destructive to those in its path. Does a rumor pose the same threat to those who know it? Can they escape it if they're forewarned? Should they try to escape it, divert it, stop it? Notice, again, how the analogy when vigorously pursued compels us to think searchingly about the nature of rumors.[7]

Below is a problem, followed by several analogies. Using the preceding example as a guide, use each analogy to investigate the problem.

Problem: Finding your way in fog

Analogies: A nearsighted person finding his way around looking for something that has been lost in a house

A traveler in a strange country trying to find the railway station

Doing a crossword puzzle

---

[7]See Edward de Bono, *Lateral Thinking* (New York: Harper & Row, 1970), pp. 168–174.

4. **The process used in the preceding question can be reversed: The same analogy can be used to frame different problems. Try to relate each of the following problems to the analogy given.**

   Analogy: Trying to start a car on a cold morning
   Problems: How to tackle a difficult math problem
              Rescuing a cat from a high ledge
              Fishing
              Getting tickets for a popular concert

5. **Identify a problem, then develop an analogy which helps clarify and provide insights into it.**

POINT/COUNTERPOINT: ESSAYS FOR ANALYSIS

Issue: *World Hunger*

Resolved: The survival of rich nations depends on their not assisting poor ones.

Background: Much of our world is hungry. Famines in Africa and Asia occur with depressing regularity. For the poor in far off places such as Ethiopia, malnutrition is a hard fact of life. Every day, thousands of such people — usually the very young and the very old — die of diseases they probably could avoid were their bodies not ravaged by hunger. The fate of the surviving hungry is also grim. Permanently damaged by malnutrition, they further drain the meager resources of their impoverished nations. Indeed, some nations have become so populated by the listless and lethargic that they are virtually incapable of making an effort to prevent future famine. The United States, among other prosperous nations, historically has provided famine relief to such countries. But not everyone thinks this is a good policy.

From: Lifeboat Ethics: The Case Against Helping the Poor[8]

Garrett Hardin

In the mid-1970s professor of biology Garrett Hardin wrote an essay that ignited a debate about the obligations of rich nations to poor ones that continues into the present. Since its publication, "Lifeboat Ethics" has been the focus of considerable criticism and some support. A portion of the essay follows. As you read the excerpt that follows, keep in mind the utility and power of a well-cast analogy for framing a problem and argument. **After carefully reading the essay, outline it, then answer the questions that follow it.**

1 No generation has viewed the problem of the survival of the human species as seriously as we have. Inevitably, we have entered this world of concern through the door of metaphor. Environmentalists have emphasized the image of the earth as a spaceship — Spaceship Earth. Kenneth Boulding (1966) is the principal architect of this metaphor. It is time, he says, that we replace the wasteful "cowboy economy" of the past with the frugal "spaceship economy" required for continued survival in the limited world

---

[8]Reprinted with permission, from the October 1974 issue of *BioScience.* © 1974 American Institute of Biological Sciences.

we now see ours to be. The metaphor is notably useful in justifying pollution control measures.

2 Unfortunately, the image of a spaceship is also used to promote measures that are suicidal. One of these is a generous immigration policy. These suicidal policies are attractive because they mesh with what we unthinkingly take to be the ideals of "the best people." What is missing in the idealistic view is an insistence that rights and responsibilities must go together. The "generous" attitude of all too many people results in asserting inalienable rights while ignoring or denying matching responsibilities.

3 For the metaphor of a spaceship to be correct the aggregate of people on board would have to be under unitary sovereign control (Ophuls 1974). A true ship always has a captain. It is conceivable that a ship could be run by a committee. But it could not possibly survive if its course were determined by bickering tribes that claimed rights without responsibilities.

4 What about Spaceship Earth? It certainly has no captain, and no executive committee. The United Nations is a toothless tiger, because the signatories of its charter wanted it that way. The spaceship metaphor is used only to justify spaceship demands on common resources without acknowledging corresponding spaceship responsibilities.

5 . . . let us look at an alternative metaphor, that of a lifeboat. In developing some relevant examples the following numerical values are assumed. Approximately two-thirds of the world is desperately poor, and only one-third is comparatively rich. Metaphorically, each rich nation amounts to a lifeboat full of comparatively rich people. The poor of the world are in other, much more crowded lifeboats. Continuously, so to speak, the poor fall out of their lifeboats and swim for a while in the water outside, hoping to be admitted to a rich lifeboat, or in some other way to benefit from the "goodies" on board. What should the passengers on a rich lifeboat do? This is the central problem of "the ethics of a lifeboat."

6 First we must acknowledge that each lifeboat is effectively limited in capacity. The land of every nation has a limited carrying capacity. The exact limit is a matter for argument, but the energy crunch is convincing more people every day that we have already exceeded the carrying capacity of the land. We have been living on "capital"—stored petroleum and coal—and soon we must live on income alone.

7 Let us look at only one lifeboat—ours. The ethical problem is the same for all, and is as follows. Here we sit, say 50 people in a lifeboat. To be generous, let us assume our boat has a capacity of 10 more, making 60. (This, however, is to violate the engineering principle of the "safety factor." A new plant disease or a bad change in the weather may decimate our population if we don't preserve some excess capacity as a safety factor.)

8 The 50 of us in the lifeboat see 100 others swimming in the water outside, asking for admission to the boat, or for handouts. How shall we respond to their calls? There are several possibilities.

9 *One.* We may be tempted to try to live by the Christian ideal of being "our brother's keeper," or by the Marxian ideal (Marx 1875) of "from each

according to his abilities, to each according to his needs." Since the needs of all are the same, we take all the needy into our boat, making a total of 150 in a boat with a capacity of 60. The boat is swamped, and everyone drowns. Complete justice, complete catastrophe.

10 *Two.* Since the boat has an unused excess capacity of 10, we admit just 10 more to it. This has the disadvantage of getting rid of the safety factor, for which action we will sooner or later pay dearly. Moreover, *which* 10 do we let in? "First come, first served?" The best 10? The neediest 10? How do we *discriminate?* And what do we say to the 90 who are excluded?

11 *Three.* Admit no more to the boat and preserve the small safety factor. Survival of the people in the lifeboat is then possible (though we shall have to be on our guard against boarding parties).

12 The last solution is abhorrent to many people. It is unjust, they say. Let us grant that it is.

13 "I feel guilty about my good luck," say some. The reply to this is simple: *Get out and yield your place to others.* Such a selfless action might satisfy the conscience of those who are addicted to guilt but it would not change the ethics of the lifeboat. The needy person to whom a guilt-addict yields his place will not himself feel guilty about his sudden good luck. (If he did he would not climb aboard.) The net result of conscience-stricken people relinquishing their unjustly held positions is the elimination of their kind of conscience from the lifeboat. The lifeboat, as it were, purifies itself of guilt. The ethics of the lifeboat persist, unchanged by such momentary aberrations.

14 This then is the basic metaphor within which we must work our solutions. Let us enrich the image step by step with substantive additions from the real world.

15 The harsh characteristics of lifeboat ethics are heightened by reproduction, particularly by reproductive differences. The people inside the lifeboats of the wealthy nations are doubling in numbers every 87 years; those outside are doubling every 35 years, on the average. And the relative difference in prosperity is becoming greater.

16 Let us, for a while, think primarily of the U.S. lifeboat. As of 1973 the United States had a population of 210 million people, who were increasing by 0.8% per year, that is, doubling in number every 87 years.

17 Although the citizens of rich nations are outnumbered two to one by the poor, let us imagine an equal number of poor people outside our lifeboat—a mere 210 million poor people reproducing at a quite different rate. If we imagine these to be the combined populations of Colombia, Venezuela, Ecuador, Morocco, Thailand, Pakistan, and the Philippines, the average rate of increase of the people "outside" is 3.3% per year. The doubling time of this population is 21 years.

18 Suppose that all these countries, and the United States, agreed to live by the Marxian ideal, "to each according to his needs," the ideal of most Christians as well. Needs, of course, are determined by population size,

which is affected by reproduction. Every nation regards its rate of reproduction as a sovereign right. If our lifeboat were big enough in the beginning it might be possible to live *for a while* by Christian-Marxian ideals. *Might.*

19 Initially, in the model given, the ratio of non-Americans to Americans would be one to one. But consider what the ratio would be 87 years later. By this time Americans would have doubled to a population of 420 million. The other group (doubling every 21 years) would now have swollen to 3,540 million. Each American would have more than eight people to share with. How could the lifeboat possibly keep afloat?

20 All this involves extrapolation of current trends into the future, and is consequently suspect. Trends may change. Granted: but the change will not necessarily be favorable. If—as seems likely—the rate of population increase falls faster in the ethnic group presently inside the lifeboat than it does among those now outside, the future will turn out to be even worse than mathematics predicts, and sharing will be even more suicidal.

21 The fundamental error of the sharing ethics is that it leads to the tragedy of the commons. Under a system of private property the man (or group of men) who own property recognize their responsibility to care for it, for if they don't they will eventually suffer. A farmer, for instance, if he is intelligent, will allow no more cattle in a pasture than its carrying capacity justifies. If he overloads the pasture, weeds take over, erosion sets in, and the owner loses in the long run.

22 But if a pasture is run as a commons open to all, the right of each to use it is not matched by an operational responsibility to take care of it. It is no use asking independent herdsmen in a commons to act responsibly, for they dare not. The considerate herdsman who refrains from overloading the commons suffers more than a selfish one who says his needs are greater. (As Leo Durocher says, "Nice guys finish last.") Christian-Marxian idealism is counterproductive. That it *sounds* nice is no excuse. With distribution systems, as with individual morality, good intentions are no substitute for good performance.

23 A social system is stable only if it is insensitive to errors. To the Christian-Marxian idealist a selfish person is a sort of "error." Prosperity in the system of the commons cannot survive errors. If *everyone* would only restrain himself, all would be well; but it takes *only one less than everyone* to ruin a system of voluntary restraint. In a crowded world of less than perfect human beings—and we will never know any other—mutual ruin is inevitable in the commons. This is the core of the tragedy of the commons. . . .

24 If the argument of this essay is correct, so long as there is no true world government to control reproduction everywhere it is impossible to survive in dignity if we are to be guided by Spaceship ethics. Without a world government that is sovereign in reproductive matters mankind lives, in fact, on a number of sovereign lifeboats. For the foreseeable future survival

demands that we govern our actions by the ethics of a lifeboat. Posterity will be ill served if we do not.

1. Paragraph 1 functions to
   A. state the thesis.
   B. introduce the topic.
   C. offer a re-refutation.
2. Explain how paragraph 1 suggests the general usefulness of analogies in framing problems.
3. What practical difference does it make if we view the problem of world hunger in terms of "spaceship earth" as opposed to "cowboy economics." (In answering, try developing these analogies and apply them to the problem of world hunger.)
4. Precisely what does the author find objectionable about the spaceship analogy?
5. Exactly how does the author attempt to discredit the spaceship analogy *(paragraph 2)?*
   A. By raising disanalogies
   B. By extending the analogy
   C. By pointing out an unacceptable underlying generalization
   D. By citing dissimilarities
6. Paragraphs 3 and 4 attack the spaceship analogy by
   A. pointing out an untrue generalization on which it's based.
   B. raising weakening differences.
   C. identifying dissimilarities.
   D. extending the analogy to the point it boomerangs.
   E. identifying the resemblances.
7. Pick out the emotive label in paragraph 4.
8. One could reasonably infer from paragraph 4 that the author
   A. has contempt for the UN.
   B. believes that the UN provides needed world leadership.
   C. believes that UN members are more interested in their own interests than in their global responsibilities.
   D. A, B, and C.
   E. A and C.
9. "A true ship always has a captain," says the author in paragraph 3. He thus offers a/an _____ definition.
   A. lexical
   B. interpretive
   C. stipulative
   D. persuasive
10. According to the author, rich nations can be likened to
    A. lifeboats.
    B. well-stocked lifeboats.
    C. a spaceship.
    D. a well-stocked spaceship.

11. In paragraph 5, the author uses the lifeboat analogy to frame a/an _____ problem.
    A. historical
    B. economic
    C. logistical
    D. political
    E. ethical

12. Jose responds to paragraph 6 as follows: "The author says that a nation, like a lifeboat, has a limited carrying capacity. But we don't know exactly what the limit of a nation is. In fact, the author admits as much, but downplays that fact. Instead, he calls on popular sentiment — 'more people everyday believe we're overburdened' — to justify his claim. He needs to prove this, not just base it on what a lot of people think." What do you think of Jose's criticism?

13. Refer to paragraphs 4–11 to explain how the author uses the analogy to investigate the problem.

14. Karen expresses the following opinion of the lifeboat analogy: "The very existence of occupied lifeboats implies a shipwreck. But I'm not clear about what the ship is in the author's analogy. Is it planet earth? And how did the ship get wrecked? And how come some of us are in better stocked lifeboats than others? Apparently the author considers this irrelevant, or too trivial to mention. But I think it's important. For example, the 'ethics of a lifeboat' decrees that the least able to fend for themselves are allowed to abandon ship first. We roundly condemn the crew that jump a sinking ship before their passengers. In fact, we customarily condemn the man who crowds out a woman or child to ensure a place in a lifeboat." Does Karen's extension of the lifeboat analogy relevantly probe the problem at issue, or not? Explain.

15. The author believes that refusing to admit the swimmer into the lifeboat
    A. is just.
    B. is the best available alternative.
    C. will make some lifeboat occupants feel guilty.
    D. A, B, and C.
    E. B and C.

16. Express the conditional syllogism implicit in sentences 4 and 5 *(in parentheses)* of paragraph 13. Is it valid? Is it sound?

17. The *innuendo* of paragraph 13 is that
    A. some people on the lifeboat will feel guilty.
    B. guilt is counterproductive.
    C. people who benefit from others' self-sacrifice do not feel ⸰ about it.
    D. A, B, and C.
    E. B and C.

18. Which of the following ethical principles most closely corresponds author's?
    A. Do unto others as you would have them do unto you.
    B. Do what likely will benefit most people.

    C. Always look out for your own best interests.

    D. Obey God's laws.

19. Irma is intrigued by the lifeboat analogy. "Let's suppose," she says, "that two of the people in the lifeboat are severely injured—they probably even will die before reaching shore. Keeping them aboard will drain the boat's scarce supplies. Approaching the boat are two very strong swimmers, who obviously are quite fit. They reach the craft and, despite the efforts of its passengers, muscle their way aboard. By the author's thinking, it seems to me that the passengers should jettison the two injured parties, and not feel a bit guilty about it. Even if one of the passengers 'escorted' off is the author!" How is Irma answering the author's analogy? Do you think her answer has merit?

20. What is the function of paragraph 14?

    A. It serves as transition to the practical implications of the author's analogy.

    B. It repeats the thesis.

    C. It forecloses any criticism of his analogy.

    D. It admits the weakness of the analogy.

21. Paragraphs 15–20 serve to

    A. enrich the analogy.

    B. provide evidence for the thesis.

    C. establish reproduction as a sovereign right.

    D. A and B.

    E. A, B, and C.

22. The author implicitly assumes (paragraphs 15–19) that

    A. birth rates cited will hold in the future.

    B. there are no relevant distinctions to be made within the category "rich nations" or within the category "poor nations."

    C. sharing resources will in no way affect the birth rate.

    D. A and B.

    E. A, B, and C.

23. What is the second principle analogy, besides the lifeboat, that the author uses?

    According to the author, Marxism and Christianity are alike in their general approach to the problem of world hunger.

        ·sic moral ideas.

        ·ing a prescription for catastrophe.

        C.

        ' C.

        ·aragraphs 21–22 suggest that Christianity is

        ·t Marxism is not.

        ·ponsible land management.

        ·r says, "If *everyone* would only restrain himself, all *only one less than everyone* to ruin a system of ·· implied conclusion of this fragment syllogism? Is

        ·nal paragraph reaffirms the author's thesis?

From: **Population and Food: Metaphors and the Reality**[9]

William N. Murdoch
Allan Oates

One of the earliest attacks on Hardin's position was expressed in the following essay, authored by two of Hardin's colleagues, also biologists at the University of California Santa Barbara, William N. Murdoch and Allan Oates. **Read the essay carefully, outline it, then answer the questions that follow it.**

1 [Hardin's] "lifeboat" article actually has two messages. The first is that our immigration policy is too generous. This will not concern us here. The second, and more important, is that by helping poor nations we will bring disaster to rich and poor alike:

> Metaphorically, each rich nation amounts to a lifeboat full of comparatively rich people. The poor of the world are in other, much more crowded lifeboats. Continuously, so to speak, the poor fall out of their lifeboats and swim for a while in the water outside, hoping to be admitted to a rich lifeboat, or in some other way to benefit from the "goodies" on board. What should the passengers on a rich lifeboat do? This is the central problem of "the ethics of a lifeboat."

2 Among these so-called "goodies" are food supplies and technical aid. Hardin argues that we should withhold such resources from poor nations on the grounds that they help to maintain high rates of population increase, thereby making the problem worse. He foresees the continued supplying and increasing production of food as a process that will be "brought to an end only by the total collapse of the whole system, producing a catastrophe of scarcely imaginable proportions."

3 What arguments does Hardin present in support of these opinions? Many involve metaphors: lifeboat, commons. These metaphors are crucial to his thesis, and it is, therefore, important for us to examine them critically.

4 The lifeboat metaphor seems attractively simple, but it is in fact simplistic and obscures important issues. As soon as we try to use it to compare various policies, we find that most relevant details of the actual situation are either missing or distorted in the lifeboat metaphor. Let us list some of these details.

5 Most important, perhaps, Hardin's lifeboats barely interact. The rich lifeboats may drop some handouts over the side and perhaps repel a boarding party now and then, but generally they live their own lives. In the real world, nations interact a great deal, in ways that affect food supply and population size and growth, and the effect of rich nations on poor nations has been strong and not always benevolent.

6 First, by colonization and actual wars of commerce, and through the international marketplace, rich nations have arranged an exchange of goods that has maintained and even increased the economic imbalance

---

[9]Reprinted with permission, from the September 9, 1975, issue of *BioScience.* © 1975 American Institute of Biological Sciences.

between rich and poor nations. Until recently we have taken or otherwise obtained cheap raw material from poor nations and sold them expensive manufactured goods that they cannot make themselves. In the United States, the structure of tariffs and internal subsidies discriminates selectively against poor nations. In poor countries, the concentration on cash crops rather than on food crops, a legacy of colonial times, is now actively encouraged by western multinational corporations (Barraclough 1975). Indeed, it is claimed that in famine-stricken Sahelian Africa, multinational agribusiness has recently taken land out of food production for cash crops (Transnational Institute 1974). Although we often self-righteously take the "blame" for lowering the death rates of poor nations during the 1940s and 1950s, we are less inclined to accept responsibility for the effects of actions that help maintain poverty and hunger. Yet poverty directly contributes to the high birth rates that Hardin views with such alarm.

7 Second, U.S. foreign policy, including foreign aid programs, has favored "pro-Western" regimes, many of which govern in the interests of a wealthy elite and some of which are savagely repressive. Thus, it has often subsidized a gross maldistribution of income and has supported political leaders who have opposed most of the social changes that can lead to reduced birth rates. In this light, Hardin's pronouncements on the alleged wisdom gap between poor leaders and our own, and the difficulty of filling it, appear as a grim joke: our response to leaders with the power and wisdom Hardin yearns for has often been to try to replace them or their policies as soon as possible. Selective giving and withholding of both military and nonmilitary aid has been an important ingredient of our efforts to maintain political leaders we like and to remove those we do not. Brown, after noting that the withholding of U.S. food aid in 1973 contributed to the downfall of the Allende government in Chile, comments that "although Americans decry the use of petroleum as a political weapon, calling it 'political blackmail,' the United States has been using food aid for political purposes for twenty years—and describing this as 'enlightened diplomacy.' "

8 Both the quantity and the nature of the supplies on a lifeboat are fixed. In the real world, the quantity has strict limits, but these are far from having been reached (University of California Food Task Force 1974). Nor are we forced to devote fixed proportions of our efforts and energy to automobile travel, pet food, packaging, advertising, corn-fed beef, "defense" and other diversions, many of which cost far more than foreign aid does. The fact is that enough food is now produced to feed the world's population adequately. That people are malnourished is due to distribution and to economics, not to agricultural limits (United Nations Economic and Social Council 1974).

9 Hardin's lifeboats are divided merely into rich and poor, and it is difficult to talk about birth rates on either. In the real world, however, there are striking differences among the birth rates of the poor countries and even among the birth rates of different parts of single countries. These differences appear to be related to social conditions (also absent from lifeboats) and may guide us to effective aid policies.

10 Hardin's lifeboat metaphor not only conceals facts, but misleads about the effects of his proposals. The rich lifeboat can raise the ladder and sail away. But in real life, the problem will not necessarily go away just because it is ignored. In the real world, there are armies, raw materials in poor nations, and even outraged domestic dissidents prepared to sacrifice their own and others' lives to oppose policies they regard as immoral.

11 No doubt there are other objections. But even this list shows the lifeboat metaphor to be dangerously inappropriate for serious policy making because it obscures far more than it reveals. Lifeboats and "lifeboat ethics" may be useful topics for those who are shipwrecked; we believe they are worthless — indeed detrimental — in discussions of food-population questions.

12 Throughout the lifeboat article, Hardin bolsters his assertions by reference to the "commons". The thesis of the commons, therefore, needs critical evaluation.

13 Suppose several privately owned flocks, comprising 100 sheep altogether, are grazing on a public commons. They bring in an annual income of $1.00 per sheep. Fred, a herdsman, owns only one sheep. He decides to add another. But 101 is too many: the commons is overgrazed and produces less food. The sheep lose quality and income drops to 90¢ per sheep. Total income is now $90.90 instead of $100.00. Adding the sheep has brought an overall loss. But Fred has gained: *his* income is $1.80 instead of $1.00. The gain from the additional sheep, which is his alone, outweighs the loss from overgrazing, which he shares. Thus he promotes his interest at the expense of the community.

14 The "commons" affords a handy way of classifying problems: the lifeboat article reveals that sharing, a generous immigration policy, world food banks, air, water, the fish populations of the ocean, and the western range lands are, or produce, a commons. It is also handy to be able to dispose of policies one does not like and "only a particular instance of a class of policies that are in error because they lead to the tragedy of the commons."

15 But no metaphor, even one as useful as this, should be treated with such awe. Such shorthand can be useful, but it can also mislead by discouraging thought and obscuring important detail. To dismiss a proposal by suggesting that "all you need to know about this proposal is that it institutes a commons and is, therefore, bad" is to assert that the proposed commons is worse than the original problem. This might be so if the problem of the commons were, indeed, a tragedy — that is, if it were insoluble. But it is not.

16 Hardin favors private ownership as the solution (either through private property or the selling of pollution rights). But, of course, there are solutions other than private ownership; and private ownership itself is no guarantee of carefully husbanded resources.

17 One alternative to private ownership of the commons is communal ownership of the sheep — or, in general, of the mechanisms and industries that exploit the resource — combined with communal planning for

management. (Note, again, how the metaphor favors one solution: perhaps the "tragedy" lay not in the commons but in the sheep. "The Tragedy of the Privately Owned Sheep" lacks zing, unfortunately.) Public ownership of a commons has been tried in Peru to the benefit of the previously privately owned anchoveta fishery (Gulland 1975). The communally owned agriculture of China does not seem to have suffered any greater over-exploitation than that of other Asian nations.

18 Another alternative is cooperation combined with regulation. For example, Gulland (1975) has shown that Antarctic whale stocks (perhaps the epitome of a commons since they are internationally exploited and no one owns them) are now being properly managed, and stocks are increasing. This has been achieved through cooperation in the International Whaling Commission, which has by agreement set limits to the catch of each nation.

1. What is the function of the first three paragraphs?
   A. To state the author's thesis
   B. To introduce the topic
   C. To refute Hardin
   D. To support the thesis
   E. To provide historical background
2. Do you think the authors have fairly represented Hardin's position (paragraphs 1 and 2)?
3. Do you think that in paragraph 1, the authors make fair use of the Hardin quotation?
4. In paragraph 3, the authors claim that the analogies (that is, metaphors) Hardin makes are "crucial to his thesis." Do you agree? If so, explain in terms of the relationship between an analogy and a problem.
5. The authors believe that the lifeboat analogy
   A. oversimplifies the problem of world hunger.
   B. masks important details.
   C. on first look is unappealing.
   D. A and B.
   E. A, B, and C.
6. In paragraph 5, the authors
   A. extend Hardin's analogy.
   B. raise what they believe are disanalogies.
   C. make a hidden generalization explicit.
   D. None of the preceding.
7. What is the overriding purpose of paragraph 6?
   A. To show that lifeboats interact
   B. To show that rich nations contribute to world hunger
   C. To show that nations interact
   D. To show that rich nations sometimes exploit poor nations
8. Which of the following patterns most closely corresponds with the author's reasoning in paragraphs 5–7?
   A. A is not like B.

B. A is not like B because of X.

C. A is not like B because of X, which is supported by Y.

D. A is not like B because of X, which is supported by Y and Z.

9. Cite four examples of appeal to authority that the authors use.

10. By *innuendo,* paragraph 7 suggests that

    A. Americans are hypocritical.

    B. the United States largely supports reduced birth rates.

    C. Hardin is naïve about U.S. policies toward repressive regimes.

    D. A, B, and C.

    E. A and C.

    F. A and B.

11. Why are the following terms "pro-Western," "political blackmail," "enlightened," and "diplomacy" (paragraph 7) placed in quotations?

12. Political Blackmail : Enlightened Diplomacy : : Propaganda :

    A. Freedom

    B. Life

    C. Manipulation

    D. Truth

13. In paragraph 8, the authors

    A. point out a dissimilarity.

    B. raise a disanalogy.

    C. extend Hardin's analogy.

    D. identify an unacceptable generalization that underlies the lifeboat analogy.

14. In paragraph 9, the authors *(choose one of the answers from the preceding question):*

15. In paragraph 10, the authors *(choose one of the answers given in question 13):*

16. What is the main idea of paragraph 11?

    A. The United States should aid poor nations.

    B. Lifeboats should never be used in analogies.

    C. Food-population questions should never involve analogies.

    D. Hardin's analogy is faulty.

17. In paragraph 13, the authors

    A. illustrate the problem of the commons.

    B. refute Hardin's commons analogy.

    C. make Hardin's point.

    D. A and B.

    E. A and C.

    F. A, B, and C.

18. The authors contend that the commons analogy

    A. can be useful.

    B. has no redeeming value.

    C. can be used to conceal relevant details.

    D. A and B.

    E. B and C.

    F. A and C.

19. In paragraph 15, the authors attack the commons analogy by
    A. raising a disanalogy.
    B. questioning an underlying generalization.
    C. extending the analogy.
    D. pointing out dissimilarities.
20. In paragraph 16, the authors in effect accuse Hardin of
    A. setting up a straw argument.
    B. introducing a red herring.
    C. neglecting relevant evidence.
    D. posing a false dilemma.
21. Do the authors make any attempt to justify this fallacy charge?

State whether the authors and Hardin are in basic agreement or disagreement on the following points (22–29).

22. The relationship between rich and poor nations needs to be addressed.
23. The United States must develop a strategy for dealing with poor nations and specifically with world hunger.
24. The United States cannot really do much to affect the plight of poor nations.
25. The quantity and nature of the world's supplies have strict limits.
26. The world is very near its agricultural limits.
27. Analogies can be useful in framing problems.
28. Analogies can be dangerously misleading.
29. Future generations will best be served by the "sharing ethics."

RELATED THEME TOPICS

1. During World War I, the French used the "method of triage" in treating their wounded. This consisted in sorting the wounded into three categories. Those with the slightest injuries were given quick first aid. Those who could not be helped were allowed to die. Those in between received intensive care. *Write an essay in which you apply the method of triage analogously to world food problems.*
2. "People are besieged by all sorts of charities. They cannot and do not give to all. In fact, some people probably do not give to any. Although we might praise those who give to charities, we do not condemn those who do not. That is because we recognize that there is nothing wrong with not giving. Feeding the world's hungry is the same thing. Yes, it might be nice to, but we do not have any obligation to, any more than we have an obligation to contribute to the heart or cancer funds." *Write an essay in which you evaluate this argument from analogy.*
3. Assume for the sake of argument that the nations of the world can be saved. *Write an essay in which you defend one of these choices:*
    A. Deliberately discontinue aid to those least likely to survive in order to ensure the survival of the others
    B. Continue aid despite our awareness of the consequences that will probably follow

11

Causal Arguments

INTRODUCTION

"Is Vitamin E good for the heart?" "What will be the ultimate results of the Persian Gulf war?" "Did Lee Harvey Oswald act alone in assassinating President Kennedy?" How we answer such questions depends largely on what we understand by "cause," for each implies that something may be the cause or the effect of something else.

In many everyday situations, we do not have to look far for a cause of something—the type appears faint because the typewriter ribbon is worn; Main Street is closed to traffic because of the Independence Day parade; I didn't receive your telephone call because I wasn't home. Understanding why something occurs in other situations can be far more complicated—am I chronically tired because I don't get enough rest, because I'm depressed, or because I'm sick? Did Dan flunk the test because he didn't study, because he panicked, or because he has an unconscious desire to fail? Did the plane crash because of mechanical failure, human error, or possibly both? The common phenomenon in these examples that cuts to the heart of much of our empirical knowledge involves the relation of cause and effect.

Asserting cause and effect relationships between things seems so basic to human perception and reason that most people probably consider it a rather obvious mental procedure. We not only believe that an effect must have a cause, but that the cause can be discovered simply by retracing antecedent events. We further believe that, having arrived at a cause, we can then accurately predict outcomes given similar antecedents.

Although such suppositions immensely influence the practical aspects of everyday life, they have long been discredited in many areas of philosophy, physics, and psychology, where belief in causation is considered "a relic of a bygone era," as philosopher Bertrand Russell once put it. Although adopting the modern physicist's attitude toward causation would be impractical in everyday life, it does generally alert

491

us to the pitfalls that lie in the path of sound cause-and-effect interpretation and construction. Since many of the essays that we read and write include causal relationships, it is well worth our time to explore this subject.

MODULE 11.1

CAUSAL ARGUMENTS AND EXPLANATIONS

Let's start by noting that the word *cause* has many "cousins" that convey the idea of causation. For example, *produce* means "to cause something to happen"; *prevent* or *deter* means "to cause not to happen"; *kill* means "to cause to die"; *vaporize* means "to cause things to change into vapor." Such terms—and there are hundreds of them—appear in causal statements.

A causal statement is a general statement that relates two things in such a way that one is claimed to bring about the other; or, alternatively, one results from the other. A causal statement, then, reduces to the assertion "A causes B" or "B is the effect of A." Here are some examples of causal statements:

Vitamin B *prevents* beriberi.
Capital punishment *reduces* crime.
TV violence *leads to* real-life violence.
A high fat diet *increases* one's cholesterol level.
The car won't start if the battery is dead.

All of these statements can be reduced to "A causes B," including the last one which contains no causal word but clearly implies causation: A dead battery will *cause* a car not to start.

If you are thinking: "But the meanings of *cause* are not identical in all these statements," you are right. Before we can verify causal statements, we need to know what they mean. This, in turn, requires a knowledge of the different meanings of *cause.* We will address this important issue, but first let's examine causal arguments and explanations.

Recall that when we were discussing analogies, we noted that some analogies are used merely to clarify or illustrate; others carry the additional function of attempting to convince or persuade. In a similar way, some cause-and-effect relationships are offered strictly as explanations, whereas others are used argumentively.

Arguments in support of causal statements are termed causal arguments. It is easy to imagine, for example, an argument that attempts to establish that alcoholism is caused by a biochemical abnormality, that a high-fat diet affects a woman's chances of getting breast cancer, that TV violence contributes to real-life violence, that abused children become abusive adults, and the like. In such arguments, the conclusion ordinarily is equivalent to a causal statement, which is supported by the evidence offered.

Causal arguments frequently appear as part of the body of evidence offered for a conclusion which itself is not a causal statement. In other words, the causal relationship functions as a miniargument within the main argument.

For example, the famous defense attorney Clarence Darrow (1857–1938) vigorously championed the abolition of capital punishment on grounds that it was unjust to execute a person. Why is it unjust? Because, said Darrow, the murderer is always a victim of heredity and environment — or, as he put it, "Back of every murder and back of every human being's act are sufficient causes that make the human machine beyond their control." Darrow was in effect arguing:

> *Forces beyond a person's control compel him to murder.*
> It is unjust to execute a person for doing something that is beyond his control.
> ———
> Therefore, it is unjust to execute a person for murder.

Clearly the force of this argument hinges on the controversial cause-and-effect relationship asserted in the italicized *premise.*

Notice that embedded in Darrow's argument is an explanation. That people are compelled to murder by forces beyond their control helps to account for the fact that people commit murder. Causal explanations are an integral part of causal arguments. But a causal explanation is not necessarily a causal argument. In order to understand this, we need to distinguish between causal arguments and explanations.

IN BRIEF   Causal statements are statements of the form "A causes B" or "B is the effect of A." A causal argument attempts to support such statements.

Cause and effect statements are not confined to argument. Consider for example this passage:

> Of all the powers of birds in the air probably none has caused more wonder than their soaring ability. To see a bird in the air and sail on motionless, flying into the distance until at last it disappears from sight, gives one a sense of magic. We now know how it is done, but it is still difficult to realize what is happening as we watch it. Actually, the bird is coasting downhill in relation to the flow of air. *It rises because of a rising current of air which is ascending faster than the bird is sinking in the current.*

The italicized statement is a causal *explanation.* Its object is mere understanding, not persuasion. Its point is not to establish the fact that a bird soars or that a bird's flight inspires wonder. It is merely to help us understand what makes the flight of birds possible. Notice that the author has framed the explanation in terms of aerodynamic principles. A biologist, on the other hand, might account for it more in terms of the bird's structure and evolution. We will return to the importance of viewpoint in causal explanations presently. At this point, it is enough to keep in mind that in a causal explanation the result (for example, the bird's soaring) usually is a well-established fact or something that is noncontroversial. At the same time, it is a "phenomenon," an unusual, significant, or unaccountable fact or occurrence. The object of the causal explanation is to account for the phenomenon, but not to convince or persuade anyone of the phenomenon.

As another example of a causal explanation, consider the *phenomenon* that after World War I a sudden and dramatic change occurred in baseball. For fifteen seasons prior to 1919, major league batters as a group averaged about .250. By 1921 that figure had jumped to .285, where it remained through the 1920s. Accompanying the increase in batting average was an increase in scoring. Rarely before 1920 did two or more players a season bat in 100 runs. In 1921, fifteen did, and the average for the 1920s was for its time a stunning fourteen a season. Earned-run averages—the measure of a pitcher's run suppressing ability—similarly escalated. Before 1919, the average annual ERA was about 2.85. In 1921, it climbed to 4.00 where it hovered through the decade. What caused this phenomenon? How to account for it? Here's one attempt:

> Babe Ruth was the most exciting aspect of the 1919 season, even more than the pennant race. The fans bubbling into the ballparks could not begin to appreciate the austere beauty of a well-pitched game, but they thrilled vicariously to the surging erectile power of the Ruthian home run. They wanted more. They wanted hits and they wanted runs, lots of hits and lots of runs. They wanted homers. . . .
>
> Too, Ruth's full free swing was being copied more and more, and so was his type of bat, thinner in the handle and whippier, in principle something like a golf club. . . . Strategy and tactics changed. A strikeout theretofore had been something of a disgrace—reread "Casey at the Bat." A batter was supposed to protect the plate, get a piece of the ball, as in the cognate game of cricket. In Ruth's case, however, a strikeout was only a momentary, if melodramatic, setback. Protecting the plate declined in importance, along with the sacrifice and the steal (the number of stolen bases in 1921 was half the pre-war average). . . . The big hit, the big inning blossomed. . . .
> (Robert W. Creamer, *Babe: The Legend Comes to Life.*)

Of course, other factors could have been included in the explanation, for example, the outlawing of the batter-befuddling "spitball" and other "trick pitches," and perhaps the introduction of the "lively" ball. More important, *non-baseball*-related explanations could be offered. A social historian, for example, might cast the phenomenon in terms of general social conditions and tendencies that marked the post-war era; an economist in terms of owners who saw big profits in the public appetite for spectacle; a psychologist in terms of a pervasive desire to return to a more innocent, pastoral time.

Although causal arguments and explanation can be distinguished in theory, in practice the theoretical dividing line often is blurred and indistinct. Thus, what on first look may appear to be a causal explanation, on closer inspection is also a causal argument. This is especially true of debatable "results" of the cause-and-effect relationship as with:

The United States is well on its way to relinquishing its leadership role in world affairs.

The object of providing a cause-and-effect relationship that leads to this evaluation could easily be both to explain and persuade. The same could be said of these statements:

Today Americans are paying a high price for the economic policies of the 80s.
Prisons do not rehabilitate prisoners.
Parental notice laws result in fewer teenage pregnancies.
The U.S. government should subsidize its technological industries.
Prohibitions against offshore oil drilling threaten U.S. security.

Moreover, a causal explanation that is debatable or controversial invites the same kind of critical response that a causal argument does. The following episode illustrates this point.

In 1990, powerful planners of Japan's "economic miracle" discovered that their nation's birthrate had plummeted to an all-time low of 1.57 during 1989. Averse to importing foreign workers, they expressed deep concern about what Japan's population decline might mean for its future economic growth. At a high-level government meeting, Finance Minister Ryutaro Hashimoto suggested that Japanese women were having fewer children because they were too well educated.

In one sense, there is nothing remarkable about his statement—as a group, more highly educated women do have fewer children than poorly educated ones. So, there is nothing unusual about the Japanese experience. On the other hand, it is likely that the minister was also wanting the audience to accept a view that education is the main cause of the lower birthrate and, by implication, to formulate counteracting measures—for example, discourage or even prevent females from attending college. This was exactly the interpretation of one anthropologist. Notice how in the first two paragraphs of the following excerpt from her reply, Sheila K. Johnson accepts the explanatory nature of the minister's statement as nondebatable, but she challenges both the assumption that education is the main cause of the birthrate decline and the policy implications of that assumption.

> I am not disputing the finance minister's observation that highly educated women usually have fewer children than poorly educated ones. It is also true that urbanized, middle-class women have fewer children than rural women, and that industrialization in general brings with it a decline in a nation's birthrate.
>
> These things are so well-known that many nations today are trying to reverse the equation by reducing their birthrate—either by educating or forcing (if necessary) couples to bear fewer children—so that the economic climate will improve. These nations are where the current population growth rate threatens to overwhelm poten-

tial development. Thus the Chinese government has tried to mandate the one-child family, and the Indian government at one time wanted to perform vasectomies on all men who had fathered three living children. But just as it is not easy to change the proclivities of peasants, who see another child as a form of old-age insurance or as an extra field-hand, so it is not easy to persuade a modern, well-educated couple to have more than one or two children.

To begin with, raising children in a highly industrialized country like Japan is expensive. There are school fees, computers, sports equipment, special classes, even cars to pay for. Responsible parents who want to see their children well-educated and well-launched into the middle class cannot afford to do it very often.

The customary retirement age—as early as 55 in some sectors—also contributes to reducing a family's size. Japanese are now marrying in their mid-to-late 20s and having their first child when the husband is perhaps in his early 30s; that child may still be in college when his or her father retires. Once they turn 40, few Japanese men are eager to expand their families.

The high cost of living also has an impact on mothers, many of whom return to part-time work when their children reach school age precisely in order to buy for them the advantages a single income may not be sufficient to provide: the "cram school," the piano lessons, the travel abroad, the lavish wedding and honeymoon.

If Minister Hashimoto is serious about Japanese couples producing more children, he should also anticipate that these children will be less well-educated and provided for than the current crop. . . .[1]

The author is attacking what she views as a most tenuous connection between education and birthrates. She is thus challenging the cause-and-effect relationship asserted by the minister, by suggesting alternative causes of which, as a social anthropologist, she is especially mindful.

One's frame of reference—where a person is "coming from" on a problem—helps shape causal explanations. The very selection of cause, therefore, says a good deal about a party's methods, predisposition, and interests. Thus, what a child considers a harmless experiment with a drug, a parent might view as the first step on the road to degradation. What an advertiser considers harmless "puffery," a government regulatory agency might consider deceptive advertising. Whereas an economist might base an analysis of the collapse of savings-and-loan institutions on the effects of deregulation, a moralist might frame it in terms of unethical behavior.

So, who is "right"—the finance minister or the anthropologist? In complex occurrences such as a declining birthrate, there is no one single cause that of itself accounts for the occurrence. This does not mean, however, that we are "at sea" when it comes to evaluating expressed cause-and-effect relationships. One thing we can do to sharpen our evaluative faculties is to clarify the various meanings of *cause*. Another is to avoid confusing cause with other things. The remainder of this chapter engages both these matters.

---

[1]Sheila K. Johnson, "Japan's Hard Sell: Motherhood," *Los Angeles Times,* June 27, 1990, p. B7. Copyright 1990, *Los Angeles Times.* Reprinted by permission.

EXERCISES ON CAUSAL ARGUMENTS AND EXPLANATIONS*

1. Do you think that an answer to each of the following "why" questions would probably be strictly an explanation or conceivably an argument as well? Explain.
   A. Why does iron rust when exposed to oxygen?
   B. Why can't camelias take much direct sunlight?
   C. Why should the United States provide financial aid to Latin America?
   D. Why did Dukakis lose the 1988 presidential election?
   E. Why did Iraq annex Kuwait?
   F. Why are there relatively few female physics majors?
   G. Why should we maintain a vigorous space program?
   H. Why are we running out of fossil fuels?
   I. Why is nuclear power a desirable source of energy?
   J. Why are offspring always of the same species as their progenitors?
2. Some of the following passages seem not only to offer a causal explanation but an argument as well. Which are stricly causal explanations, which are causal arguments? For any causal arguments, identify premises and conclusion. In all cases, indicate cause and effect.
   A. One seldom expects a country's president to adequately note the passing of a rocker, but Jimmy Carter's assessment of Elvis Presley's appeal—"energy, rebelliousness, and good humor"—is remarkably close to the mark. When he started in the 1950s, he looked like a hood, he sang sensually. Part of his appeal in the 1970s was our remembering what we thought was "sex" back then. Underneath the greasy hairdo, he had the profile of a Greek god. Besides, our parents didn't like him, what could be better? And the music? Well, the music can be left to the music critics, who by and large seem to think it's pretty good. A teenage foot that never tapped to "Heartbreak Hotel" in the 50s probably belonged to a hopeless grind. . . .
   (Molly Ivins, "Why They Mourned Elvis Presley")
   B. Messy business, argument. But, more often than not, it clears the air. Opens up minds to conflicting ideas. Makes proud intellectuals and ordinary folks ask themselves if their cherished assumptions are based on real knowledge or on prejudice, fashion, and rote response. Discussion, even when heated, tends to lead to rational judgements.
       Which is why Mobil provokes, needles, challenges, and even tickles the funny bone of America to stir freewheeling dialogue in the public print. Saying what we think needs saying on issues that matter to people. Inflation. Jobs. Energy. Environment. The sad state of commercial TV.
       Sure, we're a special interest. But what's wrong with that? As Walter Lippmann put it, "All principles are the rationalization of some special interest." The point is, voices of business balance other voices. Stifling any voice distorts the democratic process. The people must be able to weigh *all* the evidence, some to their own conclusions, and press their views on our national leaders. So future decisions in our participatory democracy will be based on the noble wisdom of the past—the First Amendment.
       (An ad prepared by the Mobil Oil Company entitled "Imagine Tomorrow Without Argument")

C. . . . . Boys and girls may be born alike with respect to math, but certain sex differences in performance emerge early according to several recent studies, and these differences remain through adulthood. They are:
1. Girls compute better than boys (elementary school and on).
2. Boys solve word problems better than girls (from age thirteen on).
3. Boys take more math than girls (from age sixteen on).
4. Girls learn to hate math sooner and possibly for different reasons.

    Why the differences in performance? One reason is the amount of math learned and used at play. Another may be the difference in male-female maturation. If girls do better than boys at all elementary school tasks, then they may compute better for no other reason than that arithmetic is part of the elementary school curriculum. As boys and girls grow older, girls become, under pressure, academically less competitive. Thus, the falling off of girls' math performance between ages ten and fifteen may be because:
1. Math gets harder in each successive year and requires more work and commitment.
2. Both boys and girls are pressured, beginning at age ten, not to excel in areas designated by society to be outside their sex-role domains.
3. Thus girls have a good excuse to avoid the painful struggle with math, boys don't. . . .

    (Sheila Toias: *Overcoming Math Anxiety*)

D. The ethnic communities that developed in early 20th-century America were essentially adaptive and transitory. They developed to buffer the economic and cultural shock of adjusting to a new host society. They were aids to assimilation, not barriers. And they succeeded.

    What is remarkable about 20th-century America is the rapid rate of assimilation of immigrant groups into the mainstream of social life.

    Chauvinistic intellectuals, by emphasizing those who remain "unmelted," shift the focus from the vast majority who assimilate to those few still remaining in ethnic neighborhoods, although the actual behavior of the majority of those remaining is in the direction of assimilation.

    The Jews, often regarded as among the most ideologically and socially cohesive of modern ethnic groups, exhibit increasing rates of out-marriage and secularism and tend more and more to live in non-Jewish neighborhoods. The same is true of all those of Eastern European origins. And despite the talk about black "soul" and separatism, every poll of the black community indicates that the great majority of blacks favor assimilation and would prefer to live in integrated neighborhoods.

    This ethnic revival then is largely an ideological revival wrought by alienated and disenchanted intellectuals and activists in a dangerous alliance with conservative political demagogues. It is the *idea* of ethnicity that is being celebrated, in much the same way that the much talked about religious revival is largely a commitment to the idea of religion. . . .

    (Orlando Patterson, "Hidden Dangers in the Ethnic Revival")

E. . . . [T]he basic reason for the energy crisis is that nearly all the energy now used in the United States (and in the world) comes from nonrenewable sources. As a nonrenewable energy source is depleted, it becomes progressively more costly to produce, so that continued reliance on it means an intending escalation in price. This process has a powerful inflationary impact: it increases the cost of living, especially of poor people; it aggravates unemployment; it reduces the availability of capital. No economic system can withstand such pressures indefinitely; sooner or later the energy crisis *must* be solved. And this can be done only by replacing the present nonrenewable sources — oil, natural gas, coal, and uranium — with renewable ones, which are stable in cost. This is what a national energy policy must do if it is to solve the energy crisis, rather than delay it or make it worse. . . .

(Barry Commoner, *The Politics of Energy*)

F. In the past, permanence was the ideal. Whether engaged in handcrafting a pair of boots or in constructing a cathedral, all man's creative and product energies went toward maximizing the durability of the product. Man built to last. He had to. As long as the society around him was relatively unchanging each object had clearly defined functions, and economic logic dictated the policy of performance. . . .

    As the general rate of change in society accelerates, however, the economics of permanence are — and must be — replaced by the economics of transience.

    First, advancing technology tends to lower the costs of manufacture much more rapidly than the cost of repair work. . . . It is economically sensible to build cheap, unrepairable, throw-away objects, even though they may not last as long as repairable objects.

    Second, advancing technology makes it possible to improve the object as time goes by. The second generation computer is better than the first. . . .

    Third, as change accelerates and reaches into more and more remote corners of the society, uncertainty about future needs increases. Recognizing the inevitability of change, but unsure as to the demands it will impose on us, we hesitate to commit large resources for frigidly fixed objects intended to serve unchanging purposes.

(Alvin Toffler, *Future Shock*)

G. Numerous factors contribute to the acceptability of ideas. To a very large extent, of course, we associate truth with convenience — with what most clearly accords with self-interest and personal well-being or promises best to avoid awkward effort or unwelcome dislocation of life. We also find highly acceptable what contributes most to self-esteem. Speakers before the United States Chamber of Commerce rarely denigrate the businessman as an economic force. Those who appear before the AFL-CIO are prone to identify special progress with a strong trade union movement. But perhaps most important of all, people approve most of what they best understand. . . . Economic and social behavior are complex and mentally tiring. Therefore, we adhere, as though to a raft, to those ideas which represent understanding. This is a prime manifestation of vested interest. For a vested interest in understanding is more preciously guarded than any other treasure. It is why men react, not infrequently with something akin to religious passion, to the defense of what they have so laboriously learned.

(John Kenneth Galbraith, *The Affluent Society*)

MODULE 11.2

CAUSES AS ANTECEDENT CONDITIONS

Somewhere along the line, all of us have had to meet certain conditions in order to attain some goal—be advanced from one class to the next, get a driver's license, be admitted to college, declare a tax deduction, enter a profession, marry, and so on. These conditions are prerequisites, or things that are indispensable to the occurrence of some event. Sometimes, all we have to do is meet a single condition to attain some end. When a mentally competent person reaches the age of majority, the person may enter into a legally binding contract. Other times, many conditions need to be met. Before receiving a bachelor's degree, students must complete many different kinds of courses. Completing the prescribed courses is a sufficient condition for the degree. Looked at another way, each of the conditions must be met—it is necessary—for graduation. Our common experience with antecedent conditions for the occurrence of events provides a helpful way for considering causal arguments.

Sometimes in argument, cause is asserted in the sense of a *necessary* condition, that is, *one that must be present for the effect to occur.* Thus, if in "A causes B," the term "causes" (or some synonym) implies a necessary condition, then it is being asserted that A must be present for B to occur. When we say, then, that A is a necessary condition for the occurrence of B, we are claiming as an empirical fact that in the absence of A, B never occurs. For example, in the absence of oxygen, we never have fire. Oxygen, therefore, can be considered a cause of fire in the sense of a condition that is necessary for fire to occur. How do we know that oxygen is a necessary condition for fire? By experience. Only through observed specifics do we know what the condition is, the absence of which is followed by the absence of the event.

Of course, the presence of oxygen of itself is not enough to bring about fire. In other words, oxygen is not a *sufficient* condition for fire—*a sufficient condition being an occurrence which invariably brings about an occurrence of the effect.* If in "A causes B," the word "causes" (or some synonym) implies a sufficient condition, the presence of A invariably will bring about B. When we say that A is a sufficient condition for B, then we are asserting as an empirical fact that in the presence of A, B always occurs. Thus, rain falling on your unprotected car is a sufficient condition for the car being wet. It is not necessary, of course—the car can get wet in the absence of rain falling on it (for example, by you hosing it off).

In some cases, a single condition is sufficient for the occurrence of an event, but in the vast majority of cases, the conditions that constitute the sufficient condition are far more numerous. Even the simple case of combustion involves three conditions: fuel, the right temperature, and oxygen. In the presence of these three conditions, a substance burns. Taken *together* these conditions are sufficient for fire; considered separately, each condition is necessary but not, of itself, sufficient for fire.

Of course, not all cases are as simple as combustion. What is sufficient for your VCR (video cassette recorder) to work properly? Many more things than we can identify here—power, proper connection of the power cord and the antenna, clean video heads, and so on. In fact, the list of necessary conditions for the proper functioning of so complex a piece of machinery runs into the hundreds, even thousands, and each would have to be listed as *part* of the *sufficient* condition. Anything less than *all* of these would be not sufficient for the proper functioning of the VCR.

As complex as the case of a VCR is, it pales by comparison with other cases we can think of. What set of conditions must be fulfilled for a person to enjoy a movie? to get a headache? to fall in love? Cases drawn from everyday experience, and from the natural, life, and social sciences, can provide such a staggering complex set of conditions that even a lengthy list of them could fall short of the *sufficient* condition for the occurrence of the event. This is why, in general, it is easier to identify necessary conditions — something in whose absence an event will not occur — than sufficient conditions.

Although sufficient conditions usually are quite complex, ones that cause "negative outcome" often can be easily stated. For your VCR *not* to work properly, it is sufficient to pull the plug out of the socket. In fact, we could think of many conditions, any *one* of which is sufficient to produce this negative effect. But to get the VCR to work properly — that is, for this positive event to occur — the set of conditions is so complex as to defy common knowledge. Of course, someone knows the whole set of conditions on which the proper functioning of the VCR depends; otherwise it could not be repaired when broken. Implicit in the repair of a defective VCR, then, is that the whole set of sufficient conditions for its proper functioning have been fulfilled. In many realms, of course, we simply do not know or understand the whole set of conditions that is sufficient for an event, as with cancer, an economic collapse, or a war. In fact, we are not even sure how to produce some negative outcomes, for example, with cancer.

Is it possible for a thing to be causally related to an occurrence, but be neither a necessary nor sufficient condition? If it is possible, what kind of condition is that?

To answer these questions it is useful to introduce the notion of *contributory condition, which can be considered a factor that in some unspecified way helps create the total set of conditions necessary or sufficient for an occurrence.* For example, when the lights suddenly go off in your room during a violent storm, you are apt to say, "The storm caused a power failure." Clearly you do not mean that the storm was a sufficient condition for the power outage, since the power can remain on during the most violent of storms. And you do not mean that the storm was a necessary condition, since the power obviously can fail in the absence of a storm. What you probably mean is that the storm *helped create* the sufficient conditions for the negative outcome, the power failure. Your analysis of the situation is based correctly on the causal assumption that power is more likely to fail in the presence of a violent storm than in its absence. To say that A is contributory to B, then, is to say that B is more likely to occur in the presence than in the absence of A.

Even from this brief discussion, it should be clear that the notion of cause can be tricky.[2] It continues to be an important and difficult philosophical problem, and its

---

[2]The preceding discussion follows a traditional interpretation of cause. It should be noted, however, that according to some contemporary views, necessary and sufficient conditions are correlational and hence definable independently of cause and effect.

complexity underlies many of the problems associated with causal reasoning. Examining some of these problems in the light of the preceding discussion will prepare us to do effective causal analysis.

Speaking of. . .

Cause

Mill's Methods of Causal Discovery

The English philosopher John Stuart Mill (1806–1873) formulated a number of methods which lead us to believe we have discovered the cause of a phenomenon. The three key ones are called: *the method of agreement, the method of difference, and the method of concomitant variation.*

The method of agreement attempts to establish the single sufficient condition that occurs in every instance of the phenomenon under investigation. Suppose, for example, that ten students became sick after eating lunch in the college cafeteria. Suspecting food poisoning, investigators find that the only common factor among the ten students is that each had eaten shellfish. There is reason to *suspect* that the shellfish is the cause of the food poisoning—or at least that the cases are related to it in some way.

The method of difference works the opposite way. Rather than looking for the causal factor in successive instances of the same occurrence, two situations are compared—one that represents the occurrence, another that does not—and a point of difference between them is sought. Thus, if students who did not get sick have every relevant factor in common with the victims except one—they did not eat shellfish—there is a good *chance* that the shellfish is the cause of the food poisoning.

This method is used by scientists in conducting experiments where they set up identical conditions except for one—the suspected causal agent. It's also used in what is termed "comparison-group testing." For example, to measure the effectiveness of a new drug for reducing cholesterol levels, researchers set up two groups of subjects—a "target" or "experimental group" and a "control" group. Every attempt is made to make the two groups as similar as possible—in age, sex, diet, activity, cholesterol levels, and so on—except for the administration of the drug. If the cholesterol levels of the members of the target group are lower than those in the control group at the end of a predetermined period, then there is the *possibility* that the drug helped make the difference.

The third method, termed concomitant variation, trades on the simultaneous occurrence of two conditions. That two events occur simultaneously does not of itself establish causation. But if two conditions are *independent*— that is, *not the effects of the same cause or parts of a single process*—and one condition varies proportionally with the other, then there might be

continued

continued

a causal connection between them. For example, a farmer might suspect a causal connection between the application of a fertilizer and crop yield by applying different amounts of the fertilizer to different parts of a field and noting that the parts to which more fertilizer was applied yielded a more abundant harvest, all other things remaining equal. When the demand for a particular product remains constant, if an increase in its supply is accompanied by a decline in its price, this inverse relationship suggests that there *might be* a causal connection between supply and price.

It is important to note that Mill was more interested in building a foundation for scientific proof than for discovering causal relationships that people seek in everyday living. Rarely can we set up strictly controlled laboratory conditions for investigating human problems.

EXERCISES ON CAUSES AS ANTECEDENT CONDITIONS

1. In the following pairs of terms, is the relation of A to B that of necessary, sufficient, contributory, or noncausal?

A	B
1. moisture	growth of crops
2. overeating	illness
3. a bullet penetrating the heart	death
4. a baseball hitting a window	the window breaking
5. friction	heat
6. infection	fever
7. unscrewing a light bulb	no light
8. increase in consumption	increase in prices
9. capital punishment	decrease in crime
10. cigarette smoking	heart disease
11. communication skill	job success

2. Cite a condition for the occurrence of each of the following events. Then indicate whether the condition is necessary, sufficient, or contributory.
   A. insomnia
   B. weight loss
   C. AIDS
   D. increase in adrenaline
   E. an economic recession
   F. earning potential
   G. rain
   H. acquiring a driver's license

3. A car skids while cornering, rolls over, and explodes into flames. Identify a possible antecedent condition for this event from the viewpoint of the car's driver, the county surveyor, the police, the car's manufacturer.

MODULE 11.3

CONFUSION IN CAUSAL REASONING

A conventional approach to the problems of causal reasoning usually entails a list of what are termed causal fallacies, which are errors in causal reasoning. But the list is lengthy and the distinctions among the fallacies can be subtle and fugitive. One alternative approach is to place the more prominent of these errors in the broader context of confusing cause with something that resembles, but is not, cause.

Confusing a Cause with an Antecedent

Obviously, causes precede effects. But simply because A occurred before B is no reason to assume that A caused B. A headache may precede a fever, but it did not produce it; the crime rate may go up after Jones' election, but that does not mean that Jones is to blame; that your grades improve after you acquire a word-processor should not convince you that the computer accounts for the improvement. Logicians call the confusion of a cause with an antecedent the *post hoc* fallacy.

Post hoc, **which is a Latin phrase for "after this," is shorthand for** *post hoc, propter ergo hoc,* **"after this, therefore because of this." The** *post hoc* **fallacy, then,** *consists in assuming that event B must have been caused by event A merely because A preceded B.* Someone observes that crime among American youth has increased since "punk rock" was imported from England; thus, the person infers that punk rock caused the increase in juvenile crime. A reading of history indicates that every war in this century followed the election of a Democrat as president; thus, it is inferred that the Democrats are a "war party."

Why we sometimes confuse cause with antecedents is not difficult to understand. Since causes produce effects, it is tempting to draw a cause-and-effect relationship based on chronological relationship. But a chronological relationship is only one of several possible indicators of a causal relationship. Neither immediate nor remote temporal succession is ever a sufficient reason for establishing a causal relationship. If the fact that event A preceded B were sufficient for establishing that A caused B, we could argue that any event that preceded B was the cause of it. It is precisely this kind of thinking that gives rise to superstitions, for underlying all superstitions is what lies back of most false judgments of causation: misinterpretation of evidence. The superstitious confuse relevant with irrelevant evidence, as, for example, with the belief that the mere boast of good health is enough to bring on illness. However, misinterpretation of evidence as it relates to *post hoc* thinking is hardly confined to superstitions. Any answer to an interpretive problem is susceptible to the confusion of cause with antecedent.

Consider, for example, the defeat of the Spanish Armada in 1588, which preceded the fall of the Spanish empire and the rise of the British empire. The chronological relationship between these events has led some historians to suggest a cause-and-effect relationship, such that the defeat of the Armada was the principal cause of the decline of the Spanish empire and the rise of the British empire. Similarly, the fact that the explosion of literary genius that marked the last fifteen years of Elizabeth's reign followed the defeat of the Armada has led some to suggest a cause-and-effect relationship between these events. But, as historian Garrett Mattingly points out, the sole basis for either interpretation is "the method of *post hoc, propter ergo hoc.*"[3]

IN BRIEF   The *post hoc* fallacy occurs when someone cites two past events and insists that because one happened first, it necessarily caused the second. Whenever anyone implies a causal relationship by saying something such as: "It wasn't too long after A occurred that B occurred," ask: "But what's the exact connection between these two events?"

Confusing Cause with the Whole of Which It Is a Part

We noted earlier that most events cannot be explained by appeal to a single condition or antecedent. A set of conditions consisting of *many* antecedents can make up the sufficient condition for an event. If we forget this, it is easy to confuse what may be an important causal antecedent with a larger aggregate of antecedents of which it is a part. **This results in the fallacy of causal oversimplification, which consists in overemphasizing the role of one or more causal antecedents of an event.**

One form of oversimplification occurs when a necessary condition is treated as a sufficient condition, as in:

If you water the plant, it will grow.

or

Change your car's oil every 3,000 miles, and you'll never have trouble with the engine.

Watering a plant may be *necessary* for the growth of a plant, but it is not sufficient; and changing a car's oil at regularly prescribed intervals may be necessary for proper engine maintenance, but it is not sufficient.

Another version of causal oversimplification occurs when a contributory condition is treated as sufficient for an event. Thus:

If corporate taxes are reduced, employment will increase.
If you practice "safe sex," you won't contract AIDS.

---

[3]Garrett Mattingly, *The Armada*. (Boston: Houghton Mifflin, 1959).

Speaking of . . .

Confusing Cause with the Whole of Which It Is a Part

Environmental Illness May Be Mental

For those who find every wafting chemical of the urbanized, industrialized world to be more than their bodies can bear, the syndrome known as environmental illness or multiple-chemical sensitivity is as real a medical condition as diabetes or thyroid disease.

But now researchers assert that some, if not all, symptoms of environmental illness, from fatigue to headaches, confusion to nasal congestion, are probably the results of a mental disorder.

In a report being published today in the *Journal of the American Medical Association*, Dr. Donald W. Black and his colleagues at the University of Iowa College of Medicine said they found that when they evaluated a group of patients in whom environmental illness has been diagnosed the patients were much more likely to meet the criteria of a current or past psychiatric problem than were a group of normal people selected from the community.

Many of the patients in whom chemical sensitivity syndrome was diagnosed were likely to be depressed, anxious, obsessive-compulsive or to display some other mental ailment, Dr. Black said.

"It's my belief that people diagnosed as having environmental illness in most cases do have something wrong: a garden variety emotional disorder,'" he said.

But doctors who insist that environmental illness is real argued that the Iowa study has been naïvely conceived and sloppily executed.

"I don't think there's ever been a study done comparing healthy community members with a group of patients who suffer from a chronic illness that hasn't found more psychopathology among the patient group," said Dr. Leo Galland, an internist in New York who treats many people with environmental illness. "Being sick tends to make people depressed."

Dr. Galland said the study might have been worthwhile had it compared patients in whom environmental illness has been diagnosed with people who suffer from asthma or some other disease considered to be organic by the medical community. As it is, he said, "the study is a waste of time."

Nobody knows how many people suffer from environmental illness, but the disorder has gained extensive attention lately and is increasingly being taken seriously by doctors and others.

People with the disease, and the specialists, called chemical ecologists, who treat them, say that the condition results when chemicals or substances in the environment or in food disrupt the immune system, leading to nausea, respiratory problems, headaches, dizziness, rashes, fatigue and many other afflictions.

continued

continued

Some people go to extremes to eliminate hostile chemicals from their lives, avoiding newspapers because of the newsprint, shunning deodorants, perfumes and synthetic fabrics, and even lining their homes with aluminum or moving to remote spots where the contemporary, toxic world is less likely to intrude.

But those with the syndrome often do not display the typical signs of an organic disorder. In contrast to people who suffer from allergies, the bodies of those people in whom environmental illness has been diagnosed may not make antibodies that signal a misguided immune reaction to an external substance. Hence, some doctors have been skeptical of the assertions of the chemical ecologists.

Dr. Black, a psychiatrist, admits he began his study on the premise that the syndrome was not a true medical disease. "Anyone who proposes the existence of a new disorder bears the burden of proof," he said. "The researchers must demonstrate through standard scientific methods that the disorder proposed actually has some validity. But chemical ecologists have never been able to demonstrate lab abnormalities in their patients, nor have they shown that their treatments have any particular efficacy."

In the study, Dr. Black and two coworkers interviewed a group of 23 people in whom the environmental syndrome has been diagnosed by chemical ecologists. Using standard psychiatric methods, the researchers determined that 15 of the patients, or 65 percent, had symptoms of a mental disorder.

"It's clear just from talking with some of them that they had ordinary depression," he said. "If they were offered standard antidepression treatments, their symptoms would probably go away very promptly."

When the researchers applied the same interview procedure to 46 community members, 13, or 28 percent, showed signs of psychiatric distress.

Dr. Black said he thinks a diagnosis of environmental illness or multiple chemical sensitivity can have grave consequences. "Patients become fanatical about the diagnosis," he said. "Their whole life revolves around the illness, some of them rebuilding their homes according to environmentally 'acceptable' standards, or moving from one part of the country to another."

Critics of the study said that nearly all people with environmental illness had sought psychiatric help, only to find their symptoms lingering, or even getting worse, from antidepression medication.

Other experts said that even if many of the symptoms of the syndrome are caused by depression or some other mental illness the depression itself may well have been touched off by toxins in the environment.

"I don't think any psychiatrist can tell me what causes mental illnesses like depression and neurosis," said Dr. Max Costa, professor of environmental medicine and pharmacology at New York University Medical School.

Reduced corporate taxes may contribute to higher employment, but it is not sufficient, and practicing "safe sex" increases your chances of not contracting AIDS, but does not guarantee it. In each of these cases, a number of antecedent conditions, not just one, constitutes the sufficient condition for the event. To emphasize the role of one or more, we oversimplify the cause-and-effect relationship and thus fail to provide adequate grounds for the causal inference.

It is human nature to ascribe simple causes to events, to reduce complexity to simplicity, diversity to uniformity. If our reasoning is to be sound, however, we need to avoid this tendency. Of special note in this regard is the causal explanation that is constructed like a single arch vaulting over a chain of complexity.

Recall the legendary battle that was lost for the want of a horseshoe nail:

For want of a nail, the shoe was lost.
For the want of the shoe, the horse was lost;
For the want of the horse, the rider was lost;
For the want of the rider, the message was lost;
And alas, for the want of the regiment, the battle was lost.

To be sure, the legend teaches important lessons about the importance of anticipation, preparation, attention to detail, and the like. But can the loss of the battle be attributed solely or mainly to the want of a nail? Although, perhaps, the *validity* of the causal interpretation cannot be questioned, there is some question about whether the nail fairly and fully accounts for the loss.

An analogous line of causal reasoning can be seen in pervasive accounts of the famous — or infamous, from the South's viewpoint — battle of Antietam. If you are a Civil War buff, you may recall that prior to this 1862 engagement, the Confederate army under Robert E. Lee had crossed the Potomac River and was threatening Baltimore, Washington, and Pennsylvania. Would Lee invade? If so, precisely where? The Union command did not know. In fact, Lee's plans called for a march on Pennsylvania, of which he so informed all his commanders in a document called Special Orders No. 191. As it happened, one copy of these orders slipped out of the pocket of a staff officer and into the hands of Union general, George B. McClellan. Acting promptly on his good fortune, McClellan readied the Union forces for what turned out to be, by the reckoning of some, the bloodiest battle of the Civil War and a disaster for the Confederate army, leaving Lee and his troops little choice but to retreat into Virginia. For many historians, Antietam was *the* decisive battle of the war. They believe it precluded pro-Confederate European intervention, allowed Lincoln to muzzle his domestic opposition, and emboldened the beleaguered president to issue his preliminary Emancipation Proclamation.[4]

Can we, then, say that *the* cause of the Northern victory in the Civil War was the loss of Special Orders No. 191? That depends on whether the question can be fairly and fully met by such a causal explanation. About that there is considerable doubt, as there inevitably is with all attempts to isolate *the* antecedent in a *complex* chain of antecedent conditions that produce some effect. (In this case, the meteorologically minded might seek *the* cause of Union victory in the weather. The copy of Special Orders No. 191 that McClellan found was wrapped around a pack of cigars. It seems

---

[4]See David Hackett Fischer, *Historians' Fallacies.* New York: Harper & Row, 1970, p. 173.

that the staff officer had used it to preserve his cigars against a damp and dewy September morning in Maryland. If only the weather had been dry and hot! . . .)

School children unwittingly can form a similarly suspect causal inference about the beginning of World War I. Given a sketchy account of antecedent events, they might conclude that the assassination of Archduke Ferdinand at Sarajevo in 1914 was *the* cause of World War I. In fact, the fuse lit by this event was a long and complex one. Events as complicated as that war pose a labyrinth of causes.

Since a causal explanation rarely includes *all* the antecedents of an event, it can always be questioned on some level. But it is unreasonable and inefficient to expect a complete listing of antecedents. A fairer and more direct approach is to look for undue bias and scant reflection in the explanation. Ask whether the explanation adequately accounts for the events, whether it overemphasizes one or more facts when there are other equally worthy or even more significant factors.

Proposing as a main cause a single antecedent in a complex series of antecedents finds a counterpart in overemphasizing the role of an occurrence in producing some *future* event. Perhaps you have heard someone object to something, A, on grounds that it will lead to a series of undesirable consequences—B, C, D, and so on, finally culminating in some horrible Z. The person's point is that if you do not want Z, then you should not permit A. In this case, the complex series of events is forecast; it has not happened. It stretches foward into the anticipated future, not back into the historical past. But forecasts of future events are as susceptible to part-whole confusion as causal analyses of past events are. Confusing a cause with the whole of which it is a part, then, often underlies another fallacy in casual reasoning termed slippery slope (or domino theory).

The slippery slope fallacy consists in assuming without appropriate evidence that a particular action if taken (or event, if it occurs) will ignite a series of actions (or events) that will lead inevitably to some occurrence. From the arguer's viewpoint, the ultimate occurrence ordinarily is undesirable and that forms the basis of his opposition to the action or event. For example, a father warns his son not to take the first drink because then he will have another, and another, and ultimately the boy will end up a drunk. Granted, the boy cannot become a drunk without taking the "first drink," that is, without first consuming alcohol. But is a first drink *sufficient* to make him a drunk? If it were, the vast majority of people would be alcoholics.

If, on the other hand, the father said: "If you don't take the first drink, you won't end up a drunk," he would have a point. The negative outcome—*not* becoming an alcoholic—would be effected by never taking a drink. In other words, not taking a drink is a *sufficient* condition for not becoming an alcoholic, but taking a drink is *not* a sufficient condition for making one an alcoholic.

Consider a case where a person opposes a national health insurance program because, if it is enacted, it will not be long before the government will take over other aspects of our lives and soon we will be living in a socialistic state. In another case, someone opposes permitting terminally ill patients to decline life-sustaining measures (that is, passive euthanasia) on grounds that, once permitted, it is unavoidable that people will be put to death against their will.

In each case, the arguer hypothesizes a chain of events. On the basis of the final, undesirable link, the arguer rejects the first link. Since the ultimate horrors are not inevitable, the appeals are fallacious. This is not to say that instituting national health insurance, for example, would not in any way make us more receptive to other government programs, or that permitting passive voluntary euthanasia would not in any way predispose us to consider other forms of euthanasia. However, making us more receptive to similar programs and policies is a far different consequence from the one forecast. In chain-of-events arguments like these, each causal claim requires a separate argument.

IN BRIEF   In a chain-of-events argument, where some objectionable final outcome is forecast on the basis of an event, ask yourself whether the chain can be broken at any link between the first and last. If it can be — if the chain lacks inevitability — then the argument is a slippery slope. Alternatively, look for independent causal explanations for each event in the series. The absence of these typically marks the slippery slope.

Confusing Cause with Correlation

Suppose that sixty percent of adult American females support strict gun control and forty percent of adult males do. These facts would allow us to say that gender and position on gun control are statistically correlated in the population of adult Americans. This statistical correlation could be pictured as follows:

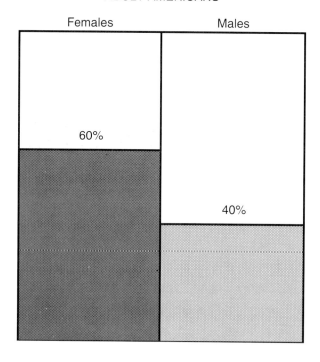

ADULT AMERICANS

We could go on to say:

Support for gun control is *positively* correlated with being a female.

The correlation is "positive" because the percentage of gun-control advocates among women *is greater than* the percentage of non–gun-control advocates among women. With respect to men, the correlation could be expressed:

Support for gun control is *negatively* correlated with being a male.

The correlation is "negative" because the percentage of gun-control supporters among men is *less than* the percentage of non–gun-control supporters among men. (If the percentage of gun-control supporters and non–gun-control supporters were exactly the same for men, we could say that there is *no correlation* between supporting gun control and being a male.)

It is almost impossible to get through a day without being accosted by some such statistical correlation. Correlations are drawn in occupations, for example, between males and engineers, or females and secretaries, or between salaries and gender. They abound in health care, as, for example, between fluoride and cavities, or Vitamin A and Alzheimer's disease, or body shape and disease. Economists remind us of the correlation between government spending and interest rates, the price of bonds and the price of stocks, consumer confidence in the economy and personal savings. You probably have formed more than one correlation based on your personal experience—between studying and grades, the amount of sleep you get and your mood, how much money you spend on a date and how much fun you have. Whatever the statistical correlation, it always involves a relationship between properties that exist in some *actual* population, not a hypothetical one. The correlations drawn between positions on gun control and sex, for example, reflect the expressed views of women and men in the actual population. They are, as it were, statistical "photographs."

It can be said that in all cause-and-effect relationships there is also a correlation between cause and effect. The occurrence of one thing in some way leads to the occurrence of the other things. That is what cause means—causes and effects are mutually related.

The fact that two things are mutually related, however, does *not of itself* establish a cause-and-effect relationship between them, no more than being an antecedent of an event makes something the cause of the event. Thus, simply because there may be a correlation between smoking pot and grades, or between living in a region of the country and lung disease, or between a female going to college and her chances of remaining unmarried, there is not necessarily a causal relationship between any of these things. *Causation always implies correlation, but statistical correlation, of itself, does not imply causation.* To assert a causal relationship between the things in the preceding pairs implies far more than that merely a simple statistical correlation exists between them. To say that cigarette smoking *causes* cancer, for example, is to state more than that there *actually* are more cases of lung cancer among smokers than among nonsmokers, which would be a simple correlation. *Cigarette smoking causes lung cancer* means that there *would be* more cases of lung cancer in the population if everyone smoked than if no one smoked, other factors remaining constant.

Statistical correlations such as the preceding involve relationships between things in an *actual* population. Their causal counterparts involve connections between *hypothetical* versions of the real population. Obscure expressions such as *linked to* and *associated with* confuse this distinction. For example, to say that "There's a *link* between taking Vitamin C and not getting colds" could simply mean that it *has been observed in the actual population* that there are fewer incidents of colds among Vitamin-C users than among people who do not use Vitamin C. Many people, however, interpret (and are encouraged to) the expression *linked to* as an expression of cause, that is, "Vitamin C *prevents* colds." They would probably be less inclined to, however, if they understood what that claim means: "If everyone took Vitamin C, there would be fewer cases of colds, than if no one took Vitamin C." The simple statistical correlation between Vitamin C and cold prevention is not enough to justify that *causal* generalization.

Sometimes, we frame correlations in terms of simultaneity of occurrences. We notice that changes in one thing reflect changes in another, so we correlate the two. A simple example would be the correlation between driving speed and stopping distance. As the speed increases, so does the distance needed to stop. As the speed decreases, so does the distance required to stop. As air pollution increases, we observe an accompanying rise in respiratory diseases. So we correlate air pollution with respiratory problems. Sometimes the correlation is inverse: as one thing increases (or decreases), the other is observed to decrease (or increase). Thus, it is observed in a particular community that, as the employment rate increases, the crime rate decreases; or as the employment rate decreases, the crime rate increases. As with all correlations, it is erroneous to infer a cause-and-effect relationship solely on the basis of simultaneity of occurrences.

When we forget this, we are likely to assume that, because two things occur together, one must be the cause of the other, when in fact both may be explained by some common cause. As an illustration, suppose a person is suffering from both alcoholism and depression. It is tempting to infer that one causes the other—the depression causes the drinking, or the drinking causes the depression. But perhaps both are the effects of something else—a chemical imbalance, for example. **Failing to recognize that two seemingly related events may not be causally related but the effects of some common cause results in the fallacy of neglect of a common cause.**

An amusing example of neglecting a common cause can be seen in a story told about Abraham Lincoln. It seems that while whiskey-swigging General Grant was handily winning battles in the West, Lincoln was receiving lots of complaints about the general's drinking. One day a delegation confronted Lincoln: "Mr. President, the general is hopelessly addicted to whiskey." To which Lincoln is reported to have replied: "I wish General Grant would send a barrel of his whiskey to each of my other generals."

Of course, cases of neglecting a common cause do not always have a humorous intent. As an example, consider the sober comments of a former Los Angeles police chief on the possible "link" between sex crimes and pornography:

Speaking of . . .

Confusing Cause with Correlation

The Hawthorne Effect

As early as the 1920s, researchers began to realize that workers would be more productive if management met those needs that money cannot buy. Managers at the Western Electric factory in Hawthorne, California, were conducting experiments to determine the effect of work environment on worker productivity. In the literature of work motivation, these studies have become known as the Hawthorne studies. What they discovered has been termed the Hawthorne effect.

Researchers in the Hawthorne studies chose a few employees to work in an experimental area, apart from the thousands of employees in the rest of the factory. Every effort was made to improve working conditions, from painting walls a cheerful color to making lights brighter. Worker productivity increased with each improvement, thus suggesting a correlation. Then something curious occurred.

The experimenters decided to reverse the process. Lights were made dimmer, walls were dulled, and so on. Fully expecting productivity to fall along with the changes in work environment, researchers were amazed to find that workers actually produced more.

It was ultimately concluded that workers were producing more because of the *attention* they were receiving. Instead of feeling like cogs in the organizational wheel, they felt important and recognized and, in turn, worked better. Discovery of this Hawthorne effect signaled the beginning of what we today know as the science of human relations.

> I had a meeting with a bunch of my policemen recently and I asked them how many had arrested rape suspects, and all of them had. How many of them had found any unusual quantity of pornographic literature in the rape suspects' homes? All of them had.

The implication is that in some way pornography *causes* the rapists to rape, but maybe some kind of sexual dysfunction accounts for both the rapes and the rapists' use of pornography. Taken on face, the chief's comments imply a causal relationship between pornography and rape that is tantamount to saying: "If all men used pornography, there would be more rapes, than if no men used pornography." A convincing case has yet to be made for that statement. Taking another tack, one could ask: "What's the percentage of males in the actual population who use pornography but don't rape?" It is a safe bet that the percentage will be far greater than those who use pornography and rape. We are, therefore, left questioning the significance of the chief's correlation.

IN BRIEF   Every cause-and-effect relationship implies a correlation, but a statistical correlation does not necessarily imply a cause-and-effect relationship. A simple correlation may reflect a causal relationship, but it does not establish it. After a cause-and-effect relationship has been established, a statistical correlation has confirmatory value. Thus, having established that smoking contributes to lung cancer, we would expect to find an increase in lung cancer among women that correlates with the increase in female smokers, and we have.

EXERCISES ON CONFUSION IN CAUSAL REASONING*

Identify and explain the kind of confusion that is present in each of the following statements of cause and effect. Where an author is identified, discuss the connection between the cause and the author's likely perspective—in other words why the author would be predisposed to see things as he or she does. Also, try to suggest alternative causal explanations that could account for the phenomenon.

1. Asked by Senator James A. McClure (R-Ida.) why he had participated in drafting a "false and misleading" version of events in the Iran-Contra affair, former National Security Adviser Robert C. McFarland blamed such factors as a weak public school program, campaign financing, military ineffectiveness, and the nation's preoccupation with domestic issues.
2. Editorial comment on the colorization of classic black-and-white films, such as *Casablanca* and *Citizen Kane:* "Let this sort of thing go on, and somebody will want to put a mustache on the *Mona Lisa.*"
3. The Yoruba people of western Nigeria believe that the birth of twins is lucky. "Twins are delivered to poor people to make them rich," says Kehinde Eghobamien, 30, a twin who works as a clerk in Lagos, Nigeria. "Within three months you will see the parents of the twins building a house, and so on. The twins have brought them good luck."
4. News Item: "Parole officials argue that they must have the freedom of action to release prisoners whenever they choose, not according to the dictates of individual communities. If one county is allowed to bar a former convict from residency, others will follow suit, raising the possibility that there would be no place available to parole some convicts."
5. Letter to the editor: "To the neighborhood, the 'Stay in School' program has meant fewer daytime crimes. Kern County Sheriff Sgt. Larry Hamilton tracked crime in the neighborhood for the winter months in 1985–1986 and again in 1986–1987. Thefts decreased by 37 percent. Vandalism was down by 35 percent. This was during a time when other parts of the county witnessed a 12 percent increase in those crimes. I just don't think anyone would argue that keeping juveniles off the street doesn't affect those crimes. Juveniles on the street are looking for things to do."

6. Economic professor Ravi Batra says that past economic cycles mean that a depression is "inevitable" and that the exact date can be pointed. His research, he says, demonstrates that great depressions follow a "third-decade/sixth-decade" pattern. For example, the 1780s witnessed a depression, the 1810s didn't. The 1840s had a terrible depression, and so did the 1870s. But the 1900s (1900–1910) escaped a depression. Then the 1930s experienced a crippling depression. Thus, since the 1960s avoided a depression, the 1990s is in for the "worst economic crisis in history."

7. "Congress is exacting its ton of flesh for having been deceived, ignored, and lied to by the Reagan administration. That's why the Iran-Contra hearings drone on, focusing on the delicate balance between the White House and Congress on war making powers."
(Jim Fain, conservative syndicated columnist)

8. South Africa Zulu leader Mangosuthu Buthelezi, an influential black moderate, warned American business persons that if American firms completely pull out of South Africa "South Africa will be thrust into the cauldron of revolution and be reduced to Third World chaos."

9. Cleveland Indians manager Pat Corrales, explaining why Boston Red Sox rookie Ellis Burks hit a grand slam home run off his Indians: "If we'd gotten the scouting tapes on time, we probably would have pitched Burks differently. But we got the tapes two days later because the mail was delayed by the holiday." (A wag replied: "I guess the Indians need a special delivery to get Burks out.")

10. "The British election of 1987 *[in which Conservative Prime Minister Margaret Thatcher won her third term]* may have been as important to America as the American elections of 1988 were. Thatcher defeated a man *[Labor party leader Neil Kincok]* whose ascension to power would have begun the dissolution of NATO, the denuclearization of Europe, and the rise of American isolationism."

11. A Saudi warplane was in the area during the Iraqi attack on the U.S. frigate *Stark,* in which thirty-seven American crew members were killed. In the absence of instructions from his superiors on the ground, the pilot took no action to stop the Iraqi fighter. Shortly thereafter, the Administration withdrew its request for congressional approval to sell U.S. "Maverick" missiles to Saudi Arabia. Secretary of State George Shultz blamed the collapse of the sale on "misinformation" surrounding the *Stark* attack.

12. News Item: "The jailed owner of a pit bulldog that fatally mauled a 2½-year-old boy has blamed the child's parents for leaving the boy unattended. 'If the parents had kept tabs on this kid, this never would have happened,' said the owner. The child was savagely torn apart when he walked past two pit bulls, tied to a post on one side of the owner's home, and across the front yard."

13. "Once again the Reagan Administration has sabotaged a compromising attempt to achieve a negotiated peace in Central America. Last weekend, just as special envoy Philip Habib was leaving El Salvador — and as Assistant Secretary of State Elliott Abrams was in the neighborhood for 'brief consultations' — El Salvador President José Napoleon Duarte announced that he could not attend the long-planned June 25–26 summit meeting of Central American presidents. Immediately Honduras

also pulled out, citing some vague lack of readiness for the meeting, which had been planned since January."
(Jorge C. Castaneda, professor of political science at the National Autonomous University of Mexico)

14. A study by the federal Office of Technology Assessment found that, under the narrowest type of inquiry, polygraph tests incorrectly label as liars an average of ten percent of truthful people. In response, William J. Scheve, Jr., president of the American Polygraph Association, blamed problems on the polygraph operator, not the test or the machine. "It is not the polygraph itself that is potentially abusive but the few unskilled or unethical examiners who cause isolated instances of polygraph abuse."

15. Letter to the editor: "I remember a time when the cities of New York, Chicago, and Los Angeles were cities where you could go to the neighborhood delis and not worry about whether you would be there when a robbery would take place. You could sit outside in the day and evenings. When the weather got hot and muggy you could leave the doors and windows open! No more. Why? Because of the kind of people that Bernard Goetz *[who shot several youths who accosted him in a New York subway]* took action against."

16. News Item: "After declining to a nine-year low of about 9 percent in late March, fixed-rate mortgages shot up to a high of 10.8 percent in May. They have retreated slightly since then and now stand at 10.35 percent. The sharp sales decline during May demonstrates that housing is still an interest-rate sensitive industry."
(James Fischer, president of National Association of Home Builders)

17. Letter to the editor: "How come our city, county and state representatives, and our national representatives are not interested in sponsoring a simple bill that would give them access to available funds that: (1) balance the budget, (2) do away with income tax, (3) reduce inflation and the Consumer Price Index to zero, and (4) finally pay off the national debt? How? By legally tapping the banker's excess profits."

18. "Our private system of health care has one central flaw. It is not available to everyone. Because our health care is so good, it is expensive. . . ."
(Ben Wattenberg, senior fellow at the American Enterprise Institute)

19. While Washington D.C.'s government staggered under a barrage of scandals involving everything from fraud, bribery, and extortion to cocaine use, philandering, and faulty snow removal, its mayor, Marion S. Barry, Jr., became enmeshed in a sensational sex and drug trial. "They're picking on Barry because he's black," said one of his honor's defenders. "If you're talking about scandal, talk about (the late Chicago Mayor Richard J.) Daley or (New York Mayor Edward I.) Koch."

20. "The Japanese didn't get rich just through hard work; they got rich through open access to our markets while we allowed them to shut us out of theirs."
(Chrysler President Lee Iacocca)

21. "I call upon the Reagan Administration to double its request for aid to the Nicaraguan democratic resistance (a.k.a. *Contras*) from $105 million to $210 million. It's not enough to give the freedom fighters enough to fight with — they must have enough to forge a victory for democracy."
(Former Representative Jack Kemp)

22. Admiral Poindexter, addressing the Iran-Contra committee: "... I frankly don't think in the whole scheme of things it's that important a decision *[that is, not informing the President of the diversion of profits to the Contras from the sales of arms to the Iranians]*. It obviously is a controversial one. The thing that made it important in your eyes, in my mind, is the reaction of the media to it, and members of Congress have to react to the media."

23. Editorial: "Last year's dramatic fall in the price of oil—reflecting worldwide glut in production—led to sharp drops in the price of gasoline. This in turn was followed by a dramatic acceleration in gasoline demand, as motorists topped off their tanks and took to driving farther and more frequently. At the same time, America increased its imports of oil. It's clear, therefore, that the fall in oil prices caused the nation's trade deficit to climb to the highest level on record in May of this year."

24. "We're not wise enough to use the machines we were smart enough to invent. Machines sustain bodily functions long after any meaningful life has gone. Given another open-ended program (e.g., health insurance for the elderly) to health providers, we shall soon have large numbers of Kafka-like Medicare warehouses where machines keep corpses alive while we simultaneously are forced as a society to shut down well-baby clinics and illness-prevention programs." (Colorado former Governor Richard D. Lamm)

25. "In the 1970s . . . members of Congress competed to write the tightest restrictions to keep the United States from having its fingers soiled by actions that could serve as text for a sermon on heavenly grace (i.e., Congress put limits on covert actions by U.S. intelligence agencies). The driving force behind this was the growing army of secular televangelists—the correspondents, commentators, and anchor people who presented the evening news as a morality play. Brandishing moral calipers they nightly measured the postures of public officials against simplistic scales of righteousness and tagged them saints or sinners accordingly. . . ." (Syndicated conservative columnist Raymond Price)

26. In 1922, Hungarian physicist Roland vos Eotvos was trying to prove that gravity has the same effect on all materials. Using a torsion balance because he had no way of measuring the acceleration of a falling object, Eotvos tested various materials—including metals, asbestos, and talc. He concluded that gravity exerted the same pull on all of them, *within the limits of experimental error.* (Hint: Some physicists today hypothesize a "fifth force," called hypercharge, in addition to the four forces thought to explain all things in nature: gravity, electromagnetism, and the strong and weak forces that govern the structure of an atom.)

27. Letter to the editor: "The recent reported 5 percent increase in inflation for the first six months of this year is absolutely outrageous and very frightening. With this rate of inflation, you, Mr. and Mrs. America, will be paying the following prices in the future: $1.63 for a head of lettuce; $1.39 a pound for chicken; $1.82 a dozen for small eggs; $2.50 for a pack of cigarettes; and last but not least $2.89 a gallon for gasoline!"

28. News Item: *(Moscow)* "The government accused U.S. diplomats Thursday of fomenting demonstrations by Crimean Tatars, and Soviet authorities moved on several fronts to suppress public demands by the Tatars for their lost homeland.

The Foreign Ministry, accusing the U.S. Embassy of improper diplomatic conduct, charged that a senior political officer had incited the Tatar protest, 'Soviet citizens to commit illegal actions.' The charges against the diplomat, Shaun Byrnes, and other unnamed U.S. representatives were reported on the evening television news, which showed two photographs of Byrnes meeting with people identified by the authorities as Tatar protesters."

29. News Item: "According to Rep. Les Aspin (D-Wis.), Deputy Defense Secretary William H. Taft IV has told the committee that he was asked by Kuwaiti officials in October, 1986, about a month before the Iran initiative became public, whether the United States was selling arms to Iran. Taft denied it. Aspin noted that this incident preceded by only a month the Kuwaiti requests to both the United States and the Soviet Union to protect their oil tankers in the Persian Gulf. It was Taft's story that convinced Aspin of a link between the Iranian arms sales and the Kuwaiti request for U.S. naval escorts in the Persian Gulf. He said that news of the arms sales, particularly after Taft denied it, must have caused 'enormous unease' among those gulf states like Kuwait that are aligned with Iraq."

30. On the event of the alignment of the planets and constellations dubbed the "Harmonic Convergence" by New Age spiritualists, record flooding hit Chicago and torrential rains battered Louisiana and Florida. Some true-believers attributed the disaster to the planetary alignment.

31. Letter to the editor: "I am an employer in a service profession, who has conducted job interviews with recent graduates for many years. About ten years ago I began to notice that the first questions applicants asked dealt with pay, vacation, and benefits. Before then they used to ask about the job, opportunities for growth, responsibilities, and so on. The discernible shift in priorities has led me to reflect on something: television. It was during the period of 1950–1955 that TV became generally available to consumers. By mid-1970s and following, graduates represent the first generation in the work force which has been raised from infancy in a household with a television."

32. A disgruntled federal official commenting on the October 19, 1987, 508-point decline in stock prices: "This is a computer-generated drop, caused by 29-year-old technicians with three years of market experience."

33. News Item: *(Rome)* "The Vatican's Congregation for the Cause of Saints decided that a St. Louis nun was cured of a serious neurological disorder 27 years ago as a result of the intercession of 18th century Franciscan friar Father Junipero Serra, who is known as the 'Apostle of California.' Sister Mary Boniface Dyrda and fellow members of the Franciscan Sisters of Perpetual Help — at the urging of the order chaplain — asked Serra to intervene with God to save Dyrda from a life-threatening disease lupus erythematosus, a chronic and debilitating inflammatory disease of the connective tissue. She subsequently showed no signs of the ailment."

34. News Item: *(Norfolk, Va)* "With all this pressure to appear beautiful or at least attractive, psychologist Thomas F. Cash is ready with help for those who can't stand to look at themselves. His beauty therapy started two years ago with a study involving 32 women who were unhappy with their appearances even though they were of average weight. Those who went through the therapy (which mainly involved joining support groups and exercise) increased their self-esteem,

Cash said, while the women who went without therapy kept their negative attitudes."

35. Approximately two weeks before "Super Tuesday," the day on which key presidential primaries were held, televangelist Marvin Gorman reportedly gave Assemblies of God leaders photographs showing Assemblies' televangelist Jimmy Swaggart with a prostitute. When the results of "Super Tuesday" wrote an end to his presidential aspirations, former televangelist Pat Robertson said it was no accident that the news of Swaggart's difficulties broke when it did. At a news conference in Columbia, South Carolina, Robertson said that to think the timing of the Swaggart disclosures had not been by design "would stretch the credulity of almost anybody."

36. "As society can increase its competitive power many times over by exporting its own economical defects to a rival, human exports can play a decisive role in this process because the most serious defects in our economy are people. Not the workers who improve the country by making and doing . . . but the yuppies—the lawyers, MBA's, management consultants, and corporate raiders—everybody who makes millions tying knots in the coils of progress. As a group, these professionals have had a devastating effect on our competitive position. Studies show that with every explosive increase in their numbers, all our economic indicators have plunged—productivity, value of the dollar, you name it. . . ."
(Michael J. O'Neill)

MODULE 11.4

WRITING WITH REASON: DEVELOPING CAUSAL ARGUMENTS

The preceding observations should be kept in mind when writing causal arguments. They are especially important to remember when writing an argumentative essay whose presentation relies primarily on the development of a cause-and-effect relationship, as, for example, with theses such as these: "Light sentences mean more crime," "Sex education encourages sexual experimentation," "Computers have created as many problems as they've solved." In developing this kind of essay, always:

1. Review all available data and support evidence. Failing to do this, you can easily make faulty connections between events, overlook the real cause, or leave a true causal relationship unestablished. Analyzing data is especially necessary when arguing social policies or issues, for example, "Making condoms available to students makes a lot of sense," "Unless we conquer poverty, we won't reduce urban crime," "Frivolous classroom activities are preventing children from learning how to read and write," "Unless we develop a national energy policy, we'll remain hostage to the wiles and whims of Middle East politics."

2. Re-examine your argument to see whether there are other possible causes and effects.   Again, this is especially important when developing theses such as the aforementioned. Even when there is strong evidence of causal connection, be sure to indicate the kind of connection it is — necessary, sufficient, contributory. Where appropriate, also say whether the cause is proximate or remote. Never leave the interpretation of cause up to your readers, for confusion usually results.

3. Offer support for your causal assertion.   As in any other argumentative essay, support can take the form of examples, fact, informed opinion (authority), statistics, and so on. No matter the kind of evidence, never leave debatable or controversial causal statements unsupported.

4. Avoid confusing a cause with something else.   Confusing a cause with an antecedent, the whole of which it is a part, or a correlation, can torpedo an entire paper.

Beyond these guidelines, a few other points are worth mentioning. We noted in this chapter the influence of purpose, interest, and perspective on the selection of a cause. These factors also impinge on the expression of cause-and-effect relationships.

Imagine, for example, that you are a reporter analyzing a fire. Your job is to explain this event to readers in a cause-and-effect essay. Certainly, the complexity of the event and your depth of information will help shape your presentation, but so will your purpose and intention. Perhaps you will focus on a *single cause* leading to a *single effect*. Thus, when you learn that the fire was started by an arsonist, you peg your essay to that single cause. *The single-cause–single-effect pattern is commonly used when the purpose is to establish blame* (or, where appropriate, praise): "Who or what caused X?" which is usually answered by "This is who or what caused X."

On the other hand, you might take the tack of showing the single cause producing *multiple effects*. Thus, you pinpoint arson as accounting for the fire, then show how the fire was not merely a single effect but one among many losses and tragedies.

You could take still another approach, keying on *multiple causes* leading to *single effect*. The fire, you write, was not only the result of arson, but also of high winds, extremely arid conditions, failure to clear brush, and so on. In this perspective you are viewing the fire as the consequence of many interlocking factors.

Finally, you could develop *multiple causes* leading to *multiple effects*. In this case, you would analyze the fire as a number of separate effects (death, property loss, recrimination, dislocations, and so on) produced by multiple causes (human, natural, institutional, and so on). These four formats are employed in causal arguments, as well as in causal explanations.

Of course, after you have decided which of these formats best suits your purpose, you must organize your material. Ordinarily, when writers attempt to trace the conditions that have produced some effect, they will first state the problem, then identify the major causes, and then summarize or conclude. More specifically, there are two main ways to order the causes: by chronology or relative importance.

Chronological Order of Causes

One way to arrange the conditions producing the effect is by presenting the major ones in chronological order, as when treating some historical event. Thus, the thesis is stated in the form of some problem, the major causes are presented in chronological order, and a summary is made. Of course, since we are speaking of causal argument here, remember that your thesis must assert an *arguable* claim—it cannot be merely a causal explanation. The following example shows how a causal argumentative essay might be developed following a chronological order:

Statement of Problem and Thesis: It is commonly acknowledged that, on the whole, we Americans are no longer as gullible about our government as we once were. We are less accepting and more skeptical, less trusting and more suspicious. When George Bush broke his campaign promise not to raise taxes, few Americans expressed surprise. We've come to expect such "flip-flops" of our leaders. And with good reason. In the last three decades, we have been lied to with metronomic regularity.

Major Cause 1: Perhaps the immediate roots of our disillusionment with government can be traced to the U-2 incident of 1960, which was shrouded in governmental lies. Recall that the U-2 was a highly sophisticated surveillance plane that was shot down over Russia. . . .

Major Cause 2: But the U-2 was just a sign of things to come. Ahead of us lay Vietnam, a notorious example of governmental deceit. . . .

Major Cause 3: No sooner did the Vietnam War end than Americans again faced the specter of deceit at the highest levels of government: the Watergate scandal. . . .

Summary: Numerous other social, political, and cultural events also figure in the calculation. But who can deny that the U-2, Vietnam, and Watergate were watersheds in the making of a nation of skeptics?

Order of Importance

A second way to develop a causal argumentative essay is to present the causes in their order of importance, typically leaving the most important for last. This pattern proceeds much as the former does. Additionally, in this kind of essay, the writer often tacks on some remedy for the problem. The following example shows an essay developed by arranging causes in their order of importance. (In this case, the topic but not the thesis is identified at the opening.)

Statement of Problem: College professors often complain that today's students can't follow a lecture, indeed not even a monologue that goes beyond ten or fifteen minutes. Why can't they?

Major Cause 1:   For one thing, many lectures and professors are simply boring. Although it may be possible to feign interest in the face of a bore, it's difficult to stay tuned in. . . .

Major Cause 2:   In addition, students easily get distracted. Many young people lack the self-discipline required to sit still and follow the meanderings of a lecture. Students are also beset by other pressing concerns, some academic, some social. . . .

Major Cause 3:   But the biggest factor in the equation is television. Whether we like it or not, this generation has been raised on a steady diet of TV, which has equipped it more to receive visual messages than auditory ones. Just as important, television viewing has accustomed young people to receive information in nice, digestible chunks — no longer than ten minutes before a commercial break for a snack. . . .

Conclusion with
Remedy: No doubt, maintaining student attention and interest will continue to challenge the classroom lecturer. One way for professors to meet this challenge is to brighten the lectures with anecdotes and entertaining asides — that is, comic relief. Another way is to integrate visuals into classroom activities. Still another way is to punctuate the lectures with class discussion.

In each of these models the argument proceeds from *effect to cause.* But many essays move from cause to effect. The cause-to-effect essay can be patterned in much the same way as those we have just outlined. The following example shows the order-of-importance format.

Thesis Statement of
Problem: Given how simple it is to get a divorce today and how many of us get divorced, it is easy to overlook the personal and social impact of divorce. Indeed, the potential effects of divorce are so pernicious that we should do everything possible to make a marriage work.

Major Effect 1:   Divorce most obviously affects the partners themselves. The often-seen gallant posturing notwithstanding, divorced people do feel a profound sense of loss and disappointment, even failure. In fact, studies indicate. . . .

Major Effect 2: When a family is involved, divorce can send emotional shock waves through every child, regardless of age, sex, and emotional stability. Again, studies of children from broken homes indicate. . . .

Conclusion with Remedy: There is no easy solution to the problem of divorce and its sinister personal and social effects. Making marriage counseling more accessible to couples might help. Also, courses in marriage and family at the high school level seem warranted.

IMPROVING PERFORMANCE

SUMMARY-TEST QUESTIONS FOR CHAPTER 11

1. Construct five questions that imply a causal relationship.
2. Which of the following, if any, does not imply causation: *cure, produce, increase, pulverize, instigate, offend.*
3. Which of the following statements, if any, is not a causal statement?
   A. The patient died from cardiac arrest.
   B. You won't be admitted unless you have a ticket.
   C. Formula X Grows Hair!
   D. Apple trees flourish in the state of Washington.
4. Is it true that cause has a uniform meaning?
5. What is the difference between a causal explanation and a causal argument?
6. Which of the following statements is/are true?
   A. Causal arguments imply explanation.
   B. Causal explanations imply causation.
   C. Causal statements are generalizations.
   D. A and B.
   E. B and C.
   F. A, B, and C.

Questions 7–12 are based on the following passage:

A second grade class of seventeen students scored higher on a standardized reading test than an equivalent class of thirty students. An equivalent class of twenty-three students scored somewhere between the other two, while an equivalent class of ten students scored the highest. Thus, class size influences students' reading ability.

True or false?

7. This could be considered a causal argument.
8. The conclusion is a causal argument.
9. A cause-and-effect relationship is part of the evidence.
10. The speaker is applying the method of concomitant variation.
11. The speaker is confusing a correlation with a cause.

12. The speaker employed the method of difference.
13. Purpose and perspective influence selection of cause. True or False?
14. Which of the following terms, if any, does not belong with the others?
    A. Difference
    B. Controlled experiment
    C. Comparative-group testing
    D. Agreement
    E. No exceptions
15. Watching TV appears to have a negative effect on grades of high school students. At Taft High last year, nearly seventy percent of students with "D" averages and lower reported watching twenty-five or more hours of TV per week, about fifty percent of the "C" students watched TV twenty or more hours per week, while only thirty-two percent of "B" students watched that much TV. As for students with an "A" average, fewer than ten percent said they watched as many as twenty-five hours of TV per week.
    The method used to discover cause here is:
    A. agreement
    B. difference
    C. concomitant variation
16. A large number of professional basketball players over the past ten years have come from Midwestern and Southeastern colleges. Something about the basketball program that Midwestern and Southeastern colleges share but which sets them apart from other collegiate basketball programs must account for this phenomenon. The _____ method of discovering cause seems to be operating in this claim.
    A. agreement
    B. difference
    C. concomitant variation

Fill in the blanks in the following passages (17–21) with one of the following:
   A. necessary   B. sufficient   C. proximate   D. remote   E. contributory

> An insurance company sends out an investigator to determine the cause of a mysterious fire that destroyed a policyholder's home. The investigator reports that the fire was caused by the presence of oxygen in the structure. Officials at the home office are furious with his report. And yet the investigator is right, in the sense of ____17____ condition; for had there been no oxygen, there would have been no fire. But clearly the insurance company had something else in mind when it dispatched the investigator. Several weeks later the investigator reports that although he has proof that the policy-holder had deliberately set the fire, he hadn't as yet assembled all the ____18____ conditions, and so can't determine the ____19____ cause of the fire. Company officials are fit to be tied. "Don't you realize that we're interested in why the fire occurred when ordinarily it wouldn't have?" they ask the investigator. "In other words, we want the ____20____ cause of the fire." "But," the investigator objects, "the policyholder was desperate because his company was threatening to fire him because sales had dropped

owing to foreign competition that's soared ever since Congress removed tariffs on imported products." "So what are you saying?" the officials demanded to know. "Congress caused the fire?" "Well," replied the investigator, "in the sense of a _____21_____ condition for it, they did." "Fine," said the officials, "now you can blame Congress for the fact that you're fired!"

22. The number of accidents at an intersection declines markedly after a traffic light is installed there. The city council decides to install lights at all other dangerous intersections, fully expecting a comparable reduction in traffic accidents. The council might be confusing a cause with
    A. a correlation.
    B. an antecedent event.
    C. the whole of which it is a part.
    D. None of the preceding. In fact, the council's is solid causal reasoning.

23. You are part of a transportation committee charged with reducing the commuting time for people who must travel into a city from outlying areas. One committee member proposes the installation of toll booths along the highways leading into the city. Having to pay to drive to the city, it is argued, will discourage commuters from driving into town and encourage them to use public transportation instead. During the ensuing debate, the following points are made. Which would *not* interfere with the predicted outcome?
    A. Almost all inflow traffic is commercial, which would not be deterred by the tolls.
    B. Some drivers will carpool rather than take public transport.
    C. A significant improvement in traffic flow will attract more cars.
    D. The public transportation system cannot handle a significant increase in the number of commuters.
    E. A and D.
    F. B and C.
    G. A, B, and D.

24. "A study recently published by the Department of Education shows that inner-city school children do not read as well as their counterparts in the suburbs and rural areas. The report blames this differential on overcrowded classes in city schools. But I think that the real reason is that city children don't get enough fresh air and sunshine." Which of the following best describes the form of the speaker's reasoning?
    A. It questions the reliability of the study.
    B. It attacks the methodology of the study.
    C. It tries to show that inner-city schoolchildren read as well as suburban and rural schoolchildren.
    D. It submits an alternative explanation for the differential.
    E. It argues from analogy.

25. Which of the following would *least* strengthen the speaker's point in the preceding passage?
    A. Medical research which shows a correlation between air pollution and learning disabilities.

B. A widely accepted study that discredits the claim that there is a relationship between the size of a class and a student's ability to read.

C. A subsequent amendment to the study by the Department of Education which, in effect, retracts the part dealing with overcrowding as the reason for the differential.

D. The results of a federal program that indicate city students show marked improvement in reading skills when they spend the summer in the country.

E. A federal government proposal to fund inner-city schools for the specific purpose of reducing overcrowding in classrooms.

26. A study by a leading university shows that increases in the salaries of police officers are accompanied by increases in the nationwide average of beer consumption. From 1975 to 1980 officers' salaries increased on the average 12 percent and beer sales grew by 11.5 percent. From 1980 to 1985, the average salary rose by 15 percent and beer sales by 16 percent. From 1985 to 1990 beer sales increased by 6 percent and so did the average salary. Which of the following is the most likely explanation for the findings cited here?

A. When police officers have more disposable income, they spend it on beer.

B. When police officers are paid more, they tend to work less which in turn gives them more time to drink.

C. Since the general population grew during this time, more beer was consumed.

D. The general standard of living increased from 1975 to 1990, which accounts for both the increase in beer consumption and average salaries.

E. The major breweries strictly limited the production of beer during the period cited.

27. WILL: If space creatures ever visited earth, it was because they were looking for other intelligent creatures to communicate with. But we haven't been contacted by any such creatures. So, it's obvious that none of them have ever visited earth.

JILL: Maybe they don't think we're intellligent.

How is Jill's reply related to Will's argument?

A. It questions a correlation.

B. It challenges an assumption of necessary condition.

C. It challenges an assumption of sufficient condition.

D. It challenges an assumption of contributory condition.

28. "If Britt graduated from State U. after 1985, then she was required to take Computer Science 101." This statement can be logically deduced from which of the following?

A. Before 1985, Computer Science 101 was not a required course at State U.

B. Every student who took Computer Science 101 at State U. graduated after 1985.

C. No one who graduated from State U. before 1985 took Computer Science 101.

D. All students graduating from State U. after 1985 were required to take Computer Science 101.

E. Before 1985, no student was permitted to graduate from State U. without having taken Computer Science 101.

29. TED: The phone always rings when I'm in the shower and can't hear it.
    TESS: That's ridiculous. You must be able to hear it; otherwise, you couldn't know it's ringing.

    Tess' response shows that she is supposing as a necessary condition the fact that
    A. the telephone is not ringing.
    B. the phone is ringing.
    C. Ted is not hearing the telephone ring.
    D. Ted is hearing the phone ring.
    E. Ted is taking a shower.

30. An independent medical research team recently did a survey at a health-and-fitness club specializing in helping smokers kick the habit. Eighty percent of two-pack-per-day smokers were able to cut down to one-half-pack-per-day after they began to take "Smoke-Out," a product designed to suppress the urge to smoke. The product's manufacturer uses the results in an ad crowing about how "Smoke-Out" can help anyone cut down on smoking. Which of the following would be a legitimate criticism of the ad?
    I.   Heavy smokers may be psychologically as well as physically addicted to smoking.
    II. A product that is effective for very heavy smokers may not be effective for the general population.
    III. A survey conducted at a health-and-fitness club may yield different results from one conducted under other circumstances.
    A. I only
    B. II only
    C. III only
    D. II and III only
    E. I, II, and III

Evaluate the cause-and-effect claims (31–35) in the following with respect to:

    A. Slippery slope
    B. Causal oversimplification
    C. *Post hoc*
    D. Neglect of a common cause

31. How to deal with the drug problem? Easy—just say "No!"

32. "Everybody I talked to there *[in Vietnam]* wants to know why they can't go in and finish it, and don't let anybody kid you about why we're there. If we weren't, those Commies would have the whole thing, and it wouldn't be long until we'd be looking off the coast of Santa Monica at them." (Bob Hope, during the height of the Vietnam War)

33. MAX: If a person wants to get rich, they should go to an Ivy League college.
    MOM: Why's that?
    MAX: A study just released shows that twenty years after graduation Ivy League graduates have an average income five times that of graduates of other colleges who are in the same field.

34. "I always reckoned that looking at the new moon over your left shoulder is one of the carelessest and foolishest things a body can do. Old Hank Bunker done it once, and bragged about it: and in less than two years he got drunk and fell off the shot-tower and spread himself out so that he was just kind of a layer, as you may say; and they slid him in edgeways between two barn doors for a coffin, and buried him so, so they say, but I didn't see it. Pap told me. But anyway it all come of looking at the moon that way, like a fool."
(Mark Twain, *Huckleberry Finn*)

35. ELLIE : I think it'd be dreadful if the state legalized gambling.

 J.R. : Oh, I don't know, mama — a little gamblin' now and then is good for the circulation.

 ELLIE : Maybe so, J.R. but do you want drugs, prostitution, and organized crime?

 J.R. : No, I can't say as I do, mama — I like my crime *disorganized.*

 ELLIE : J.R.!

CRITICAL THINKING APPLICATIONS

1. Imagine that you are a physician who writes a daily health column for a newspaper. You receive the following letter from a reader:

> I would like to know why some doctors look for complex answers to what is actually a simple problem. As a longtime reader of your column, I know that people who get headaches every day have a wide variety of medications to choose from. You once wrote that even a medication that is ordinarily used to treat depression could be helpful. Why, then, would a doctor start talking about exercise with someone who comes to him complaining of headaches? That's what mine did recently. All it did was turn me off.

Write a one-paragraph reply that will appear in your next column.

2. While leafing through a magazine you are drawn to the following item:

> While children might prefer mother's presence, they are not damaged by the lack of it. In fact, we have learned a great deal recently about the mental representation of mother — that evoked companion — that every child carries inside him and which sustains her or him in a situation such as a mother having to leave a sick child. The tremendous power this image exerts over a boy's or girl's thinking was demonstrated in a recent study conducted by Daniel Stern, M.D., a professor of psychiatry. Dr. Stern had noticed that while most infants and toddlers are wary of adult strangers, every once in a while, a two- or three-year-old will meet a new adult with whom he clicks immediately. His findings indicate that because something about the stranger — her voice, her look, and above all, her sensitivity — reminds the child of his mother, he is instantly at ease in interacting with this new face. On some level, the youngster sees himself interacting with Mother.

Compose a letter to the editor pointing out some problems with the way this causal hypothesis was formulated.

3. A study conducted by the National Center for Health Statistics finds that between 1967 and 1980 the smoking rate during pregnancy increased among younger, less-educated women. It is concluded that smoking during pregnancy is a function of education. **Would you accept this conclusion? Explain.**

4. According to the California Highway Patrol, motorcycles represent only 3.6 percent of all vehicles, but account for 16 percent of highway fatalities; and, according to a study released by the University of California at Davis, 82 percent of medical care for cycle-accident victims is handled through tax-based or state-run medical facilities. Figures from the Insurance Institute for Highway Safety report that more than 500 excess deaths occurred in states that repealed or weakened helmet laws. Those accidents generated costs of $180 million nationwide. When Louisiana reinstated its helmet law in 1981, fatalities dropped from 38 to 29 per thousand and accident costs dropped 43 percent. **(1) State precisely the kind of legislation that these statistics could be used to support. (2) Illustrate how those opposing the legislation might counter these statistics.**

5. If Marcus introduces an amendment to Edwards' bill, then Jergensen and Larsen will both vote the same way. If Edwards attacks Larsen's position, Jergensen will support anyone voting with him. Marcus will introduce an amendment to Edwards' bill only if Edwards speaks against Jergensen's position.[5]
   If these conditional statements are true, each of the following can be true except:
   A. If Edwards attacks Jergensen's position, Larsen will not vote with Jergensen.
   B. If Marcus introduces an amendment to Edwards' bill, then Edwards has attacked Jergensen's position.
   C. If Edwards attacks Jergensen's position, Marcus will not introduce an amendment to Edwards' bill.
   D. If Marcus introduces an amendment to Edwards' bill, then Jergensen will not vote with Larsen or Edwards did not attack Jergensen's position.
   E. If either Edwards did not speak against Larsen's position or Marcus did not introduce an amendment to Edwards' bill, then either Jergensen did not defend Larsen or Marcus spoke against Jergensen's position.

POINT/COUNTERPOINT: ESSAYS FOR ANALYSIS

Issue: Drugs

Resolved: Decriminalization is the way to stop the escalating drug problem.

Background: How big is the illegal drug market in the United States? Estimates vary, but most agree it is over $100 billion. Profits are huge, several thousand times the cost. Drug use reportedly saps our economy of $60 billion. According to the Federal Reserve, of the $125 billion in currency that is unaccounted for, much of it is buried underground in the drug trade. It has been calculated that between 35 and 50 million Americans—possibly

---

[5]Arco's LSAT (Law School Admission Test) offers a treasure trove of logic puzzles like these, which have inspired a variety of exercises throughout this text.

twenty percent of the entire population — consumed an illegal drug in 1988. Of those, 6.5 million are said to be severely dependent.

Of course, a problem as massive as drugs does not escape people's attention — at least not for long. More and more of us, according to the polls, feel that illegal drug use is the country's No. 1 problem. In the fall of 1989, a CBS/New York Times survey found that fifty-four percent of Americans feel that way. Four years earlier, only one percent did.

The problem has not escaped the eye of Congress either. In 1989 it added $1.1 billion to President Bush's revised request for drug-war money — in all, $3.2 billion above the president's original request. In 1990, the federal government spent $9.5 billion on the drug war, including $1.3 billion to build or expand its prisons. Of the 1.2 million drug-related arrests in 1988, about seventy-five percent were for possession, typically of marijuana.

But the more attention the drug problem gets, the more money poured into the war against it, the stricter the penalties, the worse it seems to grow. What to do?

It was not long ago that the thought that the United States might legalize cocaine and heroin was pure fantasy. Not any more.

From: **Nothing Else Has Worked: Abolish the Prohibitions[6]***

Robert W. Sweet

Robert S. Sweet, a federal judge in New York, is one of a number of respected figures in the political mainstream who have embraced decriminalization as the way to stop the escalating drug problem. In the following essay, he tells why. **Read the essay carefully, outline it, then answer the questions that follow it.**

1 The present policy of prohibition has not diminished the drug-abuse problem.

2 What has created this frustrating, debilitating and destructive situation is money, or the lack thereof. One of every four youngsters in America will experience poverty in the 1990s. A decade ago, one in nine faced similar economic circumstances. The loss of hope signified by this trend is our real problem. It is this outlook that breeds cocaine, crack and heroin addiction and its associated culture. Riding shotgun to a drug deal, or acting as a lookout while the deal comes down can make a teen-ager $50, $100 or $300 — immediately. It is the risk of capture — or death — that creates this extraordinary reward.

3 Drug prohibition thus produces two outcomes that directly undercut its goal: It creates an economic incentive for drug dealers to increase narcotics use, and by forbidding use, it enhances the appeal of certain chemicals.

---

[6]Robert W. Sweet, "Nothing Else Has Worked: Abolish the Prohibitions," *Los Angeles Times,* March 12, 1990. Reprinted by permission of the author.

4 If what we are doing is not working, it is time to abolish the prohibition, to stop treating mind alteration as a crime.

5 Decriminalization would take the profits out of illegal drugs, eliminate a major reason for gang violence and killings and remove drug dealers from street corners, much as the repeal of Prohibition ended bootlegging and its related crimes. Users could be identified and helped. The billions of dollars now spent on enforcement and imprisonment could be channeled into drug research, education and treatment.

6 Decriminalization would also have to be accompanied by a renewed government commitment to job creation, education, health care and housing to create hope where it does not now exist — principally in the inner cities. If we are unwilling to be our brother's keepers, we will have to become our brother's jailers. That's unacceptable in a nation that prizes personal liberty above all else.

7 Continued prohibition, it is now clear, will not prevent the development of a potentially more potent, addictive and dangerous drug than crack, itself the successor of heroin, angel dust and powder cocaine. Indeed, there is evidence that "ice," a synthetic drug, is fast becoming the drug of choice in some areas.

8 The existence of crack babies and the abandonment of parental responsibility demonstrates the failure of prohibition as well. Keeping crack illegal, the evidence shows, will not break this vicious cycle of dependence and abandonment.

9 After appropriate study, then, Congress should set federal standards for dispensing and taxing drugs, help state and local governments identify users, pay for research on alternative blocking agents for addicts and make some treatment available for every addict, including medical intervention. Resale and distribution of drugs outside legal channels would be a federal crime. And since ending wide-scale prohibition would proportionally free up more enforcement and court resources, punishment for violators would be swifter, surer and equally — or perhaps even more — punitive than today.

10 The young, up to age 21, would be prohibited from buying or using drugs. More than the threat of imprisonment would probably be needed to enforce this prohibition. Anti-drug education and special outreach programs would be necessary, including hefty stipends for athletic, academic and vocational achievement.

11 Since people who currently want to use drugs don't have much difficulty in finding them, perhaps abolishing prohibition would not add to the number of users. But even if the number of addicts were to increase, there is still the moral question of whether it is right to prohibit individuals from using mind-altering substances. Nineteen years of Prohibition showed that it was morally wrong to prevent Americans from drinking a mood-altering substance that has been part of our heritage throughout Western civilization.

12 Lester Grinspoon of the Harvard Medical School puts it another way: "We have to believe that, in the long run, people will respond in a rational way to the availability of substances with a potential for destruction. There will always be casualties with alcohol. There will always be death."

13 In the end, the moral issue pivots on questions of self-control and responsibility. Government must punish those who do unto others what others abhor. When government gets involved in protecting people from themselves, the opportunities for mischief are plentiful.

14 The drug problem cannot be solved by guns and tanks and by the rhetoric of war. Rather, faith, moral suasion, family commitment and individual responsibility are far more likely to produce the goal we seek: a drug policy that is consistent with our principles and ideals.

15 We must think anew, reallocate our resources and be willing to sacrifice so that dignity and ability can alter the mind of our youth instead of crack, ice and heroin. In short, abolish prohibition.

1. Is the author in a position to know about the drug problem?
2. The author believes a main cause of the drug problem is
   A. character weakness.
   B. poverty.
   C. soft-hearted judges.
   D. poor education.
3. Identify the sequence of conditions that the author believes leads to the drug problem.
4. Would it be fair to say that the author believes that if poverty can be eliminated, then so would the drug problem? If this is what the author is saying, then he must believe that eliminating poverty is a _____ for eliminating the drug problem.
   A. necessary
   B. sufficient
   C. contributory
5. Paragraph 2 implies the method of _____ .
   A. agreement
   B. difference
   C. concomitant variation
6. In paragraph 2, the author says: "Riding shotgun to a drug deal or acting as a lookout while the deal comes down can make a teen-ager $50, $100 or $300 — immediately. It is the risk of capture — or death — that creates this extraordinary reward." Which of the following questions is this an explanation for?
   A. Why do teenagers risk their lives in a drug deal?
   B. Why are drugs so expensive?
   C. Why can teenagers make so much money in a drug deal?
   D. Why do teenagers use drugs?
7. Spike, who comes from a heavy-drug urban area, says that most of the kids he knows do not do drugs, even though they are mostly poor and face a grim future. So, in his view, that disproves what the author is saying. Do you agree with Spike's analysis or do you think he is confused?

8. According to the author, drug prohibitions
   A. make drug sales highly profitable for dealers.
   B. enhance the appeal of drugs.
   C. create judicial bottlenecks.
   D. A and B.
   E. A, B, and C.
9. Which of the following patterns most closely corresponds with the author's reasoning in paragraphs 3 and 4?

   A. If A, then B.   B. If A, then B.
      Not A.   Not B.
      ——————   ——————
      Therefore, not B.   Therefore, not A.

   C. If not A, then B.   D. If not A, then B.
      Not A.   Not B.
      ——————   ——————
      Therefore, B.   Therefore, A.

10. Is the author's reasoning in the preceding argument valid?
11. Which of the following, if any, would weaken the preceding argument?
    A. In Washington there is a comprehensive national strategy in place that includes use of armed forces and diplomatic initiatives to fight the drug war.
    B. The Columbian government has re-established its control over the Medellin cartel, a major drug supplier to the United States.
    C. Six-thousand police officers are in classrooms across the nation daily teaching millions of kids the DARE (Drug Abuse Resistance Education) curriculum.
    D. A and B.
    E. B and C.
    F. A, B, and C.
12. Identify four effects of decriminalization, according to the author.
13. After reading paragraph 5, Lance says: "Sure decriminalization would take the profit out of 'illegal drugs,' because there wouldn't be any *illegal* drugs any more—they'd be legal. But the profit would still be there, the same as it is with alcohol and tobacco." What do you think of Lance's point?
14. Paragraph 6 suggests that the author views jobs, education, housing, and health care as _____ conditions for solving the drug problem.
    A. necessary
    B. sufficient
    C. contributory
15. Which of the following does paragraph 6 imply?
    A. Without jobs, there is no hope.
    B. With education, there is hope.
    C. There is no hope unless there is health care.
    D. A and B.
    E. A and C.
    F. A, B, and C.

16. Which of the following would be a relevant counterpoint to paragraphs 7–8?
    A. Will legalization prevent the development of more potent drugs?
    B. Will legalization break the cycle of dependence and abandonment?
    C. Will legalization lower the number of crack babies?
    D. A and B.
    E. A, B, and C.
17. Explain the possible inconsistency between paragraphs 5 and 10.
18. In paragraph 11, the author offers
    A. an argument based on authority.
    B. an argument from analogy.
    C. a causal argument.
    D. a causal explanation.
19. We can infer from paragraphs 10 and 11 that the author
    A. does not consider an increase in the number of drug users significant.
    B. believes it is immoral to prohibit individuals from using mind-altering substances.
    C. believes it is not immoral to prohibit teenagers from using mind-altering substances.
    D. A and B.
    E. A, B, and C.
20. Paragraph 12 represents
    A. an appeal to authority.
    B. an analogy.
    C. an appeal to tradition.
    D. A and B.
    E. A, B, and C.
21. The innuendo of paragraphs 11–12 is that Grinspoon
    A. is an authority on drugs.
    B. favors decriminalization.
    C. believes that alcohol will inevitably injure some people.
    D. A and B.
    E. A, B, and C.
22. Are paragraphs 9 and 10 fully consistent with paragraph 13?
23. Does the essay give any basis for speculating about the author's likely position on suicide? prostitution? voluntary euthanasia? pornography?

From: **Legitimizing Enslavement Will Not Reduce Its Harm**[7]

Midge Decter

Despite their growing numbers, advocates of decriminalization remain in the minority, opposed by a variety of figures across the political spectrum. One of

---

[7]Midge Decter, "Legitimizing Enslavement Will Not Reduce Its Harm," *Los Angeles Times,* March 12, 1990. Reprinted by permission of the author.

these is Midge Decter, who has written widely on American mores. **Read her essay carefully, outline it, then answer the questions that follow it.**

1 There is something truly seductive in the argument for legalizing drugs. Just when we, as a society, are feeling ever more helpless in the face of the drug problem, we are being told that it can be "solved," so to speak, by definition. Decriminalize the use of drugs, runs the argument, and not only do you wipe out a whole class of criminal users, you also, with one stroke, knock the bottom out of the vast and evil international industry that so profitably battens *[sic]* on them. Like all would-be engineers of human conduct, the drug legalizers sorely tempt us with their images of some clean and manageable fix (pun very much intended).

2 Only one problem upsets the neatness of this kind of thinking. The trouble with drugs is not that they are illegal but that they destroy people. First, of course, they destroy their habitual users morally, physically and socially. Next, they inflict great harm on the users' loved ones, especially the children, and most especially the children of using mothers, the mental and physical brutality of whose lot in life we have only just begun to fathom. And they destroy neighborhoods, communities — who knows, perhaps whole cities may soon go down.

3 The reason for the galloping chaos of drugs, it need hardly be pointed out, is that the people who use them will not — or as they tend to insist, cannot — stop. Drugs, after all, begin as a source of totally effortless and absolute euphoria. Of nothing else on earth, not even (to name some other popularly acknowledged addictions): alcohol or gambling or sex, can this be said. Once such euphoria has been tasted, it clearly cannot, without a great deal of moral strength — indeed, precisely the brand of moral strength whose absence leads to addiction in the first place — be put out of mind.

4 From where, then, would drug users gather the energy and discipline to undergo the suffering of renunciation if the surrounding community refused to support them by imposing its standards upon them?

5 In the 1960s, let us remember, hordes of children of the enlightened middle class were left to molder in a hallucinogenic purgatory, some never to return, because the community in which they were being reared refused to penalize, or even just voice disapproval of, them. No one speaks well of drugs any more; but for the ghetto and barrio youngsters whose lives are daily sacrificed to the Moloch of feel-good, something not all that different from approval is offered them by the social welfare intellectuals — apology for their behavior on grounds of poverty, unemployment, etc.

6 Thus the people who, for instance, like to make fun of the "Just Say No" campaign do not understand the importance, especially when it comes to resisting the siren call of instant ecstasy, of being socially and culturally affirmed in one's efforts.

7 By the same token, people who say that the outlawing of drugs should be repealed — because it has failed to solve the problem and has, on the contrary, only created more crime — do not really understand the role of the law. Many laws, to be sure, are merely instrumental; like traffic laws,

they expedite and smooth daily commerce. But laws are also the means by which a society both declares and teaches its moral assumptions, its understanding of the way people are supposed to live and arrange their affairs. Laws are enacted, therefore, not only to define and punish guilt but also to confirm the virtue of law-abiding.

8 What would happen if drugs were to be legalized? Perhaps dealers would have to confine themselves to gambling, prostitution, and selling protection. Just perhaps — and perhaps from the point of view of the law-enforcers — that would be an improvement.

9 As far as the addicts are concerned, however, particularly the young ones, the legitimization of their enslavement would hardly serve to lessen it. Moreover, along with suffering the consequences — in some, possibly many, cases unto death — of a murderous out-of-control pursuit of nirvana, these kids would be receiving society's ultimate message of indifference to their fate. As it is, their lives and the lives of their unfathered and unmothered children are already forfeit to the idea that they are not responsible for themselves. Remove all sanctions against their addiction, and you might as well be inviting them to put bullets through their brains.

10 Then there are all those other kids, the ones who don't do drugs, who are afraid to, or think it's wrong to. What message will they get? That being strong is no better than being weak, being good no better than being bad? They are neglected enough in all our social theories these days, the children who behave themselves and do what their society asks them to do. We would deliver another blow to their self-evaluation, such as the legalization of drug use, at our peril.

1. Why is the word *solved* in quotation marks (paragraph 1)?
2. In paragraph 1, the author accuses decriminalizers of
   A. introducing a red herring.
   B. raising a straw argument.
   C. oversimplifying the issue.
   D. making a false analogy.
3. In paragraph 2, the author makes a number of causal connections, each of which is
   A. sufficient.
   B. necessary.
   C. contributory.
4. The author believes that the basic cause of drug addiction is
   A. poverty.
   B. deficient moral character.
   C. poor education.
   D. A and B.
   E. A and C.
5. Paragraph 3 implies
   A. any euphoric drug experience is enough to cause addiction.

    B. drugs offer a unique escape from reality.

    C. anyone who would experiment with drugs lacks moral strength.

    D. A and B.

    E. A, B, and C.

6. Paragraph 4 implies that

    A. the author believes society should not support drug users.

    B. drug addicts need social censure.

    C. there is no hope for drug addicts.

    D. social censure is not enough to cure drug addicts.

7. Explain the analogy in paragraph 5.

8. Paragraph 5 is most vulnerable to the charge of which causal fallacy?

    A. *Post hoc*

    B. Slippery slope

    C. Oversimplification

    D. Neglect of common cause

9. Bernie takes exception to paragraph 5: "I happen to think that drug use takes root in poverty, illiteracy, and despair. But I'm not *defending* drug use or users. I'm simply trying to account for the problem, not *apologize* for it. The author misses this distinction entirely. She muddles things by confusing an explanation with an apology or defense." Do you agree the author is confusing the issue?

10. Bernie's friend, Toy, doesn't much care for the sentiments expressed in paragraph 6. "I think the 'Just Say No' campaign oversimplifies the drug problem, and is a lame excuse for a workable drug policy. That's why I ridicule it, not because I don't recognize the importance of social support of individual effort. In fact, the author has it backwards—it's the 'Just Say No' people who don't understand the importance of social support. If they did they'd be offering something besides slogans." Do you think Toy's comments have any merit?

11. Hilda thinks she sees an irrelevant point in paragraph 7: "I agree with the author that in general laws don't only define and punish, but express a society's highest ideals. But that doesn't mean every individual law is so noble, or that the people proposing them are virtuous. Plenty of laws insult our nation's highest ideals—presumably that's why they're found unconstitutional. More to the point, the moral *purpose* of a law is completely irrelevant. All sorts of laws have been passed and will continue to be passed by people convinced that they are right on one matter or another. The issue isn't whether these offer prescriptions for living—clearly, that's what all laws are intended to do. The question is whether those prescriptions accord with constitutional rights. So, 'moral assumptions' that drug laws teach is totally irrelevant. Are such laws constitutional or not—that's the issue. And the author misses it." Do you agree with this criticism?

12. Paragraphs 9 and 10

    A. appeal to fear.

    B. present a slippery slope.

    C. beg the question.

    D. A and B.

    E. A, B, and C.

13. Identify the rhetorical question in paragraph 10.

14. Is the rhetorical question used fairly?
15. Paragraph 10 seems to present an argument that might be reconstructed as follows:

> If society decriminalizes drugs, it is neither approving nor disapproving of their use.
> If it neither approves nor disapproves of drug use, it says to young people: "Avoiding drugs is not necessarily better than using them."
>
> Therefore, if society decriminalizes drugs, it is saying to young people: "Avoiding drugs is not necessarily better than using them."

Since we do not want to send this message to youth, we should not decriminalize drugs. Is the argument valid? **Is the argument acceptable? Explain.**

Indicate where possible whether the authors of the preceding essays are in basic agreement on the following points (16–26). If they disagree, indicate the nature of the disagreement: verbal, factual, interpretive, evaluative.

16. Drugs kill.
17. Drugs are profitable for those who sell them.
18. Drug laws serve a worthwhile purpose.
19. Minors should not have access to drugs.
20. Laws express social disapproval.
21. Adults should be permitted to use drugs if they want.
22. Drugs are probably a good thing for some people.
23. Drug laws work.
24. Drug users are weak-willed.
25. Improving social conditions won't have much of an impact on the drug problem.
26. A young person is likely to think that a society is indifferent to what it does not outlaw.

RELATED THEME TOPICS

1. *Write an essay in which you argue for or against decriminalizing drugs.*
2. Some people who ardently support drug education in public schools just as ardently oppose sex education programs. They believe that sex education belongs in the home and that teaching it in the classroom will have the effect of encouraging kids to experiment. *Write an essay in which you: (1) argue that it is logically inconsistent to want drug education but not sex education in public schools; (2) argue that it is logically consistent to want drug education but not sex education in public schools; or (3) argue that neither drug nor sex education has a place in public school curriculums.*
3. Imagine that you are a member of a committee that has been formed to deal with a serious drug problem at school. *Write an essay in which you show the beneficial*

effects of adopting three *policies or programs dealing with drugs. Your proposal will be submitted to the school board for its approval and action.*

4. "Before the 1970s, most of the drug users in black communities were musicians and a small group of street-corner junkies. Among whites, drug abuse was largely confined to Skid Row dropouts and a handful of wealthy entertainers. Vietnam and Watergate changed that — lawbreaking and the arrogance of power by business and government officials bred deep cynicism in American society. To escape the feeling of a growing sense of discontent, millions of Americans turned to drugs as an attractive means of escape and fulfillment. The drug crisis, then, is a product of the profound social, economic, and spiritual void in present-day America, and more police, prisons, tougher laws, or even legalization will not solve the problem." *Write an essay critiquing this argument.*

Suggested Answers to Starred Exercises

CHAPTER 1

EXERCISES ON ARGUMENTS

1. A. Statement
   B. Explanation
   C. Argument:

   <u>Not voting is un-American.</u>

   Therefore, we should vote.

   D. Argument
   E. Argument
   F. Non-argument: a group of propositions related only by their subject matter of trees growing in the United States

EXERCISES ON LOCATING THE MAIN IDEA

1. A. _____P_____ and _____P_____ . So, _____C_____ .
   B. _____C_____ , because _____P_____ and _____P_____ .

C. Inasmuch as _____P_____ , _____C_____ , for _____P_____ .

D. Since _____TC_____ , as _____P_____ , _____C_____ ; for _____P_____ .

E. _____TC_____ , for the reasons that _____P_____ and _____P_____ . Thus, because _____P_____ , _____C_____ .

2. A. Capital punishment should be legalized because capital punishment deters crime.

   B. Since pornography doesn't contribute to sex crimes, pornography shouldn't be restricted.

   C. A college education affects one's earning potential, for research shows that college graduates make more money in a lifetime than do noncollege graduates.

   D. No diet I've ever tried has worked. So, this diet won't help me lose weight.

   E. People who use condoms run less risk of getting AIDS than people who don't because sexually promiscuous people have a greater chance of getting AIDS than do people who aren't sexually promiscuous and AIDS is a sexually transmitted disease.

   F. Laws prohibiting suicide are indefensible because it's no business of the government if a person wants to commit suicide; whether or not people choose to inflict harm on themselves is strictly their own affair.

   G. (The statements are properly ordered.)

   H. Since the rights accorded persons vary from society to society and even within a society over a period of time, as social anthropologists report, it follows that there are no natural rights.

   I. Whatever progress blacks, and women for that matter, have made in attaining rights equal to those of white males, they can thank the Supreme Court for because without its resolute backing there would have been no civil-rights revolution as we know it because Congressional leadership in the assault on racial discrimination (would have been) highly improbable because, when the movement began in the early 1950s, the South had a lock on the U.S. Senate.

EXERCISES ON PRECISELY DEFINING THE MAIN IDEA

1. A. "Some" — quantifier
   B. "might be" — qualifier
   C. "considerable" — intensifier
   D. "perhaps" — qualifier
   E. "A lot" — quantifier
   F. "must" — intensifier

2. Strong version: Many Americans are highly materialistic.
   Stronger: *Most* Americans are highly materialistic.

3. "could," "may"

4. "some," "a lot of"

5. "possibly," "maybe"

6. "The United States has to reduce its trade imbalance"; "It's imperative that the United States reduce its trade balance."

7. Stronger: "*Most* U.S. citizens don't vote."
   Weaker: "*Some* U.S. citizens don't vote."
8. (Conclusion is in bold print; premise that also functions as a transitional conclusion is in italics.)
   A. Main argument:

   Capital punishment should be abolished *because it does not deter crime.*
   Subargument:
   It does not deter crime. This was recently demonstrated by an exhaustive university study.

   B. Main argument:

   Capital punishment should be legalized *because it does deter crime.*
   Whatever deters crime should be legal.
   Subargument:
   It does deter crime, as many would-be murderers have themselves said.

   C. Main argument:

   The longer elected officials hold office, the more likely it is that they will become corrupt. **Therefore, there should be a limit to the number of years any elected official may serve.**
   Subargument:
   The longer elected officials hold office, the more likely it is that they will become corrupt. The reason is that power corrupts, and over time office holders become more and more powerful.

   D. Main argument:

   Smoking can kill. *But it's also expensive and offensive.* **So, the prudent person shouldn't smoke.**
   Subargument:
   But it's also expensive and offensive. Statistics show that nonsmokers increasingly object to the smoker's violation of their right to breathe smoke-free air.

   E. Main argument:

   And so they will make mistakes. Since mistakes are unintentional, **it's clear that human fallibility often mocks our best-laid plans.**
   Subargument:
   Humans are fallible, *so they will make mistakes.*

   F. Main argument:

   Societies are necessary. But societies cannot survive without compromise and cooperation. **Hence, each of us must strive to see things from the other fellow's viewpoint.**
   Subargument:
   None of us left to ourselves can attain all we desire. *That's why societies are necessary.*

   G. Main argument:

   The United States is a republic. The only way to preserve and enrich democratic freedoms in a republic is for the people to be educated enough to select representatives wisely. **There's no question, therefore, that Americans ought to take education most seriously.**

Subargument:

> In a democracy, the people exercise government in person. But in a republic, they express their will through representatives. *Clearly then, the United States is a republic.*

EXERCISES ON VALID AND INVALID ARGUMENTS

1. A. Valid. Under certain circumstances, the right to life *can* be and is revoked, as when a state administers capital punishment. So, the statement "The right to life is irrevocable" isn't true. It is, therefore, unsound.

   B. Invalid. There's no way of knowing for certain that "philanthropists" refers to the same group of people in each premise; therefore, we have no firm grounds for concluding that some politicians are businesspeople.

   C. This argument can be translated:

   > **No musicians use drugs.**
   > **All poor and uneducated persons are drug users.**
   > ———
   > **Therefore, no musician is poor and uneducated.**

   The premises do provide conclusive support for the conclusion. Therefore, the argument is **valid.** But since the premises are false, the argument is **unsound.**

   D. The argument may be rewritten:

   > **If Sally were qualified, she should have passed the test.**
   > **But she didn't pass the test.**
   > ———
   > **Therefore, Sally can't be qualified.**

   If the premises are true, this argument is **sound.** If one is untrue, the argument is unsound, but it would still be **valid** because the premises make the conclusion absolutely certain, logically speaking.

   E. This argument may be written:

   > **Either the battery or the ignition is faulty.**
   > **The ignition works.**
   > ———
   > **Therefore, the battery must be faulty.**

   The premises provide absolutely conclusive support for the conclusion. So the argument is valid. But if it has not been determined previously that the problem lies with the battery or the ignition, then the argument is unsound because other factors could account for the car not starting. If every other conceivable factor has been eliminated, then the "either . . . or" statement would be true, and the argument would be sound.

   F. If we accept that the streets become wet only from rain, then, yes, it must have rained because the streets are wet. The premises, then, do provide conclusive grounds for accepting the conclusion; the argument is valid. But, of course, streets become wet in other ways, for example, by being hosed down. So, the argument is not sound.

   G. This argument is invalid because the premises cite a condition (threatening society) in the presence of which pornography should be strictly controlled, but it doesn't say anything about when pornography should *not* be strictly controlled. Therefore, it doesn't offer conclusive support for the conclusion. It's possible that although pornography doesn't threaten society, it should be *strictly* controlled for some other reason. So, even if the premises are accepted, they don't logically entail the conclusion.

H. This one is tricky because every statement is true and because it "sounds logical." But the argument is **not valid**. Even if some fruits are green and some fruits are apples, it does not *necessarily* follow that some fruits are green apples. The reason is the same as in argument D: We aren't certain that the same fruits are referred to in each premise. This logical problem can be illustrated through an analogy:

Some fruits are sweet.
Some fruits are lemons.
_____
Therefore, some fruits are sweet lemons.

2. A. C
   B. B
   C. C
   D. A
   E. B
   F. C
   G. C
   H. B
   I. B
3. Answers will vary.

SUMMARY-TEST QUESTIONS FOR CHAPTER 1

1. False. Sequence is irrelevant.
2. A. Propositions don't have to be true; arguments can have *false* propositions.
3. A true or false statement
   Claim (or statement)
4. All except D
5. D
6. No, an explanation
7. A. False
   B. True
   C. False
   D. True
   E. False
   F. No. For example, in "All humans are mortals, *therefore,* since John is a human, **he's mortal,**" the conclusion (bold) is separated from the signal "therefore" by a premise statement.
   G. True

H. False. Premises are, because they are what the arguer is *assuming* to be true. Conclusions are statements whose truth someone is attempting to establish.

I. True

J. False. Often they're the most significant part of the argument because, being unexpressed, they hide errors.

8. "Hence" is a conclusion signal; the others indicate premises when used in arguments.

9. True for both

10. D

11. Yes. For example:

> **All clocks are trees.**
> **All cars are clocks.**
> _____
> **All cars are trees.**

A relatively strong argument can also have false premises. For example:

> **Just about every American is bilingual.**
> _____
> **Therefore, being an American, Fresca's probably bilingual.**

12. "Logically justified" refers to inductive probability; the others refer to deductive certainty.

13. No. The premises don't foreclose the possibility that Jane is a female who is not a mother.

14. whose premises provide *some,* but not conclusive support, for the conclusion.

15.
A. 10	F. 7
B. 9	G. 4
C. 5	H. 8
D. 3	I. 1
E. 6	J. 2

16. From context. Ask: "What is the arguer attempting to demonstrate, prove, or convince me of?" (Conclusion signal words are helpful.)

17. 4. 3 is a transitional or intermediary conclusion.

18. Subargument. Statements 1 and 2 lead to the mini- or transitional conclusion, statement 3.

19. A democracy can only work if the people are informed; otherwise, there can't be an intelligent expression of the popular will. That's why a political campaign should be issue oriented. TV coverage, however, focuses on what's visually appealing and dramatic. A case in point: the 1988 presidential elections. Recall Dukakis riding atop an army tank and Bush nuzzling babies and flanked by police officers. **TV isn't an effective medium for conducting a political campaign.**

20. D. A is irrelevant. B is stronger ("inevitably") than the qualified conclusion demands ("we can expect"). C is too weak ("some") to provide sufficient support for the high probability implied in the conclusion. E is irrelevant—the issue is whether the critical thinking skills will produce better readers and writers.

21. A. True

B. True

C. False

D. True

E. True
F. False. An acceptable argument has these features, but a justified argument can have unacceptable premises.
G. True

23. A. C. Compare:

> **All oranges are fruits.**
> **Some fruits are bananas.**
> ———————
> **Therefore, some oranges are bananas.**

B. C. The premises are only strong enough to support a *probable* forecast about the marriage.
C. A. Do females usually make better elementary teachers than do males? There certainly have been more female than male elementary teachers. But does that mean they're better? Not necessarily.
D. C. Maybe the creature is a dog.
E. B. That people support capital punishment has nothing whatever to do with whether or not capital punishment deters crime. On the other hand, the deterrent effect of capital punishment could bear directly on whether or not a person supports capital punishment. But that would be a different argument.

24. Answers will vary.

CHAPTER 2

EXERCISES ON IDENTIFYING THESIS PROPOSITIONS

1. A. "Threats to the environment are threats to national security."
   B. "The educational system takes over where cultural myths, Freudian folklore, and the media leave off in depressing a girl's aspirations and motivations."
   C. "Detailed examinations of micro-thin sections of bone from nestling and juvenile dinosaurs, modern birds and crocodiles, reveal a remarkable similarity between bird and dinosaur bone."

EXERCISES ON UNEXPRESSED THESIS PROPOSITIONS

1. A. 4
   B. 3
   C. 3
   D. 4
2. A. Topic: education
      Attitude: in favor of
      Thesis proposition: A good education is necessary and desirable.
   B. Topic: undercover police
      Attitude: opposed to

Thesis proposition: Undercover police undermine the basic function of the police.
  C. Topic: advertising
     Attitude: convinced of its persuasive effect
     Thesis proposition: Advertising must work.
  D. Topic: Fairness Doctrine
     Attitude: in favor of
     Thesis proposition: The Fairness Doctrine ensures that the public interest is served.
  E. Topic: censorship of teenage music
     Attitude: opposed to
     Thesis proposition: Teenage music shouldn't be censored.

EXERCISES ON IDENTIFYING MAIN POINTS

1. A. Examples; cause and effect situations
   B. Cause and effect situations; facts
   C. Examples
   D. Cause and effect situations
   E. Comparison/contrast
   F. Sequence of events
   G. Cause and effect situation; facts
   H. Comparison/contrast
   I. Facts; examples
   J. Comparison/contrast; facts; examples
   K. Comparison/contrast
   L. Examples; facts
2. A. Thesis: Ethical decision-making in an organization doesn't occur in a vacuum.
      Main points (premises): rest of paragraph
   B. Thesis: Swanscombe man represents a distinct advance over his fossil predecessors, although the extent of the advance has been debated.
      Main points (premises): rest of paragraph
   C. Thesis: Even when the historical tide is low, a particular group of doers may emerge in exploits that inspire awe.
      Main points (premises): example of the Vikings
   D. Thesis: Bright children and nonbright or less bright are very different kinds of people.
      Main points (premises): (1) The bright child is curious; the dull child is less so. (2) The bright child likes to experiment; the dull child is afraid to try.
   E. Thesis: Many more inmates should be paroled.
      Main points (premises): Prison experience unquestionably boosts the chances that an offender will break the law again. (The rest of the paragraph is backing for this main point.)

F. Thesis: Our system of justice is not as civilized as we think it is.
Main points (premises):   (1) Due process plays no role in the vast majority of cases. Not too long ago alcoholic beverages were outlawed. (2) Most states austerely limit sexual conduct. (The rest of the paragraph could be considered backing for this claim.)

SUMMARY-TEST QUESTIONS FOR CHAPTER 2

1. False. A main point is a premise. The other three items are synonymous, as used in this text.
2. A
3. topic, author's attitude toward it.
4. A thesis proposition is a statement of the thesis. It's not always stated in the essay. It can be determined by making use of the details, including the verbal expressions, the writer provides.
5. B, D, and E are sufficiently debatable to make good thesis propositions. A and C are facts.
6. B. The other terms refer to the premises.
7. Comparison
8. Introduction (necessary background, statement of issue or problem, approach to issue or problem, thesis proposition); body (main points and other details in support of the thesis, possibly a refutation of opposing viewpoints); conclusion (summary or restatement of thesis).
9. Only E is necessarily true.
10. The first two assertions are true. The third is false — in fact, a mix of deductive and inductive development is typical of an extended argument.
11. The Declaration of Independence
12. *Thesis Proposition*
    I. Main point
        A. Support + (unexpressed support)
        B. Support
13. No, only when it's not obvious or is questionable.
14. A. The first warrant is definitely worth expressing because it's a controversial assumption. In other words, the arguer will have to make a case for its acceptability. The second isn't worth expressing because if the study is known to be unreliable you can so indicate when assessing the main point.
    B. Definitely worth expressing. The sweep of the generalization makes it highly questionable.
    C. This warrant is worth expressing because it cuts to what may be a questionable use of authority ("leading university"). So what if the study was conducted at a "leading university." That doesn't, of itself, make the results reliable.
    D. This warrant is worth expressing because it involves a debatable value judgment.

E. Definitely worth expressing because it isn't true and therefore is unacceptable as a premise.

CRITICAL THINKING APPLICATIONS

1. E. Notice that the exercise, in effect, calls for identifying the thesis, which is unexpressed.
2. D
3. D
4. E. The author offers no evidence for A or B. Since he's speaking only of his own office, C and D are unacceptable.
5. C. Notice how C picks up on the notion of "rights."
6. B. Discount is called for.
7. D
8. C. The key issue — expressed in the opening sentence — is the smoker's claim to a veritable, absolute right to smoke. By clarifying what a "right" is, the writer refutes the smoker's claim. The "evils of smoking" cited (B) supports the main idea that the right to smoke is a limited right.
9. C, which is supported by A. B, D, and E are support for the argument's second main point or premise, which is "people can be injured in ways other than the obvious ones just cited."
10. C. The definition of a "right" is the argument's linchpin. It's the warrant that permits the arguer to move from data to conclusion.
11. C
12. E
13. C
14. D
15. B

From: **Freedom Inside the Organization**

1. Thesis proposition: It is becoming increasingly obvious that Americans, old and young alike, object to the no-privacy-is-good policy tradition.
2. Kind of statement: factual
3. Main point: "Many national legislators are disturbed by reports that there are nearly 900 federal data banks containing more than 1.25 billion records with personnel information about individuals."

    The next two sentences of this paragraph also can be considered main points. (The last sentence seems to support the claim that various groups have been studying ways to control the situation.) "Universities and schools face a similar change in attitudes." (The rest of the paragraph supports this statement.) "In the business sector the wind has been blowing in the same direction." (The rest of the paragraph supports this statement.)
4. Facts, authority, and examples
5. Except for summary

6. The author moves from facts and details to judge the national mood on privacy. (That the conclusion or thesis is stated early is irrelevant.)
7. Suggested outline:

THESIS: It is becoming increasingly obvious that Americans, old and young alike, object to the no-privacy-is-good policy tradition.

I.   Many national legislators are disturbed . . . about individuals.
II.   The U.S. Senate . . . among federal agencies.
III.   Various groups of experts have been studying ways to control this situation.
   A. The Pentagon . . . alcoholics.
IV.   Universities and schools face a similar change in attitudes.
   A. Congress, in 1974, enacted a law giving students the right to inspect their records.
   B. In the same year, a pregnant school teacher's right to privacy was upheld.
V.   In the business sector, the wind has been blowing in the same direction.
   A. Reacting to employees' complaints about alleged invasions of their privacy, unions have been protesting more vigorously. (The rest of the paragraph seems to provide some useful background.)

Alternatively, I, II, and III might be considered backing (A, B, and C) for an implied main point (premise) to the effect: "The federal government is taking a hard look at the privacy issue."

From: **"The Best Insurance against Problem Workers"**

1. THESIS: The best way to ensure honest, reliable workers is by subjecting them to a pre-employment personality test. (Both value statement and policy statement)
2. Paragraph 1 contains necessary background, statement of the problem, and the thesis proposition — all part of the introduction. Paragraphs 2–5, the body, offer main points and raise some common concerns and objections. The last paragraph restates the thesis.
3. The author moves from facts and details to a general conclusion based on them.
4. Suggested outline:

THESIS: The best way to ensure honest, reliable employees is by subjecting them to a pre-employment personality test.

I.   Pre-employment personality tests are legal.
   A. The EEOC guidelines permit them.
   B. Section 703(h) of Title VII of the Civil Rights Act of 1964 permits them.
II.   They are valid and reliable.
   A. In one test, dishonesty, violence, and drug-use scales correlated highly with actual admitted behavior involving these workplace problems.

   B. In another test, scores from attitude scales reliably correlated with college students' admitted weekly alcohol consumption, semi-annual intoxication rates, and the number of alcohol-related problems they had on the job.
   C. In another test, the violence scales of a personality test accurately predicted the amount of on-the-job damage and waste and correlated with the number of arguments with and assaults on managers, co-workers, and customers the employees were involved in.
 III. They're cost-effective.
   A. A good psychological test will pay for itself in no time by reducing the 2–5% of gross sales lost annually to internal theft.

5. D

(B) In one, dishonesty, violence, and drug-use scales correlated highly with actual admitted behavior involving these problems.

(B) In another, scores from attitude scales reliably correlated with college students' admitted weekly alcohol consumption rates . . . on the job.

(B) In still another, the evidence scales of a personality test accurately predicted . . . employees were involved in.

⟶

(C) Such tests are valid.

CHAPTER 3

EXERCISES ON THE FUNCTIONS OF LANGUAGE

1. A. Informative
   B. Informative
   C. Directive
   D. Informative
   E. Informative
   F. Informative
   G. Directive
   H. Probably ceremonial
   I. Expressive
   J. Performative
   K. Informative, directive
   L. Informative
2. Answers will vary.

EXERCISES ON CATEGORIES OF ARGUMENT LANGUAGE

1. Premise indicators: *for one thing, in the second, for*
2. Qualifier: *some*
   Discount: *but*
   Premise indicators: *as, since*
   Intensifier: *well* demonstrates
   Conclusion indicator: *therefore*
3. Conclusion indicator: *it can be concluded*
   Premise indicators: *inasmuch as, beyond this*
   Intensifier: *must* (could be considered an intensifier)
   The examples given are evidence.
4. Premise indicators: *for, and, furthermore*
   Qualifier: *if* the energy is available
   Aside: *incidentally*
   Conclusion indicator: *hence*
   I'm inclined to view the examples as support because of the word "for."
5. Premise indicators: *also, further, and* that themselves . . .
   Qualifer: *may*
   Conclusion indicator: *thus*
6. Intensifer: *quite*
   Discount: *but* (which interestingly precedes the *conclusion*)
   Premise indicator: *and* (in last sentence)
7. Discounts: *but* (in all sentences)
   Premise indicator: *and* (in last and next to last sentences)
8. Premise indicator: *because*
   Conclusion indicator: *thus*
9. Discount: *and yet*
   Intensifier: *on the contrary*
   Conclusion indicator: *hence*
10. Intensifier: *indeed*
    Discounts: *but, yet*
    Premise indicator: *since*
    Conclusion indicator: *therefore*
11. Premise indicators: *for, and*
    Conclusion indicator: *wherefore*
12. Discount: *but*
    Intensifier: *surely*
    Conclusion indicator: *then*

SUMMARY-TEST QUESTIONS FOR CHAPTER 3

1. Argument is expressed in language. The language used to express an argument provides clues about the argument's structure.

2. A. Informative
   B. Ceremonial
   C. Informative
   D. Ceremonial
   E. Informative
3. False. It may function informatively too.
4. A lecture may be primarily informative, but also expressive of the speaker's contagious enthusiasm.
5. A, B, D (including mixed functions)
6. "For" is a premise indicator; the others indicate conclusions.
7. They are intensifiers.
8. False
9. A. P, C, B
   B. C, P, B
   C. P, P, B, C
   D. C, P, P, B
   E. P, B, B, P, P, C
10. C simply connects two events in time, or it possibly may be explanatory.
11. C
12. B (*yet* discounts the length)
13. Asides
14. C
15. The use of transitional words and phrases, repetition of a key word, pronoun reference, and the clear movement of ideas.

CRITICAL THINKING APPLICATIONS

1. D
2. E
3. A. False. The item speaks only of *Japanese* males.
   B. False. Maybe their countrymen are drinking other kinds of alcohol.
   C. False
   D. True, assuming they're drinking alcohol.
   E. False. We aren't certain that the beer is *causing* the cancer.
   F. False
   G. False
   H. Probably, because it implies a cause-and-effect connection between daily beer drinking and colon cancer, but this is only a statistical correlation. Such misleading headlines are typical of statistical news items.
4. E. This is an ingenious ad that merely touts the active ingredient. In fact, there is nothing in the ad that precludes that pediatricians *never* prescribe *Jelly Belly.*
5. B. The "at least" quantifier for both the number of employees and expenses means that a revision upward cannot contradict these entries, which cannot be

said of the other entries owing to their more restrictive quantifiers (for example, "only," "no more than," "not quite").

6. Answers to first question will vary. Then:
   A. "But" discounts the preceding sentence. "Probably" qualifies. "Especially" intensifies. "Even if" qualifies. "May" qualifies. "Sit-ups . . . these muscles" repeats a key word. "But unless" discounts and qualifies. "But" discounts. "Especially" intensifies. "(We recommend . . . program.)" qualifies.
   B. Answers will vary.
   C. Answers will vary.
   D. Version 2. It is more detailed, pinpoints the audience, refutes an alternative exercise, and allays audience concern about their capacity to do the exercise. It accomplishes all this succinctly by making effective use of verbal expressions.
   E. Answers will vary.

7. *Group 1*
   A. False
   B. False. He says the reader *may* be so inclined.
   C. False
   D. False. He says it *may* lead them.
   E. True
   Group 2
   A. "For" is a premise indicator
   B. The first sentence
   C. 3

8. A. 1, 2, 3
   B. 2, 5
   C. A–2, B–2
   D. In paragraph 2, Orwell attempts to show that we can do something to improve the state of the English language, which, therefore, refutes paragraph 1.
   E. "most," "generally," "rather," "if one is willing to take the necessary trouble," "if one gets rid of . . . think more clearly."
   F. It merely clarifies Orwell's point.
   G. D

9. A. Argumentative
   B. "Directed" emotions may make a difference in our health.
   C. Essential, because it provides some support for his thesis
   D. "Still in progress," "number," "may be," "limited basis," "may make"
   E. From paragraph 3:1
      From paragraph 4:1
   F. Inductively
   G. Paragraph 1 is the introduction. Paragraph 2 is the body. Paragraph 3 is the conclusion. Paragraphs 4 and 5 can be viewed as a mix of thesis reemphasis and, in the case of paragraph 4, a refutation.
   H. 1. In fact, he says that there *may* be a connection. This criticism is itself an oversimplification of Cousins' article.
      2. This criticism is well worth heeding. In Cousins' defense, his "conclusion" is so qualified (read: "watered down") that, *as stated,* it borders on the trivial, although its implications are intriguing.

3. Not true. Cousins, to his credit, anticipates this objection in paragraph 4.
4. An excellent criticism, which, by the way, can be generalized from newspaper headlines. A more accurate title might have been: "Can Hope Make You Well?" or "Emotions May Affect Health," but these aren't as "sexy" — they're not as seductive as the "Hope Can Make You Well."

THE LOGICAL STRUCTURE OF THE ARGUMENTS

From: **"Humans Learn Violence"**

1. Suggested outline:

THESIS: Humans' propensity for violence is culturally conditioned, not innate.

I.   Humans aren't by nature killers.
A.   Soul-searching and protests generated by recent tragedies show this.
B.   So do the countless humans who find it difficult to kill another person or to exhibit aggressive behavior.
C.   So does the fact that it takes a great deal of conditioning to prepare a nation for war.
II.   The manifestations of all genetic potentialities are shaped by past experiences and present circumstances.
A.   There's no genetic coding that inevitably results in aggressiveness, only a set of genetic attributes for self-defense that can become expressed as aggressiveness under particular sets of circumstances.
III.   The instinct for self-preservation can generate violent behavior in a species.
A.   The behavior of rabbits and mice shows this.
IV.   Social forces can make humans behave as killers.
A.   Comparative observations of animals living in zoos suggest this.

2. (D) In abolishing private property, we have not altered the differences in power and influence which are misused by aggressiveness.   → (C) The psychological premises on which communism is based are an untenable illusion.
(D) Nor have we altered the nature of aggressiveness.
(D) Aggressiveness was not created by property.
(B) It existed in primitive times when property was scanty.
(B) It exists in the nursery before property has given up its primal form.

(D) If personal rights over
material weath are abolished,
aggressiveness will assert
itself in sexual relationships.

(D) If sexual freedom is permitted,
aggressiveness will manifest
itself in ways yet unknown.

3. Yes
4. Yes, when he attempts to refute the psychological basis of communism.

CHAPTER 4

EXERCISES ON DEFINITION

1. Lexical
2. Lexical
3. The first is persuasive. The second is lexical. The third is denotative.
4. "Life . . . negotiations" is persuasive; "and I take 'negotiation' . . . agreement" is stipulative.
5. Stipulative
6. Theoretical
7. Theoretical
8. Persuasive
9. Stipulative
10. Persuasive
11. Persuasive
12. "All well-meaning people . . . elections" and "A truly big man' . . . choice" are persuasive.

SUMMARY-TEST QUESTIONS FOR CHAPTER 4

1. Logical
2. "Automobile," "flavor," and "brick" are probably neutral; "apple pie" is probably positive; "rat," "I.R.S.," "mortgage," "permissive," and "bureaucrat" are probably negative; "feminist" may be positive or negative.
3. Answers will vary. (Sample: "Politician" often is negative, whereas "statesperson" is positive, although both could be used to refer to the same person.)
4. A
5. C
6. C is stipulative; the others are persuasive.
7. D
8. A and C are stipulative; B and D are persuasive.
9. Lexical
10. Theoretical

11. E
12. A. True
    B. False. Freudian psychology, for example, contains many theoretical definitions; so do the various branches of philosophy. (Indeed, definitions of "philosophy" often are theoretical.")
    C. False. Words often are *used* ambiguously.
13. No. The context could make the intended meaning of "house" clear.
14. Yes. Their extensional meanings are not clear.
15. Ambiguous; "construction" could refer to the *building* under construction or the *act* of construction.
16. Verbal; "same" needs to be clarified.
17. Possibly both—you could disagree, for example, on the statistics (a factual dispute); or you could disagree on what constitutes "headed by a female" or even "American households."
18. Evaluative
19. Interpretive
20. Theoretical

From: **"On Liberty"**

1. Stipulative
2. The distinction, probably of necessity, is vague.
3. Vague
4. A drug addict might think that "shooting up" is in his best interests.
5. Does the state have a right to limit a woman's choice to have an abortion? or a terminally ill patient's desire to be allowed to die, or even to be assisted to die? In the economic realm, taxes—income, sales, excise, and so forth—pit the interests of the state against an individual's economic and even *moral* freedom because tax revenue might be spent to implement policies that the taxpayer finds immoral.
6. Finding the common element

THE ORGANIZATION AND DEVELOPMENT OF THE ARGUMENTS

From: **"The Opinion"**

1. Suggested outline:

    THESIS: A person may not be prosecuted for burning the U.S. flag as a peaceful protest.

    I.   The First Amendment forbids the abridgement of "speech," which can take the form of flag burning.
         A. Many decisions have recognized the communicative nature of conduct relating to flags.

II. There's no convincing evidence that flag burning disrupts the peace (which was one of the reasons for Johnson's conviction).

III. The government may not prohibit the expression of an idea simply because society finds the idea itself offensive or disagreeable — not even when the flag is involved. (This can be viewed as tantamount to saying: "The government may not criminalize flag burning to preserve the flag as a symbol of national unity," which was the second reason given for Johnson's conviction.)

    A. The case of *Street* v. *New York* makes the point.

IV. The government may not compel respect for the flag.

V. Permitting the government to designate symbols to be used to communicate only a limited set of messages invites serious violations of the First Amendment.

    A. It could be used to justify prohibitions against the burning of state flags and copies of presidential seals.

VI. There's no reason to think that the flag was ever intended to be excepted from the First Amendment.

    A. The framers of the Constitution didn't especially revere the Union Jack.

    B. The First Amendment makes no exceptions of concepts we hold sacred, such as the principle of discrimination.

CHAPTER 5

EXERCISES ON SEMANTIC AMBIGUITY AND ABUSE OF VAGUENESS

No inferences should be drawn because:
1. "Typical liberal" is vague.
2. "Average American" is vague.
3. "Traditional values" is vague (so is "great").
4. "Heck of a deal" is vague.
5. "Progress" is vague.
6. "Kill her" is ambiguous, intentionally so, presumably.
7. The entire passage is riddled with obscurity.
8. "East of the sun, west of the moon," "succulent," "sizzling" are vague.
9. "Value of your holdings" is ambiguous.

Speaking of . . . Jargon and Euphemism

1. C	10. L	19. R
2. F	11. G	20. E
3. I	12. M	21. A
4. N	13. D	22. Z
5. O	14. P	23. X
6. T	15. Q	24. W
7. U	16. S	25. AA
8. J	17. B	26. Y
9. K	18. H	27. V

Speaking of . . . Labels

What applies to labels can also apply to names. Compare your additional answers with those of other class members.

EXERCISES ON BEGGING THE QUESTION

1. "Wrong" means "immoral"; so the premise is a restatement of the conclusion.
2. That taking drugs is wrong is even more suspect than the conclusion it supposedly supports (pot smoking is wrong).
3. Obviously, nations wouldn't have dispatched their troops had they not considered the Mideast of vital interest. But why is it? That's what the arguer needs to explain in order to defend the intervention.
4. That rich people make so much money doesn't account for their superiority to poor people. It simply is another way of saying they are rich people. This argument is like saying, "Rich people are superior to poor people because they are rich people."
5. This argument asks us to accept (1) the existence of God and (2) that God has a purpose for everything. But when we're puzzled by tragedies, it helps us precious little to rationalize and understand these misfortunes by appeal to assumptions even more mysterious.
6. The circular reasoning should be obvious.
7. The circular reasoning should be obvious.
8. Saddam's premises that opposition is traitorous and that traitors should be executed are even more suspect than his conclusion that these soldiers deserved to die.
9. If not liking his wife talking with other men isn't jealousy, then what exactly is it? This is the sort of person who would say: "It's not that I'm a speeder. I just don't like to drive within the speed limit."
10. Here the premise ("for . . . sentiments") is a more generalized version of the conclusion.

Speaking of . . . Question-Begging Definition

I agree with Dr. Gagland that Dr. Friedman is attempting to defend the earlier studies by means of a question-begging definition. Let's imagine the following exchange between Friedman and Gagland:

Friedman: Type-B personalities never have a heart attack before age 60.

Gagland: But Mr. Smith, a 55-year-old type-B personality, just suffered a heart attack.

Friedman: Mr. Smith could not have been a type-B personality because a *true* type-B personality cannot have a heart attack before age 60.

SUMMARY-TEST QUESTIONS FOR CHAPTER 5

1. False
2. Fact: 50,000 illegal aliens are inhabiting empty buildings along Telegraph Avenue.
   Sentence 2 makes use of the rodent-like metaphor: "holed up" and "warrens." It's difficult to say exactly what impression this would make on a reader. On the one hand, it might imply that these people in some way pose a threat to society. On the other hand, it might elicit a sympathetic reaction owing to the subhuman conditions under which these people have to live. Whatever its impact, the sentence certainly is communicating more than the simple fact expressed in the first version.
3. C
4. They obscure and confuse.
5. A label can lead us to overlook relevant and important aspects of a thing.
6. "freeloaders," "malingerers," "cheats," "crooks," and on and on
7. E
8. D
9. A. D (It's an unloaded question.)
   B. B
   C. C (The question assumes there is a "best way.")
   D. A
10. D
11. Begging the question
12. Yes, because the premise—that the Pentagon best knows the nation's military needs—is more suspect than the conclusion.
13. This question is a complex question if it has not been demonstrated that support should be given to Eastern European nations. Like any other complex question, this one, then, would be *begging* the audience to concede a dubious assumption.
14. Question-begging definition
15. Each begs the audience to accept a dubious assumption or at least one that has not been accepted but that needs to be demonstrated.
16. distinction without a difference
17. Begging the question. The premise is merely a generalized version of the conclusion.
18. Begging the question. The premise restates the conclusion.
19. Begging the question. The premise is more suspect than the conclusion.
20. A rhetorical inconsistency is the use of contradictory terms or phrases in an argument.

CRITICAL THINKING APPLICATIONS

1. D. The others in one way or another are evasive. For example, A uses euphemism ("misspoken") and vagueness ("poetic license," "a detail or two") to downplay the charge. B seems to beg the questions, and C seems to slant through emotive

language. As for E, it begs the audience to accept the dubious proposition that a candidate leading in the polls would never distort or mislead. In contrast, D responds directly to the charge in clear, unambiguous language.

2. C
3. Rousseau seems to provide a subtle case of inconsistency. After all, if we assume that social institutions are established by humans, then we can rightly ask: "How could such naturally sympathetic creatures erect exploitative institutions?"
4. The student's response is a complex question because it assumed that Zen writings lacked clarity. The professor makes this assumption explicit by suggesting that the student isn't perceptive or discerning enough to understand the writings. Thus, C.
5. D
6. A. The author's conclusion is, in effect, that no generalization is ever absolutely true. But that means that the generalization itself—"no generalization is ever absolutely true"—is not absolutely true. The argument isn't circular (B) because it doesn't seek to establish the conclusion by assuming it. There's nothing ambiguous or vague about the argument (C). The argument can't be valid (D) because the premises don't provide conclusive support for the conclusion. It's true that the argument could be considered inductive (E), but it can't be "strong" owing to the internal inconsistency.
7. D. "Freedom" presumably refers to more than merely economic freedom. In fact, when Americans boast of "freedoms," they typically mean those expressed or implied in the U.S. Constitution, such as the freedoms of speech and religion. "Freer" in the conclusion refers to *economic* freedoms.
8. A. Each of these statements is consistent with the ad.
   B. "More powerful" is ambiguous because in this context it could mean that OMNIPOTENT is the most powerful, or more likely one of several equally powerful pain-relievers. The name itself—OMNIPOTENT—is an assumption-loaded label.
9. D
10. Reduce the size of the snack food.
11. A. "No Catholic can responsibly take a 'pro-choice' stand."
    B. "Aggressive" is vague.
    C. Bernardin (in par. 4) assumes a key assumption—"There is no choice to take a human life"—that needs to be established in order to support the conclusion that "it is not correct to speak of pro-choice." Paragraph 11 assumes another key assumption—the unborn constitutes "human life" (in the same way, for example, that a newly born baby does)—that needs to be verified in order to establish the conclusion that abortion is immoral and that the public should demand its prohibition.
    D. The comparisons with the Nazi holocaust and Nazi physicians are highly inflammatory.
    E. Sullivan rightly senses that the polarizing, inflammatory rhetoric can easily mischaracterize a "pro-choice" position as a "pro-abortion" one. It also encourages a reflexive response to any pro-choice advocate, namely, that the person is advocating murder, regardless of what the person's reasons may be.

F. If there can never be a *moral* choice to abort (par. 4), then what is there to "debate"? What is there to "really hear the issues, the struggles and the anguish of women who face issues in a way that we never will" (par. 12)? The Cardinal's ingenious plea (par. 12) is rather like the old saw out of the wild and wooly West: "Let's give her a trial before we hang her."

G. Both "pro-life" and "pro-choice" call up powerful feelings toward two key rights: the right to life and the right to free choice.

H. Evaluative

12. Philo is saying that the cataloguing of endless evils in the world will not shake the belief of the person who assumes the existence of an all-good, all-powerful God. The reason is that the person will systematically chalk up any such evidence to the incapacity of the human intellect to comprehend how the appearance of evil is compatible with an all-good, all-powerful God. Thus, no matter the kind or amount of evils you might point to, the "true-believer" would remain unmoved because her definition of God as all-good and all-powerful rules out any counterevidence.

13. A. Main Points Pro
    1. It's in the interests of the United States.
    2. The United States supported the Contra revolution.
    3. Chamorra promised U.S. aid if elected.
    4. No aid will invite a resurgence of Communism.
    5. The United States has special obligations owing to its part in Contra blunders and cruelties.

    B. Main Points Con
    1. The United States needs to lower its profile in Latin America.
    2. The United States is not the financial savior of every politically akin nation.
    3. Left alone, Nicaragua will become a vital and self-sufficient economy (which it will not if United States subsidized).

    C. Basically an evaluative dispute

    D. Agree: 1, 2, 3, 4, 8
       Disagree: 5, 6, 7

    E. Some emotive language: "freedom fighters," "Communist-sponsored, oppressive Sandinista rule," "Stalinist dictatorship," "Soviet puppet," "freedom-loving governments"

       Persuasive definition: "only serious aid can truly atone . . . central player."

       Begging the question: "The United States should financially support all these revolutions, including Nicaragua's, because it's in our interests to."

       Some abuse of vagueness: "owe something," "massive financial aid," "vital and self-sufficient"

       Rhetorical question: "Isn't it time the United States gave up its addiction to domination of the countries south of the Rio Grande?"

       False dilemma: The con position seems to exploit the false dilemma that U.S. aid must be either massive or nonexistent.

       Rhetorical inconsistency: The con side says that the United States can be rightly proud of helping overthrow Ortega. But then, it condemns U.S. interventionism in Latin America. The argument would have more rhetorical and logical force if, at the outset, the arguer had condemned the U.S. role in Nicaragua and then went on to suggest that we should not compound our unjustifiable interventionism by remaining financially enmeshed in Nicaragua's affairs. As is, the opening paragraph provides the pro-side with ammunition. Thus: "If we acted 'righteously' in overthrowing Ortega, then perhaps there will be other opportunities for such righteous interventionism in Latin America."

From: **"Deserved Retribution"**

Suggested outline:

THESIS: Capital punishment is justified on grounds of retribution.

I.   Retribution is different from revenge.
   A. Revenge is private; retribution is a legally imposed social institution.
II. Retribution serves to limit and regulate revenge.
III. Retribution provides the feeling of justice that's necessary for you to have social support.
IV. Christianity traditionally has supported social retribution in the form of capital punishment.
   A. *Romans,* chapters 12–13
V.   The Romans supported capital punishment on retributionist grounds.
VI. Retribution in the form of capital punishment underscores the value of life. $+$ (Whatever underscores the value of life in cases of murder should be permitted.)
   A. Imprisonment blurs the distinction between murder and lesser crimes.

  1. D
  2. A
  3. Probably stipulative
  4. Genuine
  5. A clearer, more precise distinction would help.
  6. C
  7. Possibility. However, given the author's position, he'd probably accept a permissibility interpretation as well.
  8. Lowell seems to have a point. But the author thinks that the distinction between, say, personal and social or legalized revenge (that is, retribution) is significant. The author isn't at all shy about embracing revenge, so long as it's institutionalized.
  9. Some example probably would help to show exactly how and who is compensated and repaired by capital punishment.
  10. C. (Notice that he says that "perhaps" revenge isn't as good as forgiveness and that revenge *can be,* not *always is,* psychologically healthy. So B and C are overstatements.)

11. A

12. It doesn't necessarily contradict his earlier attempt to distinguish between retribution and revenge. In fact, the earlier paragraphs seem to show—perhaps unintentionally—how difficult it is to define retribution.

13. B

14. The last sentence probably is intended to be the premise.

15. It's rather vague.

16. "Supported" and "protected" at "taxpayers' expense" slants through bias language. (Compare an alternative version of this sentence that ended with "to him." And substitute "not do to" for "promise." Do you think the resulting sentence would have the same emotional punch?)

17. Fact. Some churchmen deny it and so on.
    Judgment. These churchmen are trendy.

18. C. If we don't approve of something new, we devalue it by calling it "trendy" or "fashionable." If we approve, we might call it "progressive," "innovative," or "enlightened."

19. Ronna seems to have misinterpreted the author. He, in fact, doesn't believe that the *Biblical* teaching proscribes revenge. Quite the contrary, he finds Biblical support for the institutionalization of it. Ronna apparently doesn't. They're probably engaged in an interpretive dispute, which, of course, is quite common in Biblical matters.

20. Again, Milt's observation underscores the inherent interpretive problems in Biblical analysis. In a sense, he's correct—the quoted passages, technically speaking, don't directly address capital punishment, but rather *who will exact punishment.* But the author apparently finds in the language implicit approval of the harshest penalty that can be imposed on a human outside divine judgment, death.

21. D, as the previous two answers imply. Whether one considers some churchmen "trendy" (C) is a trivial and, ultimately, irrelevant matter.

22. I think she makes a relevant distinction in reminding us that societies and institutions so evolve and change that historical comparisons typically provide a weak basis for a proposition.

23. A. The author says that capital punishment deters crime. B and C raise questions about fairness, the equal application of capital punishment. However, the author never says that capital punishment is administered fairly or more fairly than any other alternative.

24. "Entitle" implies a right, but a right is not something that the possessor has that he is obligated to act on. (For example, simply because you have a right to vote doesn't mean you must vote.) Thus, when the author says that wrongdoing doesn't "entitle" someone to rehabilitation, he means the wrong-doer has no right or claim to rehabilitation. When he then says that murder "entitles" the murderer to execution, presumably he means the murderer has a right to be executed. If the murderer does have this right, then, by the same token, he does not have to exercise this "right," an option the author presumably would oppose and, in so doing, would deny the murderer the right to be executed. At the least, the author needs to explain how capital

punishment is a right or entitlement that a murderer has. Absent that explanation, the author seems to be using the word in two different senses: "entitles" in the sense of "has a right to" and "entitles" in the sense of "deserves to be" (as in, "The murderer is entitled to, that is, deserves to be, executed").

25. No. At best, it suggests that rehabilitation *is* not society's aim, but that doesn't mean it *should* not be.
26. Inconsistent
27. Why would a life sentence without the possibility of parole necessarily cheapen life? Or, on the other hand, might not maiming or doing a frontal lobotomy on a murderer better demonstrate the sacredness of life than capital punishment? Paragraph 12 does appear to pose a false dilemma.
28. C. The author seems to be saying: "You took his life. Therefore, you don't deserve to live." D is not as good a choice because the suggested punishment isn't as severe as C. It allows the car thief to continue to drive, just not to *own* a car.

CHAPTER 6

EXERCISES ON EQUIVOCATION

1. The "rights" are not identical. The hunter has a *legal* right to hunt on the lands; the animal lovers have no *legal* right to interfere. The animal lovers probably believe they have a *moral* right to interfere, but that's another issue. They do not have "as much right as the hunters to do what they please on public lands" if that means interfering with the hunters' legal right. (Of course, this defense is also a palpable distortion because no one, hunters included, have a right to do what they please on public lands.)
2. "Expiring" in this case means that the Fairness Doctrine was about to exceed its term of enforcement. To remain in force, it needed to be "renewed," as it were. "Expire," of course, can also mean to die. It's this sense of the word that the writer shifts to in evaluating Congress' action.
3. The first use of "politics" refers to the art or science of political government; the second refers to partisan or factional intrigue within a given group, as in "party politics."
4. Roughly the same distinction between "political issues" and "politics"
5. Shultz seems to have shifted Reagan's intended meaning of "citizen-hostage" to citizen in general or in the abstract.
6. Moving news via satellites for ultimate publication is not the same use of airwaves as broadcasting directly into a receiver, a television or radio. Presumably, the FCC's "Fairness Doctrine" referred to the means for broadcasting radio and television transmissions to the public. It did not refer to the means for expediting the transmission of information to an editorial desk. In the first sense, there's a finite number of "airwaves"; in the second, there is not.
7. Yes

EXERCISES ON COMPOSITION AND DIVISION

1. Composition
2. Division. As a team, the Steelers may be the best, but that doesn't necessarily mean that it has the best individual players.
3. Division. The nation as a whole overwhelmingly may approve Bush's action, but that doesn't necessarily mean that every community does.
4. Composition. That individuals have minds doesn't mean that the "general public" has a mind. There is, of course, something called "public opinion," but this is no more or less than the expression and quantification of personal opinions in something like a poll or survey. And perhaps that's all this passage is intended to mean. If so, fine. The ghostlike "American public mind" and the "general public mind" don't add anything. In fact, they tend to confuse by attributing to society a characteristic of its members: minds.
5. Division
6. Composition
7. Composition
8. Composition. Even if some individuals profit on misfortune and misery, that doesn't mean that society as a whole would exhibit "unparalleled prosperity" if misfortune and misery were pervasive.

SUMMARY-TEST QUESTIONS FOR CHAPTER 6

1. Equivocation. Example: Logic is the study of argument. But there's too much argument in the world. So, the world would be better off if people didn't study logic.
2. In semantical ambiguity, it's not clear which of several meanings a term is intended to carry. In equivocation, the meaning of a word has actually shifted in the argument. In amphiboly, the sentence structure suggests multiple interpretations.
3. True
4. Example: Racing down the street, the tree fell in my path. Revised to clarify: As I was racing . . .
5. A. Smith's about to be fired.
   B. The current administration is dishonest.
   C. Today's woman is not really liberated, doesn't have a right to abortion, and is misguided about who is sexist.
6. Composition, division
7. A. Accent on "playing"
   B. Hypostatization of "national security"
   C. Accent on "men"
   D. Division. "Diamonds" are considered collectively rather than distributively.
   E. Equivocation on "right"
   F. Division. America as a nation to individual Americans
   G. Composition. Individual atoms to matter, which is composed of individual atoms

H. Division. The family to its members
I. Division. The university as a whole to a department within the university
J. Equivocation on "happens almost every day": occurs versus predictable
K. Composition. Individual businesses to business as a whole
L. Equivocation on the collective and distributive senses of "a person is mugged once a year"

From: "The Dangers of Antipornography Legislation"

THESIS: Pornography should not be censored.

I. No sane person can
    believe it harmful if
    sexual feelings stirred   +
    by the "obscene" lead to
    normal sexual behavior.

    (Sexual feelings
    stirred by the
    "obscene" do lead
    to normal sexual
    behavior.)

    A. The survival of the
       race depends on acting
       on sexual feelings.

II. There are no reliable data that show that reading and viewing pornography lead to seriously harmful sexual conduct.

III. That pornography *might*
     produce sexual misconduct
     isn't persuasive.

     A. Virtually anything
        might stimulate   +
        irregular sexual
        conduct in some people.

        (Virtually anything
        would be subject to
        censorship, which is
        unacceptable.)

IV. Competent research, informed opinion, and common experience indicate that "obscene literature" is not a significant factor in causing sexual deviation from the community standard.

    A. The Alpert report (1920s)
    B. Macaulay and Walker testimonies
    C. New Mexico doesn't
       have a proportionately
       greater incidence of   +
       sexual misconduct even
       though it has no
       obscenity statutes.

       (If pornography did
       lead to sexual mis-
       conduct, then states
       without obscenity laws
       would have a higher rate
       of sexual misconduct than do
       states with such laws.)

V. There's no reliable evidence to infer that obscene books and pictures influence children's behavior adversely.

VI. If pornography does adversely affect children's conduct, then we need to censor lingerie ads or admit that they have created a cultural atmosphere for children in which pornography would have only a trifling effect.

A. An eminent psychiatrist says that ads emphasizing sex appeal and depicting scantily clad women can be more alluring than pictures of naked bodies.

VII. "Classics" could be   ("Classics" shouldn't
censored.   +   be censored.)
A. There's no significant distinction with respect to obscenity between books of "literary distinction" and ones that are "dull and without merit."

VIII. Unless "obscenity" is   (Prior restraint is
narrowly and precisely   +   unconstitutional.)
defined, obscenity laws
allow federal prosecutors
to exercise prior restraint.
A. Fear of punishment
(that is, prosecution) restrains
publication.

IX. Government censorship is alien to democracy.
A. Both Milton and Mill observed how government censorship, once allowed, spreads insidiously.
B. Government censorship was the basis of colonial Virginia Governor Berkeley's "undemocratic doctrine."
C. Plato, no friend of democracy, proposed a class of rulers to control what people heard and read.

1. D
2. All of these phrases are vague. That's why obscenity prohibitions continue to be difficult to enforce.
3. Frank does imply that there's no significant difference between an obscenity test related to the thoughts of "those whose minds are open to . . . immoral influences" and one related to the thoughts of average adult normal men and women as determined by "the average conscience of the time." The key point for him is whether sexual thoughts lead to antisocial conduct.
4. Paragraph 3 discounts paragraph 2.
5. B
6. C
7. (D) No sane person can   (C) It doesn't follow
believe it socially   ———————————→   that that conduct
harmful if sexual   will be antisocial.
desires lead to
normal sexual behavior.
    (B) Without such behavior,
the human race would
soon disappear.
        (W) (Sexual desires do lead to
normal sexual behavior.)

8. Answer A comes closest to weakening the position. However, of itself, it doesn't mean much because people who commit sex crimes may be drawn to pornographic material. Certainly, answer A provides no compelling grounds for

concluding that "reading or seeing those publications probably conduces to seriously harmful sexual conduct."

9. The author extends the principle that whatever could possibly produce sexual misconduct ought to be censored. By drawing out the absurd implications of such a principle, he effectively discredits the principle and with it the claim that pornography should be censored because it might *possibly* produce sexual misconduct.

10. D. The innuendo is probably that "obscene" has not been satisfactorily defined.

11. I'm inclined to disagree with Laura given the entire context of the argument. The author is not foreclosing opposition by appeal to definition, which is how persuasive definition typically is illegitimately used. If, for example, when the author is presented with what appeared to be respectable research that suggested a causal connection between pornography and sex crimes, he replied, "The researchers must be incompetent because no truly competent researcher would draw such a conclusion," then he'd be employing illicitly a persuasive definition. But he's not. In fact, he implies elsewhere that if "reliable data" based on "genuine research" were available, then he'd be amenable to obscenity laws. This is a legitimate demand for good science as opposed to pseudo-science.

12. Enrique, in my view, raises an interesting point. Clearly, communities sometimes limit freedom of expression for reasons other than that the expression will lead to antisocial conduct. If that's so, then, seemingly, either communities shouldn't do that or the fact that pornography does not lead to antisocial conduct should not, of itself, argue against censoring it. In fairness to Frank, however, the claim that pornography leads to antisocial conduct is one raised by censorship proponents. He's merely responding to it.

13. I don't think the author is saying this. He's simply pointing out that, as far as he knows, there's no substantial evidence to support the assumption that "obscene" literature significantly contributes to sexual misconduct. He never infers from this that pornography, therefore, does not contribute to sexual deviancy. Indeed, elsewhere (for example, paragraph 10) he implies he's open to data that substantiate the alleged pornography-misconduct link.

14. B. Their interpretations of the Jahoda report differ.

15. Part of Frank's point is that "dealing with sex" is open to interpretation. If "dealing with sex," in part, means "displaying women in what decidedly are sexually alluring postures," then lingerie ads do "deal with sex." Unless "dealing with sex" can legitimately be defined in other terms, then Frank would say that lingerie ads could qualify as "obscene."

16. I think the dilemma is genuine only if one assumes that such ads don't significantly differ from so-called pornography. However, if that assumption is challenged, then one isn't left on the horns of a dilemma.

17. Yes. He's in effect discounting as insignificant any esthetic criterion that separates the obscene from the nonobscene.

18. Yes. Because not knowing the exact scope and limit of the definition of obscenity, publishers will be reluctant to publish material that might in any way be construed by a federal prosecutor as obscene.

19. Carol makes a most curious point: The First Amendment seems to curb public opinion when expressed in a law that restricts freedom of expression that probably won't lead to undesirable conduct. In that sense, the First Amendment (and Judge Frank) appears to be undemocratic. Anticipating just such a point, Judge Frank wrote elsewhere in his ruling: "The paradox is unreal: The Amendment ensures that public opinion – the 'common conscience of the time' – shall not commit suicide through legislation which chokes off today the free expression of minority views which may become the majority public opinion of tomorrow."
20. B and D
21. B

CHAPTER 7

EXERCISES ON AD HOMINEM APPEALS

1. Two wrongs (*tu quoque* is okay)
2. Well poisoning
3. Probably both abusive (raising suspicions) and common practice
4. Abusive
5. Abusive
6. Abusive
7. Two wrongs (*tu quoque* is okay)
8. Common practice
9. Well poisoning
10. Well poisoning
11. Circumstantial
12. Ad hominem
13. Well poisoning
14. Well poisoning
15. Well poisoning
16. Well poisoning
17. Abusive
18. Abusive
19. Common practice
20. Abusive
21. Abusive
22. Well poisoning on the part of the Pharisees

EXERCISES ON DIVERSION

1. Red herring
2. Straw argument
3. Red herring

4. Straw argument
5. Straw argument. Darwin, in fact, explained the phenomenon that the letter writer raises.
6. Straw argument. The real issue is whether or not the commission's policies are in keeping with their mandate. The straw issue is "an agency usurping power" and "failing in our responsibility to the president and our commitment to America's form of government."
7. Straw argument. Exaggeration
8. Red herring. Whether or not a respectable period of mourning has elapsed has nothing whatever to do with the Lindners' charges.

SUMMARY-TEST QUESTIONS FOR CHAPTER 7

1. C is the best answer because the arguer implies that any proposal sponsored by the wealthiest interest is necessarily at odds with the general welfare.
2. C
3. E. The others are forms of *ad hominem.*
4. A is best.
   B shows contempt.
   C is genetic.
5. E
6. D
7. Answers will vary.
8. D
9. E
10. E
11. D
12. In the circumstantial, an attempt is made to persuade someone of a position on the grounds that rejecting it would be inconsistent with some aspect of his or her life. In the *tu quoque,* the charge is that the accuser is acting in a way that is inconsistent with the very position that he or she is advancing.
13. C. The others were treated as emotional appeals.
14. E
15. False
16. False. Passion that *substitutes for good reason or evidence* should have no place in argument.
17. Playing to our deepest needs and arousing culturally conditioned prejudices
18. No. The dermatologist provided the information that happened to frighten the patient. The dermatologist probably would be relying on fear had she said something like: "Stay out of the sun, or get another doctor."
19. Well poisoning. This argument attempts to foreclose any appraisal of Galileo because of the special circumstance of the appraiser—namely, that the person is still alive!
20. Pity
21. Straw argument through distortion and exaggeration

22. Red herring. What do these countries have to do with aid for Romania and Czechoslovakia?
23. What are some emotional appeals?
24. What are some examples of culturally conditioned prejudices?
25. What's a red herring?
26. What's a form of straw argument?
27. What's another form of straw argument?
28. What are fallacies of irrelevance?
29. What's a good example of mob appeal?
30. What are two other names for the appeal to fear or threat?
31. Where or how did the expression "red herring" originate?
32. What's the fallacy of pity?
33. What is *tu quoque?*

From: **Closed: 99 Ways to Stop Abortion**

Suggested outline:

THESIS: Extreme tactics are justified.

I. We're trying to save lives.	+	(If a tactic is intended to save lives, it's justified.)
II. We're helping to preserve the physical, mental, and spiritual health of women.		
III. Abortionists are doing evil.	+	(Abortion is murder, and murder is evil.)
IV. The pro-life movement is based on altruistic love.		
A. It's trying to save individuals from going to hell.	+	(Saving individuals from going to hell and converting people from evil to good both define an act of altruistic love.)
B. It's trying to convert people from evil to good.		
V. Some abortionists know we're right.		
A. An abortion clinic operator admitted as much.		
B. The Trulsons converted.		

(NOTE: There is, of course, a variety of other unexpressed moral and theological assumptions embedded in the argument: Hell exists; pro-lifers are right, everyone else is wrong; pro-lifers know what's best for others, especially women, and so on.)

1. C
2. C
3. B
4. C

5. E
6. "Pro-life" has positive connotations. It identifies the movement as supporting life as the overarching value and right. "Abortionists" has sleazy connotations dating back to the days when abortions were illegal and, thus, were frequently performed by the unsavory and unqualified. The author probably wishes to reinforce this image in the minds of the audience. Certainly, he doesn't wish to give those who perform abortions the professional status that "physician" and "abortion practitioner" imply.
7. B
8. C
9. A
10. A
11. D
12. B
13. D
14. 5 and 7 come pretty close to judging abortionists as hell-bound, whereas 10 seems to strike a nonjudgmental pose.
15. E
16. C
17. It would be, since intention can and has been used to justify all sorts of morally questionable practices.
18. Probably genetic
19. Probably a straw argument owing to exaggeration
20. E
21. E
22. B. The issue is not whether extreme tactics are well intentioned, but whether they are legal and moral.
23. D
24. Yes. It could be considered a side issue because it might provide some support for a claim like "Women should consider the psychological impact of abortion before having one" or "An abortion can leave a woman feeling guilty and depressed." However, the issue is whether extreme tactics are morally and legally justified; that some women have "unhappy" abortions does not speak to this issue.
25. They are all vague or ambiguous.

CHAPTER 8

EXERCISES ON FORMING AND APPLYING GENERALIZATIONS

1. Applying the inductive generalization "Most chain smokers run a considerable risk of getting lung cancer."
2. Applying the noninductive generalization "Children should be seen, not heard"
3. Forming the inductive generalization "Such drivers are probably a greater driving risk than those over twenty-five."

4. Applying the inductive generalization "As Maine goes, so goes the nation."
5. Forming the inductive generalization "Females probably outnumber males at this college."
6. Applying the noninductive generalization "Only Christians will be saved."
7. Applying the noninductive generalization "There's nothing normal about being a homosexual."
8. Forming the noninductive generalization "You should vote for my crime bill."
9. Applying the inductive generalization "There's a high probability that atmospheric conditions similar to Earth's exist elsewhere in the universe."
10. Forming the inductive generalization "The median price of a house is probably higher here as well."

EXERCISES ON DISJUNCTIVE SYLLOGISMS

Where valid, it's because one of the disjuncts is denied in the premise and the other is affirmed in the conclusion. Where invalid, it's because one of the disjuncts is *not* denied in the premise, thereby precluding a valid basis for denying the other in the conclusion.

1. Valid
2. Invalid
3. Valid
4. Invalid
5. Valid
6. Invalid. Conclusion should be "non-X."
7. Invalid. "X is the case" *affirms* the disjunct "not non-X."
8. Valid. "Non-Y is the case" denies the disjunct "not non-Y." Therefore, we may validly affirm the other disjunct "not non-X."
9. Valid. "Not A" denies the disjunct "A and B."
10. Invalid. Since "A is not the case," then B must be the case. However, if B is the case, then "X or Y" *may* or *may not* be the case. View it as consisting of two arguments:

   A or B.
   A is not the case.
   _____

   (Therefore, B is the case.)

   Either X or Y, or B.
   (B is the case) *affirming a disjunct.*
   _____

   Therefore, X or Y.

11. Valid. Symbolizing the statements, we have:

   Either J and L.
   or
   S or Spvsr.
   Not L (a denial of the first disjunct).
   _____

   Therefore, either S or Spvsr (an affirmation of the other disjunct).

12. Invalid:

> **Mr. Quayle is either slow or clever.**
> **Mr. Quayle is not clever.**
> _____
> **(Therefore, Mr. Quayle is slow.)**
>
> **Mr. Bush is either insecure or brilliant.**
> **Mr. Bush isn't brilliant.**
> _____
> **(Therefore, Mr. Bush is insecure.)**
>
> **Mr. Quayle is slow and Mr. Bush is insecure, or maybe this entire analysis is biased.**
> **There's good reason to suspect that this entire analysis is biased *(affirming a disjunct)*.**
> _____
> **So, we can conclude that Mr. Quayle isn't slow and Mr. Bush isn't insecure.**

EXERCISES ON FILLING IN WARRANTS

1. A. 2
   B. 4
   C. 4
   D. 4
   E. 3
   F. 4
   G. 1
2. A. We should do what purifies our souls.
   B. Any time other nations are out-competing them, U.S. companies need to modernize their management techniques.
   C. Students should study what's fundamental to survival.
   D. We shouldn't consume things that harm us.
   E. Not being convicted of taking bribes establishes a politician's honesty.
   F. A nation without a conscience is a nation without a soul.
   G. Mr. Bronson always accompanies his wife to football games.
   H. Increasing at a greater rate than means of subsistence results in occasional struggles for survival.
   I. Freedom in a philosophical sense requires freedom from both external compulsion and inner necessity.
   J. What we have no experience of we cannot know.

SUMMARY-TEST QUESTIONS FOR CHAPTER 8

1. True
2. D is universal; the others are nonuniversal.

3. B
4. Generalization
5. An inductive generalization
6. A universal general statement
7. True
8. True
9. What's a noninductive generalization?
10. What's a valid argument?
11. What's a test of validity?
12. What's a formal fallacy?
13. What's a syllogism?
14. Fewer specifics are needed to confirm a qualified general statement.
15. A
16. Answers will vary.
17. False
18. Valid, conclusive, invalid, some, conclusive
19. Morality, religion, politics
20. E
21. True
22. True
23. True
24. False
25. False
26. False
27. B
28. True
29. False
30. True
31. True
32. True
33. False. We can't say for sure that no Y is an X.
34. D
35. B
36. False
37. A valid argument is one whose premises, when assumed true, provide conclusive support for the conclusion. This is a valid argument. To be acceptable, a deductive argument must not only be valid but must contain premises that are, in fact, acceptable. If it hasn't been verified that all members of M.A.D.D. are mothers, the argument is not acceptable. If being a mother is a prerequisite for membership, then the argument is acceptable.
38. A. Valid
    B. Valid
    C. Invalid. The first premise asserts that all individuals who'll be admitted are ticket holders (*not* that all ticket holders will be admitted). It doesn't

discount the possibility of a ticket holder *not* being admitted. Therefore, even if Bart is a ticket holder, that's no guarantee that he will be admitted.

   D. Invalid. The second premise does not exclude the possibility that some Supreme Court justices *are* Republicans. Therefore, it's possible that some Republicans *are* elected officials, which proves that the conclusion is in doubt.

   E. Invalid. Nothing in the premises logically rules out the possibility of a woman who was a U.S. president. Another way to view this is to key on the term "U.S. presidents." The conclusion is asserting something of every U.S. president (that is, *no* U.S. president is among those "some" women the arguer has in mind). However, the first premise is talking about only *some* U.S. presidents, not all. Therefore, the conclusion is saying more than the evidence supports; it's speaking universally about U.S. presidents, whereas the premise is speaking nonuniversally about U.S. presidents. (In fact, no valid conclusion can be drawn from these premises.)

39. D
40. E
41. D. A repeats, B overstates ("never"), C and E are irrelevant.
42. D. A is disconnected from the argument because it allows the possibility that Debbie is a thin and muscular nonathlete. B repeats, and C is irrelevant.
43. C. A repeats. B means that anyone in the directory has a license. But what about people who aren't in the directory? They could have licenses. So, B doesn't properly bridge or connect the expressed premise to the conclusion. D and E are irrelevant.
44. "Any time Jack takes his briefcase, he goes to work," or "Only when he goes to work does Jack take his briefcase." A common error is to express the warrant as "Every time Jack goes to work, he takes his briefcase," "Whenever he goes to work, Jack takes his briefcase," or some equivalent statement. Such versions don't provide the *conclusive* connection between stated premise and conclusion because they don't preclude the possibility that Jack sometimes takes his briefcase when he does *not* go to work.
45. "If a defendant produces an alibi, he *may* not be guilty" or a logical equivalent. (Note the word "may," which is necessary to reflect the qualified conclusion "*may* not be guilty.")
46. "Anyone not paying the late fee usually (or 'typically' or 'probably' or 'generally') is detained."
47. "The aggressive aren't meek" or a logical equivalent.
48. "Only disloyalty justifies a dismissal" or a logical equivalent.
49. Valid, denying the consequent of a conditional syllogism
50. Invalid, affirming the antecedent, which is "If it isn't raining. . . ."
51. Valid, denying the consequent
52. Valid, denying the consequent
53. Invalid, affirming the consequent

CRITICAL THINKING APPLICATIONS

Answers will vary.

From: **"Safeguarding the Welfare of Young Women"**

Suggested outline:

THESIS: There should be parental notification laws.

I.	A young woman can't be expected to decide for herself what to do about an unintentional pregnancy.	+	(If a young woman can't decide for herself what to do about an unintentional pregnancy, at least one of her parents must be informed.)

II. Society sends out a mixed message when it inhibits parent–child communication in cases of pregnancy but encourages it in a variety of other instances. + (There's nothing so significantly different between cases of pregnancy and other adolescent concerns that society should blunt parent–child communication in the former but urge it in the latter.)

III. Abortion clinic personnel don't make good counselors for young pregnant women.
  A. They stand to profit from performing abortions. + (Those with a financial interest in an outcome can't or won't give objective counsel.)

IV. Parents almost always have the best interests of their children at heart.

V. The absence of parental notice laws strain intrafamily relations.
  A. Parents inevitably find out about a child's abortion.
  B. When parents do find out, they become estranged from the child.

VI. The burden on social services will be reduced.
  A. Parents will have to assume a greater responsibility for their children.

VII. Many young women need a weapon against peer pressure to have sex. + (Whatever provides many teenagers with an excuse to avoid sex should be made law.)

1. Qualified—"probably"
2. Formulating the generalization
3. In choice 1, the author assumes that the unborn is a child, and in choice 2 that an abortion is murder. Both of the assumptions, of course, are at the heart of the abortion issue.

4. E
5. D
6. E
7. I think Cindy makes a good point.
8. The author does suggest that not requiring parental notice is tantamount to telling young women not to inform their parents. What it would in fact do is to give them a choice, which is not the same thing as discouraging disclosure. It's also important to note, as Joanne implies, that the absence of restriction cannot and should not be automatically construed as an endorsement of the unrestricted activity. Simply because there's no law restricting one from not aiding the fallen pedestrian does not put society on record as inviting callous disregard for the welfare of one another.
9. Yes. The next question cites the confusion and fear as reasons that the author believes the decision can't be free and informed.
10. All informed choice requires calm and mature reflection.
    A young woman carring an unintended baby cannot exercise calm and mature reflection.

    Therefore, a young woman carrying an unintended baby cannot make an informed choice.
11. Valid. However, the argument is unacceptable because the second premise is questionable.
12. Abortion clinic staff are money grubbers.
13. A
14. Noninductive
15. It helps make the author's point about the centrality of the family in such cases.
16. Yes, in paragraphs 7, 8, and 10.
17. Answers will vary, but one problem might be a time delay. Another might be the young person's fear, anxiety, and embarrassment of making her circumstances public.
18. (D) Parents sooner or later find out.

    (B) The case of the young woman who needs surgery owing to post-abortion complications.   ⟶   (C) The absence of parental notice laws strains intra-family relations.

    (D) When they do find out, parents can feel estranged from their children.
19. I'm inclined to view it as evidence for the point that parents sooner or later find out, because the claim doesn't really need any clarification or illustration for that matter. It's perfectly clear, although questionable. Do parents, in fact, almost always find out? The author seems to be offering the example as compelling evidence for the claim that they do inevitably find out. Furthermore, the example sets up the further observation about how parents in these circumstances feel,

which is an important part of the author's argument at this stage. So, I'd say the example is being used to make a point, but that, of itself, it's not enough evidence to conclude that parents always find out.

20. I think Roberto makes a good point. A few well-placed qualifiers would have helped blunt such a criticism (for example, "*often* when parents are left out of a child's important decision. . . ." or "when included in a child's decision, *most* parents. . . .").

21. E

22. Generalization formulated: "Parental notice laws also appear to reduce the number of unintentional pregnancies."
Generalization extended: "All of us think twice before doing something whose consequences we know we'll be held accountable for."

23. E

24. In paragraph 8, the author claims that parents "find out sooner or later." If this is true, then why couldn't a teenage girl resist sexual advances with "the time-honored excuse of parental discovery," even if there were no parental notice laws? Paragraph 11 seems to clash with paragraph 8.

CHAPTER 9

EXERCISES ON HANDLING STATISTICAL EVIDENCE

1. The sample size was okay, but its typicality of the female population is in question. Excluded from the sample were significant subgroups (for example, Roman Catholics and orthodox Jews) whose religious beliefs presumably could influence their sexual behavior. The regionalism also is a problem. Beyond this, since amount of education can influence sexual behavior, a study that purports to generalize about sexual behavior in the human female should, in its sample, accurately reflect the educational level of the population. This one didn't. Also, always lurking in the background of studies of intimately personal behavior is respondent bias. This doesn't imply that the results were inaccurate. It's entirely possible, of course, that a seriously flawed study can yield accurate results. The issue is methodology, not outcome.

2. D. The argument is based on the dubious assumption that financial contributions exclusively or at least mainly determine the population's measure of political interest. But other factors — general political awareness, involvement in political campaigns, contact with one's representatives — are arguably better indicators of people's political interest. They're certainly as relevant as financial contributions. One of these "other factors" could be voting statistics or patterns, which are more relevant than financial contributions, especially when the contributions cited refer to *total*, not *per person* contributions. Answer A does speak of individual contributions and thus might weaken the argument, but not as much as E. B isn't a good answer because it neither explains why, as a whole, political contributions have increased, nor informs us about individual contributions. C is irrelevant because, even if total campaign contributions did reliably reflect

the degree of general political interest, it confuses corporate and individual contributions.

3. The ad assumes that the presence of PAIN-EZ in medicine cabinets proves that it's effective. Not necessarily. What if the neighborhood had recently received free samples? So, the presence of the product in households isn't significant without additional information. Another problem concerns the "typicality" of the neighborhood. Exactly how was it determined to be a "typical American neighborhood" in contrast to an "atypical" one? Finally, we need to look to more objective sources to determine the effectiveness of the product.

4. Misleadingly precise. No one can know precisely how many jobs were lost as a direct result of the trade deficit.

5. At minimum, we need to know more about the sample size and the procedure used.

6. Statistically speaking, the claim doesn't mean much until we find out what is meant by "die of poverty." Does it mean, for example, die of starvation that resulted from being impoverished? Does it refer to the death of a child who lives in a poverty-stricken area and was killed in a random drive-by shooting? Also, what is meant by "poverty," and exactly how is that being determined? For example, most families in the United States that fall below the so-called poverty level would be, by the standards of many other countries, rather well off. Furthermore, raising or lowering the level can dramatically affect the official number of poor households and individuals.

7. Clearly, we need to know how these figures were generated. How large was the sample? Were the agents sampled typical of the agents as a whole? Were the questions answered incorrectly typical of the kinds of questions agents reasonably might be expected to field? When was the study conducted? (For example, more inaccuracies might be expected immediately after an overhaul of the tax code than at some later time when individuals have processed the data and consensual interpretations have formed.) Beyond this, the objectivity of the IRS is in question. The same might be said of whoever conducted the report. This is why it's always important to determine the source of a poll or survey.

8. The letter-writer certainly is at liberty to believe that postal rates are too high. However, that they're objectionable because they've increased faster than the national inflation rate is not of itself a significant argument. What if, for example, prior to 1968 postal rates lagged behind inflation rates? What if they'd been kept artificially low? If that's the case, then it's understandable that in the past twenty years or so they might be outpacing the general inflation rate. Furthermore, what if a lot of the Postal Service's expenses are for things that have increased in recent years? Gasoline, for example. Also, what if it has had to update obsolete technology in order to be more efficient and productive?

EXERCISES ON NEGLECT OF RELEVANT EVIDENCE

1. A, B, C
2. A, B. C could be indirectly relevant if explained.

3. Without the additional facts, Moakley's appeal is persuasive. With them, one wonders what makes El Salvador and Nicaragua so unique as to justify special treatment.
4. The "Briggs instruction" probably would induce a fence straddler to return a death penalty sentence. The additional fact probably would balance the instruction.
5. The original question distorts through innuendo. Many respondents probably interpreted it as meaning *any*, or a commonplace government, restriction could amount to the "taking" of private property. In fact, the Court's ruling pertained to the most rare of cases, those in which the government blocks all use of land (for example, by preventing you from even developing beach front property that you own). Respondents might have been less enthusiastic about the ruling had they been explicitly informed of its most narrow application. Higher court rulings typically have narrow scope, which may subsequently be broadened. This point is worth remembering when public opinion polls are conducted on the heels of a "controversial" court ruling. Likely as not, the question asked of respondents misleads by concealing information about the scope of the ruling.
6. Probably "yes" to both questions.
7. The announcement makes Bradley and the Pentagon appear exquisitely concerned about public health and safety. It also makes Bradley appear extraordinarily effectual ("Wow! He can influence the Pentagon"). Those impressions probably would nosedive to a more realistic level with the additional information.

SUMMARY-TEST QUESTIONS

1. A
2. "Scientific method" is a way of investigation based on collecting, analyzing, and interpreting data in order to determine the most probable explanation. Observation is the heart of this method of inquiry, which is used to formulate generalizations whose probability is so strong that, in practice, they can be treated as if they were certain.
3. True
4. E
5. False
6. Size, typicality
7. D
8. It lacks randomness.
9. To help determine whether it's representative of the populations
10. One spoonful of milk, for example, is enough to indicate whether a gallon is sour.
11. A is loaded. B is a false dilemma (perhaps you believe in a penalty less severe than life in prison). D is vague ("tough"). E would be okay, I think, if it added "under certain circumstances." Then those circumstances could be nailed down. But as formulated, it's inviting multiple interpretations of "convicted drug dealers," from someone growing marijuana in his backyard for sale, to members of the Medellin drug cartel. Thus, there's no way of knowing whom respondents

had in mind when answering. In my view, C is the only unbiased question of the bunch.

12. When respondents answer questions, they're often thinking about how others will perceive them. They're concerned with their "image" and thus answer in a way that will receive approval. However, their answers may not reflect how they truly feel. The person who approaches life from the standpoint of being who he is, without undue concern with how others perceive him, is what Buber calls "essence man." The point is that when asked to reveal ourselves in controversial areas, likely as not we'll disclose more "image" than "essence," thereby introducing respondent bias into the sample.

13. D

14. Objectivity is the quality of viewing ourselves and the world without distortion. Our emotions, unexamined assumptions, or personal prejudice can get in the way of objective observation. Lack of objectivity can distort polls, as, for example, when a pollster "loads" a question to elicit a predetermined response. The same applies to statistics: Unwilling to confront or to allow you to confront all of the statistical data available, I select those that support my view and ignore those that don't. As for authority, if I lack objectivity, then I'm inclined to select, present, and quote from only those experts who support my viewpoint while systematically discounting counter authority.

15. B (How did the rest of the products do?)

16. D

17. Yes

18. False

19. B

20. Neglect of relevant evidence; also, accent

21. Misapplied generalization

22. "Would I be less inclined to accept the conclusion if I knew this additional information?"

23. Disagree

24. B is strictly informative, although not necessarily true. Each of the others expresses or implies what someone considers to be of worth.

25. Less inclined

26. C

27. Is the authority actually an expert in the field?

28. A

29. D

30. Tradition

From: **Withhold Consent**

Suggested outline:

THESIS: "Living wills" should be enhanced by adding provisions appointing a family member to carry out the patient's wishes if the patient can no longer communicate.

I.   Living will statutes (a.k.a. "natural death acts") limit the preparation of binding advance directives.
  A. The directive generally is only operative when the patient is determined to be terminally ill by more than one physician.
  B. In some states, it's legally binding only if the patient reaffirms the directive after the onset of the terminal disease and before the onset of incompetence.
  C. Many of the model directives aren't clear enough about which forms of care may be foregone.
  D. Living wills can't   (Such provisions
      anticipate all the   +   can anticipate
      treatment decisions   these decisions.)
      that may have to be
      made.
II. Several states already have enacted these provisions.
III. Physicians would avoid the treatment uncertainties they currently face.
  A. Family members, as opposed to the traditionally appointed "guardian," better know what the patient would want.
IV. More formal legislative mechanisms probably would rely on the family anyway.
V.   Appointing a family member would avoid the "shortage of precedent" problem, which is one reason judges often find it difficult to resolve treatment controversies.

1. Who conducted the poll? Who participated in it? Exactly what were the participants asked? How extensive was the poll? and so on.
2. D because the author is reporting the *views* of legal and medical authorities, and the general public. "Virtually" because the author identifies an exception. Also, B. (See sentence 3 of paragraph 1.)
3. The author uses experts in the field and popular sentiment.
4. As a professor of law, she could be expected to have considerable familiarity with the issue.
5. B
6. Disagree. The paragraph points up what the author believes are inadequacies in the living will. But there's nothing in the paragraph, expressed or implied, to indicate that patient autonomy in these matters (which the living will is intended to ensure) does not enjoy widespread support.
7. H. According to the author, "many of the model directives . . . fail to make clear which forms of care may be foregone. . . ." Thus, there's no way of knowing for certain whether the patient's pneumonia would (or should) go untreated.
8. A discussion of the limitations of existing statutes (paragraph 3), which prepares the reader for the author's alternative ("therefore")
9. Yes. Delegated authorities would be empowered to make decisions that the patients would if they could.
10. "Without a doubt"
11. Noninductive
12. Paragraph 4 provides some indirect evidence for the first generalization, as does the author's subsequent discussion of the value of delegating a family member.

If this generalization is unacceptable—and I believe it is—then it would provide support for the second generalization.

13. "Likely" and "probably" are used several times. "Although this claim . . . has never been competent" (last sentence) also functions as a qualifier.

14. I disagree with Ellie. In fact, those cases in which a family member was never expressly delegated as the patient's proxy support the author's point. Had the Quinlans and Cruzans been able to demonstrate that they were doing what their daughters would want, the courts would not have prolonged the cases. The author's point is that a formal delegation of authority, in effect, would provide compelling evidence of the patient's wishes.

15. I'm inclined to view it as a noninductive generalization inasmuch as the author considers the establishment of such a precedent a "virtue." In contrast, if the author were merely claiming that there is no legal precedent in such cases, that would be an inductive generalization.

16. The first sentence of the paragraph represents a premise that directly supports this conclusion. Sentences 2 and 3, additional premises, provide indirect support for the conclusion by implying that, since family members typically play a central role in these cases, a reliable presumption of family knowledge already operates. These premises do provide a basis for the conservative conclusion "the family is *likely to be as skillful. . . .*"

17. If the first sentence is taken as a qualified generalization (as it should be), then the last sentence merely specifies an exception and thus would be consistent with it.

18. Evaluative

19. It is significant insofar as, if the reasoning is circular, then one of the author's premises fails to support the conclusion. (The others, of course, could still provide the conclusion with adequate support.)

20. I'd be inclined to side with Phyllis. The basic point is that if judges are provided explicit direction, they can better honor the wishes of the patient. Phil miscasts the argument by claiming that formally delegating a patient's proxy ahead of time is primarily intended to expedite judicial procedure. It isn't. It's intended to ensure that comatose patients will have their wishes carried out. Without a patient–delegate authority, judges must employ other means—sometimes painfully slow ones—to ascertain the patient's wishes.

21. Yes, in paragraphs 8, 9, and 11.

22. Problems involving the imprecision of the term "family" aren't resolved, probably because they can't be (paragraph 8). Also, we're likely left wondering what would constitute a "good reason" for an administrative override of a family decision (paragraph 10).

23. The author deserves praise for raising problems that are embedded in her proposal. I think she helps her cause by perhaps getting readers to think more in terms of refining her proposal than rejecting it. For example, delegating a specific family member might sharpen the meaning of "family," although admittedly it wouldn't preclude "bad faith" decisions. In any event, anticipating objections implies that, in the final analysis, an author finds the common counter-arguments unconvincing, which in turn burdens the opposition to prove otherwise.

CHAPTER 10

EXERCISES ON FAULTY COMPARISONS

1. A. Pain relievers for arthritis

Bufferin		*Anacin, Bayer, Tylenol*
_____	amount of pain relief	_____
_____	stomach protection	_____
_____	anti-inflammatories and anti-swelling ingredients	_____

    Are identical dosages being compared? Are other over-the-counter products available that are better? Is the comparison being drawn with the arthritis or nonarthritis versions of the other products? Is the cost comparable?

   B. Textbook profiles of girls and boys

Girls		*Boys*
_____	achievement	_____
_____	emotions	_____
_____	activities	_____
_____	life involvement	_____

EXERCISES ON ANALOGY PROBLEMS

1. D. A canary is yellow, and a polar bear is white.
2. C. You wear a hat, and you drink milk.
3. A. A donkey is the symbol of the Democratic Party, and an elephant is the symbol of the Republican Party.
4. A. A racket is used in racketball and badminton and in tennis and lacrosse.
5. C. Yen is the currency of Japan, and the ruble is the currency of Russia.
6. D. "Terrestrial" refers to earth, and "celestial" refers to heaven.
7. D. Air pressure is measured by a barometer, and mileage is measured by an odometer.
8. D. Anesthesia prevents you from feeling, and blindness prevents you from seeing.
9. C. Hail is frozen rain, and ice is frozen water.
10. D. Nature refers to heredity, and nurture refers to environment.
11. A. A cowardly person is called "yellow," and a gloomy person is called "blue."
12. B. A biography is written in the 3rd person, and an autobiography is written in the 1st person.
13. A. A lobbyist attempts to influence a legislator, and a lawyer attempts to influence a jury.
14. D. "Actual" means "in fact," and "virtual" means "in effect."

15. A. A megaphone is shaped like a cone, and a tornado is shaped like a funnel.
16. D. Black is the absence of color, and a vacuum is the absence of air.
17. B. Emeralds are found in mines, and oysters are found in shells.
18. D. "Part" is "trap" spelled backward, and "tar" is "rat" spelled backward.
19. A. *Hamlet* was written by Shakespeare, and $E = mc^2$ was formulated by Einstein.
20. B. Palm Springs and New York are cities.

EXERCISES ON ARGUMENTS FROM ANALOGY

1. A. **Children have to be trained and taught how to behave.**
   So do puppies.
   Puppies also need to be swatted occasionally.
   ———
   Therefore, children need to be spanked occasionally.
   Additional resemblance: Both children and puppies function on a reward/punishment level.

   B. **Both children and sick people need attention.**
   Women are well equipped to meet children's needs.
   ———
   Therefore, women probably are well-equipped to meet the needs of sick people.
   Additional resemblance: both children and sick people require time and patience.

   C. **Library books and textbooks contain information, help satisfy curiosity, and enrich people's lives.**
   But there's no charge for withdrawing books from libraries.
   ———
   Therefore, textbooks should be free.
   A dissimilarity: Textbooks are always required reading, but library books are not.

   D. **Earth and Venus have roughly the same diameter and the same mass.**
   But life exists on Earth.
   ———
   Therefore, life probably exists on Venus.
   Additional similarity: Both Earth and Venus are planets in the same solar system.

EXERCISES ON RESPONDING TO ANALOGIES

1. A. Disanalogy: Clearly, human learning mechanisms are far more complicated than the canine's. When infants soil their diapers, should they be "house-broken" the same way puppies are?

   B. Disanalogies: The sick and infirm have social needs owing to their illnesses and infirmities that children don't have.

C. Disanalogy: The public has already purchased library books.
Untrue generalization: Textbooks should always be treated the way library books are. Since we're not permitted to write in library books, we shouldn't be permitted to write in textbooks either.
D. Disanalogy: Venus is closer to the sun.

SUMMARY-TEST QUESTIONS FOR CHAPTER 10

1. A
2. Isolating two categories of the same subject and isolating common features of the two categories.
3. E
4. E
5. D
6. True
7. E
8. D
9. E
10. In an argument from analogy, the known similarities between two things are intended to provide some support that the two things are similar in some additional way. Example: "I'll probably like Woody Allen's latest movie because I liked the previous two." A nonargumentative use of analogy typically intends to clarify or illustrate. Example: The human brain resembles a computer.
11. True
12. **X has characteristics a, b, c.**
    Y has characteristics a, b, c.
    But X also has characteristic d.
    ——————
    Therefore, Y has characteristic d.
13. R-1: Extending the analogy
    R-2: Irrelevant response
    R-3: True, but precisely how is it different?
    R-4: A disanalogy
    R-5: Irrelevant response
    R-6: Identifying an untrue generalization
14. A
15. D
16. F
17. G
18. B
19. E
20. C
21. The moral and the biological are obviously quite different. Even if prostitution, adultery, and homosexuality somehow threatened the existence of the state, the threat is not the same as the one posed by gangrene to the body. The threat posed

to the body by gangrene is clear and demonstrable. Not so with prostitution, adultery, and homosexuality.
22. B, E, H, and I are arguments from analogy.

CRITICAL THINKING APPLICATIONS

1. Poker and business differ in many ways. In poker, only the participants are ordinarily affected by outcome. However, business decisions can affect parties far removed from the decisions. In poker, the participants know the rules or can find out easily enough. In business, the rules of condut can be vague to the point of one party "playing the game" perhaps by the golden rule, while another pursues self-interest. Poker is a game, business is an economic practice and, viewed in a social context, a social institution which intersects with other institutions and individuals to comprise a social system.
2. Compared: A law and graduate school with public grade and high school.
   Assumed resemblances: Qualities that are incapable of being objectively measured—ability to study, engage in discussions, exchange views, learn a profession.
   Inferred resemblance: Children in grade and high schools should not be racially segregated.
   A strong analogy
3. Answers will vary.
4. Answers will vary.
5. Answers will vary.

From: **Lifeboat Ethics: The Case Against Helping the Poor**

Suggested outline:

THESIS: The survival of rich nations depends on their ignoring poor ones.

I.   The earth is not like a spaceship.
   A. It lacks unitary control.
      1. It has no captain or executive committee.
      2. The U.N. is ineffectual.
   B. Survival on earth requires the acceptance of responsibilities, not merely the exercise of rights and utilization of common resources.
II.   Each rich nation is like a well stocked lifeboat which the people of poor nations are trying to get into.
III.   If the people inside the life boats of the wealthy nations admit those poor outside trying to get in, the rich nations' lifeboats will capsize, and all will perish.
   A. The poor population is increasing much faster than the rich population.
IV.   The sharing ethics (which is opposed to the ethics of a lifeboat) is fundamentally flawed.

A. It leads to the "tragedy of the commons" that is mutual ruin resulting from overloading.

1. B
2. The author notes how metaphor has been used to consider the problem of the survival of the species.
3. "Cowboy economics" implies an unplanned, undisciplined, and unlimited use of resources." "Spaceship Earth," in contrast, implies natural limits and ecological sensitivity.
4. He finds the spaceship metaphor preferable to the cowboy comparison, but "suicidal" for promoting rights without responsibilities.
5. B
6. B
7. "toothless tiger"
8. E
9. D
10. B
11. E
12. Score one for Jose.
13. Having framed the ethical question in terms of the lifeboat metaphor, the author then sets up three possible solutions to the problem of admitting those trying to get aboard the well-stocked lifeboat. He then refutes solutions 1 and 2 and endorses solution 3. The rest of the essay functions as a defense of his choice.
14. Karen's extension is a good way to press the analogy because it coaxes from it other ethical issues, such as fairness and justice. (Are we in the well-stocked lifeboat because we earned a place in it, or do we find outselves so fortuitously located as an accident of birth? Are these "outsiders" morally accountable for being adrift, or is their plight the result of nothing that they themselves personally did?)
15. D
16. **If the needy person outside the lifeboat felt guilty, he would not climb aboard.**

    He will climb aboard.

    ─────────

    Therefore, he doesn't feel guilty.
    Valid, but I don't think the argument is sound or acceptable because it seems to be based on the illicit use of a persuasive definition. Thus, "If the needy person outside the lifeboat *truly* felt guilty. . . ." By this account, the mere performance of an act establishes that the performer feels no guilt for it. But can't we feel guilty about doing even things that we feel justified in doing? Guilt is a psychological phenomenon that can't always be eradicated by rational analysis. What do you think?
17. B
18. C
19. Irma is trying to extend the analogy until it boomerangs.

20. A
21. D
22. D
23. Earth is compared to a commons.
24. E
25. B
26. Implied conclusion: All won't be well. On first look, this appears to be invalid, denying the antecedent. Probably, however, the author means "If and *only* if. . . ." in which case the argument would be valid.
27. "For the foreseeable future . . . of a lifeboat."

CHAPTER 11

EXERCISES ON CAUSAL ARGUMENTS AND EXPLANATIONS

1. A, B, H, and J probably would be explanations in the strict sense.
2. B really consists of the explanation:

> Argument clears the air, opens minds, questions examined assumptions, and leads to rational judgments.
> This is why Mobil provokes, needles, etc.

and the argument:

> **Voices of business balance other voices.**
> **Stifling any voice distorts the democratic process.**
> **The people must be able to weigh *all* the evidence so that future decisions in our participatory democracy will be based on the noble wisdom of the past — the First Amendment.**
>
> **Therefore, it's all right, even desirable, for us, an admitted special interest, to offer arguments.**

Numerous cause-and-effect relationships are asserted in the premises.

D. The basic argument goes as follows:

> **Chauvinistic intellectuals, by emphasizing those who remain "unmelted," shift the focus from the vast majority who assimilate to those few still remaining in ethnic neighborhoods.**
> **In fact, the actual behavior of the majority of those remaining is in the direction of assimilation, for example, the Jews, Eastern Europeans, and blacks.**
>
> **Therefore, the ethnic revival is largely an ideological revival wrought by alienated and disenchanted intellectuals . . . political demagogues.**

   Cause: alienated and disenchanted intellectuals, together with conservative political demagogues
   Effect: the ethnic revival

E. **Nearly all the energy now used comes from nonrenewable sources.**
   Once depleted, nonrenewable energy becomes more expensive.
   The more expensive it is, the more powerful its inflationary impact; higher

cost of living, more unemployment, and diminishing capital.
No economic system can withstand these pressures indefinitely.

Therefore, in order to solve the energy crisis, the United States must have a
national energy policy that replaces nonrenewable sources with renewable
ones, which are stable in cost.
Note the chain of cause-and-effect relationships in the premises. The conclusion
offers an alternative to this slippery slope.
F. It's economically sensible to build cheap, unrepairable, throw-away objects
that don't last as long as repairable objects.
The reason is that advancing technology tends to lower the costs of manufacture much more rapidly than the cost of repair work.
Advancing technology makes it possible to improve the object as time
goes by.
We hesitate to commit large resources for rigidly fixed objects intended to
serve unchanging purposes because we recognize the inevitability of change.

Therefore, the economics of performance, of necessity, are replaced by the
economics of transience.
Note the cause-and-effect relationships in the premises.
(A, C, and G are probably explanatory.)

EXERCISES ON CONFUSION IN CAUSAL REASONING

1. McFarland seems to be groping for remote causes or conditions that will get him
   off the hook. Rather than oversimplifying, he's overcomplicating.
2. Slippery slope
3. *Post hoc.* Perhaps they're building a new home because they need more room
   owing to the birth of the twins.
4. Slippery slope
5. A possible case of confusing a cause with a statistical correlation. Although it's
   obviously true that juveniles can't commit street crimes if they aren't on the
   streets, perhaps other factors help account for the crime decline.
6. Confusing cause with correlation. How about first isolating the conditions all these
   periods shared, and then offering a causal generalization about depressions? From
   this, one could cautiously infer that should the same conditions hold in the 1990s,
   then, in the absence of any countervailing conditions, a depression is probable.
7. Oversimplification. More likely Congress viewed the lies and deceit as part of a
   systematic attempt by the executive branch to abuse its power and thwart the will
   of the legislative branch in ways that were unconstitutional.
8. Slippery slope
9. Oversimplification
10. Slippery slope
11. Probably *post hoc,* and a convenient one at that; for at the time, the Israelis were
    pressuring the Reagan administration to deep-six the missile deal. Certainly, this
    is an oversimplification.

12. Causal oversimplification. Yes, the parents could have acted more prudently, but they didn't tear the child apart — the man's dogs did. The man is, in effect, treating the alleged parental neglect as a necessary condition of the tragedy. At most, it was contributory.

13. *Post hoc*

14. Presumably, the Office of Technology Assessment's study accounted for unskilled or unscrupulous polygraph operators. Shreve is saying that the 10% inaccuracy rate can be attributed to operator error, that the polygraphers themselves are totally to blame. That is, to say the least, a causal oversimplification. In fact, given the history of polygraphs, it's probably a causal misrepresentation. Clearly, the head of the American Polygraph Association could be expected to defend the infallibility of the polygraph even at the expense of polygraphers.

15. The causes of urban crime are frustratingly complex as to make attribution to those "kinds of people" an oversimplification.

SUMMARY-TEST QUESTIONS FOR CHAPTER 11

1. Answers will vary.
2. They all imply causation.
3. Each implies causation.
4. No
5. In a typical causal argument, someone is attempting to establish that B is caused by A. In a typical causal explanation, someone is trying to help an audience understand how B can be accounted for or explained in terms of A.
6. F
7. T
8. T
9. F
10. T
11. T
12. F
13. T
14. D
15. C
16. B
17. A
18. A
19. B
20. C
21. D (E isn't a good choice because that would imply that in the presence of such congressional action people are more likely to set their homes ablaze than in the absence of such action.)
22. B
23. B
24. D

25. E
26. D
27. B
28. D
29. D
30. D
31. B
32. A
33. D. Might not the same qualities account for both success in Ivy League colleges and occupational success?
34. C
35. A

From: **Nothing Else Has Worked: Abolish the Prohibitions**

Suggested outline:

THESIS: Drugs should be decriminalized.

I.   Drug prohibitions create economic incentives for drug dealers and enhance the appeal of certain chemicals.
       A. Poverty and despair drive youngsters to pursue the fast buck.
       B. Drug prohibitions offer youngsters an opportunity to make big money for taking big risks.
II.   Decriminalization would take the profits out of illegal drugs, eliminate a major cause of drug violence, and remove drug dealers from street corners.
       A. The elimination of Prohibition ended bootlegging and illegal crimes.
III.   Decriminalization would allow users to be identified and helped.
       A. Billions of dollars would be available from savings on law enforcement and imprisonment.
IV.   Prohibition is not working.
       A. Crack babies exist.
       B. Parental responsibility has been abandoned.
       C. More and dangerous drugs continue to appear.
          1. "Ice" is fast becoming the drug of choice.
V.   If prohibition isn't working, we should abolish it.
VI.   Decriminalization could be implemented effectively.
       A. Congress can and should set standards for dispensing and taxing drugs: assist states and local government in identifying users; support appropriate research; and make treatment available for every addict.
       B. Freed up resources would make punishment for violators swifter and perhaps more punitive.
       C. Minors up to age 21 would be prohibited from buying or using drugs.
VII.   Prohibiting individuals from using drugs is of questionable morality.
       A. Nineteen years of Prohibition showed it was morally wrong to prevent Americans from consuming alcohol or substances that have been part of the heritage of Western civilization.

B. People have a right to decide for themselves whether to use potentially dangerous substances so long as they aren't injuring others.

C. Governmental paternalism invites governmental abuse.

1. Yes
2. B
3. Poverty breeds despair, which in turn breeds the extraordinarily profitable drug culture that at once offers immediate rewards and the hope of escape.
4. He probably believes that the drug problem can't be eliminated if poverty isn't eliminated. On this interpretation, eliminating poverty would be a necessary condition for eliminating the drug problem. A stronger interpretation would be to view the elimination of poverty as sufficient for eliminating the drug problem. There likely is enough evidence in the essay to support either of these interpretations, which suggests that the author may consider the elimination of poverty as both a necessary *and* sufficient condition for eliminating drugs.
5. C
6. C
7. Spike is incorrectly interpreting the judge's statements as strong, exceptionless generalizations.
8. E
9. C
10. Yes, affirming the antecedent
11. I'm inclined to think that none would weaken his argument since the prohibitions would remain in effect, and it's the prohibitions that the judge believes make drugs lucrative and appealing to the impoverished.
12. Decriminalization would take the profits out of illegal drugs, eliminate a major reason for gang violence, remove drug dealers from the streets, and free up money for education and rehabilitation.
13. The profit might still be there, but, according to the author, there would be more control of the drugs and less crime associated with them.
14. A
15. F
16. D
17. It's not exactly clear how prohibiting youngsters up to age 21 from buying or using drugs is consistent with the claim that decriminalization would eliminate a major reason for gang violence.
18. B
19. E
20. A
21. D (C isn't an innuendo since Grinspour actually says that alcohol will injure some people.)
22. There's still plenty of government intervention in the author's proposal, including, presumably, substantial taxation for exercising free choice (as there is, of course, with alcohol and tobacco).
23. Given the author's commitment to minimal government intervention in largely personal affairs, one would expect the author to favor decriminalization or fewer restrictions in these areas as well.

Index

Abuse of euphemism, fallacy of, 183-186
Abuse of vagueness, fallacy of, 176-177
Abusive *ad hominem*, fallacy of, 265-268
Accent, fallacy of, 233-234
Acceptable arguments, 34-39
Ad hominem appeals, fallacies of
  abusive ad hominem, 265-268
  circumstantial ad hominem, 268-269
  two wrongs make a right, 272-274
  well poisoning, 269-271
Adler, Alfred, 149-150
Adler, Mortimer, 91
Agreement, method of, 502
Altick, Richard D., 91, 355-356
Ambiguity
  definition of, 144-145
  semantic ambiguity, 174-176
Ambiguity fallacies
  accent, 233-234
  amphiboly, 230-232
  composition, 238

Ambiguity fallacies (*cont.*)
  division, 239
  equivocation, 227-229
  hypostatization, 241-242
  innuendo, 234-236
American Civil Liberties Union, 374-378
Amphiboly, fallacy of, 230-232
Analogy
  analogy problems, 458-459
  arguments from, 334-335, 462-463
  developing the argument from, 470-473
  introduction to, 457-458
  responding to, 465-468
  uses of, 460-461
Anderson, Jack, 419
Angler, Natalie, 506-507
Appeal to fear, fallacy of, 285, 287
Appeal to pity, fallacy of, 284-285, 286-287
Appeal to popularity, 414, 416-417
Aquinas, Thomas, 344
Archimides, 460
Areen, Judith, 434-437

Arguable statements, 70-71
Argument language
  asides, 106-109, 112
  categories of, 97-109
  challenges of, 89
  coherence of, 112-115
  discounts, 104-106, 112
  examples, 107-109
  intensifiers, 103-104, 112
  internal coherence, 109
  nonlogical use of standard premise and conclusion indicators, 99-100
  premise and conclusion indicators, 98-100, 112
  qualifiers, 102-103, 112
Argumentative essay. *See* Extended arguments
Arguments. *See also* Analogy; Causal arguments; Comparison; Extended arguments; Generalizations
  acceptable arguments, 34-39
  analogous argument, 334-335, 462-463

Comparison; Extended (*cont.*)
conclusions as main ideas
in, 11-23
deductive arguments, 27-29
definition of, 7, 10
evaluation of, 34-39
examples of, 3-7
explanations compared
with, 10
features of, 7-8
inductive arguments, 28-29
justified arguments, 32
logical function of premises
in, 23-27
of opinion, 425-428
persuasion compared with,
48-50
premises in, 11-12
propositions and, 9
purpose of, 49
sound versus valid argu-
ments, 30, 32
strong versus valid argu-
ments, 31-32
subarguments, 18-19
validity of, 27-32
"what" and "why" of,
11-12
Aristotle, 48, 238
Asides, 106-109, 112
Aspin, Les, 518
Assumption without good reason, fallacy of, 347
Assumption-loaded labels, fallacy of, 186-189
AuCoin, Les, 302-303
Authority
appeal to popularity, 414,
416-417
appeal to tradition, 417-418
evaluation of, 412-414,
415-416
as evidence, 412-418
fallacy of false or questionable authority, 414
Ayer, Alfred J., 476

Baber, Rab E., 456
Backing, as premise support,
27
Bafnet, Richard J., 235
Bakker, Jim, 292-293
Baldridge, Malcolm, 295
Bandwagon effect, 414,
416-417
Barbie, Klaus, 273, 404
Barry, Marion S., Jr., 516
Batra, Ravi, 515
Beauchamp, Tom, 107
Begging the question, fallacy
of, 193-195

Bell, T. H., 232
Bemba, Jean Martin d', 404
Berkowitz, Leonard, 159
Bernardin, Cardinal Joseph,
208, 209
Berns, Walter, 263
Biaggi, Mario, 405
Biden, Joseph, 269, 274, 290
Birk, Genevieve, 38
Birk, Newman, 38
Bishop, Jerry E., 197
Bismarck, Otto Von, 151
Blotnick, Srully, 152
Bohr, Niels, 460
Bonellie, Helen-Janet, 469
Boorstin, Daniel, 105
Bork, Robert H., 191-192, 266,
269, 277, 290, 405
Botha, P. W., 202
Bradley, F. H., 239
Bradley, Tom, 411
Brenkert, George, 423
Brennan, William J., Jr.,
163-166, 237
Brinton, Crane, 144
Brownmiller, Susan, 144
Buber, Martin, 393, 456-457
Buckley, William F., 290
Burnley, James IV, 240
Bush, George, 160, 269, 282,
283, 290, 298-299, 395,
420
Buthelezi, Magosuthu, 288
Byrd, Robert C., 289

Campbell, C. Arthur, 345
Camus, Albert, 108, 111,
184-185
Carnegie, Dale, 279
Carr, Albert Z., 449n
Casey, William J., 422-423
Cash, Thomas F., 518-519
Castaneda, Jorge, 193, 516
Categorical syllogisms, 330-334
Causal arguments
and causal explanations,
493-496
causes as antecedent conditions, 500-503
chronological order of
causes, 520-521
confusion in causal reasoning, 504-514
definition of, 492-493
development of, 519-522
introduction to, 491-492
order of importance,
521-522
Causal explanations, 493-496
Causal oversimplification,
fallacy of, 505-509

Cederblom, Jerry, 469
Ceremonial function of lan-
guage, 92
Chapman, Stephen, 62
Chase, Stuart, 267
Christensen, F. M., 152-153
Chronological order of causes,
520-521
Churchill, Winston, 51
Circumstantial *ad hominem*,
fallacy of, 268-269
Cleveland, Grover, 267
Cohen, Morris, 108
Coherence
in argument, 112-115
in rhetoric, 113
Common opinion, fallacy of,
414, 416-417
Common practice, fallacy of,
272-274
Commoner, Barry, 498-499
Comparison
and contrast, 450-453
developing the argument
from, 470-473
false dilemma, 455
faulty comparisons, 453-455
incomplete comparison,
453-454
point-by-point method for,
472-473
selective comparison,
454-455
subject-by-subject method
for, 471-472
Complex questions, fallacy of,
198-199
Composition, fallacy of, 238
Compton, Lynn, 294
Conclusions. *See also* Thesis
definition of, 11
indicators for, 98-100, 112
location of main idea, 13-19
as main ideas, 12-23
nonlogical use of indicators
for, 99-100
precise definition of main
idea, 20-22
words signaling, 14
Concomitant variation, method
of, 502-503
Conditional syllogisms, 339-344
Confusion. *See* Fallacies
Connolly, Francis, 113
Connotation, 135
Consequences, statements
about, 71
Consistency, checking for,
421-424
Contrast, and comparison,
450-453

Copernicus, 460-461
Cousins, Norman, 123
Cox, Archibald, 405
Cox, Louise, 369-372
Creamer, Robert W., 494
Critical thinking, 6

Darrow, Clarence, 493
Darwin, Charles, 294-295
Data, definition of, 24
Davis, Kenneth, 240
Decatus, Stephen, 151
Declaration of Independence, 65
Decter, Midge, 534-536
Deductive arguments, 27-29
Deductive organization, of extended arguments, 63-66
Definitions. *See also* Meaning and definition
 denotative definitions, 136
 extended definitions, 153-156
 fallacy of question-begging definition, 196-198
 lexical or logical definitions, 136
 persuasive definitions, 137
 stipulative definitions, 137-138
 theoretical definitions, 138, 140-142
Deliberative oration, 48-49
Dembart, Lee, 415-416
Democritus, 138, 140
DeMoss (Arthur S.) Foundation, 152
Denotative definitions, 136
Denotative meaning, 135
Deukmejian, George, 417
Difference, method of, 502
Directive function of language, 90-92
Disconnectedness, in construction of warrants, 350-352
Discounts, 104-106, 112
Discourse
 evaluation of, 96-97
 intended functions of, 95-97
Disjunctive syllogisms, 345-348
Disputes
 evaluative disputes, 148
 factual disputes, 147-148
 interpretive disputes, 148
 theoretical disputes, 148-151
 verbal disputes, 147

Distinction without a difference, fallacy of, 203-204
Diversion, fallacies of
 red herring, 291-293
 straw argument, 293-294
Division, fallacy of, 239
Dole, Robert, 405, 420
Donaldson, Sam, 237
Dornan, Robert K., 302
Drawing an affirmative conclusion from a negative premise, fallacy of, 336n
Dressler, Alan, 150
Dubos, René, 127-130
Dugan, Ann, 120
Dukakis, Michael, 240, 283, 431-432
Dunne, Brenda J., 415-416
Dworkin, Andrea, 256

Eastman, Richard M., 109
Ehrenreich, Barbara, 177-178
Eliot, T. S., 92
Emerson, Ralph Waldo, 237-238
Emotional appeals, fallacies of
 appeal to fear, 285, 287
 appeal to pity, 284-285, 286-287
 introduction to, 278-279
 mob appeal, 279-284
Emotive language, slanting through use of, 178-181
Emphasis, in rhetoric, 113
Eotvos, Roland vos, 517
Epicurus, 111-112
Equivocation, fallacy of, 227-229
Erasmus, Desiderius, 152
Euphemism, abuse of, 183-186
Evaluation
 of arguments, 34-39
 of discourse, 96-97
 of generalizations, 382-385
 of pools and surveys, 392-394
Evaluative disputes, 148
Evidence
 authority as, 412-418
 fallacy of neglect of relevant evidence, 405-410
Ewing, David, 84-85
Examples, 107-109
Exclusive premises, fallacy of, 337n
Explanations, 10, 493-496
Expressive function of language, 92

Extended arguments
 arguable statements and, 70-71
 construction of, 69-76, 75
 deductive and inductive organization of, 63-66
 definition of, 5
 elements of, 50
 examples of, 5-6
 formulation of thesis proposition, 70-71
 goal of rational persuasion, 6-7
 internalized reader and, 75
 main points of, 59-66
 organization of, 63-66
 outlining of, 66-69
 persuasion compared with, 48-50
 support materials for, 76
 thesis of, 52-56
 thesis proposition, 54-55
 unexpressed thesis propositions, 55-56
 writing the thesis proposition, 72-74
Extended definitions, 153-156

Faber, Sandra, 150
Fact, statements about, 71
Factual disputes, 147-148
Fain, Jim, 267, 515
Fallacies
 abuse of euphemism, 183-186
 abuse of vagueness, 176-177
 abusive *ad hominem*, 265-268
 accent, 233-234
 ad hominem appeals, 265-274
 of ambiguity, 227-243
 amphiboly, 230-232
 appeal to fear, 285, 287
 appeal to pity, 284-285, 286-287
 assumption without good reason, 347
 assumption-loaded labels, 186-189
 begging the question, 193-195
 causal oversimplification, 505-509
 in causal reasoning, 504-514
 circumstantial ad hominem, 268-269
 complex or loaded questions, 198-199

Fallacies (*cont.*)
  composition, 238
  distinction without a differ-
    ence, 203-204
  diversion, 291-294
  division, 239
  drawing an affirmative con-
    clusion from a nega-
    tive premise, 336n
  emotional appeals, 278-287
  equivocation, 227-229
  exclusive premises, 337n
  false dilemma, 189-191, 455
  false or questionable au-
    thority, 414
  false precision, 397-398
  hasty generalization,
    400-401, 402
  hypostatization, 241-242
  illicit end term, 337n
  incomplete comparison,
    453-454
  innuendo, 234-236
  of irrelevance, 264-294
  misapplied generalization,
    401-403
  misuse of jargon, 182-183,
    185-186
  mob appeal, 279-284
  neglect of a common
    cause, 510-514
  neglect of relevant
    evidence, 405-410
  popularity, 414, 416-417
  post hoc fallacy, 504-505
  question-begging definition,
    196-198
  rhetorical inconsistency,
    201-202
  rhetorical questions,
    199-201
  selective comparison,
    454-455
  semantic ambiguity,
    174-177
  slanting through use of
    emotive language,
    178-181
  slippery slope, 509-510
  straw argument, 293-294
  tradition, 417-418
  tu quoque, 272-274
  two wrongs make a right,
    272-274
  undistributed middle term,
    336n
  well poisoning, 269-271
False dilemma, fallacy of,
  189-191, 455
False or questionable authority, fallacy of, 414

False precision, fallacy of,
  397-398
Falwell, Jerry, 292-293
Farragher, John Mack, 451-453
Faulty comparisons, 453-455
Fear, appeal to, 285, 287
Ferraro, Geraldine, 277
Fischer, David, 239
Fischer, James, 516
Fitzwater, Marlin, 404
Fleming, Alexander, 461
Forensic oration, 48-49
Frame of reference, 387-388
Frank, Jerome, 249-253
Franklin, Benjamin, 461
Freud, Sigmund, 125-127
Friedman, Milton, 275
Fries, Peter H., 57

Galbraith, John Kenneth, 499
Galsworthy, John, 419
Gann, Paul, 199
General statements
  definition of, 321-323
  invalidity and misapplied
    general statements,
    334-338
  supporting and extending,
    358-363
  as warrants, 349-356
Generalizations
  authority as evidence,
    412-418
  checking for consistency,
    421-424
  conditional syllogisms,
    339-344
  definition of, 321, 323
  development of argument
    of opinion, 425-428
  disjunctive syllogisms,
    345-348
  evaluation of, 382-385
  evaluation of polls and sur-
    veys, 392-394
  fallacies of missing
    evidence and,
    400-410
  forming and applying,
    328-329
  general statements and,
    321-323
  general statements as war-
    rants, 349-356
  hasty generalization,
    400-401, 402
  inductive generalizations,
    323-324
  invalidity and misapplied
    general statements,
    334-338

Generalizations (*cont.*)
  misapplied generalization,
    401-403
  neglect of relevant
    evidence, 405-410
  noninductive generaliza-
    tions, 324-327
  observation and, 385-389
  reliable generalizations,
    382-385
  representativeness and,
    389-394
  sample size and, 390
  statistical evidence and,
    394-398
  supporting and extending,
    358-363
  syllogisms, 330-338
  tracing implications,
    424-425
  typicality and, 391-392
  universal versus nonuniv-
    eral general state-
    ments, 322
Getty, J. Paul, 237
Gibbs, Lawrence B., 288
Ginsburg, Douglas, 278, 405,
  421-422
Goffman, Erving, 112
Gorbachev, Mikhail, 419
Gorman, Marvin, 519
Gorney, Roderic, 130-132
Gray, George W., 461
Greenwood, Noel, 275

Haag, Ernest van den, 213-215
Haig, Alexander M., Jr., 182-
  183, 202
Hairsplitting, 203-204
Hamilton, Lee H., 235
Hardin, Garrett, 478-482
Hart, Gary, 274
Hartmann, G. W., 278
Hasty generalization, fallacy of,
  400-401, 402
Hatch, Orin G., 289-290
Hawthorne effect, 513
Hente, Karl, 161
Hess, Elizabeth, 177-178
Hewitt, Don, 230
Hoared, John A., 275
Hodel, donald, 295
Holmes, Oliver Wendel, Jr.,
  325
Holt, John, 62
Hook, Benjamin, 290
Hume, David, 209-210
Hussein, Saddam, 181, 235,
  281
Hypostatization, fallacy of,
  241-242

Iacocca, Lee A., 273-274, 516
Illicit end term, fallacy of, 337n
Implications, tracing of,
     424-425
Incomplete comparison, fallacy
     of, 453-454
Inductive arguments, 28-29
Inductive generalizations,
     323-324
Inductive organization, of ex-
     tended arguments, 64,
     66
Informative function of lan-
     guage, 90
Innuendo, fallacy of, 234-236
Inouye, Daniel K., 192
Intensifiers, 21-22, 103-104, 112
Internalized reader, 75
Interpretive disputes, 148
Invalid arguments, versus valid
     arguments, 27-32
Irrelevance, fallacies of
     abusive ad hominem,
        265-268
     ad hominem appeals,
        265-274
     appeal to fear, 285, 287
     appeal to pity, 284-285,
        286-287
     circumstantial ad hominem,
        268-269
     definition of, 264
     diversion, 291-294
     emotional appeals, 278-287
     mob appeal, 279-284
     straw argument, 293-294
     two wrongs make a right,
        272-274
     well poisoning, 269-271
Ivins, Molly, 58, 497

Jacobs, Gloria, 177-178
Jahn, Robert G., 415-416
James, William, 160
Jargon, misuse of, 182-183,
     185-186
Jeffers, Robinson, 93-94
Jefferson, Thomas, 65
John Paul II, Pope, 419
Johnson, Sheila K., 495-496
Joyce, James, 206
Justified arguments, 32

Kamisar, Yale, 248
Kant, Immanuel, 104, 111
Kelly, John H., 235
Kemp, Jack, 516
Kendall, George A., 439-442
Kennedy, Edward, 266, 421-422
Kerr, Richard, 290
Kilpatrick, James, 237

Kinsey, Alfred C., 399
Kirkpatrick, James, 192
Knickerbocker, K. L., 94
Krauthammer, Charles,
     267-268
Krull, George, 161
Kurtz, Howard, 287
Kytle, Ray, 75

Labels, assumption-loaded,
     186-189
Lacy, Dan, 455-456
Laing, R. D., 110-111, 271
Lamm, Richard D., 517
Language. *See also* Argument
     language
     ambiguity and vagueness,
        144-146
     ceremonial function of, 92
     definition of, 139-140
     definitions, 136-143
     directive function of, 90-92
     disputes, 147-151
     evaluation of discourse,
        96-97
     expressive function of, 92
     functions of, 90-97
     informative function of, 90
     intended functions of
        discourse, 95-97
     mixed functions of, 93-94
     performative function of,
        92-93
     word meaning, 134-146
Lanton, Tom, 235
Lattin, Don, 209
Lee, Irving, 187
LeHave, Beverly, 194-195
Leiser, Burton M., 317
Levin, Gerald, 113
Levine, Judith, 161
Lexical definitions, 136
Liman, Arthur L., 289, 404, 420
Lincoln, Abraham, 267, 431,
     512
Linguistic confusion. *See* Falla-
     cies
Loaded questions, fallacy of,
     198-199
Locke, John, 345
Logical definitions, 136
Lutz, William, 185

MacDougall, Malcolm, 192
Mack, Connie, 295
MacKinnon, Catharine, 256
Main idea
     conclusions as, 12-23
     intensifiers in, 21-22
     location of, 13-19
     precise definition of, 20-22

Main idea (*cont.*)
     qualifiers in, 21
     quantifiers in, 20-21
Main points
     definition of, 59
     of extended arguments,
        59-66
Marans, David, 469
Marshall, John, 413
Marshall, Thurgood, 225-226
Marx, Karl, 111
McClure, James A., 514
McFarland, Robert C., 514
McGrory, Mary, 237
McGurn, William A., 232
Mead, George Herbert, 110
Meaning and definition
     ambiguity and vagueness,
        144-146
     definitions, 136-143
     denotative meaning, 135
     disputes, 147-151
     extended definitions,
        153-156
     objective connotation, 135
     statements about, 70
     subjective connotation, 135
     word meaning, 134-146
Meese, Edwin, 423
Mill, John Stuart, 162, 240,
     502-503
Miller, Janella, 257-260
Miller, Jonathan, 456
Misapplied generalization, fal-
     lacy of, 401-403
Missing evidence, fallacies of
     hasty generalization,
        400-401, 402
     misapplied generalization,
        401-403
     neglect of relevant
        evidence, 405-410
Misuse of jargon, fallacy of,
     182-183, 185-186
Moakley, Joe, 411
Mob appeal, fallacy of, 279-284
Montagu, Ashley, 53
Montaigne, Michael de, 240-241
Moore, George Edward, 344
Morse, Joseph J., 419
Multiparagraph argument. *See*
     Extended arguments
Murdoch, William N., 485-488

Nagel, Thomas, 408-409
Neglect of a common cause,
     fallacy of, 510-514
Neglect of relevant evidence
     fallacy of 405-407
     guidelines for uncovering,
        407-410

Neill, A. S., 289
Newton, Lisa, 64
Nietzsche, Friedrich, 278
Noninductive generalizations, 324-327
Nonuniversal general statements, 322
North, Oliver, 184, 193, 228-229, 269-270, 289-291, 404, 411, 420, 421

Oates, Allan, 485-488
Objective connotation, 135
Observation, 385-389
O'Neill, Michael J., 519
Opinion-generalization
  adjusting of, 427-428
  defending of, 425-426
Organization
  definition of, 63
  of extended arguments, 63-66
Ortega Saavedra, Daniel, 144
Orwell, George, 121-122, 229, 469
Outlining, of extended arguments, 66-69
Overstatement, in construction of warrants, 352-353

Panandreous, Andreas, 287
Parenti, M., 453
Parrington, Vernon, 239
Patterson, Orlando, 498
Paulsen, David W., 469
Peirce, Neil R., 295
Perceptual defense, 388
Performative function of language, 92-93
Persona, 49
Persuasion
  argument compared with, 48-50
  example of logical persuasion, 51
  purpose of, 49
Persuasive definitions, 137
Pfeiffer, John E., 61
Pity, appeal to, 284-285, 286-287
Plato, 278, 344
Podesta, Anthony, 59
Poindexter, John M., 196-198, 230, 423, 517
Point-by-point method, 472-473
Polls, evaluation of, 392-394
Popesel, Howard, 469
Popper, Karl, 149-150
Popularity, fallacy of, 414, 416-417

Post hoc fallacy, 504-505
Powell, Lewis F., Jr., 225, 290
Premises
  acceptability of, 35-37
  adequacy of support for conclusions, 39
  backing as premise support, 27
  definition of, 11
  indicators for, 98-100, 112
  logical function of, 23-27
  nonlogical use of indicators for, 99-100
  relevancy of, 37-38
  words signaling, 14-15
Price, Raymond, 192, 274, 517
Pronoun reference, 115
Propositions, differences in, 9
Public self, 393
Pugsley, John, 39

Qualifiers, 21, 102-103, 112
Quantifiers, 20-21
Quayle, Dan, 274-275
Question-begging definition, fallacy of, 196-198
Questionable authority, fallacy of, 414
Quinn, Archbishop John, 208-209

Rachels, James, 424-425
Rand, Ayn, 476
Random sample, 391
Reading
  critical reading, 38, 91
  internalized reader, 75
Reagan, Ronald, 179, 181, 196-198, 202, 229-230, 232-233, 235, 237, 266, 277, 287, 288, 289, 404, 405, 410, 421, 422
Red herring, fallacy of, 291-293
Rehnquist, William H., 166-167, 248
Reninger, H. Willar, 94
Repetition, in construction of warrants, 353-354
Representativeness, and generalizations, 389-394
Resolution, definition of, 84n
Rhetoric, basic elements in, 113
Rhetorical fallacies
  abuse of euphemism, 183-186
  abuse of vagueness, 176-177
  assumption-loaded labels, 186-189

Rhetorical fallacies (*cont.*)
  begging the question, 193-195
  complex or loaded questions, 198-199
  distinction without a difference, 203-204
  false dilemma, 189-191
  introduction to, 173-174
  misuse of jargon, 182-183, 185-186
  question-begging definition, 196-198
  rhetorical inconsistency, 201-202
  rhetorical questions, 199-201
  semantic ambiguity, 174-177
  slanting through use of emotive language, 178-181
Rhetorical inconsistency, fallacy of, 201-202
Rhetorical questions, fallacy of, 199-201
Rice, Berkeley, 40
Roark, Anne C., 142-143
Roberts, Paul, 139-140
Robertson, Pat, 519
Rooney, Dan, 240
Roth, John K., 180-181
Rousseau, Jean-Jacques, 206
Rowan, Ford, 59
Ruby, Lionel, 325, 384, 402
Russell, Bertrand, 107-108, 151, 384
Rutherford, Ernest, 460

Sagan, Carl, 57, 475
Sampling technique
  random sample, 391
  sample size, 390, 392-393
Santayana, George, 278
Scheidler, Joseph M., 304-306
Scheve, William J., Jr., 516
Schlauch, Margaret, 244
Schlesinger, Arthur, Jr., 182, 277
Schurz, Carl, 151
Sciaroni, Bretton G., 432
Selective comparison, fallacy of, 454-455
Semantic ambiguity, fallacy of, 174-176
Shakespeare, William, 296, 475
Shaw, David, 275
Shelley, Percy Bysshe, 476
Shively, Charley, 247
Shultz, George, 230

Slanting through use of emotive language, fallacy of, 178-181
Slater, Philip, 111
Slippery slope, fallacy of, 509-510
Social policy, statements about, 71
Solomon, Gerald, 411
Sound, versus valid arguments, 30, 32
Spender, Stephen, 121
Statements
    arguable statements, 70-71
    about consequences, 71
    about fact, 71
    about meaning, 70
    about social policy, 71
    about value, 70
Statistical evidence, 394-398, 510-512
Steinbrenner, George, 419
Stevens, John Paul, 167-168, 225
Stewart, Justice, 225
Stipulative definitions, 137-138
Storr, Anthony, 158-159
Story, Joseph, 413
Straw argument, fallacy of, 293-294
Strong, versus valid arguments, 31-32
Style, in rhetoric, 113
Subarguments, 18-19
Subject-by-subject method, 471-472
Subjective being, 393
Subjective connotation, 135
Sullivan, Bishop Joseph, 209
Support materials, 76
Surveys, evaluation of, 392-394
Sweet, Robert W., 530-531
Syllogisms
    categorical syllogisms, 330-334
    conditional syllogisms, 339-344
    definition of, 330
    disjunctive syllogisms, 345-348

Syllogisms (cont.)
    invalidity and misapplied general statements, 334-338

Tacitus, 152
Taft, William H., IV, 518
Tartikhoff, Brandon, 419
Theoretical definitions, 138, 140-142
Theoretical disputes, 148-151
Thesis
    definition of, 52
    of extended arguments, 52-56
    identification of topics, 52-53
    thesis proposition, 54-55
    unexpressed thesis propositions, 55-56
Thesis proposition
    arguable statements and, 70-71
    definition of, 54-55
    formulation of, 70-71
    unexpressed thesis propositions, 55-56
    writing of, 72-74
Thoreau, Henry David, 475
Toffler, Alvin, 499
Toias, Sheila, 498
Topics
    definition of, 52-53
    identification of, for thesis, 52-53
Tradition, fallacy of, 417-418
Trow, Charlie E., 236
Tu quoque, fallacy of, 272-274
Tuchman, Barbara, 62
Twain, Mark, 470
Two wrongs make a right, fallacy of, 272-274
Typicality, and generalizations, 391-392

Understatement, in construction of warrants, 352-353
Undistributed middle term, fallacy of, 336n

Unexpressed thesis propositions, 55-56
Unity, in rhetoric, 113
Universal general statements, 322

Vagueness, 144-146, 176-177
Validity, of arguments, 27-32
Value, statements about, 70
Van Celeve, George, 420
Verbal disputes, 147
Vergas, Jacques, 273
Vodicka, John Cole, 218-221

Waldheim, Kurt, 419
Warner, Jim, 235
Warrants
    definition of, 349
    disconnectedness in, 350-352
    general statements as, 349-356
    overstatement or understatement in, 352-353
    premises functioning as, 24-25
    repetition in, 353-354
    things to avoid when reconstructing, 350-354
Washington, George, 151
Watson, George, 276
Watt, James, 144
Wattenberger, Ben, 191, 516
Webber, Alan M., 200
Well poisoning, fallacy of, 269-271
Wicker, Tom, 278
Wilde, Oscar, 151
Will, George, 58
Woard, John A., 246
Wohl, Lisa Cronin, 309-313
Word meaning, 134-146. See also Meaning and definition
Wright, Jim, 405

Yonas, Gerold, 270